6e

At-Risk Youth: A Comprehensive Response

For Counselors, Teachers, Psychologists, and Human Service Professionals

J. Jeffries McWhirter
Arizona State University

Benedict T. McWhirter
University of Oregon

Ellen Hawley McWhirter
University of Oregon

Anna Cecilia McWhirter
University of Oregon

CENGAGE
Learning·

Australia • Brazil • Mexico • Singapore • United Kingdom • United States

CENGAGE
Learning·

At-Risk Youth: A Comprehensive Response for Counselors, Teachers, Psychologists, and Human Service Professionals, Sixth Edition
J. Jeffries McWhirter, Benedict T. McWhirter, Ellen Hawley McWhirter and Anna Cecilia McWhirter

Product Director: Jon Goodspeed

Product Manager: Julie Martinez

Content Developer: Rita Jaramillo

Product Assistant: Stephen Lagos

Marketing Manager: Jennifer Levanduski

Art and Cover Direction, Production Management, and Composition: Lumina Datamatics, Inc.

Manufacturing Planner: Judy Inouye

Cover Image: ©Don Bayley/E+/Getty Images, ©stokkete/Fotolia, ©donatas 1205/Fotolia, ©annedehaas/iStockphoto, ©shironosov/iStockphoto

Unless otherwise noted all items © Cengage Learning®

For product information and technology assistance, contact us at
Cengage Learning Customer & Sales Support, 1-800-354-9706

For permission to use material from this text or product, submit all requests online at **www.cengage.com/permissions**
Further permissions questions can be emailed to **permissionrequest@cengage.com**

Library of Congress Control Number: 2016933265

Student Edition:

ISBN: 978-1-305-67038-9

Cengage Learning
20 Channel Center Street
Boston, MA 02210
USA

Cengage Learning is a leading provider of customized learning solutions with office locations around the globe, including Singapore, the United Kingdom, Australia, Mexico, Brazil, and Japan. Locate your local office at **www.cengage.com/global**

Cengage Learning products are represented in Canada by Nelson Education, Ltd.

To learn more about Cengage Learning, visit **www.cengage.com**

Purchase any of our products at your local college store or at our preferred online store **www.cengagebrain.com**

Printed in the United States of America
3 4 5 6 7   25 24 23 22 21

DEDICATION

This book is dedicated to the next generations of the McWhirter clan: Mary Veronica, Paul John, Mark Thomas, Luke Robert, Monica Clare, Marielena Rose, Joseph Benedict, Jacob Nicholas, Jeffrey Joaquim, Robert Anthony, Ryan Alexander, Gabriel Adam, Thomas Daniel, Benedict Leo, Dominic Croix, Vincent Rock, and Katherine Elizabeth. May we find ways to prevent all children from being at risk. May we find ways to help all children grow and develop into healthy, happy adults with people to love and important work to do. Albert Camus wrote, "Without work, all life goes rotten, but when work is soulless, life stifles and dies." And what matters most is having people to love all along the way.

CONTENTS

v

9   Juvenile Delinquency and Youth Violence   199

14 Family Interventions 349

PREFACE

More than 30 years ago, the U.S. National Commission on Excellence in Education issued its report, *A Nation at Risk*, regarding the status of serious social problems our nation's youth face. Ever since then, educators, counselors, and many other professionals within and outside of the human services fields have used the term *at risk* to identify a wide range of social–psychological problems young people face. The term *at risk* can be useful for describing many adolescents whose potential for becoming responsible and productive adults is limited by challenges within the ecology of their lives. These include problems at home, in schools, and in communities; problems with some cultural norms and social messages that contribute to risk in children's lives; and problems within children and adolescents themselves.

Our goals for this book, now in its sixth edition, continue to be to provide the reader with up-to-date information and research on the problems experienced by at-risk youth and to provide the reader with effective interventions for these problems. Along with extensively updated statistics and research related to youth at risk, we continue to present our long-standing conceptual framework for the categories of problems and the evidence-based prevention strategies and interventions useful for problem solution. This framework includes discussions of all levels of the ecology of problem development and resolution related to youth at risk. We present a variety of practical educational, psychological, and counseling interventions for the prevention and treatment of the problems. We continue to describe empirically supported approaches and to focus on both teens and younger children along with their families and peers.

The information we present and interventions we suggest are used by a broad range of professionals, including counselors, psychologists, social workers, juvenile detention workers, nurse practitioners, many other human service professionals, and teachers. We direct our work primarily to students in counseling, social work, education and special education, applied psychology, and other human service disciplines at both the pre- and in-service levels. However, we also write for teachers-in-training as well as for undergraduate students in psychology, social work, justice studies, nursing, community psychology, and human services. Finally, given the increasing number of Human Service Departments and the recent revision of standards by the Council for Standards in Human Service Education (CSHS), coverage of new human service material has been integrated throughout. Many of the prevention and treatment methods we present here may also be used by school and community health, direct-line human service, and mental health personnel—some directly and some with modification—in a wide range of settings, from birth-to-three enrichment programs to juvenile detention to family counseling.

This book is intended as a textbook for courses in counseling, education, psychology, social work, special education, and human services. It is especially appropriate for developmental counseling courses, such as principles of counseling, school guidance, and agency counseling interventions. This book is also applicable to courses related to counseling students with special needs, maladjusted children, and, of course, at-risk children and adolescents. It may also be useful as a supplemental or primary text in courses in child and youth care, case management, child/adolescent behavioral and emotional problem management, educational administration, and community agency administration. Feedback we have received indicates that school and agency counselors as well as special education teachers and human service workers find this book very useful.

In many ways this book reflects our belief about pedagogy, which is that three domains are important to learning: cognitive, affective, and behavioral. Whenever we plan a seminar, develop a workshop, or teach a class, we ask ourselves three questions: What is the most important information we want our students to know about the subject? How can we engage our students on an emotional/affective level? What new skills can we help our students learn to use? In this book we attend to the cognitive domain by providing up-to-date facts, research findings, and a theoretical and practical information base to stimulate thinking. We focus on the affective domain by presenting short readings at the beginning of each chapter and by presenting real-life case studies and sidebar stories to describe struggling young people and their families. We also include many specific behavioral strategies throughout the book to provide concrete and specific intervention skills to use with young clients and families. Although in Part 3 of the book we apply specific interventions to specific problems, nearly all of the interventions presented can be applied to a broad variety of problems and concerns experienced by children and adolescents.

This book may be used in a number of ways. We have used the entire text in a standard semester or quarter graduate counseling course at Arizona State University and New York University as well as at the Universities of Oregon, Hawai'i, Texas–San Antonio, Southern Maine, and Alaska–Anchorage. At the University of Oregon, this book is used as the principal text for a quarter-long undergraduate course in the human services. Educators can use parts of it as the basis for modular units elected by students in social sciences, human services, education, and psychology. For example, at Arizona State

University, we have offered several modules on a variety of topics within an upper-division educational psychology course taught by graduate assistants, with various chapters providing the major content for the modules. This text has also been useful for training workshops and other forms of continuing professional education.

NEW TO THIS EDITION

As in earlier editions, the chapters provide a wide variety of prevention and treatment intervention suggestions. These include, but are not limited to, refusal and resistance training; an Adlerian/Dreikurs intervention model; Glasser's reality therapy; crisis intervention strategies; parent training models; solution-focused interventions; and peer programs (such as cooperative learning, peer support networks, cross-age peer tutoring, conflict resolution, and peer mediation strategies). We have highlighted prevention strategies, especially antibullying programs and our own GOPEP (Group-Oriented Psychological Education Program). In this edition we have added new information about and evidence supporting these useful approaches. Also, we have moved the chapter on legal and ethical issues in working with at-risk youth (previously Chapter 3) to be part of the web-based supplement to this book. Students and instructors still have full access to that chapter and content but now in an online format.

Beyond supplementing existing material, this edition has gone through an extensive revision process. For example, we have completely revised all chapters to reflect the most current information and statistics of each problem presented. We have replaced out-of-date references and added about 40 or 50 pages of new references from 2011 and after. We have added new material on lesbian, gay, bisexual, transgender, and queer (LGBTQ) youth in various chapters, especially in Chapter 10, which deals with youth suicide, because so many LGBTQ youth are particularly vulnerable to suicide risk.

Further, we expanded material on Stages of Change, Motivational Interviewing, and the Family Check-Up, including the overarching model of Family Check-Up—the EcoFit. We also enhanced the material on Empowerment and critical consciousness, as well as on Bronfenbrenner's ecological model, by providing more examples and text. We have enhanced our presentation on cognitive-behavioral interventions and present resources and interventions related to mindfulness. We have revised and updated current educational policy changes since the administration of President Obama and social and educational policy information (such as Deferred Action for Childhood Arrivals or DACA) related to immigration that affect millions of youth in the United States. We have added information on the Race to the Top act, charter schools, English as a second language, and a description of Travis Hirsch's control theory.

We have included new discussions on areas such as Positive Action, Functional Family Therapy, and Communities That Care (CTC); on the 40 Assets framework from the Search Institute; and on the Good Behavior Game.

Sections were added on incarcerated families, child abuse, intimate partner violence, and dating violence, as well as on nonsuicidal self-injury as a contrast to suicide behavior. We have considerably expanded our discussion of digital technology and social media that contribute to risk and social problems. For example, we have added sections in appropriate chapters on virtual cyber technology applied to victimization, harassment, sexting, and gang activity, and we expanded the section on media influence to include a section on cyber bullying, including legal issues. We have also included discussions on the positive educational benefits of electronic media, including specific resources such as the Khan Academy, to illustrate Internet resources that can be of great help to at-risk youth.

Based on feedback from instructors and students, we have also added several features to this edition that are available via the website. In each chapter, we refer to further readings to supplement the information in the text. We have also provided course instructors with an array of teaching materials—ideas, stimulus questions, exercises, test questions, PowerPoint presentations, YouTube links helpful in teaching, and other aides. Concurrently, the student companion website contains useful handouts and worksheets that help to make the book more vivid. Students can access the student site at http://www.cengagebrain.com, while instructor supplements are available at login.cengage.com.

The book is divided into four major sections. In Part 1, we provide information on the background factors that contribute to risky behaviors. We focus on the ecology of children's lives, including the community and neighborhood environments that increase risk for children and adolescents. In Part 2 we turn to the family, school, and individual characteristics that provide a more prominent and direct influence on youth. In Part 3 we present data about the five at-risk categories and we discuss major treatment and prevention approaches for each. In Part 4 we incorporate more prevention strategies that focus on the family, the school, peer groups, and the individual. We suggest how and when prevention can be applied to meet the developmental needs of children, young teens, and families.

Throughout the book we have used case studies to highlight, apply, and personalize the information in the text. Early in the book, we introduce the Andrews, Baker, Carter, and Diaz families. These families represent various ethnic/cultural groups from diverse socioeconomic and educational backgrounds and with different individual attitudes and behaviors. Each of the children in these families presents some risk of problem behavior. The background and circumstances of each family are described, and each highlights and illustrates environmental, family, and school issues and concerns. The family members introduced in these case studies reappear throughout the book to illustrate specific issues. Readers will also find vignettes throughout the text that help to personalize and exemplify the issues being discussed.

It seems clear that if we do not confront the issues our young people and their families face, our society will lose nearly a quarter of its youth to life-long difficulty who might otherwise become productive, successful, and happy adults. We hope that this text increases the awareness of the problems youth face and contributes to their solution.

ABOUT THE AUTHORS

Any book with four same-name authors seems bound to arouse curiosity, so perhaps we'd better explain who we are. Jeff is the father of Benedict, Benedict and Ellen are married, and Anna Cecilia is Benedict and Ellen's daughter.

Jeff McWhirter holds a diplomate in counseling psychology from the American Board of Professional Psychology (ABPP) and is a Fellow of the American Psychological Association (Divisions 17, 48, 49, and 52), the American Psychological Society, the Association for Specialists in Group Work, and the Academy of Counseling Psychology. He is a professor emeritus in the Counseling and Counseling Psychology Programs and a founding member of the Emeritus College at Arizona State University. A former teacher and school counselor, Jeff received his Ph.D. in counseling psychology from the University of Oregon in 1969 and was awarded the UO College of Education Outstanding Alumnus Award in 2006. He has maintained a small private practice for more than 40 years and consults regularly with schools and agencies that work with at-risk individuals. He has published over 130 chapters and articles in refereed journals; written or edited 24 books; and produced numerous training manuals, research reports, and monographs. He has been a Fulbright-Hays Senior Scholar to Turkey (1977–1978), has been a Fulbright Senior Scholar to Australia (1984–1985), and has also participated in a Fulbright Intercountry Exchange to New Zealand. He was awarded a Fulbright Senior Specialist grant to return to the same department and university in Turkey 29 years after his first Fulbright. He was awarded the 2010 Lifetime Achievement Award from the International Section of APA's Society of Counseling Psychology.

In 1989 Jeff received the Arizona State University Distinguished Teacher Award. He has taught summer sessions or courses at 25 other universities in the United States and internationally. He has been the principal investigator of several externally funded projects, including a large Safe and Drug Free School and Community grant and a violence reduction grant for an alternative high school. His other areas of interest include group counseling, family counseling, learning disabilities, international aspects of counseling psychology, and grandchildren—not necessarily in the order listed.

Benedict McWhirter is a professor of counseling psychology at the University of Oregon, Department Head of the Counseling Psychology and Human Services Department in the College of Education, a Fellow of the American Psychological Association (Division 17), and a licensed psychologist in Oregon. He received his Ph.D. in counseling psychology from the Arizona State University in 1992 and was on the faculty in the Department of Educational Psychology at the University of Nebraska—Lincoln from 1993 to 1997. He has taught at Arizona State University and at the *Universidad del Desarrollo* in Chile and has been a teacher for seventh and eighth grades in

Peru. He has consulted with alternative high schools on developing psychoe-ducational curricula for high-risk youth, and, with Ellen, he has developed and delivered an after-school program for fostering critical consciousness and enhancing advocacy skills for Spanish-speaking adolescents. For 15 years both Benedict and Ellen conducted workshops with couples and provided counseling services to members of the community of Peñalolen in Santiago, Chile (1998–2012). He was named a Fulbright Scholar to teach and conduct research in Chile (2004), was funded by the Spencer Foundation to conduct school-based research in impoverished and high-risk communities in Chile (2007–2009), and continues to engage in collaborative research with colleagues at the *Universidad de Chile* in Santiago. He publishes extensively and routinely presents his research at national and international conferences. His scholarship focuses on understanding family, school, and culturally embedded risk and protective factors for preventing problem behavior among at-risk youth, for improving college success for underrepresented students, and on the experience of connectedness as a protective factor in adolescents and emerging adults. During his tenure as Director of Training of the Counseling Psychology Program, the program received the American Psychological Association Suinn Minority Achievement Award for contributing to the training of psychologists of color. As a department head, Benedict envisioned, planned, and helped to create a new masters' program and Ph.D. program in Prevention Science, expanded the Human Services undergraduate program, and supported improved training in integrated health for drug and alcohol counselor training as well as a new graduate specialization in Spanish language research and practice to support student competencies in providing bilingual counseling and evaluation services to the community.

Ellen Hawley McWhirter is the Ann Swindells Professor of Counseling Psychology in the College of Education at the University of Oregon. Ellen received her Ph.D. in counseling psychology from Arizona State University in 1992, and from 1993 to 1997 she was an assistant professor of counseling psychology at the University of Nebraska—Lincoln. She is a Fellow of the American Psychological Association (Division 17), has served as the chair of the Society for Vocational Psychology, and is a licensed psychologist in the state of Oregon. Her dissertation research on Latina career development was funded by a fellowship from the American Association of University Women. Her early teaching experience includes two years with Maricopa County Head Start. She has also taught and counseled Spanish-speaking children and parents. She routinely presents her research and scholarship on adolescent vocational development at national and international conferences, with a focus on Latino/a adolescents' supports, barriers, school engagement, postsecondary plans, and critical consciousness development. She is the author of *Counseling for Empowerment* (1989, American Counseling Association Press). Ellen was awarded the 2001 Fritz and Linn Kuder Early Career Scientist Practitioner Award, the 2008 John Holland Award for Outstanding Achievement in Career or Personality Research, and the 2015 Distinguished Achievement Award from the Society of Counseling Psychology of the

American Psychological Association. She was honored with the University of Oregon 2016 Reverend Martin Luther King, Jr., Award. With Benedict, she developed and delivered an after-school program for fostering critical consciousness and enhancing advocacy skills for Spanish-speaking adolescents. Ellen was named a Fulbright Scholar to teach and conduct research in Chile (2004) and with Benedict has conducted research and training workshops in Chile for more than 15 years.

Anna Cecilia McWhirter is a new McWhirter author to this edition. Anna Cecilia received her bachelors' degree in Ethnic Studies from the Clark Honors College at the University of Oregon and her masters' degree in Prevention Science at the University of Oregon and is currently pursuing a Ph.D. in school psychology at the University of Oregon. She is a research assistant on numerous federally funded research projects through the University of Oregon Prevention Science Institute and is a specialist with the Women with Infants and Children (WIC) Program for Lane County. Anna Cecilia has extensive experience conducting home-based developmental and parenting assessments in both English and Spanish and has had two year-long cultural immersion experiences, one in Chile and one in the Dominican Republic. In the Dominican Republic Anna Cecilia was engaged in a community-based service-scholar program. Her research interests include enhancing family–school relationships and early childhood parenting interventions.

Our previous fourth author (for editions 3–5) and current contributor to the web-based companion chapter on legal and ethical issues in working with at-risk youth is Robert J. McWhirter, Benedict's brother and Jeff's son. Robert has been a practicing attorney with the Federal Public Defender's Office in Phoenix, Arizona; with the Maricopa County Legal Defender's Office; with the Pima County Public Defender's Office in Tucson, where he also served as Training Director; and as a Supervising Attorney with the Arizona State University Alumni Law Group. In 2011–2012 he implemented a USAID contract for improving the Justice System in El Salvador, working with the Salvadoran Supreme Court to reform court procedures, the Attorney General's Office to train prosecutors, the National Civilian Police to develop community policing, and the Public Defenders to improve the quality of representation. Robert received his Juris Doctorate from Arizona State University in 1988 and clerked with Vice Chief Justice Stanley G. Feldman of the Supreme Court of Arizona until 1989. Robert specializes in criminal immigration law. He has been a visiting professor of law at Catholic University of Chile and at the University of Chile, and he has taught many seminars in Spanish for public defenders and judges on judicial reform in Venezuela, Chile, Nicaragua, and Columbia. Through support from the U.S. Department of State, Robert has also served as an advisor to the Venezuelan Constitutional Assembly, drafting the new Venezuelan constitution. Related to his teaching and consulting, Robert has also published articles in the *Georgetown Immigration Law Review* and the *Criminal Practice Law Reports*. He is the author of *The Criminal Lawyer's Guide to Immigration Law: Questions and Answers* (2nd ed., 2006; American Bar Association Press), *Criminal Law of*

Arizona (2001; State Bar of Arizona Press), and *Strangers in an Even Stranger Land: Aliens and Immigration Law after September 11th* (2002; American Bar Association Press). Robert just completed another major book: *Bills, Quills, and Stills: An Annotated, Illustrated, and Illuminated History of the Bill of Rights* (2015, American Bar Association Press).

ACKNOWLEDGMENTS

Although we four are the most visible in this family project, other members of the clan contributed in many ways. We would like to thank our daughter and sister, Anna Marie McWhirter, for her contributions as a fourth author for the first and second editions of this book. Anna Marie is a tenured professor of language and reading in the Maricopa Community College System in the Phoenix metropolitan area, Arizona. We also particularly thank our daughter and sister, Dr. Paula McWhirter, a professor of counseling psychology in the professional counseling program at the University of Oklahoma, who was a source of great ideas and resources in the preparation of this book. We especially thank Mary McWhirter (Jeff's wife, Benedict's mother, and Anna Cecilia's grandmother) who has been a source of tremendous support over the years and who has consistently cared for all the grandchildren so that we can write. Many thanks also to the reviewers who provided valuable input and suggestions: Karen Marr (St. Clair College of Applied Arts and Technology), Sandra Todaro (Bossier Parish Community College), Duane Isava (Marymount University), Robert Ivy (NOVA Southeastern University), Reggie Jones (Community College of Philadelphia), Norma Gaines-Hanks (University of Delaware), Rebekah Byrd (Old Dominion University), and Mary S. Jackson (East Carolina University).

CONCLUSION

This book is one of many McWhirter family projects that always seem to begin quite innocently around the breakfast bar but often takes us far from home as they unfold. Such kitchen conversations led us to spend an intensive and exhilarating year in Turkey and another in Australia, both years as a Fulbright family. These discussions have also led us to pursue other international experiences along the way, most recently helping develop a center for family enrichment in Peñalolen, Santiago, Chile, one of the poorest communities of that great city, where we conducted training workshops in Spanish on family communication, parent training, couples conflict resolution/mediation, and strategies for working with young people, families, and groups for 15 years. This book has not taken us nearly so far geographically, but it has been a richly rewarding process.

At-Risk Children and Youth: The Ecology of Problems

Part 1 consists of two chapters. In Chapter 1 we discuss and define the term *at risk*, provide an overview of the book, describe a metaphor, and present an ecological model for unifying various concerns for children and adolescents who are at risk. In Chapter 2 we provide an overview of environmental and societal issues that impact young people and families. We also present two family case studies in Chapters 1 and 2 (and another two in Chapters 3 and 4 of Part 2). These case studies are used throughout the book to illustrate specific problems and issues.

CHAPTER

An Introduction to At-Risk Issues

Rather than the hasty tinkering of the mechanic, the nurturing of life requires the patience of the gardener. The fast technological rush of society leads us to be mechanics. We must preserve the long patience of the gardener.

The well-being of our society depends on our ability to prepare well-adjusted, responsible, well-educated young people to step forward as the older generation passes. A nation's continuing stability and strength depend on the ability to ensure that youth are prepared to fill the courtrooms, boardrooms, classrooms, and industries of tomorrow. Young people will only be prepared to meet the demands of the future if schools, families, and communities are involved: Schools and school districts must provide optimal learning and social environments that are academically demanding, positive, and nurturing for all children; families must provide children and adolescents with security, affection, and discipline; and communities must support access to quality child care, education, health care, living wages, and opportunities for young people to work not only for their own welfare but also for the welfare of others.

CHAPTER OUTLINE

In this chapter we highlight the problems that threaten children and youth and that put young people at risk. We present data to illustrate the severity of problems and personalize these data by describing one family. We then provide an overview of the entire at-risk arena, using the metaphor of a tree as an organizational device. The tree with all its parts—the soil (environment); the roots (family, peer, and school issues); the trunk (high-risk versus low-risk attitudes and behaviors); the branches (specific at-risk categories); and the foliage, fruit, and flowers (individual young people)—together with the gardener (counselors, social workers, psychologist, and other human service professionals) who provides pruning (intervention) and nurturing (prevention) is a conceptual metaphor for understanding the complex interrelationships of risk and protective factors related to the problems that youth face. Finally, we review the ecological model as a conceptual framework for understanding environmental forces and their effect on young people's development.

THE SCOPE OF THE PROBLEMS: AN OVERVIEW OF THE ECOLOGY OF AT-RISK YOUTH

The improvements in the lives of children in the United States in the late 1990s and very early 2000s, by and large, have not been sustained in many areas (Annie E. Casey Foundation, 2015; Centers for Disease Control and Prevention [CDC], 2015; Federal Interagency Forum on Child and Family Statistics, 2015; Kann et al., 2014; National Gang Center, 2013). The scope of the problem continues to be enormous; so many children are at risk for psychosocial difficulties that it is reasonable to say that society itself is at risk. The data presented here are discussed in detail in later chapters, but for now they provide a reminder of the problems that confront young people in the United States and elsewhere. Professionals who work with young people already know the pervasiveness of these problems.

Facts of an At-Risk Society

- In 2013, over 16 million U.S. children lived in poverty, a large increase of children in poverty since 2000. From just under 20% in 2008, 22% of children under the age of 18 lived in poverty; 10% of children lived in extreme poverty, defined as a two-adult, two-child family with an annual income of $11,812 or less.
- In 2012, 22% of children lived in households classified as "food insecure" by the USDA.
- African American, Latino, and Native American children are disproportionately poor. Poverty rates for White children and for Asian and Pacific Islander children are 14%, compared to 39% for Black, 33% for Latino, and 37% for Native American Indian children.
- In 2013, one in three children (23 million) in the United States lived in families in which no parent had full-time, year-round employment. On any given day, over 375,000 American children and youth were living away from their families in foster care, generally prompted by neglect or abuse.
- In 2013, 9% of teenagers between the ages of 16 and 19 were not in school, enrolled in school, or working; African American, American Indian, and Latino teens were considerably more likely to be in this situation than were Asian and White young people.
- Rates of obesity among high school students have quadrupled, increasing from 5% to nearly 21% between 1980 and 2012. Obese children and adolescents are at higher risk for prediabetes, bone and joint problems, and sleep apnea, as well as social and psychological problems. More serious risks include adult obesity, type 2 diabetes, heart disease, stroke, several types of cancer, and osteoarthritis.
- Only 15.7% of high school students reported eating vegetables three or more times per day in the past week (an increase from 13.2% in 2007) and 6.6% reported eating *no* vegetables in the past week. Nearly 14% of teens reported not eating breakfast for the past week and only 38% ate breakfast every day. Over 11% reported drinking three or more non-diet sodas every day.
- Relative to 2009, high school students were more likely to report spending 3 or more hours per day playing video or computer games (25% versus 41%) and less likely to attend a physical education class (56% versus 48%) than in 2013.
- Violent youth crime occurs most often between 3 p.m. and 6 p.m. when most children are at home alone; a child's chance of being a victim of crime triples after school.
- Adolescents with severe conduct problems are over four times more likely to be arrested in early adulthood, and over three times more likely to have a conviction.
- Young people who have been victimized are twice as likely to be unemployed and 65% more likely to be receiving welfare.

- In 2007, 23% of students reported gangs were present in their schools. This decreased to 20% in 2009 and 18% in 2011, with higher prevalence in urban (23%) areas than suburban (16%) or rural (12%) areas.
- In 2011–2012, 10% and 9% of elementary and secondary teachers, respectively, reported that they were threatened with injury by students, and 8% and 3% of elementary and secondary teachers, respectively, reported being physically attacked by a student.
- In 2013, nearly 18% of 9th- to 12th-grade students carried a weapon (e.g., a gun, knife, or club) during the previous 30 days and 5.2% carried a weapon on school property.
- About 7% of students were threatened or injured with a weapon on school property and 8% of students were in a physical fight on school property during the previous 12 months.
- In 2013, over 7% of students reported not going to school on at least one of the past 30 days due to feeling unsafe at school or between home and school. A multistate CDC survey found these numbers to be considerably higher for gay, lesbian, and bisexual teens, with 11% to 30% staying home at least 1 day in the past 30 days.
- Nearly 15% of all high school students reported being electronically bullied; nearly 20% reported being bullied on school property, in the prior 12 months.
- In 2007, nearly 6,000 young people were murdered—an average of 16 each day. In 2010, the CDC announced a 30-year low in youth homicide with 4,828 youth ages 10 and 24 years old murdered in 2010. The rate per 100,000 was 12.7 for males and 28.8 for Black youth. Among homicide victims, 80% were killed with a firearm.
- Over one in five (22%) of students were offered, sold, or given an illegal drug on school property during the previous 12 months.
- While 46% of public high school students report gangs or gang members at their schools, only 2% of private high school students report the presence of gangs or gang members. Gang activity has increased since a low point in 2001, with the most gang activity occurring in larger urban areas.
- Gang involvement remains a powerful predictor of ongoing and future violence.
- According to the CDC, just over 10.3% of dating high school teens had been hit, slammed into something, or injured with an object or weapon on purpose by someone they were going out with one or more times during the prior 12 months, with girls (13%) more likely to experience dating violence than boys (7.4%).
- Among the 73.9% of students nationwide who dated or went out with someone during the 12 months before the survey, 10.4% of students had been kissed, touched, or physically forced to have sexual intercourse when they did not want to by someone they were dating or going out with one or more times during the 12 months before the survey (i.e.,

sexual dating violence), with higher sexual dating violence among females (14.4%) than males (6.2%).

- Sexual dating violence occurred more frequently among White (14.6%) and Hispanic (16.0%) females than among Black female (8.8%) high school students.
- Teen pregnancy rates are at a record low, dropping 18% between 2007 and 2010, and another 6% between 2011 and 2012. The pregnancy rate for Black and Latino teens remains more than double that of White teens, accounting for 57% of 2012 U.S. teen births.
- In 2013, 47% of high school students had had sexual intercourse, 15% had had four or more sex partners, and over 40% of sexually active students did not use a condom during their last sexual intercourse.
- Over 22% of sexually active high school students used alcohol or drugs prior to having sex, and nearly 14% did not use any method to prevent pregnancy.
- According to 2013 data from the CDC, young people aged 15 to 24 years acquired half of all new STD diagnoses, and one in four sexually active adolescent females have an STD. Among young women aged 16 to 24 participating in the National Job Training Program, 11.7% had chlamydia. A sexually active teen who does not use contraception has a 90% chance of pregnancy.
- Each year, there are 19 million new sexually transmitted diseases (STDs), and almost half of them are among youth. Of new human immunodeficiency virus (HIV) infections diagnoses in 2010, one quarter were among youth; 57% of these were among Black youth, and 20% among both Latino and White youth, respectively.
- The United States continues to have much higher rates of teen pregnancy and teen STDs than Canada or Western Europe.
- Between 1999 and 2013, heavy drinking and recent illicit drug use among youth declined. However, in 2013, 22% of high school seniors reported heavy drinking and 26% reported illicit drug use in the past 2 weeks. The 2013 percentages of high school students reporting they had ever used the following substances *decreased* since 1999 for inhalants (8.9%), PCP (7.1%), cocaine (5.5%), methamphetamines (3.2%), and ecstasy (6.6%) and stayed the same for heroin (2.2%). Reported current marijuana use decreased from a high in 1999 of 26.7% to 23.4% in 2013. Substance abuse continues to be a problem.
- In 2013, 17% of high school students reported seriously considering suicide in the prior 12 months, over 13% reported having made a plan, and 8% reported that they had attempted suicide. Suicide continues to be the third leading cause of death among youth ages 10 to 24. Youth victimization by peers (bullying, physical violence, dating violence) is a significant predictor of suicide attempts.
- Child and teen mortality has improved by 43% between 1990 and 2011, and these gains include all racial/ethnic groups. Gains are attributed to

medical advances and improvements in the use of safety features such as bike helmets, car seats, and seat belts.

• Finally, federal budgets demonstrate limited priorities and investments in prevention. Bush's last U.S. federal budget included $70.4 billion for the Departments of Health and Human Services, Education, Housing and Urban Development, and Justice—dollars allocated for education, training, employment, and social services combined. The same budget included $660.6 billion for the Department of Defense and for the Global War on Terror.

• Interestingly, the financial cost of the Iraq and Afghanistan Wars are appropriations and not part of the defense budget at all. Of course, that would make the contrast even greater. President Obama faced a severe economic downturn at the beginning of his administration, which also constrained allocations to departments influencing risk reduction in the United States. The budget enacted in 2014 included $208 billion for the Departments of Health and Human Services, Education, Housing and Urban Development, and Justice combined, relative to $496 billion for the Department of Defense, $39.9 billion for Homeland Security, and an additional $85.2 billion for Defense via other funds (Office of Management and Budget, 2015).

This gloomy catalog of the problems American children and adolescents face reflects millions of personal stories, some of which are reported under dramatic headlines about abandoned infants, battered and sexually abused children, suicides, and drug overdoses. The catalog also reflects millions of less "newsworthy" stories of troubled, depressed, and anxious young people: children who suffer at home and at school; young people afraid, bored, or angry; adolescents bewildered by family conflict, divorce, or absentee parents; and young people afraid of violence while at home and at school.

The Use of the Term *At Risk*: Definition Problems

During the past two decades the term *at risk* has appeared frequently in the literature on education, psychology, medicine, social work, and economics as well as in the legislation of various states and in federal government reports. Its origins are obscure, and its use in various contexts indicates a lack of consensus regarding its meaning. Psychologists, social workers, and counselors use the term to denote individuals who suffer emotional and adjustment problems. Educators use it sometimes to refer to young people who are at risk of dropping out of the educational system, sometimes to refer to youth who are not learning skills to succeed after graduation, and sometimes to refer to children whose current educational mastery makes their future school career uncertain. Medical workers use the term to refer to individuals with health problems. Economists and the business community label at risk those workers who do not have the requisite literacy and numeracy skills to obtain employment or to succeed at their jobs.

We use a definition of at risk in the context of working with children and adolescents that we believe attends to the most salient aspects of risk across these professional concerns:

> At risk denotes a set of presumed cause–effect dynamics that place an individual child or adolescent in danger of future negative outcomes. At risk designates a situation that is not necessarily current (although we sometimes use the term in that sense too) but that can be anticipated in the absence of intervention.

For example, young people who use tobacco are at risk for alcohol use; young people who use alcohol are at risk for illicit drug use. Children and adolescents who use illicit drugs are at risk for drug abuse. Thus, a specific behavior, attitude, or deficiency provides an initial marker of later problem behavior. Conduct disorders, aggression, and low achievement in elementary school become markers that predict later delinquent and antisocial behavior in adolescence. This is why the term *at risk* does not necessarily designate a situation that is current, but rather one that can be anticipated in the absence of intervention.

Perhaps even more important, being at risk must be viewed less as a discrete, unitary diagnostic category than as a series of steps along a continuum. Figure 1.1 illustrates this continuum from minimal and remote risk to personal behavior that anticipates imminent risk and finally precipitates the activities associated with being engaged in one or more types of risky behavior. The following definitions outline some of the descriptive characteristics that correspond to different levels of risk along this continuum. Although not all characteristics in each category are always predictive of outcomes, in general these clusters of risk and protective factors help determine each child's potential level of risk.

Minimal Risk

Young people who are subjected to few psychosocial stressors, who attend good and well-funded schools, who have loving, caring relationships, and whose families are of higher socioeconomic status are generally at minimal risk for future trouble. Because of the complex ecology of stressors that young people face, we do not use the term *no risk*. Young people in all circumstances may have to cope with a death, family discord, incapacity, or unpredictable family factors such as bankruptcy, divorce, or loss of home. Such stressors can appear at any time regardless of existing protective factors. Depending on the young person's age, developmental level, and personal characteristics, the environmental resources available, and a host of other factors, the consequences may or may not be negative in the long term. Further, neither favorable demographics nor "good" families and schools provide invulnerability. Affluent adolescents may reject positive adult values and norms. Neither money nor social status guarantees meaning and purpose in life. Finally, some "perfect" families harbor secrets—alcoholism, incest, depression—that stem from and perpetuate dysfunction.

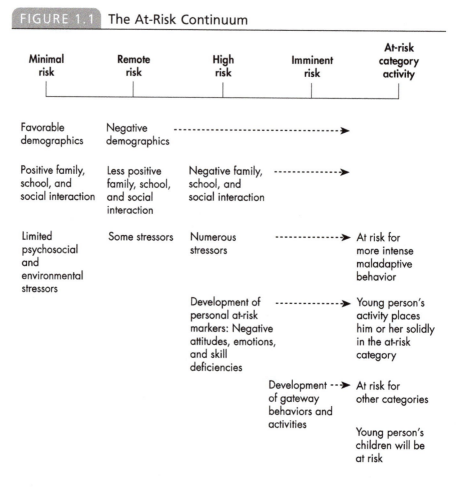

FIGURE 1.1 The At-Risk Continuum

In addition, there is mounting research evidence of studies of the adolescent brain that suggest that young people are still developing their capacities to "think like an adult." Two areas that are especially notable are the ability to understand another person's perspective and an increase in risk-taking behavior. Both of these place young people in at least "minimal risk."

Remote Risk

The point on the continuum at which risk, although still remote, seems increasingly possible is reached when markers of future problems appear. The demographic characteristics of low socioeconomic status, poor economic opportunity, poor access to good education, and membership in an ethnic minority group are associated with greater dropout rates, teen pregnancy, vulnerability, participation in violence, and/or other problems. Clearly risk factors do not emerge due to a person being a person of color, but membership in an ethnic minority group often suggests experiences of oppression, economic marginalization, and racism that negatively influence children and adolescents. That is, children of color who are poor are overrepresented in the at-risk behavioral categories. Of course, most poor African American, Latino, and Native American young people survive such difficulties and function well. Thus, even though these background factors are important, they do not determine risk for an individual child.

It is important to note that risk factors are also multiplicative. A young person who is from an impoverished, dysfunctional family and who attends a poor school in an economically marginalized neighborhood is potentially farther along the at-risk continuum than children who do not experience these conditions, especially if there are additional major psychosocial stressors. This is particularly the case when the individual child demonstrates personal characteristics that place him or her at even greater risk.

High Risk

Although dysfunctional families, poor schools, negative social interactions, and numerous psychosocial stressors nudge a young person toward higher levels of risk, the final push is supplied by the person's own negative attitudes, emotions, and behaviors. Characteristics that suggest a child is at "high risk" include aggression and conduct problems, impulsivity, anxiety, affective problems such as depression or bipolar disorder, and hopelessness, as well as deficits in social skills and coping behaviors. Of course, these characteristics both emerge from and enhance the negativity of the environment around the child; the causal pathway is dynamic. These personal markers signal the internalization of problems and set the stage for participation in gateway behaviors.

Imminent Risk

Individual high-risk characteristics often find expression in participation in gateway behaviors. Gateway behaviors are mildly or moderately distressing activities, frequently self-destructive, which often progress to increasingly deviant behaviors. A child's aggression toward other children and adults, for example, is a gateway to juvenile delinquency. Cigarette use is a gateway to alcohol and marijuana use, which can be a gateway to use of harder drugs. Although progression through each gate is neither certain nor predictable (for example, some evidence suggests that early use of marijuana among girls is actually a precursor or gateway to chronic cigarette smoking in adulthood and not the other way around), evidence linking gateway behaviors with more serious activities is so strong that such behaviors must be recognized as placing young people at imminent risk.

At-Risk Category Activity

The final step in the continuum is reached when the young person participates in those activities that define the at-risk categories. Here we confront the conceptual problem with the term *at risk*. Although the literature in this area continues to refer to young people at this level as "at risk," they have passed beyond risk because they are already engaged in the problems that define the category. Of course, activity in any at-risk category can both escalate as well as generalize to other categories. The young person who uses drugs can begin to abuse them and become addicted. The youthful delinquent can go on to commit violent crimes as a later teen and adult. Category activity by the adolescent can lead to lifelong involvement in self- and other-destructive behavior. Generalization means that individuals who participate in one category activity are at risk for engaging in others. The teen who drops out of school, for example, is at great risk for drug dependence and delinquency. Consequently, we continue to apply the term *at risk* to behaviors and characteristics along the entire continuum, using the appropriate points along the way to anchor our discussion.

Assess the Context of Problems, Such as Poverty and Racism

The use of the term *at risk* has some potential problems although some objections are resolved by viewing risk as a continuum that denotes future possibilities. Nevertheless, there is the possibility that the term emphasizes a deficit model by locating problems and pathology in the victim. The use of the term in the media, in casual conversations, and even by human service workers hints that risk is inherent in individual children and families. As will become abundantly clear (see especially Chapter 2), we place the blame for child poverty rates, which have ranged from 15% to 23% for the past four decades, firmly in the public domain. Adequate parental leaves, affordable child care, more accessible housing, increased employment opportunities, living wages, full funding of Women, Infants, and Children (WIC) and Head Start initiatives, universal preschool, and accessible health care will go a long way toward reducing risk. Equally problematic is the fact that children labeled at risk frequently are children of color from low socioeconomic environments. Rearing children and adolescents in the context of economic disparities, political marginalization, and a cultural and social milieu steeped in racism provide the soil that nurtures risk.

Chapters 1, 2, 3, and 4 each contain a case study describing a particular family to illustrate the social context and family dynamics related to the data presented here. We use these case descriptions to help clarify educational and counseling intervention strategies as well. The first family we present is the Andrews family.

AT-RISK PROBLEMS AND ISSUES

Cyber Technology

In the last few decades, there has been a virtual explosion in electronic media, computer, and mobile phone technologies. This explosion has impacted families, neighborhoods, schools, and society in diverse ways. It has also had a major impact on young people, which is likely to continue into the future. Ironically, this impact is for good and ill, both a blessing and a curse. In

CASE STUDY • The Andrews Family

The Andrews family consists of Jack, Alicia, and two children from Alicia's previous marriage. All are European American or "White." Mr. and Mrs. Andrews have been married for 8 years, and this marriage is the second for both. They live in a modest and rundown house in a working-class neighborhood of a major city.

Jack Andrews is a 46-year-old semiskilled laborer who was once employed as a technician in an electronics plant. About 5 years ago the plant was computerized, and the new technology reduced the labor force by 40%. Jack lost his job and has held a series of short-term, part-time jobs since that time. He currently has a part-time position pumping gas at a local service station. Thus, the family income, which was never very high, fell drastically. Jack is an angry, hostile man with limited insight and a blustering, aggressive style in his interactions with his family.

Jack was an only child. He alludes to a stormy relationship with his own father, who apparently was quite strict and harsh. Jack is especially critical of his mother, with whom he had a very poor relationship. When he was 13, his mother had a "nervous breakdown," and he lived with his aunt for about a year because, as he said, "My mother didn't want me." He graduated from high school and served approximately 10 years in the army. He married during this time but divorced a few months later. He maintains no contact with his first wife. He met Alicia about 9 years ago, and after a brief courtship they married.

Alicia is the third of four children. She lived with her parents until they divorced when she was 6. Her mother could not support the children, so Alicia spent the next 2 years with her grandparents. She then moved in with her father and his new wife. Alicia dropped out of school after the ninth grade and never finished high school.

Alicia went to work in a factory and married John Steiner at age 18. This marriage was difficult and stormy, beginning with Alicia's almost immediate pregnancy with Allie. John, who had probably been sexually and physically abused as a child, had dropped out of school, was a heavy drinker as a young man, and continued to indulge in periodic drinking binges. The drinking escalated after Paul was born. John physically abused the children and Alicia.

When Alicia discovered that he was also sexually abusing Allie, the tensions in the family reached the breaking point, and she divorced him. Alicia retained the house as part of their divorce settlement. John was convicted of sexual abuse and served a prison sentence, and neither Alicia nor the children have had any contact with him since the trial. Alicia believes or hopes that Allie has "gotten over" the sexual abuse and forgotten it. Neither one ever brings it up or acknowledges that it happened.

After divorcing John, Alicia worked as a waitress in a coffee shop until she married Jack. She is now 34 years old and works the lunch shift (11–2) at the same coffee shop. Alicia appears shy, unassertive, and somewhat depressed. She seems to be worried about the family interactions and often attempts to mediate family disputes and conflicts.

Mr. and Mrs. Andrews describe their marriage as an average one. They are somewhat hesitant to talk about their marital conflicts, but Jack has expressed his dissatisfaction with Alicia's complaints about his "laziness." Alicia says he is unwilling to do housework and neglects home maintenance, and she voices frustration about his limited income. They believe themselves to be fairly strict parents, and Alicia sometimes fears they are too strict.

Allie Andrews, 16, is in her second year of high school. She is an attractive girl of average ability. About 3 years ago Allie went through what her mother refers to as a "sudden transformation," changing from an awkward girl into a physically mature young woman. At the age of 14, she expressed a desire to date. Her interest in boys was reciprocated, and she seemed to be popular among the older boys in high school. Her parents reluctantly gave in but firmly stipulated the time she was to be home, the places she could go, the boys she could go out with, and so forth. During this time, her relationship with her parents became increasingly conflicted. Recently she has begun to violate her curfew and hang out with a "bad crowd." When she is grounded, she sometimes sneaks out to join her friends. Her school grades have been dropping, although she continues to pass all her courses. She became a cheerleader this year. Allie is currently dating several different boys, including an African American classmate. She has been expressly forbidden to date African Americans, so she meets him away from home.

Allie is sullen around her stepfather. She believes that Jack blames her for most of the tension in the family, and she shows her hurt by constantly defying him. Days go by without a word between them. Their mutual dislike is a consistent part of their interactions. Jack uses the same harsh, authoritarian child-rearing style that he resented in his own father. He is the unquestioned decision maker and controls the children primarily through shouting, threatening to throw them out of the house, and grounding. Alicia is worried about Allie, blames herself for the sexual abuse that occurred, and wants Allie to be "happy" and have a "normal family." Alicia absorbs conflict between the other family members, attempting to mediate and keep everyone calm. Over the past 2 years, Allie's parents, in particular her stepfather,

CASE STUDY • The Andrews Family *(Continued)*

have become increasingly suspicious and fearful. They suspect that Allie may be sexually active and fear she is not responsible enough to prevent pregnancy. They also suspect that her friends are drug users and fear that she will become addicted. Several times a week these issues erupt into loud arguments between Allie and Jack, or between Alicia and Jack. In the end, Allie, faced with her parents' lack of faith in her, feels hurt and misjudged. She responds with defiance, which invokes even more anger, and Jack tightens the restrictions. Lately she has threatened to run away if Jack doesn't let her choose her own friends, set her own timetable, and quit suspecting her of being a sexually promiscuous drug user. The most recent confrontation occurred when Jack discovered Allie's dating relationship with her African American friend. This discovery has provoked a family crisis. Jack has threatened to "disown" Allie if she does not break off the relationship. Allie is sulking and threatening to run away. Alicia is frustrated and depressed about the antagonism between the two people to whom she feels most closely connected. Allie feels deeply hurt and sees running away as a means to hurt back. Her stepfather, in his own way, feels deeply hurt that his once compliant stepdaughter is now so

rejecting of his authority and protection. He expresses a strong dislike of his stepdaughter and is quite angry about her behavior.

Paul Andrews, 12, is a short, stocky eighth grader with an air of bravado. Underneath the bravado, however, he appears to be a very depressed and angry child. His parents' main concerns are Paul's dislike of school and his aggressive behavior, although Jack often tries to convince Alicia that Paul's behavior is "how boys are." Paul says he feels very sad at times for no reason. His aggressive behavior is a problem in the classroom, and he is suspected of stealing other children's lunch money. His behavior at home is no better. Two months ago he "accidentally" set fire to one of Alicia's dresses. He shows an intense interest in bloodshed, accidents, fires, and violent crimes. Between the incidents of aggression he seems overly controlled, and unless he gets help now, he may become increasingly violent or self-destructive as a teenager. He is also reaching the stage of development at which questions of personal and sexual identity are assuming some urgency for him. He seeks acceptance while at the same time rejecting pressures to conform. His relationship with both parents fluctuates from lukewarm to cold and back again several times a week.

---

earlier editions of this book, we made reference to the apparent influence of media on conduct disorders, youth violence, and school shootings. The influence of violent television, movies, and music continue to be present, and are increasingly accessible due to new and rapidly evolving technologies.

While they have many benefits and conveniences, computer and mobile phone technologies have had a downside as well, with increasing reports of "cyber abuse" among young people. Cyber abuse includes a wide range of dangerous, negative activity that includes pornography, child pornography, sexual solicitation, stalking, bullying, and online harassment. Adolescent drug dealers use cell phones and other technology devices to negotiate and confirm illegal drug sales. Social network sites too often elicit oversharing and provide access to private data that provides young—and not so young—perpetrators information that puts young people in jeopardy. Sexting and other forms of electronic communication have serious ramifications for both the sender and the recipient.

Media attention tends to concentrate on the more dramatic, sensational, and dangerous aspects of cyber technology. Nevertheless, such technologies have many extremely positive and beneficial components that have the potential of reducing risk factors and increasing protective ones among young people. We will discuss many of these in more detail in the chapters that follow. Some examples include computer-based reading programs that help students develop and strengthen skills for successful reading and learning; the O*NET

OnLine, a freely available website that contains a comprehensive array of career exploration options, extensive educational and occupational databases, and solid resources for counseling research and practice; the Khan Academy, another free site with the mission of providing a solid education to anyone, includes over 1,600 videos posted on YouTube covering topics from basic arithmetic to advanced calculus to biology to chemistry (we discuss the Khan Academy later in Chapters 4 and 6 as a useful resource in itself and as an adjunct to the flipped classroom); and information on the use of cyber technology to delivery prevention and intervention programs online.

Vulnerable and Underserved

We know that the physical and mental health needs of many children and adolescents in the United States in general are underserved (e.g., Garbarino, 1998), but some children are treated even less equitably than others. Four groups of youth are particularly vulnerable and underserved. Children and adolescents of color usually do not receive culturally sensitive, relevant, and appropriate interventions and are more likely to be educationally and economically marginalized. Students of color also often must manage issues of acculturation, ethnic identity, and second language challenges along with all the other challenges of adolescence. The second group is gay, lesbian, bisexual, and transgender youth, who are particularly vulnerable to misunderstanding and bias, and then subsequent marginalization and violence. The third group is youth with disabilities. Youth with disabilities are vulnerable to experiencing marginalization, misdiagnosis, and to having their rights and needs underserved in our schools and communities. Finally, immigrant youth face significant academic, social, and linguistic barriers that jeopardize their school success and subsequent trajectories.

Children and Adolescents of Color

Demographics in the United States are changing rapidly. By the year 2020 people of color will make up the majority in the United States. Asian and Latino populations are the fastest growing in the United States, and ethnic minority children were projected to be 51% of public school children and 48% of public high school students in fall of 2014 (Brown, 2015). As many as 32 different Asian American ethnic groups are now identified in the United States. Soon, Filipino Americans will be the largest Asian group, followed by Chinese, Korean, Vietnamese, Indian, and Japanese. Nearly 60% of Asians in the United States are foreign born, often recently immigrated. Similarly, the U.S. Latino population is highly diverse, growing, and includes many children and adolescents for whom English is a second language. There are significant disparities in mental health care and mental health care access for ethnic minority group members in the United States (Holden et al., 2014). Our society is rich in cultural diversity, and this diversity is growing in virtually every region of the country.

The historical and contemporary marginalization of people of color continues an ethos of racism and inequitable opportunity in the United States.

There are continuing, pervasive disparities in health care and mental health care access, education, as well as disproportional representation of youth of color in the juvenile justice system (Fong, Dettlaff, James, & Rodriquez, 2015). This has contributed to youth being at risk. Many of the conditions that predict negative outcomes for youth, such as poor living conditions, poor-quality and underfunded schools, and lack of economic opportunity, are correlated with being a child of color. To respond to this, existing prevention, early intervention, and treatment efforts need to be adapted to be valid for families and young people of color, and new intervention strategies need to be developed that take into consideration issues such as ethnicity, acculturation, religious norms, and the cultural and linguistic needs of specific communities in order to be effective.

Lesbian, Gay, Bisexual, and Transgender Youth

Although considerably fewer in number than children and adolescents of color, youth who are lesbian, gay, bisexual, or transgender (LGBT) are particularly vulnerable. LGBT youth are ignored in most professional writing about children and adolescents. The increased social visibility of homosexuality, bisexuality, and transgenderism has not been paralleled by greater attention to LGBT youth in the research or treatment literature. This lack of attention is particularly problematic because young people who are "sexual minorities" are disproportionately at risk for negative outcomes.

Most LGBT youth experience stress associated with their sexual orientation or sexual identity. They commonly experience disapproval, anger, and rejection from family and peers when they disclose same-sex attraction or when they express sexual identity in a manner inconsistent with their biological being. Denial of same-sex attraction directly interferes with self-exploration and the ability to form healthy relationships critical to identity formation. Misperceptions, prejudices, social pressures, and sometimes hate-motivated behaviors from others hinder the complicated process of recognizing and accepting a transgender identity. "Living a lie" or "passing" can lead to incredible isolation and loneliness.

LGBT young people are particularly vulnerable to alcohol and drug abuse, depression, and a higher rate of suicide than heterosexual youth as they seek to cope with the isolation and rejection they experience (Grossman & D'Augelli, 2007; Hatzenbuehler, 2011). LGBT youth and adults are frequent targets of hate crimes and suffer disproportionate criminal justice punishments (Himmelstein & Brückner, 2011). Educators do little to support them or are prohibited from doing so; LGBT youth often leave school before graduation, often being expelled (Himmelstein & Brückner, 2011). LGBT youth may face chilling and sometimes hostile school climates, which adversely affects their grades, emotional well-being, attendance, and pursuit of postsecondary education (Chisler, Smischney, & Villarruel, 2014; Kosciw, Greytak, Bartkiewicz, Boesen, & Palmer, 2011). Although LGBT young people receive services from multiple systems, service providers frequently have not addressed their special needs (Bertram, Crowley, & Massey, 2010; Kitts, 2010; Liu & Mustanski, 2012).

Youth with Disabilities

Youth and young adults with disabilities face health and other disparities, with higher likelihood of childhood obesity, victimization by violence, unintended injury, unemployment, underemployment, and lower levels of academic attainment relative to young people without disabilities (Krahn, Walker, & Correa-De-Araujo, 2015). Young people with physical, intellectual, emotional, and developmental disabilities are more vulnerable to bullying victimization. One analysis of a national longitudinal data set of elementary and middle school children found that students with disabilities were one to one-and-a-half times more likely to be bullied than students without disabilities, with the highest rates of victimization across all school levels for students with emotional disturbance (Blake, Lund, Zhou, Kwok, & Benz, 2012). Adolescents with learning disabilities are disproportionately represented in the "school-to-prison" pipeline (Mallett, 2014).

Immigrant Youth

Immigrant children and children of immigrants are the fastest-growing segment of the U.S. population. The U.S. foreign-born population is expected to constitute 18.8% of the population by 2060 (Brown, 2015). They face numerous challenges including poverty, language barriers, and the demands of adaptation to a new culture. Oh and Cooc (2011) suggest replacing the terms assimilation, adaptation, and acculturation with the term *transculturation* to better capture the complex, dynamic, and bidirectional process navigated by immigrant youth. Newcomer immigrant youth face complex challenges that increase their risk of school failure and lower their educational achievement; risk factors include segregated schools, high-poverty schools, single-parent households, separation from mother or father, low English proficiency, and low academic engagement (Suárez-Orozco et al., 2010).

The At-Risk Tree: A Metaphor

One of the difficulties in trying to understand at-risk problems is fragmentation of knowledge. Decades ago, the cultural anthropologist Becker (1981) observed that information accumulated in the last half of the 20th century has become "strewn all over the place, spoken in a thousand competitive voices. Its insignificant fragments are magnified out of all proportion while its major and world historical insights lie around begging for attention" (p. 14). Becker's statement continues to be true today. Information about at-risk children and youth is indeed "strewn all over the place." What is cause, and what is effect? How does one situation relate to another? What is the relationship between various aspects of a child's problem? What are the underlying connections? Efforts to solve the problem often involve dividing intertwined and complex issues into manageable parts. School dropout, drug and alcohol abuse, risky sexual activity, juvenile delinquency, youth suicide, and other problems are usually studied separately. Programs to reduce school failure, for instance, are isolated from efforts to prevent juvenile delinquency. Strategies to ameliorate teen pregnancy may ignore problems of substance abuse.

In the real world, however, these problems interact, reinforce one another, and cluster together. Not only do problems cluster but so do the young people who have these problems; they tend to live in the same neighborhoods and to be exposed to many of the same influences. In addition, the problems reverberate within the community and frequently are intergenerational. Researchers and policy makers chip away at what remains unknown but often do not identify what is known. We attempt to determine the impact of narrowly defined interventions and strategies and ignore the powerful effects of a broad combination of strategies.

Much of the empirical research on at-risk youth has been correlational in nature. That two factors correlate does not mean that one is the cause of the other. Parent depression is correlated with child antisocial behavior, but the direction of causality is unclear. Perhaps the child's negative behavior contributes to the parent's depression, or perhaps the underlying depression of the parent results in inconsistent parenting that contributes to the child's predelinquent behavior; more likely, both affect each other and are influenced by other factors as well. Circular or dynamic causality is operating—each problem and risk factor contributes to the other—so our knowledge of families like the Andrews illustrates that those at-risk families and at-risk young people influence each other in many ways. In recent years, longitudinal research that tracks individual and contextual factors over time has assisted in answering some questions about "which came first," but overall it demonstrates the multidirectional influencing nature of community, school, family, and individual characteristics. In later chapters we identify the relationships between variables that contribute to risk and resilience and identify causal factors when it is possible to do so. Here we present a metaphor and an important ecological model to help structure the connections related to risk.

In this book we lay out a systematic framework to guide the reader toward an understanding of the scope and range of problems for which children and adolescents are at risk. The following metaphor is a conceptual and organizing framework. This metaphor integrates the various at-risk categories and intervention strategies and allows us to pull together information and knowledge that is "strewn all over" and focus on specific at-risk categories in a unifying framework.

We turn to horticulture for our metaphor. The analogy of a tree permits us to consider a range of issues that relate to at-risk children and youth. The soil of this tree is the individual's societal environment. The roots of family, school, and peer group connect the tree to the soil (i.e., the environment) to provide support and nurturance. The trunk serves as the conduit of developing attitudes and behaviors of each individual child that lead to specific at-risk categories, which are the branches of the tree (see Figure 1.2).

FIGURE 1.2   The At-Risk Tree

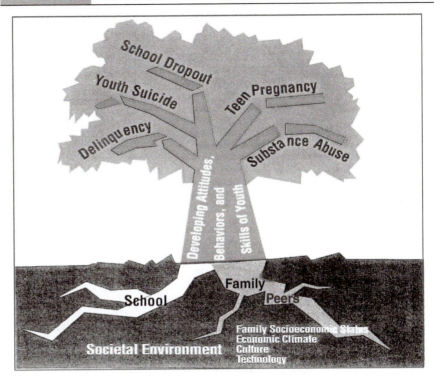

The Soil

Various aspects of the environment, such as socioeconomic status, political realities, economic climate, and cultural factors, must be considered if we are to fully understand at-risk issues. The environment/soil also includes dramatic social changes. Urbanization, the feminization of poverty, the threat of violence and terrorism, and changes in technology are parts of the soil that nourish or fail to nourish at-risk children and adolescents. The "soil" of the Andrews family is the low socioeconomic status of the family, the limited access to mental health providers, the change of job status because of technological advances, and the racist attitudes expressed by Mr. Andrews; all indicate environmental pressures that mold this family and affect its members. This environment, this soil, potentially contributes to at-risk products—Allie and Paul.

The Roots

The at-risk tree has three primary roots: family, school, and peer groups. Just as the roots provide a network that anchors and nourishes life, so the family and the schools transmit culture and along with the peer group mediate young people's development. These primary social environments provide the structures through which the children assimilate their experiences.

The family is the taproot. In the Andrews family the conflict, friction, and vastly differing parenting styles contribute to Allie and Paul's dysfunctions. Jack's anger and hostility and Alicia's depression and placating behavior limit the nurturance and support that the children receive. Multiproblem families such as the Andrews present a challenge because of the variety of issues they experience.

The school is another major root. Society looks to schools for help: to provide a secure environment for children, to foster appropriate learning experiences, and to attend to learning and emotional problems. Increasingly, schools teach essential life skills that families and churches taught in the past. The role of the school in the future of the Andrews children is critical. How the school handles Allie's and Paul's situations will have both short- and long-term effects on their attitudes toward school, learning, and life.

Peers are another major root. Although the peer group as a major influence usually starts later in a child's life—generally by preadolescence—it can be enormously powerful in transmitting culture, values, and norms that influence behavior. Failing to consider peers in understanding and intervening with young people has a high probability of leading to interventions that are ineffective.

The Trunk

The trunk is the support and brace for the tree's branches and the conduit from the soil and roots up to the leaves, blossoms, and fruit. The trunk of the at-risk tree consists of specific behaviors, attitudes, and skills of individual children and adolescents. It represents young people's strengths and weaknesses, talents and disabilities, and personal risk and protective factors. These behaviors, attitudes, and skills are also conduits to the branches, because specific characteristics such as inability to delay gratification, depression, anxiety, low self-esteem, and impulsivity lead directly to at-risk behaviors. In the Andrews family, Allie's oppositional and self-defeating behavior and Paul's anxiety, depression, and aggressiveness lead to specific at-risk behaviors.

The Branches

The branches of the tree represent children and youths' adaptation to society. Many young people are doing well. They are healthy and sound; they are integrated into society and preserve their cultural heritage; they will be productive as workers, as parents, as members of the community. Young people with this healthy adaptation contrast strikingly with those who isolate themselves through destructive attitudes and behaviors from their cultural heritage, from their families, and from society, ending up in specific at-risk categories.

The five branches that produce the most damaged fruit—that is, the five specific at-risk categories that seem most central to our concerns—are school dropout, substance abuse, risky sexual behaviors, delinquency and violence, and suicide. Both Allie and Paul are approaching school dropout. Further,

Allie is at risk for teen pregnancy and drug abuse; Paul is at risk for delinquency and violence, and possibly for suicide.

Foliage, Fruit, and Flowers

The fruits of the tree are individual and specific young people, such as Allie and Paul Andrews. Some young people are whole and healthy; others are bruised and damaged; still others drop from the tree. Although broken branches sometimes produce good fruit and healthy branches sometimes produce damaged fruit, the fact remains that certain branches—the maladaptive behaviors in the five major at-risk categories—increase the probability that at-risk behavior will escalate. Perhaps even more tragic is the probability that at-risk young people will themselves be the seeds of future generations of at-risk trees.

The Gardener

Like all growing trees, the at-risk tree needs pruning, staking and trimming, sun, water, and nurturing. Hence, this book is for the "gardeners"—the counselors and teachers, psychologists and social workers, youth recreation and juvenile justice personnel, and other human service workers—who nurture the Pauls and Allies of our society. Nurturing must be directed sometimes toward the soil, sometimes toward the roots, sometimes toward the trunk or branches; but always the intent is to improve the fruit of the tree. Throughout this text we recommend useful strategies for working with youth that will help you to be a better gardener.

The tree metaphor is a useful but informal framework for understanding and working with at-risk youth. A more extensive and elegant theory is the ecological model of human development.

THE ECOLOGICAL MODEL

The ecological model articulated by Bronfenbrenner (1989, 1994) posits that individual human development occurs within interconnected and embedded ecological systems. The model provides a good foundation to understand the impact of culture, politics, relationships, social interactions, and life experiences on the attitudes, behaviors, and competences of children, adolescents, and their families. The model has been used to frame culturally relevant counseling and assessment with adolescents, multicultural personality development, and multicultural counseling processes in general. (Mobley, 2001; Ponterotto, 2010; Yeh & Kwon, 2010). In addition, the model has been applied to the Columbine High School shootings (Hong, Cho, Allen-Meares, & Espelage, 2011) and to the role of the school counselor (McMahon, Mason, Daluga-Guenther, & Ruiz, 2014).

Bronfenbrenner's (1994) ecological model rests on the thesis that humans develop and grow within the context of a number of reciprocal systems. These systems are the micro-, meso-, exo-, macro-, and chronosystem, with the individual at the center (see Figure 1.3). The model can be visualized as

FIGURE 1.3   Bronfenbrenner's Ecological Model

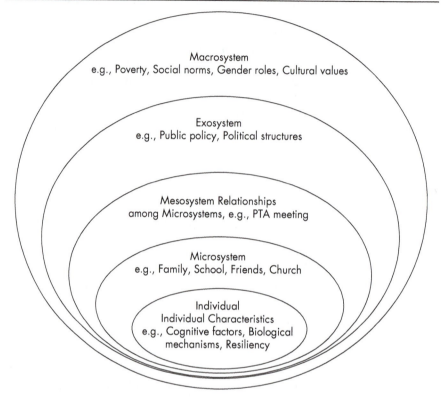

including concentric circles capturing various levels or degrees of interactive and reciprocal experiences.

At the inner core we can place individuals with their genetic predispositions, evolutionary and biological components, unique personality characteristics, and the ongoing process of behavioral, cognitive, and affective experiences. Much of this book focuses on the individual child or adolescent and the risk and protective factors that create more or less difficulty for the youth and for society. Obviously, Allie and Paul Andrews, described in Case Study, and Carrie, in Box 1.1, represent the "Individual" in the ecological model.

The microsystem consists of the people with whom an individual comes into direct contact and refers to immediate, proximal interactions in the person's world. For example, the family is the child's primary microsystem. In the case of Allie Andrews, her mother Alicia, her brother Paul, and her stepfather Jack consist of a major microsystem for her. Another microsystem is the child's school—including teachers, staff, and classmates. For Carrie, her move from a small rural school to a wealthy, high-pressured, suburban one constituted an unfortunate shift from one microsystem to another. Clearly, each microsystem influences the child's development.

Box 1.1	Carrie

Several years ago one of us was asked to work with a distressed, disturbed young girl named Carrie. At the personal level, 13-year-old Carrie was very self-defeating, angry, and fearful. She was obstinate and oppositional—a problem to her family, her school, and herself. Her behaviors and attitudes were more easily understood, however, when we analyzed the shifting ecology of her life.

Prior to moving into her father's household, Carrie had been raised in a rural community by a mother who worked part time as a waitress and received a modest monthly check for child support from Carrie's father. The mother was periodically anxious and depressed, and during these episodes Carrie assumed responsibility for herself, for her mother, and for their modest house. The living arrangements provided by both her mother and her other relatives (many of whom lived close by) could best be described as permissive and unstructured, with a high tolerance for a wide range of behaviors.

Carrie attended the small local school and had known most of her classmates for years. In spite of a documented learning disability, Carrie's schoolwork was generally adequate, perhaps because the school's expectations were not high.

When her mother went through a particularly acute depressive episode, it was determined that Carrie should go to live with her father. Overnight she went from her small home in a peaceful, rural community to her father's huge house in a wealthy suburban neighborhood. Carrie's father, a self-made millionaire, had become successful as the owner and chief executive officer of a chain of drugstores. He worked long hours, drove himself very hard, and had high expectations of everyone with whom he had contact—suppliers, tradespeople, employees, school personnel, and family members.

Carrie suddenly found herself in a household that included her father, his woman friend (who was shortly to become Carrie's stepmother), a housekeeper, and a live-in nanny hired to support, tutor, discipline, and provide companionship for her.

Carrie enrolled in the local public school. Because of the high socioeconomic status of the neighborhood, the academic expectations and achievement norms were high. Her classmates were the sons and daughters of university professors, physicians, and business executives. Most students in this school went on to graduate from college, a large proportion of them from the most prestigious universities in the country.

Carrie might be considered a very "lucky" girl, rescued from a mother unable to care for her and provided with "every advantage" and a clear pathway to success. Her "ungrateful" behavior might be confusing from a perspective that narrowly focuses on socioeconomics. Considered from an ecological perspective, the deviant and pathological behaviors that brought Carrie to our attention are a logical and obvious reaction to her environmental change. Carrie was like a fern that is transplanted from a shaded corner of the garden into the hot, glaring sun. The fern cannot thrive; neither could Carrie.

The mesosystem refers to the embedded interconnections between the different microsystems, as well as the impact of the reciprocal interactions. Mesosystemic influences include the relationships between a child's parent and teacher and between the child's school and the surrounding neighborhood. The ecological model assumes that an individual's development is enhanced if the mesosystem—that is, the relationships among the microsystems—is consistent and positive (Bronfenbrenner, 1979, 1989). Carrie, for example, moved into a new home in a new neighborhood and a new school. The connections between her new school and her father and tutor are consistent and positive. Unfortunately, the move itself and the influence of previous microsystems such as her former school and the low expectations of teachers continue to affect Carrie, disrupting the mesosystem and making her a poor fit for her new living situation.

The exosystem consists of the interconnections between one or more settings that are more distal and do not directly involve the individual. Public policy is an excellent example of an exosystemic factor. Public policy decisions regarding educational standards, teachers' wages, health care, or school lunch programs have an impact on an individual and his or her microsystems (e.g., family, community, and school), but the individual may not be present in the environments in which public policy decisions are made (e.g., city council or state legislative sessions). Again, Carrie provides an example: The school boards in both districts set policy and provide resources for the education of district children. The impact for most young people in Carrie's new school is very positive, promoting high academic achievement and eventual enrollment in good universities. The exosystem influence on Carrie has an indirect impact that is not so positive.

The macrosystem represents a social blueprint: cultural values, belief systems, societal structure, gender-role socialization, race relations, and national and international resources (Bronfenbrenner, 1994). The macrosystem includes social and cultural worldviews that influence and give framework to the preceding systems. Research that examines the relationship between children's aggressive behavior and exposure to violent television is an example of studying macrosystemic influences on the individual. Jack Andrews's rejection of Allie's dating an African American classmate partly is a result of the influence of the macrosystem.

The final concept in the ecological model is the chronosystem. The chronosystem is the sociohistorical circumstances and transitions that occur during the course of the individual's life over time. It is the interconnection and interaction among individuals and the different levels of their environments. Jack and Alicia Andrews' life experience growing up, their earlier marriages and subsequent divorces, and the sexual and physical abuse of Allie's birth father, and his subsequent sexual and physical abuse of Allie—are all examples of the chronosystem.

Three explicit assumptions are inherent in the ecological model (Bronfenbrenner, 1989, 1994): The individual and the environment are interacting and constantly changing; the individual is an active participant; and changes in one ecological system influence changes in others and vice versa. Each assumption is discussed in turn.

First, the ecological model assumes that individuals and their environment are continually interacting and exerting mutual influence and, as a result, are constantly changing. The environment influences individual development and, in turn, the individual changes the environment. There is a bidirectionality to person–environment interactions. Jack Andrews's harsh parenting contributes to Allie's defiance and negativity, which in turn leads to even more insensitive discipline.

Second, the ecological model assumes that individuals are active participants in their own circumstances and development. That is, the individual is not merely acted upon by the environment but also exerts influence on the environment. Allie Andrews is actively (and passively) making choices that will significantly influence her present and future.

Third, the ecological model assumes bidirectionality, or the idea that changes in one ecological system may influence changes in systems that are both more proximal and more distal to the individual. For example, public policy decisions affect human development in more immediate or proximal ecological systems. In the same way, individuals, families, and communities in the microsystem and mesosystem influence public policy decisions (exosystem), for example, via letters to government representatives, participation in public forums, or protesting. This example illustrates bidirectionality and how factors in every system within the ecology can effect change in another system. Throughout this chapter, as in the entire book, many examples of risk and protective factors are located within these embedded and interacting systems.

HELPER INTERFACE

Counselors, human service workers, psychologists, teachers, and other helping professionals employed in both public and private settings can incorporate in their practice the prevention and intervention strategies we present. The best interventions are ones that are fully integrated into other services provided by agencies and schools. To implement strategies presented in this text on a day-to-day basis effectively requires a high degree of professional collaboration with coworkers and administrators, as well as a sensible understanding of the specific agency culture and school climate (Massey, Armstrong, Boroughs, Henson, & McCash, 2005).

A teacher can use many of our suggestions with an individual child, a group of children, or an entire classroom. These interventions, with appropriate modifications, lend themselves to both individual and group work. They are most effective when concerned adults work together. When teachers, human service professionals, and parents collaborate in their efforts, putting the needs of an individual child or one classroom uppermost on their agenda, they increase the effectiveness of their work. Teachers, especially those in special education and in alternative schools, can incorporate in their classrooms aspects of the suggested programs that we present here. Human service workers in juvenile justice settings, in recreation centers, in day treatment programs, and elsewhere can utilize the strategies we present as well. There is an increasing need for adults to serve as mentors, to become positive role models for young people, and to provide practical information about communication and human relationships. Comprehensive life-skills training programs (discussed in Chapter 12) effectively meet this need. Teachers, perhaps in collaboration with counselors and trained parents, are in an excellent position to implement these programs. They need training, time, encouragement, and support in their efforts to do so.

The school or agency counselor or psychologist and other human service professionals are in a good position to consult with teachers about implementing life-skills programs. Counselors have the training to apply cognitive-behavioral approaches, small-group processes, and other developmental, cognitive-behavioral strategies to improve young people's social skills. The developmental and educational role of the counselor is crystallized in the concept of the counselor as a psychoeducator. Psychoeducational group interventions are applicable in a wide variety of problem areas and are especially useful for at-risk children and youth and their parents.

CONCLUSION

This chapter highlights the severity of the problems U.S. children and adolescents confront as they progress toward adulthood. The concept of an at-risk continuum is useful to teachers, counselors, psychologists, and human service professionals interested in identifying the nature and level of risk faced by the young people with whom they work. The ecological model provides a way of analyzing how varied dimensions of the environment support or decrease the likelihood of risk and risk-category behaviors. The Andrews family, whom we will meet again in later chapters, demonstrates the complex interrelationships of family, school, and social problems that young people frequently experience. This book is intended to clarify the problems of youth at risk and to set the stage to help you provide multifaceted, comprehensive, practical, and ethical prevention practices and treatment interventions.

Environmental/Societal Factors that Contribute to Risk

CHAPTER

2

If we put the same effort, worry, and bother into improving our society

That we do in propping up some fool over his people, Or in selling cat food,

Or in putting pink stripes into toothpaste,

We would have solved many of our social problems long ago.

If we put the same effort, worry, and bother into societal reform

That we do in building bombs,

Or in advertising cigarettes and booze,

Or in putting white back into collars,

We would have solved most of our social problems long ago.

CHAPTER OUTLINE

Heraclitus is credited with saying that "nothing is permanent except change." Perhaps at no time in history has this insight been clearer than it is today. Children and youth face the challenge of growing into mature, responsible, healthy adults amidst a maelstrom of economic, political, social, and technological change. Technological advances are occurring more rapidly than ever before in history. The resulting highly specialized systems of production and service, communication and transportation, add complexity to lives that are already complex. The World Wide Web, for example, connects our world, makes it smaller, and provides information for the "knowledge age," yet at the same time it provides children and adolescents with rapid exposure to information and social influences that are difficult to monitor and sometimes risky. The continuing mobility of the population, the declining influence of the extended family, the movement of industries from the North to the South,

outsourcing of jobs to overseas locations, extensive automation in the workplace, and the Great Recession and its aftermath make our society one in which very little seems certain. In addition, terrorist attacks, international instability, two major wars, and the nuclear capabilities of an increasing number of nations add to people's sense of threat, change, and insecurity, especially in this "post–September 11th" era. Our economy is globally interdependent, and the social and economic forces that affect other parts of the world also affect our young people.

In this chapter we review some environmental influences that place young people at risk for poor outcomes. We discuss current economic trends, with particular attention to poverty, and describe the complex interactions between socioeconomic status, ethnicity, the recession, national trends, and public policy. Later, we provide several policy proposals and suggestions designed to ameliorate the negative effects of poor economic trends.

THE ECONOMY

A major exosystemic influence in children's lives is the economy. One economic phenomenon that greatly affects at-risk young people is poverty, which particularly threatens the well-being in several "types" of families: working poor families, vulnerable and underserved families, young single-mother families, and homeless families. Of course, families often have multiple group identities, such as a working poor, young single mother forced to leave her home for the street. The intersection of multiple identities can lead to more or less risk to the children depending upon the particular combination of family status and identity (Garcia & McDowell, 2010). We note here that, as yet, the vast majority of national or regional data sources on indicators of employment, poverty, and other aspects of the economy do not allow for describing the status of same-sex parents and their children. Now that same-sex marriage is legal throughout the United States, future data on "married" and "single" parents is more likely to allow accurate portrayal of the status of families headed by same-sex couples.

Poverty

Poverty is the risk factor most closely associated with family stress, and it is highly correlated with school failure, delinquency, and other problems, even though some children from poor economic backgrounds fare well. Child poverty rates have ranged from 15% to 23% over the past four decades (Ratcliffe & McKernan, 2010). Among all children under age 18 in the United States, 44% live in low-income families and 22% live in poverty (Jiang, Ekono, & Skinner, 2015). This is an increase from 2007, when 39% of children lived in low-income families and 18% in poverty. Children of color are more likely to be raised in low-income families, with 63% and 65% of all Latina/o and Black children, 55% of children of immigrant parents, and 31% of White children living in low-income households, respectively. Similarly, while 13% of White children live in poor families, 32% and 39% of Latina/o and Black children are poor. Poverty rates vary by family structure as well, with 12% of children living with married parents and 42% of children living with a single parent living in poverty (Jiang et al., 2015).

Rural child poverty rates (26.2%) remain higher than those of most urban children (21.6%) with the exception of some inner cities (U.S. Department of Agriculture, 2015). Child poverty rates in some of the largest cities of the United States, for example, are 67% (Detroit), 57% (Cleveland), 49% (Miami), 48% (Milwaukee), 43% (Fresno), and 43% (Atlanta) (Annie E. Casey Foundation, 2012). Although the number of children living below the poverty line dropped to a 20-year low of 11.6 million in the year 2000, many low-income families remained poor. Promising news of fewer children living in poverty was an artifact of the late 1990s boom in employment. A decade later that boom and that promise were over. Since the Great Recession and economic downturn in 2008, the United States has faced sharp rises in childhood poverty that resemble the increases in child poverty that accompanied recessions in the early 1980s and early 1990s.

Working Poor Families

Work reduces poverty. Seventy-two percent of children who have no employed parents live in poverty, compared with 48% of children who have at least one parent who works part time (Jiang et al., 2015). However, work alone is not sufficient to avoid poverty: Half of all low-income families and 30% of all poor children live in households in which at least one parent is employed full-time, year-round (Jiang et al., 2015). In some families, both parents must work simply to keep the family out of poverty, and young families are increasingly stressed to provide for their families. People of color are especially affected. In 2013, one third of all working families were of low-income, and racial/ethnic minority parents headed nearly half of those families (Povich, Roberts, & Mather, 2014–2015).

What employment indices fail to reflect is that during a recession, workers who lose their jobs and then are reemployed typically earn less than they had earlier. For adults aged 25 to 34 who lost their jobs and were reemployed during the Great Recession, their new median monthly income was 11% lower. For adults aged 50 to 61, their new median monthly income was 23% lower (Johnson & Butrica, 2012).

The economic problems faced by working poor families influence a child's development through parental attitude, disposition, and behavior. For example, parents with financial stress are more tense, irritable, and explosive and become increasingly arbitrary and punitive in child discipline (Ponnet, 2014; Schliebner & Peregoy, 1994). Further, adult mental health is affected by economic problems. Unemployment is associated with a decrease in mental health (Paul & Moser, 2009; Wanberg, 2012). Lower socioeconomic status, neighborhood disadvantage, and poverty-related stress are associated with higher anxiety and depression in both parents and children (Santiago, Wadsworth, & Stump, 2011). Financial stress increases parental depression and decreases positive parenting behaviors, contributing to externalizing behavior in adolescents in low-income families (Ponnet, 2014).

Unemployed parents are more dissatisfied with themselves and with their lives, feel victimized, and are more anxious, depressed, and hostile than employed parents. The incidence of neurosis, psychosis, and suicide is higher among unemployed parents; they have more sleeping, eating, and somatic problems and consume more alcohol (Smith, 2002). These changes in attitude, disposition, and behaviors strain family relationships and harm children's development (Solantaus, Leinonen, & Punamaki, 2004).

In Chapter 1 we introduced the Andrews family. Recall that technological changes resulted in the loss of Jack's electronic technician job, and that he now works part time in a service station. This change in his employment status and income level undoubtedly contributes to his feelings of anger, hostility, and powerlessness. These feelings in turn cause him to be less nurturing with his stepchildren and more punitive and arbitrary toward them. Allie Andrews's sullenness and defiance reflect her heightened stress and lowered self-esteem. Her sexual acting out (if indeed her parents' suspicions are correct) can be at least partially explained as a reaction to her stepfather's harsh and abrasive behavior. Similarly, Paul's depression, anger, and low self-esteem are exacerbated by his stepfather's situation. Paul's destructive behavior and poor school adjustment are among the consequences.

In short, the Andrews family illustrates several characteristics common to working poor families in the United States. Because of the parents' part-time work schedules, they do not require child-care services, which is an advantage many do not have. However, the low minimum wage and Alicia's and Jack's limited employment opportunities are important factors in the short- and long-term problems faced by this family.

Vulnerable and Underserved Families

In the Great Recession of 2008 to 2010, poverty rose among all racial and ethnic groups, but stood at higher levels for Black and Latina/o individuals. The number of Latina/os in poverty increased from 23% to nearly 31%; for Blacks it increased from over 24% to over 35%. In contrast, the number of poor Whites increased from 8.6% to 11% (FIFCFS, 2010). Besides being hardest hit by the recession, families of color have experienced a disproportionate share of income and job loss, due to structural changes in the economy (Economic Policy Institute, 2015a). This has been exacerbated by the shift of manufacturing employment from the cities to outlying areas, including outsourcing to China and other countries. Because families of color reside in inner-city areas in disproportionate numbers and are overrepresented in the blue-collar jobs that have been disappearing, they are much more likely to be affected by displacement and unemployment. The problem is likely to be prolonged as the United States continues its transformation from a goods-producing economy to a service economy.

Workers of color continue to be overrepresented in less-skilled jobs. For example, Latina/os make up only 16% of all employed workers, but account for 50% of the workers in agriculture, 45% of the workers in grounds maintenance, and 44% of maids and housekeeping cleaners (Bureau of Labor Statistics, 2014). African Americans constitute 11% of employed workers but are 36% of the workforce in nursing, psychiatric, and home health aides, 27% of bus drivers, and 27% of security guards and gaming surveillance officers. The highest paying major occupational category is management, professional, and related occupations, in which 50% of workers are Asian, 39% are White, 29% Black, and 20% Latina/o. This pattern is also seen in the armed forces. For example, in 2014 among the Army's main combat units of infantry, armor, and artillery, there was not a single Black officer in leadership, and only one Black officer scheduled for 2015 (Brook, 2014).

Poverty rates among African Americans and Latino Americans are consistently higher than among European Americans. Female-headed households with children are particularly vulnerable to poverty, especially among ethnic minority groups. In 2012, African American, Hispanic, and American Indian children were significantly more likely to live without securely employed parents than were their Asian and non-Hispanic White counterparts (Annie E. Casey Foundation, 2014). Black children are far more likely to be *persistently* poor than White children. Being poor at birth is a marker for future poverty status. Over 30% of White children and nearly 70% of Black children who are poor at birth will spend at least half their childhoods living in poverty (Ratcliffe & McKernan, 2010).

The Great Recession of 2008 to 2010 has seen workers—regardless of race or ethnicity, age, gender—experience a steep increase in long-term unemployment. Half of the unemployed—the largest proportion since World War II—have been looking for work for 6 months or more. Black and Latino workers as well as older workers and blue-collar workers experience the largest median duration of unemployment. Of course, long-term unemployment impacts family's finances, emotional well-being, and career prospects much more deeply than short-term unemployment (Morin & Kochhar, 2010). Native Americans are less affected by national economic cycles, including unemployment, because they *consistently* suffer high unemployment, especially on most reservations.

Young Single-Mother Families

If Allie Andrews continues her presumed sexual behavior, becomes pregnant (which is probable), and marries the father (which is less probable), and if she keeps her baby (also probable), she is setting herself up for a limited income and a heavy workload. She will assume most of the care for her baby and most of the household chores. She will probably also work outside the home, if she can find a job and if she can find child care for her baby. Young female-headed families are at the greatest risk of poverty and its co-occurring problems. Over 39% of single-parent, female-headed families were living in poverty in 2013, compared with about 20% of single-parent, male-headed families and 7.6% of married couples with children (Economic Policy Institute, 2015a). Children in families headed by a single parent are also more likely to be poor (Wu & Eamon, 2011). Indeed, the economic plight of families headed by single mothers has worsened in the last 25 years (Economic Policy Institute, 2015a).

Adolescent childbearing can have long-term negative effects on both the teenage mother and on the newborn (American Academy of Child and Pediatric Psychiatry, 2012). Babies born to teen mothers are at higher risk of being born preterm and with low birth weight. When young teens become pregnant and carry their babies to term, many do not receive prenatal care, placing their child at risk for future problems. Lack of prenatal care influences the child's future health, well-being, and learning ability; and the consequences are borne by our schools and health care systems. They are also far more likely to be born into families with limited economic and educational resources. All of these factors function as impediments to future success.

The U.S. teen birthrate has declined almost every year since 1991. Between 2012 and 2013, the teen birthrate dropped 10%, to 26.5 births for every 1,000 adolescent girls (Martin, Hamilton, & Ventura, 2015). Though it has dropped, this rate is higher than in most other developed countries. Teen birthrates remain higher for African American and Latina teens, at 39 and 41.7 births per 1,000, respectively (Martin et al., 2015).

In addition to affecting the family structure, a mother's marital status impacts the economic security of her children. Births to unmarried women rose sharply between 2002 and 2008. Since that time, among unmarried women under age 35, births have decreased, while for those older than 35, births have increased. Currently, about 4 in 10 U.S. births are to unmarried women (CDC, 2015). Among Latina and Black women, birthrates to unmarried women dropped 28% and 11% between 2007 and 2012, to 73 and 63 per 1,000, respectively. The risk of negative outcomes is higher among unmarried women, and includes low birthweight, premature birth, and infant mortality (CDC, 2015). Increasing numbers of young unmarried mothers are members of the workforce out of necessity, some because of the decline in real family income.

Homeless Families

Poverty, unemployment, low-paying jobs, and lack of affordable housing are primary causes of homelessness. The national rate of homelessness in the

United States decreased overall between 2005 and 2013, as did rates of homelessness for families and veterans (National Alliance to End Homelessness, 2014). These national rates mask changes in homelessness across different areas of the country. Thirty-one states reported decreases in homelessness while twenty states reported increases between 2012 and 2013. Another source, the U.S. Conference of Mayors (2014), reported that homelessness among families increased in survey cities by an average of 3%, with 22% of cities reporting no change in homeless families, 35% reporting a decrease, and 43% of survey cities reporting an increase in the number of homeless families. The number of families seeking shelter increased by about 3% across cities, and 73% of the cities had to turn away homeless families with children due to lack of beds. A particular concern is that school-age children and independent homeless youth represent one third of the homeless population.

The U.S. Conference of Mayors report also noted:

- Among those requesting emergency food assistance, 56% were persons in families and 38% were employed.
- About 27% of the demand for emergency food assistance went unmet in the past year. In the majority of cities, the emergency food providers had to reduce the amount and frequency of emergency food provision.
- Eighty-four percent of the cities expect the need for emergency food assistance to increase in the coming year, and forty-four percent expect a decrease in resources that support emergency food assistance.

Lack of affordable housing is the most commonly cited cause of homelessness. Families have to wait an average of 2 years for public housing assistance (National Center for Family Homelessness [NCFH], 2015). A report cited by the NCFH indicated that for every 100 very low-income families seeking rental housing, there are only 30 available, affordable units. One study of housing costs and minimum wage in every county in the United States concluded that a full-time, minimum-wage worker could not afford a one- or two-bedroom apartment anywhere in the United States (National Low Income Housing Coalition [NLIHC], 2013). This leads to the phenomenon of "doubling up" or temporarily sheltering homeless families with other families in single-family dwellings.

Homelessness creates many barriers to children's well-being and school success. In many cities, homeless families in emergency shelters have to spend their daytime hours outside of the shelter, and families often are forced to separate in order to obtain shelter. These conditions make studying, having a quiet place to complete homework, access to necessary school supplies, and obtaining parent assistance with school work very challenging. Homeless children also face problems with transportation to school, lack of official school records, immunization requirements, residency requirements, and providing birth certificates.

In the Andrews family we see the effects of the first two trends we have discussed: job and income loss leading to economic stagnation, and young families. Two other areas of concern are now illustrated via the Baker family: single motherhood and homelessness.

CASE STUDY • The Baker Family

Sally Baker is a 28-year-old African American woman. She is legally married to George, the father of her 9-year-old son, Tyrone, and her 7-year-old daughter, Daniella, although she has not lived with George for 5 years. A boyfriend whom she has not seen for over a year fathered her 3-year-old son, Jerome. During most of her 9 years of motherhood, Sally's primary means of support has been Aid to Families with Dependent Children (AFDC). For several months she and her children have been residing at the Andre House, a shelter for homeless families.

Sally was born in rural Alabama. She never knew her father. When Sally was 8, she and her mother moved to Dallas with her brother and sisters. Sally remembers that her mother was not working and that "she couldn't afford to keep me and couldn't afford to send me back." As their situation became increasingly strained, her mother's frustration spilled over into abuse. After several years of intermittent abuse, at age 14 Sally refused to take any more of it and left home. She lived for several weeks in a local park but was then arrested for curfew violation and possession of alcohol and sent to a detention facility for status offenders. From there she went to the first of several foster homes. She indicated that after being sexually abused in this foster home, she went back to living on the streets. This became the pattern of her life over the next few years. She lived on the streets for several weeks or months until the police picked her up again and sent her to a detention facility, which placed her in another foster home. Her siblings were also eventually placed in foster care, and they maintained sporadic contact. When she was 18, she met and married George Tucker. For the first several months, Sally's marriage to George provided companionship and a home base. However, these elements were short lived. After 4 years of conflict and frequent separations, George availed himself of a "poor people's divorce": He walked out and never returned, leaving Sally to parent their two small children alone.

In the year before their arrival at Andre House, the Baker family's lifestyle mirrored Sally's earlier life—a chronic pattern of lurching from crisis to crisis. Sally had been living on AFDC in a Housing Authority complex in a small city. Because the Housing Authority subsidized her unit, she was paying hundreds of dollars less than she would have had to pay for a private unit, but she had to contend with drug dealers, gang activity, and considerable neighborhood violence. When Tyrone started to wear the "colors" of one of the local gangs, Sally decided to move in with her sister-in-law in a neighboring town. The safety of this new living arrangement was offset by the crowded conditions; there were now two adults and seven children in a two-bedroom apartment. Sally was able to stay for 3 months and saved some money, but not enough to get a place of her own.

Sally and her children moved back to Dallas to live with her sister, who also had a two-bedroom apartment. The sister and her boyfriend slept in one bedroom, the sister's three children slept in the other, and Sally and her three children slept on the living-room floor. Again there were problems. Her sister's boyfriend used and sold crack cocaine. Sally contributed a share of the monthly rent, but a few months later both families were evicted because the boyfriend was not paying the rent.

Sally and her children moved in with a friend, but once again drugs were a problem—this time because friends of the friend were using her apartment to make their deals. The police frequently came to the house because of the drug activity and finally threatened to take Sally's children away from her unless she got them out of the house.

Bit by bit Sally had been saving money from her AFDC checks, but the $100 she had managed to put aside was still too little to pay the first and last months' rent on a place of her own plus a security deposit. In any case, the fruit of her prudence and foresight disappeared when the drug-dealing friends of the woman with whom she was staying robbed the apartment. Sally was beaten, her life was threatened, and even her children were threatened. The elderly couple living next door called the paramedics and they took her to a clinic. After all the threats to her life, she was too frightened to let anyone call the police. The counselor at the clinic found a shelter that had room for them and gave her money for the bus. And so the Baker family found themselves at Andre House.

Sally's children reflect the type of chaotic life she has led. Ty especially seems to have been negatively affected by his experiences. His behavior is highly impulsive. His attention shifts rapidly from one object or activity to the next. At school he is an "attention-starved" child. He must be first in line, the one to sit next to the teacher, the first to play with a new toy. At times he hurts other children and is destructive. Sometimes conflict with his mother erupts into aggressive outbursts and he lashes out at his 3-year-old brother.

Daniella, by contrast, has more self-regulation and relationship skills. She and Sally talk frequently, and Daniella is able to ask for what she wants and needs. Her calm, sweet disposition endears her to adults and apparently helps her with both of her brothers, even Tyrone. She is especially helpful in caring for Jerome. Even though this task is sometimes frustrating to her, she is quite responsible and affectionate with him.

Jerome is a shy, passive, sickly child who is fearful of strangers. He prefers to be left alone and makes few demands. He is apathetic and disinterested and when left alone mostly watches television. He seems indifferent to Tyrone's temper outbursts, even when they are directed at him. He tends to cling to Daniella, though, and follows her about closely.

Like poverty, homelessness is often explained at the individual, personal level. Sally Baker must be lazy or imprudent or unlucky. She didn't want to work. She should have put her savings in the bank. These simplistic arguments fail to account for the complex realities that have shaped her opportunities for decades. Homelessness, at the aggregate level, is caused by a lack of low-cost housing, which means many thousands of families will not have access to any housing. In these circumstances, poor people pay more for housing if they can afford to, or move in with friends or family members until they wear out their welcome, or become homeless. Basic arithmetic demonstrates that the Sally Bakers of this country have very limited choices.

Research on homeless families shows that they are disproportionately likely to be families of color, to be young, to be composed of parents who are more likely to have been abused as children and battered as adults, and to have limited social support networks. Women caring for children are exceptionally well represented among the nation's homelessness (Paquette & Bassuk, 2009). Life in shelters or on the streets for homeless children and adolescents is linked to depression, anxiety, behavioral disturbances, and an assortment of educational problems (Anooshian, 2005) and mental illness (Bassuk, Richard, & Tsertsvadze, 2015). Of course, children of homeless families perform poorly in school and have more erratic attendance records (Murphy & Tobin, 2011). Here again the Baker family exemplifies the problems of homelessness. Sally's early physical and sexual abuse, chaotic and stressful living arrangements, and her lack of purpose and hope place Sally and her children at risk.

Poverty's Contributions to At-Risk Youth

The conclusion that family poverty and children's cognitive development are linked is nothing new; several decades of research have established this beyond doubt. Impoverished children also are far more likely to experience poor and inadequate education and health care.

Among the detrimental effects, neuroscientists have found that children from very poor families with economic deprivation and low social status experience unhealthy levels of stress. This impairs language development and memory, reducing the likelihood that the child will ever escape poverty (Krugman, 2008). In addition, the "social toxicity" of poverty increases the risk of exposure to violence, racism, unstable care arrangements, and community insecurity. Some of the by-products of these "toxins" are academic failure, learning disabilities, and child abuse. Children growing up in poor households are more prone to delayed intellectual development. Even by the young age of 3, over a quarter of children living in persistent poverty show signs of cognitive delay (Kiernan & Mensah, 2009). The social and economic environment in which children grow is a significant exosystemic predictor of their overall well-being. Almost all available data support the conclusion that children's education, later employment, future earnings, and health greatly depend on their families' socioeconomic status (SES; Duncan, Kalil, & Ziol-Guest, 2015). Membership in the lowest SES group—that is, families in extreme poverty—is especially problematic. Children and adolescents from impoverished families have an increased risk of health problems (Bauman, Silver, & Stein, 2006; Reynolds, Rolnick, & Temple, 2015). Children who come from low SES families usually grow up with highly stressed immediate environments or microsystems (Evans & Cassels, 2014). They live in disorganized and impoverished neighborhoods, and their microsystems often involve socially isolated and very young mothers, minimal support from other family members, and a lack of healthy male role models. Low SES status is associated with mental health problems, impaired parent–child relationships, and a high incidence of child abuse and neglect. Low SES is the strongest predictor of school dropout, teenage pregnancy, and juvenile delinquency. The cumulative stresses of being born and raised in poverty adversely affect mental health in emerging adulthood (Evans & Cassels, 2014). We will examine the relationship between SES and each at-risk category behavior more fully later in this book.

The Income Gap

The number of people below the poverty line has grown over the past two decades. For many reasons related to the changing economy as discussed above, most U.S. workers are finding it more and more difficult to meet their financial needs.

The gap between rich and poor has also grown (Economic Policy Institute, 2015b; OECD, 2010). Poor and middle-class people are losing ground to the wealthy. The income earned by the top .1% of Americans was less than 3% in 1970; it increased to more than 12% in 2007. Since 1913, the only time that this share was higher was in 1928—just before the stock market crash that led to the Great Depression (Hacker & Pierson, 2010).

The average family income in the middle and lower brackets has decreased while the income for the wealthiest families has increased. It was a terrible economic year in 2009 for most Americans; for some it was a very good year. On Wall Street, 38 firms earned a total of $140 billion. Goldman Sachs, for example, had its best year since 1869, with its employees making an average of $600,000 per person (Hacker & Pierson, 2010). This increasingly wide gap did not begin with the Great Recession. For instance, salaries for major executives jumped 571% between 1990 and 2000. Salaries for CEOs rose even in the year 2000, a year in which the S&P 500 suffered a 10% loss, and CEO salaries increased dramatically even in companies that experienced major layoffs. The explosion in CEO pay over the decade dwarfed the 37% growth in worker pay (Anderson, Cavanagh, Hartman, & Leonard-Wright, 2001). Stated another way, if the average annual pay for production workers had grown at the same rate since 1990 as it has for CEOs, the workers' 2000 annual earnings would have been $120,491 instead of $24,668. The top 20%, those making more than $100,000 each year, received nearly 50% of all income in the country. This compares with 3.4% made by the bottom 20% of workers. More recently, the top 1% of the wealthiest Americans control 40% of the wealth in the United States, and 95% of the gains in income after the

Great Recession have gone to the 1% (Stiglitz, 2011). The median net worth of U.S. households shows the racial nature of this inequality: $113,149 for Whites, $6,325 for Hispanics, $5,677 for Black households (Pew Research Center, 2011). Because much of the shifting redistribution of wealth upward is based on income-producing assets—bonds, trusts, and business equity—this trend will likely continue. This increasing gap between the rich and the poor contributes to an increase in at-risk youth in at least two ways: ennui from lack of purpose and social comparisons.

Ennui, Anomie, Affluenza, and Purpose

The economic conditions of a major portion of our population contribute greatly to increasing risk factors for children and adolescents. It would be a mistake, however, to conclude that only poverty creates risk. Many young people from affluent backgrounds are also at risk, with some affluent youth engaging in higher substance use than national samples (Luthar & Barkin, 2012). In a certain sense, some very well-off children are "poor little rich kids." They have extensive material "things"—often too many and too much—but may lack discipline, support, and connection. Affluent children typically spend a great deal of time on their own and often seek peer support and nurturance instead of parental and familial support (consider Carrie in Box 1.1). In fact, these young people give rise to a newly defined "malady": affluenza. Affluenza is a figurative illness resulting from too much material wealth. It exists among upper-middle class, white-collar families whose children show elevations in various maladjustment areas such as substance use, depression, and anxiety, indicating the urgent need for preventive interventions (Luthar & Barkin, 2012). Among other problems, children and youth with "affluenza" and without family presence and adult support experience a great deal of "ennui."

Ennui refers to an emotion of noninvolvement and boredom that comes from a lack of connectedness and a lack of life purpose. It is closely related to anomie or a personal state of isolation, alienation, social instability, and normlessness. Many young people—including those from affluent backgrounds—suffer from ennui or anomie, a lack of connectedness with others, themselves, and their own sense of future, which increases the possibility that they will be at risk for problems (Townsend & B. T. McWhirter, 2005). Ennui can occur in children from all types of families; it both causes and is affected by aimlessness, alienation, and lack of direction.

Too much affluence can contribute to other risk factors. In one study, students who were of a higher social and economic status demonstrated lower empathy than nonaffluent youth (Kraus, Côté, & Keltner, 2010). The researchers observed that people living in more challenging economic circumstances are more likely to have their lives affected by their environments (including other people). For less well-off young people, self-involvement is a luxury and their lives are enhanced because their emotional antennae and social sensitivity are more acute. Further, huge income inequality provides the underlying conditions for scorn, distain, and blame-the-victim attitudes on the part of the rich toward the poor (Fiske, 2010). Positive psychology research indicates that it is not material things that make life rich and fulfilling, but rather work and play, love and service to others (Chamberlin, 2010).

Social Comparisons

Many of us have heard people, especially those who went through the Great Depression, say: "We were poor. But we didn't know we were poor." This is often followed by the comment that everybody was in the same boat, which lessened the perception of being disadvantaged. Those days are long gone. Professional athletes who negotiate salaries of millions of dollars a year, movie stars who are paid enormous sums for just one movie, and TV shows such as "Rich Kids of Beverly Hills" provide a constant reminder for poor children and adolescents about just how much they do not have. Social comparison is inevitable, even as it divides, stresses, and depresses people.

In 2008, 53% of Americans identified themselves as middle class, but in 2014 this percentage dropped to 44%, while the proportion identifying themselves as lower or lower-middle class rose from 25% to 40% in that same time period (Kochhar & Morin, 2014). Young people have been the most adversely affected by the global recession and have experienced the fewest benefits in the "recovery" (OECD, 2015). When rising inequality is combined with daunting challenges, lack of hope that things will improve, and lack of purpose, conditions are created in which young people from disadvantaged backgrounds might more easily become disengaged at school and drop out, or justify the use of drugs, risky sex, delinquency, and violence.

POLICY PROPOSALS AND SUGGESTIONS

What can be done? In later chapters we try to provide some of the answers. Here we suggest several measures that may help to nurture the soil. These policy areas focus on child care, comprehensive preschool programs, before- and after-school community learning centers, empowerment, and community/neighborhood involvement. Each of these suggestions requires the collaborative efforts of families, schools, and communities.

Child Care

Child care requires the joint efforts of families, communities, and state and national government to provide healthy and beneficial choices for children and their parents. The number of children who are cared for by people other than their parents during work hours continues to rise. Access to adequate child care enables parents to work, and to work without undue stress and concern for the welfare of their children. When both parents work, some of the socioeconomic limitations of their children's environment are likely to be overcome. Lack of affordable child care is a major obstacle for mothers moving off of welfare.

Children in high-quality child care and early learning programs demonstrate better cognitive and noncognitive outcomes, particularly children from low-income families. While good day care provides benefits for the less poor, the largest and most cost-effective gains are realized with the poorest children (Dearing, McCartney, & Taylor, 2009). The better the quality of the early care, the more marked the benefits, although the best is not necessarily critical (Vandell et al., 2010). Apparently, "above average" quality child care seems to deliver benefits sufficiently well (Dearing et al., 2009). Less than 10% of U.S. child care is estimated to be of high quality, with 80% of "fair" quality. The quality of early child care predicts cognitive-academic performance even in adolescence, and this benefit applies both to well-off and to poorer families. The negative effects of low-quality child care are more pronounced among children from low-income families (Child Care Aware America, 2014).

Lack of "affordable" child care, defined by the U.S. Department of Health and Human Services as 10% of a family's income, is a nationwide problem. Center-based child care costs an average of 40% of the state median income for single mothers across the 50 states (Child Care Aware America, 2014). In 2013, the cost of 1 year of tuition and fees at a public 4-year college was *less than* the average annual cost for center-based infant care in 31 states, and *less than* the average annual cost for care of 4-year-olds in 20 states (Child Care Aware America, 2014). For families at poverty level, the average cost of center-based child care for an infant ranges from 28% to 85% of their annual income, depending on state of residence.

Fears and biases about the adverse effects of child care have resulted in the failure to develop constructive social policies that ensure affordable, accessible, quality child care to people of all economic means. There is nearly complete consensus among developmental psychologists and early childhood experts that child care per se does not constitute a risk factor in children's lives; rather, poor quality care and poor family environments can together produce poor developmental outcomes. Thus, research on the effects of child care must account for variations in the type of care provided (from in-house caretakers to centers that care for more than 100 children), for the family/home environment (from abusive to highly supportive), and for the qualifications and training of care providers (from minimal attention by untrained caretakers to programmatic enrichment by highly trained child-care professionals). Factors that contribute to quality of child care include the ratio of children to caregivers; the number of children cared for in the setting; the caring and responsiveness of caregivers; and the training, experience, and stability of caregivers. Unfortunately, many child-care workers cannot survive on the low income that the position provides, resulting in a high turnover rate for this occupation (Whitebook, Phillips, & Howes, 2014).

A national policy to shape and direct child-care services would help resolve this problem. A commitment from workplaces to reevaluate personnel policies that create difficulty for employees with families would also contribute to its solution. Currently, the social values that prevail in the United

States generally require families to adjust to the demands of the workplace rather than expecting workplaces to modify policies to meet the realistic demands of families. In schools, teachers, counselors, and parent support volunteers can help foster parent advocacy by informing them of procedures for reaching their legislators. In addition, teachers and counselors might devise ways to facilitate exchanges of information on child care and to link parents interested in sharing child-care arrangements. Currently, many communities have nonprofit organizations that serve as clearinghouses for child-care service information, but even these services may involve at least a nominal cost to families.

The lack of adequate child care is a persistent problem, particularly for the working poor. Parent employment options may be highly constrained due to inadequate child-care options. Often, mothers out of work due to child-care problems are poorly educated, with lower potential to earn a wage that might allow them to purchase the very child care they need. And because of daily hassles, these parents do not access available child-care subsidies (Johnson, Martin, & Brooks-Gunn, 2011). Thus they are stuck in a vicious cycle.

The federal government subsidizes some day care through the dependent-care tax credit, Child Care and Development Block Grant (CCDBG) programs, Temporary Assistance for Needy Families (TANF), Head Start, and Social Service Block Grant programs, but the majority of poor people do not benefit from these services. For example, only about one out of six eligible children receive assistance through CCDBG, and CCDBG funds have not increased since 2002 (Child Care Aware, 2014). Head Start and the block grant program that focus on social services are typically underfunded. This leaves the dependent-care tax credit as the major federal support for child care. A family may deduct a portion of annual child-care expenses from their federal income tax, but the very poor rarely owe enough income tax to qualify. Thus poor and single mothers whose children are at risk and who most need quality child care are least likely to receive any benefit from this policy. The child-care tax credit primarily benefits middle- and upper-income families. Securing safe and affordable child care remains a major obstacle for mothers moving off of welfare.

Comprehensive Preschool Programs

Another effort that requires collaboration on the part of communities, schools, and families is the provision of comprehensive preschool programs for children who are identified as at risk. Evidence suggests that overcoming deficits in skills needs to begin early, so preschool is extremely important. The following results have been documented as a result of participation in early childhood education: increased learning in language, math, and reading skills; emotional development; and health.

Though there is evidence that test score differences between children who did and did not receive preschool dissipate in later years, the long-term benefits of preschool include higher high school graduation rates, more years of education, and lower crime and teen pregnancy rates (Yoshikawa et al., 2013). Poor as well as middle-class children realize these benefits, with the greatest benefits seen among children living in or near poverty. Other research shows that interventions, including preschool programs: increased cognitive and emotional development, improved parent–child relationships, improved educational outcomes for children, increased economic self-sufficiency for parents and later for the child, decreased criminal activity, decreased child abuse and substance abuse, and increased maternal reproductive health (Karoly, Kilburn, & Cannon, 2005). There are major economic costs of childhood poverty and there are considerable benefits of intervening early. The logic is as follows: Children from poor families are more likely to struggle when they start school; the disadvantages persist as they progress through school, aggravated by lower achievement in most school subjects, especially reading; their limitations impact their prospects when they eventually enter the job market; the disadvantages follows them into adulthood.

Providing high-quality comprehensive preschool programs helps to break this damaging family cycle. Preparing children from low-income backgrounds for school helps narrow the success gap between them and their more advantaged peers.

Head Start, a nationwide, federally funded program for economically disadvantaged prekindergarten children, is an example of one comprehensive preschool program. Head Start programs vary from locale to locale, but each provides a classroom-based, multicultural learning experience for 4-year-olds. Through Head Start, children with little limited home stimulation and lack of exposure to the resources of the middle class are given a "head start" on kindergarten. They learn school-related vocabulary and norms in a relaxed, cognitively rich environment. Children are assessed for a variety of developmental problems and may be provided access to speech therapists, psychologists, and other professionals as the need arises. Head Start provides enrichment for the rest of the family as well. By actively participating in the daily events of the classroom and by receiving specific training in parenting, life skills, and health and employment issues, parents become engaged in an empowering process that extends beyond the 9 months of the school year (see Box 2.1).

Head Start programs have helped children from challenging economic backgrounds to persevere, graduate from high school, and eventually find employment, though the success of Head Start varies with the quality of its implementation. Some research has suggested that Head Start does not affect socioemotional skills, but Bierman et al. (2014) found that an enhanced Head Start curriculum was associated with higher learning engagement, reading achievement, and positive social behavior in kindergarten compared to Head Start participants who received the usual curriculum.

Preschool programs have had a positive impact on children's cognitive and social development. Another comprehensive preschool program, the High/Scope Perry Preschool Project began examining the lives of 123 low-income, 3- and 4-year-old African American children. Randomly divided into two groups, with one group receiving a high-quality preschool program and

Box 2.1	Mother Gets a Head Start

When her first child was 4, she shyly volunteered to help out in the classroom. Just for an hour. Over the weeks it became 2 and 3 hours and she even started looking children in the eyes. She was quiet, worked very hard, and seemed quite bright in a clandestine kind of way. When her next child turned 4 a year later, she was working on her GED. Her home, she told me, had been a smelly, dirty shack; her children were always barefoot and always hungry. When they weren't hungry, it was because she had given them change for candy bars and pop. "I weighed 250 pounds and I was still growing," she said, laughing. "I was disgusting even to me." And she had bruises and permanent nerve damage in her left hand, and a husband who got mean when he drank.

She had bruises on her arm the first time I met her, when her third child was enrolled, and a welt under her eye, and she had been a Head Start teacher's assistant for 3 months. She was bringing her youngest to work and taking home a paycheck for the first time since she got married at age 18. Her husband didn't much like it but he had a little more beer money now. He really got mean when she insisted on cooking carrots one night. For the first time, she pressed charges. One incredible year, 82 pounds, and a divorce later, she was considering a community college course, "so I can be a teacher someday." And several years after she left Head Start, I heard she had done it.

the other no program, the now-adult participants demonstrate the value of preschool. Although results from the initial program were modest in the early years, lasting effects, both in the original study and in additional randomized controlled trials, found improved adult outcomes on employment, income, and arrest records. With an initial investment of a little over $15,000 per student, preschool participants had committed fewer crimes, were more likely to have graduated from high school, earned higher salaries, and were more likely to hold onto jobs. In addition, both child-care assistance and comprehensive preschool programs have contributed to the effects of welfare-to-work programs (Dearing et al., 2009).

Stated in simple monetary terms, every dollar invested in early childhood education interventions is estimated to save two to seven dollars in later costs (Washington State Institute for Public Policy, 2014; Whitebook et al., 2014), making failure to invest in early childhood interventions a strikingly foolish choice. The combination of inadequate child care and pervasive deficits in adult skills contributes to the stagnation of the poor and leaves our children at risk. If Sally Baker had adequate child care for her children, a reasonable wage, and support to enhance her work-related skills, she and her children might emerge from their cycle of instability. Unfortunately, the safety net our society provides for Sally and others like her has huge holes and is badly in need of repair.

Before- and After-School Educational Centers

Some years ago, Zigler (the developmental psychologist most associated with Head Start) suggested that a given community owns its public school buildings by virtue of having invested one to two trillion dollars in these properties. Based on this premise, Zigler advocated keeping schools open from 7 a.m. to 6 p.m. and establishing child-care centers for 3- to 5-year-olds as well as before- and after-school care for 6- to 12-year-olds. The centers would provide developmentally appropriate recreation and enrichment activities in a safe and well-staffed setting. These school-based centers would also offer home visits to all parents of newborns and organize and coordinate family day care for infants from birth to 3 years. Early childhood educators trained to bridge the gap between home and school would administer the center.

The 21st Century Community Learning Centers implemented some of Zigler's ideas. Federal legislation provided federal grants that allowed schools to stay open before and after school hours, as well as on Saturdays and during summer. Most of the centers are organizational hybrids that include school-, city-, and community-based nonprofit organizations, each of which draws funding from a variety of sources. This decentralized arrangement leads each center to provide programs and services tailored to its unique combination of funders, constituencies, and youth (Moore, 2005).

Evaluations of the 21st century centers find few gains in academic outcomes (Public Agenda, 2005), and a more recent meta-analysis of after-school programs also did not find significant benefits with respect to school attendance or externalizing behavior outcomes (Kremer, Maynard, Polanin, Vaughn, & Sarteschi, 2014). However, students enrolled in such programs are more likely to be supervised by adults after school and report feeling safer. Middle school participants missed one less day of school per year and were more likely to say they expected to graduate from college (James-Burdumy et al., 2005). Policy makers tend to focus on the educational value of out-of-school programs. Interestingly, only 15% of parents and 12% of young people reported that academic achievement is the best reason to be involved in out-of-school, organized activities. Developing interests and hobbies and keeping young people engaged in positive activities and out of trouble were much more important outcomes according to parents and participants (Public Agenda, 2005). Unfortunately, limited academic achievement is often used as a basis for funding cuts or program elimination.

This is extremely unfortunate because pre- and after-schools centers provide a structure to enhance the educational experiences of young people. Feeling safe, having adult supervision when parents are working, missing less school, and believing that one will graduate from college are valuable qualities in themselves. There is also evidence that such programs serve a protective role in reducing delinquency (Mahatmya & Lohman, 2011). In addition, the structure provides enrichment, tutoring, and a focused educational framework that has great value in potentially confronting some of the educational problems that we face as a country. The structure also promotes the development of personal and social skills in children and adolescents (Durlak et al., 2015).

Empowerment

Facilitating youth empowerment is another way in which adults can help at-risk children and adolescents to address limiting environmental conditions. Empowerment helps people actively confront their environment rather than passively accept their conditions as unalterable (Cattaneo & Chapman, 2010; E. H. McWhirter, 1997; E. H. McWhirter & B. T. McWhirter, 2007).

The term "empowerment" is frequently used in education, social work, and counseling literature. We have elsewhere defined empowerment as "the process by which people, organizations, or groups who are powerless or marginalized (a) become aware of the power dynamics at work in their life context, (b) develop the skills and capacity for gaining some reasonable control over their lives, (c) which they exercise, (d) without infringing on the rights of others, and (e) which coincides with actively supporting the empowerment of others in their community" (E. H. McWhirter, 1994, p. 12). For young people this means learning how their lives are influenced by family, school, and the larger society; developing the skills to resist negative influences, promote positive changes, and make healthy choices for their lives; and supporting the healthy choices of others in their families, schools, and communities. The benefits of contributing to the welfare of others is consistent with Adlerian principles and supported by findings such as those associated with service learning programs that reduce the likelihood of teen pregnancy (Kirby, 2007; see Chapter 8). Here we will discuss three aspects of empowerment in more detail: critical consciousness, skill development, and social activism.

Critical Consciousness

Critical consciousness is a term coined by Paolo Freire (1970) that refers to awareness of inequity and power differences, a sense of agency to address injustices, and engagement in actions to reduce injustice and increase fairness. Critical consciousness sometimes is referred to as sociopolitical development, and its defining components of awareness, agency, and action parallel the empowerment process (Diemer, E. H. McWhirter, Ozer, & Rapa, 2015). Critical consciousness has been associated with Latina/o adolescents' academic achievement and engagement at school and at home (E. H. McWhirter & B. T. McWhirter, 2015; Luginbuhl, E. H. McWhirter, & B. T. McWhirter, 2015), and with urban ethnic minority adolescents' connection to their future (Diemer et al., 2010). Urban minority adolescents with higher critical consciousness in high school had higher paying jobs and had obtained more education 8 years later (Diemer, 2009). Thus, critical consciousness is a promising resource for young people, and especially those who experience poverty and other forms of marginalization.

Facilitating critical consciousness includes both raising awareness of the power dynamics that affect young people's life ecologies and critical self-reflection on their own actions within that ecology (B. T. McWhirter, & E. H. McWhirter, 2007). Analysis of power dynamics can focus on family systems, school and community factors, and local and national government policies; it can also be applied to racism, sexism, homophobia, poverty, ecology, nuclear weapons, pollution, and a multitude of other topics. The key is to help students critically understand how these issues affect them as individuals and as members of a community, and to foster agency for contributing to positive change.

The more immediate dynamics of popularity, peer pressure, and media influences such as advertising are especially salient to adolescents. Current reality television shows and music videos can serve as a basis for analysis and critique, when discussing classroom social politics is not warranted. For example, "Who has ideas about why (character's name) on (show) got so angry in last week's episode? What kind of power do you think she has in her social group? How do others in her social group try to influence her behavior? What messages do you think society gives her about how women are supposed to behave, and how might this affect her? Has anything happened in the past 2 weeks at school that is similar to the way (some of the characters) are treating (the other characters)?" Even young children can be taught in simple ways to examine how their behavior is influenced by context. For example, "I laughed at James when all the other kids did, even though I didn't really think it was funny" is a level of awareness many children could achieve. Adolescents are often quite willing to explore how peers, the school, and the community shape their behavior, but they need assistance developing a norm and a language for doing so. Critical self-reflection about what they contribute to peer dynamics, social pressure, family tension, or class projects requires a safe and nonjudgmental atmosphere that is free of blame. When they understand how they are influenced and influence others, and can explore the choices they have made and are making without being criticized for those choices, adolescents have a basis for choosing different attitudes and behaviors.

Power analysis and critical self-reflection contribute to the awareness component of critical consciousness and can be integrated into a variety of standard subjects, including history, language arts, government, creative writing, and literature. Building adolescent skills for taking positive action contributes to the agency and action components of critical consciousness. Fostering critical consciousness helps young people identify social influences and inequities, develop agency for promoting changes within their ecologies, and take action with others to improve their lives (E. H. McWhirter & B.T. McWhirter, in press; Watts, Diemer, & Voight, 2015).

Critical consciousness about disability issues among young people could be manifested in learning about the accessibility (or inaccessibility) of their school and local stores, developing awareness of how students with disabilities are treated as "less than" and marginalized, exploring and confronting their own stereotypes about disabilities, and working with other students to raise awareness, advocate to increase accessibility, and enhance school policies so that bullying of students with disabilities is prevented, identified early if it does take place, and addressed effectively.

Skill Development

Empowerment also involves development and utilization of the concrete skills necessary for enacting responsible choices. Teaching children more effective social skills increases their power in their personal environment. Learning cognitive-behavioral skills helps them manage and cope better with their internal processes. Providing them with learning strategies facilitates their intellectual growth. Decision making and assertiveness training, imagery and relaxation techniques, and other psychological tools, which we cover in later chapters, enhance people's ability to negotiate the barriers and take advantage of the opportunities in their environment. Training in other skills, such as conducting research, writing letters, organizing meetings, and public speaking, enable at-risk youth to take more active roles in negotiating various power structures influential in their lives.

Much of the discussion in the following chapters is designed to help teachers and counselors empower young people through the development of important skills. Unfortunately, some social skills programs do not work when they are characterized by poor teaching of the skills, inadequate reinforcement of skills over time, and negative or poor modeling. Conducting an unstructured counseling group populated with aggressive, conduct-disordered boys may reinforce negative modeling. A classroom teacher who instructs students on social skills and at the same time is disrespectful to them violates the basic principles of the skills that are being taught. Promoting skills development requires understanding components of the skill, the ability to model the skill, and providing consistent opportunities for students to practice the skill.

Enhancing critical consciousness begins with helping at-risk youth realistically appraise the forces of socialization, economic stratification, inequity, and discrimination on their lives, as well as the more immediate influences of peers and family members. To ignore the political, economic, and social context within which the young person operates and survives is to risk identifying the source of the problems as the individual. It is the responsibility of the teacher or counselor to help individuals identify contributing factors, for many young people are all too willing to shoulder all the blame themselves. If young people are led to believe that a "system" caused all of their problems, however, their apathy and withdrawal may simply increase. The awareness component of critical consciousness must be accompanied by the development of concrete skills and, equally important, the motivation and encouragement to utilize the skills, to resist negative influences, identify new alternatives, and to engage in new behaviors. When the norms for behavior change within a classroom or a school, the child's environment is significantly affected.

Empowerment suggests that although problems are often rooted in and replicated by systems, individuals and collective groups can share the responsibility for addressing and alleviating problems. Identifying how problems are sustained by systems, identifying possibilities for resistance, and engaging in new choices and behaviors are essential, as is providing students with opportunities to practice and implement new behaviors and choices. Otherwise, teachers and counselors will leave their students and clients feeling even less in control of their lives. Social activism is a natural outgrowth of the empowerment process.

Social Activism

One hindrance to the development of adequate services for youth is the fact that so many of the solutions require fundamental sociopolitical and economic changes (Albee, 1995; Prilleltensky, 1997; Romano, 2014). Poverty, inadequate nutrition, substandard housing, discrimination, and prejudice cannot be prevented with crisis-oriented programs. Prevention requires changing the environment that fosters such problems. Thus prevention must involve critical analysis of the structure of society and reflect the results of such analysis in planning, programming, and action.

Empowerment, by its very nature, requires not just reflection and change on the part of those served by human service professionals but on the part of service providers themselves. Empowering helpers cannot facilitate critical consciousness in others without becoming aware of how they themselves participate in maintaining systems that perpetuate inequity, injustice, and ongoing community and individual problems. Effective helpers are aware of existing community organizations, support groups, neighborhood action committees, and other channels of collective effort. They inform their clients and families, their communities, and colleagues of opportunities to participate in social and community affairs.

We and others have long argued that advocacy for individuals should be accompanied by advocacy for change in the policies, systems, and structures that perpetuate risk and marginalization of young people. Counseling competencies now include attention to advocacy skills not just for individuals, but also for addressing systemic and policy change (Toporek, Lewis, & Crethar, 2009). With the growing acknowledgment of the role the environment plays in human development, social activism is the natural arena into which counselors and teachers must move if they are to remain faithful to that advocacy. Counselors can urge adoption of effective mental health programs that address specific environmental circumstances, limitations, and inadequacies. Teachers can advocate for evidence-based curricula that promote learning, growth, and competencies among diverse students. Teachers and counselors can advocate for implementing effective preventive interventions that alter the trajectories of young people at risk and improve quality of life. All can work to be more aware of how local politics affect mental health policy in their communities and take action through voting, writing letters, publications, and community education seminars.

The social and economic risk factors in the larger society can be directly modified only modestly at the grassroots level by individual mental health and school personnel. Collective voices offer greater possibilities for system change, and educational and mental health policy and practice at every level of government, pre-service training, school district and building, and agency service can be modified to improve the health and learning of students at risk.

Resources for advocacy efforts are numerous and include, for example, Counselors for Social Justice. The mission of this group is to "work to promote social justice in our society through confronting oppressive systems of power and privilege that affect professional counselors and our clients and to assist in the positive change in our society through the professional development of counselors" (http://counseling-csj.org/). Berkovich (2014) presents a framework for social justice advocacy in educational leadership of schools and the challenges and limitations of varied approaches; Evans and colleagues (2014) describe how mental health and human service professionals can engage in "critical community practice" that addresses systemic inequities and injustices.

Although we use the terms *social activism* and *advocacy*, what we are referring to could also be described as citizenship: working conscientiously to make society better for all of its inhabitants, and especially for those who are most vulnerable.

Communities that Care

Adequate child care, good comprehensive preschool programs, and before- and after-school learning and enrichment centers primarily influence the individual and the microsystem, the soil and roots of the tree. Empowerment of individuals, neighborhoods, and communities potentially influences the entire ecosystem, the entire tree. Another way to impact the entire ecosystem is to provide prevention and treatment interventions on a broader scale. Systemic strategies that encourage client-family-community-helper partnerships have great potential to enhance direct client services, increase advocacy to remove barriers, and promote mental health (Bryan, 2009; Nakkula, Foster, Mannes, & Bolstrom, 2010). One such strategy is the Communities that Care (CtC) model (Hawkins et al., 2009; Hawkins, Oesterle, Brown, Abbott, & Catalano, 2014; Oesterle, Hawkins, Fagan, Abbott, & Catalano, 2013).

Communities attempting to prevent delinquency, substance abuse, teenage pregnancy, school dropout, and other problems of at-risk youth have applied numerous evidence-based programs (EBPs) addressing such issues. Unfortunately, their overall impact is usually low. Perhaps this limited impact is because there are few models of broad community-level planning and action. Programs that are designed to focus on one problem might be effective with that problem but not touch other problems.

CtC is one of the most effective available models for developing community partnerships. CtC provides materials and training to form, mobilize, and empower community coalitions to identify needs and effect change to meet those needs. CtC supports the new partnerships with an "overview framework" or "operating platform" that communities can use to select from a menu of evidence-based interventions to address identified problems. The community members then decide to promote the adoption of EBPs that target different populations. Thus, CtC is a model that attends to different parts of the at-risk tree with built-in flexibility so that different communities based on perceived local needs target different ecosystems.

Community coalition members under the CtC umbrella might choose many of the interventions that we describe in later chapters. For example, in one study (Hawkins et al., 2009), menu choices included family-focused interventions such as Strengthening Families, Guiding Good Choices, and Family Matters; school-based curricula such as All Stars, Life Skills Training, and Olweus Bullying Prevention; and community programs such as Big Brothers Big Sisters. Thus CtC does not focus on a single outcome, but on addressing common protective and risk factors that predict various later problems such as risky sexual behavior, delinquency, or drug abuse.

Developed by David Hawkins, Richard Catalano, and their colleagues (Hawkins et al., 2009; Oesterle et al., 2014) from the University of Washington, Seattle, CtC has been found in randomized controlled trials to reduce risk factors and enhance protective factors for adolescent behavior problems. Matched communities were randomly assigned by a toss of a coin to implement the CtC system, or to carry on as usual. In over 20 towns, CtC reduced smoking, alcohol abuse, and delinquent behavior among children between the ages of 10 and 14. Students in comparable towns where CtC was not implemented were 79% more likely to start smoking and 60% more likely to start using alcohol between ages 12 and 14. Students in communities without the intervention were prone to more kinds of trouble and were 41% more likely to become involved in delinquent behavior between the ages of 10 and 14.

One large quasiexperimental study (Feinberg, Jones, Greenberg, Osgood, & Bontempo, 2010) focused on a decade-long implementation of CtC in 120 Pennsylvania communities involving over 59,000 young people. Students completed a well-validated, student self-report measure that covers a range of risk and protective factors for adolescent problem behaviors including family relations, information on the child's neighborhood, and attitudes toward school. Students demonstrated less delinquency in CtC communities than youth in non-CtC communities with the normative increase in delinquent behavior falling by 11% a year. There was also one-third less annual decline in academic performance for youth included in CtC. Further, risk factors like antisocial attitudes increased at a slower rate; protective factors such as academic performance, community cohesion, and family connectedness decreased at a slower rate among young people in CtC communities than those in the communities with which they were being compared.

As we will describe later in this book, research has demonstrated that evidence-based programs have an important and positive impact on the at-risk attitudes and behaviors of individual young people. Clearly, community coalitions that utilize EBPs can affect child and adolescent protective and risk behaviors at a population level. CtC represents an exciting and effective

model for disseminating such programs that positively influence neighborhood and other communities.

CONCLUSION

Advocating for universal and targeted prevention programs is an important
strategy to enhance the potential of youth at risk, but it is not enough.
Ultimately, prevention of the conditions and systems that place youth at risk
requires us all to be active in securing the type of public policy that benefits
families who are economically struggling and socially marginalized. In this
chapter we discussed the problems of poverty and low SES and then pre-
viewed several configurations of family life including the working poor, vulnerable and underserved, young single mothers, and homeless families. These
result in important risk factors, which we discussed. We propose that improving social policy and funding for child care, comprehensive preschool programs, before- and after-school programs, empowerment of young people,
and communitywide mobilization of evidence-based programs are some of
the first steps to take to confront the environmental, exosystemic, and macrosystemic problems that place our children and adolescents at risk for future
difficulty.

PART 2

Families, Schools, and Skills

Part 2 contains three chapters. In Chapters 3 and 4 we deal with two important microsystems that serve to reduce or enhance risky behavior in young people: the family and the school. To extend our metaphor, they are two "roots" of the risk "tree." Peer influences are another root, but because the impact of peers occurs somewhat later, we only briefly touch on issues related to peers in this section. (Chapter 13 is devoted to peers and to peer-based interventions.)

Families and schools provide important resources to offset negative behavior. In families and schools, young people learn attitudes and skills that help them to survive and thrive. In Chapter 5 we describe resiliency and identify five important constructs that contribute to healthy, prosocial behavior. The case studies presented in Chapters 3 and 4 are used throughout the book to illustrate important issues and concerns.

Family Problems of At-Risk Children and Youth

Why are some families bubbling fountains, filling goblets full of cold, clear water for thirsty people living there?

While other fountains fill cups with dark, bitter liquid.

And yet other fountains are dead dry—nothing flows and mugs remain empty?

Too many children have either dusty-dry, empty vessels or bitter-brown, sewage-filled ones.

How do we turn on the fountains so that the cold, clear water flows?

CHAPTER OUTLINE

As we saw in Chapter 2, shifting economic, political, and policy trends have created an often disturbing environment that directly affects the roots of the problems young people face.

Nowhere is this more evident than in the family. The family microsystem is a major influence on individuals, and in this chapter we focus on family issues that affect at-risk children and adolescents.

SOCIETAL CHANGES AFFECTING THE FAMILY: A CULTURAL SHIFT?

The traditional American family has undergone major changes in recent decades. In 1960, almost 90% of children lived with two married parents. In 2008, that number was 64% (Taylor, 2011). With the 2015 legalization of same-sex marriage in the United States, we expect the percentage of children living with married parents will rise. Census and most other large-scale data sources do not yet reflect this change, but in the future data will be available that more accurately reflect statistics for marriage and two-parent families. This is but one example of how the American family has changed, with more changes during the last 50 years than at any other time in history.

Children in the United States are growing up in more diverse living arrangements than a half-century ago. In a survey of "new" family arrangements, a Pew research study identified several different types of family life and tried to ascertain the public's conception toward them (Morin, 2011). There were seven different living arrangements:

- A married couple raising one or more children
- A married couple with no children
- A single parent raising at least one child
- An unmarried man and woman raising at least one child
- A gay or lesbian couple with children
- A same-sex couple without children
- An unmarried, childless man and woman who are living together

A sizable percentage of Americans viewed all of these combinations as living in a family, with children and marriage being the strongest factors in deciding what constituted family. As families have changed, so have perceptions of the family.

Mothers or fathers are more likely to be absent from the home now than at any time in history, and extended family members are also less likely to be involved in family life. In earlier generations, the majority of children were raised through the collective efforts of a network of extended family relatives, in-laws, and friends who interacted with them throughout childhood and adolescence. Today children have fewer adults to help them develop responsibility, judgment, and self-discipline, even though the task requires more understanding, care, and awareness than ever before. Most young people do not have an extended family network of in-laws, aunts, and uncles to support them and their parents. Today, when the extended family is involved in child rearing, it is typically not adjunctive—that is, supportive of the children's parents—but, in fact, replaces parental roles as primary or even sole caretakers. For example, of those children not living with a parent, over half live with a grandparent (Taylor, 2011). This is especially true since the beginning of the Great Recession in 2007 (Livingston & Parker, 2010).

Years ago the extended family provided a variety of role models, opportunities to anticipate and vicariously experience child-related problems, and individuals available to serve as resources. Today, children and their parents have less access to the extended family as they face life crises. The family, once buffered with supports, is now stretched thin. Most frequently, recreation, spiritual training, and education all take place outside the home. Among most U.S. families, children often become acquainted with the adult world through television, highlighted by programs that portray casual and unprotected sex (Kaiser Family Foundation, 2005), drinking, gratuitous acts of violence, and self-centered aggrandizement as routine behavior. Through commercials, television also sends negative messages about sacrifice, self-discipline, and patience. Many young people are unable to bond and connect with others; they lack a sense of being tied emotionally to other people, of sharing commitments to common values, and do not see themselves as part of society.

Divorce and the decline of the extended family do not necessarily result in a reduction of social networks for children and young people. Indeed, the increased complexity of family patterns may actually increase the availability of people who can serve as resources. Consider "Lisa." Her father had several children from a previous marriage with whom she interacted when they came for visits. When Lisa was 8 years old, her parents divorced. She lived with her mother but continued to see her father in the summer and on weekends. When Lisa was 13, her mother remarried. Lisa and her stepfather got along well and did many things together. Lisa continued to see her father, although less frequently, because he had moved to another state and married a woman with two children. Lisa graduated from high school and entered college. During two of her college years she lived with a man, and soon after graduation she married another man. She and her husband had a son. After several years, Lisa and her husband divorced and she was awarded custody of her son, who continues to see her ex-husband in the summer and on weekends. Three years later Lisa remarried. She and her second husband have two more children. During Lisa's life so far she has lived in nine families either part time or full time.

Lisa's situation is not typical, but neither is it unusual. Although the relationships in some of Lisa's families may not have been ideal, in each case there were people she enjoyed doing things with, wanted to continue seeing, and loved. This situation represents a substantial change from the experience of people who grew up several decades ago, when one might have been part of two or three families at the most. Some of these family experiences have the potential of enriching children's lives by providing more adults to serve as role models and by providing a greater variety of experiences. Unfortunately, for many youth these changing patterns and variable family experiences produce alienation, rootlessness, and disconnection.

Despite pervasive assumptions that poor children are at high risk and affluent children are at low risk, comparative studies of rich and poor children reveal more similarities than differences in socialization processes and adjustment patterns. Children of high socioeconomic status often manifest problems of depression, anxiety, and substance abuse. Such children often must deal with excessive pressures to achieve along with physical and emotional isolation from their parents. Family wealth does not automatically confer equanimity of spirit or wisdom in parenting. Children from wealthy families are privileged in many areas, but this does not remove potential threats to their psychological well-being (Luthar & Barkin, 2012).

ISSUES WITHIN THE FAMILY

Even in the absence of current structural changes arising from evolving societal conditions, the family normally changes over time. All changes necessitate shifts in the relationships of family members. At each stage, the family has specific developmental tasks to accomplish, which lay the foundations for later stages.

The Family Life Cycle

The family life cycle is the name given to stages that a family goes through in its developmental history (McGoldrick, Garcia-Preto, & Carter, 2015). The family group begins with each newly married or partnered couple, even though the couple continues to be a part of their two original family groups. The fact that a new family cycle begins with each new couple does not cut short the cycles of the families of origin of each partner. The couple continues the family life cycles of their earlier family groups at the same time that they begin their own family life cycle. Because this text is focused on children and adolescents, our discussion here is of families with children, but this does not exclude couples without children from the definition of families.

Duvall and Miller (1985) proposed an eight-stage model of the traditional family life cycle that remains useful today. This framework is appropriate for families that progress through certain predictable marker events or phases (such as marriage, the birth or adoption of the first child, the onset of adolescence, and so forth). Each stage is determined by the age of the oldest child, and each stage has its own set of tasks for the family to complete before it moves to the next stage. McGoldrick et al. (2015) have outlined sets of developmental tasks for nontraditional blended families and single-parent families. They also add an initial stage—the unattached young adult—to the family life cycle. The inability of the family to negotiate developmental tasks at any of the stages contributes to the child's problems. Professionals need to be aware of the family developmental tasks and help the family to develop the necessary skills to negotiate them. The following stages are derived from the works of Duvall and Miller (1985), and McGoldrick, Carter, and Garcia-Preto (2010). Movement between stages is sometimes difficult for traditional families; it can be even more difficult for nontraditional families.

Unattached Young Adult Stage

The young adult must accomplish several developmental tasks at this stage. Young people must develop responsible habits that enable them to self-direct their behavior, manage their resources (e.g., maintain means of transportation, place of residence, secure food), and secure paid employment or some means of supporting themselves. These tasks are important even when single adults continue to live at home. In addition, it is important that young adults establish close peer relationships and begin to separate from the family of origin through an ongoing process of differentiation.

Establishment Stage (Married, No Children)

This stage begins with marriage or a committed partnership. The young adult continues to differentiate from the family of origin. The major task for couples at this stage is to establish their identity as a new unit. Making rules, defining roles within the marriage, and realigning relationships with friends and family are important components of this stage. For young adults who are gay, lesbian, or bisexual, this stage may include tasks associated with affirming their identity within their family of origin; interracial couples must often devote considerable time to negotiating the effects of racism (their own as well as that of family members and society) on their relationship.

New Parent Stage (Infant to 3 Years)

These next stages apply to couples who have children. When the couple becomes parents, their duties and roles change. Their relationship as a couple must shift to accommodate the infant.

Preschool Stage (Oldest Child 3 to 6 Years)

Parents continue to develop their work and family roles. The major developmental task at this stage is learning and applying effective parenting skills to help the children learn how to interact positively with others.

School-Age Stage (Oldest Child 6 to 12 Years)

The family becomes more involved with community and school activities as the children grow and develop. Members of the family must learn to renegotiate boundaries to include the children's peer group.

Teenage Stage (Oldest Child 13 to 20 Years)

The couple is required to deal with their individual, work, and marital issues along with the developmental tasks of their children and their own aging parents. The adolescent children, who are going through the individual developmental task of establishing their own identities and independence, challenge the boundaries and rules of the family system.

Launching Stage (Departure of Children)

Children and parents must separate emotionally and physically from one another. Of course, there is tremendous variation in the extent and nature of "healthy" separation. The primary task of the family at this point is to let go. Other tasks include reestablishment of the marital system as a dyad and negotiation of adult relationships between the parents and the children. Many families must cope with the death of a grandparent.

Two Final Stages

Two final stages, the postparental middle years and the aging family, are equally important in the family life cycle, but they do not bear directly on our subject so we will not describe them here.

Normal Crises

Families undergo such profound changes as they move from one stage to another that the transitions present all families with normal family developmental crises. Most families negotiate these transitions adequately. Unfortunately, some families have such difficulty with the transitions between stages that they compromise the well-being of their children. Such families can become dysfunctional. If we are to understand dysfunctional families, we have to understand the family as a system. In addition, helping professionals need to view the cultural, ethnic, and unique aspects of families' backgrounds as resources and strengths that can be fostered and supported for their benefit. This appreciation of diversity is critical. Human service professionals need to develop and maintain an attitude that learning about culture and cross-cultural practice is an essential, ongoing, and ethical process synonymous with professionalism (Sue & Sue, 2013). The National Organization for Human Services (NOHS, 2015) standards of advocating for social justice, recognizing people's strengths and abilities, and supporting physical, mental, emotional, and spiritual health also highlight the critical importance of multicultural competencies in working with families. An ongoing commitment to learning, including consistent use of supervision and consultation from diverse colleagues, will assist helping professionals in understanding similarities and differences in family systems across various cultural and ethnic groups.

The Family System

As discussed in Chapter 1, the family is a critical microsystem in the life of every child, and within which every child learns attitudes and behaviors that influence many long-term outcomes (Bronfenbrenner, 1989). The family is a system consisting of connected components (family members) organized around various functions that interact to maintain balance and a state of equilibrium. Each element is dependent on the functioning of other elements. Giving and receiving affection, child rearing, and the division of labor are some familiar family functions. Families are interdependent in that each member of the system influences and is influenced by each other member. Understanding family systems is thought to be a way to aid parent training programs (Scott & Dadds, 2009; see Chapter 14).

As they live together from day to day, families develop systematic patterns of behavior that serve to maintain the system in a state of equilibrium. Each family member contributes to this equilibrium or homeostatic balance. Homeostasis is represented by a particular family's ongoing behaviors, habits, expectations, and communication patterns.

To see the family as a homeostatic system, consider a family in which the husband/father is an alcoholic. He serves as a scapegoat and maintains the system by receiving all the blame for the family's problems. Rather than accept the blame, he projects it onto his spouse. She internalizes the blame and enables him to continue his drinking by trying to improve her own behavior and the children's rather than confront his drinking. One child may try to keep the parents from fighting by diverting their attention to his or her own problems through drug use, pregnancy, or truancy. Another child may attempt to dissipate tension by being the family clown. These roles are not conscious attempts to keep the family in balance, however precarious this balance may be, but are patterns maintained at an unconscious level in a manner that is sometimes blatantly obvious and sometimes extremely subtle. When the patterns of behavior that maintain homeostasis are rigid and unyielding, the family system is considered "closed."

A closed system is dysfunctional because it is isolated from the environment, is less receptive to external stimuli, and is unresponsive to change. Because of its impermeable boundaries and unreceptiveness to change, a closed system tends to move toward increasing disorder. Open systems, by contrast, interact with the environment and so may be capable of both adaptation and flexibility. Adaptation depends on maintaining enough stability to permit the family members to develop coherent, separate identities as they make the necessary accommodations to environmental changes.

Closed-system families contribute a disproportionate share of troubled children and youth to society because problem behaviors emerge more in closed family systems. Closed family systems typically demonstrate one of two major types of problems: detachment or enmeshment.

Detachment

A detached family is one in which the individual members function separately and autonomously with little family interdependence. When one family member faces a time of stress, the family hardly seems to notice or respond at all. Detached families tend to be unresponsive because each member is isolated within the system. In such families, the boundaries are so rigid that only a high level of individual stress may activate support from other family members. The family members cannot get their social and emotional needs met within the family, nor do they learn appropriate ways to meet the needs of others. Although family members are not nourished or supported within their family, they often remain together because they seem to have no alternatives. Unfortunately, detached families produce young people who form inadequate or dysfunctional relationships outside the family because they have not learned how to have good relationships within the family. They do not know that other kinds of relationships are possible. Obviously, such youth are at risk for a variety of problem behaviors.

Enmeshment

Enmeshed families demonstrate such intensity and closeness in family interactions that the members are overly involved and overly concerned with each other's lives. In enmeshed families, the children in particular experience a distorted sense of involvement, attachment, and belonging. They fail to develop a secure sense of individuality, separateness, and autonomy. When a member of an enmeshed family encounters a stressful situation, the family is likely to respond by rescuing rather than teaching constructive problem solving. Subsystem boundaries are weak, easily crossed, and poorly differentiated; children may act like parents, and parental control may be ineffective. The young person's distorted sense of belonging and attachment interferes with his or her capacity to negotiate developmental tasks successfully. For example, a child may remain isolated from classmates and repeatedly feign illness so as not to "threaten" the mother–child relationship.

In the case study, the Carter family demonstrates the difficulties of negotiating the family life cycle and illustrates one kind of dysfunctional family. As you read this case study, take a few minutes to reflect on the family life cycle, the family as a social system, and issues of detachment and enmeshment.

The Carter family is at the transition point leading to the teenage stage of the family life cycle. Jason's underlying problems are intensifying precisely because adolescents begin to challenge rules and boundaries as they seek to establish their own identities. As the family is struggling to negotiate this transition, both Mr. and Mrs. Carter are attempting to cope with their own midlife transitional periods.

The Carters illustrate not only the family life cycle but also the family as a social system. The presenting problem—behavior difficulties at school—is an extension of Jason's role in his family. His "angelic" younger sister supports this role; his angry and depressed mother maintains it; and his isolated father covertly encourages it. Everyone in the family maintains homeostasis. Even though each of them is in some pain, the unknown (if Jason's position should change) is more anxiety provoking than the status quo. In other words, although Jason is the catalyst that prompts the Carters to seek an outside helper, the underlying causes of his behavior are embedded within the family's interaction. Each family member maintains equilibrium in the closed system of the family because each is vulnerable. Christie is vulnerable because she builds her self-esteem on being the model child. If things shift, she may become the bad one—the "devil"—in the family. She does not know how to disagree or express negative emotions in a healthy way. She appears to be enmeshed in the family system. Mrs. Carter is vulnerable to a change in the homeostasis: If she loses the reasons for her depression (if Jason becomes cooperative and constructive), she might need to feel more guilt and be self-punitive to maintain her depression. Jason provides her with a scapegoat on which to vent her emotions. She would also have to develop a new relationship with Christie and begin to confront her husband, and such changes appear threatening. Mr. Carter might have to confront directly his anger and resentment toward his wife. He might also have to redefine Christie's role and change his behavior toward Jason. Jason is vulnerable because if his role changes, he might have to improve in school, risk failing when he is actually trying (instead of failing on purpose), and he will have fewer excuses for acting out. These shifts in perception, roles, and behavior are inevitably threatening. Thus each family member has a vested interest in maintaining his or her current functioning.

Cultural Variations

Family life cycle and family system theories are useful constructs in understanding family dynamics. Although useful in understanding and helping many families, the framework must be adapted to families of color and immigrant families (Domenech Rodriguez, Donovick, & Crowley, 2009). The professional helper's multicultural knowledge, awareness, and skills in working with people from diverse backgrounds are critical.

For example, cultural variations influence the nature of the tasks within each stage in the family life cycle. In some cultural groups, for example, young people are expected to leave home at age 18 or soon thereafter, whereas other groups expect young adults to live with their parents until they marry, and in some cultures even after they marry. In any assessment of a family's passage through the stages and the completion of tasks, the cultural norms of the family must be explored.

Another specific example of cultural differences is the concept of enmeshment. What is enmeshment in the dominant culture may be collective sharing and interdependence in families of color. We must be cautious in relying on stereotypes to guide us; often families of color rely more on a larger social base and extended family support than do typical European American families. Among African American families, for example, extended family and friends are central. The role of the church community also provides a rich network of support for many African American families. Among Native American families, the extended kinship system—including uncles, aunts, cousins, and grandparents—is central in children's lives, and multiple households that include nonblood-related individuals are often incorporated into the kinship circle. Many American Indian groups even have formal rituals to induct significant individuals into the family system. Asian American families often have close-knit and hierarchical family structures, with particular authority being invested in the father and elders. Asian American relatives may participate in family life and in family decisions. And for traditional Latino families, the family structure is extended by formalized kinship relationships to the godparents. The term "cousin" may include many people—often same-age peers who are not biologically related. With many families of color and immigrant families, loyalty to family and to their extended family takes priority over other social demands and dominant culture expectations. Clearly, there are cultural variations, group differences within ethnic groups, and individual differences within families of color as well as within European American families.

Parenting Issues

Another area in understanding within-family characteristics is parenting. Parents have different values, characteristics, temperaments, and skills that influence their children for good or bad. Four basic dimensions of child rearing with fundamental bipolar dimensions include permissiveness/restrictiveness; hostility/warmth; anxious, emotional involvement/calm detachment; and inconsistency/consistency.

The permissiveness/restrictiveness dimension incorporates the constructs of control and power; permissiveness refers to low control and low power in parents' behaviors, whereas restrictiveness refers to high control and high power. The hostility/warmth dimension ranges from low to high levels of affection. The anxious, emotional involvement/calm detachment continuum ranges from high anxiety to low anxiety and reflects the emotional engagement or connectedness of the parent. The inconsistency/consistency dimension reflects stable and predictable rules, rewards, and punishments and steady follow through. These four dimensions appear to be relatively independent of one another and provide a key to understanding child rearing.

Note that the two end points of each dimension represent the extremes of parental behavior. The behavior of most parents tends to fall near the middle rather than the extremes on most dimensions. That is, a father is not likely to be either completely hostile or overwhelmingly warm; most mothers neither permit nor restrict everything their children want to do. It is typically parents who react at either extreme who place their children at greater risk. This is even true with the dimension of consistency. At the extreme end of consistency are often parents who are rigid, inflexible, and unyielding. They limit the necessary give and take atmosphere that allows their children practice in decision making and problem solving. Of course, besides extreme parenting behaviors, the at-risk child's family life is most often characterized by parental inconsistency. Generally, consistent behavior by parents increases the child's ability to predict the environment and leads to more stable behavior patterns. Inconsistency has negative effects on children and may take various forms. Clear evidence of the deleterious effects of inconsistency emerges from the research literature on delinquency, which has repeatedly demonstrated a strong connection between inconsistent and erratic discipline (both between parents and within an individual parent) and a youth's antisocial behavior. Interventions that help parents balance parenting styles and especially respond with more consistency are of great help to at-risk youth. Equally

CASE STUDY • The Carter Family

The Carter family came to our attention after Jason, a thin, pale, and intense 13-year-old, got into a particularly vicious fight. The other members of this middle-class family are Jason's parents, Doug and Lois Carter, and his 10-year-old sister, Christie. Jason was referred by his teacher because of fighting and other behavioral difficulties. He frequently disrupted his classes by harassing and fighting with other children and by talking back to teachers. His short attention span and apparent inability to sit still were the focus of a subsequent neurological examination, but no neurological impairment was indicated. Next Jason underwent an evaluation at school, consisting of a standard social history, psychological tests, and an intake interview.

The findings suggested that poor family communication and ineffective discipline might be the source of Jason's problem behavior. On the basis of this information, family therapy was strongly recommended. Referral to the neurological clinic, contact with school personnel, the social history, and the intake interview were all accomplished by a school social worker assigned to the case. She was also responsible for the family casework and referred Jason and his family to a mental health clinic that provided individual and family therapy.

Lois Carter, a chronically depressed European American woman, was torn by guilt over her perceived failure to rear a child who could function adequately at home and in school. She also seemed to have considerable unspoken anger, which was frequently directed at Jason. Mr. Carter, an engineer, was also a cauldron of unexpressed anger. Emotionally locked out by his wife's depression, he seemed to resent Jason and to continually put the child in a double bind by subtly sending the message that his acting out was just a case of "boys will be boys" and at the same time reprimanding him for his behavior. He seemed unwilling or unable to follow through with punishment. In part, this behavior was an acting out of his own angry feelings toward his wife.

Mrs. Carter was the second daughter in her family of origin. She described her parents, who live only a mile from the Carters, in ambivalent terms. Her father was a chronic drinker, and he physically and emotionally abused his wife and children. He suffered brain damage as a result of drinking and had mellowed considerably in recent years. Mrs. Carter's mother was a passive-aggressive woman who turned to religion for comfort in her later years. Lois had an older sister who had twice married and divorced. After repeated attempts, the sister attained a college degree and now worked as an elementary school teacher. Mrs. Carter's two brothers expressed the family dysfunction more obviously. The youngest brother had committed suicide several years earlier. The other brother continued to live with his parents. At 30 he was unemployed and unmarried and existed on a small payment for service-connected emotional disability.

Doug Carter, of English and French descent, was the older of two brothers. His father, a bookkeeper for a small manufacturing firm, was a harsh, critical, and sarcastic parent. His mother was a pleasant though ineffectual woman who "adored" Mr. Carter's younger brother. A paternal grandmother, now deceased, lived in the home while Mr. Carter was growing up, and she tended to favor him. Mr. Carter and his brother had been very competitive as children and now have no contact. His parents reside in another state and contact with them is infrequent.

Christie was described by both parents as a "very good girl" who never caused any problems. She did well in school, was helpful at home when asked, and had a "nice little group" of girlfriends.

Both Jason and Christie Carter had been adopted as infants. Jason was considered the identified problem (patient), and Christie was regarded as a perfect little angel.

A counselor saw the family weekly for therapy that focused on their style of communication. During the first six sessions, the family discussed setting limits and the need for more direct communication. They reached an impasse, however, because the family members refused to listen to one another. Jason frequently pointed out, for instance, that his sister instigated many situations by teasing him. His parents refused to acknowledge that Christie could possibly do such a thing and reprimanded Jason for not listening to them and for trying to get his sister in trouble. Christie sat quietly and primly, in silent agreement with her parents. At the end of six sessions, the counselor felt that she was making little headway in helping the parents listen to Jason or to each other. Christie indicated little willingness to modify her secure position in the family structure. Jason continued to disrupt his classes and behave outrageously at school, in the neighborhood, and at home.

important is attending to cultural variations in parenting styles. For example, apparently "protective parenting" better accounts for Latina/o parenting than the four traditional parenting dimensions discussed earlier (Domenech Rodriquez et al., 2009).

FAMILIES WITH STRESS AND DYSFUNCTION

Family Problems

A focus on societal change, stages and transitions in the family life cycle, and the family as a system helps to identify stressors that may contribute to problems for young people. For example, the accumulation of family risk factors such as socioeconomic risk, parents' psychological risks, as well as marital problems and parenting risks is associated with increased internalizing problems among girls in early adolescence, and higher externalizing problems among boys within two-parent families. These risk factors are also associated with lower grades that decline over time and with adjustment difficulties (Buehler & Gerard, 2013). Therefore, specific family problems contribute to the development of risky behaviors. Some family situations place all family members, and especially children, at risk.

As we saw in Chapter 2, single-parent and poor families experience considerable stress as do blended families and latchkey families. Families with lesbian, gay, bisexual, or transgender (LGBT) members are also subjected to stress due primarily to exosystem and macrosystem influences of homophobia. In Chapter 2 we considered the impact of SES and poverty and noted the increasing numbers of single parents and mothers in paid employment. Divorce, out-of-wedlock births, the legalization of same-sex marriage, and declining marriage rates have changed the composition of the "typical" family and increased the diversity of types of families. Here we highlight a few sociological trends that influence modern family life.

Divorce and Single-Parent Families

The marked rise in the divorce rate that characterized the late 1960s and 1970s actually reversed direction (except for teen marriages) during the 1980s and then stabilized. The rate of currently divorced or separated adults rose from 5% in 1960 to 14% in 2008 (Taylor, 2011). According to the CDC, the number of marriages per 1,000 people declined from 8.2 to 6.8 between 2000 and 2012, whereas divorces per 1,000 declined from 4.0 to 3.4 (Martin, Hamilton, & Ventura, 2015). Divorce inevitably affects children.

Single-parent families face some unique stressors. Four out of ten children living with a single parent live in poverty (Jiang, Ekono, & Skinner, 2015), and seven in ten children living with a single mother are poor or low-income, compared to 32% of children living in two-parent and other types of families (Mather, 2010). African American and Latino children are overrepresented in these numbers. Hilton, Desrochers, and Devall (2001) compared children and parents functioning in single-mother, single-father, and intact families. They found that single fathers had better economic resources than did single mothers; in addition, single fathers had more positive parenting than married fathers, and they relied more on friends than did married parents.

Low-income, single mothers are more likely to be young, never married, less educated, and unemployed. Most are at a financial disadvantage due to reliance on a single household income, and for many, this is also due to difficulty in obtaining child support from absent fathers (Mather, 2010). Over the past 50 years, children born to unmarried mothers have risen dramatically—increasing from 5% in 1960 to 41% in 2008 (Martin et al., 2015; Taylor, 2011). By 2010, 24% of the 75 million children under the age of 18 were living in a single-mother family (Mather, 2010). Children living with single mothers were found to have more internalized problems, and those living with either a single mother or father had more externalized behavior problems (Hilton et al., 2001). In addition, children living in single-mother homes were more at risk for school dropout (Mather, 2010; Pong & Ju, 2000).

Blended Families

Blended families (or reconstituted or stepparent families) are families in which the remarried partners bring children into the relationship. Today, fewer and fewer children are living in a "traditional" family; 34% are living with an unmarried parent, 15% of children are living with parents who are in a remarriage, and 6% of all children are living with a stepparent. Remarriage has become increasingly common in the United States, as 23% of married individuals have already been married before, compared with 13% in 1960 (Livingston, 2014). Children in blended families face an unfamiliar network of relationships, particularly with an adult with whom they have not fallen in love. They often suffer some degree of discomfort. These children may have few resources to draw upon in their attempts to cope with a new parent, new grandparents, possibly new stepsiblings, and a new family lifestyle. As the new couple shapes and ritualizes their lives, the young people face a whole new set of expectations, procedures, and interactions. Further, these children are struggling to adjust to their new conditions while the most significant people in their lives—their parents—are themselves adjusting and are undoubtedly less available.

Viewed in the context of the family life cycle, the newlyweds must negotiate the establishment stage—a complex task in itself—at the same time that they must adopt a satisfactory and consistent system of child parenting and disciplining. The needs of the children are unlikely to coincide with those of the parents. Obviously, this situation is ripe for problems, which may be a major factor in the fragility of second marriages; they are more likely than first marriages to end in divorce.

Latchkey Families

"Latchkey" families are those in which one or more of the children are home alone before or after school and on school holidays. The increase in the number of mothers of young children in the workforce is one of the largest social changes in the last half of the 21st century (Halpern, 2005), and is an important factor in the latchkey phenomenon. The traditional arrangement in which fathers are employed and mothers stay at home with the children is no longer the case for most families, for a complex variety of reasons including financial necessity, increasing equality in women's roles, and lifestyle goals. The combination of most mothers working and few fathers staying at home with the children means that many U.S. children are latchkey children, with estimates ranging from 7 million (Taylor, 2011) to over 11 million (Afterschool Alliance, 2014). According to the Afterschool Alliance (2014), 1 in 5 children, or 11.3 million children, are without supervision between the hours of 3 p.m. and 6 p.m., which is down from the 15.1 million in 2009. Of those children, 3% are in elementary school and 19% are in middle school. After-school programs keep children occupied and supervised after school, but 55% of African American parents, 53% of Hispanic/Latino parents, 50% of White parents, and overall 54% of lower-income families have reported that the lack of a safe way to get to and from after-school programs has been a significant barrier to utilizing this type of family support (Afterschool Alliance, 2014). Many latchkey children are not able to reach a parent by phone due to their parents' work situation. Latchkey children are susceptible to accidents. They may also engage in acts of vandalism or delinquency (Dishion & Bullock, 2001). Not surprisingly, violent youth crime is most common between 3:00 p.m. and 7:00 p.m., and a child's chance of being a victim of crime is greatest after school (National Center for Juvenile Justice, 2015). Children spend an average of 7 hours a day engaged in screen time, which includes viewing computers, televisions, phones, tablets, and other electronic devices (American Academy of Pediatrics, 2015). Unsupervised use of the Internet also occurs when children are home alone, which all too often can result in viewing pornography (even inadvertently), participating in chat rooms, and the formation of unhealthy and even dangerous relationships.

Carlos Diaz (see Chapter 4) spends his afternoons taking care of his sister. He is like countless other children who carry their keys in their backpacks and return to an empty house after school. Many latchkey children are bored, lonely, and frightened. These experiences can be even more intense when children do not have a structure to follow or responsibilities to carry out. As many as one in four latchkey children may be extremely fearful—fearful enough to arm themselves with a baseball bat as they watch television. For the latchkey child, television and the Internet become the babysitters, anesthetists, and constant companions. Given that parents must work and that the number of latchkey children will rise, widespread pre- and after-school programs that extend the number of hours children receive supervision are an important part of prevention efforts (see Chapter 2). Many after-school programs function as "afternoon schools." Such programs may seem too academic after a full day in the classroom, especially for young children. However, after-school programs are helpful both for working parents and the children that would otherwise be unattended. The demand for after-school programs has been found to be higher among lower-income families as compared to higher-income families, and Hispanic and African American children are at least two times more likely to participate in these programs than White children (Afterschool Alliance, 2014). Indeed, the benefits of extra schooling and afternoon supervision may outweigh the possible excess of academia. This is particularly the case when after-school activities include games, sports, assistance with homework, counseling groups, tutoring, and opportunities to explore music, drama, and art. If schools are unable to obtain the funds to offer pre- and after-school programs, they can still meet some of the needs of latchkey students. For example, the school counselor or psychologist can conduct workshops for parents or children to help children deal with the fears they encounter during their unsupervised hours. Children can be taught what to do in case of emergency or danger and how to maximize their safety. Latchkey children can be helped to devise productive ways to fill the time until a parent returns home, such as completing specific chores, doing homework, preparing nutritious snacks, and working on creative projects.

Families of Lesbian, Gay, Bisexual, and Transgender Youth

By 2011, 63% of Americans believed that members of a parenting couple do not have to be of the opposite sex (Taylor, 2011), and they consider a gay or lesbian couple with children to constitute a family. Nevertheless, biased attitudes about homosexuality continue to put pressure on a gay or lesbian couple raising a child. The children themselves especially feel the pressure. LGBT young people in straight families often experience even more pressure.

For many youth who are LGBT, family life is not a very safe life. Some who come out, or who are "found out" by their families, are thrown out of their homes or are physically or sexually assaulted by family members (Hunt & Moodie-Mills, 2012). Many LGBT youth are rejected and blamed for the family's dysfunction, ultimately contributing to their overrepresentation in the juvenile justice system (Hunt & Moodie-Mills, 2012). In fact, the process of "coming out" is a major developmental task of homosexual youth, and LGBT youth often have a difficult time finding appropriate strategies and family support for the coming-out process (Sullivan & Wodarski, 2002). Transgender youth are those whose "innate, deeply felt psychological identification as male or female, ... may not correspond with the person's body or assigned sex at birth (meaning what sex was listed on a person's birth certificate)" (Human Rights Campaign Foundation, 2004). Society's lack of understanding of transgender individuals contributes to the enormous challenges they face within their families and communities, and these youth are at high risk for being rejected, shamed, and shunned (Harper & Singh, 2014).

Even more problematic is that the lack of support and acceptance at home usually leads to other problems. Many LGBT youth run away or are thrown out of the home. Life on the street brings even more severe problems. Young people on the streets are not attending school; many are also using alcohol and drugs; many youth become prostitutes to support addictions, secure a place to stay, or ensure their "protection." LGBT youth with unsupportive families are three times more likely to be at high risk for HIV and sexually transmitted diseases, and more than three times as likely to use illegal drugs (Society for Public Health Education, 2012). Among runaways, LGBT youth have higher levels of early onset of sex and drug use and are at exceptionally high risk for HIV infection (Moon et al., 2000). Interventions within the family must be sensitive to sexual orientation and gender identity, and should help families develop the knowledge and skills to be effective allies with their children (Harper & Singh, 2014).

Problem Families

All dysfunctional families subject children to stresses that may lead to risky behavior (Sander & McCarty, 2005). Substance abuse by the adult caretaker, parental psychopathology, and interpersonal violence involving child abuse or neglect, intimate partner violence (IPV), and dating violence are among those most likely to result in problems for young people (Reupert, Maybery, Nicholson, Gopfert, & Seeman, 2015). Most adults in such families experienced the same problems in their own families of origin and, as is common, perpetuate the same problems for their children.

Families Experiencing Substance Abuse

Children of alcoholic (or drug-using) parents are at risk for adverse childhood experiences including neglect; emotional, physical, and sexual abuse; and witnessing violence. Such children may be predisposed to become alcoholic or drug dependent themselves or to enter into relationships with alcoholics (Sterling, Weisner, Hinman, & Parthasarathy, 2010; Wilens et al., 2002). Children of substance-abusing parents are at high risk for short-term and long-term emotional and social adjustment problems, including hyperactivity, relationship difficulties, aggression, depression, school absenteeism, and drug use (Straussner & Fewell, 2015). The literature on adult children of alcoholics documents the comprehensive and long-term impact that substance-abusing parents have on their children.

Families and Incarceration

The number and proportion of incarcerated men and women in the United States is dramatic, with 2.2 million people in prison or jail in 2013, which is a 500% increase over the last 30 years (Carson, 2014). Per capita, the United States incarcerates more people than any other nation in the world. Most incarcerated adults were at one time at-risk youth. And it continues. Many inmates have left spouses, other family members, and especially children vulnerable. The human toll on the victims and families is enormous; the toll on children is immeasurable.

The bonds between family members are severely tested during an inmate's incarceration. This is particularly true with the children of inmates. In addition to the lack of parental contact and the negative impact of stigmatization, many of the children also fall into other risk categories—poverty, single parents—that we discussed elsewhere in this book. Additional problems arise when the inmate is released. Many have been subjected to violence and sexual assault with severe psychological impact. Children are forced to deal with the aftereffects with a parent who has been missing for months and years. Reconnecting within the family is often a significant challenge.

Incarceration is also a problem when it involves adolescents in the family, for a different set of reasons. The act of arresting a young person often increases the likelihood of future antisocial behavior. In one study, requiring a young person to go to court apparently boosted future criminal activity and using juvenile detention increased the chances of a negative outcome even more (Gatti, Tremblay, & Vitaro, 2009). Boys processed by the juvenile justice system were nearly seven times more likely to be arrested for a crime in adulthood than similar peers who avoided the system. Those sentenced to juvenile detention were 37 times more likely to be arrested as adults than were their antisocial peers.

The iatrogenic effects associated with the juvenile justice system present a major problem for young people and for society. Apparently, assortative pairing, that is, the process in which antisocial young people connect with each other to brag, justify, and reinforce their delinquent behavior, actually contributes to future problems (Gatti et al., 2009). This provides yet another argument for prevention programs to deal with problems before they become severe.

Families with Parental Psychopathology

Many young people are at risk because of parental mental health challenges or psychopathology (Bennouna-Greene, Bennouna-Greene, Berna, & Defranoux, 2011; Kohl, Jonson-Reid, & Drake, 2011; Reupert et al., 2015). Anxiety in mothers, for example, is highly related to anxiety in their teenage daughters (Rapee, 2009). Schizophrenia, bipolar disorders, and depression in adult caretakers seem to be particularly debilitating to young people. This can have long-term effects. For example, depressed teenagers growing up with depressed parents—especially depressed mothers—tend to have more frequent and severe depressive episodes as young adults than those with mentally healthy parents (Rohde, Lewinsohn, Klein, & Seeley, 2005). Even minimal depressive symptoms in parents across time are associated with increased risk for psychopathology in their teenagers (Mars et al., 2015). There is also a positive relationship between the degree of maternal depression and the frequency of a teenager's aggression (Pugh & Farrell, 2012). Poor marital adjustment and a low level of parent solidarity, warmth, and support usually characterize a family with depressed parents. The parents' mental illness contributes to disturbed parent–child interactions, which leads to limited cognitive, emotional, and social development in the child (Center on the Developing Child at Harvard University, 2009). Parental depressive symptoms are associated with children's reports of stress (Sieh, Visser-Meily, & Meijer, 2013). Teenagers in these families frequently have poor emotional and behavioral control and school adjustment problems. They may become easily upset, may disturb the class with unusual behavior, and have consistent discipline problems. These young people are at risk both for possible psychopathology themselves and for other risky behaviors.

When a child or adolescent exhibits risky behavior, it is important to consider the family in which the individual is being raised. The behavior of concern may be a reasonable—even if disturbing or dangerous—response to living in a dysfunctional family. The problems of the parents are sad and distressing; their effects on the children are tragic.

DOMESTIC VIOLENCE

Family Violence Correlates

In reality, the various types of dysfunctional families often overlap. Interpersonal violence, for example, is closely associated with alcohol use, drug use, or both. For women who experience interpersonal violence, the belief that alcohol and drug use will reduce stress is associated with frequency of alcohol use, the severity of alcohol problems, the severity of physical and sexual IPV, and PTSD (Peters, Khondkaryan, & Sullivan, 2012). For women who experience minor forms of violence (i.e., threats, pushing), odds of later drug use increase by a factor of 1.5 (Nowotny & Graves, 2013). Furthermore, these researchers found ethnic/racial differences in substance use when experiencing physical forms of interpersonal violence. For White and Latina women, later marijuana and drug use was associated with different forms of IPV, while this was not the case for African American women, suggesting different coping strategies across groups. Violence between spouses is often accompanied by violence toward children; parent alcohol and drug use are associated with child neglect and physical abuse (Kohl et al., 2011). As we have noted, growing up with alcohol-abusing parents significantly increases the risk of a variety of adverse childhood experiences, including interpersonal violence (Reupert et al., 2015). For example, mothers with substance use disorder (SUD) and higher depression symptoms are more likely to engage in overreactive parenting, with higher potential for child abuse (Kelley et al., 2015). Similarly, depressive symptoms in fathers with SUD were moderately associated with risk for child maltreatment. Alcoholic fathers are eight times more likely and alcoholic mothers three times more likely to abuse or neglect their children than parents who are not alcoholic (American Psychological Association Presidential Task Force on Violence and the Family, 1996).

Witnessing interpersonal familial violence is also risky for children and adolescents. Of course, violence signals general marital discord, which is also associated with problematic behavior in children. Even when the child is not a direct target of family violence, exposure to adults who verbally abuse each other and who are not in control of their explosive anger can have long-lasting repercussions. The effect of family violence on the child is wholly negative, and it can damage the child's self-esteem and confidence. Such children are more vulnerable to stress disorders and other psychological disturbances. Violence also begets more violence. Child maltreatment significantly predicts adult and juvenile–adult general violence as it is positively associated with adult and juvenile–adult violent offending (Topitzes, Mersky, & Reynolds, 2012). As violence in the family increases, it also increases the likelihood that the child will grow up to engage in violent and abusive behavior (Capaldi et al., 2009; Tolan, Gorman-Smith, & Henry, 2006). Childhood neglect increases a person's vulnerability to interpersonal violence victimization; adults with documented histories of child abuse/neglect were more likely to report having been victimized in the form of injury by an intimate partner (Widom, Czaja, & Dutton, 2014). Families with child abuse are especially distressed (Bennouna-Greene et al., 2011).

Child Abuse

As a specific form of violence, child abuse occurs in many forms: physical violence, emotional abuse, psychological abuse, neglect, and sexual abuse. Physical violence is any physically harmful action against a child, from hair pulling and slapping to beating and burning. Emotional abuse occurs when children are subjected to harsh criticism, ridicule such as name-calling, irrational punishment, and inconsistent expectations. Psychological abuse occurs when parents manipulate children by withholding affection, giving inconsistent verbal and nonverbal messages, threatening suicide in front of children, and isolating children from peer contact, including making the home environment miserable so that peers never want to come over and play. Neglect occurs when a parent fails to safeguard the health, well-being, and safety of the child. Children who are not provided with healthy food and bathed regularly, who are left unattended, or who are consistently ignored are victims of neglect. Sexual abuse is any form of sexual behavior with a child, including molestation, incest, and rape, as well as systematic and consistent exposure to explicit sexual material.

Children who grow up in such families find themselves at risk for future problems. Psychological abuse is particularly harmful. Children that have been psychologically abused suffer effects that are equal to or greater than that of children who have been physically and/or sexually abused, and children who have experienced a co-occurrence of psychological maltreatment with physical or sexual abuse experience a greater frequency of negative effects than those who suffer from physical or sexual abuse alone (Spinazzola et al., 2015). Nearly half a million children who are victims of abuse and neglect are a part of our foster care system and over time, many of these youth will cross into our juvenile justice system; many will eventually become adult offenders (Krinsky, 2010). Child abuse and neglect also has a negative impact on a person's likelihood of successfully achieving three important milestones in life—high school graduation, employment, and marriage—and the failure to attain these milestones is associated with a significant increase in the risk for adult arrest (Allwood & Widom, 2013). The correlations between child abuse, teenage pregnancy, and sexual victimization via unwanted sexual experiences are well documented (USDHHS, 2008). The age of first pregnancy is also linked to early physical or sexual abuse in the family (Feingold, Kerr, & Capaldi, 2008).

Intimate Partner Violence

IPV involves two people in a close relationship, including current and former spouses, and cohabitating and dating partners. Four types of behavior—emotional/ psychological abuse, sexual abuse, physical abuse, and threats—constitute IPV, which exists along a continuum from a single episode to ongoing battering. Notice that all four of the case studies we have presented up to this point have examples of child abuse, IPV, or both, reflecting their prevalence in the lives of at-risk young people.

Many victims do not report IPV to police, friends, or family. Nevertheless, men are the victims of nearly 3 million intimate partner assaults each year, while women experience nearly 5 million assaults and rapes. Male victims of rape had predominantly male perpetrators, while other forms of sexual violence were perpetrated predominantly by women (i.e., being made to penetrate) or were split evenly between men and women (i.e., unwanted sexual contact, noncontact unwanted sexual experiences, stalking) (Centers for Disease Control and Prevention/CDC, 2011). Lesbians and gay men reported IPV over their lifetimes at equal or greater levels than that of heterosexuals (Center for Disease Control and Prevention/CDC, 2013). Of the over 1,500 IPV deaths in 2005, 78% were women and 22% were men (Centers for Disease Control and Prevention/ CDC, 2010a). Interpersonal violence is also the leading cause of homicides for females and injury-related deaths during pregnancy. In addition, abuse of women is the single greatest cause of injury to women and the most common and frequent form of family violence (Whitaker & Lutzker, 2009). U.S. women lose nearly 8 million days of paid work and over 5 1/2 million days from household chores every year because of violence perpetrated against them by their partners. This is the equivalent of over 32,000 full-time jobs (Chronister & Davidson, 2010).

Children whose parents are involved in IPV are exposed to parental violence and are also more likely to be abused. Such exposure affects cognitive, emotional, and behavioral function and peer relationships and school adjustment (Whitaker & Lutzker, 2009; Wolfe, Wekerle, Scott, Straatman, & Grasley, 2004). Parental IPV that includes the child's observing or experiencing violence is a major risk factor for the child's future involvement in IPV, as either a victim or a perpetrator or both. Essentially, children learn how to act by experiencing how others treat them and by observing how their parents treat each other.

Two prevention programs are now described that yielded positive effects on IPV survivors (Chronister, 2006; Chronister & E. H. McWhirter, 2006; Chronister, Linville, & Palmer, 2008; P. T. McWhirter & J. J. McWhirter, 2010): Advancing Career Counseling and Employment Support for Survivors (ACCESS) and Project FREE.

ACCESS

ACCESS (Chronister, 2006) is a five-session career counseling program. It is a group intervention designed to build equity and empowerment for women survivors of IPV by increasing their self-awareness and career options. Each group session is led by one or two group facilitators and lasts 2 hours. Five career intervention components included in the program have been associated with the greatest positive outcomes in career counseling interventions (Brown & Krane, 2000): building support, individualized career skills assessment, providing world-of-work information, written exercises, and role modeling.

An essential focus of ACCESS is to contribute to survivors' critical consciousness and empowerment by increasing their awareness of the supportive and abusive power dynamics in their lives; the social, political, and economic injustices that affect their life contexts; and their occupational and life skills. Six group process components help promote the development of the women's critical consciousness: dialogue, group identification, posing problems, identifying contradictions, power analysis, and critical self-reflection.

ACCESS participation had a significant influence on survivors' vocational self-efficacy and critical consciousness and, at 5-week follow-up, increased participant's progress toward achieving their goals (Chronister & E. H. McWhirter, 2006). Further, in another study (Chronister, Linville, & Palmer, 2008), participants reported increased vocational knowledge, self-efficacy, self-esteem, and motivation. In short, ACCESS is a psychoeducation curriculum that counselors, social workers, and human service workers can use to help restore to survivors the career and economic opportunities that are diminished by oppressive partners and limited social and structural supports. Children of women survivors of domestic violence benefit significantly when their mothers become free of the cycle of violence and are able to shape and enhance their economic future.

Project FREE

This community-based program focuses on mothers who have survived domestic violence and their children who witnessed it (P. T. McWhirter, 2006, 2008a, 2008b). Project FREE includes simultaneous psychoeducational group sessions with battered mothers and their children separately, followed by conjoint family sessions with mothers and children together. Groups also met weekly for 5 weeks. Women-only group met separately for 60 minutes

60-minute conjoint family session involved children with their mothers. Each group consisted of 4 to 5 participants with conjoint groups consisting of 8 to 10 participants (children with their mothers) (P. T. McWhirter, 2008a).

Several group experiences have been developed for mothers: One focuses on mental health enhancement using cognitive behavioral and gestalt approaches; one targets economic development with an employment mentoring and networking process; another is a heavy emotional-focused, here-and-now group model; and the fourth is goal-oriented intervention. During the same time that the mothers are meeting, their children are provided with psychoeducational groups to reduce the negative consequences of violence. These children's groups are designed to address developmentally appropriate skill building, and they include dealing with stress and strong emotions, communication skills, increasing responsible behavior, identifying and making friends, and handling interpersonal family conflict (P. T. McWhirter, 2008b).

Outcomes for Project FREE have been quite positive. For mothers there is an increase in family bonding, size of social network, and an increased readiness to make meaningful therapeutic changes. There is also a decrease in social isolation and financial stress. In addition, participant mothers experience attitude and skill enhancement, allowing them to cope more effectively in stressful family environments. There are also positive effects related to the psychoeducational content of the various groups: decreasing alcohol use, reaching personal goals to decrease alcohol and other drug use, and increasing social support (P. T. McWhirter, 2007). The children's psychoeducational groups in Project FREE studies generally have increased emotional well-being, encouraged more positive peer and sibling engagement, and improved self-esteem in the children (P. T. McWhirter & J. J. McWhirter, 2010).

Dating Violence

Antecedents to IPV, and IPV itself, often manifest when young people begin dating. Although the research demonstrating that dating violence is a predictor of adult domestic violence, most researchers believe that it is likely that abuse patterns established during adolescence continue with adult partners (Foshee & Reyes, 2009; Whitaker & Lutzker, 2009).

Regardless of its influence on future behavior, dating violence is a serious problem in itself (Ortega & Sánchez, 2011). Dating violence is a type of IPV that occurs between two people in a close relationship. The nature of dating violence can be physical, emotional, or sexual and includes physical abuse ranging from pushing, to throwing objects, to attacking with weapons, as well as sexual and emotional abuse.

Almost three of four 8th and 9th graders "date." Although many teens do not report dating violence because they are afraid to tell friends and family, data indicates that of those adolescents dating, 1 in 4 report verbal, physical, emotional, or sexual abuse from a dating partner each year. In addition, nearly 10% of students report being physically hurt by a boyfriend or girl-friend in the past 12 months (Centers for Disease Control and Prevention, 2010b). Lesbian, gay, and bisexual youth are more likely to experience physical dating violence, psychological dating abuse, cyber dating abuse, and sexual coercion than heterosexual youth (Dank, Lachman, Zweig, & Yahner, 2014). These youth have also reported higher rates of perpetration of physical, psychological, and cyber dating violence and abuse than heterosexual youth. Transgender youth experience the highest rates of victimization compared to both male and female youth, as well as highest perpetration rates for everything except psychological abuse (Dank et al., 2014). Adolescent dating violence apparently is not significantly associated with socioeconomic status (SES) or with race (Jacob, Ouvrard, & Bélanger, 2011). There is, however, a link between adolescents' experience of dating violence and substance use (Chronister, Marsiglio, Linville, & Lantrip, 2014).

Intervention programs are especially important because of the developmental tasks that confront adolescents. Teens compared to adults tend to accept and conform to traditional sexual stereotypes. Their basic need to belong and be validated by peers can create a vulnerability to intimidation, control, and violence (Ortega & Sánchez, 2011). Preventive interventions and those targeting young people already experiencing dating violence should include a strong focus on targeted relationship and coping skills to reduce the negative impact of current relationships, and prevent future abusive relationships (Chronister et al., 2014).

Strategies for preventing dating abuse should begin early, and intervention approaches should be initiated upon identification of disrespectful dating interactions, including physical and psychological abuse. Most scholars recommend that an appropriate time to begin primary prevention of dating violence is in the 8th grade or about age 13 (Foshee & Reyes, 2009). Such programs could build on the effects of a bullying prevention program as a way of preventing dating violence. Primary prevention of dating abuse should focus on preventing bullying, aggression, and sexual harassment with peers, which are behavioral precursors to dating abuse.

The bully's use of aggression to assert power and dominance is likely to express itself in romantic relationships. Bullying prevention programs as early as elementary grades, when bullying behaviors are just emerging, may contribute to preventing dating violence. Research is needed on this topic. Bullying programs clearly reduce bullying, but research has not been done to show that they impact dating violence even though logic suggests that they might. Two prevention programs focusing specifically on dating violence—the Safe Dates Program and the Youth Relationships Project—have demonstrated a positive impact on adolescents' dating violence (Foshee et al., 2005, 2014; Wolfe et al., 2004).

Safe Dates Program

This program is a universal schools-based program targeting knowledge and attitudes about dating abuse. Safe Dates (SD) was designed to prevent the start of dating violence and reduce future victimization and perpetration among those who had already experienced it (Foshee et al., 2000, 2005, 2012). The program consists of a 10-session curriculum that includes a 45-minute theater production. Program goals include improving conflict management skills such as communication in response to anger, reducing acceptance of norms of gender stereotyping and acceptance of dating abuse, increasing awareness of victims' and perpetrators' need for help and community resources, and preventing or decreasing experiences of victimization and perpetration of dating violence.

Foshee et al. (2005) reported the results of long-term follow-up for students who had received the Safe Dates intervention in 8th or 9th grade. They compared Safe Date participants with students who had not received the intervention, at four different time points after the intervention, on victimization and perpetration in the following four areas: psychological abuse, moderate physical abuse, severe physical abuse, and sexual dating violence. Compared to those who did not receive the intervention, Safe Dates participants reported less psychological, moderate physical, and sexual dating violence perpetration, and less moderate physical dating violence victimization, at all four time points. Sexual dating violence victimization rates were also marginally lower among program participants. The program was found to be as effective for girls as for boys, with no differences in effectiveness between White and ethnic minority students. The program did not prevent or reduce psychological victimization or severe physical abuse victimization, and among the participants who had already engaged in severe physical abuse perpetration, the program did not have effects on subsequent perpetration. The program also positively influenced gender role norms, dating violence norms, and participant awareness of community resources. In summary, Safe Dates demonstrated both primary and secondary prevention effects up to 3 years after the intervention. Unfortunately, the program did not prevent more severe forms of dating abuse victimization. The effectiveness of Safe Dates appears to extend beyond its specific goals. In a later analysis, Foshee et al. (2014) reported that 1 year after the Safe Dates intervention, participants were 12% less likely to be victimized by peers at school and 31% less likely to carry a weapon; ethnic minority participants (but not White participants) also were 23% less likely to perpetrate other forms of youth violence.

Youth Relationships Project

Dating violence is associated with child abuse and maltreatment, including corporal punishment. The Youth Relationships Project (YRP) targeted adolescents identified by Child Protective Services as victims of maltreatment. Meeting in coeducational groups of adolescents who had been identified as maltreated with male and female cofacilitators, the young people were presented with three components: (1) awareness of abuse and power in close relationships, (2) skills development, and (3) social action.

The project, which consists of eighteen 2-hour sessions, reduced emotional dating abuse victimization, victimization from threatening behaviors, and physical dating violence perpetration over several months of the data collection. The project demonstrated reductions in trauma symptoms, but no effects on communication or problem-solving skills or on hostility (Wolfe et al., 2004).

CONCLUSION

In this chapter we considered social changes that affect today's families and the rapid changes that occur within families in response to them. Helping professionals need to understand and appreciate cultural differences in families rather than impose dominant culture assumptions. Many families are characterized by detachment, enmeshment, poor parenting practices, or are dysfunctional in other ways. The Carter family illustrates a fairly common family dysfunction. As families progress through developmental periods, or stages of the family life cycle, some of the interaction patterns that developed early, such as parenting styles, must adapt to the changing needs of the children. When they do not, young people are often at risk for engaging in maladaptive and self-defeating behaviors.

School Issues that Relate to At-Risk Children and Youth

CHAPTER

4

If families do not...

Then schools must

Provide roots for children...

So they stand firm and grow,

Provide wings for children...

So they can fly.

Broken roots and crippled wings

Destroy hope.

And hope sees the invisible,

Feels the intangible,

And achieves the impossible.

CHAPTER OUTLINE

- The Value of Education
  - Federal Engagement in Education
  - Federal Legislation: No Child Left Behind; Race to the Top
  - State Initiatives: Common Core

- Research on Effective Schools
  - Variables in Research on School Effectiveness
    Leadership Behaviors
    Academic Emphasis
    Teacher and Staff Factors
    Student Involvement
    Community Support
    Social Capital
  - Definitional Issues in Research on School Effectiveness
    School Culture
  - Case Study: The Diaz Family

    Student Climate
    Peer Involvement
    Teacher Climate

- Educational Structure: Schools and Classrooms
  - School Structure
  - School Choice
  - Charter Schools
  - Classroom Structure
  - Curriculum Issues

- Education Structure: Innovations
  - World Wide Web—the Internet
  - Flipped Classroom

- Conclusion

In education, the term *at risk* refers primarily to students who are at risk of school failure. As we discussed earlier, *at risk* actually means much more than flunking reading or math, or even dropping out of school. Yet from an educator's perspective, educational concerns define at-risk issues. School problems and dropout are linked to many other problems expressed by young people (APA, 2012; Henry, Stanley, Edwards, Harkabus, & Chapin, 2009; Rumberger & Ah Lim, 2008; Suh, Suh, & Houston, 2007). The strong relationships between school difficulties and other problems, as well as evidence that educational involvement is a protective factor influencing resilience (Search Institute, 2013; Wang & Fredricks, 2014), highlight the pivotal position of schools. In schools, prevention efforts can reach the greatest number of young people; therefore, examining the educational environment is critical.

THE VALUE OF EDUCATION

There are a number of indicators of the value placed on education in the United States. News reports compare the scores of students in the United States and in other countries on tests in geography, spelling, math, and science. These reports consistently favor students in other countries. They imply that learning in U.S. schools is somehow not quite up to par. Does a student's ability to spell reflect his or her ability to think? Does recall of dates, locations, or facts indicate a student's problem-solving skills? The answer to these questions is "No." Learning is the act of acquiring knowledge or a skill through observation, experience, instruction, or study, yet these comparisons suggest a view of learning that reduces this complicated act to an isolated and mechanical process. In addition, these comparisons often fail to note that in the United States all children are expected to attend school through high school graduation, not just wealthy or middle-class urban or college-bound students.

How learning is valued is also reflected in the following statistics. In 2000, the average household income was about $55,000 (Census Bureau, 2001). A decade later, the average teachers' salaries were less than $54,000 (NCES, 2010). This situation has not changed much since the last census. Schoolteachers and counselors, over 50% with master's degrees, continue to be paid less than the national average income and are poorly remunerated relative to other professionals. Low teacher salaries reflect the value society places on education and is one contributor to the current teacher shortage. Research on the early career patterns of beginning teachers indicates that 17% of new teachers are no longer in the classroom 5 years after they begin (Gray & Taie, 2015). First-year salary levels were related to continuing teaching. When the first-year base salary was $40,000 or more, 89% of these beginning teachers were still in the classroom 5 years later. When the first-year salary was less than $40,000, only 80% were teaching.

Being assigned a mentor for the first year was also important; only 71% without a first-year mentor were still teaching compared to 86% who had had a mentor 5 years earlier. As a society, we are indeed fortunate that so many good teachers do remain in our classrooms for other reasons than salaries.

In response to the current shortage of teachers, many states are lowering teacher standards, with many new teachers not meeting state licensing requirements. Frequently, students in high school physics, geology, biology/life science, and physical science and in ESL/bilingual education classes have teachers who are not certified. The charter school movement probably contributes to this situation because certification is not a requirement for teaching in a charter school. Students learn more from better teachers. Not surprisingly, more affluent schools attract teachers with greater academic skills (Wayne, 2002); a much greater percentage of teachers at poorer schools have poor academic and teaching skills. And the disparity between rich and poor schools is increasing (Berliner, 2001; Kozol, 2005). The richest school districts in the United States spend 56% more per student than the poorest schools. Economists, sociologists, and educators have known for decades about the link between the social and economic disadvantage and the student-achievement gap. To obtain real school reform, it is critically important to address the underlying social and economic conditions (Rothstein, 2004). Those schools serving large numbers of poor children are likely to have fewer books and supplies and more teachers with less training and experience. If U.S. schools are expected to combat the societal problems of at-risk students, we must commit to the education of our children and youth as our highest priority, which includes attracting and training enough qualified teachers and counselors, encouraging them to work in poor districts, and providing them with adequate compensation.

Federal Engagement in Education

Federal funding and policies provide further evidence regarding society's support of education. During Carter's presidency, Congress elevated the subcabinet agency of education to the Department of Education (DOE). In the 1980s, the Reagan and the first Bush administrations insisted that the DOE bring about educational reforms by "leadership and persuasion"—not by new programs or funds. In fact, during every year of Reagan's administration, educational funding was level or reduced for programs that provided aid for disadvantaged children, bilingual education, and work-incentive child-care initiatives; educational funding fell from 2.3% to 1.7% of the total federal budget (Carville, 1996). The expenditure per pupil (dollar level adjusted) in public schools rose very slowly during the 1980s and 1990s. The 1990s saw a disturbing trend in prisons versus education. For the first time, states spent more on prisons than on colleges: University construction funds decreased by almost a billion (to $2.5 billion), and corrections funding increased by almost a billion (to $2.6 billion; Ambrosio & Schiraldi, 1997; also see CNN Money, 2015).

For example, the New York State prison budget increased by $761 million at the same time that the higher education budget dropped by $615 million. And in California there was a 209% funding increase in the prison system budget, but only a 15% increase in state university funding (Taqi-Eddin, Macallair, & Schiraldi, 1998). The cost of housing an inmate per year, on average, is $31,286 (Henrichson & Delaney, 2012), a huge drain on public funds. Young Black males are the group most adversely and directly affected by the "school-to-prison pipeline" (Alexander, 2010; Dancy, 2014).

A society loses by producing nonproductive citizens. If schools do not provide a safety net for children, health and well-being are reduced. Investing in prisons instead of education and prevention is an expensive, wasteful, and failing long-term strategy. America spends more dollars on incarcerating non-violent offenders than on welfare programs and considerably more than on child care. Although the United States has only 5% of the world's population, it has 25% of the world's prisoners and the highest rate of incarceration in the world (Walmsley, 2011). Of the 10 million incarcerated people in the world, the United States, Russia, and China are detaining almost half. Yet children in the United States attend greatly underfunded schools.

The publication of *A Nation at Risk* (National Commission on Excellence in Education, 1983) has led to over three decades of bashing public school education by placing the source and responsibility of student problems primarily on schools to the exclusion of other societal factors (Mehta, 2015). By ignoring the role of external issues, the document unfairly scapegoats educators and school systems.

A Nation at Risk also launched the high-stakes testing phenomena, in which consequences for not passing standardized tests include grade retention for individual students and decreased funding for schools that fail to achieve required pass rates (Amrein & Berliner, 2002; Au, 2013). High-stakes testing contributes to the American myth of meritocracy and lends legitimacy to the structural inequality experienced by poor, ethnic minority, and immigrant communities (Au, 2013). In *The Manufactured Crisis*, Berliner and Biddle (1995) provide convincing evidence of a political agenda underlying *A Nation at Risk* and present thorough and sound data indicating that public schools in the United States have done a marvelous job of educating American children. In fact, they demonstrate that children actually know more than earlier generations, compare very favorably to students educated in other countries, and perform better than ever before (see Box 4.1).

Federal Legislation: No Child Left Behind; Race to the Top

The No Child Left Behind (NCLB) Act of 2002 was a sweeping reform of the Elementary and Secondary Education Act, and it redefined the federal role in K–12 education. Unfortunately, its promise to help close the achievement gap between disadvantaged and minority students and their peers was only moderately successful. NCLB contains four basic principles: stronger account-ability for results (e.g., decreased funding for schools that do not meet pass

Box 4.1	Separate and Unequal 15-Year-Olds

A new look at the literacy of teens living in the industrialized world shows that American students are about average. "Average is not good enough for American kids," warns former Education Secretary Rod Paige. True enough—but Paige and the Bush administration miss the point. Hidden in those results is yet one more piece of evidence that American youth attend schools that are separate and markedly unequal.

The Program on International Student Assessment (PISA) seeks to understand what 15-year-olds in 27 industrialized nations learned in reading, mathematics, and science from school and nonschool sources. PISA's goal is to assess how well we teach youth to think and solve common, everyday problems in those three disciplines. With 85% of a student's waking hours up to graduation from high school spent outside school, this is really a study of how well our society educates our young.

The answer depends on whether the teens are White, African American, or Hispanic. Overall, in the United States 15-year-olds were close to the international averages in all three areas of literacy: About 10% scored in the top 10% worldwide on all three scales. The three tests correlated so highly that national scores on any one measure of literacy were almost a perfect proxy for scores on any other measure.

In reading, our strongest area, teens in only three nations—Finland, Canada, and New Zealand—scored significantly higher than ours; in fact, 81% of U.S. teens scored at levels two and above on a five-level reading literacy scale (with Level Five being the top).

This is noteworthy because of what PISA says a "Level Two" teen can do: make a comparison or several connections between the text and outside knowledge, draw on personal experience and attitudes to explain the text, recognize the main idea when the information is not prominent, understand relationships or construe meaning within a selected part of the text, and locate one or more pieces of information, which may require inferences to meet several conditions. Only 12% of our teens, those classified in Level One, cannot reach this remarkably high standard. Even among the least-literate teens classified at Level One, almost half were able to successfully respond to the more difficult items in Level Two.

On all three tests, our youth didn't do badly overall—but we didn't shine either. Why? The answer becomes clear when the scores of different 15-year-olds are viewed separately.

PISA clearly shows we have some ill-educated 15-year-olds, and most of those are poor and minority children. On the reading literacy scale White students in the United States are 2nd in the world, but African American and Hispanic students rank 25th; in mathematics White students are 7th, African American students are 26th; in science White students are 4th, African American and Hispanic students are 26th.

Box 4.1 (Continued)

The unpleasant reality is that the United States maintains separate and unequal schools and neighborhoods. The conditions of the schools and neighborhoods for our poor, African American, and Hispanic youth are not designed for high levels of literacy in reading, mathematics, and science. We accept poverty, violence, drugs, unequal school funding, uncertified teachers, and institutionalized racism in the schools that serve these children and in the neighborhoods in which they live. These unequal conditions appear to be the major reason we fall short in international comparisons. We combine the scores of these ill-educated children with those of children who enjoy better resources. As long as we tolerate these disparities in education, we will rank about average in international comparisons.

As PISA makes clear, accepting deficient schools and troubled neighborhoods for our poor and minority students diminishes our international competitiveness. In ignoring these data about who does well and who does not, we diminish our moral authority in the world as well.

PISA exposes what we have known for too long: that we have social problems to which we pay scant attention. In every international comparison of industrialized nations, the United States is the leader in rate of childhood poverty. African American and Hispanic students attend public schools as segregated as they have ever been. Our poor and minority children are not getting the opportunities they need for the nation to thrive.

Politicians who spend their energy condemning the public schools for their supposed failure to educate American youth are ignoring what PISA tells the world: that we fail selectively, having organized our society to provide poor and minority 15-year-olds less opportunity to achieve. Shame on us.

David Berliner, Regents' Professor Emeritus
Arizona State University
Tempe, Arizona

Note: Recent reports (OECD, 2014) indicate that the U.S. average mathematics, science, and reading literacy scores in 2012 were not measurably different from average scores in previous PISA assessment years, continuing to support Professor Berliner's position.

---

rates for standardized tests), increased flexibility and local control, expanded school choice options for parents (e.g., parents can remove their children from failing schools), and an emphasis on scientifically supported teaching methods. There are significant concerns about the effects of the NCLB Act with more funding flowing away from those public schools in most desperate need and an undermining of support for public education (e.g., Meier, Kohn, Darling-Hammond, Sizer, & Wood, 2004). Another concern is the diminished attention to both above- and below-average students. Schools required to demonstrate improvement can do so most efficiently by focusing resources on those children who test just below the minimum pass rates. Those children who have very poor test scores are unlikely to raise scores high enough to increase the school's pass rate, and those students with good scores are already part of the pass rates. Both the highest and lowest achieving students are less likely to receive support or services. The NCLB focus on standardized test results has had other negative consequences including reducing the extent to which the school is engaging and creative; de-professionalization of teaching; diminishing emphases on social studies, music, and the arts; and greatly reducing attention to development of values and skills that contribute to problem solving, reasoning, cooperation, and democratic participation (Welner & Mathis, 2015). While the NCLB continues to be extended, the Obama administration introduced the Race to the Top (RTTT) Act designed to replace the NCLB. The RTTT program was designed to spur K–12 education reform and is funded by the American Recovery and Reinvestment Act. RTTT goals are to improve student achievement, improve high school graduation rates, ensure postsecondary success, and close achievement gaps between best and lowest performing schools (U.S. Department of Education, 2009). To the extent that education reforms continue to be driven by standardized test results without increasing resources, Welner and Mathis (2015) argue that achievement gaps will only increase.

State Initiatives: Common Core

In addition to federal legislation, Common Core Standards have been developed as an education reform. State school chiefs and governors from 48 states recognized the value of consistent, real-world learning goals and, in 2009, launched this effort to ensure all students, regardless of where they live, are graduating high school prepared for college, career, and life. By the early 2000s, most states had developed learning standards that specify what students in grades 3 to 8 and high school should be able to do. Also, each state had its own definition of proficiency (i.e., the level at which a student is determined to be sufficiently educated). This lack of standardization was one reason why the Common Core State Standards were implemented. Using feedback from the public, the experience of teachers and content experts, and the best state standards already in existence, the Common Core Standards have been adopted by most states (McLaughlin & Overturf, 2012).

Common Core does provide a template for educating children and adolescents. It remains to be seen whether resources will be provided to help those students at risk of dropping out or leaving school without the recognized proficiencies. Most scholars express optimism that at-risk students including those with special needs can potentially benefit greatly from these new standards, although they also caution that the demands of these standards may require a higher level of support than those commonly available for many students with learning problems (Powell, Fuchs, & Fuchs, 2013; Scruggs, Brigham, & Mastropieri, 2013). In two early studies completed on Kentucky students—one from the National Center for Analysis of Longitudinal

Data in Education Research and the other from the Brookings Institution's Brown Center on Education Policy—scores rose during the years in which many Kentucky schools implemented Common Core State Standard (Granata, 2015). However, it might be too early to tell whether there is a connection between the improvement in scores and the Common Core, and whether implementation of the Common Core contributes to reduction in achievement gaps for poor, immigrant, or ethnic minority students, or students with learning disabilities.

Most teachers work hard, are concerned about children, and try to do a good job of teaching. Teachers know that all children need support, care, and nurturing. They also know that with the decline of economic stability, the pressures parents face, and the fragmentation of neighborhoods and communities, the support and care children receive at school is even more critical. Teachers are expected to do more than ever before in classrooms that some find increasingly unsafe. Gang activity occurs around schools. School shootings leave teachers questioning whether such shocking violence could happen "at my school." Of course for some, incidents of victimization lead to disenchantment and even departure from teaching (Dinkes, Kemp, & Baum, 2009; Smith & Smith, 2006). Amidst these concerns, teachers are constantly bombarded about how "teachers are not doing their jobs," how "schools are inadequate and failing," and how teachers must "do more with less."

For public education to succeed, increased financial support is needed for struggling schools. More money is needed. School reform is critical to the development of more effective schools. However, reforming education is more than revising tests, rewriting curricula, and restructuring schools. Reform must include supporting the human resources on whom so much depends. Teachers and counselors and other "people personnel" must be better compensated, freed from bureaucratic harassment, given a role in academic governance, allowed to do what they were trained to do, and provided with the best methods and materials.

RESEARCH ON EFFECTIVE SCHOOLS

Variables in Research on School Effectiveness

A recent report identified several common elements that characterize effective schools: Teachers consistently engage students; the entire staff is dedicated and caring; both class size and student populations are small; clear ground rules set the tone for respectful behavior; high expectations and clear consequences are articulated to students frequently; both daily and classroom routines provide stability and direction (Education World, 2015). These characteristics reflect elements that are present in effective schools (Henry et al., 2009; Sadker, Zittleman, & Sadker, 2010) and can be classified into the general categories of leadership behaviors, academic emphasis, teacher and staff factors, student involvement, community support, and social capital.

Leadership Behaviors

Effective schools have autonomous staff management at the school site. Administrators, teachers, and counselors make many decisions about programs and program implementation without the need to seek approval of the school board or the district. Effective schools have a clear mission and place an emphasis on strong instructional leadership.

Academic Emphasis

Effective schools provide a rigorous curriculum. Students are expected to perform, and they are frequently monitored. Academic achievement is recognized on a schoolwide basis, instructional time is maximized, and the curriculum is consistently improved (Rumberger & Ah Lim, 2008).

Teacher and Staff Factors

Effective schools are characterized by collegial relationships among the staff, encouragement of collaborative planning, and low turnover among the faculty. Further, staff development is provided on a schoolwide basis.

Student Involvement

Students at effective schools tend to have a sense of community, a feeling of belonging, and a sense of safety at school (Khoury-Kassabri, 2011). They also are likely to have clear goals. Teachers and counselors work to help students feel connected. Student discipline is fair, clear, and consistent and neither oppressive nor punitive.

Community Support

The communities in which effective schools are located have high expectations of the schools and their students. Further, district support and supportive parental involvement are evident, and relationships between home and school are strong and positive.

Social Capital

Social capital, the network of relationships that surround an individual child, is important for development (Terrion, 2006). One of the major reasons some schools perform significantly better than others is that they are so rich in social capital (Coleman & Hoffer, 1987; Terrion, 2006). The nuclear and extended family, the neighborhood and church community, the social service agencies, and community organizations form a supportive enclave of adults who are united with school personnel around a system of similar educational beliefs and values. This network of relationships is extremely important to the education of all children. Improvements in social capital lead to reduced family stress, which results in improved child behavior. Most school systems are severely constrained today because of the general reduction of social capital in society.

Definitional Issues in Research on School Effectiveness

Most research on effective schools—partly a by-product of the NCLB Act—measures effectiveness as students' performance on standardized achievement tests. This is an extremely narrow view of learning. Other cognitive criteria, such as depth analysis, decision making, and critical thinking, are largely ignored. Most high-quality knowledge cannot be measured by standardized, machine-scored tests. To judge school effectiveness by the narrow criterion of scores on standardized tests pressures teachers and districts to carry out test-driven curriculum (Welner & Mathis, 2015). It may not be helping the educational problem anyway. In one study examining a decade of data from 18 states that implemented high-stakes testing, Amrein and Berliner (2002) found that scores on standardized tests such as the ACT and the SAT did not increase after high-stakes testing was implemented, even when the high-stakes test scores increased. Scores on the ACT, SAT, and content measures stayed the same or actually decreased.

Results of research on school effectiveness must be viewed with caution. For example, schools with higher dropout rates potentially have higher test score averages than do schools that retain their lower achieving students longer. If effectiveness is judged by performance on high-stakes tests alone, a school that fails miserably with at-risk students by pushing them out may be deemed highly effective! Alternative indices, such as students' involvement in the community, attendance rates, the incidence of school vandalism and violence, or dropout rates, are seldom measured in school effectiveness research, but these indices may be more relevant to the school, community, and country. Another dimension of school effectiveness is school culture. School culture focuses on aspects of education more directly relevant to at-risk youth. Before reading about school culture, please read the Diaz family case study.

School Culture

Every social organization has its unique culture, and schools are no exception. Student involvement, teacher factors, community support, curricular focus, and educational leadership—factors that also define effective schools—determine school culture. A culture provides its members with two things. First, it establishes a set of rules, expectations, and norms for members. Carlos's teachers encourage an English-only norm for students who are speaking Spanish, even extending to students' informal conversations with each other, but do not intervene with students speaking other non-English languages. In Lidia's school, retaining students who do poorly is the rule, and teacher expectations are not high for students in the lowest ability groups. Essentially, school culture provides an informal understanding of the way things are done. Second, culture can enhance self-esteem—or not—through shared values, beliefs, rituals, and ceremonies. Students, faculty, and staff who take pride in their school culture are likely to do better than those who do not. Many of Carlos's teachers share negative views of bilingual education; Lidia's feelings of stupidity are due in part to her exclusion from her

CASE STUDY • The Diaz Family

Enrique Diaz came to the United States from El Salvador some years ago when he was 23 years old. He was forced to flee El Salvador when his membership in a small labor union was revealed to the government authorities, and he left behind his parents, brothers, sisters, and extended family. He brought his sister's 2-year-old daughter Ramona with him because the baby's father had been killed for his labor union activity and his sister feared for her own life. A nonprofit community agency serving immigrants and a local church helped Enrique and Ramona obtain housing as well as assisted Enrique to find employment. Enrique works as a day laborer for growers and lawn maintenance companies. He met Alicia, a Mexican American woman volunteer at the community agency, during his first week in the United States. Alicia began spending a great deal of time caring for Ramona, and she and Enrique married 10 months after his arrival. One of the things that attracted Alicia to Enrique was the fact that he was a very hard worker and did not drink alcohol. Currently Enrique continues to work as hard as ever during the day, but he now consumes one or two six packs of beer most evenings. Alicia is the second child in a family of nine children. Her parents came to the United States from central Mexico as young adults. Alicia works as a motel maid and has a second part-time job doing custodial work at her church. Alicia and Enrique have raised Ramona, now 18, as their own daughter, and also have a son, Carlos, who is 13, and another daughter, Lidia, who is 5 years old. They live in a small rented home and maintain a very modest standard of living. Enrique and Ramona became naturalized citizens just before the birth of Lidia.

Enrique understands but does not speak English. Alicia was raised in a monolingual Spanish-speaking household but learned to speak English in school. Although her English skills are solid, she is very reluctant to use English unless she has to because she believes that she makes many mistakes and feels self-conscious about her accent. Both of the parents express concern about their children because family life is curtailed by the long hours the parents spend at work. They are especially concerned about their children's educational problems. Neither parent completed high school; both desperately want their children to have a better life. They view education as a necessary step toward that goal. Their communication with the school system has been complicated by language barriers and work schedules. In addition, Enrique and Alicia are convinced that the teachers think they are bad and uncaring parents because they have not learned enough English.

Upon entering kindergarten, Ramona Diaz was placed in an ESL (English as a second language) program. She was transitioned into an English-only classroom when she entered middle school because that was district policy; however, she did not seem prepared to enter this environment. Ramona associated only with other girls who were Spanish-language dominant and fell behind in all of her content areas. She resisted going to school, even skipping classes on occasion. In parent–teacher conferences, her teachers consistently said that she was not turning in her homework or would turn in work that was incomplete and inaccurate. Ramona insisted that she was turning it in but that her teachers were misplacing it and grading her unfairly because they thought she was "stupid" and didn't like her. Enrique was enraged by Ramona's attitude toward school, and they had explosive arguments two or three times per week, which were most likely to occur in the evening after Enrique had been drinking for several hours. Finally, at age 16, Ramona dropped out of school and began working five nights per week at ABC Burgers. Although Enrique and Alicia did not approve, they had felt somewhat out of control of Ramona and were unsure of how to help her in school. With Ramona out of the house at night, and because homework was no longer a constant source of tension, the fighting between Enrique and Ramona decreased. Enrique's drinking did not decrease.

Ramona tells her parents that she will eventually earn her GED. Alicia is concerned that Ramona will become pregnant and be stuck in low-paying jobs for the rest of her life. She rarely sees Ramona. Ramona arrives home from work after her parents are in bed and is still sleeping when Enrique and Alicia leave for work in the morning. Alicia suspects that Ramona has a boyfriend at work, but Ramona denies this and is very closed about her social activities. She has been contributing to the family income and is affectionate with her brother and sister when she sees them. Just last week, however, Ramona told her parents that she had lost her paycheck and would not be able to help out the family until the next one arrived.

Carlos Diaz is in the 7th grade. He has had a solid relationship with his parents, particularly his mother. Carlos has been in a regular classroom for the past 2 years. He has generally done well in his schoolwork, but he is not a model student. He has often had trouble with his peers and at times gotten into fights on the playground. Since he has moved into junior high school, his social problems have decreased somewhat. He has several teachers now, and the classes are larger than those in the primary school. He has begun to make friends, although his lack of free time outside of school has made this difficult.

Because of Ramona's job at ABC Burgers, Carlos has the responsibility of watching his little sister after school, and he has

CASE STUDY • The Diaz Family *(Continued)*

had difficulty completing school assignments. His after-school activities now include cleaning the house and helping to prepare dinner in addition to babysitting, so he has only a limited amount of time to complete the homework assigned by his five teachers. When his assignments require use of a computer, Carlos has to skip lunch and use one at school because his family does not own one. Some nights he works on every subject for at least a short time, but on other nights he is able to complete an assignment for only one of his classes. At the time the family entered counseling, Carlos was behind in every class and was falling asleep in school. Some of his teachers seem to think he is lazy, contrary, and unresponsive. Many of them seem frustrated that Carlos is not completely fluent in English "by now."

Carlos's social studies teacher, Ms. Bassett, has taken a particular interest in him. At first, she found him inattentive in class and unresponsive to her questions, and she assumed this behavior was a combination of language and lack of ability. She noticed, however, that when he did complete his homework it was usually well done and accurate. After consulting with the school counselor, she gave Carlos a more active role in his own education. She found ways to give him more responsibility for learning, provided a means for him to monitor his own progress, and generally encouraged his efforts to be more active in learning. The counselor also suggested that cooperative learning groups might be especially beneficial to Carlos, not only academically but also as a means to help Carlos develop better peer relationships. Ms. Bassett is currently struggling with ways to modify her teaching style in a school that bases

evaluations of her teaching on direct instruction, a method that typically works well for social studies recitation classes but fails to allow students to take an active role in learning. Enrique and Alicia view Carlos as a very responsible young man and hope that he will continue on in school. They are aware that he is under a lot of pressure at home and in school but do not seem to know what to do about it. In spite of their concerns, they have not responded to Ms. Bassett's invitation to meet with them or talk on the phone. They seem to fear that she will be upset about Carlos's caretaking role and that she will not understand their family situation.

Lidia Diaz is in kindergarten this year. Last year she participated in Head Start, which greatly aided her language skills and helped prepare her for kindergarten. In spite of this advantage, she is progressing quite slowly. She is one of 30 kindergartners in the classroom. Some of her classmates attended private preschools and can already read. To deal with the large number of students in her class, Lidia's teacher groups the children according to their ability in reading and arithmetic. Lidia knows that she is in the lowest group in both subjects. Like her older sister, Lidia often feels stupid. Lidia's teacher believes that Lidia has the potential for school success and wishes she could spend more time with her. Lidia's elementary school has a retention policy for kindergarten students who do not make certain gains in achievement. In spite of her teacher's belief in her abilities, Lidia fits the criteria for the district retention policy, and if things do not improve, she will probably be kept back next year.

school's culture. Participation and attendance in school activities can greatly enhance school connectedness and pride. These activities are generally hard hit when resources are scarce, and even when they are available, students such as Carlos are not able to take advantage of them. The culture of a school can be described in terms of student and teacher climate.

Student Climate

Several aspects of student climate relate directly to children and youth at risk. Children's experiences with their peers provide them with an opportunity to learn how to interact with others, develop age-relevant skills and interests, control their social behavior, and share their problems and feelings. As children get older, their peer group relationships increase in importance. The child's recognition of belonging to a group is an important step in development, and students with more friends at school feel more connected to their schools and generally have fewer problems (Karcher, 2004; SCDRC, 2010). Another important component of climate is "mattering" to others and having others that "matter" to you (Dixon, Scheidegger, & McWhirter, 2009). But belonging to a group has both benefits and costs in the child's subsequent social development and behavior. Many students who are at risk for school failure know early that somehow they are different from—less acceptable and less accepted than—other students. Lidia Diaz is one such student. Consistently grouping students by ability heightens such self-perceptions. Who of us did not know by the second grade which groups constituted the "good readers" and the "poor readers"? More important, the expectations of students depend on the group they are in. Students who succeed in school have both high expectations of themselves and a strong, positive sense of belonging to the school community. Students who are at risk for school failure are often placed in the lowest ability groups and excluded from the academic success community. Exclusion from the school community limits the potentially positive effects of school culture on students at risk for failure.

In addition to academically based groupings, the peer groups that students form influence student climate. Peers influence one another by offering support, advice, and opportunities to discuss conflicting points of view, but peers may also negatively influence others by coercion and manipulation. Peer group pressure can be either a very powerful ally or a formidable antagonist, dissuading or encouraging problem behaviors (Roseth, Johnson, & Johnson, 2008). Behaviors such as misbehaving in class, fighting, arguing, victimization (Khoury-Kassabri, 2011), and neglecting to turn in homework all interfere with learning and are related to school failure. Students are more likely to drop out in schools with a poor disciplinary climate as measured by student disruptions in class or in school (Rumberger & Ah Lim, 2008). Carlos's earlier playground fights demonstrate how poor decision making among students can hinder positive student climate. Efforts to improve students' problem-solving and decision-making skills have a positive effect on at-risk students (Shure, 2006, 2007; and see Chapter 12). Some schools have reported a marked reduction in disruptive behaviors after students have been taught to mediate disputes on their own. Significant benefits accrue when students teach and model social skills (Blake, Wang, Cartledge, & Gardner, 2000). The ability of students to solve their own problems and peacefully settle disputes directly and positively affects student climate. School mediation programs (discussed in Chapter 13) have been especially helpful in this regard (Decker, 2009; Jones, 1998; Lane & McWhirter, 1996; Smith & Daunic, 2002).

Peer Involvement

Because peers play such an important role in adolescents' risky behavior, prevention and treatment efforts should focus not only on individuals' problems but also on the peer group itself. Peer programs that emphasize training in assertiveness and other social skills have a good success rate (Herrmann & McWhirter, 1997). If these skills are not taught to the whole peer cluster (see Chapter 13), or if adolescents return to the same peer cluster after receiving treatment away from their peers, they often regress to past patterns.

Adolescent girls—especially those who are talented—experience decreases in self-confidence and more social anxiety than in earlier grades. Some have argued that there is an abrupt psychological shift at age 14 from needs for achievement to needs related to love and belonging (Neihart, Reis, Robinson, & Moon, 2002). Talented girls see more disadvantages to their abilities than do their male peers and, simultaneously, girls' self-esteem plunges between ages 11 and 17. They perceive that their achievements will threaten boys; thus, they "dummy down" and hide their abilities. In addition, girls receive inequitable instruction in the classroom, less attention from teachers, less informative responses from teachers, less detailed instructions on the correct approach to tasks, and more reprimands for calling out answers to questions and other "assertive" responses.

Other groups also experience challenges to their self-concept in the school context. For example over a 3-year time period, African American boys' school-related self-esteem dropped more sharply than that of African American girls (Dotterer, Lowe, & McHale, 2013). Another group of students who are especially impacted by the climate of schools are those whose sexual identity or sexual orientation does not conform to strict heterosexual norms (Greene, Britton, & Fitts, 2014; Russell & McGuire, 2008). They are under consistent stress. Too often other students, and sometimes teachers, demonstrate nonacceptance, rejection, and hostility. In many ways school climate is particularly important for them.

Student climate is affected by students' ability to monitor their own behavior and progress, take responsibility for their own learning, and contribute to the school community. Most learning research focuses on methods and procedures that increase desired student behaviors and center on strategies teachers and counselors can use (Crone, Hawken, & Horner, 2015; Farkas et al., 2011). More research is needed, however, on the ways teachers and counselors can modify the classroom environment and expectations in a manner that helps young people help themselves. At-risk youth are capable, thinking people who are able to see and monitor their own progress. They need to be taught how to do so. They need to be encouraged to develop a shared responsibility for learning.

Teacher Climate

The working environment for teachers and other school employees is also part of school culture. Levels of collegiality and collaboration among staff members, community support, autonomy, adequacy of funding, and the effectiveness of leadership all contribute to teacher climate within the school.

Consistent and focused meetings with teachers and support staff (psychologists, counselors, social workers) encourage stability, development, collaboration, and collegiality. Unfortunately, school personnel usually meet for curative rather than preventive reasons—ultimately a costly and inefficient procedure—largely because of heavy demands on their time combined with limited understanding of one another's efforts and strategies. Moreover, they generally have no training in a collaborative, collegial model of working

> ### Box 4.2   Teacher Climate
>
> One of the authors of this text had the experience of spending 15 minutes in two different middle school teachers' lounges in the same week during a research project. The atmosphere within the two lounges could not have been more different and provided insight into the teacher climate at each school.
>
> In the first lounge, five teachers were filling coffee cups, organizing papers, and chatting energetically about the events of the week. One teacher approached the author/researcher, asking her name and making introductions to the others. Entering teachers were greeted by name. There was some joking about the "mountains of grading" that faced several of them.
>
> In the second lounge, two teachers were silently grading papers when a third entered and immediately began talking about a student, using crude and insulting language. The other two teachers offered comparable stories about difficult students, also using language such as "asshole" and "bastard." Then the third teacher stated, "God, I can't wait to retire" and left the room; the other two teachers returned to their grading. All three teachers completely ignored the author/researcher and did not make eye contact at any time.

together to prevent problems. If Carlos's teachers were able to work as a team, as middle school teachers often do, they might gain a better understanding of his previous bilingual problems and devise potential solutions. Models of shared decision making and leadership organized around shared values, commitments, and beliefs can make a dramatic difference in teacher climate. Box 4.2 illustrates one dimension of how teacher climates can vary.

When teachers are identified as professionals, the effect on teacher climate is positive. Unfortunately, it is frequently the case that teachers are not treated as experts on learning, pedagogy, and curriculum. Teachers have a base of professional knowledge, a professional language, and bring specific skills to their job. Yet teachers often are required to simply follow mandates regarding curriculum and pedagogy. Educational practices that stifle teachers from utilizing their knowledge produce a poor teacher climate and ultimately a poor student climate. This is true for school counselors as well.

There is a need for teacher empowerment in the workplace, particularly with regard to curriculum. Teachers' knowledge about lesson preparation should prevail over the prepared lesson plans found in teachers' manuals. Teachers are capable decision makers and need to be involved in school-based management. Team-teaching is another way in which teachers can contribute to high-performance schools. Teachers in the teams receive immediate feedback from one another. The team provides teachers with a support group to help resolve educational and behavioral problems. Consequently, teachers perform better in

How do schools typically respond to increasing incidences of disruption? Often, schools respond with "zero tolerance" policies, the addition of security guards and video cameras, and the suspension or expulsion of disruptive students. Although removing disruptive students from the classroom or the school provides some immediate relief to the affected teachers and students, these short-term policies have a series of negative consequences. They shift responsibility away from the school, reinforce antisocial behavior and an environment of control, devalue the adult–child relationship, and weaken the ties between academic and social behavioral learning. Positive Behavioral Support (PBS) is an alternative that involves a significant investment of resources and time, but it provides significant long-term benefits (Crone et al., 2015; Farkas et al., 2011). PBS is a systemwide approach to school behavior management that combines a system that supports teacher behavior with data that support effective decisions and practices that support student behavior. The purpose of PBS is to increase the effectiveness, relevance, and efficiency of academic and social learning for all students, and especially for those with emotional and behavioral problems by (1) increasing time devoted to teaching (instead of managing behavior problems) and (2) increasing students' academic engagement time and achievement. That is, PBS changes individual behavior by changing the context in which behavior occurs. PBS establishes a schoolwide system for discipline with clear procedures and behaviors that are expected. There is a continuum of reinforcement for positive behaviors and a continuum of discouragement for negative behaviors. School staff are required to collaborate throughout the school (Crone et al., 2015; Farkas et al., 2011).

Initiating PBS requires a commitment of several years, with maintenance of the system a top priority. Other requirements include a team-based approach, active administrator support, proactive instructional approach, local behavioral expertise, and the use of data-based decision making. Implementation of PBS requires an enormous amount of time, resources, and energy. So why would a school select this intervention? Answer: Results. In one school, the average daily referrals in December dropped from 21 per day to 6 per day the following December. Four years later the changes were maintained, with an average of five referrals per day in December with similar effects every month. The savings of time and energy that go into dealing with office referrals, as well as the increased satisfaction and security experienced by school personnel, are enough to convince many schools to adopt this program.

EDUCATIONAL STRUCTURE: SCHOOLS AND CLASSROOMS

Two levels at which the structure of education can be manipulated are the school itself (grade configuration, type of building) and the classroom (the teacher's philosophy and teaching style, the instructional method). Reform may be needed at both levels to optimize the academic success of students at risk.

School Structure

Grade configuration has been the primary organizing principle of our system. The rapid growth of high schools in the United States after the Civil

War led some sections of the country to operate under an 8–5 schedule: 8 years of elementary school, 5 years of high school. Other areas used a 6–6 plan: 6 years of elementary school, 6 years of high school. Toward the end of the century, the 8–4 pattern became popular. In 1909 the first junior high school was introduced. Since then, grades have been configured in a variety of patterns (6–3–3, 6–2–4, 7–2–3, 5–3–4, 4–4–4) in attempts to group students by developmental needs and to increase the cost-effectiveness of education. However, evidence contradicts the widely held notion that large schools serving a small range of grades are uniformly more cost-effective than single-unit (K–12 or K–8) schools (Bickel, Howley, Williams, & Glascock, 2001). With respect to human costs, a larger size school is more damaging to disadvantaged students' achievement. After an in-depth analysis of a variety of indicators, Bickel and colleagues conclude, "If we were also interested in balancing expenditure per pupil with achievement-based equity, the best configuration seems to be a small single-unit school.... This makes the achievement advantage of small schools (where they are most needed, that is, in impoverished communities) more affordable than previously expected." It is important to engage in deeper level examination of issues such as cost-effectiveness, and to raise questions such as "beneficial to whom?" and "cost-effective with respect to what dimensions?" and "what dimensions have not been considered?"

The school-within-a-school concept is one way of structuring the school so that smaller groups of students are clustered together. For example, the school population of a specific secondary school is divided into four "houses." These houses become the major vehicles for social interaction, intramural athletics, school activities, discipline, and so forth (think of the organization of Hogwart's Academy of Witchcraft and Wizardry, featured in the popular Harry Potter books by J. K. Rowling). The main reference group can be reduced in this way from, for example, 2,000 students in the comprehensive school to 500 students in the house, increasing the sense of community. Another example of school-within-school programs are high school Career Academies, which provide academic coursework and curricula based on a career theme with work experience available through employer partnerships. They show positive effects on staying and progressing in school for youth at-risk of dropping out (Kemple, 2004). Some schools build before- and after-school supervised programs into their structure (see Chapter 2). Youth without supervision after school and who are with peers are more likely to engage in risky behaviors and to have poorer school achievement than youth who are with caretakers after school. In addition, there are significant benefits to participation in quality after-school programs (Durlak, Domitrovich, Weissberg, & Gullott, 2015). The demand for school-based after-school programs exceeds the supply, and even existing programs are constantly threatened by decreasing funds. After-school care programs could be of significant benefit to at-risk students like Carlos and Lidia Diaz.

School Choice

School choice has been offered as a solution to poor-quality schools. The proponents of school choice include political conservatives who view public education as overly controlled by the government, religious conservatives who view public schools as damaging to children because of exposure to immoral values and practices, private schools seeking increased enrollment, and activist, urban parents of color seeking a higher quality education for their children. Based on the belief that choice inspires competition and therefore higher quality, the school choice movement was supported by a 2002 U.S. Supreme Court decision upholding the constitutionality of the Cleveland school voucher program, which enabled students to attend private religious schools. In a study of the Milwaukee Public Schools (Witte et al., 2010), students who used a voucher to attend secular or religious private schools demonstrated no significant differences between math and reading achievement. The National Education Association, the National Association of School Principals, and the American Federation of Teachers maintain strong opposition to the voucher system, believing that the effects will damage public education by reinforcing and replicating inequities for lower SES, ethnic minority, and poor achieving students.

Charter Schools

The charter school movement emerged from school choice and has expanded enormously: from 1999 to 2012, the percentage of public schools classified as charters increased from around 2% to 6%; the number of students enrolled nearly quadrupled (NCES, 2014). In the 2014–2015 school year, with the addition of new charter schools and additional students, there are more than 6,700 public charter schools that enroll nearly 3 million students throughout the United States (National Alliance for Public Charter Schools, 2014). Although charter schools are public schools that offer a free education, they differ from district-controlled schools in that they are organized by a variety of different entities including private organizations. Charter schools also embody many different visions of school improvement.

Charter schools have the freedom to be innovative and to become a source of good ideas. Supporters view charter schools as a promising way to raise academic standards, empower educators, involve parents and communities, and expand choice and accountability (National Alliance for Public Charter Schools, 2014). Despite these promising possibilities, the variation in characteristics has made it difficult to evaluate and compare their effects with one another and with traditional schools. In one study (Gleason, Clark, Tuttle, & Dwoyer, 2010), charter schools students scored no differently on math and reading and they were no different on attendance, grade promotion, or student conduct than noncharter students. However, parent and student satisfaction showed significant positive results in favor of the charter schools. In another study (Tuttle, Teh, Nichols-Barrer, Gill, & Gleason, 2010), students had higher reading and math test scores than similar students in traditional public schools.

Charter schools have the potential to be an important educational innovation. However, the accessibility of charter schools must be addressed with respect to transportation, enrollment procedures, requirements, and a better understanding of who actually enrolls.

Classroom Structure

Classroom structure affects the academic experience of at-risk students. The structure of the class can give at-risk students a feeling of control over their situation. An environment in which students are treated as unique individuals who have unique contributions to make to the group yields positive results (Wubbolding, 2007). Emotional connections and interactions promote academic achievement (Reyes, Brackett, Rivers, White, & Salovey, 2012). Such an environment produces an acceptance and appreciation of differences, an increase in creativity, an enhancement of personal autonomy, an improvement in mental health, and the ultimate overall quality of learning. A caring relationship between adults and students helps meet the needs of at-risk students and influences students' perceptions of climate and community in the classroom (Doren, Murray, & Gau, 2014; Madill, Gest, & Rodkin, 2014; Mainhard, Brekelmans, den Brok, & Wubbels, 2011).

Class size also affects at-risk students. There is strong evidence (National Council of Teachers of English [NCTE], 2014; Rumberger & Ah Lim, 2008) that small classes (15:1) in grades K–3 improve high school graduation rates. Certainly Lidia Diaz's teacher would be able to meet Lidia's needs more effectively if she were responsible for fewer children. Indeed, academic achievement and connection to school have been found to be related to class size (Finn, Gerber, & Boyd-Zaharias, 2005; Rumberger & Ah Lim, 2008). In fact, 4 or more years in small classes (13 to 17 students) in early elementary school significantly increase the likelihood of students graduating from high school. This is especially true for students from low-income homes (Finn et al., 2005; NCTE, 2014).

Because Lidia's class is large, students have been assigned to smaller groups based on ability levels. Although little advantage accrues to students assigned to the high groups, students assigned to the low groups suffer great disadvantage. Educational researchers now advocate smaller heterogeneous groups that work cooperatively in lieu of homogeneous ability groups working competitively (Roseth et al., 2008). When teachers and students are encouraged to work collaboratively, there is a positive effect on the overall school environment and on student achievement (Reyes et al., 2012). Students who are at risk for school failure are usually several grades behind their age-mates; school structures that emphasize cooperation over competition meet the needs of these students better (see Chapter 13). Curricular and instructional practices also affect students who are at risk for school failure. Students have little enthusiasm for a curriculum that focuses simply on learning facts and isolated skills and over time become passive players in the schooling process. Further, controversial and sometimes very interesting content areas are being omitted from the curriculum. For example, the Mexican American Studies (MAS) curriculum was eliminated from the Tucson Unified School District in Arizona based on the passage of H.B. 2281, on the basis that it was "too political." This curriculum, based on Freirean pedagogy and "Critically Compassionate Intellectualism" (Cammarota & Romero, 2014), engaged students in a critique of traditional school curricula in which ethnic minority perspectives are absent, supported students' active engagement in their learning process, and fostered development of basic academic competencies in the context of caring relationships with teachers. The curriculum met the objectives of increasing the academic success of at-risk students. Prior to taking MAS classes, student participants had lower standardized test scores and grades than students who did not take any MAS classes, but by 12th grade those who took one or more MAS classes had higher test scores and were significantly more likely to graduate than those who took no MAS classes (Cabrera, Meza, Romero, & Rodriguez, 2013). The more MAS classes a student took, the greater the effects of the curriculum on standardized achievement tests and graduation.

Educators, as well as the parents, pass down the common values of society. Yet content associated with "ethnic pride," "values clarification," "values education," or "morals" sets off alarm bells in some segments of the community. Many districts tightly regulate classroom discussion of topics such as sexual behavior and pregnancy prevention in an effort to avoid controversy.

Curriculum Issues

A curriculum that ignores moral education, development of social skills, student dialogue, and critical thinking does not help at-risk students. We have already given an example of a banned curriculum that provided significant benefits to students in the Tucson Unified School District. As another example, making contraceptives available to teens and providing information about effectiveness has been criticized as contributing to sexual activity among teenagers. However, even though sexual activity among teenagers is approximately equal in the United States and Europe, the teen birthrate is much lower in Europe, where contraception is available. In the year 2000, a narrowly defeated bill in Oregon would have prohibited school discussion of safe sex activities that prevent AIDS because of the unsubstantiated accusation that such information "promotes homosexuality." (We return to this important issue in Chapter 8.) The argument that children and adolescents should get their information at home is a hollow one in light of the vast numbers of families that do not provide this information at all.

Measures to assess the curriculum need to be broadened as well. As mentioned earlier in this chapter, assessment of student learning should go beyond scores on standardized achievement tests to include critical thinking, decision making, and other factors. As a result of reforms in several states, students are required to pass benchmarks throughout K–12 that include social skills, problem solving, and other important career and life skills. Passing benchmarks in mathematics requires, for example, not simply providing the correct answer but being able to describe the reasoning process used to arrive at the answer, and to identify alternative strategies for finding the answer. Connecting education to the world of work is a critical element for at-risk youth and includes seven components (Bizot, 1999) that provide a connection: (1) develop a sense of competence based on genuine achievement via opportunities to attempt challenging tasks; (2) expose students to many areas of potential interest with the opportunity to develop some greater mastery; (3) foster an ability to set goals, generate alternatives, evaluate options and results, and cope with obstacles; (4) provide a framework for understanding and organizing occupational information; (5) convey respect for individual differences and an understanding of how individual values, interests, and skills lead to different choices, opportunities, and barriers; (6) provide for participation and opportunities to collaborate and contribute; and (7) impart an understanding that education and career are lifelong, ongoing processes. These key elements should be integrated into curricula. Perhaps if Ramona had been exposed to ongoing career education, and had a curriculum that made consistent connections between learning and life skills, she might have seen more benefits to staying in school. At a minimum, she may have had better-developed work and life skills when she did drop out. English as a Second Language (ESL) programs, also known as English language learner (ELL), or bilingual education programs are also an important part of school curricula for students at risk. From 1979 to 2008, the number of school-age children who spoke a language other than English at home increased from 9% to 21% or from 3.8 to 10.9 million (Kena et al., 2015). ELLs in 2014–2015 made up an average of 14% of total public school enrollment in urban areas, ranging from 9.4% in small cities to 16.7% in large cities (Kena et al., 2015). ESL students continue to have disproportionately high dropout rates and low graduation rates (Gil & Bardack, 2011). Given the shortage of ESL teachers with appropriate credentials, and the fact that they live in a district characterized by many poor families, it is likely that the Diaz children did not have qualified teachers when they were in ESL classes.

Under No Child Left Behind, federal funds support the education of ELLs with the rapid teaching of English taking precedence at every turn. Annual English assessments are mandated, and academic progress in English is expected. Even though the resources provided by NCLB are good news for schools with substantial numbers of language-minority students, the money is spread thinly—between more states, more programs, and more students. Although districts will automatically receive funding based on their enrollments of ELLs and immigrant students, the impact of federal dollars will be reduced, given the complexity and heterogeneity of the ESL population. They do not fit a single profile (Bardack, 2010). ESLs have different socioeconomic status, levels of language proficiency, academic experiences, and immigration history.

EDUCATION STRUCTURE: INNOVATIONS

World Wide Web—the Internet

It appears that the World Wide Web, the Internet, provides both an interesting curricular issue and contributes to an innovative educational structure. The information available to students and schools via the Internet is virtually limitless, and support services to assist teachers to incorporate this resource into their teaching are evolving rapidly. There has been a virtual explosion of resources available for educators to use with students.

Schools have made consistent progress in expanding Internet access in classrooms. Now virtually all public schools in the United States have access to the Internet, most with broadband wireless connections. Thus computer access at school is nearly universal among 4th grade students (95%) and very high for the vast majority of 8th graders (83%). Home computer access in 2011 for children ages 3 to 17 was 58%, in comparison to 11% in 1997 (Child Trends, 2013). These findings differ by racial/ethnic group and income level, with, for example, 91% of White and 69% of Hispanic children having access to a computer at home, and 58% of children in the lowest income group. When teachers are provided with the time and technological support to capitalize on the Internet, students benefit. And it is clear that access to and ability to navigate the Internet are critical skills for today's young people. One of the primary functions of the Internet is for communication, and many proponents have convincingly described how the Internet expands the number of people with whom someone can be in easy communication. Options include e-mail, texting, instant messaging, instagrams, blogs, twitter, online gaming, and social networking sites like Facebook. The social benefits seem obvious. The Internet is a rich resource that allows a wide variety of activities ranging from information gathering to communications to game playing, to other forms of entertainment (Lenhart, Madden, MacGill, & Smith, 2007; O'Keeffe & Clarke-Pearson, 2011).

For some adolescents, the Internet relieves social anxiety and social isolation. However, Internet use raises some serious questions. Does use of the Internet decrease family communication? What happens to the size of the user's social circle? Might the social media actually increase loneliness and depression? As children and youth experience increased access, it will be critically important to monitor the effects of Internet use on their social interaction with family and peers. Future research will need to investigate how the combination of media—television, Internet, computers, cell phones, and so forth—influence the lives of adolescents, and how the media can be used in positive ways to improve health, education, and development of young people. Researchers with the American Academy of Pediatrics (O'Keeffe & Clarke-Pearson, 2011) note the risks of social media use for children, such as cyberbullying, sexting, and depression, and recommends that pediatricians advise parents to learn about social media, discuss usage with their children, and monitor their children's engagement with social media.

Flipped Classroom

Typical elementary and secondary classrooms in this country and, indeed, throughout the world usually include a lecture by the teacher presenting new material to students. Sometimes the lectures are augmented by discussions, questions and answers, and PowerPoint presentations. Students are then given worksheets and problems to solve as homework. In the last decade, a new innovation has been developed. Referred to as the "inverted" classroom or the "flipped" classroom, the approach has been attributed to two high school science teachers, Bergmann and Sams (2012), who flipped their classes in 2006 and subsequently wrote about the innovation. Since then, the number of flipped classrooms has increased dramatically (Educause, 2012). For example, membership in the Flipped Learning Network's (2012) social media site rose from 2,500 teachers in 2011 to 9,000 teachers in 2012. After adopting flipped classrooms, the failure rate of students in one Michigan high school's 9th grade math classes dropped from 44% to 13% (Finkel, 2012).

The term *flipped* refers to the inversion of the traditional teaching process. The flipped classroom interchanges what typically is done during class with what is done outside of class (Herreid & Schiller, 2013). Students hear, see, or read the lecture content on their own and classroom time is spent completing what would have been homework in the classroom. Originally, teachers were responsible for recording lectures and providing videos. But, as we discussed earlier, the Internet has expanded so much that a large number of existing video resources are available. There are thousands of lessons and videos from which to choose, which we discuss in more detail in Chapter 6. The Kahn Academy, TED talks, and YouTube's education channel provide a rich array of possible content to utilize in a flipped classroom.

The flipped classroom has a few important key characteristics (Flipped Learning Network, 2012; Hamdan, McKnight, McKnight, & Arfstrom, 2013; Moran & Milsom, 2015).

- The first characteristic is a shift from a culture that is teacher-centered to one that is student-centered.
- Second, teachers need to be selective in what they assign students to learn on their own before class and what is best dealt with in the classroom.
- The teachers provide discussions, activities, and mini-lectures to address concepts that students may not understand and respond to questions that still exist.
- Students provide peer instruction, including peer feedback on assignments and projects.
- The flipped classroom also incorporates small group work, and it allows teachers function as facilitators and provide individualized attention.

Do flipped classrooms work? Do student learn more? Are they more engaged in school? Are high-risk children and adolescents helped with this new procedure? It appears that the flipped classroom may be a helpful response to many of the issues that affect at-risk youth. The problem is that as yet there is no strong evidence base to indicate exactly how well flipped classrooms work

(Abeysekera & Dawson, 2015). Less scientific data suggest that flipping the classroom does produce some benefits. In one survey of 500 teachers who flipped their classrooms, 99% said they would flip again the following year, 80% reported improved student attitude, and 67% reported increased test scores. There appeared to be particular benefits for students with special needs and for students in advanced placement classes (Flipped Learning Network, 2012).

There are several aspects of flipped classrooms that are especially helpful to high-risk students. The flipped classroom practice promotes better student–teacher interaction. Teachers can circulate and talk *with* students, not lecture *at* them. Recognizing and responding to students' social and emotional needs is especially important to at-risk students (Goodwin & Miller, 2013). Also, students can pace their own learning according to different needs and abilities, useful to students who may struggle academically and students who are bored with a slow pace. In addition, at-risk learners tend to check out after 10 minutes of exposure to new content. By breaking down direct instruction into more engaging, 10-minute bites of learning, students can better be engaged. Finally, completing in-class "homework" allows students to practice their skills and knowledge with corrective teacher feedback that immediately addresses student misperceptions (Greenberg, Medlock, & Stephens, 2011). In short, the flipped classroom is a promising development because it incorporates many aspects of improved school climate that have been shown to contribute to school success (Voight, Austin, & Hanson, 2013). We hope that the summary and call for research provided by Abeysekera and Dawson (2015) stimulates development of a strong evidence base for this teaching strategy.

CONCLUSION

Practitioners have control over some educational practices and policies and elements of school climate that may improve the learning potential of at-risk students. They can promote curricular and teaching practices that emphasize the entirety of students' learning and development. Second, educators can increase collaborative efforts that encourage collegial support and collaborative decision making to improve school climate. Third, student critical thinking and empowerment can be promoted, and students can be helped to approach their work and their interactions with tolerance and democracy. Teachers and counselors can be excellent models of such practices. Finally, all of us can assist in raising public awareness about the value of extended support for children and youth who are at risk. Collaboration with researchers to provide evidence of successful prevention and intervention programs (or evidence that programs are not working) is one way to help draw attention to what does and does not work. Researchers, in turn, must consult with teachers and other practitioners to draw educators' firsthand classroom experience and wisdom into the development and implementation of prevention and intervention programs. Teacher expertise is a critical component of school-based programs that provide at-risk students with the skills and resources they need to be successful in school and in life.

Individual Characteristics of High-Risk and Low-Risk Children and Youth

CHAPTER
5

What makes some young people resolute and sturdy enough to chip away at the ore, locate the diamond, and polish it ... while others weakly and feebly patter in the soil, haphazardly searching for a gem, finding only dirt?

CHAPTER OUTLINE

- Resiliency

- Factors that Contribute to Resilience
  - Social Environment
  - Family Milieu
  - Individual Characteristics of Resilient Youth

- Skills that Characterize High-Risk Versus Low-Risk Youth: The Five Cs of Competency
  - Critical School Competencies
    Basic Academic Skills
    Academic Survival Skills
  - Concept of Self, Self-Esteem, and Self-Efficacy

- Connectedness
  Communication with Others
  Perspective Taking
  Solving Relationship Problems
  - Coping Ability
  - Control
    Decision-Making Skills
    Delay of Gratification
    Purpose in Life

- Mindfulness

- Things to Do Chart: Increasing the Five Cs

- Conclusion

Within their unique family and community ecologies, young people develop individual characteristics—likes and dislikes, talents and limitations, strengths and weaknesses. These individual characteristics emerge from the societal environment and from the roots of family and school conditions. Most young people develop adequate knowledge, positive behaviors, prosocial attitudes, and other healthy characteristics with lower risk of future problems. Other children and adolescents do not acquire the knowledge, behaviors, attitudes, and skills they need to become successful adults (Crowe, Beauchamp, Catroppa, & Anderson, 2011). Such youth often exhibit interrelated dysfunctional patterns of behaviors, cognitions, and emotions early in life and especially in their early school years. If negative patterns are not reversed, they may develop into self-fulfilling prophecies. It is very important to understand young people's social functioning (Crowe et al., 2011) to prevent a downward spiral of multiple problems that could include school failure, drug use, teen pregnancy, delinquency, and suicide—what Jessor (1991, 1993) developed as Problem Behavior Theory (Donovan, 2005).

Individual characteristics exhibited by children and adolescents form the trunk of the at-risk tree, which links the soil of environment and the roots of family, school, and peers to the branches of behaviors. These characteristics can nourish positive and healthful development or

risky behavior. When studies of at-risk youth are reviewed, a "multiple-problem syndrome" becomes apparent. School dropout, drug abuse, delinquency, teen pregnancy, and youth suicide are all associated with similar sets of psychosocial variables and skill deficits. Teachers, counselors, and psychologists realize that many young people are lacking in fundamental skills. The term *skills* refers here not merely to mechanically performed actions but rather to proficiency in the behaviors, feelings, and thought patterns that are appropriately applied in specific situations and circumstances. All youth, including those defined as at risk, are capable of learning more adaptive strategies for addressing their life challenges, and the incorporation of skills acquisition into educational and counseling interventions is critical (Algozzine, Daunic, & Smith, 2010).

Some young people manage to survive extremely difficult life circumstances. Somehow they rise above poverty, chaotic families, peer pressure, and poor school conditions—in short, those environmental conditions described in earlier chapters. These young people are considered to be at risk because their circumstances clearly suggest future problems. And the greater the number of these risk factors, the greater their level of risk. But resilient youth avoid falling into drug use, delinquency, and other risky behaviors. By examining their lives and circumstances, we may learn something that will inform our efforts with young people who are not so fortunate.

RESILIENCY

Despite extremely debilitating environmental, familial, and personal experiences, many young people develop normally. They exhibit competence, autonomy, and effective strategies to cope with the world around them.

These children and youth have been called "invulnerable," "stress-resistant," "superkids," and "invincible." These terms have been subject to criticism because they imply that the well-being of these young people is due to internal or constitutional factors only, that they are successful across all domains, and that they are consistently successful across time (McGloin & Widom, 2001). The term *resilience* refers to those who demonstrate "a good outcome in spite of high risk, sustained competence under stress, and recovery from trauma" (p. 1022). Essentially, resilience is the capacity to adapt and function successfully despite experiencing chronic stress and adversity. Resilience is not a static trait, but it is influenced by both internal and environmental factors (Dishion & Connell, 2006).

Every child has a "tipping point" between doing well (having hope, positive attitudes about self, functional behaviors) and doing poorly (feeling despair, having low self-esteem, dysfunctional behaviors). No child is immune to excessive exposure to negative social, familial, and educational environments, and the idea of a tipping point may be even more useful than the concept of resilience. Another criticism of the term is that the justice system has used the notion of resilience to help punish offenders—contending that a violent and abrasive upbringing provides no explanation for violent behavior because some youth who grow up in the same environment do not engage in violence. We acknowledge the validity of these criticisms. However, we find the concept of resilience useful to distinguish between young people who do well and those who do not.

FACTORS THAT CONTRIBUTE TO RESILIENCE

The development of resiliency is a function of three related but distinct areas that provide protection to the child (McCreanor & Watson, 2004). First, the social environment can provide children with opportunities for development and support despite adverse conditions. External support systems can enhance the young person's competencies and provide a sense of meaning or a belief system by which to live. Second, the family milieu has both direct and indirect influences on a youth's resiliency. Ties within the family provide emotional support at times of stress. This is most evident when there are more robust kinship connections (Taylor, 2010). Third, there are a number of individual characteristics and attributes related to resiliency that have positive influences on at-risk children. These include, for example, cognitive skills, styles of communication, interpersonal skills, and dispositional attributes such as activity level, sociability, and intelligence.

Social Environment

Resilient children derive support from the social environment—their school, their community, and their kinship network (Taylor, 2010). The school environment is potentially a mediating milieu for children who experience numerous risk factors. When social support is low in one setting or microsystem, such as the family, other microsystems, such as school or the neighborhood, can compensate by providing support and assistance in the weakened area. Building resilience in children ameliorates the negative impact of adverse childhood experiences (Bethell, Newacheck, Hawes, & Halfon, 2014), and caring relationships increase resiliency (Laursen & Birmingham, 2003; Wolchik, Schenck, & Sandler, 2009). Supportive and encouraging teachers are particularly important. Counselors and psychologists can make a crucial difference as well. Resilient children often succeed in academic areas and may also achieve in art, music, sport, or drama. Positive contact with peers and adults in these extracurricular areas provide support.

The social support networks of the larger community also help to ameliorate the effects of stress on children. Resilient youth frequently use community networks—ministers, older friends, youth recreation workers, and others. Resilient children often have at least one adult mentor outside the family throughout their development. These adults provide emotional support, encouragement, and advice. Resilient children also have one or more close friends and confidants among their peers. These networks provide at-risk children and adolescents with resources that enable them to develop the skills necessary for survival and success.

Many young people develop specific survival skills that work in their setting. These skills provide them with mechanisms for coping with an unsupportive, negative, or destructive environment. Unfortunately, some of these survival skills are functional and effective only within the subculture of the neighborhood; using the same skills in other contexts is often ineffective or self-defeating. Creatively demeaning insults and threats of physical aggression may decrease the risk of physical assault in the neighborhood, but may lead to school suspension when carried out in the hallways.

Children of color in particular are often subjected to the stress of overt and covert racism and marginalization within the majority culture. Even though minority status is correlated with high risk, the way children learn to survive that stress makes a difference in their ability to maintain self-esteem and a positive identity. Some authors have articulated how many adolescents of color learn to navigate the traumas and stressors that they experience as systemic racism and actually transform such events into life-affirming experiences (e.g., see Holleran & Jung, 2005). Young people's collective resistance to oppression, such as protesting and walkouts, can result in positive consequences that supersede individual consequences such as being labeled as a troublemaker (Cabrera, Meza, Romero, & Rodriguez, 2013). Parents, teachers, and other school personnel should be sensitive to the differences between behaviors that are fundamentally destructive and behaviors intended to call attention to and transform oppression.

Carlos Diaz, whom we met in Chapter 5, is a potentially resilient young adolescent. His relationship with his mother has given him a secure foundation. His family responsibilities, although they interfere with schoolwork, have allowed him to develop important life skills that improve his self-concept and self-esteem such as cooking and caring for a younger child.

Even though these responsibilities are stressful, knowing that he is contributing to his family gives Carlos an important role in the family's well-being. His academic difficulties are associated with not having time and resources (e.g., a computer), but the work he completes reflects that he is learning and academically competent. Also important is the special interest his social studies teacher has shown in him. Ms. Bassett's interest and support, coupled with reasonable expectations, provides a solid relationship with a caring adult. Further, her willingness to modify her classroom and teaching style encourages responsibility for learning and contributes to his resiliency.

Family Milieu

As we have seen, family environment is one of the most important influences on the psychosocial development of young people. The characteristics of a positive family environment include a lack of physical crowding, consistently enforced rules with strict but fair supervision, and well-balanced discipline. The child who has a good relationship with even one caregiver demonstrates greater resiliency (Contreras & Kerns, 2000; Werner, 1995). Parental support and involvement are useful for autonomy and self-direction that contribute to resiliency.

Healthy communication patterns often prevail in the homes of resilient youth. The parents model such skills as attending, focusing, and sustaining tasks. Focused, flexible, well-structured, and task-appropriate communication leads to academic and social competence. Parenting characterized by warmth, affective expression, anticipatory guidance, active teaching of social skills, and involvement reduces risk and increases children's social competence. Children in families who engage in interactions that encourage the expression of independent thought and allow for give-and-take communication are more likely to exhibit psychosocial competence (Larzelere, Morris, & Harrist, 2013). Parental monitoring and control is associated with better childhood outcomes in both urban and rural neighborhoods characterized by violence and poverty (Murry, Simons, Simons, & Gibbons, 2013).

Positive parenting, parent support, and the quality of the mother–child relationship fosters resilience (Klein, Forehand, & the Family Health Project Research Group, 2000). Although there are some cultural variations in parenting behaviors and outcomes (Domenech Rodriguez, Donovick, & Crowley, 2009; Ramírez, Jorge, Manongdo, & Cruz-Santiago, 2010), these findings hold consistently across most cultural and ethnic groups in the United States.

The family also contributes to resiliency indirectly, through its influence on the children's support networks. Some parents, for example, selectively expose their children to religious and church-related organizations, community organizations such as the Girl Scouts and Boy Scouts or 4-H clubs, or culture-affirming groups focused on music or dance traditions. Adults in these organizations provide a useful support network that builds resiliency.

Christie Carter, whom we met in Chapter 3, may be resilient. She emerges in the family as a prim and slightly unpleasant little girl. Her role as the family's angel relegates Jason to the role of devil, but perhaps her adoption of this role is what will save her. She does receive a great deal of attention, support, and reinforcement from both her father and her mother. The security that this support provides may be enough to inoculate her against the family dysfunction and prevent her from engaging in risky behavior.

Individual Characteristics of Resilient Youth

Resilient children frequently possess a number of individual characteristics and skills (Alvord, Zucker, & Grados, 2011; Bethell et al., 2014; Flores, Cicchetti, & Rogosch, 2005):

- An active approach to life's problems, including a proactive problem-solving perspective that enables the child to negotiate emotionally hazardous experiences
- An optimistic tendency to perceive pain, frustration, and other distressing experiences constructively
- The ability to gain positive attention from others and to form positive relationships with others, both in the family and elsewhere
- A strong faith that maintains a vision of a positive and meaningful life
- An ability to be alert and autonomous with a tendency to seek novel experience
- Competence in social, school, and cognitive areas with better verbal communication and good social skills
- An internal locus of control, impulse control, reflectiveness, and positive self-regard
- A well-developed sense of humor, an ability to delay gratification, and a future orientation

These characteristics act as protective shields that allow the young person to avoid, regulate, or cope with aversive environmental or developmental conditions, modifying the impact of stressors and leading to less damaging results (Dishion & Connell, 2006).

Daniella Baker, whom we met in Chapter 2, has a special relationship with her mother. She has developed good communication skills and has the ability to make her needs known. Her sweet, calm temperament elicits positive reactions from her mother and from others. This is especially valuable in light of her frequent changes in living situations. Daniella also has assumed the care of her younger brother. Although this responsibility sometimes frustrates her, it enhances her self-esteem. These personality factors contribute to her resiliency and may mitigate the effects of her environment.

Resilient children and youth cope constructively with challenges by balancing short- and long-term needs of both themselves and others. This allows them to reap mostly favorable outcomes that bolster their self-image and increase their future propensity for positive coping (Bethell et al., 2014). These attitudes endear them to untroubled peers while alienating them from deviant peers.

Carlos Diaz, Christie Carter, and Daniella Baker are potentially resilient young people. All of them have personal characteristics that reflect influences from their social environment and their family milieu that may inoculate them against the stress of their current situations and help them to avoid future difficulty. The characteristics of resiliency correspond to specific skills that distinguish low-risk from high-risk children.

SKILLS THAT CHARACTERIZE HIGH-RISK VERSUS LOW-RISK YOUTH: THE FIVE CS OF COMPETENCY

As a result of our work in teaching and counseling at-risk children and adolescents, our discussions with other professionals, and an extensive review of research on resilient and at-risk children and youth, we have identified five characteristics that capture the major differences between low-risk and high-risk youth. We call these characteristics the "five Cs of competency":

- Critical school competencies
- Concept of self, self-esteem, and self-efficacy
- Connectedness
- Coping ability
- Control

These characteristics discriminate between young people who move through life with a high potential for success and those who do not do well. Low-risk individuals exhibit proficiency, strength, or potential in the five Cs; high-risk individuals are deficient in one or more of these skills. The lack of these skills is closely related to the chronic dependency, aggressive behavior, or inability to cope with life that propels young people into the at-risk categories: school dropout, substance abuse, teen pregnancy, youth delinquency and violence, and suicide.

Of course, these skills overlap. Critical school competencies, for example, may lead to connectedness and relate to skills in coping and control. Self-concept interacts in very important and powerful ways with the other characteristics. All the same, we can grasp their importance more firmly if we consider each in turn.

Critical School Competencies

Critical school competencies comprise those skills that are essential to success in school: basic academic skills, academic survival skills, and self-efficacy expectations (Arbona, 2000). Because self-efficacy expectations also relate to the second C, concept of self, we discuss here only basic academic skills and academic survival skills.

Basic Academic Skills

In a high-tech industrial society, young people must learn the basic skills of reading, writing, and arithmetic to survive. If they are to thrive, they also need information about themselves and the world around them. The lack of such skills reduces the prospects for a useful, productive life.

One of the most obvious characteristics for many at-risk students is academic underachievement. Underachievement often results from a lack of basic numeracy and literacy skills. These academic deficits are an overwhelming cause of early school leaving and are often a contributing factor in many other problems. Mastery of academic skills encourages persistence in school. A lack of basic reading, writing, and arithmetic skills is often attributable to developmental delays, specific learning disabilities, a limited grasp of English, or emotional disturbance. These problems are compounded by contextual factors such as an inadequate educational structure, an uncaring and unresponsive school culture, limited instructional programs, or poor teaching. Elementary and secondary school students at risk for academic underachievement may be withdrawn and apathetic or, conversely, disruptive and aggressive (Jitendra, Dupaul, Someki, & Tresco, 2008). Early detection and intervention is critical to the prevention of ongoing academic difficulty.

Academic Survival Skills

In addition to numeracy and literacy skills, a core of social-behavioral skills is necessary for student success (McKown, Gumbiner, Russo, & Lipton, 2010; Preston, Heaton, McCann, Watson, & Selke, 2009). The lack of these essential competencies or "survival skills" predisposes students to failure because skills such as attending to tasks, following directions, and raising hands facilitate the acquisition of knowledge. Some research indicates that these skills are actually more important than academic achievement. Fad (1990), for example, provides evidence that some social-behavioral variables are more important for students' success than academic achievement and demographic characteristics. Work habits, coping skills, and peer relationships are three important areas. She identifies 10 behaviors in each area that are highly correlated with overall functioning. Strategies for mastering these behaviors may maximize students' chances for success.

Recent research (Lemberger & Clemens, 2012; Lemberger, Selig, Bowers, & Rogers, 2015; Webb & Brigman, 2007) supports Fad's earlier work. The Student Success Skills (SSS) program was developed for school counselors to use with students in grades 4 through 10 but was then expanded to include K–12 graders. The program is counselor-delivered (Webb & Brigman, 2007) with school counselors and/or teachers introducing and teaching key skills and strategies in large classroom groups. These are continued and reinforced in counselor-led small groups. Group counseling allows school counselors to work with small groups of students identified as needing support in developing key academic and social skills beyond what can be provided by the teacher or counselor in the classroom (Webb & Brigman, 2007). In the model, group counseling provides an important direct service intervention targeting the skills.

The SSS intervention is designed to support students by exposing them to specific learning, academic, social, and self-management skills they need to be successful in school. Many of the skills taught in this program are precisely some of the skills and attributes that were identified by Fad over 25 years ago; others match up closely with some of the other five Cs that we discuss later in this chapter.

The skills included in the SSS program are based on three skill sets: (1) cognitive and metacognitive skills; (2) social skills; and (3) self-management skills. These skill sets have consistently been identified as contributing to improved academic and social outcomes for students. The specific skills within the skill sets include: (a) goal setting, progress monitoring, and memory skills; (b) interpersonal and social problem-solving skills, listening, and teamwork skills; and (c) managing anger, attention, focus, and motivation.

In more than a dozen and a half studies, researchers have found significant treatment effects for multiple components of executive functioning (see the "C" of control later in this chapter), feelings of connectedness to classmates and teachers (see the "C" of connectedness), and mathematics and reading achievement (see the "C" of critical school competencies). The program has been shown to be effective in improving K–12 students' learning skills and academic achievement (e.g., Lemberger & Clemens, 2012). It is also important to note that several studies have provided evidence that the SSS program is useful to inner-city African American elementary students (Lemberger & Clemens, 2012) as well as economically challenged, low-income middle school Latino students (Lemberger et al., 2015).

SSS program components continue to be supported by a growing body of literature tying social and emotional competence to achievement outcomes, making a strong empirical case linking social-emotional learning to improved behavioral and academic performance for students, including those at risk for academic failure. The SSS program is one of the most useful and reliable approaches for school counselors to implement (Carey, Dimmitt, Hatch, Lapan, & Whiston, 2008).

Ramona Diaz is at risk. She has not learned the basic academic skills she needs to function in society. Her lack of proficiency in English and her low connectedness with successful peers probably reduced her academic self-efficacy expectations, and her decision to drop out of high school limits her potential for acquiring academic skills and developing more positive academic self-efficacy. She is a prime candidate for the SSS program especially because of its proven effectiveness with low-income Latino students (Lemberger et al., 2015).

Concept of Self, Self-Esteem, and Self-Efficacy

The second of the five Cs refers to the self-concept. Self-concept is the view or perception that one has about oneself. Three terms that are often confused and are sometimes used interchangeably are important: self-concept, self-esteem, and self-efficacy. Although the terms seem similar, their differences are more than just semantic.

Self-concept refers to our beliefs about who we are. That is, how we define ourselves on various dimensions—traits, skills, characteristics, relationships, and so forth. Most often, self-concept carries with it an evaluative adjective. For example, a young teenager might define himself as a popular friend with really "cool" hair, a bad athlete, and an indifferent student who does really poorly at math but is okay in reading.

Self-esteem, on the other hand, refers to how good we feel about ourselves or how much we value ourselves, given our self-concept. Well over a century ago, William James (1890) indicated that self-esteem decreases following failures and increases following successes in domains that are important to the individual's self-concept. In general, self-esteem is vulnerable when people experience failure in domains upon which their self-concept is contingent.

Self-efficacy expectations refer to beliefs about how capable we believe we are in performing specific tasks (Bandura, 1993; Pajares & Urdan, 2006). Self-efficacy is domain specific, such that an adolescent girl might have very high self-efficacy expectations for tasks associated with playing basketball (dribbling, passing, shooting, guarding) but low self-efficacy expectations for the tasks associated with playing baseball (catching, throwing, pitching, batting). Another youth might have low self-efficacy expectations for playing all sports. Self-efficacy expectations are not necessarily accurate; individuals sometimes have low self-efficacy for tasks they are quite capable of doing, or high self-efficacy for tasks they do not do well. Self-efficacy expectations influence decisions about whether to attempt particular behaviors and how long to persist in those behaviors in the face of obstacles.

Consider a teenage girl who has poor ability for playing on an athletic team at school, based on her performance in gym class and earlier attempts to participate in school and neighborhood sports. Her self-concept may include the belief that she is not the "athletic type." If she and her family highly value sports participation and her closest friends are all varsity athletes, then her self-concept might be "lousy athlete" and her self-esteem may be lower. If her friends and family are not interested in sports and she herself does not enjoy them either, her self-esteem is unlikely to be negatively affected by her lack of confidence and success in athletics. Her earlier experiences led her to conclude that she cannot learn athletic skills. Because her self-efficacy is low, she is reluctant to attempt to participate in sports and is likely to give up easily if she does so. Obviously, if she never tries to develop a skill, she will not. Her self-efficacy expectations become a self-fulfilling prophecy. A young man who is not succeeding in school, lacks a sense of belonging, and does not feel good about himself might begin to experiment with disruptive or deviant behaviors. If these result in attention and admiration from deviant peers, he may shift his self-concept from "failing student" to "daring student," develop increased "skills" and more self-efficacy for disrupting class, begin to devalue school performance even more, and may actually experience increased self-esteem. A strong relationship exists between young people's self-evaluations and their performance. The environment around young people influences the value they place on something (academic success, popularity, deviant behavior, and so forth) and to whom they compare themselves. The academically average student from a family of scholars is likely to have lower self-esteem than the academically average student from a family in which no one has graduated from high school. Both self-concept and self-esteem are "global"; they are derived from numerous experiences across many domains. Self-efficacy expectations are specific to domains.

Academic self-efficacy expectations are an important influence on children's school performance (Arbona, 2000; Pajares & Urdan, 2006). When children believe they are capable of doing something, they are far more likely to successfully do it. Poor self-concept and low academic self-efficacy expectations are critical determinants of school dropout. For example, one study of African American high school students found that self-esteem, as well as perceptions of the benefits of staying in school and perceived ability to overcome barriers to school completion, was a significant predictor of intentions to stay in school (Davis, Johnson, Miller-Cribbs, & Saunders, 2002).

Low self-esteem does not predict delinquency when other factors are considered. In fact, there is little evidence that kids who bully or engage in delinquent behavior suffer from low self-esteem (Baumeister, Bushman, & Campbell, 2000). As we have mentioned, some young people may shift their self-concept to incorporate their delinquent or bullying behavior and in that way increase their self-esteem. However, Herrmann, McWhirter, and Sipsas-Herrmann (1997) found that young adolescents with more negative self-concepts were significantly more involved as "wannabes" in street gang activity than peers who possessed more positive self-concepts. Beliefs about their ability to have any impact on their world were particularly important. Middle school students who were involved with gangs had significantly less confidence in their ability to solve problems, obtain their goals, bring about desired outcomes, and function effectively within the environment. Perhaps this explains some of the confusion about whether gang membership increases a person's self-esteem. "Wannabes" who then become gang members may shift their self-concept, and through their gang involvement increase their confidence in having an impact on their world.

Seligman (1995) demonstrates that it is not low self-esteem that causes low achievement at school, but the opposite: Low achievement causes low self-esteem. Low self-esteem may reflect a realistic appraisal of negative life experiences. There is little evidence (Baumeister et al., 2000) that self-esteem influences achievement in any meaningful way. There is, however, considerable evidence to suggest that positive self-esteem should be pursued as an important outcome in itself. Opportunities to experience academic success via skill development and other supports serve to bolster a young person's self-esteem more so than praise or encouragement alone (Seligman, 1995).

Allie Andrews, whom we met in Chapter 1, feels badly about herself and her behavior in part because of her negative relationship with her stepfather. As she becomes more distant from her stepfather, she adjusts her self-concept to that of a person who does not need her stepfather's approval. She develops distorted attributions with regard to herself, to adults, and to nondeviant classmates. As she rejects her parents' (and other adults') beliefs and values, she becomes more closely aligned with and influenced by a negative peer cluster. As the value she places on parental approval decreases and the value of deviant peer approval increases, her self-esteem may actually increase. Her self-efficacy expectations for pleasing her stepfather decrease—making her less likely to attempt to gain his approval and more likely to give up quickly if her reluctant attempt to be friendly is met with suspicion. Her self-efficacy for winning her friends' admiration increases as she begins to smoke, drink, and date more frequently in spite of her father's restrictions. Unfortunately, her behavior leads her down a path to potential disaster.

Connectedness

In earlier editions of this book, we identified "communication with others" as one of the five Cs of competency. Subsequent research (see Townsend & B. T. McWhirter, 2005, for a review) has convinced us that communication is actually subsumed under the broader and more encompassing construct of connectedness. Communication with others, of course, continues to be a very important construct and is, in fact, one of the main conduits that children and adolescents use to foster connectedness.

Connectedness is a ubiquitous and enduring experience of the self in relation to the world that includes a sense of close belonging in relationships with others (Lee & Robbins, 2000). In addition to communication, connectedness includes the idea of "mattering" or knowing that one matters to others (Dixon, Scheidegger, & McWhirter, 2009). Children and adolescents who lack connectedness experience social isolation or rejection and tend to suffer psychological distress, greater mental health problems, and suicide risk (CDC, 2011a; Karcher, 2004).

Communication with Others

Connectedness requires adequate social and interpersonal skills, and they play an important role in psychological adjustment and psychosocial development (CDC, 2011; Kamps & Kay, 2001). Basic interpersonal skills are necessary for competent, responsive, and mutually beneficial relationships and are perhaps the most important skills an individual must learn. The level of a young person's interpersonal skills has been related to several areas of adjustment in later life. A high incidence of mental health problems, juvenile delinquency, dropping out of school, and other at-risk behaviors has been related to social deficiencies in children and adolescents. Good social functioning in childhood and adolescence, in contrast, is related to superior academic achievement and adequate interpersonal adjustment later in life. Further, an individual's ability to achieve and maintain positive interpersonal relationships is a prerequisite to success in work and in love.

Positive social interaction enhances social integration. Friendship is important not only for social reasons but also because it enhances positive classroom and peer relationships. Children and adolescents who have positive peer relationships engage in more social interaction, and they provide positive social rewards for one another. They also use their abilities to achieve academically and to behave appropriately in the classroom. Students with positive peer and teacher relationships adapt better to school (Roseth, Johnson, & Johnson, 2008).

Perspective Taking

Perspective taking has been broadly defined as the ability to understand the perceptions, thoughts, feelings, and actions of others. Individuals must be able to distinguish the perceptions and reasoning of other people from their own. A young person's perspective-taking ability is related to his or her cognitive development and has implications for moral reasoning and empathy. Children with greater emotional knowledge are more empathetic and popular with peers and less likely to experience peer social problems (Schultz, Izard, Ackerman, & Youngstrom, 2001).

At-risk children not only have distorted perceptions but also lack the core abilities that make for satisfying social relationships. For example, kindergarten children with low cognitive ability and inattention had deficits in prosocial skills, were aggressive, and were rejected by peers (Bellanti & Bierman, 2000). These children were at higher risk for poor peer relationships in elementary school.

Solving Relationship Problems

The ability to solve interpersonal problems is an important skill. Shure (2006) describes problem solving as the integration of two skills: thinking of alternative solutions and understanding the consequences of behavior. Interpersonal problem-solving ability is related to interpersonal functioning in adults, adolescents, middle childhood, and children as young as 4 years old. Children usually develop this skill in the early grades (Shure, 1992a, 1992b, 1992c, 2007; Youngstrom et al., 2000). Even though Shure (1992a, 1992b, 1992c) has emphasized that the number of alternative solutions generated is most important, the work of Youngstrom and colleagues (2000) demonstrated that the quality of children's interpersonal problem-solving solutions was at least as important as the quantity of solutions. That is, the ability to generate two prosocial solutions is better than the ability to generate eight aggressive, hostile, or withdrawing solutions.

Jason Carter, whom we introduced in Chapter 3, is not connected. He has not developed adequate communication skills. He is at risk precisely because he cannot communicate his wants and needs without resorting to explosive, impulsive, and ultimately self-defeating behavior. His poor peer relationships, his lack of respect for adults, and his aggressive outbursts suggest serious deficiencies in communication skills. He has not learned those fundamental social skills that might help him deal more effectively with his dysfunctional parents, his competitive sister, his rejecting classmates, and his upset teacher.

Core skills for students encompass communication, perspective-taking, and problem-solving skills. They include: (a) classroom survival skills (e.g., asking for help, ignoring distractions, bringing materials to class), (b) friendship-making skills (e.g., beginning a conversation, joining in, apologizing), (c) skills for dealing with feelings (e.g., knowing and expressing one's own feelings, showing understanding of another's feelings, dealing with anger), (d) skill alternatives to aggression (e.g., asking permission, responding to teasing, problem solving), and (e) skills for dealing with stress (e.g., deciding what caused a problem, being a good sport, reacting to failure, dealing with group pressure). These skills help to foster connectedness, and effective skill training (e.g., the SAFE model: sequenced, active, focused, and explicit) provides good learning outcomes (Durlak, Weissberg, Pachan, 2010). In Chapters 12 and 13 we discuss teaching social skills in more detail.

Coping Ability

The ability to cope effectively with anxiety and stress is another skill that differentiates low-risk from high-risk young people. All individuals confront situations that cause conflict and stress. All young people sometimes feel disappointment, rejection, fear, and anger in their interactions with others. How they cope with these emotions determines their adjustment.

Coping skills influence an individual's response to stress, which in turn affects the way that person deals with conflict. Some young people cope with humor and altruism, others by focusing their attention elsewhere. These methods result in a more relaxed and positive view of the situation. When young people are in a positive, relaxed state of mind, they are able to process information more objectively, exercise better judgment, and use common sense. They also demonstrate more effectiveness and competence in solving personal problems.

Some young people, unfortunately, are exposed to more stress and have greater difficulty coping with it, placing them at greater risk. They use evasive strategies such as compulsive acting out, withdrawal, and denial. Or they succumb to one of the twins of mental health problems: anxiety or depression. Anxiety interferes with the learning process, social judgment, and interpersonal relationships and often leads to aggressive and destructive reactions. Depression can lead to suicide, suicide ideation, and other self-defeating behaviors (B. T. McWhirter & Burrow-Sanchez, 2004). Both anxiety and depression in children and adolescents are associated with cognitive distortions, negative self-talk, and anticipation of more negative future outcomes. Anxiety and depression may be logical responses to young people's astute awareness of their adverse family, school, and societal conditions. Anxiety and depression place children at risk for learning problems, academic underachievement, conduct problems, and poor social problem solving, none of which ameliorate adverse conditions in their environments. Fortunately, a number of programs have demonstrated effectiveness in enhancing children's skills for coping with stress, anxiety, and depression (Durlak et al., 2010; Rishel, 2007). Later in this chapter, we introduce mindfulness as a major coping skill.

Paul Andrews, Allie's brother, exhibits problems coping with stress. His bravado, aggressiveness, and destructiveness appear to mask considerable anxiety. His inability to modify his aggressive outbursts and his destructive hostility are a problem to him both at home and at school. His lack of skills in coping with the stress he feels foreshadows serious problems as he moves into adolescence.

Control

Lack of control—over decisions, over the future, over life—is a common characteristic of high-risk young people. Indeed, social control theory (Hirschi, 2004; Hirschi & Gottfredson, 2004) provides an explanation for delinquency and crime. External barriers combined with an inability to generate options and follow through with sound decisions relates to failure to consider consequences, unwillingness to delay gratification, and an external locus of control. These problems influence the setting and achievement of goals. Many young people have an even more fundamental problem: Their sense of a purpose in life is limited, distorted, or lacking. Low-risk young people, by contrast, exert control over their environment and their behavior in developmentally appropriate ways.

One theory of motivation, self-determination theory, incorporates aspects of control, connectedness, and self-efficacy or competence (Deci, Vallerand, Pelletier, & Ryan, 1991). According to self-determination theory, young people have three innate, universal needs: relatedness (connectedness), autonomy (control), and competence (self-efficacy). When these needs are satisfied in family and school contexts, young people develop autonomous motivation, which in turn leads to a wide range of short- and long-term positive outcomes, including school achievement and mental health (Deci & Ryan, 2000; Neimeic & Ryan, 2009; Ryan & Deci, 2000).

Decision-Making Skills

Decision making is a goal-directed sequence of affective and cognitive operations that leads to behavioral responses. Deficits in decision-making skills are clearly linked to at-risk behavior.

Low-risk children and adolescents have access to relevant information on which to base decisions. They more accurately perceive, comprehend, and store this information. They personalize the information by relating it to their own beliefs, values, and attitudes. They evaluate their solutions by considering the consequences. They demonstrate behavioral skills in their efforts to implement these decisions in social situations, and they believe in their personal competency. Young people who have high control and important goals exhibit more mastery-oriented behavior, and they have higher levels of achievement and satisfaction (Bandura, Pastorelli, Barbaranelli, & Caprara, 1999).

High-risk youth make poor and often impulsive decisions. Information or knowledge about good solutions is only part of the problem. Deficits in working memory are associated with two types of impulsivity: acting without thinking and "delay discounting" (Khurana et al., 2013). Delay discounting (DD) refers to the extent to which consequences of behavior have less and less influence on behavior the farther in time those consequences are from the behavior. For example, adolescents higher in DD will be less likely to apply sunscreen to prevent skin damage, or leave the party early to get better quality sleep before tomorrow's exams, than adolescents lower in DD. Acting without thinking and DD have been found to account for adolescents' early initiation of sexual behavior (Khurana et al., 2012) and alcohol use (Khurana et al., 2013). Another problem lies in the ability to set constructive and attainable goals, which is related to alcohol and drug use, delinquency, and low academic achievement. Further, high-risk youth are less likely to consider consequences fully and they manifest an external rather than an internal locus of control. That is, they feel that forces outside of themselves control the events in their lives and even their own behavior and that they have no power to shape their own lives. Adolescents transitioning to middle school who did not believe they had control over their success in school and were not invested in success experienced significantly more school stress and depression (Rudolph, Lambert, Clark, & Kurlakowsky, 2001). Finally, many problems with decision making are related to an inability or an unwillingness to delay gratification.

Delay of Gratification

Individuals vary in their capacity to delay gratification even as early as preschool. Low-risk individuals voluntarily postpone immediate gratification, maintain self-control, and persist in behavior directed toward a larger goal to be reached when the appropriate foundation has been laid. At-risk young people value immediate gratification and behave in ways calculated to attain it. This behavior often becomes self-defeating. Inability to delay gratification is related to depression, limited social responsibility, conduct disorders, antisocial behavior, and a variety of addictive disorders (Adams, 2013). An assessment of preschoolers' ability to delay of gratification, measured in seconds, has been positively associated with adolescent adjustment, SAT scores, body mass index, and a variety of other important indicators (Casey et al., 2011; Schlam, Wilson, Shoda, Mischel, & Ayduk, 2013).

Tyrone Baker, whom we introduced in Chapter 2, is a young man who is unable to delay gratification. He is impulsive and lacks self-control. The chaos in his home life, the lack of connectedness with his mother and siblings, and the absence of an adequate male role model have constrained his opportunities to learn self-control strategies that would enable him to delay gratification for the sake of a more important and more distant goal. His insistence on immediate gratification compromises his decision making and contributes to his potential for highly risky behavior.

Purpose in Life

Purpose gives life meaning. It is the positive end of a continuum whose negative end is meaninglessness or loneliness. Levels of future optimism and self-acceptance can discriminate between nonsuicidal adolescents and those who have attempted suicide (Gutierrez, Osman, Kopper, Barrios, & Bagge, 2000). Lack of a purpose in life, with its accompanying sense of boredom, futility, and pessimism, is an essential mediating factor in the relationship between self-derogation, depression, and thoughts of suicide. Further, lack of purpose in life is related to the subsequent use of alcohol and other drugs (Kumpfer & Summerhays, 2006). When life has no purpose, why worry about school or friends or goals or even life itself?

Low-risk youth have a purpose in life that is potentially attainable and that propels them forward. Their purpose in life orients them toward the future and often suggests short-term, realistic goals. Goals are important predictors of student achievement. Students who have realistic and hopeful visions or planful competence for themselves as successful in the future are more likely to be successful in school; those with weaker visions are not. For this reason, school-based career development interventions that promote "vocational hope" have been described as an important component of school dropout prevention programming for at-risk youth (Brown, Lamp, Telander, & Hacker, 2011).

Many high-risk youth lack a viable life purpose (see Box 5.1). If young people do not perceive themselves as having a viable future, "just say no" has no meaning. They need to discover what to say "yes" to. When young people feel that they have a limited future, they have little to lose by expecting little of themselves or by engaging in at-risk behaviors, including dropping out of school, unsafe sexual behavior, delinquency, substance abuse, and suicide.

MINDFULNESS

An understanding of the five Cs of competency provides a useful framework to help focus prevention and treatment efforts to aid troubled and troubling youth and their parents. Changing society, communities, neighborhoods, families, and schools are very important endeavors. Nevertheless, the fact remains that often the targets of change are the children and adolescents who are at risk. Mindfulness, similar to the Student Success Skills (SSS) program discussed earlier in this chapter, provides a tool to help the child or adolescent change and has been proven to be helpful with bolstering and increasing several of the five Cs.

People have been developing and applying mindfulness skills to easing psychological suffering for at least 2,500 years. Although originating from Eastern spiritual teachings, focusing on one's present moment experience with awareness and acceptance is not tied to a specific religious tradition. Indeed, mindfulness is a type of awareness that is universally accessible to anyone (Kabat-Zinn, 2013) and is not specifically religious or spiritual. Mindfulness involves an attitude of acceptance of ongoing experiences and developing here-and-now awareness of the present moment that includes internal thoughts, reactions, and feelings as well as external interpersonal and environmental events. Mindfulness emphasizes changing people's relationship to their experiences.

Box 5.1	One Week at a Time

Young men and women who have just left high school or are close to graduation frequently struggle with the reality of poverty. Manolo, who lives in Huascar, Peru, is one such young man. His face is alive with enthusiasm and excitement. His wide grin often gets him out of trouble, and it also covers up some of his problems.

When we spoke during his last year of high school, he said to me, "You know, Peru is a great country, but I don't think about the future too much; not more than a few days ahead, anyway."

"Why is that?"

"Because I have no idea what will happen to me after next week. There are no jobs, a university costs too much, and when I'm at home, dry bread is sometimes the only thing we have to eat."

Then I asked him, "Are your high school studies going to help you later?"

"No," he replied with resignation. "School is taking up my time now, but what's the use? I'll never study in a university. I'll probably work in a factory somewhere, if there's a job to be found."

Educational opportunities in the Peruvian barrios and in many U.S. inner-city schools are extremely limited. For many young people, a career is out of the question; even a job is unlikely. Undocumented youth who were brought into the United States without authorization by their parents or other family members are another group with constrained education and career pathways (McWhirter, Ramos, & Medina, 2013). About 65,000 undocumented students graduate from high school in the United States every year. Raised in the United States, sometimes they are unaware of their lack of documentation until they seek a driver's license or attempt to fill out financial aid forms for college. Their status blocks these and other pathways to responsible adulthood such as getting a job, attending college, or entering the military. Some states permit undocumented people to obtain driver's licenses, and some undocumented youth qualify for and have obtained temporary protection from deportation under federal legislation referred to as "DACA" or Deferred Action for Childhood Arrivals. DACA protection enables some undocumented young people to work, but they remain ineligible for federal financial aid, and participation in DACA exposes them and their families to deportation risk if DACA is overturned. Many barriers to higher education remain. Undocumented students are at risk of depression, anxiety, suicide, incarceration, and long-term or permanent separation from their family members (Gonzales, Suárez-Orozco, & Dedios-Sanguineti, 2013). What happens to purpose in life and hopes for the future for adolescents who are undocumented, impoverished, or facing other seemingly insurmountable barriers?

Mindfulness (Brown, Marquis, & Guiffrida, 2013; Kabat-Zinn, 1994) is an approach that has emerged as a major therapeutic intervention in the last two decades or so. As is often the case, most early application and studies were accomplished primarily with adult clients. The value of mindfulness is most striking in that in addition to improving empathic understanding and general well-being (Hölzel et al., 2011), it reduces the symptoms of many distressing problems, including anxiety, depression, eating disorders, binge drinking, and drug addiction (Brown et al., 2013; Mermelstein & Garske, 2014). Coupled with cognitive-behavioral strategies, mindfulness-based stress reduction has consistently demonstrated its effectiveness in alleviating stress and chronic physical pain (Goyal et al., 2014). For teachers, counselors, and other school personnel, mindfulness can be an effective means of reducing stress and promoting well-being, self-awareness, and self-regulation—important intrapersonal social and emotional competencies (Vago & Silbersweig, 2012). Mindfulness also helps teachers reappraise stressful situations more effectively and thus promote the development of effective classroom management (Jennings, Frank, Snowberg, Coccia, & Greenberg, 2013).

More recently, a growing body of evidence specific to children and adolescents has emerged (Simkin & Black, 2014) with the most researched techniques being mindfulness-based stress reduction and cognitive therapy, yoga and transcendental meditation, and mind–body techniques (meditation, relaxation, yoga poses, and tai chi movements). These techniques have been helpful in treating anxiety, depression, and pain (Simkin & Black, 2014), and some data indicate benefits across a wider range of affective and behavioral outcomes, for example, school attendance, decision making, safe sex, improved body image, maladaptive eating, and self-care behaviors (Cook-Cottone, Tribole, Tylka, & Tracy, 2013; Greenberg & Harris, 2012; Zenner, Herrnleben-Kurz, & Walach, 2014). Integrating mindfulness techniques into current school practice is acceptable and feasible. It has the potential of influencing an entire school by being applied in classroom-wide programs. In Great Britain, for example, teachers deliver the Mindfulness in Schools Programme (MiSP) as a part of the school curriculum to students who are stressed and have the potential for mental health difficulties (Kuyken et al., 2013). The MiSP is a program of nine lessons tailored to teenagers 12 to 16 years that include mindfulness-based cognitive therapy and stress reduction strategies adapted for youth. The intervention reduced depressive symptoms both immediately following the program and at 3-month follow-up.

Mindfulness allows for emotional regulation that involves awareness, identification, and monitoring. It is useful for negotiating difficult emotional experiences. All in all, mindfulness-based interventions in children and teenagers hold promise, particularly in relation to improving cognitive performance and response to stress. In short, it is a useful tool for increasing resiliency and self-control in young people.

Mindfulness practices have been critiqued for potentially minimizing or ignoring the role of systematic and structural oppressions experienced by marginalized groups. If mindfulness leads to complacency with oppression and acceptance of structural inequities, it is not healthy for anyone in the long term. One study identified factors that contributed to the helpfulness of group mindfulness interventions with people experiencing cultural oppression, including: paying close attention to participant culture and experiences of oppression, honoring participants' reactivity, creating a safe space for experiencing the reactivity, helping participants connect oppression with body symptoms, providing guidance for responding to oppression, adapting the intervention to the unique experiences and language of participants, and fostering inclusiveness and community among participants (Longoria, Adams, & Hitter, 2014). Another study found mindfulness helpful for those who experience discrimination (Brown-Iannuzzi, Adair, Payne, Richman, & Fredrickson, 2014).

THINGS TO DO CHART: INCREASING THE FIVE CS

We have included specific empirically supported interventions throughout the book that describe concrete and specific intervention skills to use with children and adolescents. Although these skills and activities are embedded in specific chapters, they usually have broader application beyond the particular problem area discussed. Most increase resiliency and relate directly to one or more of the five Cs. On the inside of the front cover is a "The Things to Do" chart indicates the location of various activities and approaches that helpers can use with at-risk children, adolescents, and their families. On this chart we have suggested the most appropriate age groups and grade level for using each of the skills, strategies, and activities listed and presented throughout this book. We hope the "Things to Do" chart (Figure 5.1) will help you locate intervention and prevention activities that work.

In addition to the interventions that are peppered throughout the following chapters, three very broad constructs are important in most of the interventions suggested in this text. The first construct is that open, honest, and nurturing relationships between adults and young people who are at risk are essential to effective interventions. Adult caring relationships are key to the development of resilience in children and go a long way in helping young people develop the five competencies important for successful functioning. One study identified seven important characteristics of caring relationships that adults need to demonstrate in relationships with youth at risk: attention, availability, affirmation, empathy, respect, trust, and virtue (Laursen & Birmingham, 2003).

The second construct is that faulty, negative, and self-defeating thought patterns that perpetuate risky behavior must be the focus of intervention when young people are mature enough to deal with their own insights (e.g., typically after fourth grade). While not totally universal, the negative spiral of faulty cognitions, poor expectations, reduced effort, and diminished performance is extremely common among many at-risk youth (see Figure 5.2). Understanding this negative spiral provides the helper with a variety of areas for focused intervention when working with youth.

A related construct is a "syndrome of negative affect." Emotional problems—anxiety, depression, and other mood problems—typically accompany risky behavior. Often, if we can alleviate negative affect, we reduce risky behavior. Over half of all lifetime cases of mental illness begin by age 14, but many people do not receive treatment until years after the first onset of symptoms of a mental or emotional disorder (Kessler, Wang, & Zaslavsky,

FIGURE 5.1 Things to Do

Grade level:

	Preschool & Kindergarten	1	2	3	4	5	6	7	8	9	10	11	12
Parent effectiveness training (Chapter 14)	▓	▓	▓	▓	▓	▓	▓	▓	▓	▓			
Premack principle (Chapter 14)	▓	▓	▓	▓	▓	▓	▓	▓	▓	▓			
Logical consequences (Chapter 8, 14)	▓	▓	▓	▓	▓	▓	▓	▓	▓	▓			
Optimism training (Chapter 12)	▓	▓	▓	▓	▓	▓	▓	▓	▓	▓			
Adlerian/Dreikurs (Chapter 8)	▓	▓	▓	▓	▓	▓	▓	▓	▓	▓			
Interpersonal problem solving (ICPS) (Chapter 12)	▓	▓	▓	▓	▓	▓	▓	▓	▓	▓			
Communities that Care/CtC (Chapter 2)	▓	▓	▓	▓	▓	▓	▓	▓	▓	▓			
IPV prevention/Project FREE (Chapter 3)	▓	▓	▓	▓	▓	▓	▓	▓	▓	▓			
Family check-up/EcoFit (Chapter 14)	▓	▓	▓	▓	▓	▓	▓	▓	▓	▓			
Cooperative learning (Chapter 13)		▓	▓	▓	▓	▓	▓	▓	▓	▓	▓	▓	▓
Conflict resolution (Chapter 9, 13)		▓	▓	▓	▓	▓	▓	▓	▓	▓	▓	▓	▓
Good behavior game (Chapter 13)		▓	▓	▓	▓	▓	▓	▓	▓	▓	▓	▓	▓
Student Success Skills (Chapter 5)				▓	▓	▓	▓	▓	▓	▓	▓	▓	▓
Assertiveness skills (Chapter 12)				▓	▓	▓	▓	▓	▓	▓	▓	▓	▓
Crisis management (Chapter 9, 10)				▓	▓	▓	▓	▓	▓	▓	▓	▓	▓
Anti-bullying programs (Chapter 11)				▓	▓	▓	▓	▓	▓	▓	▓	▓	▓
Comprehensive, competency-based guidance (Chapter 6)				▓	▓	▓	▓	▓	▓	▓	▓	▓	▓
Peer and cross-age tutoring (Chapter 13)					▓	▓	▓	▓	▓	▓	▓	▓	▓
Peer support networks (Chapter 13)					▓	▓	▓	▓	▓	▓	▓	▓	▓
Anger reduction (Chapter 11)					▓	▓	▓	▓	▓	▓	▓	▓	▓
Peer mediation (Chapter 13)					▓	▓	▓	▓	▓	▓	▓	▓	▓
Reality therapy (Chapter 9)					▓	▓	▓	▓	▓	▓	▓	▓	▓
Flipped classroom (Chapter 4, 6)							▓	▓	▓	▓	▓	▓	▓
Mindfulness (Chapter 5)							▓	▓	▓	▓	▓	▓	▓
Life skills social competency training (Chapter 12)							▓	▓	▓	▓	▓	▓	▓
Resistance and refusal skills (Chapter 12)							▓	▓	▓	▓	▓	▓	▓
Cyberbully prevention training (Chapter 12)							▓	▓	▓	▓	▓	▓	▓
Benson's relevation response (Chapter 12)								▓	▓	▓	▓	▓	▓
Cognitive change strategies (Chapter 12, 14)								▓	▓	▓	▓	▓	▓
Relaxation and imagery training (Chapter 12)								▓	▓	▓	▓	▓	▓
Solution-focused counseling (Chapter 6)								▓	▓	▓	▓	▓	▓
Suicide assessment (Chapter 10)								▓	▓	▓	▓	▓	▓
Dating violence reduction (Chapter 6)								▓	▓	▓	▓	▓	▓
Motivational interviewing (Chapter 7)									▓	▓	▓	▓	▓
Student assistance programs (Chapter 7)									▓	▓	▓	▓	▓
Khan academy/TeDtalk/YouTube (Chapter 4, 6)									▓	▓	▓	▓	▓
IPV prevention/ACCESS (Chapter 4)									▓	▓	▓	▓	▓

FIGURE 5.2 The Spiral of Self-Defeating Cognitions

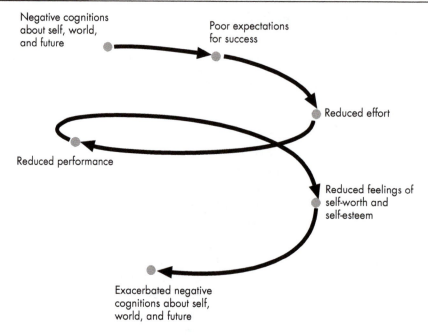

Negative cognitions about self, world, and future

Poor expectations for success

Reduced effort

Reduced performance

Reduced feelings of self-worth and self-esteem

Exacerbated negative cognitions about self, world, and future

2005). We clearly want to help young people change self-defeating behavior and make better choices. To be optimally effective, it is critical to understand emotions and the potential "negative affect syndrome" in developing and implementing prevention and treatment strategies.

Each of these three constructs needs to be considered when working with at-risk youth and when implementing the interventions presented in later chapters.

CONCLUSION

In this chapter we highlighted an important issue that we emphasize throughout this book: The problems faced by children and youth are mediated not only by their social, family, and school environments but also by the skills the children possess—skills they can develop to overcome their difficulties. One way we can assist young people is by recognizing how some of them have developed resiliency and by teaching these skills to those who are at risk. Professionals who can recognize the characteristics of high-risk versus low-risk youth are in a position to identify young people who are at greatest risk and to design well-focused interventions. They can reduce the risk to young people by helping them develop the competencies we have presented in this chapter. The five Cs of competency are attended to in greater detail in Part 3, in which we describe problems in the at-risk categories and treatments for them, and in Part 4, in which we suggest strategies for prevention.

At-Risk Categories

In Part 3 we consider five specific categories that reflect some of the principal problem areas for at-risk youth: school dropout, substance use, risky sexual behavior, delinquency and youth violence, and youth suicide. Although these topics represent a substantial portion of child and adolescent problem areas, they do not reflect all areas of concern. Nevertheless, we believe these central topics are highly representative of other problems as well. In each chapter we provide (a) a conceptualization of the problem, (b) a discussion of the scope of the problem, (c) characteristics of the problem and strategies to identify and assess it, (d) consequences of the problem, and (e) specific intervention approaches that helpers need to know to reduce the problem. In addition, for each category we examine a major prevention and intervention strategy or two that address the specific areas described. Of course, the intervention ideas provided in each chapter can be applied to other areas as well.

School Dropout

Long day coming

where any corner I turn

any door opening

any hallway minute

can end up with everyone watching

all those eyes seeing

and no one is there

Later you'll say "just ignore them"

like it would be so easy,

like breathing

You'll tell me stories

listen to my plans

nod and then smile

and look at your watch

like I'm not even talking

like I'm not really there

We'll sit in your office

with posters of baby animals

on the endangered list

(they aren't the ones who belong on that list)

but you'll pretend, and then we'll both pretend

that our little talks make it better

that I will bravely endure

that this story has a nice quiet ending

and that I will be OK.

CHAPTER OUTLINE

I n this chapter we concentrate on young people who leave school before they graduate. In the following pages we (a) discuss changing literacy standards that define the term *dropout*, (b) discuss the scope of the dropout problem, (c) outline some of the roots of the problem, (d) highlight the economic and social consequences of dropping out, (e) present information to identify potential dropouts, and (f) describe pragmatic ideas and interventions designed to reduce dropout.

DEFINITIONAL ISSUES OF THE DROPOUT PROBLEM

Literacy Standards

To understand the apparent decline in academic proficiency of students, we must note the changes that have taken place in educational standards. In 1890 only 6.7% of the nation's 14- to 17-year-olds attended high school. By the late 1990s, more than 95% attended high school. In 1890, 3.5% of America's 17-year-olds graduated from high school. By 1970, 75.6% did so, and by the late 1990s, 89% were graduated. In 2014, 91% of adolescents had completed high school or its equivalent (Kena et al., 2015). In addition, the criterion for functional literacy has risen steadily from 3 years of schooling in the 1930s, to 6 years in the 1950s, to the completion of high school in the 1970s. These climbing standards have placed increasing demands on students with some unintended effects; one analysis revealed that more stringent high school math and science requirements resulted in higher dropout rates for all students, and decreased the likelihood that Black women and Hispanic men and women would enroll in college (Plunk, Tate, Bierut, & Grucza, 2014). The nation-wide application of Common Core standards, discussed in Chapter 4, is likely to increase demands even more.

Many more children with widely diverse backgrounds are being educated than ever before in our history. High schools of 100 years ago were mainly open to the most privileged children, and only a handful of them were expected to graduate. Schools today are called upon to serve vastly larger numbers of children and to serve children from very different social, cultural, and language backgrounds. Schools also are expected to deliver many more services and to reach children with a much greater ability range. Today's students who drop out of high school are a major concern for educators and for society, and there are strenuous efforts to reduce the high school dropout rate to zero. Despite these challenges, the American educational system has been enormously successful.

Definition of a Dropout

A dropout is a student who leaves school before graduation and before completing a program of study. The U.S. Department of Education (DOE) has two classifications of dropout: event dropout and status dropout. Event dropouts are youth who withdraw from school within a specific time frame—during a given school year, for example. Status dropouts are nonenrolled youth ages 16 to 24 who are out of school without a high school diploma. The DOE also tracks two types of school completion rates: status completion rates (all completers, ages 16 to 24) and the 4-year completion rate (Aud & Hannes, 2010). These definitions provide consistent criteria for counting those who drop out. However, educators, state governments, policy makers, and school district personnel sometimes use additional and inconsistent criteria, leaving us with statistics that are often imprecise and sometimes contradictory.

The quality of dropout data varies as a function of adequacy of school staffing; consistency of definitions of illnesses, leaves, and transfers; family transience; and specific state criteria for calculating dropout. For example, some states count students with equivalent high school degrees (General Educational Development, GED) as graduates; others do not. Many schools have a vested interest in keeping dropout rates low, at least at the beginning of the year, because their state funds are tied to student counts. In many cases, for example, per student funding is tied to the number of students enrolled on the one hundredth day after fall classes begin.

Even statistics based on common criteria rarely include students who dropped out before entering high school. For example, figures cited for Latino high school sophomores who drop out by their senior year may actually understate the dropout rate among Latinos. In one large secondary school district in Arizona, for example, eighth-grade students who do not register for high school are never counted in the high school census, and therefore they are not counted in the dropout rate. Latino students are especially affected by this practice (Aud & Hannes, 2010).

SCOPE AND CHARACTERISTICS OF THE PROBLEM

Despite ongoing inconsistency in tallying dropout, educators and researchers have made headway in their attempts to profile the student who drops out of school. Research has identified both individual and institutional risk factors for school dropout (De Witte, Cabus, Thyssen, Groot, & van den Brink, 2013). And, of course, teachers know from their own experience that students who drop out are likely to be those who are unmotivated by their class work; who have had problems with either the school authorities, the police, or both; who skip classes or are often absent; who are pregnant or married; who are poor and must work; who have family problems; who have drug or alcohol problems; who are students of color; or who have fallen behind their grade level. The latter group includes many students who are learning English as a second language (ESL), also called second-language learners (SLL) or English language learners (ELL). The percentage and number of ELL students were larger in the school year 2012–2013 (over 9.2% or 4.4 million) than in 2002–2003 (8.4% or 4.1 million, Kena et al., 2015). Students from non-English-speaking homes drop out in much higher numbers than do students from homes where English is the only language spoken (Gil & Bardack, 2011). Recall that Ramona Diaz (Chapter 4) gets poor grades and dislikes school. She does not think school is meeting her needs, and she feels as though she does not belong there. Her family's economic situation is difficult, and Ramona feels strongly that she should work to help support her family. She also feels badly about herself and does not believe she has the ability to compete at school. Ramona has little social involvement with the school, partly because of the family's economic situation and partly because of her struggle with the English language. These factors made Ramona a prime candidate for dropping out.

In 2000, 11% of 16- to 24-year-olds were out of school without a high school diploma. Although the status dropout rate remained fairly consistent from 1992 to 2000, it declined for young people as a group between the early 1970s and mid-2000. The rate of this decline, however, varied for European Americans, African Americans, Latinos, and American Indians (Chapman, Laird, & KewalRamani, 2010). American Indians/Alaska natives have the lowest high school graduation rates. In 2012, African American students had only a 69% graduation rate and Hispanic students had a 73% rate, while Asian students had an 88% graduation rate and White students had an 86% rate (Layton, 2014). State variation in graduation success (or failure) is high; only 37% of Black males graduate from high school in 4 years in the state of New York, and only 45% in Nebraska (Schott Foundation for Public Education, 2012). The high dropout rate of Latino students reflects dropout among immigrant and undocumented Latina/o students as well as Latino students whose parents are undocumented.

Immigrant Students

Although all countries have experienced immigration, the United States has an especially high immigration rate. The number of new immigrants has remained steady at around 1 million per year for the last 5 years, according to the Department of Homeland Security, down from a high of nearly 2 million in 1991 (Wade, 2015). Public school systems reflect these demographics, with children of immigrants accounting for a large percent of all U.S. schoolchildren. Most of the parents of these children arrived in the United States from Latin America (42% from Mexico as of 2014) and Asia.

The dramatically lower educational attainment of immigrant adolescents from Latin America has adverse implications for their later employment, income, health, marriage, and housing (Wade, 2015). This problem is likely to get worse as California, Arizona, and other states drop bilingual education programs in favor of state-mandated English immersion programs, putting a substantial proportion of immigrant children at even more risk. The English immersion approach assumes that immigrant children, and others whose first language is other than English, learn English very quickly—generally within a year's time—under conditions of total immersion. Interestingly, studies have indicated that the development of oral English proficiency takes an average of 3.31 years, ranging from 1 year to 6.5 years. Only 2.25% of students demonstrated English proficiency in a year's time; most achieved English proficiency in 2 to 5 years (MacSwan & Pray, 2005). In English immersion programs, all subjects are taught in English regardless of whether the student understands. In effect, these students lose a number of years of instruction. For youth who immigrate as adolescents rather than as young children, acquisition of English language skills takes longer and is further complicated by lower levels of academic and language support, more complex academic demands, and higher stakes assessment requirements (Carhill, Suárez-Orozco, & Páez, 2008).

Immigrant children from Mexico and from Central America—Guatemala, Honduras, El Salvador—are often fleeing from drug violence and gang activity in their home countries (Assessment Capacities Project/ACAPS, 2014). Children who have experienced fear, isolation, and trauma are subject to a variety of mental health challenges and psychological stressors, with a number of children developing depression, anxiety, and posttraumatic stress disorder (PTSD) (Collier, 2015; Landale, Hardie, Oropesa, & Hillemeier, 2015). Latino students with undocumented parents often exhibit behavioral problems in reaction to their parents' possible or actual arrest and deportation (Landale et al., 2015). Such conditions, of course, interfere with learning and with reasonable school success.

Latino Students

Between 2000 and 2011, the status dropout rate for Hispanics dropped from about 27% to about 14%, and the decline is especially apparent among younger Hispanics (Fry & Taylor, 2013). This positive trend is accompanied by a significant increase in college enrollment among Latinos, with the class of 2012 surpassing the college enrollment of White high school graduates. Nevertheless, Hispanics remain far more likely to drop out of high school and less likely to complete a bachelor's degree than their White and Asian counterparts (Fry & Taylor, 2013). The extensive literature on Latino dropout rates indicates that there is not a single cause associated with the decision to leave school. Foreign-born Latinos dropped out at a higher rate than native-born Latinos (Aud & Hannes, 2010). For immigrants, the stress, confusion, and anxiety when first entering a U.S. school, combined with language problems, are issues. Other factors are poverty, pregnancy, poor academic achievement, parents' educational attainment, lack of motivation, low aspirations, disengagement from learning, and single-parent families (Chapman, Laird, & KewalRamani, 2010). A growing body of literature also points to school-related or institutional factors that play an important role in the dropout process, including lower teacher expectations, teacher expression of stereotypes, and discrimination by school personnel and peers (Conchas, 2001; McWhirter, Valdez, & Caban, 2013). Undocumented students, of which the greatest proportion are from Mexico, may drop out when they realize the legal barriers that can prevent them from pursuing higher education and work (Abrego & Gonzalez, 2010; McWhirter, Ramos, & Medina, 2013). While Deferred Action for Childhood Arrivals (DACA) legislation has provided some undocumented students with the opportunity to attend college and work without fear of deportation, many barriers remain, including costs, restrictive criteria on who qualifies for DACA, and fear of exposing undocumented family members to the risk of deportation. This is especially problematic because DACA legislation could be revoked under a new administration (see http://www.dhs.gov/deferred-action-childhood-arrivals).

Exceptional Students

In addition to students of color, immigrant, and English as a second-language students, dropout statistics include many students with disabilities. The dropout rate for students with emotional/behavioral disabilities is considerably higher than that of general education students, despite the school's legal obligation to provide students with disabilities a free, appropriate education until they reach age 21 or receive a high school diploma, as mandated by the Individuals with Disabilities Education Act (IDEA) and the Americans with Disabilities Act (ADA). Students with specific learning disabilities and with attention deficit hyperactivity disorder (ADHD) who drop out of school are more socially alienated from classmates and teachers than are similar students who complete school. Girls with disabilities are at greater risk of dropout and have more negative long-term economic trajectories than boys with disabilities (Lindstrom, Harwich, Poppen, & Doren, 2012). Mental disorders are estimated to account for 5.8–11% of high school dropout (Mojtabai, Stuart, Hwang, Eaton, Sampson, & Kessler, 2015). Young people with disabilities face numerous and complex challenges to complete their high school education.

Gifted students, who often demonstrate high ability and intelligence, high creativity, and a strong drive to initiate and complete a task, drop out of school more often than one would think. In fact, they drop out more often than their nongifted peers, perhaps because they are confronted with many concerns that giftedness does not resolve (Foley-Nicpon & Assouline, 2015).

Black male students are disproportionately identified as having learning disabilities and emotional/behavioral disorders, and highly underidentified as gifted and talented, both of which contribute to their marginalization in school systems and ultimately their risk of dropout (Dancy, 2014). All of these exceptional students must be kept in mind when we discuss the scope of the dropout problem.

Lesbian, Gay, Bisexual, and Transgender Students

Another group of students who are particularly at risk of dropping out of school are lesbian, gay, bisexual, and transgender (LGBT) students. We use the umbrella term *LGBT* to also include intergender and genderqueer youth, while recognizing that there are many unique characteristics and challenges for subgroups of students within this larger group. Many of the school problems of these adolescents are related to the pervasive physical and verbal abuse they receive from peers. According to the 2013 National School Climate Survey (Kosciw, Greytak, Palmer, & Boesen, 2014), 55.5% of LGBT students felt unsafe at school because of their sexual orientation, and nearly 39% felt unsafe due to their gender expression. Over 60% of LGBT students avoided school events and extracurricular activities due to feeling unsafe or uncomfortable. LGBT students also reported verbal harassment (74% for sexual orientation, 55% for gender expression), physical harassment (36% for sexual orientation, 23% for gender expression), physical assault (16.5% for sexual orientation, 11% for gender expression), and 49% of LGBT students reported experiencing some form of cyberbullying. Such harassment has significant consequences. The LGBT students who experienced higher levels of harassment and victimization associated with their sexual orientation or gender expression were more likely to miss school, had lower GPAs, were less likely to plan to pursue postsecondary education, and had lower self-esteem and higher depression (Kosciw et al., 2014). Nearly 60% of LGBT youth did not report the incidents of harassment or abuse that they experienced, fearing inaction or an action that would make things worse. Of those who did make a report, over 60% said that the school staff did not respond or take any action. This illustrates that peers are not the only, or even the primary, problem for LGBT students. Teachers and other school personnel convey biases and negative attitudes that implicitly or explicitly condone inappropriate behavior from peers, and often fail to respond or even notice when such behavior happens right in front of them (Greene, Britton, & Fitts, 2014; Kosciw et al., 2014; Russell, Toomey, Ryan, & Diaz, 2014).

School policies often explicitly convey intolerance of LGBT youth, for example, being disciplined for expressions of affection that are not the subject of discipline for heterosexual students, being prohibited from forming an LGBT-affirmative support group, or being prohibited from wearing clothing that is inconsistent with their biological or birth-assigned sex. Making school safe for LGBT youth is the responsibility of all educators.

LGBT youth consistently report significant stress associated with school and related activities, which contributes to alienation from school and dropout (Russell et al., 2014). LGBT youth are susceptible to depression and are at higher risk for suicide because of internal turmoil and environmental harassment (see Chapter 10).

Adjudicated/Incarcerated Youth

Adjudicated young people are less likely to graduate from high school. More than two-thirds of juvenile offenders of high school age fail to return to school following their release from custody. These adolescents are often alienated from school by below grade level academic performance, a lack of necessary high school credits, school reenrollment procedures, chronic truancy, and a need for special education services (Office of Program Policy Analysis & Government Accountability, 2010; U.S. Office of Juvenile Justice and Delinquency Prevention, 2005). These young people present a particularly thorny problem because in addition to their potential for dropping out of school, incarcerating young people incurs short-term costs of over $100,000 yearly, with even greater long-term costs to themselves and society (Justice Policy Institute, 2015). Eight in ten incarcerated juveniles suffer from learning disabilities. Nearly four out of five youth arrested for juvenile crimes in 2000 were involved with drugs or alcohol, and 92% tested positive for marijuana. Unfortunately, only a very low number of these youth receive substance abuse treatment once they enter the juvenile justice system. Up to three quarters of all incarcerated juveniles had a diagnosable mental health disorder. Most often educational programs fail to meet state standards, and mental health services are scarce (National Center on Addiction and Substance Abuse, 2005). Finally, the system does not affect all young people equally. Hispanic/Latino youth are adjudicated/incarcerated at a rate twice as high as Whites, and African American youth at a rate nearly five times higher than White teenagers (Justice Policy Institute, 2015). Racial inequity in the U.S. justice system and the incarceration of African Americans is well documented in Michelle Alexander's *The New Jim Crow: Mass Incarceration in the Age of Colorblindness*.

On a related note, social language analyses in one study (Kayama, Haight, Gibson, & Wilson, 2015) indicated that school personnel used criminal justice language to send a strong and consistent message about the connection between student misbehavior at school and the criminal justice system. The authors suggested that such language impacts some students' perspectives of their misbehavior that is relevant to a criminalized self-identity and is one potential mechanism in the school-to-prison pipeline.

THE CONSEQUENCES OF DROPPING OUT

Dropping out of school has a significant impact on the life of the individual, but the costs go far beyond individual consequences. School dropout rates have serious economic and social repercussions for society as well as various forms of social exclusion and other disadvantages. Flexible, holistic, and intensive support approaches tend to be more attractive and beneficial to the participants.

Economic Consequences

Students who drop out of school are at an economic disadvantage and will be throughout their lives: Unemployment and underemployment rates are high among high school dropouts; they earn significantly less over their lifetimes than high school graduates and less still than those graduates who attend some college. In 2008, a student with a bachelor's degree earned 28% more than one with an associate's degree, 53% more than a high school completer, and 96% more than a young person without a high school diploma (Aud & Hannes, 2010). In addition to lower income, the unemployment rate of those who drop out is considerably higher as well. Detachment from school by teenagers puts youth at increased risk of having lower earnings and less stable employment than peers who stay in school (U.S. Department of Education, 2010). A high school diploma no longer ensures gainful employment as it did in the past.

The economic consequences of the dropout problem include loss of earnings and taxes, loss of Social Security, and lack of qualified workers. A high school diploma is the minimum qualification for participation in the U.S. economy. A worker without one can find work in only the most menial occupations, which often pay quite poorly. The factory jobs that once allowed workers to make a good income without a high school diploma are diminishing or are being transferred out of the country; the educational requirements for jobs in general are increasing. The high school dropout is not easily absorbed into the workforce due to this ever-increasing demand for highly trained workers. Students who drop out of high school will lack the necessary skills to participate in the high-tech job market and are likely to be destined for marginal employment or outright dependence on society. The poverty rate for those who drop out is over twice as high as college grads, and the unemployment rate is generally 4 percentage points higher than the national average (Lynch, 2015).

The economic consequences of dropping out will continue to worsen as jobs for low-skilled workers dry up. And this affects the nation as well. If the 1.3 million dropouts from the class of 2010 had graduated, the nation would have seen $337 billion more in earnings over the course of the students' lifetimes (Campaign High School Equity/CHSE, 2015). Those who drop out pay half as much in taxes as do high school graduates. They receive larger government subsidies in the form of food stamps, welfare payments, and housing assistance. They have higher rates of criminal activity and are more likely involved in crime, which dramatically increases the probability of prison, and they have worse health outcomes and lower life expectancies, and thus have a higher reliance on Medicaid and Medicare.

Not long ago, the Social Security checks of retirees were paid for by as many as 17 employed workers; currently, however, the ratio is 2.8 workers paying taxes per each recipient drawing upon Social Security (Social Security Administration/SSA, 2014). From a purely economic perspective, schools, communities, and legislators must ensure that adolescents at risk graduate in increasing numbers both to meet the needs of the national labor market and to ensure continuity of our Social Security system.

Social Consequences

Students who leave school before completing their program of study are at a disadvantage in other ways as well. Dropping out of school often has an impact on an individual's psychological well-being. Dissatisfaction with self, with the environment, and with lack of opportunity is also associated with lower occupational aspirations among young people. When high school dropouts are unemployed or earn less money than their graduated peers, their children also experience negative consequences because they live in lower socioeconomic conditions. Proportionately few of these homes provide the study aids that children of graduates can expect to have. Parents who are poor are less likely to provide non-school-related activities for their children than parents of higher socioeconomic status. Further, low wages require parents who dropped out to work such long hours that it is difficult for them to monitor their children's activities. Because high school dropouts have lower occupational aspirations than their graduated peers, they typically also have lower educational expectations for their own children. The Andrews, Baker, and Diaz families (of Chapters 1, 2, and 4) are prime examples of this situation. In each of these families, at least one of the parents did not complete high school, and the children must bear the consequences.

Dropping out of school truncates educational and vocational development in a manner that dramatically increases the probability of a downward spiral into greater physical, emotional, and economic problems. Those who dropout are in worse health than other adults. High school dropouts report poorer health at age 40 than those with college educations at age 70 (Zajacova, Montez, & Herd, 2014). Less-educated adolescents are more likely to become pregnant outside of marriage and to abuse alcohol and drugs. In short, health-risk behaviors—substance use, violence, physical inactivity—are consistently linked to academic failure (Centers for Disease Control and Prevention, 2011a). Dropouts also make up disproportionately higher percentages of the nation's prison and death row inmates (Chapman et al., 2010).

The idea that "dropouts beget dropouts" conveys an unnecessary hopelessness. Not all dropouts have children who want to drop out, and not all students at risk for school failure today are children of dropouts. Nevertheless, a continuing cycle of leaving school early seems likely if schools do not take action. Schools can break the cycle in a variety of ways.

PREDICTIVE INDICATORS AND TYPE OF DROPOUT

According to a recent report by Rosen and Chen (2015), close to 3% of the 2009 ninth graders had dropped out of school by spring of 2012, most in the eleventh grade. There was some variability of the dropout rate by student ethnicity: African Americans (4.3%), Latino (3.5%), European American (2.1%), and Asian (0.3%). Close to 5% of students in the lowest fifth socioeconomic status dropped out compared to about a half a percent of students in the highest fifth. Of course, effective implementation of dropout prevention programs requires a more precise identification of students at risk than merely ethnicity or socioeconomic status. To facilitate this, we turn to research that teachers, counselors, psychologists, and other human service professionals may find useful in their daily work with students (Dynarski et al., 2008; Suh, Suh, & Houston, 2007; and especially, Ekstrom, Goertz, Pollack, & Rock, 1986).

Differences Between Stayers and Leavers

About 30 years ago, Ekstrom and her colleagues (1986) focused on a sample of high school sophomores over a 2-year period. They found that those who stayed in school (stayers) differed significantly from those who left (dropouts) across a variety of dimensions: socioeconomic status, race/ethnicity, parent support for education, family structure, school behaviors, and attitudes/abilities toward schoolwork. Students who left school were more likely to be poorer, older, male, and ethnic minorities. They tended to come from homes with fewer study aids and fewer opportunities for non-school-related learning than students who stayed in school. Dropouts were less likely to have both birth parents living in the home, were more likely to have employed mothers (who had less education and lower educational expectations for their children), and had less parental monitoring of their activities.

The students who dropped out of school also differed from the stayers in a variety of behaviors. The dropouts were less likely to be involved in extracurricular activities and had lower grades and lower test scores than the stayers. Interestingly, the gap between stayers' and dropouts' grades was greater than the gap between their scores on achievement tests. Those who dropped out did less homework: an average of 2.2 hours a week as opposed to the 3.4 hours reported by the stayers. The dropouts also had more discipline problems in school, were absent and late more often, cut more classes, got suspended from school more often, and had more trouble with the police.

Differences between dropouts and stayers also emerged in the affective domain. Many of the dropouts reported feelings of alienation from school. Most were not involved in clubs, sports, or student government. Not surprisingly, few dropouts reported feelings of satisfaction with their academic work. Dropouts did not feel popular with other students, and their friends were also alienated from school and had low educational expectations.

Finally, the dropouts worked more hours than the stayers, and their jobs were more enjoyable and more important to them than school.

The question arose: What had happened to the students who had dropped out of school between their sophomore and senior years. Ekstrom et al. (1986) found that 47% of them were working either full or part time (more Whites and males reported working for pay than did minorities and females), 29% were looking for work, 16% were homemakers, 10% were enrolled in job-training programs, and 3% were in military service. Of these dropouts, 58% hoped to finish high school eventually, and 17% reported that they had already enrolled in an educational institution. Fourteen percent had already obtained a GED high school equivalency certificate. Very little has changed since Ekstrom's original report (see, e.g., Dynarski et al., 2008; Rosen & Chen, 2015; Suh et al., 2007), except poorer pay and lack of jobs are more severe problems. It is probable that at least 50% of a similar cohort today would not be employed or would be underemployed. This is especially so because of the increasing demands on the labor force. In the workplace, 85% of current jobs and 90% of new jobs require some or more college or postsecondary education (Alliance for Excellent Education, 2015).

Predictive Variables and Dropout Types

Although the profile developed by Ekstrom et al. (1986) tells us some of the characteristics of young people who drop out of school before graduation, it does not tell us enough about the complex interaction of variables or about why younger students leave. Indeed, dropping out of school is a culmination of a developmental process that involves a complex ecology. Dropping out is a process that begins early in development, typically before a child even enters school, and continues through the time a student formally withdraws. For example, a third-grade student who reads at the appropriate reading level compared to a third-grade student who does not is four times more likely to graduate by age 19. Furthermore, a student living in poverty is 13 times less likely to graduate on time (Sparks, 2011). In one study, the quality of early care giving, the early home environment, peer competence, and problem behaviors predicted high school status 15 years later (Jimerson, Egeland, Sroufe, & Carlson, 2000). Early experiences may affect a student's sense of agency and self-concept. These may directly influence school performance and later decisions to stay in school. Diemer (2009) found that urban minority high school students who had higher critical consciousness, or awareness of and motivation to address social inequity, were more likely to graduate from high school, and obtain further education or be in the workforce 8 years later relative to their less critically conscious counterparts. Early experiences also lay foundations for relationships with teachers and differential interactions with peers that further propel the individual along the pathway toward dropping out. Success in school requires numerous capacities for behavioral control and self-regulation that are formed in earlier years.

In a study designed to test five theories of early dropout behavior, Battin-Pearson and her colleagues (2000) identified poor academic achievement as assessed by standardized achievement tests and grade point averages as consistently one of the strongest predictors of dropping out of high school early. Engaging in deviant behavior such as substance abuse or delinquency, having close connections to antisocial peers, and coming from a poor family increased risks for leaving school by age 14, even when the student had not experienced academic failure or difficulty. Clearly, dropout prevention efforts should be focused directly on improving academic achievement at early ages, but prevention programs should also focus on poor families, youth who associate with deviant peers, and those who participate in aggressive behavior and drug use.

Good dropout prevention programs have the ability to closely match their methods and content to the specific strengths, vulnerabilities, and needs of the participants. One helpful typology of dropouts comes from the work of Janosz and his colleagues (2000). Combining three axes of school-related behavior—academic achievement, school commitment, and behavioral maladjustment—Janosz and colleagues identified four basic, reliable, and valid dropout types: disengaged type, low-achiever type, quiet type, and maladjusted type. Each type has unique characteristics to consider in designing interventions.

Disengaged Type

Although they believe that they are less competent than other students, disengaged type dropouts obtain surprisingly high achievement scores considering their lack of school involvement. These young people care little about school grades and have few educational aspirations, generally do not like school, do not recognize the importance of education, and accord little value to both school and education in their lives.

Low-Achiever Type

Although they have relatively few behavior problems, low-achiever type of dropouts have a very weak commitment to education, experience poor grades, and learn little. Of all the dropout types, low achievers are distinct in their lack of ability to fulfill minimal course requirements.

Quiet Type

Young people who fit this dropout category have few external problems, although they exhibit poor school performance. They hold positive views about school attendance, appear to be involved in school activities, and do not create disciplinary trouble. They do not get very good grades but also do not misbehave much and do not react openly to school difficulties. They generally go unnoticed until they drop out.

Maladjusted Type

Dropouts in this category have high levels of misbehavior. They demonstrate a weak commitment to education, have poor school performance, invest little in school life, and frequently are in disciplinary trouble. Due to the variety and severity of difficulties, these students have the most negative school profile of the four types.

Knowing these dropout types will assist counselors and educators to identify potential dropouts. Clustering variables that predict dropout types will improve interventions to reduce dropouts because prevention efforts can target specific behaviors and attitudes.

We must also consider another contributing factor: the student's instructional environment. The instructional environment can seriously magnify a student's dislike for school, lack of motivation, and low self-concept. For example, at-risk, low-achieving students are often treated differently from high-achieving students, and this kind of differential treatment can literally "push" them out of school. Differential treatment of at-risk students includes that they are called on less, given less wait time to answer questions, given less praise, and given less eye contact and other nonverbal communication of responsiveness. It also includes disproportionately severe discipline, a phenomena that especially affects Black students. At-risk students sense the teacher's lower regard for their personal worth as learners, come to believe it, and then conform to those expectations. Equally important is the need at the district level to deal with schools that are not performing well with respect to at-risk students (Knudson, Shambaugh, & O'Day, 2011).

Balfanz (2007) identified four categories of dropout that are parallel to those presented by Janosz and colleagues, and also include the notion of being "pushed out." He describes students who drop out due to *life events* (e.g., pregnancy, a death or disability in the family, deportation of a family member, being arrested or the arrest of a family member, becoming homeless), students who *fade out* (invisible students who do not call attention to themselves, who are "making it" but are bored, frustrated, and/or do not think a diploma will make a difference), students who are *pushed out* (those who have engaged in or who are *perceived* to engage in behavior that is dangerous or too challenging to manage in the classroom, and may be overtly or covertly encouraged to drop out), and students who *fail to succeed* (those who need more academic or more socioemotional support than they are receiving, fall behind in class work, do poorly on tests, skip classes, may act out, and eventually, fail). These categories, similar to those of Janosz and colleagues (2000), incorporate attention to the ecology of students' lives and the multidimensional nature of those factors that constrain learning, erode motivation, and for too many, lead to dropping out of school.

SPECIFIC INTERVENTION STRATEGIES FOCUSED ON SCHOOL DROPOUTS

Students at greatest risk for dropping out of school are identifiable, although many disengage from school and drop out for a variety of reasons for which there is no one common solution. School districts and specific schools can improve their retention rates by organizing programs that directly address the personal and idiosyncratic issues of individual dropouts in their region. At a minimum, though, efforts to prevent students from leaving school should include methods to reduce antisocial behaviors, increase academic achievement, improve connection with other students and adults, and in other ways encourage positive school commitment. Insufficient attention is paid to alienated, lonely, and disliked students (Thomas & Smith, 2004). The teenager who speaks to us in Box 6.1 (a possible quiet or disengaged dropout) expresses concerns that are common to many high school dropouts: a lack of relevance between the school's curriculum and the circumstances of students' lives and a lack of a sense of belonging. This teen, however, at least has a goal: She is going to help her mother manage a restaurant. Clearly she is interested in learning, but the school she attends is not where most of her learning takes place. Because she seems to be so eager to learn science, to read, and to use math skills, it is indeed a shame that she does not see the school curriculum in these areas as relevant to her life. Curricula that highlight the connection between learning and the "real world" should be selected whenever possible, with support for teachers to promote those connections. She would also benefit from a curriculum that encompasses goal-setting techniques. Identifying and writing down long-term goals, developing a plan to implement those goals, and periodically reviewing the actions taken to achieve the goals are useful skills. Tyrone Baker, for example, would benefit from such a curriculum. (We discuss problem-solving techniques in Chapter 12 and use of cooperative learning to foster group goal achievement in Chapter 13.)

Schools can also organize programs to bring truant students—disengaged, quiet, or maladjusted potential dropouts—back to the classroom. For example, requiring a daily after-school study group might enable truant students to catch up, work at their own pace, and receive credit while increasing connections to people at school. These last-resort study sessions could be a key element in a dropout prevention program.

Social interaction, especially with antisocial peers, influences the decision to leave school; it can also help keep young people in school. An opportunity to get involved with a social group and to work with the other members in a positive manner might be beneficial to the quiet potential dropout. Perhaps if 9-year-old Tyrone Baker could get involved in healthy social activities run by the school, he would not be so susceptible to gang activities. School arts, music, and athletic programs provide support and opportunities for disadvantaged students to participate in sports, clubs, and activities. Most school arts programs provide valuable outlets for young people and give them a sense of accomplishment, as does participation in the school band or choir. Too often, when funding is tight, the prevention value (in human and economic terms) of school arts programs is ignored.

Peer and cross-age tutoring, mediation, leadership, and facilitation (counseling) programs can also help young people at risk for dropping out of school. Such programs have great potential because they blend learning and responsibility with the development of social skills and a positive self-image. In Chapter 13 we provide an extensive discussion of the use of peer and

Box 6.1	Reflections of a Future Dropout

I wish I could leave school. It's so boring that I just daydream all day anyway. Why can't they just let me leave now, instead of waitin' till I'm 16?

When I leave, I'm gonna help Mama in her restaurant. It's her own business and she runs it, but she also has to take care of my little sisters. We have it all worked out. I already help her every night when I get home from school. This week she let me work in the kitchen. I figured out a new way to make salad dressing, and it's really good. Mama says it's gonna be a house specialty. The first time we served it, I had to figure out how to make a batch for 100 people without messing it up.

Mama also lets me do the books. She don't have time for everything. If I didn't have to go to school, I could help her a lot more. Three weeks ago, we had a taxman in here checking through the books. He said he was impressed with the figures. We couldn't let him know I did them cuz I'm too young to work. Mama brings 'em home for me, and I do 'em at night. I'm usually right. I wish I could be like that in school. But man, those questions in my homework just get me all confused. I mean, once I was s'pose to figure out when two trains would meet if they was goin' toward each other and leavin' at different times and stuff like that. I mean, who cares? Someone's already got the train schedule all figured out so they don't run into each other, and I ain't never gonna be a train engineer, so why ask me? Usually, though, it don't make much difference cuz I'm so busy addin' up customers' bills that I don't have time to set down and figure out what some smart guy has already done. Mr. Larson is sorta gettin' used to me not turning in my homework. So is Mr. Poland. He says I better start thinkin' about what I'm gonna do for the science fair or I'm gonna flunk his class. Well, excuse me, but I just don't have time to figure out how to make an atom bomb. I wish he'd just get off my case and stick to buggin' the smart kids.

If I didn't have to go to school, I could help Mama by takin' the kids to the library. They have story time, and my little sisters like to hear it sometimes. I just set and read the encyclopedias. The other day I was readin' that a kangaroo can have as many as three babies suckin' on her tits at once. There can be an embryo that attaches itself to the nipple, a newborn inside the pouch, and an older baby (they're called "joeys," in case you weren't aware) that hops in for some chow. I really like the library. Especially in summer cuz the air conditioner works real good. Some of those librarians are real nice to me. Mrs. Bishop is my favorite. She always asks me about the books I check out, if I liked 'em, and then she says here's another good one to read. One librarian there is kinda mean, but she's nothing like the one at the school library. Man, that lady won't even let you read the inside cover flaps cuz it'll mess up her nice clean shelf. She looks at me like I'm lookin' to take something all the time. Mama says she must have a board up her butt. I just hate goin' in there. Anyway, it doesn't matter much cuz we're only allowed to go to the library with our English class, and I never finish my work in that class. I just can't get into prepositions and garbage like that. I mean, who cares anyway? In Mama's restaurant, nobody says I'm not talkin' right, and I know I never heard anybody discussin' conjugatin' verbs while they was eatin' a French dip roast beef sandwich. I sure wish I could leave school so I could start learnin' something.

cross-age programs. In addition, classroom techniques that provide students with the opportunity to communicate with each other in a positive manner help to improve their social relationships and connectedness. Jason Carter and Ramona Diaz would benefit greatly from working with other students in supportive groups. Some specific classroom practices are discussed in Chapter 13, including peer support networks and cooperative learning groups.

The more effective dropout intervention programs identify and track young people at risk for school failure and maintain a focus on students' progress toward educational achievement. They are designed to influence enrollment status and to address various indicators of student engagement. They address issues related to student mobility, alternate time lines, and routes for school completion that often include alternative education programs (Christenson & Thurlow, 2004; Dynarski et al., 2008; Knudson et al., 2011).

Specific Intervention: Cyber Technology

We hear much about the negative impact of technologies, often focusing on potential harm related to addiction, aggression, risky sexual behavior, and lowered school performance although much of this concern fits a pattern of media-based moral panic (Ferguson, 2010). Nevertheless, as we indicated in Chapters 1 and 4, cyber technology can be for good or ill, both a blessing and a curse. Technology and the World Wide Web include dangerous, negative, and destructive activities: pornography and callous television, violent movies and music, sexual solicitation and stalking, bullying and harassment, drug sales and other illegal activity. We discuss some of these negative implications in other chapters. But the fact remains that cyber technology is a tool. And tools can be used in diverse ways—good and bad—after all, iron and steel can be fashioned into either swords and guns or plows and pruning hooks.

Today's youth are digital learners, and technology has become something that youth depend upon. The constant access and convenience provided by smartphones and other mobile devices is reflected in the fact that 92% of teens report being online daily. A fourth of the teens surveyed by the Pew Research Center reported going online almost constantly (Lenhart, 2015). Teachers must consider that each student has a different learning style and technology opens up new methods to respond to those differences. At-risk youth are easily bored and unmotivated by traditional teaching practices. But many at-risk youth are comfortable with technology such as laptops and play stations, Xboxes and IPads, PCs and MACs. These technologies can provide problem-based learning challenges that help students learn how to learn; they can help students work cooperatively in groups to seek solutions to real-world problems; they can also be used as adjuncts to enhance ongoing counseling or psychotherapy. Biofeedback, mobile phones, Skype, and personal digital assistants can supplement or enhance traditional counseling (Clough & Casey, 2011).

Public schools have made consistent progress in expanding Internet access in classrooms. Now virtually all public schools in the United States have access to the Internet, most with broadband wireless connections. The ratio of students to computers was 12 to 1 in 1998 and then 4.5 to 1 in 2003 to about 2 to 1 a decade ago (National Center for Education Statistics, 2006). Thus computer access at school continues to expand and is nearly universal among grade schools and very high for the vast majority of secondary schools. School-based computer access continues to vary, however, with schools in poor areas far less likely to have wireless network access within the whole school and inadequate student-to-computer ratios.

Previous research reports have shown that household computer ownership and Internet use have both increased steadily over the years. For example, in 1984, only 8.2% of all households had a computer, and in 1997, 18% of households reported home Internet use. In 2013, data indicated that household computer ownership had increased to 83.8% and 74.4% for household Internet use (File & Ryan, 2014). This is an important progression because increasing evidence points to the value of the Internet in helping youth. Some solid evidence supports an online learning approach. A meta-analysis (U.S. Department of Education, 2010) of rigorous published studies that compared online learning with traditional instruction provided a key finding. Students who took all or part of their course online performed better than those taking the same course in a traditional way.

Access to computers in the home is associated with better education outcomes, higher reading scores, and overall higher GPAs among low-income children (Brown & Marin, 2009). Students who used computers at least once every few weeks had higher scores than students who rarely used computers. This was especially true in science classes (U.S. Department of Education, 2009).

Computer video games have aided the development of some types of cognition (Spence & Feng, 2010), have been applied to health-related problems (Kato, 2010) and to the development of "serious" games to help educate youth (Annetta, 2010), and have been used in the new research field of video games applied to therapy with youth (Ceranoglu, 2010).

YouTube EDU and TED Talks

YouTube EDU and TED Talks are beneficial and positive tools available on the web for working with at-risk youth. Although neither of these sites was developed for dropouts, both provide important aids that can be important for dropout prevention and for providing educational content to those who have dropped out.

Most readers are familiar with YouTube as a video-sharing website that allows users to upload, share, and view video clips, music videos, and video blogging. YouTube EDU is an educational section that features a large number of educational videos. The viewer has access to a broad set of educational videos that range from academic lectures to speeches and presentations. It contains inspiring videos, and full course lectures from top teachers and top-tier university faculty. In addition to university material, YouTube EDU has a large collection of short lessons and material for elementary and secondary school students. YouTube videos can enrich classroom lessons and make theoretical concepts come alive. They are especially helpful to the visual learner. Thousands of educational videos are available by signing up for YouTube for Schools.

TED Talks are another entity that makes use of YouTube. From 1984, TED was developed after a conference where Technology, Entertainment, and Design came together (hence the name, "TED") and was conceived to encourage ideas, most often provided as short talks (usually less than 20 minutes). Currently, this nonprofit organization includes talks on a wide range of topics: science, business, entertainment, education, and world issues. TED's endeavors have also expanded to include the TED Conferences, TED Books, the TED Fellows Program, and the TED Open Translation Project. TED-Ed has an extensive library of educational videos made specifically accessible to teachers and very appropriate for those who have flipped their classrooms.

Khan Academy

We mentioned the Khan Academy in Chapter 4 when we discussed the flipped classroom. The Khan Academy grew from YouTube video tutoring sessions in algebra that Salman Khan provided for his young cousin who lived in a different city. This has grown into "the largest school in the world" (Noer, 2012). As of this writing, Khan Academy has over 4,000 videos from which to select. Because of the nice fit between the Khan Academy and the idea of the flipped classroom, it might appear that they were developed concurrently, but this is not the case. Interestingly, in a TED Talk on YouTube, Salman Khan describes how and why he created the Khan Academy and discusses its relationship with the flipped classroom.

As indicated, both TED Talks and the Khan Academy are major resource to schools and teachers who want to flip their class. Here we devote more spaces to this resource because of its great potential for reforming education, improving achievement for high-risk students, and for possibly reducing the dropout rate. The Khan Academy (http://www.khanacademy.org), a completely free site, has the mission of providing a solid education to anyone who has access to a computer. It consists of over 6,500 videos and more than 100,000 interactive exercises posted on YouTube. These short 10- to 12-minute lessons, developed by Salman Khan, cover basic arithmetic to advanced calculus, biology to chemistry, humanities to history.

Initially designed to be used by individual students, the Khan website reports serving over 1,000,000 students worldwide. For students struggling to understand specific course content or required to participate in a daily after-school study group, the Khan Academy provides a rich resource for study. The site provides an extensive video library, practice exercises, and assessments. After completing self-paced learning tools, students can profile their progress and receive points and badges to measure their progress. Students can work for "streaks" which are obtained when a certain number of consecutive math problems are answered correctly, for example. Badges are accumulated as students build streaks and work through the different levels of specific content.

The material presented online can be used by teachers to supplement their curriculum. Also, teachers can track what students are learning and doing, allowing them to have better information for doing targeted interventions. And, of course, the lessons are ideal for use in a flipped classroom.

Perhaps most important for potential dropouts is that the format allow students to repeat and review information. When students do not understand, they can replay the material. The Khan Academy along with the YouTube TED Talks can be an excellent supplement to augment alternative education programs.

The What Works Clearinghouse (WWC) has released a number of research reports that review specific and targeted dropout prevention programs. The following seven were judged to show positive or potentially positive effects (Dynarski et al., 2008): Achievement for Latinos with Academic Success (ALAS), Career Academies, Check and Connect, High School Redirection, Talent Development, Talent Search, and Twelve Together. Next we describe some universal strategies for reducing dropout.

Specific Intervention: Comprehensive, Competency-Based Guidance

Most students who leave school before graduation do not receive interventions to help them stay in school (Dynarski et al., 2008). More than 60% indicated that no one on the school staff had tried to talk them into staying. Less than one-fourth saw a counselor or social worker to discuss their troubles or dropout plans. For many of these students, it was clear that they were struggling with academic and other problems in their final 2 years, and no one caught the problem early enough to prevent dropout. A major factor in this problem is that school counselors are scarce, with a U.S. national average of 1 school counselor in elementary and secondary schools for every 400 or more students, leaving counselors with very little time to dedicate to individual students at risk of dropping out.

Beginning in the early 1990s and continuing to the present, the American School Counseling Association and other concerned groups have pushed to encourage schools to adhere to the national standards for school counseling programs. These national standards are closely aligned to the Comprehensive, Competency-Based Guidance (CCBG) model. CCBG programs are rapidly becoming the programs of choice for managing guidance and counseling in schools (Gysbers & Henderson, 2012). It is estimated that more than half of the states promote the use of CCBG programs.

CCBG programs are developmentally focused and are designed to provide all students with systematic experiences to help them grow and develop in academic, career, and socioemotional arenas (Gysbers & Henderson, 2012). These programs change the traditional responsibilities, roles, and contributions of school counselors. Although counselors continue to meet the immediate counseling and crisis management needs of students, they also engage in assessment, information sharing with teachers and parents, consultation, prevention (small-group, large-group, or classroom-level interventions), referral, placement, and follow-up work with children and youth and their families. Their major task, however, is to provide planned activities on a regular basis to assist students to achieve specific competencies and to learn new skills in academic, career, and social/personal domains. Developmentally appropriate competencies in each of the three domains are identified at all levels, pre-K through 12. All students are systematically provided with opportunities to develop competencies through classroom and small-group presentations according to the master calendar developed by the counseling staff. Academic development refers to acquiring the knowledge and skills that contribute to effective learning in school and across the life span. Career development refers to knowledge and skills to explore, set goals, and achieve future work and career success and satisfaction. Personal/social development refers to acquiring the attitudes, knowledge, and interpersonal skills to help students understand and respect themselves and others.

In the CCBG model, school counselors are more fully engaged in implementing prevention and intervention activities for all students. They move out of marginalized positions and into roles that more effectively promote essential education and career objectives for students. Substantial research (e.g., see Gysbers & Henderson, 2012) indicates that implementation of CCBG programs is associated with improving student success and safety.

In later chapters we provide a wide range of programs, strategies, and interventions that fit extremely well with the CCBG model. For example, in Chapter 11 we present two universal prevention strategies—the Group-Oriented Psychological Education Prevention (GOPEP) program and a bullying prevention model—both of which can be used in a CCBG counseling program.

In the traditional school counseling model, not every student receives the same quality or quantity of information from the counseling staff regarding postsecondary educational opportunities, career opportunities, or life-coping skills. Students with the most obvious personal difficulties and students with top academic skills receive the most attention from counselors. In this traditional counseling model, counselors are passive and wait for students to contact them, which is particularly disadvantageous to the potential school dropout. In the CCBG model, potential dropouts are receiving systematic support for the development of academic, career, and social/personal skills, whether they seek support or suffer in silence. Of course, because of the increase in the school counselor's job responsibilities, there are fewer opportunities for long-term counseling of individual children in the school setting, and more outside referrals to appropriate counselors, social workers, or psychologists in the community. The CCBG model provides more support and guidance to more students, and adoption of such a model can be a significant step toward dropout prevention.

Specific Intervention: Solution-Focused Counseling

How can a school be transformed from a problem-focused environment into a solution-focused environment that fosters and highlights positive change? Solution-focused counseling is a positive and competency-based response to the problems experienced by children, adolescents, adults, and even organizational systems (Macdonald, 2011; Nelson & Thomas, 2012). Rather than focusing on what is wrong and how to fix it, this approach looks for what is already working and how to use and augment it. Its usefulness within the school system and its effectiveness with school problems have been well reported (Murphy, 2015). The limited time frame of the solution-focused approach and its positive, competency-based, goal-oriented emphasis make it very well suited for counselors operating in a comprehensive, competency-based guidance model.

Our focus here is on the use of a solution-focused approach within the context of counseling. However, the techniques are also useful to administrators working with teachers, parents, and students; in administrative meetings; and in case conferences. Teachers have found many of the strategies, skills, and concepts to be helpful in working with parents and students.

There are several key assumptions of solution-focused counseling:

- Change can occur rapidly, and often a small change is all that is needed to prompt other changes.
- Problems are usually not pervasive; there will be times when the problem is less intense or not present at all.
- Students are more likely to change when they have a clearly defined goal and are able to generate solutions that fit.
- People have strengths and resources and are already doing some things to solve their problem.
- The problem is the problem, not the student, teachers, or parents.

Consistent with these assumptions, encouraging a student to make small changes in behavior has the potential to lead to bigger changes in behavior. Encouraging a student to complete a small portion of her English paper rather than complete the entire assignment is based on the idea that he or she needs success and encouragement to get some momentum started in his or her life. In addition, small shifts in role by one person in a relationship have the potential to cause the role shift of others in that relationship. Initially, the counselor's job is to push for small changes.

Using solution-focused questions helps the client identify exceptions and potential solutions to the problem. The counselor helps the client identify those times when the problem is not present or is less intense ("Can you describe a time in the past week when your teacher was not angry with you? What were you doing?"). These exceptions can be transformed into solutions. Next, the counselor builds on asking the client how the exception happened and how the client could make it happen more often.

The following pragmatic points appeal to clients' common sense:

1. If it works a little, try to do more of what is working.
2. Build on and add behaviors to what works.
3. If it is broke, stop what's not working and do something different to fix it.
4. "If it ain't broke, don't fix it."

In solution-focused counseling, goals are stated in positive and observable terms. Clients do better in achieving goals that are specific and quantifiable. For example, the goal of "study harder" is inferior to the goal of "complete one homework assignment per day in study hall." Time in the counseling session is devoted entirely to increasing exceptions (doing more of what works) and identifying and pursuing specific goals. No time is spent trying to determine the cause of a problem, describing the history of a problem, or rehashing old, past experiences.

One simple strategy that counselors can use to implement solution-focused counseling is the "miracle question" (De Shazer, Nolan, & Korman, 2007). The miracle question is a future-oriented question that is very useful in goal setting and in shifting from focusing on the problem to focusing on the solution. In essence, clients are asked to visualize what life would be like if the problem was suddenly solved. For example, "Suppose a miracle occurs tonight while you are sleeping. When you wake up, you realize that your problems are solved. What would things be like? What would you be doing that would let you know that the miracle had actually taken place?" A form of the miracle question useful for children is, "If I were to wave a magic wand and all of your problems went away, what would you do? If we could videotape you for one day, what would we see?" Older children and adolescents might respond better to a visualization of what their life would look like 6 months or a year from now if the problem were solved. "If we were to meet in a year and the problem we are talking about didn't exist anymore, what would you be doing differently and how would you know that things were okay?"

The miracle picture is elaborated through the use of solution-focused questions, such as "What else?" "What will others see?" "How would that make you feel?" and "How would that happen?" By engaging in this process, students are essentially able to explore the positive change they would like to see occur and come up with possible solutions that they would like to implement.

Solution-focused counseling is nonblaming and emphasizes normalizing young people's experiences and problems. Solution-focused counseling may be especially effective with youth at risk for early school dropout for the following reasons:

- Students are less likely to feel that the counselor is attacking or blaming them for the problems they are experiencing.
- Students feel empowered knowing that the counselor believes they are capable of becoming their own agents of change.
- Students are able to recognize that they have many options besides dropping out of school.
- Counselors hone in on realistic solutions that can be readily implemented, thereby maximizing the effects of their brief encounters with each at-risk student.

Counselors should keep in mind the following principles when working with at-risk youth from a solution-focused perspective (Macdonald, 2011; Nelson & Thomas, 2012):

- Make the most of each brief encounter with a student, as it may be the only one that you have.
- Honor and respect students, especially the resources and strengths they already have, because these are the ingredients for positive change.
- Help students to transfer what they've heard and learned in their counseling interactions with you to the hallway, lunchroom, gym, the bus or subway, and so on.
- As much as possible, engage in a collaborative, nonconfrontive exchange with students and their families.
- Instill in students a reason to be hopeful because hope fuels change, and change is always possible.

Solution-focused brief counseling (SFBT) is uniquely suited to the school setting (Murphy, 2015). It emphasizes resources and strengths and natural forces within the environment, and it uses effective, simple, and positive strategies to help students change behavior.

Research on the efficacy of SFBT is limited; much of what is known is from anecdotal reports of SFBT. However, the research that is available demonstrates that brief counseling has been effective when applied to students with behavioral disorders, anxiety, depression, and suicide risk (Macdonald, 2011; Murphy, 2015). SFBT has also improved behavior, somatic, and cognitive difficulties in young people in foster care (Cepukiene & Pakrosnis, 2011). This approach allows a busy counselor to have an impact on a larger number of students and is of great potential value in limiting risky behavior.

CONCLUSION

As literacy standards rise along with the demands of our increasingly technological society, we expect more from our young people than ever before. Unfortunately, these demands come at a time when economic resources are more unequally distributed than ever before, and many schools, communities, and families are unable to meet young people's educational and motivational needs. When we recognize the family, school, social, and personality issues involved, as well as the effects of the experience of failure, we are in a better position to understand why young people drop out of school. We must attempt to effect changes in all of these areas if we are to make any headway against the dropout problem and its wide-ranging consequences.

If at-risk children and adolescents do not stay in school, they move beyond the reach of effective prevention and intervention strategies that can be administered by and through the schools. And if young people do not develop the fundamental skills that schools can provide, they will continue to be dependent, unproductive, and discouraged members of society.

Substance Use and Addiction

There is an assumption that perhaps should be argued out rather than taken for granted. It is that the self is worth being.

There is a philosophical dialogue that turns on the question of whether people are born good and become corrupted or are born evil and become civilized.

My own opinion is that each is equally true.

Thus, I cannot claim that if you strip yourself of the encrustation of attitudes and defenses, you are going to expose an angelic, euphoric, and expansive person.

But, certainly, neither are you going to find the cretinous and willful monster that most of us fear is lurking underneath.

There will be a human being, with the assets and limitations inherent in the definition of human being but, for the first time and most importantly, with the choice not to be ugly and cruel and stunted. ...

To give the self permission to be the self, a leap must be taken across the chasm of dread that the self may be little and mean and nasty toward a certain faith that the self is a good thing to be and that spontaneous behavior can be trusted.

J. J. McWhirter, *Seek Wisdom*, 2nd ed.

CHAPTER OUTLINE

- Definitional Difficulties and Assessment
- The Scope of the Problem
- Some Determinants of Substance Use and Common Characteristics of Users

- Environmental and Social Correlates of Substance Use
- Peer Influence on Substance Use
- Family Correlates of Substance Use
- Personal Correlates of Substance Use

In this chapter we describe substance use by children and adolescents, the problems associated with it, and potential solutions to this widespread problem. This discussion is especially pertinent because in the United States youth have a high rate of tobacco, alcohol, and extraordinarily high levels of illicit drug use (Johnston, O'Malley, Miech, Bachman, & Schulenberg, 2014). Throughout this chapter, we use the terms *substances* and *drugs* interchangeably and include tobacco and alcohol as examples of drugs. In the following sections, we (a) describe some of the definitional and assessment problems associated with substance use, (b) illustrate the scope of substance use among adolescents, (c) outline personal and social determinants leading to drug use and addiction, (d) discuss some of the consequences of alcohol and drug consumption, and (e) highlight child and adolescent substance use treatment and prevention approaches found to be effective.

DEFINITIONAL DIFFICULTIES AND ASSESSMENT

To determine the abusive nature of drug use, one must consider the context, frequency, and purpose for which a drug is used. There is often a fine line between *drug use* and *drug abuse*. The causes of substance *use* are often linked to social influences (e.g., peer drug use), whereas *abuse* may be more tied to internal processes, for example, using drugs as self-medication against persistent emotional distress. Yet for adolescents and preadolescents, most of the correlates of substance use are identical to those of abuse. The term *substance abuse* is also an ideological term, suggesting that the results of drug use are always negative or harmful, which can be misleading. We use the term *substance use* throughout this text because it does not negate the harmful consequences of drug use nor does it exaggerate them.

We are also in line with the newest version of the *Diagnostic and Statistical Manual of Mental Disorders* (DSM-5; APA, 2013), the primary classification system for psychological disorders in the United States. The DSM-5 uses the new "Substance Use Disorder" terminology and no longer distinguishes between substance dependence and substance abuse that had been in effect in previous editions. Criteria have been established for identifying 10 substance use disorders. There are no separate provisions for children and adolescents.

Drug Use Disorders involve the physiological responses of tolerance (increasingly larger doses of a particular drug are needed to maintain its physiological effects) and withdrawal (painful physical and psychological consequences result when the drug is withheld from the body). Substance use is maladaptive in DSM terminology if the use of a particular substance causes impaired social, school, or occupational functioning (DSM-5, 2013). Drug use is also identified as being "with or without physiological dependence," and the specific courses of drug use are identified as "early full remission," "early partial remission," "sustained full remission," or "sustained partial remission." Although not specifically listed as DSM criteria, substance abuse can be determined by examining (a) the frequency of use, (b) the quantity typically used, (c) the variety of substances used at the same time (polydrug use), (d) the social context in which drugs are used (Is the user being dared to try drugs? Does the user usually use drugs with friends, alone, or with strangers?), and (e) the emotional state of the abuser (Is the user typically depressed or feeling positive before engaging in drug use?). Examining these factors helps to clarify the nature and extent of substance use problems among children and teenagers. The issues are also useful in identifying dual-diagnosis problems in which the young person is using substances as self-medication. Studies have found a high prevalence of psychiatric disorders in youth with substance use disorders, including major depression (DiCola, Gaydos, Druss, & Cummings, 2013), bipolar disorder (Stephens et al., 2014), and trauma (Garland, Pettus-Davis, & Howard, 2013).

Although tobacco products, alcohol, and in some states marijuana are accepted and legal for adults, they can have severe negative consequences even when they are used in relative moderation. Alcohol and tobacco use is responsible for significant physical and personal problems and has greater social costs than all other drugs *combined*. In the United States, the cost of alcohol misuse is well over a billion dollars a year. Smoking, drinking, and illicit drug use are leading causes of death, both during adolescence and later in life (Johnston et al., 2014). Cigarette smoking is estimated to account for a large number of premature deaths each year, with over 480,000 deaths annually among men and women age 35 and older (U.S. Surgeon General Report, 2014). Nevertheless, we do not define the occasional smoker or drinker as an abuser of substances although in some ways this is ironic. Tobacco is highly addictive and directly kills half of its users, as well as many nonsmokers exposed to secondhand smoke (Prochaska, 2013).

THE SCOPE OF THE PROBLEM

The overall use of drugs in the United States by young people has continued to decline over the last few years, providing some encouragement. However, this has not been true of all substances and their use fluctuates by cohort, type, and time. Since the mid-1960s, when drug use exploded among youth, illicit drug use has remained a major concern for the nation. The National Institute on Drug Abuse (NIDA), through its Monitoring the Future study (MTF), is a long-term, 35-year study of American adolescent drug use (Johnston et al., 2014). The MTF points out that beliefs, attitudes, and usage rates vary greatly by grade level for different drugs.

Generally, alcohol use is declining among U.S. teens, with significant decreases in alcohol use among all grades and down to under 37.5% of 12th graders. In 2014 there was also a significant drop in binge drinking. About 20% of high school students had engaged in binge drinking within 2 weeks of the MTF survey, compared with a high of 31.5% in 1998 (Johnston et al., 2014).

Experimentation with tobacco during adolescence is also quite prevalent. Many children experiment with tobacco as early as age 9. Daily use rates began declining in the middle years of the 2000s; for example, cigarette smoking has decreased almost 50% over the last 5 years (Johnston et al., 2014). Nonetheless, 15% of high school boys use smokeless tobacco such as chewing tobacco, snuff, or dip (U.S. Department of Health & Human Services, 2015). The use of tobacco and alcohol is critical because both are often considered "threshold" or "gateway" substances, meaning that use of tobacco and alcohol typically precedes use of illicit drugs such as methamphetamine, inhalants, and other "hard" substances. Consistent with the "gateway" concept, most of these substances, excepting marijuana, have demonstrated a decline in use as well. Marijuana use has remained steady overall, though use of edible forms of marijuana has increased, and the perceived risks associated with marijuana use have declined.

Thus, substance use and abuse prevention and intervention programs for America's youth seem to be working as evidenced by encouraging news about children and adolescent drug use. This includes decreasing use of cigarettes, alcohol, and prescription pain relievers; decreasing use of inhalants and synthetic drugs; a steady decline over the last 20 years in the use of illicit drugs; and no increase in the use of marijuana (National Institute on Drug Abuse, 2015). At the same time, there is a growing concern over increased hookah use and especially the rate of use of electronic cigarettes (e-cigarettes), which is high among young people.

While society has made good progress in reducing cigarette use, other forms of nicotine consumption are growing. Nearly 9% of 8th graders, over 16% of 10th graders, and over 17% of 12th graders (National Institute on Drug Abuse, 2015) report using e-cigarettes in the past month. The nicotine in e-cigarettes is not smoked but vaporized and inhaled. It is not clear what the health impact is of e-cigarette use. It is also not known if e-cigarettes use increases the probability of transitioning to conventional cigarettes or other tobacco products. Perhaps equally important is that only 14.2% of 12th graders view regular e-cigarette use as harmful.

Increasing numbers of youth are smoking tobacco with hookahs, also known as a "waterpipe," "nargile," "goza," or "hubble bubble." Hookahs are instruments used to smoke flavored—strawberry, cappuccino, cotton candy—tobacco, which is called *shisha*. Young hookah smokers believe that smoking a hookah carries less risk than cigarette smoking. However, hookah smoking is dangerous. Its smoke contains many of the same toxins as cigarette smoke and delivers 4 times the nicotine, 11 times the carbon monoxide, and 100 times more tar than one cigarette. Hookah smoking has been associated with respiratory illness, lung cancer, low birth weight, and periodontal disease (Morris, Fiala, & Pawlak, 2012). Perhaps the biggest danger for long-term risk is the belief that hookahs are not dangerous.

This finding mirrors the changing of attitudes about the perceived risk of harm associated with marijuana use. The majority of high school seniors do not think regular marijuana smoking is harmful. This softening of attitudes toward e-cigarettes and marijuana use may signal future problems. Lower perceptions of harm and increasing acceptance toward the use of a substance often precede changes in reported use. The reduced perceived risk of harm of regularly using marijuana could indicate that the use of the drugs could begin to rise again in future years (National Institute on Drug Abuse, 2015).

Perhaps just as troubling as actual use are changing perceptions about use and attitudes toward friend and peer use. Young people who perceive underage drinking as "normal," and who see early and heavy use as not much of problem, are likely to be at greater risk of future problems. Interestingly, teens who begin drinking before age 15 are much more likely to have alcohol problems as adults. In fact if drinking begins prior to age 15, a person is 4 times more likely to develop alcohol dependency than if drinking starts at 20 years of age. Most teens (73%) report that they have a friend who drinks alcohol at least once a week. Less than a third of them strongly disapprove of peers of their age getting drunk, and almost half do not see a "great risk" in heavy daily drinking (Feliz, 2011). Drinking alcohol—even heavy drinking—was viewed as less risky than using other substances.

One important cause for optimism is that in spite of these softening attitudes, there has been no evidence of increase in the early onset of drug use. As mentioned earlier, the use of most illicit drugs decreased or was stable through 2014, and perceptions of risks associated with smoking and using *most* illicit substances were increased (Johnston et al., 2014). Although these data are positive, drug and alcohol use among U.S. children and adolescents continues to be a serious behavioral, social, and health problem. In addition, the continuous introduction of new drugs, as well as the tendency for youth to "forget" the dangers associated with "older" drugs such as heroin, requires ongoing effort to educate the public.

The often-held stereotype that adolescents of color abuse substances more than European American youth is not fully supported by research. African American youth are significantly less likely to use cigarettes, alcohol, and illicit drugs than European American youth (Johnston, O'Malley, Bachman, & Schulenberg, 2011). In 8th grade, Latino youth have the highest rates of using all substances except amphetamines. In 10th and 12th grades, it is European American youth who tend to have the highest rates of using all substances (Johnston et al., 2011). Native American adolescents use alcohol, tobacco, and other drugs significantly more than other ethnocultural minority groups, resulting in problems that include a high incidence of fetal alcohol syndrome (Plunkett & Mitchell, 2000).

Adolescents who are lesbian, gay, bisexual, or transgender (LGBT) are at high risk of substance abuse because of an increase in suicidal ideation, levels of depression and hopelessness, and experiences of victimization (Mayer, Garofalo, & Makadon, 2014). Estimates suggest that more than a third of LGBT youth are frequent and problematic users and are more likely to engage in polysubstance use, with marijuana and alcohol used most. Of course, gay and lesbian teenagers abuse drugs for the same reasons as straight youth, but the additional challenges and oppression they experience as members of a sexual minority group may drive many LGBT youth to use drugs as a way of buffering the social exclusion, ridicule, and torment that they experience (Mayer et al., 2014). Clearly, a better understanding of substance abuse among LGBT youth can help the development of targeted prevention and treatment programs, and a greater awareness and sensitivity to this underserved community can improve our prevention and intervention efforts right now.

SOME DETERMINANTS OF SUBSTANCE USE AND COMMON CHARACTERISTICS OF USERS

Family and peer influences, individual behavior, and personality characteristics consistently relate to child and adolescent substance use. Counselors and human service professionals can use the knowledge of these factors to assess the likelihood of drug use and to provide appropriate interventions. Correlates and predictors of child and adolescent drug use influence one another in a variety of ways (Mulvey, Schubert, & Chassin, 2010). Understanding the complex ecology of children's lives and how each aspect of their environment—social policy, media advertising, parenting practices, family and peer drug use, and individual characteristics—combines to predict substance use and its outcomes is important. Although correlates of adolescent drug use are presented here in discrete categories, these variables are highly interrelated and mutually influential.

Environmental and Social Correlates of Substance Use

A variety of environmental factors contribute to drug use. The soil that nurtures drug use (see Chapter 2) includes poverty, racism, community and interpersonal violence, lack of educational and job opportunities, the dissolution of communities, and interpersonal and family problems. In economically depressed communities, young people often use drugs in response to the bleakness of economic and social conditions, as we see in the Andrews and Baker children (Chapters 1 and 2). Traumatic events, poor neighborhoods, adverse school conditions, and negative peer influences also contribute to increased use of substances (Nakkula, Foster, Mannes, & Bolstrom, 2010) and to aggression (Mason & Mennis, 2010). Consistent with such environmental adversity, drug use is typically heavier among lower socioeconomic groups.

The U.S. "war on drugs" has been unsuccessful in large part because it has been a military/geopolitical response to what is fundamentally a social and public health issue. The "war" also underscores that the United States focuses much effort on dealing with drugs and their related problems through the criminal justice system, contributing to the U.S. status as the most incarceration-oriented country in history (Alexander, 2010). This is a war that is not winnable. This response does not address the reasons adolescents turn to drugs in the first place. Drug use is also reinforced through the media, which inundate the market with images of drug use as a helpful solution to all physical complaints and psychological problems. Alcohol is portrayed as necessary to lead the "good life." Movies depict marijuana use either in a positive way (52%) or as a neutral substance (48%) (Gunasekera, Chapman, & Campbell, 2005). These messages of drug acceptability further communicate to young people the usefulness of drugs as part of mainstream U.S. culture. The profit motive also leads advertising to glamorize products to appeal to and entice young people, such as using cartoon characters to advertise cigarettes or attractive, well-dressed models to sell vodka. Finally, modeling by older siblings, parents, and peers is highly correlated with drug use among children and adolescents (Mares, van der Vorst, Engels, & Lichtwarck-Aschoff, 2011). The most important and direct predictors of adolescent drug use are peer drug use and low parental monitoring; that is, parents who are disconnected from the everyday activities of their child's life. Interestingly, there is a significant relationship between recreational music downloading and social media computer use and adolescent alcohol use (Epstein, 2011).

Peer Influence on Substance Use

Peer groups strongly influence a young person's decision to use drugs, and they predict the age of initial drug use, especially alcohol, marijuana, and tobacco (Lewis, Neighbors, Lindgren, Buckingham, & Hoang, 2010). Peers who endorse pro-alcohol attitudes, model alcohol use, provide drinking opportunities, and exert pressure have a particularly strong impact (Schwinn & Schinke, 2014). Thus interventions that focus on the peer group may be the most effective for preventing and treating substance use and associated problems. Unfortunately, "peer group" and "peer pressure" have been used so loosely that their meanings are ambiguous. Peer cluster theory (Lewis et al., 2010), which we discuss in greater detail in Chapter 13, provides a specific framework for understanding and explaining the influence of peers on a young person's decisions and decision making. Peer cluster theory emphasizes that drug use is linked to peer relationships. Peers provide information about drugs, shape attitudes toward them, create a social context for their use, give rationales for using them, and make them available (Schwinn & Schinke, 2014).

Peer cluster theory has been tested and supported by a series of research studies that highlight the importance of attending to peer clusters in both prevention and treatment (Beauvais, Chavez, Oetting, Deffenbacher, & Cornell, 1996; Lewis et al., 2010). This theory has also enjoyed some support in describing problem behavior among adolescents in other cultures (P. T. McWhirter, 1998), suggesting that the theory may be culturally sensitive and broadly applicable.

Adolescent drug use is also a function of positive reinforcement. When children and adolescents use certain substances, they frequently experience not only physiological reinforcement (e.g., euphoria, stimulation) but also social reinforcement by peers who bestow attention and status on the using adolescent. Such reinforcement is a powerful force for maintaining substance use and for experimenting with more potent drugs.

Family Correlates of Substance Use

Research consistently identifies family factors, such as parenting style, as central to the etiology of multiple problem behavior outcomes, including early-onset substance use (Mares et al., 2011). Lower socioeconomic status and parental substance use are predictors of early onset of alcohol and tobacco use (Kirisci, Vanyukov, & Tarter, 2005) as is observing an intoxicated parent (Rüütel et al., 2014). Low parent monitoring, in particular, predicts early alcohol, tobacco, and marijuana use. Therefore, increasing parental monitoring serves as a key protective factor for reducing substance use among children exposed to it by their siblings or peers (Bargiel-Matusiewicz, Grzelak, & Weglinska, 2010). Poor parent–child relationships, deficient parental limit setting, and weak problem solving and communication skills within families all predict higher use as well. Conversely, parental rules against drinking, monitoring of children, and support may buffer children from the strong influence of their peers. Indeed, in one study parental rules against drinking were associated with limited alcohol use and less binge drinking (Schwinn & Schinke, 2014). Of course, the parent's alcohol-related problems as well as lenient attitudes about alcohol are directly related to alcohol-related problems in adolescents and to excessive drinking (Mares et al., 2011).

Authoritarian and punitive approaches in schools and in families also tend to contribute to higher drug use among children and adolescents. Teens are more likely to use drugs if their family environments are disruptive or disorganized, include an adult who uses drugs, or have no family religious affiliation (Webster-Stratton, Reid, & Hammond, 2001). Thus the children in the Andrews, Baker, and Carter families are at serious risk. Jason Carter's dysfunctional family, his poor school adjustment, and his underlying emotional distress provide particularly fertile ground for the development of drug-use problems. Because family factors are central to the risk of adolescent drug use, it is not surprising that family-based approaches are quite promising for reducing early-onset substance use and would be quite helpful to each of our described families.

Personal Correlates of Substance Use

Although some adolescents never experiment with drugs, and others experiment briefly and never use them again, others develop long-term patterns of use. Drug dependence may be associated with the inability to cope with psychological pain. Psychological pain can emerge from pervasive self-criticism and a chronic sense of failure that often leads to lower self-esteem and to young people believing that they are hopelessly responsible for the problems they experience. Many adolescents internalize these attributions for problems and experience subsequent depression and anxiety (B. T. McWhirter & Burrow-Sanchez, 2004). Adolescents with poor coping skills are vulnerable to this intense emotional pain; drug use can become a relief-seeking behavior aimed at alleviating both internal problems (frustration, stress, depression, feelings of low self-worth) and external problems (poor school performance, family discord, violence). Such pain can be overwhelming and draw many young people into substance use as a form of self-medication (see Box 7.1). But because relief through drugs is only temporary, drug use itself becomes part of a downward spiral and is ultimately self-defeating. Jason Carter of Chapter 3, for example, is experiencing considerable psychological pain, and his coping methods are ineffective and exacerbate his distress. He is a prime candidate for potential chronic drug abuse and dependency.

Pervasive substance use, rather than experimentation, is associated with a variety of other personality characteristics. Among these are pleasure- and sensation-seeking (SS) behaviors (Burrow-Sanchez & Hawken, 2013) such as rebelliousness; nontraditionalism, tolerance for deviance, adventuresomeness, and need for excitement (Kirisci et al., 2005); and an acute desire for independence and autonomy, along with low interpersonal trust and low impulse control with poor ability to delay gratification (Mulvey et al., 2010). Indeed, increasing evidence suggests that adolescents' brains are less developed than previously believed, and impulsive and risky behavior may result (Rosser, Stevens, & Ruiz, 2005).

Some research has suggested that impulsivity, characterized by strong reward-seeking tendencies, *and* weakness in executive control (such as working memory) are more strongly related to the escalation in drug use than other dimensions, like SS alone (Khurana, Romer, Betancourt, Brodsky, Giannetta, & Hurt, 2014). Impulsivity can be defined as the tendency to act prematurely, with little forethought for the consequences of one's behavior (Eysenck & Eysenck, 1980). Impulsivity includes (a) acting without thinking (AWT) and (b) delay discounting (DD), or the inability to delay the gratification of a small immediate reward in favor of a larger deferred reward (think of the marshmallow experiment) (Madden & Bickel, 2010). Impulsivity also shares characteristics with SS (Buckholtz et al., 2010; Pattij & Vanderschueren, 2008; Zald et al., 2008), but what distinguishes SS from AWT and DD is the level of executive control involved, especially working memory (WM). Adolescents who are high in SS also tend to have stronger WM. WM is a higher-order cognitive ability that facilitates flexible, goal-directed behavior. Individuals with strong WM have been shown to exert control over impulses and to consider adaptive alternatives, thus making them less prone to engage in impulsive and potentially risky behaviors (Khurana et al., 2014). Research has suggested that drug-abusing populations have greater weaknesses both in executive control (such as WM) *and* greater impulsive tendencies (Ersche, Turton, Pradhan, Bullmore, & Robbins, 2010). So, adolescents with weaker WM tend to engage in progressively worse drug use over time, while those with stronger WM do not (Khurana et al., 2014).

Box 7.1   Joe

One of us worked with a 13-year-old boy named Joe for 2 months after Joe's mother requested that he receive counseling. She and her husband, Joe's stepfather, were concerned about Joe's poor school performance, his acting out, his group of "delinquent" friends, and his alternately hostile and completely withdrawn behavior at home.

Joe's stepfather was a machine operator who provided severe yet inconsistent discipline. Joe disliked his stepfather, and he reported that the dislike was mutual. He described his mother as "nicer" but complained that she did not permit him to do what he wanted. His mother was primarily a homemaker, but occasionally she did temporary office work. She frequently placated her husband so that he would not get angry with Joe. She felt Joe needed to change, however, and believed that counseling might "fix" him. Joe's parents refused to come in for counseling as a family because they insisted that Joe was the problem.

Joe spent a great deal of time with his friends both during and after school. He reported smoking marijuana and cigarettes fairly regularly. Shortly after our first counseling session, he was arrested for possession of drug paraphernalia. His parents refused to let him see any of his friends after the arrest.

Joe's school performance and effort were poor. Joe probably had a mild learning disability, but a recent psychoeducational evaluation had been inconclusive. Joe's primary problem at school was his acting out. Unfortunately, when Joe got into trouble with a teacher, he was inadvertently rewarded for his disruption. He could effectively avoid the schoolwork that he found so difficult and distasteful by sitting in the assistant principal's office "listening to stupid stories." Joe was doing so poorly at school and misbehaving with such frequency that his stepfather threatened to send him to a strict boarding school unless his behavior improved. Joe said that would be fine with him because he had heard that the work was easier there. His stepfather's threat to cut his hair short was the only consequence he seemed concerned about.

Joe primarily used marijuana, which did not change during the 2 months he was in counseling. We don't know whether Joe experimented with more powerful substances because he showed a great deal of resistance to coming to counseling and seemed very disinterested in changing himself, although he did want his stepfather to move out. Joe was a frustrated and angry adolescent who resented his parents and received little direction or consistent structure from them. He was unsure of their expectations, hated school, felt isolated from his friends, and could see no solution to his problems. He directed his anxiety and poor self-esteem inward and acted out by skipping school, talking back to his teachers, or roaming the streets with his friends.

Like many other young people, Joe faced difficult challenges in life and had few resources for coping with them. He had never learned to delay gratification, he did not know how to relate to others in a healthy and positive way, he received no consistent discipline and failed to develop a sense of responsibility for his actions, and he felt mistreated and betrayed by the school and by his parents. Drug use was simply a means for Joe to escape from the problems that troubled him so much.

Joe's parents did not accept that his difficulties might be symptomatic of larger family problems. They refused to enter family therapy and eventually withdrew Joe from counseling.

Why? Perhaps because adolescents high in SS tend to have stronger WM, they tend to learn from their experiences, especially the negative consequences associated with drug use, and thus stop themselves from developing a pattern of engaging in negative behaviors (Romer, Duckworth, Sznitman, & Park, 2010). Preventive interventions should target underlying weaknesses in executive control during younger years. Strengthening young people's executive control could help at-risk adolescents to exercise greater self-restraint when they are presented with the rewards (social and physiological) for using drugs or drinking.

Developmental Changes in Reward vs. Control Systems

Drug interventions should focus on the problematic aspects of personal risk factors (Castellanos-Ryan & Conrod, 2011). Some of these characteristics (e.g., high risk-taking behavior, acting without thinking, delay discounting, and adventuresomeness) are not necessarily a problem and, in fact, can be used in treatment. Some prevention and treatment programs use adventurous activities to help adolescents channel their SS energies in a positive direction along with building self-efficacy and appropriate trust in self and in peers.

Finally, cognitive dissonance and personal attribution make abstention from drugs difficult for adolescents. Cognitive dissonance is a result of conflicting internal messages. For example, the statements "I don't smoke anymore" and "After 3 months without a cigarette, I just smoked most of a pack" are inconsistent. They create dissonance, which brings on feelings of guilt, depression, and failure. These feelings are relieved when the internal messages are made harmonious: "I just smoked most of a pack" and "I'm a smoker." Personal attribution is the act of placing responsibility for a break from abstention on personal weaknesses and inadequacies. Despite situational factors that may greatly influence their behavior, such as unusually strong peer pressure or the actual addictive properties of the drug, people blame themselves for using substances again after they have decided to quit. The feelings of loss of control, failure, and guilt that result from both of these cognitive processes can lead abstainers to turn again to substances in an effort to cope, to alleviate their negative feelings, and to engage in behaviors consistent and congruent with their self-concept.

Effective child and adolescent drug prevention and intervention may need to address many of these fundamental contributing factors to be successful. The most effective interventions do attend to underlying problems, skills deficiencies, and systemic problem deficiencies (such as poor family life, lack of school programs) that are core to successful intervention and prevention programs.

SOME CONSEQUENCES OF SUBSTANCE USE

The long-term consequences of substance use require additional research, but some of the physiological and psychosocial consequences are clear. Examples of each are briefly presented here.

Physiological Consequences

The physiological consequences of drug use vary with the drug. Most substances (alcohol, nicotine, marijuana, narcotics, hallucinogens) have relatively immediate physical effects with alterations in one's sense of reality, judgment, and sensory perceptions. These effects are caused by interference with the normal functioning of the central nervous system. The effects may be felt for hours (as with alcohol) or for days (as with marijuana). Part of the difficulty with communicating the physiological risks of substance use to young people is that not all substances have severe or immediate consequences. Although marijuana impairs perception and judgment, for example, it is not physiologically addictive when it is used in moderation (although its ability to become psychosocially addictive is quite high). Focusing exclusively on the short-term negative effects of marijuana actually reduces the perceived truthfulness or knowledge and therefore the effectiveness of the helper.

Although short-term feelings associated with use of a substance are obvious, the long-term consequences of drugs are more severe. Alcohol is a factor in many adolescent deaths (i.e., motor vehicle crashes), and long-term alcohol misuse is associated with liver disease, cancer, cardiovascular disease, and neurological damage. In one study in Mexico (Miller et al., 2011), use of tobacco and abuse of alcohol and other drugs were a strong predictor of subsequent suicide ideation, attempts, and completion among adolescents. One of the most troublesome effects of marijuana smoking is impairment in brain development. When marijuana users begin using as teenagers, the drug often reduces thinking, memory, and learning functions. It may also affect the brain building connections between areas necessary for these functions (National Institute of Drug Abuse, 2015). Like tobacco, marijuana use also has adverse respiratory effects including chronic cough, recurrent bronchitis, and irritation of the respiratory tract.

Physiologically addictive substances (cocaine, crack, methamphetamines, heroin, other narcotics) used over a long time can cause severe impairment of the nervous system and internal organs. Addiction is typically defined as a physiological state in which the body needs increased amounts of a substance to maintain homeostasis (physiological balance). Users become tolerant of a drug and need increasing amounts of it to achieve the desired effect. Withdrawal is a painful physical experience that occurs when the drug is withheld from the system and the body reacts. Abuse of drugs or alcohol produces increased tolerance and withdrawal, often requiring inpatient detoxification to overcome. Physical dependence on the drug needs to be eliminated as a first step of effective behavioral and psychological interventions.

Psychosocial Consequences

Typically, drug use during childhood and adolescence leads to more serious problems in early adulthood. High levels of drug use are associated with early and risky sexual involvement, failure to pursue educational opportunities, early entrance into the workforce, and unemployment or underemployment (Burrow-Sanchez & Hawken, 2013). Alcohol use has been linked to physical fights, academic failure, occupational problems, and juvenile criminal behavior (Mulvey et al., 2010). Drug use contributes to HIV/AIDS and to infant morbidity and mortality (Johnston et al., 2011). Moreover, adolescents who enter early into adult roles before they are ready, without critical life skills, demonstrate poorer outcomes for themselves and their offspring (Gragg & McWhirter, 2003).

Adolescent cigarette smoking is associated with poorer achievement on standardized tests (Jeynes, 2002). Interestingly, moderate use of alcohol in the later teen years tends to increase a young person's sense of being integrated with others, positive self-perceptions, and emotions, along with less loneliness and self-derogation (Shedler & Block, 1990). But heavy use of more serious drugs (e.g., intravenous drugs, cocaine-based derivatives such as crack and methamphetamines) during adolescence increases loneliness, depression, and suicide ideation and decreases social support (Johnston et al., 2014).

SPECIFIC INTERVENTION STRATEGIES FOCUSED ON DRUG USE

School Intervention Programs

Prevention programs are a common form of drug use intervention because many young people have not yet experimented with drugs or alcohol. In addition, treatment to deal with the use of tobacco and alcohol as gateway drugs is also considered prevention for use of other drugs. Because some children experiment with drugs early, universal and indicated prevention programs should begin in the early school grades, commensurate with the prevention–intervention framework we present in Chapter 11. Drug use prevention programs generally have two goals: To delay age of first use and to reduce the use of gateway substances. Delaying the age of initial drug use is associated with better social, academic, and economic outcomes. Prevention programs are significantly related to reduced susceptibility of gateway substances, although some research (Wiehe, Garrison, Christakis, Ebel, & Rivara, 2005) suggests that there is little evidence to support that prevention programs reduce smoking among youth. Nevertheless, the role of schools in prevention programs is extensive and varied. For example, evidence (Andrews, Hampson, & Peterson, 2011) suggests that cognitions in middle school about students' social images and perceptions of peers' use of alcohol predict subsequent heavy drinking in high school. The need for middle school prevention programs targeting such cognitions is important. In addition, recent research (Lemstra et al., 2010) indicates that comprehensive programs that include antidrug information combined with social-skills training that includes refusal and self-management skills are the most effective primary prevention programs for reducing alcohol and marijuana use among teenagers.

Some very effective school programs have demonstrated positive substance abuse prevention results by focusing on broader social and character development issues rather than substances themselves. One such program is the Good Behavior Game (GBG) (Kellam, Reid, & Balster, 2008), which we describe in some detail in Chapter 13. Used in grades 1 and 2, the GBG resulted in a wide variety of positive behavioral and mental health outcomes. For example, participating students at age 13 were 26% less likely to have started smoking; less than half had used cocaine, crack, or heroin. Young adult males especially benefited: 59% had lower smoking rates; 35% lower rates of alcohol abuse; and 50% lower rates of illicit drug abuse.

Another "indirect" approach to substance abuse prevention is Positive Action (Beets et al., 2009), which is another example of a comprehensive program that involves a social and character development curriculum. All the children from 5 or 6 to age 10 in 20 elementary schools in Hawaii received daily classroom sessions that used role plays and activities focusing on self-improvement, self-management, and cooperating with others. Children who received the program were much less prone to sexual activity, violence, and drug abuse. The more involved children were in the program, the more their behavior improved. Four factors seemed to account for the positive impact of the program. First, positive interactions were encouraged between students and teachers. Second, the program provided an intensive "dose," with children receiving about an hour a week of the curriculum. Third, positive action encourages more effective interactive teaching methods than traditional ones. Finally, the program was implemented in every classroom at the same time across the entire school. Consequently, all the children as well as school staff and parents were involved simultaneously. This created a supportive school-wide environment.

Some school intervention programs provide alternative activities, such as adventurous recreational activities and service-related community projects. Others offer better opportunities for drug education, increase teachers' awareness of drug use, provide more substance use counseling, and support law enforcement efforts to limit drugs on the school campus. Some schools enlist family and community organizations. Indeed, most successful programs are ecological in nature; they include work to strengthen the relationships between families, schools, and communities (Hawkins et al., 2007, 2009, 2014).

Family Interventions

Inconsistent parents who do not monitor their children's activities contribute to high risk for drug use (Dishion & Stormshak, 2007). Thus efforts targeting parents' management practices and family norms regarding adolescent substance use are promising for preventing substance abuse (Bamatter et al., 2010). Parent training in improving monitoring of their children is particularly important. In Chapter 14 we review a variety of examples of family interventions.

Community Intervention Programs

Most juvenile programs are patterned on the traditional drug-free treatment models developed for adults in the 1960s, but programs early in the last decade began to respond more to the developmental needs of youth. Although more research is needed, programs tailored to youth have demonstrated promise in reducing adolescent drug use as well as other problems (Hawkins et al., 2015). A serious shortage of programs for adolescents is a major problem in most communities, perhaps one of the reasons Communities that Care (CtC), which we discussed in Chapter 2, has shown such great promise (Hawkins, Oesterle, Brown, Abbott, & Catalano, 2014). That program—a framework really, for combining a number of individual programs—is implemented within a community, matching proven interventions to community needs. Relative to comparable communities that did *not* use the CtC model, those that implemented CtC reported a 33% reduction in those beginning tobacco use, a 32% reduction in those beginning alcohol use, and a 25% reduction in delinquent behavior community-wide (Hawkins et al., 2014). Effects on initiation of these behaviors were sustained throughout high school (Hawkins et al., 2014).

Examples of community intervention programs for youth include the following:

- Drug-free programs offer outpatient counseling and use no medication. Some offer drop-in services; others are organized around activities, such as camping trips or challenge experiences.
- Therapeutic communities are residential programs that utilize a structured environment relying on peer influence and confrontation to change self-destructive values and behavior.
- Psychiatric residential programs are operated by profit-making corporations that operate on a mental health residential rehabilitation model.
- Day-care programs provide alternative schooling, counseling, recreational, and social activities for several hours daily and include greater attention to ecological factors such as families and neighborhoods.
- Aftercare programs incorporate therapeutic elements such as professional contact, and participation in self-help groups like Alcoholics Anonymous or Narcotics Anonymous after the young person has been discharged from a residential facility.

Student Assistance Programs

Because of the limited programs for young people, school-based Student Assistance Programs (SAPs) have great advantages. Originally begun to help substance-abusing youth, SAPs have expanded to include other behavioral problems. Here we will focus on their original intent because they deal directly with two major problems that confront substance-using students. First, students involved with alcohol and other substances are hesitant to seek counseling services. Second, the illegal nature of substance use contributes to the reluctance of adolescents to seek assistance and accentuates the denial of problems associated with abuse. The typical SAP has a team that includes representatives from the school-administrators, teachers, counselors, and parents along with a substance abuse specialist. SAPs have a structure and process for identifying substance-abusing students, a network to community resources that provide treatment and recovery interventions, and a reentry program that includes case management and follow-up for students returning to school after treatment.

One particularly important component of follow-up is the school recovery support group. The type of support received when a young person leaves a treatment center and reenters the "real world" is extremely important in preventing relapse. Unfortunately, teens who take a leave of absence from school for drug treatment are faced with pressure to use drugs again very quickly after returning to school. The recovery support group provides an opportunity for students to discuss emotional difficulties of being clean and sober. Because they include students who are "working a program," they accentuate a prosocial peer cluster. In fact, it is detrimental to a school recovery support group to include students who are not actively engaged in their own recovery. Other types of interventions should be available to drug-using adolescents who choose not to be committed to a drug-free lifestyle.

The above interventions are all very important in helping young people make positive change. The fact remains, however, that change is difficult; it almost always requires some degree of commitment from the individual. It is useful to the helper to have some idea where the individual is in the change process. An important tool to do this is the Stages of Change (SOC) model.

Stages of Change

SOC, sometimes referred to as the Transtheoretical Model of Change, is conceived as a framework that bridges all theoretical approaches (Prochaska, 2013). The SOC model suggest that individuals change when they are ready and that the change process is dynamic: People move through established stages from one to the other, but they also can move in and out of stages depending on a variety of circumstances and the specific nature of the problem. Therefore, interventions help people progress through the stages, develop their readiness to change, and provide the skills needed to effect and maintain change. The model has been used as a guiding framework to help reduce high-risk behavior and to adopt less risky behavior (Ryan, Lynch, Vansteenkiste, & Deci, 2011). Thus, the model suggests that youth can be located along a continuum of stages reflecting the motivation or readiness for change.

In their movement toward positive change, the individual progresses from precontemplation (not considering change at all), to contemplation (weighing pros and cons), to preparation (getting ready to make the change), to action (making the change), and finally to maintenance (consolidating positive change). Using substance abuse as an example, the stages are described as follows:

- *Precontemplation.* Not considering quitting drug or alcohol use
- *Contemplation.* Considering quitting within a specific time frame, such as within the next month

- *Preparation.* Characterized by making active plans and attempts to quit drug or alcohol use, sometimes characterized by following through with at least one quit attempt
- *Action.* Being engaged in and actively involved in treatment
- *Maintenance.* Typically defined as maintaining abstinence for a specific time period after treatment

These stages of change describe the discrete steps in the process of an individual's intentional behavior change during treatment. Assessment of where people are along this sequence may also help to monitor and guide substance use treatment and prevention planning in adults and adolescents (Prochaska, 2013; Prochaska & DiClemente, 1992; Werch & DiClemente, 1994). The appropriateness and potential impact of any given intervention is contingent upon the young person's readiness to change. For example, the clinically appropriate response to a relapse is qualitatively different when an adolescent is in an initial stage of the change process (i.e., internally more at the preparation stage) than at the final stage (maintenance) (Ryan et al., 2011). Fundamentally, interventions designed to enhance readiness to change may be necessary before people engage in and benefit from other active treatment strategies (Prochaska, 2013). For example, young people in the preparation stage were 25 times more likely to quit smoking than those in the precontemplation or contemplation stages (Dino, Kamal, Horn, Kalsekar, & Fernandes, 2004).

SPECIFIC INTERVENTION: MOTIVATIONAL INTERVIEWING

Motivational interviewing (MI) is a counseling approach that was originally developed to address substance use disorders—smoking, alcohol use, and a wide range of other drugs—and has been proven extremely helpful and efficacious (Miller & Rollnick, 2012). In addition, MI has been tested across a wide range of other target behavior changes and found to be effective in promoting adaptive behaviors (e.g., exercise, diet, medication adherence), in reducing negative behaviors (e.g., gambling, HIV risk behaviors, overeating), and helping with psychological problems (Arkowitz, Miller, & Rollnick, 2015).

A growing body of research has demonstrated that MI is equally useful with juveniles as well with both substance use and abuse (Hall, Stewart, Arger, Athenour, & Effinger, 2014; Naar-King & Suarez, 2011) and other problematic conditions. For example, in one meta-analysis of 15 studies, medical professionals using MI, compared to other treatments, had positive treatment effects on adolescent health behavior: diet, exercise, asthma management, diabetes management, and sexual behavior (Cushing, Jensen, Miller, & Leffingwell, 2014). Positive treatment effects were seen on average after only five sessions and in some in as few as two. Some evidence exists that suggests that MI is also useful to children precisely because it acknowledges both the for-and-against sides of ambivalence, relies on self-direction, and encourages self-motivated change that are likely appealing to youth. In another meta-analysis of 37 studies evaluating the use of MI for child health behaviors such as asthma, diabetes, obesity, sleep, infant health, and HIV/AIDS, MI resulted in small but significant changes and outperformed alternative treatment (Gayes & Steele, 2014). MI was most effective in the treatment of asthma, type 1 diabetes, and calcium intake. It was most effective as a standalone treatment when parents were included with their children.

Even though MI is increasingly helpful to a range of youth health problems, it remains a major intervention for addiction. MI has been applied extensively to drug abuse and alcohol use problems with adolescents including school-based curriculum demonstrating significant reductions in cigarette smoking, alcohol use, and hard drug use (Sussman, Sun, Rohrbach, & Spruijt-Metz, 2012). It is supported by research and includes the fundamental components of best practices. Equally important, the mechanisms of change in MI and the counseling style employed seem to have a general positive impact on young clients. Further, MI can be used to assist adolescents in highlighting their unique reasons for wanting to avoid substance use, increasing their confidence to resist peer influence, and draw on family support to assist in making better decisions (Schwinn & Schinke, 2014).

Using the "Stages of Change" model (Prochaska, 2013), MI is based on the idea that people proceed through a process of preparing to make a change before actually doing so. This preparation process is characterized by ambivalence about change. MI helps to resolve the ambivalence and motivate clients to both desire and prepare for making a life change. The assumptions of MI are that people, especially young people, who are abusing alcohol or drugs, will not change their behavior (i.e., quit drinking or doing drugs) unless they are ready. The MI intervention focuses on helping the individual realize that the negative consequences outweigh the positive effects of drug use and understand how the costs are greater than the benefits. Thus, instead of the confrontational approach traditional in drug and alcohol intervention, MI provides clients with personalized feedback and focuses on pointing out discrepancies and inconsistencies in a client's self-view with their actual behavior. The counselor is always supportive throughout the process. Studies (e.g., Naar-King & Suarez, 2011) indicate that MI is effective in reducing adolescent smoking by increasing adolescents' motivation to change and by increasing their interest in participating in smoking cessation programs compared to students who received a school-based tobacco education group intervention. In one randomized study, MI reduced young people's use of cigarettes, alcohol, and marijuana, with greater reductions among heavier users of these substances. Reduction in marijuana use was also greater among teenagers at high risk in other areas, with a single session of MI proving useful in reducing marijuana use (McCambridge, Day, Thomas, & Strang, 2011).

In addition to other substance use studies Baer et. al (2008), MI has been used with children, adolescents, and their parents in pediatric settings (Erickson, Gerstle, & Feldstein, 2005). MI has also been used in school settings. Project

READY, an eight-session school-based intervention using MI, was developed to reduce adolescent substance use. Results demonstrated that motivational self-efficacy is predictive of adolescents' substance use outcomes.

An application of MI, Motivational Enhancement Therapy (MET), coupled with Cognitive Behavioral Therapy (CBT), has demonstrated long-term efficacy among depressed teens who also had alcohol problems. In fact, CBT/MET was more effective than other drug treatment approaches (Cornelius et al., 2011). Relying on the SOC model discussed earlier, MI is designed to motivate people to progress along the change process, regardless of where they are in the process (Cushing et al., 2014).

MI includes core intervention components, and one MI-like system referred to as FRAMES provides a good model. Each letter stands for one of the following important, but not sequential, aspects of counseling:

- *Feedback* of personal status allows the counselor to simply reflect back behavior to an individual without judgment or pressure to change. Sometimes showing a mirror to a client can be very powerful.
- *Responsibility* for change is an emphasis that keeps counseling focused on the choices, consequences, and personal responsibility of the adolescent for changing and reduces the focus on external excuses that adolescents may make for engaging in behaviors that they have chosen.
- *Advice* to change allows the counselor to simply suggest that the adolescent may be much better off if he or she considers and follows through with a behavior change. Advice always comes after developing a trusting relationship with the client.
- *Menu* of change options allows counselors to suggest treatment alternatives to teens and to parents. As opposed to narrowing options, this method lets adolescents and families choose what they believe will work for them at any given time. Providing a menu of treatment options is central to the idea of allowing adolescents and families to make choices about the treatment they receive.
- *Empathetic* counselor style is something that occurs from the very outset of counseling and highlights the importance of accepting people where they are, being nonjudgmental about their behavior, and accepting them as people who are struggling. Acceptance facilitates change, and skillful reflective listening is a powerful intervention for understanding clients and for helping them to feel heard.
- *Self-efficacy* for change means that adolescents develop the skills needed to quit or reduce use, find and enter into more positive social and support environments, and develop the confidence that they can quit.

An underlying spirit of MI is a crucial component of its effectiveness. The MI spirit is collaborative not authoritarian, evokes motivation rather than trying to impose it on the client, and respects the client's autonomy. Early evidence for the linkage of MI spirit with change talk and favorable outcome is found in a wide range of studies (see Miller & Rollnick, 2012; Naar-King &

Suarez, 2011). Some of the fundamental principles and the spirit of MI are well integrated into the FRAMES list.

Expressing empathy is paramount and a major component of the approach. There are positive relationships between therapist empathy and counselor interpersonal skills and measures of client involvement and drinking outcomes (Miller & Rollnick, 2012).

Helping clients develop discrepancies is also critical. This involves helping clients see for themselves the consequences of their actions, and that the consequences of their actions are often in conflict with stated goals. By pointing out discrepancies, clients present their own arguments for change rather than the counselor doing it for them as is more common in traditional interventions.

Avoiding argumentation is important because arguments are counterproductive. Pushing a position (e.g., "Abstinence is the only way to improve your life!") nearly always breeds defensiveness in clients and enhances their resistance to change.

Rolling with resistance means that instead of "boxing, wrestling, or fighting with" clients, it is best to "dance with" them. Trying to get clients to see the counselor's point of view often creates a power struggle with them. It is better to see their resistance as a coping strategy, which suggests that clients have some important strengths that the counselor and the client can utilize.

Finally, supporting self-efficacy means communicating to clients a belief that they have the ability to change. Providing clients with hope and with a range of available behavioral alternatives that they might use to act differently—if they choose to—is a powerful motivator. Supporting self-efficacy means communicating clearly to clients that responsibility for personal change rests solely within them and that they have the capacity to make the change.

MI meets the core components of best intervention practices. It is multimodal. It is well adapted to include individual counseling, can be applied to family counseling, can involve peers in the treatment process, and is sensitive to cultural and individual differences. MI also highlights the notion of perceived choice. Adolescents make their own decisions about change, and interventions are based on where an adolescent is along the change path (Naar-King & Suarez, 2011). Using the stage model framework (Prochaska, 2013), therapeutic interventions at each stage incorporate stage-appropriate strategies to motivate and prepare the adolescent for the next stage. These interventions increase the adolescent's intrinsic sense of choice throughout treatment. MI is also sensitive to individual, cultural, and ethnic group differences (Villanueva, Tonigan, & Miller, 2007). This is essential because studies show that the reasons adolescents use drugs vary according to their ethnicity. Youth of color may have a higher risk of post-treatment relapse due to the greater number of environmental and contextual risk factors they face such as greater availability of drugs within their communities. MI accounts for potential, cultural, and environmental differences and is flexible enough to integrate specific risk and protective factors.

Fundamentally, MI is very respectful of clients' worldview, helps clients to identify their own strengths, and supports their own decisions of what changes to make and when. Similar to the solution-focused brief therapy model we presented in Chapter 6, we encourage you to read more about MI as an effective approach to working with adolescents who have a drug or alcohol problem.

CONCLUSION

Drugs and alcohol are widely used, and their abuse imposes great social, economic, and personal costs on individuals, communities, and society as a whole. The most effective prevention strategies involve schools and families, and treatment is most effective when families, schools, and the community collaborate. Understanding and attending to the influence and attitudes of the peer cluster are critical for both deterring and treating the problems caused by drug use. Only by helping young people to understand themselves, their motives and coping strategies, and their responsibility for their actions and for creating change in their own lives will the negative influences of alcohol and drug use among adolescents be diminished.

Teenage Pregnancy, STIs, and Risky Sexual Behavior

A young girl-woman, without education,

without resources, stressed and depressed,

rears her baby alone and

bends like the poplar.

Gentle summer rains nourish the soil ... but

where do the poplars and the waters meet?

CHAPTER OUTLINE

The personal, familial, and social challenges related to adolescent sexual activity are broad-ranging and complex, including pregnancy, sexually transmitted infections (STIs) including the human immunodeficiency virus (HIV) and acquired immunodeficiency syndrome (AIDS), abortion, sexual identity difficulties, childhood molestation and incest, and sex-related violence. No one chapter can fully attend to the interpersonal, psychological, and social implications of these issues. Therefore, we focus on two critical problems related to a young person's sexual development and sexual activity: teenage pregnancy and STIs, particularly HIV and AIDS. More specifically, we discuss (a) the incidence and frequency of teenage pregnancy; (b) incidence of HIV/AIDS and other STIs among teens; (c) background factors associated with risky sex among teens, including media influences; (d) the consequences of risky sexual activity; and (e) prevention and treatment strategies.

THE SCOPE OF THE PROBLEM: TEEN PREGNANCY

After steady increases in the teen pregnancy rate in the 1980s, the United States has made clear progress in reducing it. Currently, teen pregnancy rates are at a record low, dropping 18% between 2007 and 2010 and another 6% between 2011 and 2012 (Centers for Disease Control and Prevention [CDC], 2015b). Abortion rates in the United States have also dropped in the last two decades. The decline in teen pregnancy and birthrates is attributed to the increased use of contraceptives among teens; reform of the U.S. welfare system during the Bill Clinton administration; and success in the many, varied pregnancy and STI/HIV prevention programs that have been instituted in the past two decades. This decline can be seen not only across the nation but in every state, and crosses ethnocultural groups (Boonstra, 2014).

Nevertheless, even with the reported decreases, the United States continues to have one of the highest teen pregnancy rates in the developed world (CDC, 2015b; Guttmacher Institute, 2012). In the United States, teenage girls still give birth to over 1,200 babies each day, and this is more problematic in poor urban and poor rural areas (CDC, 2015). Although only 13% of U.S. teens have had sex by the age of 15, by their 19th birthday 70% have had intercourse (Guttmacher Institute, 2012). In 2013, 47% of high school students had had sexual intercourse, 15% had had four or more sex partners, and over 40% of sexually active students did not use a condom during their last sexual intercourse, perpetuating risk outcomes (CDC, 2015b). A sexually active teen who does not use contraception has a 90% chance of pregnancy (CDC, 2013). Additionally, teen birthrates in the United States remain high especially among African American, Latino, and southern state adolescents (CDC, 2015b). The pregnancy rate for African American and Latino teens remains more than double that of European American teens, accounting for

57% of 2012 U.S. teen births (Federal Interagency Forum on Child and Family Statistics, 2015).

Regular use of alcohol, cigarettes, and marijuana by 14- and 15-year-olds is also related to their engagement in sexual intercourse, with boys more likely than girls to be actively using alcohol or drugs during the time when they are sexually active. European American (28%) and Latino (24%) students are more likely than African American (18%) students to use alcohol or drugs at the time of sexual intercourse (CDC, 2013). Over 22% of sexually active high school students reported having used alcohol or drugs prior to having sex, and nearly 14% did not use any method to prevent pregnancy when alcohol or drugs were involved (CDC, 2014).

In the United States, the response of adolescents to becoming pregnant has changed over the past two decades as well. For all teen pregnancies in the United States, 82% are unplanned, with 59% ending in birth, and more than a quarter in abortion (Guttmacher Institute, 2012). In comparison with European American families, teens from Latino, African American, and Native American families are more likely to not end their pregnancy in abortion, and the children born to these youth are often parented or informally adopted by a member of the extended family. Trends among European teens suggest that many adolescent girls would rather have an abortion than carry an unwanted pregnancy to term and relinquish the baby for adoption (Federal Interagency Forum on Child and Family Statistics, 2015).

Of course, in addition to pregnancy, engaging in risky sexual activity (being poorly informed about the body, sex, and reproduction; having unprotected sex; being too young at first coitus; etc.) also presents danger of acquiring an STI, including HIV/AIDs.

THE SCOPE OF THE PROBLEM: HIV AND OTHER SEXUALLY TRANSMITTED INFECTIONS

Adolescents ages 15 to 24 account for nearly half of the 20 million new cases of STIs each year in the United States. In 2015, 4 in 10 sexually active teen girls have had an STI that can cause infertility and even death. Also, while rates of HIV generally are very low among adolescents, males make up more than three-quarters of HIV diagnoses among 13- to 19-year-olds (U.S. Department of Health and Human Services; Office of Adolescent Health, 2015). The United States continues to have much higher rates of teen pregnancy and teen STIs than Canada or Western Europe (CDC, 2013). Gonorrhea, genital warts, herpes, and syphilis are all too common. In a single act of unprotected sex with an infected partner, a teen girl has a 1% risk of acquiring HIV, a 30% risk of getting genital herpes, and a 50% chance of contracting gonorrhea. Chlamydia, an infection of the vagina or urinary tract, is the most frequently diagnosed STI among adolescents (Alan Guttmacher Institute [AGI], 2011). Among young women aged 16 to 24 participating in the National Job Training Program, 11.7% had chlamydia (CDC, 2013). Of new HIV infection diagnoses in 2010, one-quarter were among youth; 57% of these were among Black youth; and 20% among both Latino and White youth, respectively (CDC, 2013).

The prevalence of STIs is in part due to teenagers not receiving accurate or comprehensive sexual information in order to protect themselves. Of 177 sexual health websites used by teens for sexual education, 46% of those discussing contraception and 35% of those addressing abortion contained inaccurate information (Buhi, 2010; Guttmacher Institute, 2012). When parents and teens discuss sexual health, parental knowledge of contraception and other topics may also often be incomplete or inaccurate. Additionally, 11 out of 13 commonly used abstinence-only programs had misleading, distorted, or inaccurate information (Guttmacher Institute, 2012). Accurate and comprehensive sexual health education has been found to reduce sexual risk behaviors, pregnancy, HIV, and other STIs and increase protective sexual behaviors (Chin et al., 2012).

Teens tend to feel invulnerable to something as catastrophic as AIDS—"It can't happen to me!" or else "Even if I get it, there will be a cure before it affects me." That attitude—coupled with sexual activity; multiple sex partners; and ineffective, sporadic, or no condom use—makes teenagers very vulnerable for contracting HIV/AIDS. Sexually active adolescent gay males are particularly vulnerable to HIV infection. In 2010, gay and bisexual men (aged 13–24 years) accounted for 72% of new HIV infections among all people aged 13 to 24 and 30% of new infections among all gay and bisexual men (CDC, 2015). In 2011, among adolescent males (aged 13–19 years), approximately 93% of those with an HIV infection were from male-to-male sexual contact (CDC, 2014).

The fluctuations in adolescent risky sexual activity and subsequent STIs, pregnancies, abortions, and births can be attributed to a variety of factors. We review these next.

PRECURSORS OF RISKY SEXUAL BEHAVIOR: BACKGROUND CHARACTERISTICS

Family and social issues as well as psychological and interpersonal characteristics contribute to teen pregnancy and risky sexual behavior that can lead to STIs. In this section we discuss (a) issues related to adolescent development; (b) antecedent characteristics that set the stage for teen pregnancy; (c) interpersonal influences, such as peer relationships and family dynamics; and in the next section, we consider various forms of the media that influence risky sexual behavior.

Adolescent Development

In view of the normal challenges of adolescence, it is not surprising that many teens are involved in sexual activity or that pregnancy so frequently results. One of the primary ways in which adolescents attempt to negotiate the transition from childhood to adulthood is through sexual activity. Even though most teenage parents never expected or wanted to conceive a child, many teens see sexual activity as a way to develop adult identity, and in some ways, their own relational autonomy, apart from their families. Teens look to relationships with others for validation and approval, and sometimes these interactions become sexual. Sexual behavior also provides a means of challenging parents on the way toward independence.

Adolescence is an important time in the formation of sexual identity. Experimentation with sex is often a part of the learning experience. Young people engaging in same-sex activity often do not identify as gay or lesbian. Models of gay or lesbian identity development characterize the process of developing a positive gay, lesbian, or bisexual identity as a series of nonlinear and potentially reoccurring stages (Fassinger, 2000; E. H. McWhirter, 1994). For teens who identify as Lesbian, gay, bisexual, transgender, and queer LGBTQ and as people of color, this process of developing a positive ethnic identity may conflict with the development of a positive sexual identity. LGBTQ adolescents confront the task of forming a stigmatized identity just at a time when sameness and affiliation with peers are very important, and they may withdraw from their peers, stifle expression of their feelings and experiences, or develop an identity that is not internally genuine as a means of managing this pressure. All of these strategies create anxiety. Not surprisingly, drug use, running away, family rejection, and engaging in risky sexual activity are significant problems among LGBTQ adolescents. For instance, youth who report same-gender sexual contact, or who identify as lesbian, gay, bisexual, or questioning, are more likely to engage in a variety of sexual health risk behaviors than adolescents who do not (Kann, O'Malley, Olsen, & McManus, et al. 2011). High school students who identify as lesbian or gay are more likely (67%) than students who identify as heterosexual (44%) to have engaged in sexual intercourse. High school students who identify as bisexual are most likely to engage in sexual intercourse (69%), while students who identify as "unsure of their sexual identity" are least likely (43%) (Kann, O'Malley, Olsen, & McManus, et al. 2011).

Preparation for career, marriage or partnership, and family life are part of this developmental period for all adolescents, and sexual activity serves as a way for young people to test these future roles. When an unwanted pregnancy occurs, the developmental process is both delayed in some ways and accelerated in other, significant ways. Adolescents must cope immediately with adult roles: parenthood, finding a job, and dealing with social isolation and loneliness. In many cases they become dependent on public aid for survival. In addition, these adverse consequences for mothers and their children impose high public sector costs (CDC, 2011).

For many girls, pregnancy limits life options. However, if already restricted in opportunities, having a child may not alter their beliefs about the options that they have.

Antecedent Characteristics

Some personal and demographic characteristics place teens at risk for premature pregnancy; some serve as protective factors. For example, higher self-esteem decreases the risk of pregnancy for Latino and African American teens (Berry, Shillington, Peak, & Hohman, 2000), but delinquent activity and alcohol use often precede and are a risk factor for teen pregnancy (Hockaday, Crase, Shelley, & Stockdale, 2000). Among urban African American girls, living in a more disorganized neighborhood, being faced with low expectations for school success (whether at home or from teachers), holding values that are not prosocial (such as being a gang member, engaging in early status offenses, etc.) are the greatest risk factors for risky sexual activity and subsequent consequences. For many girls in these situations, pregnancy may represent a source of gratification and independence (Lanctot & Smith, 2001). Pregnant African American girls are proportionally more likely to participate in status offenses than their sexually active but nonpregnant peers (Berry et al., 2000). Teens at risk for pregnancy are also likely to reject social norms, to have limited knowledge of their own physiology, to have difficulty using information about birth control, to be biologically mature, and to be less religious. Finally, a young woman's socioeconomic status, perception of her own opportunity, and educational expectations are crucial determinants of pregnancy (Advocates for Youth, 2015; Berry et al., 2000; Hockaday et al., 2000).

Teens who were born to poor and less-educated teenage parents are more likely to bear children during their own adolescence (Advocates for Youth, 2015; Berry et al., 2000). Lower educational and career opportunities and coming from a single-parent family or from a family with marital strife and instability also increase risk. Students who dropout or are forced out of school are more likely to start sexual activity earlier, fail to use contraception during intercourse, become pregnant, and give birth (Advocates for Youth, 2015). Finally, early childbearing is associated with conduct disorder (CD) as well as with lower IQ, lower educational attainment, and lower socioeconomic status (Jaffee, 2002).

Interpersonal Influences

A teen's relationship with his or her parents is associated with adolescent pregnancy. Perceptions of high levels of warmth, love, caring, and connection with parents, as well as parental disapproval of teen sex, have been associated with delay of sexual activity and delay of first coitus among teenagers. Girls, more than boys, talk with their parents about "how to say no to sex" or about birth control (Guttmacher Institute, 2012; Martinez, Abma, & Casey, 2010). A close mother–daughter relationship, in particular, encourages girls to turn to their mothers for nurturance. Communication between mother and daughter about sexual issues, feelings, and behaviors can significantly help daughters learn and practice responsible sexual behavior. Girls who are close to their mothers are more likely to abstain from sex or to practice birth control (Darlington, B. T. McWhirter, & E. H. McWhirter, 2012; Dittus & Jaccard, 2000). A good mother–daughter relationship provides a girl with a model for responsible sexual behavior and for maintaining a good relationship with a future partner. However, even though most parents see it as their responsibility to talk to their children about sexuality, most do not engage in in-depth discussions with their children about sex (Byers, 2011). In fact, many teens who have had sexual intercourse have never spoken with their parents about sex (CDC, 2015b).

Families characterized by poor interpersonal relationships, ineffective communication, and limited problem-solving skills typically encourage teens to turn to peers for information and intimacy needs, which often leads to risky behavior and irresponsibility. In one study, the only significant predictor of teenage girls' attitudes about pregnancy was their boyfriends' attitudes toward having children (Cowley & Tillman, 2001). Peers can provide support, fairly clear norms, and the structure that most adolescents want. Along with the media, peers are a primary source of information about sex. Unfortunately, adolescents who confidently share information may lack knowledge and may encourage premature and irresponsible sexual decisions.

Once a girl becomes pregnant, her mother usually has the most influence on the outcome, but not always (see Box 8.1). Often the mother pressures her pregnant daughter to keep the child. In this case, the relationships between

---

Box 8.1	Daddy's Girl

When 16-year-old Susan and her father came for counseling to work on their relationship, she appeared sullen, depressed, and angry. When I met with her alone, she explained that her father had tricked her into coming by telling her he was taking her shopping. She confided that she was pregnant, that her father did not know, and that she hadn't been able to hold down food for three straight days. Susan's mother had "run off years ago." Susan reported that she had had one abortion already and was very reluctant to have another one. When I saw her father alone, he told me that he knew she was pregnant—"Well, that's why I brought her to you." He emphasized several times, "I'm a hundred percent behind her. I support Susan all the way." He told her the same thing when the two were brought together and she acknowledged her pregnancy. In the same breath he told her, "The decision is totally up to you. But, of course, if you decide not to get an abortion, you'll have to live somewhere else."

Susan did not show up for her next appointment. She sounded tearful when she answered the phone.

"Couldn't you make it in today?" I asked.

"No, I'm sick. Well ... I had an abortion this morning."

Despite repeated calls and letters to her father, he would not bring her in for additional counseling. So far as her "supportive" father was concerned, Susan no longer had a problem.

mother, daughter, and baby tend to become confused, with the new grandmother taking on primary responsibility for the infant. Although these teen mothers may indeed have family support, the decision to keep the baby in the family often restricts their educational and occupational options and opportunities. Often this choice places the babies in a similar situation of restricted future options, and the cycle of "babies having babies" can be easily perpetuated.

PRECURSORS OF RISKY SEXUAL BEHAVIOR: MEDIA INFLUENCES

Young people are bombarded with sexual messages and images in the media that reflect premature, risky, and irresponsible sexual behavior. The Internet, social media, and social network connections often encourage risky sexual behavior by flooding young people with sexual and sexually explicit content. Smartphones can give young people immediate access to porn at the touch of the finger, anywhere they are, and at any hour of the day. Media sources and technology, although a potential source of useful information and positive influence, can provide considerable misinformation and active danger that is difficult for responsible adults to manage or even know about.

Television and Other Media

Young people are influenced by commercial media. Nearly 40% of students watch television for more than 3 hours per day during an average school day, with male African American and Latino students having the highest rates of television viewing. More than two-thirds of the programming on television have some form of sexual content (Brown, Halpern, & L'Engle, 2005; The Media Project, 2015).

The effect of television on teenagers' sexual behavior increases as a teenager watches more sexual content. Exposure to high levels of sexual content on television is associated with an increased risk of initiating sexual activity and a greater likelihood of teen pregnancy (Chandra, 2008), and youth who look at x-rated or violent material are six times more likely to report forcing someone to do something sexual online or in-person in comparison to youth not exposed to x-rated material (Center for Innovative Public Health Research, 2015).

Internet Pornography, Sexual Solicitation, and Sexting

Young people have easy access to pornography on the Internet. Seven out of ten youth unintentionally come across porn online (Kaiser Foundation, 2006), and 13% of youth Internet users receive unwanted sexual solicitations (Wolak, Mitchell, & Finkelhor, 2011). In 27% of online incidents, perpetrators asked youths for sexual photographs of themselves (Wolak, Finkelhor, Mitchell, & Ybarra, 2011). Parental monitoring of children's Internet use is critical; however, sexually explicit websites may be entered even when there are no indicators of sexual content at that link. Another problem that has emerged with the development of electronic media is sexting. Sexting refers to sending from a mobile phone a sexually suggestive or explicit text message, photo, or short video to someone else, usually a current or prospective boyfriend or girlfriend. Young people are aware that sexting is a potentially dangerous behavior with 75% of teens agreeing that sending sexually suggestive content "can have serious negative consequences." Most teens (71%) indicate that sharing sexual messages or nude/seminude images of themselves leads to more sex in real life. Yet many do it anyway. A significant number of teens, one in four, have sent or posted online nude or seminude pictures or videos of themselves, and nearly 40% have sent or posted sexually suggestive messages (Albert, 2010).

The potential of these sexting messages being shared is very high and could have disastrous consequences. For example, the impact of such content becoming public could result in unwelcome sexual solicitations, bullying, and social isolation from friends. It potentially provides easy material for cyber bullying (see Chapter 11). In some cases, depending on the motive for sharing the content, sexting could result in violence. Sharing such sexual content could lead to disciplinary action by schools and legal action by state and federal authorities. Finally, the behavior could lead to serious emotional and self-esteem issues. Jesse Logan, discussed in Box 8.2, provides a tragic example of bad consequences of sexting.

The Positive Potential of Information Technology

Just as the media and information technology can encourage risky sexual behavior, it also has an undeniable potential for presenting helpful and healthy information. Although much more research is needed, interactive computer programs are a promising area to improve knowledge and attitudes about sexuality. Even though the lack of group interaction is a drawback to stand-alone instruction, this approach is inexpensive, easily replicated with

Box 8.2	A Sexting Tragedy

Jesse Logan, an 18-year-old Cincinnati high school girl sent nude pictures of herself to a boyfriend. After they broke up, he circulated the images on the Internet, including posting them to other girls in their high school. The girls harassed her—calling her a slut and whore. The ridicule made her miserable and depressed; she began to skip school. According to family reports, when the school was asked to intervene, they did very little.

Jesse agreed to appear on a television station to tell her story in the hopes that others would not have to go through what she had gone through, to warn other young people about the dangers of sending sexually explicit messages and pictures to others. Apparently, this was not enough because a short time later, Jesse hanged herself in her bedroom.

fidelity, can be used in most locations, and can be integrated into daily monitoring and journaling via mobile devices that are now almost ubiquitous among adolescents. Apparently, short, noninteractive videos and computer-based instruction alone have no effect on behavior, whereas longer interactive videos viewed several times may have some impact on improved knowledge and safer sex attitudes (Kirby, 2007).

CONSEQUENCES OF EARLY CHILDBEARING

When a teenage girl becomes pregnant, her physical, social, educational, and career development is significantly altered. An unwanted child has consequences for the mother's socioeconomic status, educational attainment, health, and family development.

Socioeconomic Consequences

A teenage girl who decides to keep her baby is likely to suffer consequences in the form of using public assistance, unemployment or underemployment, an end to her schooling, earning a lower income than those who had children later in life, and an increased likelihood of having a second child within two years of the first (Schuyler Center for Analysis and Advocacy [SCAA], 2008). Each year nationally, teen childbearing costs taxpayers at least $7 billion due to costs associated with health care, foster care, criminal justice, public assistance, and lost tax revenue (National Campaign to Prevent Teen Pregnancy, 2001; SCAA, 2008). Children of young teenagers are more likely to be born prematurely, live in poverty and suffer higher rates of abuse and neglect, are less likely to complete high school, and have lower performance on standardized tests. Additionally, sons of teenage mothers are 13% more likely to be incarcerated, and daughters are 22% more likely to become teenage mothers themselves (National Campaign to Prevent Teen Pregnancy, 2002; SCAA, 2008).

Educational Consequences

Teen pregnancy is associated with low achievement scores and limited vocational and educational expectations. Clearly, youth at risk for becoming parents are also at risk for dropping out of school and are more likely to be unemployed or underemployed throughout much of their lives.

In recent years, the proportion of teenage mothers with high school diplomas has increased, in large part because many school districts now provide alternative high schools or school programs for student mothers. Nevertheless, teenage mothers are less likely to complete school, more likely to have large families, less likely to go to college, and more likely to be single (Kirby, 2007). This, of course, increases the likelihood that they and their children will live in poverty.

The educational problems faced by adolescent parents are frequently carried over into the next generation. A disproportionate number of the children born to teenagers show more emotional and behavioral problems while growing up. These children also have more erratic attendance records, poorer school performance, and lower college expectations. As might be expected, teen parents' children have been found to have less supportive and stimulating home environments, poorer health, and lower cognitive development (Kirby, 2007).

Health-Related Consequences

Pregnant adolescents commonly experience poor nutrition, poor health, and limited access to and use of health services. One-third of pregnant teens receive inadequate prenatal care. Prenatal, perinatal, and postnatal problems are more common among younger mothers than among older mothers. More of their babies die, likely because younger mothers rarely seek prenatal care in their first trimester. Pregnant teens are at a much higher risk for serious medical issues such as toxemia, significant anemia, premature delivery, pregnancy-induced hypertension, and placenta previa (Medline Plus, 2011).

Children of teenage mothers also have serious health problems. Babies born to teen mothers are more likely to have childhood health problems and to be hospitalized than those who are born to mothers in their 20s or older. They are also more likely to have low-birth-weight babies; low-birth-weight babies are more likely to have several developmental problems during adolescence and to have lower IQs at age 20 than comparable children (Federal Interagency Forum on Child and Family Statistics, 2010).

Infant mortality is highest among younger teen mothers, especially African American teen mothers (Ventura, Matthews, & Hamilton, 2002). Low birth weight, congenital problems, and sudden infant death syndrome account for nearly half of infant deaths in the United States (Ventura et al., 2002). The challenges that adolescent mothers deal with often result in a lack of optimal development of the baby, which lays a foundation for a continued cycle of teen pregnancy.

Family Development

Few teen pregnancies actually involve marriage or committed social unions. Of the girls who do marry, nearly a third of them are divorced within 5 years, compared to 15% among couples who marry later. Most children born to teen mothers will spend at least part of their lives in single-parent homes (Advocates for Youth, 2015). Indeed, many teenage fathers never acknowledge parenthood. Some of these boys never know that they are fathers, but many do know and are simply unwilling to deal with the responsibilities of parenthood (Advocates for Youth, 2015).

Teenage mothers are at a great disadvantage when they attempt to create a healthy and stimulating environment for their children. They are often forced to work long hours and may have little time to spend with their babies. These problems may be compounded by neglect because teen mothers often know little about what babies need to thrive. Teen mothers experience a great deal of stress, and the potential for child abuse is significant (Senn, Carey, & Coury-Doniger, 2011), although the high rate of maltreatment inflicted by adolescent mothers on their children may be due to their histories as abuse victims rather than their immaturity. Moreover, psychosocial adjustment is an important predictor of a variety of outcomes for teen mothers. For example, one longitudinal study found that prenatal socioemotional adjustment (as measured by social competence, self-esteem, depression, anxiety, and attachment to mother) predicted later parenting stress, child abuse potential, and maternal socioemotional functioning, and was also the best predictor of their children's later socioemotional adjustment (Whiteman, Borkowski, Keogh, & Weed, 2001). Finally, Hunt-Morse (2002) found that teenage mothers with higher levels of psychosocial development experienced less parenting stress, reported using fewer dysfunctional parenting practices, and were more confident in their maternal role and in their ability to overcome parenting barriers.

INTERVENTION STRATEGIES FOCUSED ON RISKY SEX

Executive functioning in adolescents plays a key role in sexual risk-taking behaviors and should be an emerging area for prevention and intervention efforts. For instance, stronger working memory (a key feature of executive functioning) predicts lower sexual risk taking in adolescents, but its buffering effect on sexual risk taking depends on the impulsivity of the adolescent. Adolescents who have a greater tendency to act without thinking and who have an inability to delay gratification (both parts of impulsivity) are at higher risk of sexual risk taking than adolescents lower on impulsivity (Khurana et al., 2015).

In his reviews of the empirical literature on pregnancy prevention, Kirby (2001, 2007) divided prevention programs into separate categories that still have great relevance today: those that focus on "nonsexual antecedents" (i.e., poverty, parental relationships, school failure, depression) and those that focus on the "sexual antecedents" of pregnancy (i.e., sexual attitudes, beliefs, and skills typically referred to as sex education or HIV prevention programs). Kirby also indicated that some approaches addressed a combination of both these areas.

Nonsexual Antecedent Program and Approaches

Programs focusing on the nonsexual antecedents of teen pregnancy address such issues as poverty, school detachment, lack of parental connections, and lack of vocational aspirations. Kirby (2001, 2007) categorized these programs into several subgroups: early childhood programs, service learning programs, vocational education programs, and other youth development programs. Although more research is needed, interesting findings are that vocational education programs alone were not effective in decreasing sexual activity, pregnancy, or contraceptive use. Children and adolescents from the early school years through high school have benefited enormously from family life education programs that address health, development, information about sexuality, family life stages, family transitions, and so on. The most effective nonsexual antecedent programs were service learning programs. That is, engaging young girls and teens in service programs reduced their rate of teen pregnancy. School-based interventions for pregnant and parenting adolescents also significantly decreased the occurrence of repeat births (Key, Barbosa, & Owens, 2001).

Several broad-based interventions that have a positive impact on risky sexual behavior as well as other risks are discussed elsewhere in this book. Specifically, Communities that Care (CtC) covered in Chapter 2, and the Good Behavior Game (GBG) in Chapter 13 are examples of nonsexual antecedent programs. Of course, these nonsexual antecedent programs and others contain common elements that address a variety of risky behaviors above and beyond those of a sexual nature. Many of the recommendations for program development, as well as counselor and human service worker behaviors, that we make throughout this book involve content, attitudes, skills, and processes that are broadly helpful for many at-risk children and adolescents. To avoid redundancy, we leave the discussion of these programs to other chapters (e.g., see Chapter 12).

Sexual Antecedent Programs

Programs in this category deal with sex itself. Most target behavior is in two areas: abstinence, enabling teens to avoid pregnancy or STIs, and/or the correct and consistent use of contraception to reduce the risk of pregnancy or STIs. These apparently divergent positions are particularly controversial with people expressing very diverse views from total abstinence until marriage to free accesses to free contraceptives for sexually active teens. In addition, some believe that the opposite position detracts and diminishes the other position. This creates a difficult position for school and health agency personnel who are trying to administer sex education programs. One resolution to this impasse is to leave it to parents. Yet many young people receive little systematic information about sexuality from their parents. Many parents are intimidated by the subject, and some possess limited or inadequate information themselves. A 2013 study found that parents reported to be more accepting of oral contraceptive pills (59%) and condoms (about 50%) compared with more effective methods of birth control like intrauterine devices and implants (Hartman et al., 2013). However, parental recognition of their teen's autonomy was associated with greater parental acceptability of clinicians providing their adolescent with contraceptives (regardless of the specific type of method being offered).

Differences in ideology on sex education policy continue in the United States, regardless of the data that could and should drive decision making and help break the impasse. Abstinence-only sex education costs federal and state governments well over $1.5 billion in the first decade of the century and still has major proponents. In 2014, Congress provided $55 million for abstinence-until-marriage programs. At the request of the Obama administration, Congress also provided roughly $185 million for medically accurate and age-appropriate sex education programs. In 2014, 35 states and the District of Columbia required that public schools provide some form of sex or STI/HIV education. Most states also currently place requirements on how abstinence or contraception should be handled when included in a school district's curriculum, even when the instruction is not mandated. As of 2014, guidance was still heavily weighted toward stressing abstinence, with 19 states requiring that instruction on the importance of being married before engaging in sexual activity. By contrast, although many states allow or even require that information about contraception be covered, none require that it be stressed (Boonstra, 2014). Meanwhile, by 2010, public health centers served nearly 1.5 million teens and helped teens prevent 360,000 unintended pregnancies; 190,000 of which would have resulted in unplanned births and 110,000 in abortions if these health centers were not available. In 2013, Planned Parenthood alone averted an estimated 515,000 unplanned pregnancies and 216,000 abortions because of their contraceptive services. Thirty-four percent of Planned Parenthood health services are geared toward contraceptive services, while 3% goes toward abortion services (Planned Parenthood, 2014). President Obama's Affordable Care Act has expanded funding for public health centers (Boonstra, 2014).

Although sex education is still controversial in some communities, less than 5% of parents excuse their children from sex education classes (Boonstra, 2014). Despite sentiments to the contrary, HIV and sex education programs do not increase the frequency of sexual activity or hasten the onset of intercourse. The Center for Innovative Public Health Research (2015) reports that many sex and HIV education programs have actually been found to delay the onset of sex, reduce its frequency and number of partners, and increase contraceptive use. An overwhelming majority of Americans support providing sex education in junior and senior high schools. Most parents want students to have information to protect themselves against unplanned pregnancy and STIs and oppose the portion of the federal law that funds abstinence-only-until-marriage education (Advocates for Youth, 2015). Of course, teaching young people about contraception while denying them access to it is unlikely to be effective when young people begin to have sex. Abstinence-only education as a state policy is ineffective in preventing teenage pregnancy and may actually be contributing to the high teenage pregnancy rates in the United States (Stanger-Hall & Hall, 2011).

Abstinence, although a critical element in prevention programs, cannot be counted on as the only means to reduce unintended pregnancy or HIV/AIDS/STIs among teenagers. In fact, programs promoting both abstinence and consistent contraceptive use have demonstrated delay of initial sexual activity (a significant protective factor) if the information is provided in a culturally appropriate fashion. Longer-term intervention programs (such as longer courses in middle school) also show more lasting positive effects than short-term interventions (National Campaign to Prevent Teen Pregnancy/Child Trends, 2005), especially if they include booster sessions (Pedlow & Carey, 2004). Access to information about human sexuality, reproduction, and birth control is a prerequisite for responsible sexual behavior. At the same time, adolescent well-being is optimized when sexual intercourse occurs later versus earlier in adolescence and in the context of a personal commitment based on caring, mutual consent and respect, the exercise of personal responsibility, and includes steps to avoid both STIs and unintended pregnancy.

Risky sex prevention programs have a number of common characteristics (Kirby, 2007). There is a clear focus on reducing risky sexual behavior. They deliver and consistently reinforce a clear message about abstaining from sexual activity, and if not, then condoms and other contraception methods are essential. They provide basic and accurate information about the risks of teen sexual activity and ways to avoid intercourse or use protection. They include activities that address social pressures that influence sexual behavior. Successful programs provide examples of and practice with communication, negotiation, and refusal skills, and they tailor program goals, methods, and materials to the age, sexual experience, and culture of the students. Such programs are based on theoretical approaches that have been demonstrated to influence other health-related behavior as well. They identify specific important sexual antecedents to be targeted, employ teaching methods that involve the participants and personalize the information, last a sufficient length of time, and select teachers or peer leaders who believe in the program and provide them with adequate training. By and large, to avoid negative outcomes people need a variety of skills, such as skills in decision making, assertiveness, and learning how to regulate intimacy and how to behave in accordance with their personal values and boundaries (Kirby, 2007).

Any skill-building program designed to alter sexual behavior needs to personalize the information so that young people apply it directly and concretely to themselves. Self-understanding aids in personalizing information and increasing motivation. Awareness of the purpose and goals of one's behavior is an extremely important component of self-understanding. Young people at risk for pregnancy need to be encouraged to explore and understand why they are engaging in sexual activity, and especially why they are unwilling to use methods that prevent pregnancy and disease. Such understanding helps the young person make better decisions. Adults who work with young people at risk for pregnancy need to understand these underlying goals and purposes as well because they are in a position to help young people make better decisions. A method to expose these goals and purposes is described in the following section.

SPECIFIC INTERVENTION: AN ADLERIAN MODEL

One of the best models for understanding child and adolescent behavior is found in Alfred Adler's (1930, 1964; Ferguson, 2001) concepts of social interest, mistaken goals, and purposive behavior. Rudolf Dreikurs (1964, 1967), the foremost interpreter of Adler's ideas as they apply to the American scene, added another concept: the goals of misbehavior. These concepts are useful for understanding and dealing with a wide range of adolescent problems and issues, and we apply them here specifically as a tool for responding to teenagers in the sexual realm. The concepts are also helpful for younger children. Indeed, Adler, and later Dreikurs, developed child guidance clinics that provided education and counseling to families and parents, not infrequently with very young children. Many school counselors use these ideas to assist young children as well.

In the following paragraphs, we first present the general framework of the model, and then we detail its specific application to issues of sexuality. These recommendations are not a substitute for sexual health education but are adjunctive to it.

According to Adler, much individual behavior is directed toward finding a place or position in the group. All young people need a sense of belonging and an arena in which to contribute. Low-risk children find belonging first in their families and later in the school environment with peers and adults. In their interaction with their social environment, they find ways to contribute to the common welfare. These contributions increase their social interest, build their feelings of self-worth, and solidify their sense of belonging. Unfortunately, other young people struggle to belong and are frustrated in their attempts to contribute to the social group. But the need to belong continues, and these youth often behave in ways that are less acceptable in the mistaken belief that a particular action will fulfill a certain social need. These mistaken beliefs contribute to what Dreikurs calls the goals of misbehavior. Negative, antisocial, and self-defeating behavior has an underlying purpose—to allow the individual to fit into the group. One way to help at-risk children is to attend to the underlying purposiveness of their behavior: First, to understand their mistaken goals and to respond more appropriately to them; and second, to reveal to the young people their own underlying goals and the purposiveness of their actions.

Purposiveness of Behavior

Purpose is not the same as cause. Cause is past-oriented; purpose is future-oriented. Cause implies a need to search through past history to identify what event, person, or situation brought about the child's present behavior. It also implies that the individual has no agency or influence over his or her own behavior. Purposiveness reflects the goals the youth wants to achieve and the consequences he or she anticipates. In this sense, the young person's behavior is a means to an end and is based on his or her perceptions of reality. Young people behave in ways that they believe will lead to desirable consequences and help them avoid unpleasant ones. Purpose operates in the present and looks toward the future, toward the outcome of behavior, and therefore is more directly open to intervention. Probably, the purpose of some adolescent sexual activity is associated with an underlying tendency to nonconformity. In other cases, for girls their purpose may be self-destructive, especially when prenatal care is neglected.

Goals of Misbehavior

In the Adler/Dreikurs model, a young person's misbehavior may be designed to achieve one or more of four goals: (a) attention (the child wants service and attention), (b) power (the child wants to be boss), (c) revenge (the child desires to hurt others), and (d) inadequacy or assumed disability (the child wants to be left alone). Although young people usually do not think about their behavior in these terms, they do see their actions as logical. Whether they seek attention, attempt to assert power, take revenge, or capitalize on their inadequacy, the corresponding misbehavior is designed to get special recognition. Their behavior, regardless of their goal, results from the belief that this is the most effective way to function in the group, which includes the family and the peer cluster.

Attention

When children do not achieve acceptance and belonging through useful contributions to the family, they may seek inclusion through attention. At first they may seek attention through socially acceptable means. If these efforts are unsuccessful, they may try any of a vast array of negative behaviors calculated to get attention. The purpose of such attention-getting mechanisms (AGMs) is to engage the adult. The young person's underlying goal is to get adults to pay attention. The adult's intervention reinforces the young person's desire for attention, because it's better to be punished than to be ignored.

Attention-getting behaviors are usually negative, but overly cooperative behavior may also be a bid for special attention. It is sometimes difficult to distinguish between behavior that stems from a genuine willingness to be helpful and behavior that is aimed primarily at getting attention. If the youth's behavior seems directed to becoming the best or better than the other children (the teacher's pet), he or she is probably motivated by a desire for attention. Children and adolescents need to be able to derive satisfaction from performing positive, cooperative behaviors rather than simply from the reinforcement that follows. Consider an adolescent girl who gains satisfaction from her prosocial acts only when adults notice them. If her siblings (at home) and classmates (at school) are more successful at gaining adults' attention, she may try to gain attention by being the worst among her peers. Many youth behave negatively because the positive roles they really want are already "taken."

Recognizing when attention is the goal of misbehavior is not simple, but it may be inferred when the adult's initial reaction to the behavior is annoyance, irritation, or surface anger, and the child responds to correction by temporarily stopping the disturbing action. Essentially, the scolding, coaxing, helping, reminding, and so forth provide the desired attention, so the behavior stops—temporarily. Understanding the purpose of irresponsible sexual behavior is a more complex task because the behavior may be aimed not only at adults but at peers as well. In some cases, AGMs evoke attention and concern from permissive or indifferent parents. In other cases, AGMs derive from a desire for attention and affection from peers or a specific peer. Sometimes the AGM is directed toward the idealized infant in the hope that the baby may fill an emotional gap left by rejecting parents or the romantic partner. In each instance, the need to belong, to feel needed, to be loved, or to feel increased self-esteem underlies the AGMs.

As part of a research project, one of the authors was debriefing eighth-grade students after they filled out questionnaires about stress. One student, a 12-year-old eighth grader, offered shyly, "Well, I don't have a boyfriend, but I met a boy at the mall and I let him put it in me. I know that's how you get a baby, but he said he took it out in time. I hope he's gonna meet me there again." In the course of a subsequent conversation, it was quickly apparent that she was not interested in physical pleasure, nor did she seem to have romantic notions about babies; she simply wanted to feel special.

Boys exhibit purposiveness and mistaken goals in their sexual behavior in experiencing sexual interaction as a means of gaining affection and attention from girls. Sometimes boys establish desired reputations as their sexual exploits gain the attention of their male peers. In some subgroups, fathering a child increases the boy's status and brings him into what he perceives to be a more mature and powerful stage of development.

Power

When the goal of misbehavior is power, young people attempt to establish their position in the group by dominating, controlling, and manipulating adults and peers. They demonstrate their control and power by refusing to be commanded and by breaking rules. Many use manipulation to demonstrate to themselves and to the world that they do have power over others. If the adult responds to the power struggle by exerting more control or power to force compliance, the young person becomes even more convinced of the value of power. The goal is less to win the struggle than to get the adult involved in it. Once the adult engages in the battle, the teenager has won, regardless of the outcome.

If the adult's anger goes beyond mere annoyance and if the anger is coupled with feelings of being challenged and provoked, then the young person's goal is probably to gain power. The sentences that run through the adult's mind at this point also provide clues to the nature of this power struggle ("I'll show you who's boss around here." "I'll make you do it." "You can't get away with that."). When the adult behaves in accordance with these thoughts, the adolescent may escalate his or her actions or comply outwardly while subtly sabotaging the adult's efforts. Either way, the teenager wins the power struggle.

The underlying goal of power in sexual acting out may be directed against parents who are inconsistent, too permissive, or too strict. On the surface the young person appears to be expressing independence, but in reality the behavior is designed to establish a position vis-à-vis the parents. Willingness or unwillingness to engage in sex may provide girls and boys with perceived power over others or over a specific partner. Willingness to coerce a girl into unprotected intercourse may be based on the mistaken belief that a subsequent pregnancy would secure the relationship. Boys may use sexual activity to demonstrate independence and power over their parents. With their partner or even someone unknown to them, boys may use sex as a physical expression of domination or control through rape and other forms of sexual assault. Sometimes the boy's domineering attitude and his unwillingness to use a condom are attempts to demonstrate power. Assuming that girls are responsible for contraception and denying fatherhood when pregnancy occurs are other ways in which the young male may express domination and power over others through sexual behavior.

Revenge

The child who seeks revenge is extremely discouraged and poses the greatest problem. If children have not been able to attain and maintain a desired position by gaining attention or power, they may consider that the only other way to gain attention is to hurt someone. It is as if they conclude, "I can't be liked and I don't have power—but I can be hated." This often-violent antagonism provides them with a specific role to play in the group.

Revenge is sought only after a long series of failures has convinced the young person of his or her utter lack of belonging. Revenge is frequently the result of an unrecognized problem (depression, severe learning difficulties, CD) and of unrealistic expectations and pressures by significant adults. The unrecognized problem may prevent the young person from accomplishing a particular task. Assuming negative motives, adults punish the youth for "not trying." Young people are hurt by such encounters and want to hurt back. In taking this position, they are likely to evoke responses that justify the continuation of revenge, and the cycle escalates.

Feelings of intense anger with underlying hurt and shock in response to a young person's behavior indicate to the adult that the goal of misbehavior is probably revenge. The adult may think: "How could he possibly do that to me?" "This kid is just nasty and unlovable." "How could she be so vicious and cruel?" If the adult's response is full of anger, the adolescent will continue trying to get even. If the adult responds with hurt, sadness, and tears, the youth may actually smile (see Box 8.3).

Premature and irresponsible sexual activity is sometimes a way to get back at parents. One of the authors of this book worked with an angry father whose son had dressed in women's makeup and clothing and had sexually explicit pictures taken of himself on the family's front porch in daylight. The son left these photos for his father to find, which achieved the desired effect. Sexual behavior can also be used to obtain revenge on the partner if one feels rejected. The person who acts out sexually may intend to get back at the former partner. So, ultimately, the dynamics of revenge are played out not only within the family but also between partners.

Box 8.3	Lying for Revenge

Some years ago we were counseling with several teenagers and their families. The model we were using called for a large-group meeting that included both parents and teenagers, in which participants discussed family and school concerns. We then broke into smaller groups, the adults in one group and the young people in another.

After several weekly sessions, a girl who had a particularly stormy relationship with her mother used the large-group session as an opportunity to tell her parents that she thought she was pregnant. Her mother's horror and embarrassment were vividly evident. Later, during the session with peers and siblings, the girl reported that she was not pregnant and currently wasn't even sexually active. Her earlier false self-disclosure, she concluded, was intended to hurt her mother: a clear instance of revenge. In a later family session, this incident became a springboard that enabled us to help her look at the self-defeating aspects of her behavior and to help her family confront their own dysfunction.

Assumed Inadequacy

Children and teenagers who expect failure rely on their assumed inadequacy to escape participation in the group and family system. They want to be left alone. As long as nothing is expected of them, they can still appear to be members of the group. Some children and adolescents believe that by hiding behind a display of real or imagined inferiority they can avoid even more embarrassing and humiliating experiences. Those who feel inadequate and incapable of functioning will not try, whether their deficiency is real or merely assumed.

This goal poses serious problems for parents, teachers, and counselors because these young people realize that underachievement and lack of effort are the most effective ways to keep adults involved with them. Thus it is convenient for them to continue their lack of effort even when it is no longer necessary. Adults often fail to distinguish between a real lack of ability and a lack of ability that the child or adolescent merely assumes.

Feelings of despair, frustration, and hopelessness in the adult are good signs that the young person is operating on the assumption of inadequacy. Adults should reflect carefully upon the feelings aroused by a young person's misbehavior because whatever they feel is often exactly what the young person intends them to feel. Despair and hopelessness may be what the child wants, but when the adult responds with despair, inadequacy is reinforced. Such responses encourage continued inadequacy.

Assumed inadequacy in the sexual realm may be expressed by lack of assertiveness regarding sexual activity. The term *assumed* suggests that these adolescents have the skills to resist sexual pressure—from a partner or from peers—or to insist on protection if they do engage in sex, but that they do not use these skills. Of course, we know that some young people's inadequacy is not assumed; the lack of skill is real. In such situations the concerned adult can use specific cognitive and behavioral strategies to provide success experiences and reduce the young person's sense of inadequacy. In Chapter 11 we provide a model for building skills, and in Chapter 12 we discuss specific cognitive and behavioral strategies from which young people may benefit.

Summary

Having reviewed the four goals, we must emphasize that young people are often in pursuit of more than one goal at the same time and that their goals can shift depending on the people with whom they interact. Some young people actually pursue all four goals at one time, a situation that causes parents, counselors, teachers, and other adults a great deal of distress. Some children or teenagers may have one goal at school, another goal with their peers, and still another at home. If the misbehavior is to be understood, the child's actions have to be seen as a whole, as part of the total social environment, not as emanating solely from one situation.

Sexual behavior does not have an underlying negative purpose for all teens. Needs gratification, reinforcement, pleasure, and desire for warmth, closeness, and validation are all components of sexuality. When teens become pregnant, mixed goals are probably the rule rather than the exception. Allie Andrews, for example, appears to use sex to gain attention from boys. Further, lacking a positive position at home, she has progressed from sex-as-attention to sex-as-power to show her stepfather that she counts. Unfortunately, his criticisms and accusations have led her now to use sex to shock and hurt him. She has adopted the goal of revenge (on her stepfather) and uses her sexual behavior, at least partly, as a way of getting back at him.

Among the methods that have proved helpful in efforts to intervene with young people who are struggling with these four mistaken goals are corrective procedures, logical and natural consequences, and encouragement. We describe these techniques in the context of risky sexual behavior; however, they can be used with any kind of misbehavior.

Corrective Procedures

Corrective procedures involve (a) altering adults' responses to adolescents' risky sexual behavior and (b) helping young people to interpret the goals of their sexual activities. Altering the adult's responses (e.g., the parent, teacher, or counselor) begins with identifying the feelings aroused by the youth's behavior (anger, disgust, resentment, despair, and so forth) and then not acting on those feelings. Helping young people interpret their goals is a bit more complex. If you ask them why they didn't use a condom, the response may be an honest "I don't know" or a hindsight rationalization rather than a factual account of motives: "I just finished a period and didn't think I would get pregnant" rather than "At that moment, I didn't care what happened to me, even if I got some disease, I was so lonely." The sensitive counselor or teacher can help young people by proposing some possible goals of their behavior. Such a confrontation can be the first step toward change. To confront the behavior, however, is not to label it ("You're being stupid"). Labeling has no meaning for the young person, does not explain the behavior, and does nothing to change it. Confrontation helps adolescents understand their own motivation and gives them the option of continuing or discontinuing their behavior. Sometimes the behavior loses its appeal once the underlying intention has been brought into the open; other times the young person is able to identify more effective and less harmful ways of getting his or her needs met.

The most useful approaches are tentative, beginning with "Could it be that ..." or "I was thinking that maybe ...." All questions must be asked in a nonjudgmental way, and not during an argument. It is not enough to help young people identify their goals; it is important to provide them with alternative and less self-defeating goals. All corrective procedures should be geared toward helping young people choose more constructive goals and behaviors.

Corrective Procedures for AGMs

When the goal of risky sexual behavior is attention, the following questions may be helpful: "Could it be that you want him to see you as more special than other girls, by sleeping with him?" "Do other guys respond differently, say, with more respect or admiration, when they know you've had sex?" Recognize that punishing, giving service, coaxing, and scolding are forms of attention and may only serve to reinforce the negative behavior. Although ignoring the behavior while it occurs is normally a corrective procedure for AGMs, this strategy isn't useful in the case of risky sexual behavior because adults are not typically present. However, if the young person is bragging about his or her sexual escapades, ignoring the behavior in the moment may be the most appropriate response.

Corrective Procedures for Power

Interpretive questions for power-seekers might include, "Could it be that you want to show your mother that she isn't in control of you?" or "It seems to me as though you want her to see you as stronger and in charge, as if that will make her think you are more masculine." It is important to recognize and acknowledge that the young person does indeed have power and choices regarding sexual behavior, even though that behavior has consequences. Refrain from engaging in arguments over sexual behavior, and rather than insisting that rules be followed, put energy into being consistent about imposing consequences when rules are broken. Be willing to negotiate on issues where it is possible for you to do so. And, outside of the context of arguments, help the young person identify other means to establish a sense of power in ways that do not pose health risks to himself or herself or to others. This may include broadening the youth's circle of activities and engaging his or her leadership and responsibility skills.

In addition to interpreting goals, provide alternative goals that are less self-defeating. One of the authors worked with an adolescent male client who had been having unprotected sex with an older young woman in his father's garage. He quite readily admitted that part of him wanted to be caught, to show his father he was "practically a man" now. After several counseling sessions he decided to, at least temporarily, abandon this tactic and get his ear pierced instead. This action provoked a confrontation with his father that allowed him to express some of his resentment quite directly. When last seen, he and his father had begun a tense but hopeful process of negotiating a new set of freedoms and responsibilities.

Corrective Procedures for Revenge

It is of critical importance that the adult refrains from punishment and retaliation and does not take the young person's revenge behavior personally or show feelings of hurt. When the adult is also the parent, this can be especially difficult, and the parent will need support and time to learn better responses. Questions to help the young person identify his or her goals might include, "Could it be that you want to punish your mother for her boyfriend's behavior?" or "I'm wondering if you are consciously trying to hurt me, and if you are, I want to understand that."

Corrective Procedures for Assumed Inadequacy

When the child sees himself or herself as a failure, it may be helpful to ask, "Do you think you're going to flunk out, so you might as well have a child to take care of?" or "I wonder if you think you don't deserve to be protected against infections." It is important that the adult helper shows encouragement and optimism in the face of the young person's despair. Arranging situations in which he or she can experience success may be critical, and this may require engaging the assistance of teachers, tutors, parents, and siblings.

Some general suggestions for corrective procedures in response to risky sexual activity also include participation in skill-building groups and activities to increase self-esteem, assertiveness, and self-efficacy (see Chapter 12); individual, group, or family counseling; social competency skills building; and sex education for the young person and parents. It is important that all interventions and corrections be geared toward empowering adolescents to identify healthier ways to meet their goals of belonging, inclusion, and recognition.

Natural and Logical Consequences

Natural and logical consequences are also effective ways of dealing with misbehavior (see Chapters 12 and 14). Traditional discipline involves reward and punishment: Adults punish kids for unacceptable behavior and reward them for complying with their wishes and commands. Natural and logical consequences differ from reward and punishment in a number of ways and have certain advantages. The goal of consequences is to teach young people responsibility, cooperation, respect for order and the rights of others, good judgment, and careful decision making, and to give them a sense of control and choice. The goal is not to force submission and compliance, nor is it to obtain retribution and revenge (often the real goal of punishment). To some degree, reliance on consequences removes from the adult the function of meting out rewards and punishment, which de-emphasizes the traditional authority position of the adult. When authority is de-emphasized, young people feel more independent, and that feeling itself decreases undesirable behavior.

Natural consequences result directly from the behavior. Examples are getting an STI or becoming pregnant. Because natural consequences in this case threaten health and safety, logical consequences should be used in the hope that the natural consequences will never be experienced. Clear and unequivocal communication about the natural consequences of risky sexual behavior should be accompanied by encouragement to engage in healthier behavior. Logical consequences are determined in advance, are logically connected to the behavior, and are applied when the misbehavior occurs; for example, "If you have your boyfriend over while I'm at work one more time, you will not be permitted to have any friends over for one month." It is important that logical consequences are not arbitrary or invoked during the heat of an argument. Consequences are administered and experienced in an impersonal, matter-of-fact fashion, without moralizing, judgment, or excessive emotional involvement.

Sometimes another young person can share natural consequences in a way that communicates more effectively than adults can do so. A student of one of the authors gave a speech on how becoming pregnant earlier in high school had drastically changed her life. She did not "preach" to her classmates, nor was she dramatic in her descriptions. She simply told her story. Her straightforward, unromantic portrayal of daily life had a profound effect on her classmates and generated a lively discussion on the belief that "it could never happen to me." Although the actual effects of her speech cannot be measured, her matter-of-fact and nonjudgmental approach certainly provoked a good deal of nondefensive discussion. Exposing students to the natural and logical consequences of risky sexual behavior through other people's lives may promote some behavior change so they do not have to experience the consequences themselves.

Reliance on consequences is intended to help children develop responsibility for their own behavior. It is not meant to be a vehicle to express the adult's displeasure or anger. Care should be taken that the nonverbal aspects of the interaction do not turn it into covert punishment and thereby defeat the purpose of the entire procedure.

Encouragement

Encouragement greatly enhances the relationship between child and adult and reduces the child's need to resort to undesirable behavior to feel significant. Encouragement is the process of increasing young people's sense of worth and self-esteem by focusing on their actual strengths and assets, not on expected or potential strengths. Encouragement conveys to young people that the adult has faith in them, trusts and respects them, and values them as people despite any mistakes or flaws.

All too often children and teens are exposed to ongoing discouraging experiences. Some adults focus only on the mistakes children make, attributing them to basic defects of character or ability (e.g., "He's just lazy," or "She's always been clumsy."). Some adults set standards that are difficult or impossible to reach; they compare young people to each other in such a way that there is always a loser. The discouragement and self-doubt that arise from these practices may be manifested in misbehavior and in useless, inappropriate attempts to gain recognition.

Encouragement should be a regular aspect of interactions with all adolescents and children. When a young person is deeply discouraged, the teacher or counselor has the difficult task of counteracting a host of negative experiences. Adults can offer encouragement by recognizing effort and improvement as well as accomplishment, expressing appreciation, separating the deed from the doer when the deed is unacceptable, focusing on the child's or teenager's unique talents and contributions, and treating youth with respect and courtesy. Nonverbal messages are also important. Listening without interruption; using a friendly, nonjudgmental tone of voice; treating mistakes as opportunities for learning rather than as failures; and choosing the right moment for a remark are as important as the choice of words.

Keep in mind that some words that purport to be encouraging have the opposite effect. Some ill-advised attempts at encouragement include competitive encouragement ("See what you can do when you try?") or coupling encouragement with expectations ("You got an A; that's great. Now let's keep up that average."), expressing surprise at success ("You did? I never thought you could do it!"), using someone else as an example ("If Kristin can do it, you can too, I'm sure."), and blaming someone else for a young person's failure ("If it hadn't been for that referee, I'm sure you'd have won.").

In general, anything which perpetuates low self-esteem, which lowers confidence in a child's ability to master problem situations, or which fosters feelings of inadequacy and insignificance is discouraging. Anything that gives a sense of being an important member of the group and a feeling that the child's participation, contribution, and cooperation are valued is encouraging. Above all, it is important for young people to learn that they are good enough as they are.

CONCLUSION

Premature and irresponsible sexual activity, teen pregnancy, and HIV/AIDS/STIs are significant social problems. Understanding some of the environmental, family, and peer dynamics that young people encounter and helping adolescents change the goals of their misbehavior may help prevent some of these problems. Because of the long-term consequences of teenage sexual activity, it is critical to provide young people with accurate, comprehensive sex education, including the skills they need to carry out their own informed decisions about sexuality. The growing literature on successful prevention programs indicates that there are specific characteristics associated with reducing pregnancy and unprotected sex, increasing abstinence, and delaying first intercourse.

Young people's optimistic and positive beliefs about themselves and their capacity to set the direction of their future are an important part of a comprehensive effort to prevent pregnancy and risky sexual behavior. One of the best contraceptives is providing young people with a meaningful future, and a future requires opportunities to build academic and work-related skills, job opportunities, and life-planning skills. Providing greater funding to support prevention, education, and economic opportunity is an important method to reduce problems related to teen sexual activity.

Juvenile Delinquency and Youth Violence

CHAPTER

9

When I feel bad and can't do anything about it,

Don't even know it, maybe,

I can still pound somebody, smash a windshield, maybe.

At least I have a good reason for feeling bad.

And so what if they do too?

When I feel bad, I can do something about it.

Jacking lunch money or something from the store shelf,

or the Jacksons' yard, or even living room, maybe, helps.

The rush covers up bad feelings.

And so what if the feeling becomes me?

When I feel bad, the kids on the street help

I like colors and coats and bright-green shoelaces.

Out here, bad is good.

Being feared is better.

CHAPTER OUTLINE

- The Scope and Nature of Antisocial Behavior and Delinquency
  - Family Aggression and Violence
  - School Problems
  - Juvenile Delinquency and Vandalism
- Origins of the Problem
  - Society at Large
  - Guns
- Box 9.1 Beat the System
  - Media
    Television and Film
    Video Games
    Music: Rap and Acid Rock
    Internet Cyberspace

- Box 9.2 When Adults Fail
  - Communities and Neighborhoods Environment
  - Family Environment
  - School Environment
    Conduct Disorder

- Box 9.3 Training for Violence
  - Peer Group Environment
    Rejection by Low-Risk Peers
    Membership in a Deviant Peer Group
    Rejection of Low-Risk Peers
  - Onset of Delinquent Behavior
  - Gang Involvement

In this chapter we discuss (a) the nature and scope of conduct disorder, antisocial behavior, delinquency, and gang activity; (b) the roots of conduct disorder; (c) the development and consequences of delinquency; (d) youth gangs; and (e) school shooters. The developmental and ecological model of antisocial behavior (see Figure 9.1) has relevance here. Because society has witnessed an increasingly lethal dimension of youth violence, we include a section specifically on the school shooter and highlight differing experiences and ecological pressures that contribute to school shootings. We also present several interventions that focus on preventing youth violence, including Glasser's choice theory and Reality Therapy.

THE SCOPE AND NATURE OF ANTISOCIAL BEHAVIOR AND DELINQUENCY

Antisocial behavior refers to any activity which conflicts with social norms. Sometimes it includes criminal activity, but not always. Delinquency implies breaking the law. Not infrequently, antisocial behavior and delinquency include violence. Violence takes many forms, among them organized gang violence, school and community shootings, and self-inflicted violence (which we discuss in the next chapter). Antisocial behavior, delinquency, and violence have common roots and similar consequences. Some of the most frequently encountered antisocial behaviors are (a) expressions of aggression within the family and school; (b) problems such as vandalism; (c) nonindex crimes such as substance use and running away; (d) index crimes such as theft, robbery, and larceny; (e) gang membership; and (f) school shootings. Although these areas are related, we discuss them separately to make clear their unique characteristics.

Family Aggression and Violence

Family aggression and violence occur with alarming frequency and can lead to the development of severe antisocial behavior with children witnessing a large percentage of the nation's homicides. Violence is the leading cause of injury to women in the home, and 74% of all murder-suicides involved an intimate partner, with 96% being women killed by their intimate partner (American Psychological Association, 2015). Between 2 million and 4 million women are battered by their partners each year; perhaps, an estimated 3.5 million in their homes (P. T. McWhirter, 2008).

Chronic exposure to violence can have a detrimental developmental effect on children, including identification with the aggressor, truncated moral development, and pathological adaptation to violence. Children who observe parents using violence observe not only the violent behavior but also the circumstances, the emotional triggers, and the consequences of violence as well. These observations significantly influence behaviors.

A related problem in families is poor parental response to children who are irritable, inattentive, and impulsive (Feder, Levant, & Dean, 2010). These difficult children are often responded to with anger and hostility, followed by appeasement, leading to inconsistent discipline. When children view the world as hostile and inconsistent, they often attempt to get their way regardless of social rules. These children are potentially violent later in life. Young people who experience a negative, neglectful home environment that leads to placement in foster care also may often become engaged in youth violence (Reupert, Maybery, Nicholson, Gopfert, & Seeman, 2015). On any given day, tens of thousands of U.S. children and adolescents are living away from their families and in foster care (Annie E. Casey Foundation, 2015). Many youth leave families in which they experience emotional and physical neglect or emotional, physical, and sexual abuse. Some young people are, in effect, discarded, forced to leave homes with no alternative care and prevented from returning home (Montgomery, Thompson, & Barczyk, 2011). A lack of connection to, escape from, and rejection from families can be contributors to antisocial behavior and of all of these factors are related to future youth violence (Mikulincer & Shaver, 2014).

School Problems

Problem behavior at school is often a precursor to more severe destructive behavior and even antisocial behavior. Not surprisingly, aggression early in a child's life is one of the best predictors of delinquency in later years. The general principle is that less serious problem behaviors precede more serious delinquency. Thus disruptive and delinquent behavior generally progresses in an orderly, sequential fashion from authority conflict (e.g., defiance and disobedience), to covert actions (e.g., lying and stealing), to overt actions (e.g., fighting, delinquency, and violent behavior). Studies suggest that overall aggression in the classroom increases individual aggression (e.g., Powers, Bierman, & the Conduct Problems Prevention Research Group, 2013). Children in classrooms with higher overall levels of aggression are at increased risk of higher levels of aggressive strategies, aggressive fantasies, and hostile attributions. This higher level of classroom aggression even affects future behavior. Classroom aggression in the first grade has been shown to increase boys' risk of being aggressive in middle school. Further, the more aggressive first-grade boys who were in more highly aggressive first-grade classrooms were at a much higher risk for aggressive behavior 6 or 7 years later (Kellam et al., 2011). Early aggression patterns characterized by high frequency, intense severity, and occurrence across multiple settings predict a number of ominous outcomes later on, including victimization of others, delinquency, and violence (Farrington, Loeber, & Ttofi, 2012). Victimization can have lasting effects both for children and teachers (Morgan, Kemp, Rathbun, Robers, & Synder, 2014).

Juvenile Delinquency and Vandalism

Vandalism accounts for millions of dollars in damage to school property, parks, and playgrounds; street signs and billboards; museums and libraries; buses and trains; and numerous other venues. Such behaviors are often the first steps in full-blown delinquency. In fact, as "high-level" aggression, such as student fights, assaults on teachers, weapon violations, youth gangs, increases, vandalism diminishes. But aggression toward both property and people is learned behavior. Some children who are oppositional develop into preadolescents with conduct disorder, who may engage in delinquent behaviors as older adolescents. So, young people who engage in vandalism often begin to engage in assaultive behavior. Indeed, the motivations for vandalism suggest underlying feelings and attitudes such as disconnection from school and peers; vindication for perceived wrongs; and anger, rage, and frustration and indicate more serious future problems.

The juvenile arrest rate for offenses in the Violent Crime Index (robbery, aggravated assault, forcible rape, and murder) has continued to decrease from 1993, the peak year for youth violence (Office of Juvenile Justice Delinquency Prevention [OJJDP], 2010). Ironically, most people continue to believe that juvenile crime is increasing, perhaps because the media sensationalize crime, particularly when it is violent and involves young victims or perpetrators. Following the national trend of "get tough on youth crime," a number of states enacted laws to prosecute young juvenile offenders as adults. A 14-year-old alleged murderer being tried as an adult makes headline news, continuing reports of the trial often go on for weeks and months, and subsequent legal and sentencing ramifications—especially possible execution—go on for months and years. In addition, the public may believe that youth crime is increasing because the average age of first offense has become increasingly younger, making the problem appear worse. Finally, child and adolescent use of certain drugs, particularly methamphetamines, continues to rise and the use or possession of alcohol and other illegal drugs has also led to many youth arrests. Because drug and alcohol use is highly correlated with other law violations, their relationship highly influences social perceptions.

The decrease in youth crime rates in the United States over the past 20 years is encouraging, but it remains a significant social problem. More youth die from homicide every year than from birth defects, cancer, diabetes, flu, heart disease, pneumonia, respiratory diseases, and stroke combined (David-Ferdon & Simon, 2014). In 2008, juveniles accounted for 16% of violent crime arrests and 26% of property crime arrests; nearly 1,300 juveniles were arrested for murder, over 3,300 for forcible rape, and 56,000 for aggravated assault (Puzzanchera, 2009). In addition, the number of girls in the juvenile justice system continues to increase both in percentage and numbers. By the late-2000s, girls accounted for 30% of all juvenile arrests (Girls Study Group, 2010). Boys continue to account for more violent crime, property crime, and burglary arrests. Girls have increased status offenses (i.e., behaviors that would not be criminal if committed by an adult) such as loitering and curfew violations (150% of boys' rates) and drug violations (almost 200% of boys' rates) (Girls Study Group, 2010).

ORIGINS OF THE PROBLEM

The origins of conduct disorder, delinquent activity, and gang involvement are developmental and ecological. The model of antisocial behavior we present here provides one way to conceptualize this multifaceted and complex problem. In this model, society, community, and neighborhood are viewed as remote predictors of antisocial and delinquent behavior (see Chapter 2). As depicted in Figure 9.1, family, school, and peer influences as well as individual characteristics of youth all contribute to the ecology of the problem (Thompson & Bynum, 2016).

Society at Large

The ecological model (Bronfenbrenner, 1989) highlights the importance of the microsystems of community and neighborhood as well as other environmental influences in predicting and understanding antisocial behavior. Economic conditions—prosperity, employment rates, family income—are important and help to predict the degree and severity of antisocial behavior and delinquency. In fact, significant correlations between rates of unemployment and juvenile delinquency have been found in more than 100 American cities, and youth crime is most common in urban areas that are economically depressed (Thompson &

FIGURE 9.1 A Developmental and Ecological Model of Antisocial, Delinquent, and Gang Behavior

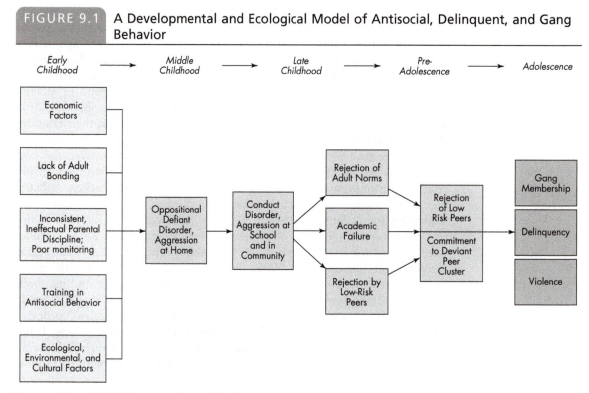

Source: Adapted from Patterson, DeBaryshe, & Ramsey, 1989.

Bynum, 2016). Other aspects of environment also play a part in the link between youth and vulnerability to delinquency (Dinkes, Kemp, & Baum, 2009). The impact of media and the access to guns are important societal components as well.

Guns

The pervasive ownership of firearms in the United States has persisted throughout American history and is unique among Western industrialized nations. In fact, the United States has more firearms than any other industrialized nation in the world. In the United States, a police officer dies by gunshot every 5 days, and a child dies by gunshot wound every 2 hours. More Americans were killed with guns between 1979 and 1997 than were killed in battle in all wars since the founding of the country in 1776.

Firearm-related death rates for both boys and girls reveal that the most vulnerable group are youth 15 to 19 years of age, a group in which the death rate from guns jump precipitously from younger teens and children. However, a child under the age of 15 in the United States is 15 times more likely to be killed by gunfire than a child growing up in Northern Ireland.

Box 9.1	Beat the System

In discussing the issue of mechanical screening for weapons with young people in an alternative high school, the adolescents we talked to scoffed at the idea of metal detectors. "Sometimes we have contests among ourselves to see who is able to sneak in a gun. You can get in trouble but if you can get it to work you get respect."

As we discussed further, they told us, "School starts at 8:15. Security people get here at 7:30; so we just get here at 7:15." When we asked them what happened if the school locked the doors until 7:30, the response was, "We just give it (the weapon) to the girls. They (the security officers) don't like to check purses."

We asked further, "Well, what if they did check the girls' purses?" "All of us get there at 8:10; they don't want us to be late to class, so we all rush by the machine." We persisted, "But what if they don't let you get by the machine and just mark you tardy?" Their response, "Oh, in that case, a friend goes in, we go to the outside fence, toss the gun over, and get it from him later."

The overall firearm-related death rate among U.S. children under 15 years of age is nearly 12 times higher than that of children in 25 industrialized countries (Prothrow-Stith, 2001). The easy and excessive availability of firearms is a major contributor to the problem. The availability of guns makes youth violence more lethal and provides school shooters with access to the means to create their mayhem. In 2007, close to 6,000 young people were murdered—an average of 16 each day—and 84% of them were killed with a firearm (CDC, 2010a). A disproportionately high number of children fall victim to homicide (and suicide and accidental shooting as well) in those areas where purchase and possession of guns is especially prevalent (Miller, Azrael, & Hemenway, 2002). A comparison of five states with the lowest gun availability compared to the five states with the highest gun availability shows the number of nongun murders is similar. Those states with high gun availability, however, have 250% more shooting murders of children. When compared to other upper-income nations, the homicide rate for U.S. children is 17 times higher (Miller et al., 2002). Among urban youth, 40% report that a gun is available in their homes. Eighty-eight percent thought it is acceptable for children and teens to have guns, yet nearly half (47%) stated that a gun had injured either a relative or themselves (Kahn, Kazimi, & Mulvihill, 2001). Youth street gangs make great use of guns to protect their "turf," establish their prestige, and to conduct criminal activity (Carlock & Lizotte, 2015).

Adults have increased gun availability to young people during the last two decades. Young people have come to believe they need handguns for their own protection. Handgun manufacturers have been quick to take advantage of this situation, making their guns more attractive to teens and marketing their product to them. In spite of efforts to raise awareness of the problem of gun accessibility, stricter gun legislation has not been passed, typically in the name of misinterpreted Second Amendment rights.

Student access to weapons is common and is especially critical for school shooters. Most of the shooters had a history of gun use, with some demonstrating a fascination with weapons and explosives. Most of the attackers had easy access to weapons and were able to take guns from their own home or from a relative or friend. Harris and Klebold, the Columbine shooters, easily purchased them. Some received them as gifts from parents. The Glock used by Kip Kinkel, the Springfield, Oregon, shooter, was a gift from his father, an attempt to demonstrate confidence in the young man who was such a concern to his parents.

Relying on metal detectors in schools to prevent weapons from entering the building provides false security. Most of the shooters made no effort to conceal their weapons. In addition, metal detectors are very expensive, require at least two operators, and are subject to relatively frequent breakdowns with high maintenance costs. Their effectiveness is very limited and at best gives a false sense of security.

Media

Television and Film

Over five decades of research on film and television viewing has documented the consistent exposure of American children to high levels of media violence. The relationship between television viewing and violence has been empirically established: There is absolutely no doubt that increased acceptance of aggressive attitudes and increased aggressive behavior are correlated with higher levels of viewing violence on television (e.g., Anderson et al., 2010; Huesmann, 2010). Further, younger children's exposure to media violence can have harmful lifelong consequences. Modern society's exposure to massive doses of violent media impacts our children. By the time the average American child graduates from elementary school, he or she will have seen more than 100,000 assorted acts of violence (e.g., rapes, assaults) and more than 8,000 murders on network television (Bushman & Anderson, 2001). If the child has access, as most do, to a VCR, DVD player, or cable television, the numbers are higher. In movies as well as television, violence dominates. Even G-rated films now contain more violence than they ever did before.

Video Games

Media games also contain violence, with 62% to 85% of the most popular video games containing violence. Even young children play violent video games. Playing violent video games—on average from 7 to 9 hours per week—can increase aggressive thoughts, feelings, and behavior in real life (Anderson & Dill, 2000), although this increased hostility and aggressiveness is more likely to be true with inconsiderate children—those low on conscientiousness and agreeableness and high on neuroticism (Markey & Markey, 2010).

Violent video games teach children aggressive solutions to conflict, and practicing aggressive strategies during the game makes it more likely that children will use those strategies when real-life conflicts arise. Although some suggest that factors other than video content may be the culprit (Adachi & Willoughby, 2011), repeated exposure to video games with violent content is associated with academic difficulties, aggression, trait hostility, and lowered empathy (Anderson et al., 2010; Bushman, Rothstein, & Anderson, 2010; Huesmann, 2010). Some of the video games are advertised by "Let the slaughter begin!" and "More fun than shooting your neighbor's cat." The games played extensively by the Columbine shooters were *Doom*, *Doom 2*, and *Duke Nukem*. Of course, Grand Theft Auto, Postal 2, Gears of War, the Manhunt series, and other, even more violent, games have replaced these. Under pressure from concerned parent groups, video game manufacturers have developed a ranking system. Unfortunately, the descriptions provide a guide to young people who seek the most violent games. It is as if the advertisements are a message to young people: "This video is of extreme violence and mayhem."

Perhaps the worst example was a nearly released game called "School Shooter: North American Tour 2012." The player of the game is the shooter, and the objective of the game is to kill unarmed students, all who happen to be people of color. The weapons used are modeled after those used in Columbine. At the end of the shooting spree, players have the option of committing suicide. Apparently, this game was never released, perhaps because its appearance created such an uproar among parent, teacher, and other citizen groups that the industry itself put pressure on the developers to cease production and release.

Music: Rap and Acid Rock

Music is another media influence that is often imbued with violence and misogynistic messages. The FBI surmised in its study that all the school shooters had listened to music lyrics that promoted violence (Band & Harpold, 1999). Youth today have access to gangsta rap and acid rock with lyrics of murder, violence, and aggression—raps about slitting parents' throats and sticking needles through eyelids—and other viciously disturbing images. Most school shooters listened to acid rock and rap more than 40 hours per week (Buchman & Funk, 1996). This overwhelming saturation by the combined media highlights aggressive and antisocial behavior and promotes an appetite for more violence. In addition, teenagers fear becoming victims, which sets the stage for "justified" violent behavior. At the same time, media violence has led to increased desensitization to violence and depersonalization toward the victims of violence.

Internet Cyberspace

As mentioned in earlier chapters, the Internet can be a positive tool for social connections and academic success for many young people. It can also have very negative effects. Gang members and other teens use cell phones and

---

Box 9.2   When Adults Fail

Megan was 13 when her neighbors fraudulently created a Myspace profile of a seemingly attractive 16-year-old boy called "Josh Evans" to cultivate a close relationship with her, with Megan informing friends that "Josh Evans" is "the kind of boy a girl would kill herself over." For over a month, "Josh" and Megan chatted and flirted in an online friendship.

But one afternoon, "Josh" turned mean. He called Megan names and they traded insults for an hour. "Josh" wrote her that he did not like the way she treated her friends. "Josh's" friends all linked to his Myspace page began to send Megan profanity-laden messages. Later, Megan and "Josh" continued to argue online. Finally, "Josh" told Megan that "the world would be a better place without you in it." She then ran sobbing to her bedroom and within the hour her mother found her hanging from a belt tied in her closet. She died the next day.

"Josh" turned out to be another mother, Lori Drew, who created an online profile to see if Megan was spreading rumors about her own daughter. The two girls had been longtime friends whose relationship soured when Megan got transferred to a different school. Lori Drew, with her own 13-year-old daughter and an 18-year-old employee, had created "Josh," and their creation drove Megan to suicide. Ms. Drew was convicted of three misdemeanors in this case (Castle, 2009; Ruedy, 2008); these convictions were later overturned (*U.S. v. Drew*, 259 F.R.D. 449).

---

texting to traffic in drugs. Some young people provide their social network sites such as Facebook with too much information that puts them at risk. Such sites along with e-mail and twitter accounts and messages are critical to cyber bullying and harassment. Victimization occurs when predators use the Internet to solicit and groom young people to participate in sexual and other harmful acts (Burrow-Sanchez, Call, Zheng, & Drew, 2011). With the continuing expansion of Internet use, it is likely that this problem will become more severe.

Communities and Neighborhoods Environment

The primary social environments for most children are family and school. Children also interact with others in their neighborhood, with peers who attend other schools, and with other adults. Children develop a set of expectations about themselves and others in their communities and neighborhoods that provides a backdrop for antisocial behavior. Public policy that fails to meet community, economic, family (e.g., accessible quality day care), and educational needs often goes along with failure of communities to meet their economic and educational expectations. This poor community response to economic marginalization contributes to high frequency of neighborhood vandalism, crime, gang activity, and violence. Because parents who are struggling with social, economic, neighborhood, and community problems are often less able to provide the structure young teenagers need, many young people are drawn to antisocial behavior, delinquency, and gangs, which provide an individual identity and structure (such as rules and norms) and a sense of group belonging.

Other social influences such as racism continue to be a major factor. Racism's effects continue to be insidious and far reaching, with large portions of our ethnically diverse communities experiencing serious violence, crime, and continued economic, social, and educational marginalization. Such marginalization is associated with poorer parenting, lower levels of parental monitoring, and less-integrated family structures, all of which have been associated with criminal behavior. Adolescents of color living in inner cities have much higher levels of personal victimization and higher frequency of social marginalization and racism, including the presence of hate groups and hate crimes.

Lesbian, gay, bisexual, transgender, and queer (LGBTQ) youth are especially affected. Most studies suggest that they have a higher incidence of negative encounters with police, including jail, than do heterosexual youth (Rotheram-Borus & Langabeer, 2001). But more important than crime committed by LGBTQ adolescents is the violence done to them. LGBTQ youth are uniquely subject to violence resulting from societal homophobia. Forms of violence in the school and in the community range from name-calling to "gay bashing" to physical attacks. There is a large number of hate crimes directed toward people who identify as LGBTQ in the United States (Klein, 2012; Langman, 2015). This amplified vulnerability to victimization of LGBTQ youth is especially problematic because of the distinctive developmental struggles encountered by this group during their adolescence.

Antisocial behavior is a developmental process that begins early in life and continues throughout childhood and adolescence and into adulthood. Chronic delinquency emerges in a series of predictable steps that place young people at increasingly greater risk for long-term criminal behavior. Unfortunately, by the time offenders come to the attention of the juvenile justice system, they may have spent several years committing minor offenses and developing serious behavior problems that eventually led to crime. Next, we will review risk factors that contribute to this developmental process.

Family Environment

Families play a key role in the development of delinquency. Parents whose discipline is harsh and inconsistent, for example, who have little positive involvement with their children, and who do not monitor their children's activities foster early aggressive behavior, which is strongly related to later delinquency. When caregivers are negative and inconsistent in their parenting styles, are explosive, and are antisocial themselves, aversive and aggressive behavior is reinforced (Forgatch, Patterson, Degarmo, & Beldav, 2009). Family stressors such as family violence, marital discord, divorce, or stresses related to acculturation or bicultural adjustment all contribute to the development of a youth's antisocial behavior as well.

Certain family demographic features are also highly correlated with delinquency. Being poor is in itself not directly related to the incidence of delinquency; but ethnicity; type of neighborhood; and parents' education, occupation, and income levels do influence the type of delinquency children exhibit. Children who live in poor communities, whose parents have limited job skills, are underemployed or unemployed, and whose schools and community economic opportunities are limited are at greatest risk for developing violent forms of delinquent behavior (Knoester & Haynie, 2005). This risk is partly attributable to the difficulty of raising children in a negative environment and to parents' lack of education, resources, and problem-solving skills. Parents in these contexts often monitor their children less, show little involvement with them, and provide less educational stimulation and positive reinforcement for prosocial behaviors.

Early parenting patterns can lead to antisocial behavior in two ways. First, a negative and hostile interaction style and inconsistent discipline lead to poor bonding between parent and child. This lack of bonding contributes to the child's failure to accept society's values and to develop internal control mechanisms. Second, coercive and violent behaviors may be modeled and reinforced by grandparents, parents, and siblings. Children learn to use aversive and aggressive behaviors to counteract the hostile and negative behaviors of other family members, and aggressiveness is rewarded. Learned aggressiveness in such an environment is functional for survival, and hitting, screaming, and other aggressive behaviors are sometimes accepted as normal early in life (Bor & Sanders, 2004).

Families that reinforce aggressive and antisocial behavior fail to provide the appropriate skills that children need for survival in the school and social environment. The significance of positive parental involvement, healthy parent–child interaction, and consistent discipline is supported by the fact that when parents change their discipline and monitoring styles to become more consistent, more positive, less physical, and more aware and observant, their children's antisocial behavior almost invariably declines significantly (Kumpfer & Tait, 2000). Conversely, when children receive training in antisocial behavior in the home, they will likely experience significant difficulties in and out of school (see Box 9.3).

School Environment

Coercive behavior learned at home usually leads to aggression at school and often to a subsequent evaluation by school personnel of Oppositional Defiant Disorder (ODD) or CD. School aggression, in turn, often leads to academic failure. Uncontrolled behavior adversely affects a child's ability to concentrate, to stick to a task, and to complete homework. The relationship between antisocial behavior and poor academic performance is strong. Further, classroom disruptions are associated with lower student achievement for the student's classmates as well as for the student exhibiting the behavior (Lannie & McCurdy, 2007).

The link between aggression and poor academic performance is due to several factors. Children who are aggressive are disruptive, and disruption itself means less on-task behavior, leading to less concentration and study. Disruptive young people are more often placed in time-out, receive more office "referrals," spend more time in a "responsibility" room, and are more often suspended. All of these consequences contribute to less learning time, which contributes strongly to poor performance. In 2007–2008, 34% of teachers indicated that student misbehavior interfered with their teaching (Dinkes et al., 2009). In a nasty cycle, limited academic achievement contributes to the student's negative self-perception, which encourages more negative behavior which, in turn, leads to even poorer academic achievement.

In addition to academic problems, young people with conduct problems cause difficulty for others and for themselves in school. Behaving aggressively, making sexual gestures, acting violently toward others, and vandalizing school property and materials cause disruption for the whole environment. These are symptomatic of more severe delinquent behavior expressed outside of school as well.

Conduct Disorder

CD and the less severe ODD outline criteria that encompass most of the antecedent and contributing behaviors that relate to delinquent and violent behavior. CD encompasses a range of behavior including disobedience, defiance of authority, temper tantrums, aggression, lying, and stealing. As it progresses,

---

Box 9.3 | **Training for Violence**

At one time I was a school counselor for two brothers, Tom, a freshman, and John, a sophomore. Almost every week one or the other or both got into a fistfight at school—sometimes with each other, more often with another student. The vice principal provided appropriate discipline, which progressed from talking to detention to more detention to in-school suspension to suspension. Because the parents refused to attend parent–teacher or parent–administrator conferences, and because I worked with the boys in a counseling relationship, the vice principal asked me to make a home visit to discuss the problem with the parents.

The boys' father was home when I arrived. It quickly became clear that the boys' problem was their dad. The overriding family value he expressed went something like this: "Don't take nothing off of nobody. If someone bothers you, hit him." In this family, aggression and violence were not only being modeled and reinforced, they were being actively encouraged through verbal instruction.

Once I understood the situation, I was able to work with the boys to help them understand their aggression, to develop different standards of behavior at school, and to learn more appropriate problem-solving skills.

CD refers to clinically severe antisocial behavior including physical aggression, fire setting, truancy, and running away (American Psychiatric Association, 2013). The effects of CD and associated delinquent behavior patterns constitute a major social problem; for example, disruptions in the classroom interfere with teaching and learning. Even more important, boys who carry a concealed firearm are more likely to be diagnosed with CD; those who carried concealed guns as adolescents are more likely to commit crimes as adults. For children with conduct disorders, the risk of crime, mental health issues, substance abuse, relationship, and parenting issues in their adult lives are between one and a half and three times greater than children without the disorder (Fergusson, Boden, & Horwood, 2009).

Some researchers (Delligatti, Akin-Little, & Little, 2003) argue that girls are underrepresented in CD research because of the focus on externalizing behaviors rather than covert relational aggression, which is often exhibited by girls. Alternatively, boys' traditional masculine socialization experiences correlate with conduct disorders and heighten their risk of engaging in acts of violence (Feder et al., 2010).

Peer Group Environment

Rejection by Low-Risk Peers

As young children become socialized to the behavioral standards and norms of society, they gradually reduce their level of aggressive and acting-out behavior. However, older children with antisocial behavioral patterns display rates of aggression that are more typical of younger children. They are usually not cooperative or helpful in their social interactions. Indeed, antisocial students seem to have a particular disinclination to cooperate with others in peer-related activities. They have difficulty entering positive peer groups: They misperceive peer group norms and inappropriately interpret peer reactions. Considerable evidence suggests that even benign actions by other students—an innocent, accidental bump in a crowded hallway, for instance—are interpreted as hostile, deliberate, aggressive attacks. Their aggression, lack of cooperation, and hostile defensiveness lead to eventual rejection by low-risk peers (Forgatch et al., 2009).

Membership in a Deviant Peer Group

Antisocial behavior ultimately leads young people to join deviant peer groups for support and acceptance. Aggressiveness and antisocial behavior learned at home are exacerbated by academic failure and rejection by normal peers and become a precursor to membership in a deviant peer group. But the relationship between inappropriate and aggressive behavior and academic failure and peer rejection may be circular. That is, school failure and social rejection may in fact stimulate behavior problems, enhance aggressiveness, and contribute to delinquent and hostile reactions by the struggling student. This relationship needs to be assessed more carefully, however. Training in academic and social skills is effective, but it is quite likely that they must be introduced early in the child's life to prevent or reduce antisocial behavior.

As we mention in Chapters 4 and 13, the peer cluster is a major training ground for the development of a young adolescent's attitudes, beliefs, and behaviors. Peers supply the attitudes, motivations, rationalizations, and opportunities for engaging in antisocial and delinquent behaviors. Furthermore, delinquent peers reinforce deviant behavior and punish behavior that is socially conforming (Cho, Hallfors, & Sanchez 2005; Kaminer, 2005). Thus, antisocial boys who are involved with antisocial peer groups are at serious risk of chronic offending through their teenage years and into adult life (Forgatch et al., 2009). Pressure from the peer cluster makes it difficult for children and adolescents to modify antisocial behavior once they have started to engage in it. Many delinquent youth actively resist efforts to change their behavior. If they adopt more positive social behavior, they may alienate themselves from their major source of companionship and acceptance.

Rejection of Low-Risk Peers

This involvement in a deviant peer cluster and the previous rejection by peers with less risky behaviors leave these young people with increasing limited options. Of course, this leads them to reject low-risk peers, which further complicates solutions to the problem. And the problem is likely to escalate into crime and violence.

Onset of Delinquent Behavior

The age of onset of aggressive and delinquent behavior is an important factor in determining its severity. Youth who begin delinquent activities early are at greatest risk for becoming chronic offenders. Boys who are first arrested before age 14, for example, are much more likely to become adult criminals (Forgatch et al., 2009) than "late starters," or those who commit their first offense in later adolescence. About one-half of conduct-disordered children become adolescent delinquents, and one-half to three-fourths of adolescent delinquents become chronic adult offenders. These data argue for the importance of early assessment and intervention.

The developmental perspective (Patterson, Crosby, & Vuchinich, 1992; Patterson, DeBaryshe, & Ramsey, 1989) and the ecological model (Bronfenbrenner, 1979) show how ecological, cultural, and economic factors place external pressure on families, schools, and children. As young people develop, their interactions with families, schools, and peer groups change. Identification with a deviant peer cluster encourages delinquent behavior and, for some, eventual membership in a gang.

Gang Involvement

A youth gang is a group consisting primarily of adolescents and young adults who interact frequently with one another, share a common identity expressed through a gang name and common symbols, claim control over a certain geographical area, and are deliberately involved in illegal activities. Researchers have identified risk factors for juvenile gang membership at a variety of levels: individual, peer group, school, family, and community (Howell & Griffiths, 2015). These risk factors range from lack of parental role models to academic failure to neighborhood drug availability.

Although down somewhat from 1998, there were still 21,500 gangs active in the United States in 2008, with all segments of the U.S. population currently reporting gang increases. Forty-five percent of high school and thirty-five percent of middle school students say that there are gangs in their schools (Arciaga, Sakamoto, & Jones, 2010; Egley, Howell, & Moore, 2010). Youth in gangs are responsible for a wide variety of offenses, including street crime, drug trafficking, and witness intimidation, and they are highly likely to use firearms in an assault crime. Twenty percent of public schools in 2007–2008 reported gang activities at their school; 23% of students reported gangs at school, with African American (38%) and Hispanic students (36%) reporting a larger number (Dinkes et al., 2009).

When one gang gains power and control in an area, rival gangs sometimes relocate to other areas, even to other cities. Divisions of power and region are frequently related to ethnicity, although a new type of hybrid gangs is emerging. Hybrid gangs are characterized by mixed racial and ethnic participation within a single gang and are driven by drug sale profits (Starbuck, Howell, & Lindquist, 2001). Economic opportunities (e.g., new markets for drug profits) also play a part in a gang's decision to relocate or expand. In addition, higher levels of gang organization increase the likelihood that gangs have a website, post videos, and recruit online (Moule, Pyrooz, & Decker, 2014). Many neighborhoods untouched by organized violence now find themselves threatened by gang activity. The proliferation of youth gangs in recent decades is of concern, and of particular concern is the spread of homegrown youth gangs to rural communities. These findings highlight the importance of continuing a systematic response in combating youth gang problems. Gangs have significant negative consequences not only for society but also for their young members. However, a gang may be the only means many young people have to satisfy their need for affiliation and affirmation (Howell & Griffiths, 2015). Gangs also provide an opportunity for economic gain and an image of success for young people who have no other means to establish it. Gangs provide security, protection, companionship, and opportunities for excitement. Thus gang membership gives young people ways to enhance their perception of their worth and their acceptance (Sharkey, Shekhtmeyster, Chavez-Lopez, Norris, & Sass, 2011).

In one of our studies (Herrmann, McWhirter, & Sipsas-Herrmann, 1997), we found that high gang involvement was associated with low competence and low self-concept. That is, those middle-school-aged students who were most involved (members) or wanted to be involved (wannabes) in gangs believed they had very little impact or influence on their environment, with adults, or with their peers. Apparently, if young people believe themselves impotent, gang membership is viewed as a way to increase their competency and power.

The consequences of gang involvement make intervention a complicated and challenging task. The best practices to deal with youth gangs include a number of strategies: community mobilization; social intervention; providing better educational, social, and economic opportunities; organizational coordination; and gang suppression (Decker & Pyrooz, 2015; Howell & Griffiths, 2015). Of course, the importance of early prevention is obvious. Youth gangs represent a particularly acute concern because gang members account for a disproportionate number of delinquent acts and for a greater number of more serious crimes. In addition, substance use and abuse, drug trafficking, conduct disorders, and gang membership are related (Castellanos-Ryan & Conrod, 2011; Decker & Pyrooz, 2015; Howell & Griffiths, 2015). Moreover, gang involvement remains a powerful predictor of ongoing and future violence (National Gang Center, 2013).

School can play an effective role in mitigating the influence of gangs. A positive school climate is negatively related to delinquent behaviors and positively related to school safety (Crone, Hawken, & Horner, 2015; Decker & Pyrooz, 2015). Effectiveness depends on the level of communication among school personnel and the speed of their response to a potential crisis or violent acts. School personnel need to be in close communication with one another, with each employee having a clearly designated response role when the threat of gang activity is present. However, because delinquency generally precedes gang membership, efforts should not be limited to gang intervention or suppression within the school.

Schools can also play a crucial role in developing communication with the community and in building coalitions with community organizations and law enforcement. A working relationship with local authorities is important before and after critical events (Daniels et al., 2010; Howell & Griffiths, 2015), a practice useful for dealing with youth gangs as well. Community groups that are recruited and educated by schools can help to minimize violence and gang activity. Youth service centers, recreational centers, and religious organizations can meet an adolescent's need for inclusion, affirmation, and acceptance and can serve to discourage gang involvement by providing a healthy alternative. Developing and nurturing school, community, and family relationships (the mesosystem level) is very important for preventing youth violence including gang activity, with proactive citizen groups developed in some communities to deal with youth gangs. This may be particularly important for young gang members who desire to leave the gang even though they still socially and emotionally enmesh with gang members (Pyrooz, Decker, & Webb, 2014). Such community groups can make a positive difference, especially when closely coordinated with schools, churches, youth agencies, and police to provide a better general environment for managing youth violence in the community. Gangs, however, do not explain a particularly violent form of youth crime: school shooters.

SCHOOL SHOOTERS

Recent massacres, especially the murder of six- and seven-year-old students and that of some of the staff at Sandy Hook Elementary School in Newtown, Connecticut, reminds us of a series of school shootings both before and after Columbine (Langman, 2015). It is noteworthy that these more recent massacres differ from earlier shootings because the killer was a young adult (versus another student) and most took place in settings different from public schools, such as churches, universities, and parking lots. In fact, recent shootings appear to be more focused on college campus settings, such as the 2015 mass shooting at Umpqua Community College in Roseburg, Oregon. Many new preventive policies, programs, and greater vigilance implemented in many public schools have likely diverted many school shooting tragedies in the last decade (Daniels & Page, 2013). There have been fairly frequent news reports—now usually a small paragraph or two on the back pages of the newspaper—that report the arrest of an individual or small group of students who were planning a shooting. These support the value of improvements and changes in safety practices in many U.S. schools.

The changes implemented in schools were prompted by the unprecedented number of school shootings in the mid-90s through the first decade of this century that resulted in the deaths of many students and teachers in Arkansas, Mississippi, Kentucky, California, Oregon, Colorado, and Minnesota. These shootings generated widespread concern about school safety. The seemingly random and irrational acts demonstrated that school violence extends far beyond poor, inner-city schools. The watershed event in U.S. school shootings was the 1999 massacre at Columbine High School in Colorado. After Columbine, school security was instituted in most school districts: locked doors, metal detectors, video surveillance, staff monitoring of hallways, identification badges, and more school resource officers. School policies also changed: zero tolerance, crisis plans, antibullying initiatives, and anger management programs were initiated (Daniels & Page, 2013).

Tragic events like the shooting at Columbine High School in Colorado captured public attention, even though most adolescent homicides were committed then, and continue to be committed, in inner cities and outside of the school setting. Most adolescent homicides typically involve a single victim and an interpersonal dispute with a clear territorial, retaliation, or economic motive. In contrast, most of the perpetrators of school shootings were from affluent and middle-class communities, and most have been from intact families. The majority of the shooters were academically able students, and most were European American. Even though mass school shootings have been curtailed, the massacres in the public arena, especially in colleges and universities, are a constant reminder of the possibility and a warning to remain vigilant.

Young people continue to not feel safe at school. Among ethnic minority teens, commonly at least 20% indicate that the threat of crime and violence have kept them from attending school, and this is even more of a problem with LGBTQ students (Klein, 2012; Langman, 2015). Other children and youth reported considerable distress because of school violence. The ripple effect of concern and fear is manifested in settings far from those in which the shootings took place. It is really not very surprising that so many members of the American public, including young people, think that school is not safe: We are all exposed to repeated televised pictures of students who have used handguns to kill their fellow students; media broadcasts and newspaper stories describing a teacher disarming a student in the classroom; or telephoned, texted, or Facebook posted weapon or bomb threats that necessitate closing down schools for a thorough search. These are powerful images that encourage the belief that schools are no longer safe regardless of the facts.

Even though school shooters share some of the characteristics described for youth with severe conduct problems or who engage in antisocial behavior, they represent a distinct subcategory of antisocial behavior (Klein, 2012; Langman, 2015). Identifying the potential shooter before tragedy occurs continues to be a major concern.

Identifying Potential Shooters

In the aftermath of violence by school shooters, professionals have taken increased steps to prevent violence. Often, efforts have focused on providing resources to schools such as funding and hiring of school security officers and increasing physical security measures with metal detectors and cameras. Schools have developed tactical plans for responding when a shooting occurs. Although some of these approaches might be moderately helpful, they do not get to the root of the problem. Two other recommended approaches consist of profiling and utilizing problem checklists to prevent a shooting.

Profiling and Checklists

Historically, profiling has consisted of carefully studying a crime scene and, based on the physical evidence, generating a set of hypotheses about the demographic, physical, personality, and other characteristics of the person most likely to have committed the crime. Profiling has been helpful in identifying suspects and solving crimes. More recently, profiling has been used in an attempt to identify perpetrators of violence before an incident occurs; it is based on studying the characteristics of past school shooters. Prospective profiles of school shooters include the "classroom avenger" profile and the FBI profile to predict an individual student's potential for violence. Unfortunately, profiling potential shooters is not an exact science. Accurate prediction requires a very high degree of concordance, and most students who fit shooter profiles do not become shooters. For example, shooters are described as moody, confrontational, angry, and have low self-esteem. This description fits almost any young person at some point in adolescence. Undoubtedly, the use of profiles will fail to identify dangerous students who share only a few characteristics with prior attackers and will identify as dangerous many students who do not actually pose a risk to others.

Checklists of warning signs are a less scientific alternative to profiles that are designed to help identify potentially violent youth without assuming that all young people fitting the description are potential shooters. Several agencies and groups, including the Department of Education, the FBI, and the National School Safety Center, have provided checklists of warning signs and risk factors. The best use of these checklists is usually to motivate schools to develop prevention and early intervention procedures, as well as safe school plans, because warning list items are so commonly found among adolescents at a given school. Most developers of checklists emphasize that the list is not intended to predict future violent behavior by otherwise nonviolent students. The Department of Education warning sign checklist explicitly cautions that their list does not constitute a profile and was never intended to serve as a predictor of violent behavior. Yet even explicit cautions are disregarded (Sewell & Mendelsohn, 2000), and many checklists are applied as profiles. This can result in the unfair labeling of students who do not pose a threat to the school, particularly students who differ from the majority with respect to sexual orientation, race, and appearance. Lonely, isolated, "weird," young people who dress "funny," have quirky personality characteristics, and otherwise don't fit the norms of their peer group are likely to receive even more harassment, rejection, and ostracism than they already do. Warning lists may actually promote the profiling concept, creating an environment of both suspicion and false security.

Predicting Versus Preventing

Predicting future incidences of school violence is fraught with methodological and practical problems. Predicting any base rate or infrequent behavior, even if reasonably accurate, results in many false positives for every true positive. Although social scientists are able to predict with some accuracy the approximate number of individuals in a given cohort group who are likely to behave in a certain way, their ability to predict which and when a specific individual is likely to engage in the behavior is poor. From a scientific and research perspective, we know a great deal about groups of people: We know very little about a specific person.

There is an important distinction between predicting violence and preventing it (Reddy et al., 2001). Violence prediction involves maximizing the accuracy of predicting who will be violent and under what circumstances the probability of violence is greatest. Some schools have had success with threat assessment teams that include a high level administrator, the resource officer/ law enforcement officer, and a school psychologist/counselor/social worker (Cornell & Williams, 2006). In one year, one school reported there were nearly 200 threats of violence, all of which would have resulted in the expulsion of students under zero-tolerance policies. In fact, the threat assessment team in this school determined that only three threats posed serious risk (Cornell, 2004). However, the best violence prevention practices emphasize not determining who and when a specific act of violence may occur, although that is critical, but identifying the common underpinnings of violence and intervening to maximize protective factors and minimize risk factors among youth more generally (Daniels et al., 2010).

Collaboration between the U.S. Secret Service and the U.S. Department of Education (Reddy et al., 2001) focused on 37 school shootings from 1974 to 2000, involving 41 attackers. Shootings that were drug related, gang related, or stemming from disputes that just happened to occur on school property were not analyzed. Rather than building a profile of attackers from a set of personality traits and demographic characteristics, the Secret Service focused on behavior and motives, tracing the shooters' thoughts and actions from the day of the attack back to when the perpetrator first developed a notion to make the attack. Based on a systematic analysis of investigative, educational, judicial, mental health, and other files, along with interviews of some of the shooters, the report provides useful information about the patterns of relationships, emotions, and attitudes of others in the shooter's environment.

Bender, Shubert, and their colleagues (Bender, Shubert, & McLaughlin, 2001; Shubert, Bressette, Deeken, & Bender, 1999) came to remarkably similar conclusions as those of the Secret Service, even though they used different data sources. Using national press reports, the researchers constructed a list of factors consistently associated with the shooter's psychological and social environment. They used the term *invisible kids* to describe the school shooters, underscoring the finding that these students were not known for overt behavior problems or aggression; indeed, they were simply unknown. They were not unknown to everybody: Retaliation for being bullied was one of the most common reported motives for planning and executing a shooting (e.g., Daniels et al., 2007; Klein, 2012).

Targets of Intervention

Drawing together the results of the reports by Reddy et al. (2001) and Shubert et al. (1999), four clusters of emotions and behaviors emerge as critical indicators of potential violence: emotional pain and confusion, aggressive hatred toward self and others, planning and leakage, and vigilante motivation. Each of these is an important target of intervention, and the four areas are the basis for intervention with young people behaving in an antisocial manner.

Boxes 9.4 and 9.5 provide a glimpse inside the mind of a school shooter in his own words. These excerpts from Kip Kinkel's (Springfield, Oregon) journal and letters were included with the documents presented at his hearing. They graphically illustrate the four target areas we now describe. Notice that these target areas do not refer to personality traits, family background, or demographic characteristics per se. Rather, they address specific thoughts, behaviors, and plans that represent the ecology common to school shooters.

Box 9.4	The Words of a Shooter: Kip's Journal

These excerpts are from a journal hidden in the loft of Kip Kinkel's home. Investigators discovered the black, hardcover book tucked away in a chest. Passages read in court are filled with violent images: with Kinkel's wishing for his own death, with visions of his classmates' deaths. The journal offers a window into Kinkel's state of mind leading up to the tragic shooting at Thurston High School in Springfield, Oregon. It also illustrates the concepts discussed in this chapter.

Aggressive Hate

I sit here all alone. I am always alone. I don't know who I am. I want to be something I can never be. I try so hard every day. But in the end, I hate myself for what I've become.

Every single person I know means nothing to me. I hate every person on this earth. I wish they could all go away. You all make me sick. I wish I was dead.

The only reason I stay alive is because of hope. Even though I am repulsive and few people know who I am, I still feel that things might, maybe, just a little bit, get better.

I don't understand any f-—ing person on this earth. Some of you are so weak, mainly, that a 4-year-old could push you down. I am strong, but my head just doesn't work right. I know I should be happy with what I have, but I hate living.

Motivational Vigilantism

Every time I talk to her, I have a small amount of hope. But then she will tear it right down. It feels like my heart is breaking. But is that possible? I am so consumed with hate all of the time. Could I ever love anyone? I have feelings, but do I have a heart that's not black and full of animosity?

Plan and Leakage

I know everyone thinks this way sometimes, but I am so full of rage that I feel I could snap at any moment. I think about it every day. Blowing the school up or just taking the easy way out, and walk into a pep assembly with guns. In either case, people that are breathing will stop breathing. That is how I will repay all you (expletive) for all you put me through.

Motivational Vigilantism

I need help. There is one person that could help, but she won't. I need to find someone else. I think I love her, but she could never love me. I don't know why I try.

End. New day. Today of all days, I ask her to help me. I was shot down. I feel like my heart has been ripped open and ripped apart. Right now, I'm drunk, and I don't know what the hell is happening to me.

I gave her all I have, and she just threw it away. Why? Why did God just want me to be in complete misery?

| Box 9.4 | (Continued) |

Aggressive Hate

Oh, (expletive). I sound so pitiful. People would laugh at this if they read it. I hate being laughed at. But they won't laugh after they're scraping parts of their parents, sisters, brothers, and friends from the wall of my hate.

Please, someone, help me. All I want is something small. Nothing big. I just want to be happy.

It is clear that no one will help me. Oh, God, I'm so close to killing people. So close.

Every time I see your face, my heart is shot with an arrow. I think that she will say yes, but she doesn't, does she? She says "I don't know." The three most (expletive) words in the English language.

I need to find more weapons. My parents are trying to take away my guns. My guns are the only things that haven't stopped me—that haven't stabbed me in the back.

Emotional Pain/Confusion

I want you to feel this, be this, taste this, kill this. Kill me. Oh God, I don't want to live. Will I see it to the end? What kind of dad would I make? All humans are evil. I just want to end the world of evil.

I don't want to see, hear, speak or feel evil, but I can't help it. I am evil. I want to kill and give pain without a cost. And there is no such thing. We kill him—we killed him a long time ago.

Anyone that believes in God is a (expletive) sheep.

If there was a God, he wouldn't let me feel the way I do. Love isn't real, only hate remains. Only hate.

Emotional Pain and Confusion

Very few school shooters had been diagnosed with any mental illness prior to the violent acts. Relatively few of them had histories of alcohol or drug abuse, but most demonstrated an incredible range of conflicting emotions and each of the students responsible for school shootings demonstrated some type of emotional trouble. More than half had a history of feeling extremely depressed, almost desperate. Most threatened to kill themselves, made suicidal gestures, or tried to kill themselves before the attack. A number did kill themselves during the attack.

School shooters have been young people bursting with anger and rage. But under the anger and rage was an enormous range of feelings including pain, fear, shame, and despondency. These conflicting emotions interfered with reasonable problem solving. Many of the shooters saw the attack as the way to solve a personal problem: a parent planning to move the family, a lost or unreturned love, or a school suspension. For these emotionally confused shooters, their problems appeared to be devastating and without solution. For those who did not commit suicide, most experienced intense regret, remorse, and guilt afterward. Developmentally appropriate life-skills training would have

Box 9.5 The Words of a Shooter: Kip's Letter

This second document is the text of a letter written after Kip Kinkel killed his parents. He left it on the living room coffee table. We have divided it into segments to provide examples of key points in the text.

Emotional Pain/Confusion

I have just killed my parents. I don't know what is happening. I love my mom and dad so much. I just got two felonies on my record. My parents can't take that. It would destroy them. The embarrassment would be too much for them. They couldn't live with themselves. I am so sorry.

Aggressive Hatred

I am a horrible son. I wish I had been aborted. I destroy anything I touch. I can't eat. I can't sleep. I didn't deserve them. They were wonderful people. It's not their fault or the fault of any person or organization or television show. My head just doesn't work right. God damn these voices inside my head!

Emotional Pain/Confusion

I want to die. I want to be gone. But I have to kill people. I don't know why. I am so sorry.

Why did God do this to me? I have never been happy. I wish I was happy. I wish I made my mother proud, but I am nothing. I try so hard to find happiness, but you know me: I hate everything. I have no other choice. What have I become? I am so sorry.

assisted them in dealing with negative feelings, disappointment, and loss, as well as learning skills in developing and maintaining intimate friendships.

Aggressive Hatred Toward Self and Others

The shooters had very favorable and narcissistic views about themselves, concurrent with very poor self-esteem. They believed that they were different from other people, and at the same time, they disliked those who were different. Along with narcissism, they were filled with self-loathing. Apparently these narcissistic young people with fragile, unstable self-esteem erupted into violence when their egos were threatened.

Almost all of the attackers had come to the attention of someone, often fellow students, for their disturbing behavior. Behind this disturbing behavior were feelings that exemplified a callous disregard for the lives of others and for their own lives. Some wrote poems about homicide and suicide. One student talked often of putting rat poison in the cheese shakers at a local pizza restaurant. One shooter claimed that he did not dislike his English teacher, whom he killed. His goal was to kill two people because killing any two people made him eligible for the death penalty. The teacher just happened to be an opportune target. Because other teens may have knowledge of potential problems, peer assistance programs and supportive, compassionate adults are important components of an environment that increases protective factors of support and belonging.

Planning and Leakage

In almost all of the incidences of school shootings, the attacker developed the idea to harm the target well before the attack, most at least two weeks earlier. The attacks were neither spontaneous nor impulsive. The attackers developed the idea, acquired weapons, and most developed a plan at least 2 days prior to the attack. These young people took a long, planned, public path toward violence.

Prior to most incidences, the shooter told someone about his plan. The FBI describes this communication as "leakage." In more than half of the incidents, the shooter told more than one person about his plans. In virtually all of the cases, the person told was a peer—a sibling, a schoolmate, or a friend. Sometimes the attackers told their friends directly, providing detailed information about the plan and the target. In other cases the information was oblique, with the peers knowing that something spectacular was going to happen at school on a particular date. In almost half the cases, the shooters were encouraged or influenced by other students.

Even though the shooter told a sibling, schoolmate, or friend about his ideas about a possible attack before it occurred, in almost no case was that information relayed to adults. Thus a few young people at school usually knew what would happen because the shooters had told them, but these bystanders didn't warn anyone. Ironically, this disturbing pattern gives hope: If shooters plan, there is time to intervene; if shooters tell peers, adults might be able to learn what is planned. Indeed, in studies (Daniels et al., 2010) focusing on averting these tragedies, school personnel must actively strive to break the code of silence and then immediately respond to students who come forward with information of a potential shooting.

Vigilante Motivation

School shooters had more than one motive, with the most frequent motive being revenge. Most of the shooters were known to hold a real or imagined grievance against the targets. Coupled with the grievance was the shooter's difficulty in coping with a major change of a significant relationship or with a personal failure prior to the school attack. These young people had built up such a huge reservoir of pain, resentment, hostility, anger, and rage that, in the end, it took relatively little to tip the scale.

A precipitating event alone did not cause the shooters to act. Rather, most had been persecuted, threatened, attacked, injured, or bullied by others prior to the incident. Shooters described experiences of being bullied in terms that approached torment. They described behaviors that, if they occurred in the workplace, would meet the legal definitions of harassment. In fact, in studies (Daniels et al., 2007) that have explored averting school violence report that most frequent motive was retribution for being bullied.

The experience of bullying has appeared to play a major role in motivating school attacks. More important, perhaps, was the common belief held by most of the shooters that they had not been safe at school. They had come to believe that adults would not or could not protect them, and they concluded that adults did not care.

We followed the sentencing hearing in Lane County Circuit Court for Kip Kinkel, a 15-year-old high school student from Springfield, Oregon. On May 20, 1998, Kinkel was suspended from school for stashing a stolen pistol in his school locker. That evening he killed his mother and father at home, and the next morning he took several guns and hundreds of rounds of ammunition to school and proceeded to shoot 26 of his high school classmates. Two were killed. At the time of his hearing, Kinkel had accepted a 25-year prison term after pleading guilty to killing his parents and two classmates. The hearing was held to help the court decide whether to add more prison time for the 26 counts of attempted murder and for trying to stab a police detective after his arrest. His final sentence was for close to 112 years without possibility of parole.

Case law from the 9th U.S. Circuit Court of Appeals and from the U.S. Supreme Court has ruled that mandatory life sentences without the possibility of parole for juveniles is unconstitutional. In September 2013, Kinkel, who was 31 at the time, requested a new sentencing hearing. A Marion County judge dismissed the appeal, ruling that the original sentence "does not violate the Eighth Amendment" against cruel and unusual punishment; thus ensuring that Kinkel would be in prison until he was 102 years of age (Bernstein, 2013).

Intervention Strategies Focused on Youth Violence

An effective plan for prevention of school shootings, as well as other types of youth violence, should target the four areas just discussed. Quiet, withdrawn, or "strange" youth who are frequently rejected, disrespected, teased, and bullied by classmates need appropriate attention from adults, especially if they have a tenuous relationship with parents. The presence of a caring and involved adult may be the single most effective school safety measure available. Developing positive connections with students, creating a safe environment, being aware of school conditions, and having school personnel visible throughout the school are variables important to successful prevention (Daniels et al., 2007b). Teachers, administrators, and other educators, as well as transportation, cafeteria, and maintenance staff, can all be taught improved skills for listening and identifying troubled students.

In almost every school shooter case, adults were not especially concerned or even knowledgeable about the behavior and feelings of the perpetrators prior to the shootings, but other students knew something was wrong. Schools can creatively use peer groups as a vehicle to identify and assist young people at risk for violence. Peer support networks, cross-age and peer tutoring, mediation, and leadership programs provide links to connect understanding adults to the youth peer culture. Through connecting the troubled teen with positive peers—in itself a great help—the responsible adult has access to adolescents who may be on the fringe in a meaningful way. What also seems clear is that students must believe that telling an adult is an appropriate and positive behavior and that telling an adult will lead to positive outcomes. If they do not believe both of these, students are unlikely to confide in adults.

Uncontrolled feelings of anger, hostility, and rage are a major factor in shootings. The anger was often connected to experiences of rejection, isolation, and persecution, and hurt and fear were underlying the anger. Although expressed in different ways, these feelings are often a component of other antisocial behaviors.

In addition to learning to deal with feelings, young people can learn to behave more responsibly if they are taught to do so. Schools in which rules and expectations for behavior are clear to children are very effective in managing school discipline. For instance, programs such as Positive Behavioral Support—a proactive, schoolwide approach for managing problem behavior (see Chapter 4)—are very important in maintaining discipline. Schools that have a consistent, clear, and graduated consequence for misbehavior and that provide recognition for positive behaviors reduce antisocial behavior and conduct disorders (Crone, Hawken, & Horner, 2015).

Analysis of research on averted school shootings resulted in a framework that provides useful directions: the Safe School Communities Model (Daniels & Bradley, 2011; Page, Daniels, & Craig, 2015). The approach includes five factors to make schools safer. Establishing and reinforcing expected student behaviors and encouraging positive adult interactions with students mirror the Positive Behavioral Support model discussed above. In addition, student self-awareness and awareness of others, along with social and interpersonal skill development instruction, provide specific tools for students. Finally, engagement with the community broadens and includes important others in the endeavor to make the school a better and safer place to be. At the same time, to deal with a specific troubled youth, a specific intervention, such as Reality Therapy, is called for.

SPECIFIC INTERVENTION: REALITY THERAPY

William Glasser and G. L. Harrington developed Reality Therapy, one of the more promising approaches to the deterrence of delinquency. When Glasser was a resident in psychiatry at the Veterans Administration Neuropsychiatric Hospital in West Los Angeles, California, in the 1950s, both he and his supervisor, Harrington, were frustrated by the inability of traditional psychotherapy to solve the problems of many of their patients. Harrington was in charge of a "back" ward that had a very low success rate. The 210 patients averaged 17 years of confinement; the last discharge had occurred 2 years earlier, and the patient had returned within a short time. Although the staff was compassionate and well intentioned, the patients were not getting better. Harrington began to confront the patients, chiding them for their unacceptable behavior and supporting them when their behavior improved. Nurses and aides began to follow suit; they became more involved with the patients and less tolerant of their "crazy" symptoms.

At this time Glasser was taking a similar approach to delinquent girls at the Ventura School for Girls, an institutional facility of the California Youth Authority. In view of the populations they were serving, both men were achieving a remarkable degree of success. Forty-five patients on Harrington's ward went home the first year. They were followed by 85 the second year, and 90 the third year. Many returned, of course, as they were encouraged to do, but only a very few remained more than a month after their return. The others reentered mainstream society immediately. Glasser obtained similar results at the Ventura School for Girls. Roughly 400 girls, with offenses ranging from "incorrigibility" to murder, were confined there for 6 to 8 months for rehabilitation. After applying the new therapy, Glasser reported that 80% of the girls were released and did not return.

Reality Therapy grew out of the experiences and discussions of Glasser and Harrington. Glasser first described this treatment in *Reality Therapy* (1965), and Glasser and his colleagues continued to elaborate and expand his approach (Glasser, 1972; Wubbolding, 2006). Glasser (1998, 2001, 2002) developed the concept of choice theory, in which Reality Therapy is embedded. Glasser (1990) also developed the Quality School Model, which shows promise in school reform (see Wubbolding, 2006, for a clear description of this program).

Assumptions of Reality Therapy

Reality Therapy and choice theory are based on the assumption that human beings must have human communication and contact to thrive, much like the notion of connectedness that we present as one of the five Cs of competency in Chapter 5. Within the context of this communication and contact, people must balance their five basic drives: (1) belonging, (2) power, (3) fun or enjoyment, (4) freedom, and (5) survival (Wubbolding, 2007). Humans have a basic desire to be with other people, to care for others, and to be cared for in return. Individuals who seek help or who are sent for help suffer from one basic inadequacy—they are unable to achieve such contact successfully.

Striving for human contact reflects two fundamental needs: to love and be loved and to be worthwhile as a person. Low-risk young people are able to satisfy these needs in an appropriate way. They develop a success identity that enables them to be involved with respected people who care for them and for whom they care. They have the capacity to give and receive love. They have at least one other person who cares about them and one person whom they care about. They also develop a feeling of personal self-worth. They believe they have a right to be in the world, and they behave in socially responsible ways.

High-risk young people are unable to satisfy these two basic needs. Instead, they either ignore or deny reality. In the process, they develop a failure identity. Young people who ignore reality cope with life by acting as if the rules do not include them (see Box 9.6). They are described as antisocial, sociopathic, delinquent, or criminal. Those who deny reality cope in one of two ways—through substance abuse or mental illness. The young person who says "The world is no good, so I must change it" and proceeds to change the world by getting "high" or "wasted" is essentially denying reality and escaping it. Withdrawing from the world through delusions and other symptoms of mental illness is another way of denying reality.

The Reality Therapist assumes that all problems result from an inability to fulfill essential needs (Brown & Swenson, 2005). Psychological problems are caused by lack of responsibility, the choice of behaviors, and toxic relationships (Glasser, 2001). Individuals must fulfill their needs without preventing others from fulfilling theirs. The person who cannot do so is irresponsible, not mentally ill or bad. Perhaps more than any other approach, Reality Therapy holds that it is impossible to maintain self-regard while living irresponsibly. The practice of Reality Therapy is based on teaching at-risk individuals satisfactory standards of behavior, praising them when they act appropriately, and correcting them when they are wrong. Self-respect comes through self-discipline and closeness to others. In learning to face reality, young people fulfill their needs. In doing so, they become socially responsible people who can achieve honest human relationships.

Theoretical Components of Reality Therapy

Reality Therapy has three basic components: involvement, rejection of irresponsible behavior, and relearning. We consider each of these components in detail as they might apply to Tyrone Baker of Chapter 2.

Involvement

Involvement is the initial and most difficult phase of counseling and requires the most therapeutic skill. Involvement, and the process of developing it, is a prerequisite to the other steps and forms a consistent theme running through the entire helping relationship. In creating involvement with young people, it is important not to give up or push too hard. In the language of choice theory (Glasser, 2001), if Tyrone is internally controlled, the adults cannot work "on" him (external control); they can only be effective by working with him. A good relationship is necessary to work with another person.

In Tyrone's case, the helper must be able to become emotionally involved with him and must be able to accept him uncritically at first. The adult cannot be frightened by or angry about Ty's behavior, thoughts, or attitudes. By demonstrating interest, warmth, and sensitivity while discussing Ty's values, interests, hopes, and fears, the adult helps Tyrone grow beyond his problems. The counselor must know and understand Tyrone and express interest in him as an individual with great potential.

Further, the helper must be open and present him- or herself as a model of transparency and integrity. Glasser says that helpers must be willing to

Box 9.6   Mikey the Menace

When Mikey arrived at the classroom door each morning, the atmosphere changed. A subtle wave of tension would pass among the children as he entered the room shouting, "Hi, everybody!" Within minutes, someone would be crying, complaining, or retreating from his awkward overtures and fast-moving fists, and he would be temporarily relocated to the time-out chair. He would beam at me from the chair. "Teacher, I'll be good." And he tried.

Mikey is the youngest of seven children. His father was in prison for selling drugs, and his mother had described her current boyfriend as a "damn scary alcoholic." Child Protective Services closely monitored the family and was close to taking the younger children away from the mother. During one home visit, I observed the mother grab Mikey roughly, pull his hair, and hit him on the head, all in response to appropriate attention-seeking behavior. Each time he was punished, Mikey scowled and then quickly turned his sunniest smile back on; each time, his mother failed to notice.

One evening I was still working in my classroom as darkness fell, and I was suddenly startled to hear him shout, "Hi, every... Where's the kids?" There was Mikey in the doorway, cheerful as ever, having just walked seven long blocks through projects so crime-ridden that the classroom mothers had warned me to "never go in there." Mikey was very disappointed to learn that "the kids" had gone home. His desperate efforts to gain affection and attention were all that a 4-year-old could do. Mikey should be 19 years old now. What new methods has he learned?

have their own values tested. The helper must be tough and able to withstand Tyrone's intense criticism and anger. In addition, the helper must be willing to admit imperfection and yet demonstrate to Tyrone that he has the ability to act responsibly. The helper, in effect, supports and strengthens Ty's conscience by demonstrating honesty, concern, and personal authenticity.

The counselor develops an "I/you" pattern of interaction. The personal "I," Glasser says, must be used instead of the more impersonal "we," "the school," and "they." The adult says, "I'd like you to do your homework for me." "It's important to me that you're here every day." "I'm concerned about you and interested in you." "I want to explain how your life can go better." Such statements emphasize the personal; they lead the adult to involvement not only as helper to client but as person to person. They communicate that the adult cares enough to risk an emotional, personal involvement. This allows Tyrone to look at his unacceptable behavior and to learn better ways to lead his life. By being responsible, tough, and sensitive, the helper shows confidence that Tyrone can change his irresponsible behavior. The counselor thus creates a sense of belonging for Ty (Wubbolding, 2000).

Rejection of Irresponsible Behavior

In the second phase of treatment, the client's irresponsible behaviors are rejected first by the counselor and later by the client. The counselor ignores the past and works in the here and now with a view to the future. The focus is on Ty's behavior rather than on his feelings and attitudes. In fact, the feelings and emotions that accompany deviant behavior are de-emphasized.

The counselor working with Tyrone insists that he recognize and assume responsibility for his own behavior. Tyrone is helped to evaluate and to judge his behavior against an established standard of social responsibility. The counselor does not accept excuses or help him justify irresponsibility. Ty is helped to "own" his behavior and to view that behavior in light of his values and needs and of society's system of values and needs (Glasser, 2001). "The skill of therapy is to put the responsibility upon the client and, after involvement is established, to ask him why he remains in therapy—if he is not dissatisfied with his behavior" (Glasser, 1965, p. 29).

Of course, emphasizing responsibility is fruitless if the client is not ready. Irresponsibility is discussed with stubborn clients only when they are ready to change. Even then, the counselor should discuss only the fact that the client's behavior is irresponsible and that only the client can do something about it. Tyrone's recognition that his current behavior is irresponsible or wrong and therefore not effective in getting his needs met provides powerful motivation for positive change. Consequently, the counselor is free to pose questions such as, "Are you taking the responsible course of action?" or "Are you doing right or wrong?" Questions of this sort underline the unrealistic aspects of negative behavior and set the stage for the next level of interaction.

Relearning

The third procedure employed by the reality therapist is to help clients learn more realistic ways to fulfill their needs. By modeling consistently responsible behavior, the counselor can guide Tyrone toward an understanding that happiness results from responsibility.

Counselors instruct clients to examine their "constructive" thinking about the present and future—in other words, to evaluate their plan for getting what they want out of their current situation so that they can be where they would rather be. By working out this plan of action with Tyrone, the counselor helps identify alternatives to his negative, self-defeating behavior. Developing a realistic plan of action that accords with Tyrone's previously articulated values serves as a means for the counselor to teach responsibility.

After the counselor and the client jointly agree on a plan, they make a mutual commitment to resolve the problem. Tyrone's plan, for instance, must lead to behaviors that will enable him to satisfy his needs for acceptance and connection with others. The mutual planning and mutual commitment demonstrate that the counselor does not accept Tyrone's negative behavior but cares about him and is willing to help him do something definite that will lead to the fulfillment of his needs. The plan and the commitment always involve much positive reinforcement for Tyrone's responsible behavior and the rejection of excuses for irresponsible, self-defeating behavior.

When Tyrone behaves irresponsibly, the counselor refrains from punishing him. The helper does, however, freely express praise when Tyrone behaves responsibly and shows disapproval when he does not. In varying degrees, then, the counselor teaches Tyrone more realistic ways to meet his needs.

The Seven Principles of Reality Therapy

Glasser has elaborated his three-stage framework by providing seven principles of Reality Therapy. These principles constitute the essential mechanics of Reality Therapy. We briefly describe each principle here with sample statements that reflect the interactions of client and counselor.

Every session does not incorporate all seven principles. Involvement is essential in every session, but the other principles emphasized will depend on the particular client, the circumstances, and the progress of counseling. Early sessions tend to focus on identification and evaluation of current behavior. Later sessions tend to deal with planning and commitment issues.

Involvement

Involvement means development and maintenance of a close, emotional relationship between client and helper. It implies a positive, caring attitude and gives the relationship a warm, personal quality. The thread of involvement is woven throughout the therapeutic process and intertwines with all other principles. (Client: "I'm going out of my head. I've got to get some help quick." Helper: "I'd really like to help you.")

There is convincing evidence of the importance of an empathetic therapeutic relationship in achieving positive outcomes in counseling children and adolescents. It is critically important for difficult and defiant adolescents especially, and a strong relationship based on mutual respect and trust is an attribute of effective prevention programs.

Current Behavior

The focus is on behavior here and now. The counselor helps the client become aware of his or her current behavior and its ramifications. The client is also helped to see that this behavior is self-selected and therefore the consequences of the behavior are self-inflicted. (Client: "My mother is always angry at me. She's always been angry at me. I never do anything right." Helper: "What are you doing now about that situation?")

Evaluating Behavior

The client is made to look critically at his or her behavior and judge whether the behavior is in his or her best interest. The counselor helps the client make value judgments about what is contributing to a lack of success. At this stage, the client realistically determines what is good for him- or herself and what is good for people the client cares about or would like to care about. (Client: "To keep her off my back, I don't stay home much." Helper: "Is that productive for you?")

Planning Responsible Behavior

The counselor helps the client develop a realistic plan to implement the identified value judgment. At this stage the counselor is strongly involved in teaching responsibility to the client. Working with the client to develop a realistic plan for changing behavior is an important step in teaching responsibility. (Client: "It's not productive because when I do come home she complains even more." Helper: "Is there a plan that we could make together that would keep your mother from complaining so much?")

Commitment

When the plan of action has been agreed upon, the client and counselor make a commitment to follow it. The commitment may be a written agreement, but usually it consists of an oral exchange. Equivocations—"I'll try," "Maybe," "I think I can do it"—are not acceptable. (Client: "Yes, I guess I could stay home a couple of nights a week." Helper: "Are you willing to make a commitment to stay home two nights next week?")

The principles of Reality Therapy are designed to help clients learn to become involved with others in a responsible way and to learn to say yes and no at appropriate times. Clients are also encouraged to try new patterns of behavior to fulfill their needs, regardless of fears that these behaviors may not work. Essentially, clients learn not only to face reality but also to fulfill their needs. They commit themselves to a plan that has no loopholes. In the process they evaluate their current behavior and develop a plan for the future.

Reality may be painful, but when at-risk young people can admit to the irresponsibility of their actions, the last phase of counseling—the relearning process—can begin. Then there is potential for growth, fulfillment, and self-worth. When at-risk young people take responsibility for their actions, they gradually find better ways to meet their needs and change inappropriate patterns of behavior. At-risk young people can learn to control themselves.

Accept No Excuses

The helper must help the client gain the experience that will enable the client to keep the commitment he or she has made. In addition, the new behavior needs time to become satisfying and thus self-reinforcing. Consequently, the helper cannot accept excuses for failure to keep a commitment. Glasser makes it clear that counselors, teachers, parents, and other adults who care about young people must not make excuses for them. Nor should adults tolerate the excuses that young people offer. (Client: "Yes, I'll stay home unless something more important comes up." Helper: "If you make the commitment, no excuses are acceptable. You have to decide now whether to commit yourself or not.")

No Punishment

A counselor will not implement sanctions that have not been agreed upon in the commitment. Punishment changes the relationship that is necessary for success and reinforces the client's loneliness and isolation. (Client: "What will happen if I don't stay home two nights?" Helper: "Well, then we'd have to restudy the plan and the commitment. I would be disappointed; you wouldn't have helped your situation. It would be better to come up with a plan you can live with than not to follow through on your commitment.")

Engaging adolescents in a process that reflects the assumptions and principles of Reality Therapy can be very helpful to counselors, teachers, and parents. Adults who use this approach can effectively confront a potential or current delinquency problem. Although the principles of Reality Therapy were developed in a structured, controlled setting, they can be applied successfully in many less-controlled environments.

CONCLUSION

Unfortunately, many young people with interpersonal, personal, and environmental pressures react to these pressures through aggressive acting out. Unless we help young people identify and manage their own behavior, and unless our interventions help modify and change school and family environments to support more positive and prosocial responses, children with conduct problems may develop antisocial behavior, engage in more severe crime, or become involved in gangs and in violent aggression as teens. Moreover, even though there has been a decrease in youth crime and school violence in the last decade, sensational incidences of school shootings—even though most have been at colleges and universities most recently—rekindle concern and fear for all communities. The characteristics of shooters are different from the characteristics of other perpetrators of youth violence, but their access to guns, emotional pain and confusion, aggressive hatred, and vigilante motives mark them distinctly as at risk.

The problems of delinquency are multifaceted, so understanding the problem as well as prevention and intervention strategies must focus not only on the individual youth but on family, school, peer group, and the community as a whole. Professionals and parents alike should develop ways to systematically listen more to young people regarding their experiences within their environments, engage peer groups in prosocial ways, reduce the incidence of bullying within schools, and provide improved training in anger management and other social skills. We have also identified more specifically how the principles of Reality Therapy can be usefully applied to help adolescents understand the consequences of their actions and form a plan for changing self-defeating and destructive behaviors.

Youth Suicide

CHAPTER
10

Wet the top of the glass and run your finger around the rim.

That's me in the shimmering squeal; the sound of glass.

Drop the vase to the floor and listen to it shatter. That's me in the piercing shatter; the sound of glass.

Crush the mirror and watch the image crack and splinter.

That's me in the crack, the splinter, the sound of glass.

There is not much left of me.

Why not just silence the sound of glass, too?

If only I could find

some meaning for myself that

death won't take away.

CHAPTER OUTLINE

- ◆ Nonsuicidal Self-Injury
- ■ Identification and Risk Assessment Strategies
    - ◆ Interviews for Suicide Lethality
    - ◆ Self-Report Inventories
- ■ Specific Intervention Strategies Focused on Suicide Crisis
    - ◆ Prevention, Early Intervention, and Postvention

- ◆ Crisis Management and Response
    Immediately After a Crisis
    Family Interventions
- ◆ Postvention and Follow-Up Treatment
    Schools
    Families
- ■ Conclusion

To prevent suicide one must understand the influences that contribute to suicidal behavior. They may range from a child's chaotic family life to not knowing how to manage relationships, from a child's perception that the future is doomed to a teenager's feeling that the present is hopeless. Media and Internet exposure have considerable influence on suicide as well, making things more difficult (Whitlock, Purington, & Gershkovich, 2009). Preventing suicide involves focusing on suicide ideation (i.e., thinking and planning) and reducing suicide attempts. This starts with knowing key warning signs and available intervention strategies.

Among the aspects of suicide discussed in this chapter are (a) the incidence of childhood and adolescent suicide; (b) precursors to suicide and the characteristics found in children and teens who are suicidal; (c) warning signs and behaviors; (d) common misconceptions of suicide, including nonsuicidal self-harm; (e) identification and assessment of suicide ideation; and (f) prevention and intervention strategies, including early intervention, crisis management, and follow-up treatment. We pay particular attention to childhood and adolescent depression and early-onset bipolar disorder. Finally, for each intervention, we focus on the potential role of the teacher, counselor, psychologist, and other human service professionals and the role of the school, family, and clinical settings in effecting change.

THE SCOPE OF THE PROBLEM

Suicide is the third leading cause of death among adolescents in the United States after unintentional injury and homicide. Every year, 16% of adolescents contemplate suicide, 13% develop a plan, and 8% actually attempt suicide. Obviously, the detection and prevention of adolescent suicidal behavior are important. In the United States, teen suicide rates tripled over several decades in the 20th century but have declined slightly from the mid-1990s to the mid-2000s (Moskos, Achilles, & Gray, 2004). In 2013, suicide was the second leading cause of death among persons aged 15 to 24 years and the third leading cause among children aged 10 to 24 years. Every day five young people under the age of 20 commit suicide; every 6 hours, a young person completes suicide (Centers for Disease Control and Prevention, 2015).

All youth are affected by suicide, but there are general behavioral differences between females and males. Girls are more likely to report attempting suicide than boys (Centers for Disease Control and Prevention, 2015) and also seem to be more likely than boys to benefit from existing prevention programming (Hamilton & Klimes-Dougan, 2015). Boys, however, are more likely to die from suicide than are girls. Between the ages of 10 and 24, boys completed 81% of suicides and girls completed 19%. An even greater number of young people, especially females, develop a plan to commit suicide. This planning rate is higher among troubled adolescents, students with disabilities, and even higher for juvenile offenders. Each year, nearly 160,000 youth receive medical care for self-inflicted injuries. In the past year, an average of three students (one male and two females) within a single high school classroom will have attempted suicide (Centers for Disease Control and Prevention, 2015).

The above percentage estimates are likely lower than reality. Many suicides are not reported as such because of the family's embarrassment or even lack of recognition, or due to the discomfort of the school and community in acknowledging that a suicide has occurred (see Box 10.1). An additional barrier to identifying accurate suicide statistics is the fact that suicide ideation falls into two categories: passive suicide and active suicide. Deaths from overdose, accidents, and reckless actions might fall under the label of "passive suicides." Consider that accidents, the leading cause of death among children and adolescents, are often associated with impulsive recklessness and use of alcohol or other drugs, both of which are related to suicide ideation and attempts. Many accidental deaths may result from a wish to be dead or a wish to no longer be alive. Similarly, drug overdoses, recorded as accidental deaths, may be unrecognized or unreported suicides. Those who entertain passive thoughts of suicide (e.g., "I would be better off dead") usually do not immediately and maybe never will experience active suicidal ideation that involves thoughts of actually killing themselves. Of course, researchers are unable to determine the number of passive suicides that occur each year.

Sex differences have also been found in the rates and the lethality of suicide attempts. Males tend to choose more violent means to kill themselves, whereas females more often use pills and poisons. Overall, firearms remain the most commonly used method, especially for boys. Firearms account for close to one-half of all suicides completed by young people. In 2013, nearly 900 youth took their own lives with a firearm, an increase for the third straight year (Brady Center to Prevent Gun Violence, 2015). Having access to a gun in the house is the single most important factor that distinguishes between adolescent males who just think about suicide, those who attempt it, and those who complete it (Bearman & Moody, 2004). Suicide by firearm topped a 12-year high in 2013, with most deaths involving a gun belonging to a family member. Clearly, access to and the availability of firearms is a significant factor in the suicide rates of youth. Indeed, some modest declines in the rate of suicide among 14- to 17-year-olds is

Box 10.1	Accidental Death

Jarrod was a senior in high school who loved to play the guitar and compose songs. He had dreamed of being a musician for as long as he could remember. It was a dream his parents did not share. Jarrod was the oldest child in the family and had hoped to study music in college, but his parents insisted that he attend a business school because they didn't want to "send good money after bad." Jarrod expected a lot of himself, and he knew that his parents also expected a great deal of him. He had few friends, but the friendships he had were quite intense. His friends looked up to him and had high expectations for his career in music. They were disappointed about his parents' plan to send him to business school and told him to "fight for his rights." Feeling unable to live up to his friends' expectations, he retreated from them. That spring Jarrod was sleeping only 3 to 4 hours a night. He alienated himself from his friends and his parents and grew increasingly distraught over his seeming inability to please the people he loved. Four days after his high school graduation, local newspapers reported that Jarrod, aged 18, had died in a car accident. Investigators could not explain why, in the absence of traffic or bad weather, he had suddenly veered off the road and crashed at high speed into a very prominent cement wall.

attributed to child access prevention laws in some states. Those states with laws that require gun owners to lock away firearms to prevent access by young people had fewer suicides (Grossman et al., 2005).

Cultural variations in suicide rates also exist. Latino children and adolescents have a higher rate of suicide and suicide attempts than European American youth (Centers for Disease Control and Prevention, 2015). For example, nearly 15% of Latino youth in grades 9 to 12 reported suicide attempts. This was considerably higher than European American, African American, or most other ethnocultural groups.

Historically, African American teenagers have had lower suicide rates than European American teens, but in recent decades, the suicide rate for Black youth has increased dramatically (CDC, 2010). Suicide attempts are nearly two times higher among Black and Hispanic youth than White youth. This is an issue for older African American female teenagers who are at an especially high risk for attempting suicide (Joe, Baser, Neighbors, Caldwell, & Jackson, 2009).

Although there is considerable variability from tribe to tribe, Native Americans/Alaskan Native young people have the highest adolescent suicide rate of any ethnic group in the United States (Centers for Disease Control and Prevention, 2015; Dorgan, 2010). The high suicide rate has been associated with factors such as substance abuse and alcoholism, child abuse and neglect, unemployment, the availability of firearms, and lack of economic options leading to hopelessness (Grossman et al., 2005). Another factor for the high rate of suicide among native young people is intergenerational trauma (Duran & Duran, 1995). The tribal variability may be due to the connectedness and cultural pride of the members of some tribes. In one study (Albright & Fromboise, 2010) young Native American middle school students who maintained their Indian cultural identity did not feel hopelessness, as compared to their classmates with a White cultural identity who felt significant hopelessness. Apparently, ethnic cultural identity had a protective effect on this particular suicide characteristic. Although few data exist for Asian American adolescents, cultural values may also contribute to lower rates of suicide among this group.

Lesbian, gay, bisexual, transgender, and queer (LGBTQ) youth are at particular risk for suicide and attempted suicide. While we utilize the term *LGBTQ* here, part of the spectrum of sexual identity development includes youth who may identify as "intergender," "questioning," or "asexual," among other self-identities. The identities and processes need to be understood to prevent suicide among LGBTQ youth. The rate of attempted suicide is considerably higher among LGBTQ youth than that for heterosexually identified youth. LGBTQ teenagers are four times more likely to attempt suicide than their heterosexual peers, and they constitute 30% of all successful adolescent suicides (Trevor Project, 2015).

Suicide attempts by LGBTQ youth are most frequent soon after they "come out" to themselves and others. Suicide attempts most likely occur when individuals begin to seriously question their heterosexual identity and after initiation of same-sex sexual activity. During this period of transition in identity and behavior, LGBTQ youth are faced with feelings of social isolation, self-revulsion, disenfranchisement, and rejection from family and peers (Commission on Adolescent Suicide Prevention/CASP, 2005).

Along with higher suicidal ideation rates and a longer history of suicide attempts, LGBTQ youth often report other problems as well, such as higher rates of intravenous drug use and higher rates of depression (Noell & Ochs, 2001). Such risk factors increase when LGBTQ youth are faced with additional difficulties, such as homelessness and/or family violence. Gay males are also more likely to report poor body image, binge eating, or purging behaviors than heterosexually identified males. Gay men who attempt suicide tend to adopt a homosexual identity at a younger age, express more feminine gender roles, and often come from dysfunctional families. LGBTQ youth who come from highly rejecting families are 8.4 times more likely to have attempted suicide than LGBTQ peers who reported no or low levels of family rejection (Trevor Project, 2015).

Disability status may also be a factor in youth suicide. Children and adolescents with disabilities often feel isolated and are frequently the only member of their family with a disability. Feelings of isolation and "differentness" can cause additional stress leading to loneliness, depression, and thoughts of suicide.

COMMON MISCONCEPTIONS OF SUICIDE: SUICIDE MYTHS

Of all the problems that counselors help young people deal with, none is more stressful than suicide or potential suicide. There are a number of common misconceptions or myths about suicide that increase that stress

(Joiner et al., 2009; Moskos et al., 2004). Here are some of the most common ones:

- *A person who has considered or attempted suicide will always be suicidal.* In fact, most children and adolescents think about suicide at some point. Most suicide attempts are a desperate means of crying out for help. If the crisis is resolved effectively, many will not become suicidal again, with those who did not actually attempt suicide at lower risk of future attempts.

- *After a suicide crisis has passed, the child is no longer at risk for suicide.* Although children may not continue to feel suicidal after an attempt, they are not out of danger. Approximately 40% of adolescents who attempt suicide make another attempt within 2 years (Miranda, DeJaegere, Restifo, & Shaffer, 2014). Because those who attempt suicide have already overcome a social taboo by trying to kill themselves once, subsequent attempts are easier for them. If parents, counselors, psychologists, and school personnel do not attend to the child and the reasons for the attempt, a subsequent attempt is possible. Suicide takes a great deal of emotional energy. A child or adolescent who displays a calm reaction after an initial suicide attempt may be gaining strength for another. Later suicide attempts frequently involve more lethal methods. This leads adolescents with a history of suicide attempts, contrasted to those with no attempts, to be more likely to actually commit suicide later.

- *Talking about suicide can make people more inclined to make an attempt.* Talking to children and adolescents about suicide can allow them to express their feelings and concerns and can lead to increased supports and coping skills. Adults should not avoid the topic of suicide; there is no evidence that this increases risk.

- *People who commit suicide always leave a note.* Actually, only a small proportion of children and teenagers who commit suicide leave a note, even though they may leave numerous clues or hints. This misconception can perpetuate a family's bewilderment after a suicide. Not only are they helpless to change what happened, but they are also uncertain about the reason for the suicide. Many suicides are classified as accidents because no note has been found and the deaths are not recognized as suicides.

- *Suicide happens without warning.* Though few people who are thinking about committing suicide actually spell out their intention directly, most do give numerous clues and hints of despair and suicidal ideation. After a young person has committed suicide, it is not uncommon for friends and family members to retrospectively identify many of the warning signs.

- *The person who talks about committing suicide never actually does it.* Nearly every suicide has been preceded by some kind of warning. Even if such threats seem to be bids for attention, it is better to respond to a child's potential risk than to regret a completed suicide. Always take threats seriously.

- *Children in poverty are more likely to kill themselves than kids with more economic support.* Suicide does not occur more frequently among lower socioeconomic groups than among the more affluent. Although age and gender differences persist (suicide is on the rise among children and adolescents) and some ethnic differences persist (Native Americans have the highest suicide rate)—as we discussed earlier, suicide is a problem in all socioeconomic and ethnic groups.

• *Suicidal people are mentally ill or severely depressed.* Suicide is an ineffective, maladaptive solution to a problem that appears unsolvable. Suicidal youth usually are not mentally ill, nor can any genetic markers for the incidence of suicide be distinguished from ineffective coping mechanisms learned from others in the environment. And even though many suicidal children and adolescents are depressed, not all are. Some children and adolescents who are not depressed consider suicide in the absence of adequate problem-solving skills.

Awareness of these misconceptions about suicide helps parents, teachers, and counselors to identify true suicidal attitudes, thoughts, and behaviors among children and adolescents. Understanding risk factors are also important.

RISK FACTORS AND CHARACTERISTICS OF YOUTH SUICIDE

To understand the causes of suicide among children and adolescents, it is helpful to recognize behaviors that are considered "normal" during development. Many adolescents of all cultures enjoy life, are happy most of the time, and are able to develop nurturing friendships. They feel positive about their development and their future. They experience physical changes and new social roles without undue trauma, even though they may regularly experience situation-specific anxiety. For the most part, they are able to cope with the changes that are taking place in their lives.

For other adolescents, however, this period of change and growth is filled with stressful events and adjustments. Depression, aggression, and divergent thinking are common during this transitional period. As discussed earlier, these characteristics can be exacerbated by low socioeconomic status, absence of parental support, and lack of educational and economic opportunity. Gay, lesbian, and other sexual minority young people confront a negative and hostile social environment (Baams, Grossman, & Russel, 2011; Hatzenbuehler, 2011). Girls tend to express more negative feelings toward themselves than boys, and report more loneliness, sadness, and vulnerability (Tang & Cook, 2001). These experiences may provide fertile ground for suicide ideation and attempts.

It is often difficult for parents, teachers, and mental health professionals to differentiate between the normal turmoil that occurs during childhood and adolescence from turmoil that is life-threatening. Many children and adolescents at risk for suicide have been mistakenly viewed as simply "going through a stage."

Most theories of suicide focus mostly on older populations. One of these, the interpersonal theory of suicidal behavior (Joiner et al., 2010; Van Orden et al., 2010), is a general theory encompassing all age groups and provides components that are particularly relevant to young people. The interpersonal theory proposes that the most dangerous form of suicidal desire is caused by two interpersonal constructs—thwarted belongingness and perceived burdensomeness. These are heightened when they occur in tandem and simultaneously with the belief that one is hopeless in changing them (Joiner et al., 2009). When these beliefs are held long enough, the individual develops a desire for death.

One other aspect to the theory: Suicide is not an easy or comfortable act and is, in fact, a frightening and painful event. Thus, the theory suggests that the young person develops less fear of pain and death through a process of repeatedly experiencing painful events. Frequent physical fights, repeated accidental injuries, previous self-injury, and other similar experiences prepare the person for suicide attempts and possible completions. Later in this chapter, we discuss so-called nonsuicidal self-injury (NSSI) experience as it relates to children and teens.

Interpersonal, Family, and Psychosocial Characteristics

A variety of interpersonal, family, and psychosocial characteristics are associated with suicidal ideation and suicide attempts. Here, we describe 14 characteristics presented in ascending order, with the more distal characteristics presented first and the more proximate ones later. Research suggests that the distal factors are somewhat more remote for a suicide attempt and the proximate ones are more immediate. In Figure 10.1 this is demonstrated as a spiral leading into the more critical and proximate characteristics toward the center. Of course, for individual young people with their specific traits, backgrounds, and behaviors, this order-of-importance spiral may not apply, nor is this an exhaustive list. Nevertheless, for most distressed young people these characteristics are important.

Substance Use, Misuse, and Abuse

Alcohol and drug use are often related to adolescent risk for suicide (Hull-Blanks, Kerr, & Kurpius, 2004). Adolescents who are chemically dependent are at higher risk for suicide. This is especially problematic for girls because they are more likely to suicide with substances than in other ways (Brady Center to Prevent Gun Violence, 2015). However, interrelated factors, such as homelessness, social isolation, and other involvement in problem behavior, can add to the likelihood of a suicide attempt (Ramey, Busseri, Khanna, & Rose-Krasnor, 2010). Substance abuse can exacerbate suicide risk in myriad ways (Substance Abuse and Mental Health Services Administration, 2012). For example, people who abuse alcohol and drugs may not seek the support they need, and when seeking treatment, the effects are diminished by their often lack of impulse control and ability to maintain treatment gains. Substance use is one factor that predicts the transition from suicidal ideation to suicide attempts (Van Orden et al., 2010). In Chapter 7 we provide detailed information about the risks associated with substance use.

Under- and Overachievement

Academic underachievement has been linked to suicide. Impaired academic functioning may be a consequence of suicide thoughts or attempts: One out of five high school students receiving mostly D and F grades attempted suicide contrasted with one out of twenty-five who receive mostly A grades (Substance Abuse and Mental Health Services Administration, 2012). On the other hand, perfectionism, overachievement, and living up to high expectations are characteristic of many academically talented suicidal children and adolescents. Talented girls with high levels of impulsivity and aggressiveness and low levels of harm avoidance may be particularly at risk for suicide (Robinson Kurpius, Kerr, & Harkins, 2005). Deterioration in the academic performance of young people, whether they are high or low achieving, can be a warning sign of suicidal potential.

Catastrophic Worldview

In addition to negative thoughts and feelings about the self, a negative or catastrophic view of the world and the future is associated with suicide risk. Some children and adolescents view the world as an unpredictable, dangerous, and hostile place. These intimations of catastrophe are exacerbated by threats of nuclear weapons, the AIDS crisis, racism, poverty, post 9/11 terrorism, Middle East wars, natural disasters, and civil violence. Consequently, some young people feel desperate and helpless and are potential victims of a suicide crisis. Unfortunately, music, video games, films, and television influence catastrophic feelings by modeling and glorifying violence and death (see Chapter 9 for media influences on at-risk youth).

Cluster Suicides

Cluster suicides are suicides that imitate or are a copycat response to a previous suicide. There are two types of copycat suicides: mass clusters or point clusters. A mass cluster is media related. For example, a mass cluster follows a television program or movie that depicts teenage suicide. A point suicide is more local. When a child or adolescent commits suicide, the act somehow becomes normalized for others. After one suicide, those who have already been experiencing despair may begin to see suicide as a viable response to their stress and feelings of hopelessness. Adolescents who are at risk for self-destructive behavior are even more vulnerable after someone they know or know of commits suicide (Cerel, Roberts, & Nilsen, 2005). Suicide reports in the media primarily affect teenagers and young adults as opposed to young children. Suicide clusters are a particular problem on American Indian reservations. For this reason, appropriate postvention or follow-up treatment after a suicide crisis is essential.

Lesbian, Gay, Bisexual, Transgender, and Queer Youth

Suicide is the leading cause of death for LGBTQ youth, primarily because of the debilitating effects of growing up in a homophobic society (Hatzenbuehler, 2011). Suicide attempts by this population are frequently linked with sexual milestones such as self-identification as homosexual, coming out to others, or resulting loss of friendship and family acceptance (Baams, Grossman, & Russell, 2015). During this period, LGBTQ adolescents are faced with additional stressors and experience feelings of social isolation, self-revulsion, disenfranchisement, and rejection from family and peers (Martin-Storey & Crosnoe, 2012). In this particularly high-risk group, special attention is required to reduce suicide attempts.

Disruptive and Violent Families

Suicidal youth often come from dysfunctional, disintegrated, and violent families, especially when there is a history of sexual or physical abuse (Gould, Greenberg, Velting, & Shaffer, 2003). Family interactions that are characterized by anger, emotional ambivalence, and rejection are also associated with self-destructive behavior in youth. The rise in single-parent households as well as lack of skill and experience in parenting, communication, and discipline (see Chapter 3) exacerbate the risk of suicide. When single parents are overloaded with work and financial obligations and have limited support from others, they have less time and energy to devote to children. "Blended" families or stepfamilies may also be at high risk for suffering from uncertain, inconsistent, and confusing family interactions.

Depressed parents, especially depressed fathers, are particularly problematic for their sons. Depressed male teenagers with depressed fathers are seven times more likely to attempt suicide as young adults than depressed male teenagers with unaffected fathers (Rohde, Lewinsohn, Klein, & Seeley, 2005).

Adolescents are more likely to have serious suicidal thoughts if they engage in fewer activities with parents (Bearman & Moody, 2004). Parental support and consistency are important protective factors against children at risk for suicide, and youth who lack family stability are at increasingly higher risk for suicide (Mazza & Eggert, 2001; Randell, Eggert, & Pike, 2001). Mattering to others is important, and when young people believe that they do not matter to people in their families they are more likely to think of taking their own life. It is an easy step from "not mattering" to being a "perceived burden" (Joiner et al., 2009; Van Orden et al., 2010).

Suicide is also more prevalent among young people whose families have a history of suicide (Gould & Kramer, 2001; Gould et al., 2003). When relatives attempt suicide, adolescents' suicide thoughts greatly increase (Bearman & Moody, 2004), and when a family member commits suicide when children are young, they are more likely to attempt suicide as adolescents.

Connectedness and Poor Communication

Children who grow up in a dysfunctional family system frequently develop inadequate communication skills. Young people who grow up in an environment where communication of their thoughts and feelings is unsafe do not learn to express their distress to others. As feelings and thoughts fester and become increasingly negative, these children may withdraw into themselves, making it difficult for others to recognize and respond to their increasing pain, depression, and possible suicidal feelings. The progressive isolation that results from poor communication skills can be a warning sign of low connectedness and belonging which is a warning sign of suicide attempts (Joiner et al., 2009).

Loss and Separation

Suicidal youth are more likely than other youth to have experienced the loss of a parent through separation, divorce, or death. Even when one has not lost a parent or other close relative, suicidal thoughts may arise in response to the loss of a friendship or dating partner. Separation and differentiation from parents is an important developmental task of adolescence, but death and divorce are life-changing events over which a child has no control. The natural feelings of grief, abandonment, and anger call for coping skills that not all children have developed. The surviving parent may be experiencing tremendous emotional adjustment as well and may be unable to provide the direction and support the child needs. In contrast with steadily nurturing autonomy, the loss of a parent may push children rapidly into adult roles before they are ready.

Intrapersonal and Psychological Characteristics

Certain intrapersonal and psychological characteristics are associated with suicide ideation, attempts, and completions. These factors are less demographic and more personal. Hence, they are further along on the spiral depicted in Figure 10.1 and they deserve specific attention.

Self-Image

Low self-esteem, poor self-concept, and feelings of worthlessness are typical of suicidal children and may predispose a child or adolescent to suicide ideation. Poor self-esteem and self-concept often lead to feelings of hopelessness and depression. A distorted view of the self can also lead to irrational and unrealistic expectations of others, the world, and the future. For example, adolescents who are underweight or overweight are only slightly more likely to report suicidal tendencies. However, teens *who perceived themselves* to be underweight and overweight were more likely to report thoughts and attempts of suicide compared to those who said they were "about the right weight" (Centers for Disease Control and Prevention, 2005)—perhaps a manifestation of self-concept or self-esteem. Children and adolescents who dislike themselves and who are unable to see themselves in positive ways require special attention from counselors, teachers, and parents. Girls are at an increased risk of problems with self-esteem, especially during middle school (Tang & Cook, 2001). Female adolescents who physically mature earlier than others and began dating at an early age may have particularly negative outlooks on their body and appearance (see Box 10.2).

Anger

Anger, aggression, and anger control difficulties are also predictors of risky suicidal behavior (Randell et al., 2001). As discussed in Chapter 9, inappropriately expressed anger is a major problem, and suicidal adolescents often

Box 10.2	She Didn't Want to Die

Jennifer was a 12-year-old girl, just finishing her sixth-grade year in elementary school. Unlike other girls her age, she began developing physically and emotionally into a young adult during the school year. Although Jennifer had a close circle of friends, she often worried about other girls teasing her and gossiping about her behind her back. She felt different than everyone else. She was ashamed to shower after gym class and uncomfortable about her rapid physical development. Jennifer often found herself hanging around boys several years older and enjoying their company. She no longer felt comfortable giggling and gossiping with her friends. She was too ashamed to tell her parents how she felt and believed her friends would not understand. Slowly Jennifer started speaking with her friends less and spending more time with her older male buddies.

One day after school, Jennifer headed home and flipped on the television as she normally did. There on the news she saw a young girl in high school who had committed suicide the previous week. The news coverage was quite extensive, showing her memorial service, her saddened classmates, and all of the flowers around the school laid out for her. It was at that moment that Jennifer grabbed a bottle of pills and swallowed over 30 of them in hopes of recovering some sense of importance and belonging. Later, in the emergency room, she told her mother that she really didn't want to die; all she wanted was to stop feeling so unbearably alone.

display increased levels of hostility. In a recent study conducted in the Rocky Mountain region, the area with the highest rate of adolescent suicide, researchers found a relationship between reported suicide risk and initiation of fights, threatening of other children, and use of weapons to assault (Evans, Marte, Betts, & Silliman, 2001). Those who act aggressively toward their peers, are victims of violence, or witness such hostility are at increased risk for suicidal behavior.

Impulsivity

Impulsivity is often related to a suicidal response in young people. Teenagers and preteens who are part of a peer cluster, for example, may attempt suicide out of an impulsive reaction to someone else's self-destructive actions. Impulsive children are also influenced by others' responses to suicide and by the impact that a suicide has on others. Of course, the restriction of firearms is very important here. As discussed earlier, the most common method for attempting suicide is through the use of firearms (Brady Center to Prevent Gun Violence, 2015). Having a gun in the home is a significant suicidal risk factor, especially for boys. Girls who attempt suicide often overdose or use poison.

Impulsivity is also related to a risk-taking style. Although young people may be ambivalent about ending their lives, an impulsive or daredevil reaction to stressors often leads to suicide. In other words, adolescents may not be intent on killing themselves, but they may attempt to gain attention or approval from others through risky behavior. High-risk behaviors and impulsivity, fairly common during adolescence, allow young people to test their fears of death against their feelings of immortality. This may be especially true when reasons for living are blurry or not clear (Salami, Brooks, & Lamis, 2015). Impulse control may be a key predictor of the outcome of a suicidal crisis: Impulsive children who contemplate suicide may attempt it before they have time to think of an alternative.

Loneliness

Loneliness and isolation are clearly implicated in suicide (Gallagher, Prinstein, Simon, & Spirito, 2014). Most suicidal children and adolescents have problems with their peers and are sensitive to rejection. Loneliness usually begins in childhood and continues into adolescence. Teenagers who feel lonely and isolated in a period marked by developing social relationships do not experience the support of friends. Without these nurturing and bonding relationships, children feel expendable and unnoticed—feelings that often lead to suicide ideation. For girls, especially, being socially isolated and having peer conflicts means that they are more likely to consider suicide (Bearman & Moody, 2004). Perhaps because it offsets loneliness, adolescence involvement in prosocial activities such as volunteering and peer support programs reduces suicide risk as demonstrated in one Canadian study (Ramey et al., 2010). The interpersonal theory of suicide discussed earlier refers to this "loneliness" factor as "thwarted belongingness" and suggests that social isolation is perhaps the strongest, most reliable predictor of suicidal ideation, attempts, and actual suicide among all populations.

Burden on Others

Another interpersonal/psychological characteristic of youth suicide is by perceiving oneself to being a burden on others (Opperman, Czyz, Gipson, & King, 2015). Apparently, feeling like a burden to "people in their lives" is a critical mechanism in explaining higher levels of depression and suicidal ideation, and a risk factor for lower meaning in life.

Most community and social support groups base their prevention/intervention efforts on decreasing social isolation rather than addressing youths' beliefs of burdensomeness even though perceived burdensomeness may be related to more lethal means of suicide among those who actually complete suicide.

Hopelessness and Despair

Despair or hopelessness is the loss of hope. Young people who experience hopelessness view the future pessimistically (Sargalska, Miranda, & Marroquin, 2011). Hopelessness is a significant sign in recognizing suicide intent and behavior. It is a solid predictor of the feeling or state that leads some young people to self-destructive behavior (Gallagher et al., 2014). As discussed, it is especially predictive of suicide when the person feels hopeless about not belonging and sees themselves as a burden on others.

Other psychological disorders, such as anxiety disorders, obsessive-compulsive behavior, hostility, and psychosis, also play important roles in some teenage and child suicides. However, recognition of the signs of depression especially may help to avert a suicidal crisis.

Depression

Depression and related psychiatric disorders are clearly a strong contributing factor to youth suicide (Gallagher et al., 2014). Studies have suggested that 14% of young people ages 12 to 17 have experienced at least one major depressed episode in their lifetimes, and about half of them thought about killing themselves (Bridge, Goldstein, & Bren, 2006). Depression is linked to suicidal thoughts and behaviors among children and adolescents in both clinical and nonclinical settings (Gould & Kramer, 2001; Mazza & Eggert, 2001). Interestingly, antidepressant medication apparently has significantly lowered the suicide rate of older adolescent boys (ages 15–19) from lower socioeconomic circumstances (Olfson, Shaffer, Marcus, & Greenberg, 2003), suggesting that depression is a component of some adolescent suicides. As we have argued elsewhere (B. T. McWhirter & Burrow-Sanchez, 2004), depression may not be present in all cases of youth suicide but remains an important and major risk factor for suicidal behavior (Vitiello et al., 2009).

Adolescents who develop depression are at increased risk for a variety of adverse outcomes later in life (Fergusson & Woodward, 2002), including subsequent depression, anxiety, suicidal behavior, nicotine dependence, difficulties in academia and employment, and unplanned pregnancy. As many as two-thirds of those between the ages of 14 and 16 showing depression will experience another episode before the age of 21 (Fergusson & Woodward, 2002).

Thinking Patterns

Faulty thinking and irrational beliefs such as cognitive rigidity and cognitive distortion are consistently found in conjunction with depression and low self-esteem and are prevalent among suicidal youth. Children at risk for suicide possess fewer positive coping strategies and often do not seek assistance for their problems (Labouliere, Kleinman, & Gould, 2015). If faulty thinking can be modified earlier, many suicide crises may be avoided. Here are some thinking patterns common to suicidal children and adolescents.

- Cognitive constriction: The inability to see options for solving problems and the conviction that the current bad feelings will never end. This leads to dichotomous thinking.
- Dichotomous thinking: The individual is able to see only two solutions to the problem: (a) continue to exist in a living hell or (b) find relief through death. (For example, "I will feel this way forever unless I kill myself.") A number of negative thinking patterns are common to suicidal children

and adolescents, but the most important one is dichotomous thinking, which is common in the critical stages of suicide ideation.

- Cognitive rigidity: A rigid style of perceiving and reacting to the environment, which restricts a person's ability to cope with stress and to formulate realistic alternative approaches to problems. Cognitively rigid individuals see the problem, their inability to solve it, and the future as catastrophic. (For example, "I have no place to live and no one to help me; there's absolutely nothing I can ever do about it.")
- Cognitive distortion: Overestimation of the magnitude and insolubility of problems. The difficulty of a problem is also generalized to all situations. Distorters assume that they are the cause of the problems they have. (For example, "I didn't get an A on that test, so I must be stupid and everything in my life is a complete mess.")

Children and adolescents with pervasive negative beliefs about the self, about the insolubility of problems, and about the future are at great risk for self-harm (Sargalska et al., 2011). These thoughts can lead to withdrawal, to an inability to create change, and ultimately to suicide. Faulty thinking patterns are self-defeating, and tend to spiral: Once young people begin to see their problems as insolvable, the problems themselves grow increasingly worse, and their ability to conceive of solutions becomes increasingly limited (see Figure 10.1).

WARNING SIGNS OF SUICIDE

Suicide Motivations

The reasons that young people attempt suicide are, themselves, initial warning signs, if they can be detected. Suicide can be a method of self-punishment to deal with guilt or shame. Self-punishment is not uncommon for a young girl who discovers she is pregnant, for a teenager who begins to have memories of sexual molestation, or for an adolescent in conflict about sexual orientation. Suicide may also seem to provide absolution for past behaviors; this motivation is not uncommon among alcoholics. Suicide may be motivated by perverted revenge, a perceived means to get back at those who caused the individual pain, such as parents who got divorced. Retaliatory abandonment is another motivation for suicide. A boy who has been dumped by his girlfriend can "retaliate" by showing her how awful she was to cause him to end it all. He would rather leave than to be left by someone. Both perverted revenge and retaliatory abandonment may have been operating in the case of the girl described in Box 10.3. Fantasy of omnipotent mastery is a desire to have absolute control over the self and others, to control life and death itself, and to be completely autonomous. Finally, children or adolescents may attempt suicide not intending to end their lives but rather as a cry for help; of course, these attempts can be just as lethal. Decreasing suicidal ideation is essential in reducing actual attempts, and being aware of suicide motivations can assist in detection and prevention.

FIGURE 10.1 Suicide Potential Spiral

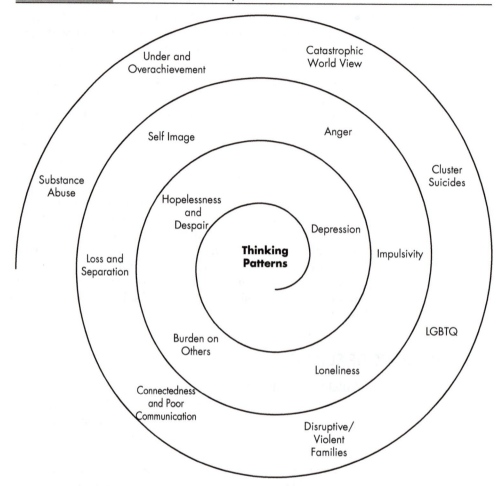

Verbal Messages

Most children who feel self-destructive give verbal hints that life is too difficult to handle and not worth living. Children and adolescents may say any of the following or similar statements:

- "I don't see how I can go on."
- "I wish I were dead."
- "There's only one way out of my problems."
- "I won't be around much longer."
- "I'm tired of living."
- "You'll be sorry you treated me this way."
- "Pretty soon my troubles will be over."

These young people are hinting or saying directly that they are considering suicide.

| Box 10.3 | The Girl Who Had Everything |

Shelley was an intelligent, beautiful, and popular high school senior. She was dating the homecoming king, earning straight A's, the star of the girls' softball team, and was liked by everybody. She seemed to have everything her girlfriends wanted without even trying. When her parents went through a sudden and angry divorce, Shelley continued to be the same smiling, fun-loving friend; her girlfriends believed that this "courage" was just another strength that their talented friend possessed.

One weekend she got into a fight with her mother just before her mother and brothers were to leave for an overnight visit with friends. In what was probably an attempt at revenge, Shelley called a large number of her friends and had a party at her mother's house. After several hours of drinking, Shelley got into another argument, this time with her boyfriend, and he broke off the relationship. Her girlfriends reported that Shelley seemed to be her "normal, laughing self" for the rest of the evening; at the time, they assumed she thought the breakup was only temporary. But when her family arrived home the next morning, the car was running in a closed garage, and Shelley had been dead for hours.

She left no note. Shelley had not done or said anything to her friends to suggest that she wouldn't be around the next day. It appeared to be an impulsive decision, carried out in haste. Clearly her outgoing high spirits and bravado were masking despair and anger. Perhaps they also masked the fact that this girl who "had everything" had never really learned how to cope with disappointment and pain.

Suicidal children also talk about death, wonder aloud what it will be like to be dead, and may be preoccupied by thoughts of others who have died. They may also joke about killing themselves. Many messages that are communicated as jokes are actually indications that a suicidal crisis is imminent; these jokes should not be taken lightly. In an effort to get help or to find out how others will respond, some children make direct threats of suicide. Verbal warnings should be taken seriously and not seen as just a "stage" that children go through. Failure to respond to a verbal warning or to a direct threat of suicide may be interpreted as confirmation that the child is worthless, expendable, and unloved. These feelings only increase the risk of a suicide attempt. Comments that reflect an orientation to passive suicide also merit serious response. The mechanism that transfers a passive view of self-destruction to an active one is unknown. From a preventive perspective, the helper needs to respond to both categories.

Behavioral Changes

Parents, teachers, and counselors can help prevent suicide attempts in children and adolescents by familiarizing themselves with behavioral changes that may suggest the risk of a suicide attempt. These include the following:

- Mood swings or fluctuations
- A change from happy and positive interactions with others to withdrawal and negativity
- Apathy or a lack of activity, such as neglect of hobbies that once were important to the person
- Changes in sleeping or eating patterns—insomnia or lethargy, lack of appetite or ravenous hunger
- Giving away prized possessions

School personnel in particular may recognize the following behavioral changes:

- A decline in the child's productivity and performance
- An increase in truancy
- More acting out in class
- Possible drug or alcohol use and hanging out with the "wrong crowd" at school and after school hours
- Higher levels of social activity than the average student if the youth is at risk for school dropout as well

General Risk Factors

As we observed earlier, suicidal children typically have a rigid and unrealistic style of thinking (Sargalska et al., 2011). The content of their preoccupations may also be a warning sign. When children seek to escape from a situation, join a dead friend or family member, be punished for their actions, get revenge or hurt someone else, control their death, or solve a problem that they see as intolerable or unresolvable, they are at risk for self-destructive behavior. A negative outlook and poor self-image are also warning signs. Most children will express their thoughts in some way. Knowing the state of mind and the style with which a child resolves or fails to resolve problems is the first step in preventing suicide. Strategies for cognitive change are discussed in Chapters 12 and 13.

As we saw in Chapter 1, Paul Andrews exhibits many of the warning signs of suicide. The conflict with his parents, although less focused than that of his sister, Allie, may be a precursor to a suicide attempt because parent–child conflict is a common prelude. Paul's stepfather, Jack, either is overtly aggressive toward him or ignores him completely. His mother passively encourages Paul not to upset Jack. Paul acts out in school, is aggressive with other children, and yet at times is very withdrawn. He also receives attention (and subsequent rejection) from other children by repeating gory news stories related to death and human pain. Paul's interactions with his peers reinforce both his aggressiveness and his feelings of guilt, worthlessness, and anger at himself and at the world. Paul demonstrates warning signs in those areas that serve as red flags—verbal messages, behavioral changes, and cognitive preoccupations. Unfortunately, his strategies for getting attention and support are not effective.

Nonsuicidal Self-Injury

NSSI is defined as behaviors where children or teenagers intentionally inflict physical harm, usually causing tissue damage, to their own body without the intent to die (Hyldahl & Richardson, 2011). Deliberately cutting one's arm or leg is a common example; burning, bone breaking, hairpulling, and other self-injurious behaviors also qualify. Usually, body piercing and self-tattooing are not considered an NSSI because the purpose is ornamentation, sometimes attention getting, or, in the case of gang or prison "tats," advertising or announcing affiliations.

Self-injurious behaviors have been relatively common in psychiatric clinical settings that deal with patients with borderline personality disorders. However, in recent years they have increased among young people who are neither hospitalized nor have a psychiatric diagnosis. Among community and school samples, about 7% of preadolescents and 12% to 40% of adolescents (Lloyd-Richardson, 2010) have engaged in NSSI, and the numbers are expected to increase (Whisenhunt et al., 2014). Just as suicide has increased among youth in the last two decades, so too have other types of self-harm, perhaps because the Internet and media have had considerable influence on other types of self-injury, as well as on suicide (Whitlock et al., 2009).

Consequently, human service professionals are being called upon to work with NSSI clients more and more frequently. Counselors have expressed their reactions to working with clients who self-injure and they conceptualized such clients by noting the external factors, the potential for harm, the conditions for treatment, and the young person's response to treatment (Whisenhunt et al., 2014). Because of the problems created by NSSI acts—self-mutilation, infections, observer shock—intervention for self-harming is important. Moreover, self-harm is symptomatic of any number of underlying issues that the young person and her/his family need to deal with.

Self-injury is a distinctly different activity from a suicide attempt. Although many who self-injure, apparently, do have some suicidal thoughts and 55% to 85% have made at least one suicide attempt (Trepal, 2010), NSSI is primarily a mechanism to relieve overwhelming negative feelings, relieve tension and cope with stress, and diminish feelings of disassociation and emptiness. Ironically, seen in this light NSSI becomes a life-sustaining act rather than an exit strategy; it is a life preserver and a means to disrupt emotional disorganization, at least initially (Hyldahl & Richardson, 2011).

Nevertheless, in addition to very real negative consequences in and of itself, NSSI contributes to later suicide thoughts and behaviors (Whitlock et al., 2013). It probably fulfills the final factor necessary for the interpersonal theory of suicide to predict suicide. It may reduce inhibition through habituation to fear and pain. Thus, NSSI prior to suicide behavior may serve as a "gateway" behavior for suicide.

IDENTIFICATION AND RISK ASSESSMENT STRATEGIES

Several useful strategies have been devised to determine whether children will act on suicidal thoughts. Recognizing signs of depression and familiarity with its various forms and manifestations can be very helpful. Two other methods are clinical interviews, which can disclose the severity and lethality of suicide ideation, and self-report measures.

Interviews for Suicide Lethality

Interviews are probably the most effective and informative way to assess suicide risk (J. J. McWhirter, 2002). Interviews are conducted with parents, teachers, and the child or adolescent who appears to be at risk of suicide (Bryan, Corso, Neal-Walden, & Rudd, 2009). Because suicidal children are typically angry at themselves, upset at the world, and caught up in emotional turmoil, it is critical to establish a professional relationship that expresses confidence, helpfulness, and trust.

The interviewer should attempt to assess (a) the history of the presenting problem (e.g., depression, anxiety, loneliness); (b) the family constellation and family relationships; (c) a developmental, medical, and academic history; (d) the status of the child's interpersonal relationships; (e) verbal and behavioral warning cues; and (f) any current stressors that may trigger a suicide attempt. Changes in behavior, in sleep and eating patterns, and in emotional status as well as any previous suicide attempts should be noted. Discrepancies between the parents' and the child's reports may indicate a problem and the parent interview can be most important (Bryan et al., 2009). The following high-risk factors should receive particular attention (Substance Abuse and Mental Health Services Administration, 2012):

- Symptoms of clinical depression and hopelessness
- Recent loss of an important relationship or life goal
- Serious family problems, such as divorce, alcoholism, physical abuse, or incest
- Personal history of physical disability, alcohol or drug abuse, or psychiatric treatment
- Interpersonal impoverishment, or the absence of friends, family, church members, or others who can provide direct emotional support in a crisis

When suicide ideation is present, the lethality of the risk must be assessed. The severity of the threat depends on the specificity and the lethality of the method of choice. Ideation alone is not a great risk, especially if it is passive. In fact, for every completed suicide, 100 to 200 attempts are made (Centers for Disease Control and Prevention, 2010). Progressively worse are (a) ideation with a plan, including a time, place, and method; (b) a lethal method (such as a gun or a leap from a tall building); (c) accessibility of a means to commit suicide (such as a loaded gun in the house); and (d) a history of previous suicide attempts. Research (Miranda et al., 2014) on previous suicide attempts is particularly revealing. Adolescents who reported a high desire to die, who planned their attempt for over an hour, and who were alone during the initial suicide attempt were at least five times more likely to make a future attempt.

Self-Report Inventories

Researchers have developed a variety of inventories to identify suicidal children and adolescents (see Thompson & Eggert, 1999, for a previous review of these). Granello (2010) has identified 12 core principles for suicide risk assessment.

The Suicide Risk Screen is a pragmatic and effective method for identifying suicide-risk students (Thompson & Eggert, 1999). In addition to his depression measures, other scales by Beck and his associates are the Beck Hopelessness Scale (BHS; Beck, Weissman, Lester, & Trexler, 1974) and the Scale of Suicide Ideation (Beck, Kovacs, & Weissman, 1979). The Scale of Suicide Ideation includes questions related to attitudes about living or dying, the characteristics and specificity of suicidal ideation, and background factors such as previous suicide attempts. These measures can help identify the risk of suicide among children and adolescents. The Columbia-Suicide Severity Rating Scale retrieved from http://www.cssrs.columbia.edu/about_cssrs.html is another measure that may assist counselors in the assessment of suicide risk.

Schoolwide screening strategies have demonstrated encouraging results in preventing suicidal behavior (Gould & Kramer, 2001). Through the use of interviews and self-report inventories such as those described here, preventive screening methods in schools can generate information about suicidal ideation, substance abuse, depression, and previous suicide attempts. This is critical for identifying those who are at risk.

SPECIFIC INTERVENTION STRATEGIES FOCUSED ON SUICIDE CRISIS

When involved with a young person who is seriously contemplating suicide, it is very important to assume a different stance than that which is ordinarily assumed by counselors. Suicide is not correctable. Counselors should become active, authoritarian, and engage other significant people in the intervention process. Two words of caution: Young people with suicidal thoughts and more severe depression before treatment are at higher risk for suicidal events while undergoing treatment (Vitiello et al., 2009) and girls are more likely than boys to benefit from existing prevention programming (Hamilton & Klimes-Dougan, 2015).

Suicide treatment is a response to a threat of suicide, and the following steps must be taken to defuse a suicide crisis:

1. Listen and show respect for the feelings a suicidal youth expresses. Suicidal youth feel that their problems are severe, and their feelings should not be brushed aside. Schools should incorporate peer assistance programs to aid in crisis intervention and decreasing suicidal behavior.

2. Reinforce the young person for seeking help. Admitting suicide ideation or attempting suicide brings shame and embarrassment. These feelings should be acknowledged. The counselor can also help the youth recognize and voice the part of him or her that wants to survive. This can help deter a later attempt.

3. Be specific about assessing lethality. Ask direct questions: "Are you thinking about killing yourself?" Be particularly specific about assessing the concreteness of the plan. Ask: "How do you plan to kill yourself?" "Do you already have the pills?" "Have you attempted suicide before?" Don't be afraid that asking such questions will increase the risk for a suicide attempt.

4. Make decisions. Children or adolescents who give indications that they will attempt suicide within the next few hours should be hospitalized for consistent care and monitoring.

5. Have the youth sign a written contract. An oral contract may be adequate, but a written contract is more powerful. Sometimes the suggestion of hospitalization is enough to persuade a child to sign a written contract. Be very careful about this tactic though. The child who feels coerced into signing a contract may feel under no obligation to abide by its terms.

6. Use the resources that are available. Community mental health agencies and private therapists are often the primary resources for helping children and their families after a suicide attempt or acute suicidal ideation.

7. Obviously, counseling for the young person is indicated. There have been only a few studies to explore the utility of treatment of suicidal thoughts and behaviors for adolescents and almost none for children. In a review of those studies (Glenn, Franklin, & Nock, 2015; Whitlock et al., 2013), six or seven were considered to probably provide efficacious treatments. Because of the dearth of research identifying a well-established treatment, practitioners should use treatments that (a) are intensive at the beginning of treatment to deal with immediate concerns and provide a safe environment, (b) focus on family to understand the circumstances and to build positive relationships, (c) contain a life skills training component to improve interpersonal functioning, (d) explore vulnerabilities for cognitive restructuring to enhance purpose and meaning in life, and (e) target other maladaptive behaviors such as substance misuse. In Chapter 12 we elaborate on these factors, especially on developing life skills and cognitive restructuring.

Prevention, Early Intervention, and Postvention

Primary prevention involves the removal or modification of environmental and interpersonal characteristics that are commonly associated with suicide. Early intervention programs target early detection and treatment of depressive disorders, anxiety, loneliness, stress, and family problems. Parents and teachers, the adults most accessible to the child and adolescent, play crucial roles in early intervention, but other school personnel and community professionals are also important. Early intervention programs in the school minimize the frequency and severity of the suicide ideation experienced by high-risk youth (Daniel & Goldston, 2009). Early detection can be managed conveniently and inexpensively through group screening devices and suicide threat can also be detected through gatekeeper training programs. In these programs, adults who come into contact with youth in school on a daily basis are trained to identify suicidal youth because suicidal children and adolescents are often not identified. Had such an early intervention program been in place in Paul's school, he might have been identified earlier and appropriate interventions could have been implemented before the suicide crisis emerged. However, school principals are reluctant to institute screening programs but are more in favor of staff training (Whitney et al., 2011).

School crisis response teams are an important part of deterring suicide and providing support when a suicide or other tragedy occurs (Substance Abuse and Mental Health Services Administration, 2012). Of course, a crisis response team also deals with other tragedies, such as school shootings or localized terrorist attacks. Response teams are made up of trained teachers and administrators, school counselors, school nurses, social workers, and educational paraprofessionals (Allen & Ashbaker, 2004), as well as parents and community members (Maples et al., 2005). Although response teams are designed for crisis intervention, part of their purpose is to provide education and intervention before an actual crisis emerges.

Several early intervention activities are central to the response-ready crisis team (Brock, Sandoval, & Lewis, 2001). The school must develop a prevention and early intervention plan. Referral resources should be prepared and procedures established so that team members can take direct, immediate action when it is needed. Schools should involve families and parents in this program. In addition, schools must incorporate the unique experiences of diverse populations into their early intervention plan.

- Teams coordinate their activities with those of mental health agencies and other organizations that serve families and children in the community. They may also engage law enforcement agencies, private therapists, medical professionals, and church and hospital personnel. Developing a network is critical for preventing suicide and for dealing with attempts.
- Response teams can participate in education and training. Continuing education on suicide risk and response should be provided to teachers, other school personnel, and parents (Daniel & Goldston, 2009). Response teams can also maintain appropriate audiovisual materials and a library of information on suicide and intervention resources. In one study, researchers found that after viewing videos on suicide, parents' knowledge increased regarding suicidal signs, responses toward suicidal youth, and appropriate help-seeking and prevention strategies (Maine, Shute, & Martin, 2001). This is particularly important in light of the finding that family- and community-based programs have the greatest protective effect at addressing suicide risk (Brutsch, 2015).

- Response teams should review and maintain the program to ensure that referral resources are updated, procedures are efficient, and the prevention and early intervention activities are appropriate for the students.

Finally, response teams should consider the following recommendations when instituting suicide prevention and early intervention procedures:

1. Plan your response before a crisis.
2. Deal with suicide issues openly and honestly. Don't avoid talking about suicide.
3. Prepare significant adults first, especially teachers and other school personnel, to deal with a suicide crisis. This will help to prepare students to deal with suicide.
4. Always prepare adults about suicide issues and discuss the content of educational films about suicide before showing them to students. Be sure to reserve time after showing an educational film on suicide to discuss the content and to allow students to share their thoughts and feelings about it. The same is true for parents.

Crisis Management and Response

A suicide crisis is managed with the same concern and immediacy as any other emergency. Counselors, teachers, and administrators who are members of the response-ready crisis team should free themselves from normal duties to respond to such an emergency. Mental health professionals, such as school counselors, play primary roles in a crisis response.

First, counselors need to assess the lethality of the suicide threat (J. J. McWhirter, 2002). If a suicide plan is specific and lethal or if an attempt has been made, counselors must assess whether the child or adolescent is stable, using referral procedures as needed. Hospitalization may be called for.

Second, a written contract is developed between the student and the counselor. This contract establishes an agreement that the student will not attempt suicide before talking to or seeing a counselor again. Most children who sign a contract comply with it. Providing the child with an emergency crisis number is also important. Crisis hotlines have been used for decades to prevent suicidal behavior (Gould & Kramer, 2001). Suicidal behavior is often related to a crisis, and trained workers at crisis centers can handle "cries for help." Two national hotlines are available for support: (1) National Suicide Prevention Lifeline [1-800-273-TALK (8255)], and (2) The Trevor Project (1-866-488-7386). The Trevor Project is a 24-hour free and confidential crisis and suicide prevention helpline specifically for LGBTQ and questioning youth (http://www.thetrevorproject.org for more information) (Heilbron, Goldston, Walrath, Rodi, & McKeon, 2013). Although hotline resources may be especially important for at-risk teens, few studies have examined their efficacy.

Third, observation is critical. The child or adolescent must be monitored during the crisis for a period of at least 24 to 72 hours. This may involve arranging for hospitalization or a "suicide watch," during which family members and friends keep constant track of the youth's affect and behavior. Counseling should be action oriented, directive, and aimed at dealing first with the danger of suicide. Once a young person is stabilized, the underlying causes of the suicide crisis can become the focus of intervention.

Finally, counselors must notify parents of the danger of suicide when they are aware of suicide ideation. Parent–counselor contact is often the first step of a crisis response. Although this contact may break confidentiality, it is an ethically and legally appropriate response to a child's suicide threat. The counselor must make clear to all minor clients and to relevant adults the limits of confidentiality at the onset of the relationship. The counselor who informs others of the danger of suicide shows concern for the youth's welfare.

Immediately After a Crisis

After a nonfatal attempt, school personnel or the crisis team should attend to a number of other issues. Because most suicide attempts are not made at school, a member of the crisis team should call the parents to verify the suicide attempt. The call also provides an opportunity to offer assistance to family members. After this call, a team member should notify teachers and administrators, emphasizing confidentiality. It is also important to monitor the attempter's friends, follow up on others who are perceived to be at risk for suicide, and respond to friends who may be traumatized by the attempt. While the student is recovering, a team member should keep the student informed about what is going on at the school and encourage the parents to report on the child's progress.

This collaborative relationship is continued when the student returns to school. Members of the crisis team should help to make the student's return to school as comfortable as possible. Teachers should also remain aware of the appropriate steps necessary when a student returns to school after a suicide attempt. Both individual and group counseling have been effective in helping a child deal with the aftermath of a suicide attempt, although group counseling should be postponed a few months so that the attempter is not the primary focus of the group. Medications for depression and anxiety may also be effective after a suicide attempt and may be used in conjunction with therapy. It is important that the prescribing physician is aware of the young person's suicide attempt.

Family Interventions

After a suicide attempt, family treatment is often recommended in place of or in addition to individual interventions. An attempt at suicide by any member of the family is very stressful for all the other members, particularly when the family is already struggling. Even when the family is relatively healthy and functioning well, normal nurturance and family care may not be adequate to deal with a child's stress, anxiety, depression, and suicide ideation.

When working with families, counselors must emphasize certain key issues (Daniel & Goldston, 2009). First, counselors must establish the significance of the problem. Although parents may see their child's concerns as minimal, they may be overwhelming to the child. Parents must understand that a suicidal child's problem is a family problem. The involvement of Paul's parents, for example, is critical because much of his despair is rooted in family problems and dynamics.

Second, counselors must deal with the shame, guilt, and anger that parents often experience when their child is suicidal—and with the denial that may be operating within the family. Oftentimes, individual meetings are helpful after a suicide attempt in a family.

Third, the family must begin to recognize that the problems that led up to the suicide crisis have developed over a long time and recognize the extent to which they reflect family dynamics. Families should be encouraged to recognize, understand, and modify these dynamics as a means of managing a suicide crisis and of effecting long-term change. Finally, counselors should assess for suicide ideation among each member of the family.

Family counseling is probably the most effective method for dealing with the primary causes of self-destructive behavior. For example, modifying the communication styles and helping each family member to clarify and modify his or her role in keeping the dysfunctional family in balance would be useful for Paul and his family. Unfortunately, many suicidal children and adolescents do not live with their birth family, and interventions should involve alternative caretakers. Family counseling interventions are discussed in Chapter 14.

Postvention and Follow-Up Treatment

If a young person completes suicide, the focus shifts to damage control. A great deal of suffering is felt in the aftermath of a teen or child suicide. Surviving family members, friends, and schoolmates of the suicide victim often need follow-up treatment, or postvention. Individual, group, or family counseling may be needed to help them deal with the event. Sharing information about the suicide and discussing it with community members and with fellow students helps to prevent cluster suicides. Indeed, mental health professionals and school personnel have important responsibilities after a successful suicide. Most postvention efforts involve the school and the family.

Schools

The school is the major setting not only for prevention and early intervention but also for attention to the aftermath of a student's suicide. School personnel can provide information about suicide, help survivors cope with their loss, and offer counseling to students who may need special attention. Suicide should be discussed because a fear of discussing self-destructive behavior actually increases the risk to other students. In discussions of the suicide, the deceased child should not be glorified or romanticized, but students should be allowed to grieve. For example, the school should not hold a memorial for the student or plant a tree in honor of the student. However, students should be allowed to miss school if necessary to attend the funeral service of the deceased student. Neglect of these factors may increase the possibility of cluster suicides and complicate the grieving process for students.

Postvention, like crisis intervention, is the responsibility of the crisis team. The response team should take the following steps after a student has committed suicide (Substance Abuse and Mental Health Services Administration, 2012):

- Administrators should call an emergency faculty meeting to relay the facts and to give teachers "talking points" for class discussions.
- Designated team members call parents and offer assistance, contact the district counseling department, and prepare written information for parents about the event, the school response, and how to support their children and secure outside support as needed.
- The school should not hold an assembly to announce the suicide or issue a public statement about it. Some students may perceive these actions as positive consequences of suicide. In addition, the school must prepare for possible media coverage of the suicide.
- The school should not hold a memorial service, nor should it prepare a memorial statement for publication in the student newspaper. These activities can increase the perception that suicide is an acceptable form of death.
- Opportunities should be provided for friends and schoolmates to meet to share their grief, and emergency or crisis hotline numbers should be made available to students. The school may need to enlist community resources to manage these groups and to provide emergency and information services.
- Depending on the nature of the event, the school should hold a critical incident stress debriefing (CISD) of staff members (Juhnke, 1997; E. H. McWhirter, 1994). This process includes a structured review of the event and allows personnel to ventilate their feelings, fears, and frustrations. Although the usefulness of CISD has been questioned (Mayou, Ehlers, & Hobbs, 2000; Rose, Bisson, & Wessely, 2001), its use very soon after the incident and its continuing use (Campfield & Hills, 2001) suggest it has value in preventing future problems.
- The school should identify and monitor the well-being of close friends of the student who committed suicide.

Families

Some of the strategies used in working with families after a suicide attempt are also useful for postvention. Families may experience feelings of guilt, shame, and embarrassment after a suicide, but family members also feel grief, loss, and helplessness. Those who deal with a youth suicide must pay particularly close attention to the needs of the surviving family after the death.

CONCLUSION

Suicide attempts and completions can have a catastrophic effect on children and adolescents and on those around them. The prevention of suicide using early interventions for suicide ideation is essential. Because teachers, school counselors, and other school personnel play primary roles in the lives of children and adolescents, their knowledge of the symptoms, causes, misconceptions, warning signs, and related problems of adolescent and child suicide is of particular importance. Understanding child and adolescent risk factors can help prevent suicide. Prevention and early intervention strategies help minimize the likelihood and long-lasting effects of self-destructive behavior.

Prevention, Intervention, and Treatment Approaches

In Part 4 we provide a wide range of empirically supported and evidence-based prevention and intervention strategies to help young people. In Chapter 11 we describe a systematic conceptual framework and model of prevention, early intervention, and treatment of children and teenagers at risk. We conclude the chapter by describing two universal prevention programs. In Chapter 12 we return to resiliency and the five Cs of competency listed in Chapter 5 and discuss helpful interventions for decreasing negative behaviors and improving prosocial ones, including social skills, cognitive-behavioral strategies, and other approaches. In Chapter 13 we describe several intervention programs that can be used to help young people by harnessing prosocial peer group influences. In Chapter 14 we focus on family-based interventions. Thus we conclude the book with a presentation of interventions that have been found very helpful for working effectively with children, youth, and families.

Prevention, Early Intervention, Treatment Framework, and Other Environmental Considerations

CHAPTER

11

Ten old men gather for an evening of conversation and drink. They each bring their own bottle of Chinese wine, to be mixed together, warmed up, and shared.

One of them thinks: "Why should I bring wine? The other nine will. I shall fill my bottle with water instead," which he did.

Unfortunately, so did the other nine. And the old gentlemen suffered the evening, silently and ruefully, drinking warm water.

This vignette comes from an old Cantonese story. A family, school, or community is greater than the sum of its members. How often do we, as parents, educators, counselors, human service professionals, and as a society bear only "water" instead of bearing "wine"?

From Seek Wisdom by J. J. McWhirter and B. T. McWhirter

I n this chapter, we introduce a multifaceted prevention and treatment framework that integrates the concepts addressed throughout the book and provides an overall context for interventions. To provide background for this framework, we first clarify the relationship of prevention, treatment, and risk. Then we discuss a brief history of prevention strategies and define prevention. After a thorough description of the prevention and treatment framework, we address two universal programs that can reduce child and adolescent risk.

A COMPREHENSIVE PREVENTION, EARLY INTERVENTION, TREATMENT FRAMEWORK

What serves as a treatment intervention for one problem frequently serves as a preventive strategy for a more advanced problem. Problem behaviors exist along a continuum. If we involve Tyrone Baker (of Chapter 2) in a smoking-reduction group, for example, we are providing a treatment for his cigarette smoking; but because cigarette smoking puts Ty at risk for the use and possible abuse of alcohol, marijuana, and other drugs, our treatment also serves as a prevention strategy. If we engage the Carter family (of Chapter 3) in therapy for their troubled family system, we are providing treatment for their ongoing negative interactions. We are helping Jason Carter deal more effectively with both his maladaptive and self-defeating behaviors, and we are also potentially preventing Jason's further progression toward one or more of the at-risk categories.

Risk also forms a continuum, from remote risk to imminent risk. Factors that contribute to risk include demographic characteristics such as social class and economic conditions; family, community, and school stressors; and personal characteristics, attitudes, and behaviors. As discussed in Chapter 5, some young people are resilient enough to flourish even though their environment and context place them at risk. Other youth are fortunate in having enough protective factors to counterbalance the risks. Unfortunately, some young people develop specific personal behaviors that interact with poor family and social contexts to increase their potential for problems and place them at further risk for even more severe problems. As risk factors increase without a concurrent increase in protective factors, children and adolescents become increasingly likely to be at imminent risk. Our continuum framework incorporates the relationship between prevention and treatment as well as the continuum from remote to imminent risk.

In understanding risk, it is especially important to consider protective factors. Clearly, protective factors serve to buffer or protect young people who might otherwise be at greater risk. Just as risk factors can be thought of with respect to individual characteristics, family, community, and other contextual characteristics, so too are protective factors potentially present at each level. Individual protective factors include but are not limited to social skills and intelligence; familial factors include authoritative parenting and strong attachments between parents and children; community factors include accessible resources such as social and medical services and parks, as well as strong linkages between family and community. Prevention efforts that support and maximize protective factors while reducing risk factors are more likely to be successful (American Psychological Association, 2014; Hawkins et al., 2015).

Any model that incorporates prevention, early intervention, and treatment raises complex issues. The role of the school/agency/clinic, the linkage between the problems of young people and prevention, and the interplay between treatment and prevention are important considerations in formulating such a model (Conyne, 2015). To improve current interventions, it is also important to understand previously successful and unsuccessful efforts at prevention.

HISTORY OF PREVENTION PROGRAMS

During the 1960s, drug prevention programs emerged with a focus on providing information. Early efforts were based on scare tactics, moralizing, and often inaccurate information; many programs contained fear-arousal messages regarding the social and health consequences of drug use. The emphasis was on the drugs themselves rather than on the reasons people used them. Perhaps even more significant, youth reported that the information lacked credibility, and drug use actually increased among adolescents during this time. A consensus emerged that relying on information about drugs alone to change problem behavior is misguided.

By the 1970s, drug prevention programs began to address the personal and social factors that correlate with drug abuse and to provide more accurate information. Affective education became the major preventive approach. Rather than focusing on drug abuse, educational efforts focused on apparent factors associated with the use of drugs and attempted to eliminate the presumed reasons for using drugs. Affective education programs targeted self-esteem on the assumption that if young people understood their motivations for drug use and had greater self-esteem, they would not want to use drugs.

This approach also failed to lower substance abuse rates. Indeed, trying to eliminate most problem behaviors by focusing on self-esteem alone is not effective.

During the 1980s, prevention efforts began to emphasize behavioral strategies. These programs focused on developing social competency and prosocial coping, often subsumed under the rubric of "life skills." Following the behavioral tradition that includes a strong empirical foundation, research was conducted across some at-risk areas to test the efficacy of prevention and early intervention programs. The results of this research were promising, and life-skills education and social emotional learning began to be adopted around the world as an important prevention tool (Durlak, Domitrovich, Weissberg, & Gullotta, 2015).

The 1990s built on these previous efforts. Models developed in the 1990s began to systematically incorporate affective, cognitive, and behavioral areas and emphasized development of both skills and prosocial attitudes. Programs became more comprehensive and broad-based. Some efforts were made to develop programs to increase protective factors, but the main focus continued to be on eliminating risk. This began to shift during the first decade and a half of the 2000s. Risk factors continue to be targeted, but emotional education (Goleman, 1995) and positive psychology (McKown, Gumbiner, Russo, & Lipton, 2010; Seligman, Schulman, DeRubeis, & Hollon, 2010) contributed to a shift to a much greater focus on developing protective factors.

Concern with program effectiveness began to emerge in the 1990s and continues into the 2000s and 2010s. Unfortunately, relatively little is known about the effectiveness of the hundreds of commercially marketed youth prevention and intervention programs currently used in communities and schools throughout the United States. As serious attempts have been mounted to evaluate program impact, it has become evident that many well-intentioned prevention programs are ineffective and may even have negative effects on their young participants.

To deal with this concern, some university institutes (e.g., Blueprints Program at the University of Colorado) and a number of federal agencies (e.g., National Institute of Mental Health, Substance Abuse and Mental Health Services Administration, and the Office of Juvenile Justice and Delinquency Prevention) have utilized expert panels to consider the level of evidence for classifying empirically supported programs. Six such evaluation programs are as follows:

- Blueprints for Healthy Youth Development identifies a range of model and promising programs (**http://www.blueprintsprograms.com**).
- California Evidence-Based Clearinghouse for Child Welfare (http://www.cebc4cw.org) provides scientific ratings for child welfare settings.
- The Campbell Collaboration Library of Systematic Reviews (http://www.campbellcollaboration.org/library.php) focuses on critical reviews of criminological, educational, psychological, and social programs.

- National Registry of Evidence-based Programs and Practices, established by the Substance Abuse and Mental Health Services Administration (SAMHSA), reports on interventions aimed at substance abuse and mental health problems (http://nrepp.samhsa.gov/Search.aspx).
- Office of Juvenile Justice and Delinquency Prevention's (OJJDP's) Model Programs Guide (www.ojjdp.gov/mpg) provides a list of effective programs by a variety of outcomes and type of intervention.
- What Works Clearinghouse (http://ies.ed.gov/ncee/wwc) of the Institute of Education Sciences identifies effective educational policies, practices, programs, and products.

The need for these panels has come about because state and federal agencies are mandating that practitioners spend public funds only on effective programs. Most states are now moving to a policy of legally mandating that interventions used in clinical settings are mostly (although not completely) evidence-based strategies. Lists of acceptable scientific programs help facilitate the use of more effective programs. The highest level of evidence is usually based on the Chambless and Hollon (1998) criteria, which in turn are based on the American Psychological Association Task Force on Psychological Intervention Guidelines (1995). It is the gold standard for defining empirically supported therapies—ones that are supported by at least two randomized control trials by two independent teams of investigators. Unfortunately, practitioners are not implementing these evidence-based interventions routinely, compared with practitioner-developed or commercially marketed programs, which often have no tested outcome results. There are probably very good reasons for this, not the least of which is the gulf that exists between researchers and school and community practitioners. Some programs are very expensive because in addition to materials, workbooks, and audio- and videotapes they require considerable training to implement. In restricted school and community budgets, the practitioner looks elsewhere. Some programs are not particularly user-friendly, and most have to be adapted anyway to accommodate local community and school norms and circumstances.

To confuse the issue further, the federal agencies use somewhat different criteria to produce incompatible lists and different qualifying terms—*exemplary, model, promising, best practices, evidence-based,* and so forth—and also differ in how they define the level of evidence of effectiveness.

Nevertheless, programs with research-supported evidence of success are likely to be more helpful to children and adolescents. Understanding how programs are identified as effective should be helpful. Almost always, the procedures include establishing a set of evaluation standards for selection. This most often includes an experimental design, evidence of a statistically significant effect, replication of the original study with an experimental design that demonstrates effects, and—sometimes—evidence that the effect was sustained for at least 1 year post-treatment. Based on adherence to criteria, programs are designated by evaluative category. For example, the Safe and Drug Free Schools and Communities (SDFSC) program of the U.S. Department of

Education (2000), although it is currently not being funded, had a rigorous process for identifying prevention and intervention programs that have evidence of being successful. Using expert field reviewers, programs are submitted, reviewed, and evaluated according to the criteria. Evidence of program efficacy is a critical dimension of their evaluation; other criteria include program quality, educational significance, and usefulness to others. After a series of field reviews, the full expert panel then meets to consider all of the reviews and to make recommendations to the Secretary of Education on those programs successfully meeting the criteria. Programs are designated as Best Practices or Promising Programs. In this text, we offer descriptions of many of the programs that have been deemed valid and effective through this process or a very similar one.

PREVENTION DEFINED

Commensurate with this brief history of prevention programs, definitions of prevention have varied over time and across disciplines (e.g., Caplan, 1964; Conyne, 2004; Gordon, 1987; Mrazek & Haggerty, 1994; O'Connell, Boat, & Warner, 2009; Romano & Hage, 2000). Literally, prevention means to stop something before it happens (Romano, 2014). In 1964 Caplan added the categories of primary, secondary, and tertiary prevention. These terms refer to the reduction of new incidence rates of a disorder (primary), prevalence rates for those at risk of developing a disorder (secondary), or the harmful effects of an existing disorder (tertiary). In 1987 Gordon created a different classification system, making distinctions among universal, selected, and indicated prevention. This classification system identified targeted populations, including everyone in a population (universal), an individual or subgroup of a population (selected), or only individuals and groups at high risk (indicated). This system is currently used; most descriptions of target populations in prevention research, grant applications, available programs, and articles use these concepts.

There are several criticisms regarding the applicability of these definitions and classification systems to the prevention of mental disorders. Caplan's (1964) and Gordon's (1987) prevention definitions, for example, were originally created to classify prevention efforts for physical disorders. Unlike most physical disorders, however, it is more difficult to identify the cause or origin of a psychological disorder and to classify complex mental disorder prevention efforts into a single category such as primary or universal prevention. Similarly, the Institute of Health's prevention definition (Mrazek & Haggerty, 1994) has been criticized for using a disease-based prevention model, excluding social and political change and health-promoting interventions as part of prevention. Researchers addressed these criticisms and created a new definition for the prevention of mental disorders (Romano, 2014; Conyne, 2015).

Currently, in counseling and psychology, prevention efforts have at least one or more of the following five dimensions: (1) stops (prevents) a problem behavior from ever occurring; (2) delays the onset of a problem behavior; (3) reduces the impact of an existing problem behavior; (4) strengthens knowledge, attitudes, and behaviors that promote emotional and physical well-being; and (5) supports institutional, community, and government policies that promote physical and emotional well-being. This definition of prevention encompasses the goals of primary, secondary, and tertiary prevention practices and also includes strategies for risk reduction and promotion of protective factors. Moreover, this definition includes prevention efforts within larger social systems and acknowledges counselors' and other human service professionals' role as agents of social change (Conyne & Horne, 2012). To engage in prevention efforts along any of these dimensions, however, practitioners are challenged to determine which prevention practices and implementation strategies will be most effective with what individuals and communities at what time. This requires consideration of individual and context-specific factors as well as the interaction among these components in the creation and implementation of interventions (Bronfenbrenner, 1979, 1989; also see Conyne & Horne's [2012] *Prevention practice kit* for an application of factors). The framework we describe next is designed to assist in connecting some of these areas.

DESCRIPTION OF THE FRAMEWORK

This comprehensive framework is conceptualized as operating along several continua and provides intervention components that encompass society and community, family, and schools. Universal primary prevention, secondary prevention and treatment programs (i.e., early intervention and selected programs), and second-chance treatment intervention strategies are included. Figure 11.1 shows the several continua that comprise the framework.

FIGURE 11.1   Risk, approaches, and prevention continuum

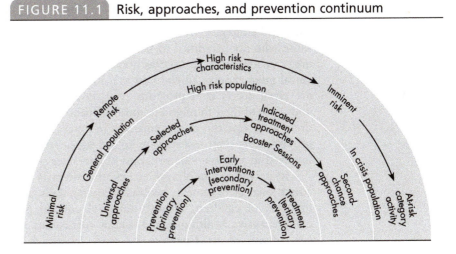

The Risk Continuum

The risk continuum introduced in Chapter 1 is at the top of the figure. Problems faced by young people are conceptualized as following a continuum from minimal risk to actual participation in an activity in one of the at-risk categories. Beginning at the left of Figure 11.1, a remote degree of risk is associated with certain demographic characteristics. As young people develop and mature, personal characteristics that lead to increasingly higher risk may become evident. If these personal characteristics are not modified, young people may soon be beyond remote risk and high risk and considered at imminent risk for many problems. The end of this continuum describes children or adolescents who are already engaged in one or more of the risk behavior categories discussed in earlier chapters.

The Approach Continuum

The second strand in the arch in Figure 11.1 identifies various intervention approaches to the problems that may appear at each level of risk: universal approaches, selected approaches, indicated treatment approaches, booster sessions, and second-chance approaches. We use the terms *universal*, *selected*, and *indicated* broadly to help conceptualize the continuum of possible interventions for at-risk youth. The relative placement of each approach between the anchors of the risk continuum above reflects the relation of the approach to the level of risk. Thus a universal approach is the most appropriate type of intervention when a child exhibits minimal or remote risk. As a child moves from remote risk to high risk, a selected approach is more appropriate. As a young person moves from high risk to imminent risk and then to at-risk category activities, an indicated treatment approach and then a second-chance program are appropriate. Each of the approaches in the second strand of the arch can operate in the domain of the community, family, or school, but we focus on the school setting for our examples.

Universal Approaches

Universal strategies are considered to be appropriate for all children, not just those who are presumed to be at risk. All children within a given catchment area (a community, a neighborhood, a school) may receive a common or universal intervention. All children in a low-income neighborhood, for example, are given access to a program even though some are at only minimal risk and some of their families are more affluent (Goodnight et al., 2012). All children in a classroom are engaged in interactive and cooperative learning groups rather than just those who are educationally deficient; all children are involved in a schoolwide program of character education or bully prevention.

In universal school approaches, the intent is to maintain or increase the educational achievement, prosocial coping skills, and mental health of large numbers of children. Ideally, universal content is integrated throughout a comprehensive health-oriented school curriculum. Basic life-skills competencies (discussed in Chapters 12 and 13)—such as problem-solving and decision-making skills, communication and other social skills, and impulse control—help young people respond to a variety of social situations. Developmentally appropriate personal, social, and cognitive skills are important components of a universal life-skills program. These programs can be beneficial at any time in the life of a young person, but they have the greatest influence early in life. Ideally, universal programs should be an integral part of preschool, elementary, and middle school curriculums.

Selected Approaches

Selected approaches are aimed at groups of young people who share some circumstance or experience that increases the probability that they will develop problems in the future. Demographic parameters, specific environmental stressors, and skill deficits indicate the need for target prevention programs. The children from low-income families who qualify for a Head Start program are perhaps the best example of a selected group defined by demographic factors. Because of their economic situation (which presumes other stressful circumstances), they are provided with an enriching preschool experience that increases their chances for later academic success.

Specific environmental stressors also provide a useful way to target young people either when they appear to be in a vulnerable situation or during specific developmental stages. Children from families in which there has been an acrimonious divorce, mental health problems, or drug abuse or alcoholism, for example, are quite vulnerable. Individual or group counseling or school support programs are very useful interventions for these students. The transitions from elementary school to middle school and from middle school to high school are stressful developmental periods. When these transitions are followed by a significant increase in absenteeism, increased susceptibility to substance use or delinquency, and a sharp decline in psychological well-being, selected approaches are needed. A third group of children appropriate for selected programs are those whose behaviors indicate deficits in skills. Sometimes these children are identified in psychological terms, such as *lonely*, *depressed*, *anxious*, or *aggressive*; sometimes by educational categories, such as learning disabled or behavior disordered; and sometimes in terms of their limitations in the five Cs (critical school competencies, concept of self, connectedness, coping, and control skills, discussed in Chapter 5). Most often, these children are identified and referred because of behavior disruptions. Unfortunately, many classroom interventions designed for these children focus on reducing behaviors that disrupt the class but do not attend to behaviors such as increasing literacy skills that are also vital to the child's ability to succeed in school in the long run. As we discuss elsewhere, increasing protective factors is equally important as reducing risk factors. Often the same social and cognitive skills that are addressed in universal approaches are used in selected approaches. Sometimes some students need increased attention, more intense emphases, and more applied practice to learn those very important skills. The risks, problems, and needs of the selected group must be identified before an appropriate intervention can be designed and implemented. This is the case in any learning situation, but school personnel need to give particular attention to students with special education classifications. Social skills competency interventions for children with emotional and behavioral disorders need to address the following components: skill acquisition, skill performance, removal or reduction of competing problem behaviors, and generalization and maintenance of skills (Durlak et al., 2015). Because of their emotional, behavioral, and learning problems, children identified for special education are especially suited for selected approaches.

Booster Sessions

Prevention efforts should be intensive, sequential, and comprehensive, with continued involvement over a long time period. One-shot prevention efforts are not very effective because program effects dissipate in a relatively short time. Short-term interventions usually achieve, at best, short-term results. Consequently, our framework includes periodic and sequential "booster" follow-up sessions to help potentially maintain the effects of the initial intervention. Bundy, P. T. McWhirter, and J. J. McWhirter (2011) demonstrated that five-session booster lessons for the SCARE program and for the SOAR program (Bundy, 2004; described later in the chapter) administered to randomly assigned participants nearly a year after the original interventions were extremely useful in maintaining and extending the positive effects of both programs. Usually, programs with booster sessions boost support over the initial intervention and are more likely to achieve positive long-term results (Tolan, Gorman-Smith, Henry, & Schoeny, 2010). More research is needed on the impact of boosters. For example, in one study (Sussman, Sun, Rohrbach, & Spruijt-Metz, 2012) the researchers employing a motivational interviewing booster component failed to achieve significant incremental effects above and beyond the initial results.

Indicated Approaches

On the right-hand side of the middle continuum in Figure 11.1 are indicated treatment approaches for individuals who are at imminent risk for problem behavior or who have actually begun to engage in the behavior. Indicated treatment approaches must be developed for young people whose underlying characteristics, problems, and behaviors are associated directly with at-risk activity. An anger reduction treatment group, for example, is an indicated treatment for hostile teens, and it is also a prevention strategy for fighting or other violence. Attitudes and skills that are particularly relevant for each at-risk category are addressed in indicated treatment approaches. Alternative behaviors and coping skills specific to the problem are also taught in indicated treatment. This is less restricted than appears. A number of interventions that are initially directed to one problem or issue often impact other areas positively (Hale, Fitzgerald-Yau, & Viner, 2014).

Second-Chance Approaches

Finally, "second-chance" interventions are needed for those children and adolescents who are already engaging in substance use, have dropped out, have become pregnant, or are engaging in violent and aggressive behaviors. Young people who have made poor choices need an opportunity to change those choices to more constructive ones; they need a second chance. The five chapters of Part 3 provide concrete examples of specific treatment interventions for specific at-risk categories.

The universal, selected, indicated, and second-chance approaches address, in sequential order, those risk factors that are the most salient contributors to young people's problems. These intervention efforts are most successful when they are comprehensive and cover a broad range of risk and protective factors. The problems of children and youth at risk have multiple antecedents, and interventions must focus on many causal factors if they are to be effective. The intent of such approaches is to set individuals on new paths as early as possible, to open opportunities, to modify life circumstances, and to aim for long-term change.

THE PREVENTION–TREATMENT CONTINUUM

Prevention, early intervention, and treatment programs also form a continuum, which is represented by the bottom strand of the arch in Figure 11.1. Conceptually, these three terms are closely aligned with the four-decade-old formulation of primary, secondary, and tertiary prevention that Caplan (1964) used to define prevention in the psychiatric field. As we mentioned earlier, Caplan used these terms to describe efforts for "reducing (1) the incidence of mental disorders of all types in a community (primary prevention), (2) the duration of a significant number of those disorders which do occur (secondary prevention), and (3) the impairment which may result from disorders (tertiary prevention)" (pp. 16–17). Caplan's terms are included on the continuum for some grounding; however, we use the prevention, early intervention, and treatment designations to more appropriately anchor our framework.

ENVIRONMENTAL SETTINGS

In the comprehensive framework, we attend to the environment by including society–community, family, and school settings, and we acknowledge the relationship between these components. Intervention in each of these settings is also conceived as following a continuum from (a) early broad-based prevention to (b) early intervention efforts to coordinate support and training activities, and ultimately to (c) treatment approaches. The three rectangles in Figure 11.2 represent the three settings, and each is divided by a diagonal line to indicate that some strategies and programs are best implemented earlier in the risk continuum and some are more appropriate later. Research indicates the importance of both the timing of interventions (Tolan et al., 2010) and the setting (Goodnight et al., 2012). The diagonal line also suggests that some aspects of prevention need to be maintained and supported throughout the model. In some circumstances treatment begins early and may accompany prevention. Early intervention falls in the middle of Figure 11.2 and has elements of both prevention and treatment.

Society–Community–Neighborhood

The society–community–neighborhood continuum interacts with both family and school continua but encompasses the neighborhood, the community, and the larger society. Prevention efforts in these arenas consist of improving socioeconomic conditions; increasing the supply of low-cost housing, child care, job opportunities, and career options; providing community social support programs; and developing healthy community norms and values.

Along the early intervention portion of the continuum are community programs that involve family members and school personnel. That is, there is a need to provide social support and coordinated programs that enable community members and neighborhoods to assist young people (Goodnight et al., 2012). There is a need to strengthen existing support for families in the schools and in community organizations. There is a need for schools to work with the community. Below the diagonal line are treatment strategies that include system-level interventions such as empowerment and social activism. Empowering young people and helping them to develop plans for social action are a preventive approach on the individual level, but they serve as treatment on the society–community level. The target here is not individuals or even groups of individuals but rather the norms, structures, and practices of organizations, communities, society, and the nation.

Family

Prevention, early intervention, and treatment for families form a continuum that begins with strategies designed to strengthen families—strategies that encourage interaction, consistency, communication, stability, support, and prosocial values (Healy & Sanders, 2014). Prenatal and health care programs are included as well. As family problems increase, social and emotional support programs and training in parenting skills are implemented. Counseling is critical for dysfunctional families. At the extreme end of the continuum, programs designed to address child abuse and neglect, parental dysfunction, and family violence are especially important (see also Chapter 14).

School

Prevention in schools begins with adequate comprehensive preschools, compensatory programs (such as Head Start), and before- and after-school programs (Durlak, Weissberg, & Pachan, 2010). And prevention continues on throughout the elementary and secondary years. The fact remains: Schools continue to be a critical setting for preventing behavioral and mental health problems (Bradshaw et al., 2012; Weist, Lever, Bradshaw, & Owens, 2014).

All school-based efforts are enhanced and the effects prolonged if there is a strong level of collaboration between school and home. Such collaboration is difficult to achieve due to parents' anticipation of being treated with cultural insensitivity, being patronized by school personnel, or being blamed for their children's difficulties. In addition, teachers may anticipate that parents will not respect their expertise, will not participate, or will blame their children's problems on the teachers. Indeed, these fears are all too often realistic, and the presumed common goal of serving the child is often not enough to overcome these barriers. Rather, multicultural competence, communication skills, time, resources, empathy, and patience are also required. The development and implementation of parent–teacher partnerships help prevent problem development among children at risk for behavioral and emotional disorders. One important element of good programs is the inclusion of parent liaisons, paraprofessionals from the local community who support parent–teacher interactions and facilitate and direct the meetings.

Universal school programs for teaching social and life skills to all children begin early in this model, although the diagonal line indicates that they can be implemented at any point (see Figure 11.2). In Chapter 12 we provide detailed information about teaching these skills. The need for selected

FIGURE 11.2 Environmental settings for a prevention, early intervention, treatment framework for at-risk children and youth

Environmental settings	Prevention		Early intervention	Treatment
Society/ community	Adequate socioeconomic conditions with housing, child care, and job opportunities and career options	Programs to increase low-risk community values and norms Community social support programs	Coordinated programs that link community, family, and school efforts Community programs and strategies	
Family	Programs that encourage family interaction, communication, and stability Programs that increase supportive and pro-social values in families Prenatal and other health care provisions		Social and emotional support programs Parent training	Family counseling and therapy Specific treatment programs for child abuse and neglect, parental dysfunction, and family violence
School	Preschool and compensatory educational programs (e.g., Head Start) Before- and after-school programs	Universal programs that develop social and cognitive skills Selected programs	Booster sessions Treatment for specific at-risk activities	Second-chance programs

programs increases chronologically; specific early intervention is necessary for targeted children in specific problem situations or for those who exhibit problem behavior.

Figure 11.3 presents early intervention and treatment concepts for each of five at-risk categories (discussed in Chapters 6 through 10). The universal programs specified at the left in each box of Figure 11.3 represent the preventive efforts that are directed toward all young people. As children develop, efforts shift from universal approaches to programs aimed at selected groups or individual children experiencing the specific problem areas listed.

Selected interventions should begin by grade 3 or earlier for children who engage in risky behavior (e.g., aggressiveness, withdrawal) or who exhibit such negative emotions as depression, anxiety, or hostility. In a given third-grade classroom, quite accurate predictions can be made as to who will drop out of school before graduation. Evidence also suggests that delinquency in adolescence can be predicted on the basis of early behavior patterns. A pattern of antisocial behavior established by fifth grade or even earlier often characterized by high impulsivity and lack of self-control is a strong predictor of subsequent antisocial behavior and is the single best predictor of criminal behavior in adolescence and adulthood (Hirschi, 2004;

FIGURE 11.3 Early intervention and treatment for five at-risk categories

	Selected programs			Indicated treatment programs	Second-chance programs
	Demographic factors	Environmental stressors	Skill deficits		At-risk activity
			Underlying characteristics	At-risk behavior	
Dropout prevention	Universal programs for all children		CCBG Solution-Focused Counseling Mastery learning; cooperative learning; learning strategies		Alternative school programs; GED/apprentice programs; Job Corps
Substance-abuse prevention	Universal programs for all children			Decision making, assertiveness, and refusal skills training Motivational interviewing	Drug rehabilitation programs
Pregnancy prevention	Universal programs for all children			Peer relationship and self-esteem programs	Community- and school-based health clinics; programs for pregnant girls
Delinquency prevention	Universal programs for all children			Prevention programs for aggression and conduct problems; anger reduction and anti-bullying programs	Reality therapy and restitution programs; school security and postvention
Suicide prevention	Universal programs for all children			Suicide-prevention programs; school crisis team	Direct-action interventions, postvention
Grade level	Preschool 3 4 5	6 7 8 9			10 11 12

Hirschi & Gottfredson, 2004). This is especially the case if the antisocial behavior occurs in a wide variety of settings and involves more than one type of act.

As young people progress through school, indicated treatment programs are required to assist those with more specific and serious concerns. Figure 11.3 also highlights second-chance programs for adolescents who have already engaged in risk category behavior.

A universal life-skills curriculum modified and adapted for developmental skill level, cultural appropriateness, and social class variables should be provided to all students as they move through school. Curriculum should include information on study skills and time management, how to prepare for tests, how to make friends, how to manage emergencies when home alone, how to avoid or report abuse, and, as the young adolescent matures, how to prepare for intimate relationships, how to prevent pregnancy and STDs, how to avoid drug use, how to resist peer and media pressure to engage in behavior that has negative consequences, and other life events. To be effective, these programs should be ongoing components of the curriculum rather than one-session classes. Training in problem solving, decision making, empathy, communication, assertiveness, and coping skills should also be ongoing. Teachers, with support from and in consultation with school counselors, psychologists, and social workers, should be prepared to teach cognitive and life skills, avoidance of substance use and delinquency, and sex education. Implementing such a model will have far-reaching effects for young people and for society as a whole.

PRACTICAL CONSIDERATIONS

Would such a comprehensive program be expensive? Certainly. But it is useful to consider the social costs if certain behaviors are not prevented. The costs of comprehensive prevention and intervention programs must be weighed against the costs of future residential treatment programs, medical bills, long-term incarceration, property damage, and welfare programs. When we calculate all of these costs, the expense of comprehensive prevention and early intervention becomes a bargain (Jones, Greenberg, & Crowley, 2015). To illustrate, in 1996 the federal government spent more than $38 billion to provide services and support to families that began with a birth to a teenager. In that same year, the federal government invested $138.1 million—less than one-seventh of one billion dollars—to prevent teen pregnancy (Bess, Leos-Urbel, & Green, 2001). That is more than 275 times less than the amount the federal government spent to support families begun with a birth to a teen. Of course, the long-term costs of teen mothering calculated here did not include lost wages (and lost taxes) associated with limited education or costs associated with the increased likelihood that sons born to adolescent mothers will spend at least some time in prison. In Chapter 4 we described the parallel increases and decreases in funding for prisons and educational institutions, respectively. An Urban Institute study on the costs of protecting vulnerable and abused children found that for every $1 states spend on "other services" (including prevention, child protective services, and case management activities) more than $3 is spent to cover interventions such as out-of-home placement, adoption, and administrative costs (Green, Waters Boots, & Tumlin, 1999). Several years later, a follow-up report from the Urban Institute indicated that prevention funding is still dramatically lower than intervention funding. Whereas at least $1.5 billion was expended on other services, of which prevention services only constitute one part, $9.4 billion was spent on maintenance payments and services for children in out-of-home placements (Bess et al., 2001). Of course, simply withdrawing money from intervention and investing in prevention does not solve our problems. We need to continue to assist those who are already struggling while dramatically increasing our investment in prevention. Unfortunately, when the economy is depressed, money for public services often takes the biggest hit. Resources are clearly more restricted in tough economic times and there is always a push to do more with less (Domitrovich, Gest, Jones, Gill, & DeRousie, 2010). Nevertheless, as we indicated in Chapters 1 and 2 especially, poverty continues to negatively impact the mental, emotional, and behavioral health of children, adolescents, and their families (Yoshikawa, Aber, & Beardslee, 2012).

TWO UNIVERSAL PREVENTION PROGRAMS

Universal programs are implemented to an entire population of intact groups. They are presumed to be helpful to all young people regardless of where they happen to be on the at-risk continuum, from remote risk to category behavior. That is, the populations served range from those doing well, to risky groups, to those already experiencing some level of impairment. In this section we provide examples of and discuss two broad-based programs that are helpful to all young people. The scope of both these prevention programs ranges from universal (i.e., promoting positive development for all) to targeted interventions for at-risk groups. The first is a school-based antibullying program, and the second is a classroom-based psychoeducational group program. Desired outcomes include the enhancement of social competencies and the reduction of problems and risk factors. The terms *school-based* and *classroom-based* are used for convenience only. In addition to school settings, these programs can be used in preschool and after-school settings, juvenile detention facilities, and recreational and day care programs.

Antibullying Interventions

The bullying that students, parents, and educators face today differs from that of earlier years in part because of young people's access to more lethal forms of aggression. Even when a bully is not actually accessing weapons, the perception of threat and the psychological effects are intensified. Evidence suggests that high school bullies and bully victims have higher criminal thinking and demonstrate more aggression than victims and control students (Ragatz, Anderson, Fremouw, & Schwartz, 2011).

Bullying is a specific subset of hostile aggression in which: (1) there is an imbalance of power with a more powerful person or group attacking a less powerful one; (2) the behavior is intended to disturb or harm; and (3) the behavior occurs repeatedly over time. The aggressive behavior may be verbal (e.g., threats, name-calling), psychological (e.g., exclusion, rumors), or physical (e.g., hitting, kicking). Bullying can be done directly in the classroom, hallway, or playground or indirectly and sometimes anonymously through e-mail and text messages, Facebook posts, and other Internet-based social networks and social media. The power differential may be psychological or physical. Thus, bullying can take many forms but retains the same essential spirit. Bullies are characterized by the need to dominate others through hostile means, and they show little or no empathy for their victims. In fact, students who bully and students who are victims (discussed later) both have higher levels of neuroticism and extraversion and lower level of agreeableness and conscientiousness. Only bullying behavior was associated with diminished affective and cognitive empathy (Mitsopoulou & Giovazolias, 2015). Thus, an important tool in reducing bullying is to teach empathy and other socioemotional skills (McKown et al., 2010).

Of particular concern is frequent bullying, typically defined as bullying that occurs once a week or more. Frequency of bullying is rather widespread and is higher in middle school grades than in high schools. Males were more likely than females to be both the victims and the perpetrators of bullying. However, relational aggression has emerged in the last few years as a serious problem (Low, Frey, & Brockman, 2010). Much of girls' aggression is not captured in many studies of bullying. Girls often bully their victims using relational aggression, which is characterized by high frequency and invisibility to teachers, and girls are often reluctant to acknowledge that it occurs. The Internet, with many forms of social media, is a perfect medium for relational aggression.

Cyber Bullying

Technology has afforded young people a new, and particularly insidious, method of bullying; electronic bullying or cyber bullying is a mode of bullying using chat rooms, text messaging, social network sites such as Facebook, and e-mail. The Internet allows users to maintain anonymity when communicating with a victim. Much less research has been done on this form of bullying although research has been increasing in the last decade and anyone familiar with e-mail can readily see the problem. A victim can receive dozens of electronic messages, perhaps from the same bully, and assume that virtually everyone at school believes him or her to be a jerk, a loser, or anything else the bully chooses to call the targeted individual. Options for practitioners directly dealing with youth, however, are a bit less sweeping, although they include a "multifaceted approach" to dealing with the behavior (Hinduja & Patchin, 2015a).

First, given the power of the cyber world, especially among young people, practitioners must try to set both limits and good examples of how to behave online. This is especially important given that it is more common for teachers and even counselors to communicate with students via the Internet than ever before.

Second, it is important to develop educational campaigns for parents and guardians (Hinduja & Patchin, 2015b, 2015c). Caretakers need to know what their children face. With practitioner support, parents need to learn to spot the dangerous Internet behaviors, patrol their child's online space, and to set limits with their own children. Parents and guardians can create their own Facebook and Instagram profiles and "friend" their child so they can look out for them online. They should also know their child's Internet passwords. These ideas will help a great deal, but unfortunately will not save every child.

Third, develop education campaigns for students that relate to spotting cyber bullying, dealing with cyber bullies, and communicating to students how not to be a cyber bully. This should include developing student anti–cyber bullying contracts. Chaffin (2008) presents a sample contract that includes the following: Teachers must discuss cyber bullying in all computer classes. Encourage victims of cyber bullying to bring offending material to the attention of schools and practitioners. Practitioners for their part must fully investigate all reports. Sanctions may include taking away offender's computer privileges, detention, suspension, separation, or expulsion. Schools can also block access to social networking sites on school equipment and prohibit students from accessing them on campus. A harassment-free environment must become the group norm for students (Chaffin, 2008; Hinduja, & Patchin, 2015a). This is just as important in the cyber world as it is in the noncyber world.

Fourth, build coalitions to police the "halls" of cyberspace. Practitioners and parents should collaborate to monitor websites and create an "Internet watch" similar to neighborhood watches to identify offensive material and ban offending users. Contact Facebook by using the "report abuse" button to note offensive material for removal. Schools and parents should keep web providers accountable for removing cyber bullying content (Chaffin, 2008).

Research examining personal characteristics of young people involved in bullying has consistently found that both the victims and the bullies demonstrate poorer psychological functioning than their peers and more negative academic competence (Ma et al., 2009).

Bullies generally demonstrate greater dislike of school, higher levels of conduct problems, and have an increased risk of having a criminal record as adults. Most research indicates that people who bully feel more comfortable in the social environment of school, are often at least moderately popular, and hold relative high status with their peers (Juvonen, Graham, & Shuster, 2003; Pelligrini, 2002). They also have low empathy skills and are impulsive

---

Box 11.1   Mean Classmates

When 13-year-old Ryan got his computer in seventh grade his parents gave him a detailed list of house rules. They included "no chatting with strangers; no giving out personal information; no secret passwords from parents." But, his parents did not imagine Ryan's own classmates were the most dangerous predators. An online bully, whom Ryan first faced in the schoolyard, took a funny story out of context to spread the rumor Ryan was gay. Ryan's father later described the "feeding frenzy at school" against Ryan. A popular girl pretended to like him and then humiliated him by spreading the details of their online conversations. She later told him she "would never want anything to do with such a loser." Despite his parents' conscientious attempts to protect him from online predators, Ryan killed himself (Chaffin, 2008).

(Farrington & Baldry, 2010; Mitsopoulou & Giovazolias, 2015). Most young adolescents who were bullied, on the other hand, believed that the victimization caused them significant problems, including the loss of friendships, feelings of isolation, hopelessness, and thoughts of ending their life (Rivers & Noret, 2010). Young people who are bullied generally show higher levels of anxiety, depression, and unhappiness, and they display significant behavioral difficulties years after the bullying. Bullying intensifies depression and the victims of bullying are more likely to self-injure than others (Claes, Luyckx, Baetens, Van de Ven, & Witteman, 2015).

Bully victims, young people who are victims and then turn around and bully others, appear to suffer from more severe social and psychological problems than either bullies or victims (see Jimerson, Swearer, & Espelage, 2009). Fortunately, actions taken by school personnel and others can significantly reduce the occurrence of bullying (Newman-Carlson & Horne, 2004) if they attend to the problem. On average, antibullying programs are effective at decreasing bullying by 20% to 23% and victimization by 17% to 20% (Farrington & Ttofi, 2010). Unfortunately, school personnel underestimate the prevalence of bullying, and they intervene in only one-third of bullying incidents brought to their attention (Rodkin & Hodges, 2003).

Schoolwide Plan

Although individual efforts can be helpful, developing a systemwide plan is necessary to significantly reduce bullying. Begin with a clear, agreed-upon definition of bullying, and make a plan for action. This plan for action should include answers to these questions:

- Does the plan develop an effective way to eliminate or reduce student-to-student put-downs?
- Are there as many opportunities for students to be recognized for prosocial, positive behaviors as opportunities to be recognized for antisocial, negative behaviors? How would the students answer this question?

- Does the plan include recognizing and promoting students' prosocial behavior and their random acts of kindness?
- Does the plan establish ways to recognize and support positive and kind acts done by staff and faculty?

Faculty and staff must be backed up in their efforts to identify and halt bullying. Inconsistent application of the plan or administrative failure to support the efforts of those implementing it will reduce student confidence and decrease effectiveness.

The purpose of the schoolwide plan is to change the context in which bullying occurs (Bradshaw, 2015; Gendron, Williams, & Guerra, 2011). Norms of looking the other way, intermittent punishment, and classroom Darwinism must be changed to norms of attending to bullying incidents, consistent application of consequences, and fostering a strong sense of community within every classroom (Newman-Carlson & Horne, 2004). In addition to responding systemwide, the plan needs to consider interventions with the specific people involved in the bullying. This includes victims, bullies, bystanders, "toadies," and parents.

The Victim

Concerned adults need to consider the bullying victim's realistic options given the particular situation and persons involved. The coping skills and support network of students who are bullied may need to be strengthened, especially for those children and teenagers who are quiet, unobtrusive, and socially unskilled, before the student can act more assertively on his or her own behalf. Victims of bullying often feel a great deal of shame and mistrust, which may make it harder for them to attempt to use the skills they do have. Identifying behaviors and strategies that will reduce their risk of further bullying can sometimes help students. The assertiveness training program described in Chapter 12 attends to one dimension that may be important for students who are bullied.

There is another type of victim, referred to as the "provocative victim," who provokes the bully with aggressive comments and hostile challenging behavior. While these victims can also benefit from assertiveness training, they need to learn more appropriate ways to meet their needs for importance, validation, and esteem.

The Bully

Incidences of bullying should not be ignored, but they do vary widely in seriousness and severity. Thoughtless teasing might merit an informal discussion; group harassment with threats might need formal procedures, including interviews with perpetrators and parents and possible disciplinary action. One promising approach, the Method of Shared Concern (Rigby, 2011), involves a two-stage process. In the first stage, perpetrators are identified and spoken to individually. The adult shares his or her concern with the bully for the person being victimized and invites the bully to act in a constructive and responsible way to remedy the situation. No threats are used, but the adult carefully monitors subsequent behaviors. In the minority of cases where this approach is not successful and the bullying continues, the second step includes sanctions and application of consequences.

The Bully Victim

An even more serious problem is those young people who are both victims and bullies. These bully victims (Cook, Williams, Guerra, Kim, & Sadek, 2010) perform poorly academically and have both externalizing and internalizing problems with significantly negative attitudes and beliefs about self and others. They are low in social competence and problem-solving skills and are not only rejected by most peers but are also negatively influenced by those peers with whom they interact.

The Bystander

Observers of victimization and bullying often receive little attention. This is unfortunate because they contribute to the problem and are negatively affected themselves. Many want to help but are insecure and afraid that they themselves will be targeted next. Remaining silent leads to guilt and anxiety and those students who were involved in bullying with multiple roles (victim, bully, and bystander) were significantly more likely to report having had thoughts of ending their life (Rivers & Noret, 2010). Encouraging bystanders to discuss their feelings, along with the provision of assertiveness skills and exploration of various options for responding, can encourage them to become more active in reducing bullying. Bystanders can provide personal support to victims, show their concern, encourage the victim's efforts and accomplishments, and refuse to reinforce the bully with verbal encouragement or laughter. More direct intervention might take the form of protecting the victim and confronting the bully during the incident.

Toadies

There is another type of bystander who is more interested in encouraging bullying and the bully. Indeed, bullies are sometimes bolstered by the presence of "passive bullies." These participants in bullying behavior support the primary aggressor by expressing approval and encouragement, reinforcing the perpetrator. These passive bullies should be dealt with in the same way as the overtly aggressive bully.

Parents

Parents/guardians are essential allies in implementing a schoolwide antibullying program. Understanding the problem of bullying, the prevention program, and the definitions of bullying used by the school is all-important in parental acceptance and support of the program (Bradshaw, 2014). In the process of learning about the program, parents may realize the importance of exploring bullying with their children in a more focused way, which may lead to surprises for the parents of both victims and bullies. Many children suffer, and dole out suffering, in silence. The parents of bullied children need information and support to help their child. The parents of students who bully may respond in numerous ways to their child's behavior: denial, blaming the victim, the school, or society, or requesting assistance with an out-of-control child. Blaming the bully—or his or her parents—is not helpful.

A developmental and comprehensive approach to reducing bullying is important. The most positive programs are those that adopted a whole-school approach, firm discipline and classroom management, improved playground supervision, and information about bullying and victimization for parents (Bradshaw, 2014). Thus, prevention programs that are supported throughout the school building, that include consistent responses to individual behavior, and that incorporate aspects of the social context of bullying are most likely to reduce the number of young people victimized by bullying. We describe such a program next.

Group-Oriented Psychological Education Prevention

This second universal program was developed around themes and suggestions offered by Phoenix area high school students who were asked to respond to the question: "How can we decrease violence in the schools?" These students were participants in a citywide essay contest conducted by the City of Phoenix and Prudential Securities. Students from 14 high schools submitted essays with a winner selected from each school. A cash prize was given to each winner, and an overall citywide winner received an additional cash prize. In addition to providing the prize money, Prudential Securities also provided a small grant to the City of Phoenix and, subsequently, to Arizona State University to analyze the essays and to develop a violence reduction program based on the winning suggestions. Although some of the students' solutions were not applicable—psychologically, politically, or economically—the suggestions were concrete, interesting, and always thought provoking.

We (J. J. McWhirter, McWhirter, B. T., McWhirter, A. M., & McWhirter, E. H., 1995) used a content analysis procedure for reviewing the winning essays, which we confirmed and validated by a similar analysis for all the submitted essays at one randomly selected school. The content analysis identified common themes regarding strategies and programs to prevent or reduce school violence. The content analysis resulted in four basic themes:

1. Increase support and encouragement through positive peer models (e.g., conflict resolution and peer mediation programs).
2. Change the structure of the school environment.
3. Increase positive adult role models, and provide better communication between school and home.
4. Develop specific classes that deal with student emotions underlying issues leading to violence (e.g., stress, turmoil, and difficulties young people face).

Students highlighted one other factor that led to developing the Group-Oriented Psychological Education Prevention (GOPEP) program. Almost all the students mentioned the need for prevention. This group of young people saw a need to begin violence reduction and other programs early and to continue them on into high school.

We completed an extensive review of prevention programs and discovered a host of training resources and materials on conflict resolution and peer mediation. This fact made the first suggestion superfluous. It seemed redundant to develop such a program when abundant material on this topic is already available. Suggestions two and three, which have been the focus of many prevention efforts and are important considerations, were beyond the scope of this specific project. We strongly recommended to school personnel that steps should be taken to implement them.

Because so many of the essay winners suggested the possibility of using the classroom structure to deal with underlying violence issues, and because so many believed that underlying emotional issues were often the cause of violence, we decided to focus our efforts on developing programs to help young people understand and then manage their negative emotions and behavior and increase their positive ones. Thus the students' fourth suggestion led to the development and validation of an anger management program.

SCARE (Student Created Aggression Replacement Education; Herrmann & McWhirter, 2001) is designed to help young adolescents manage feelings of hostility, aggression, and anger. The SCARE program teaches young people methods to control impulsive emotions, encourages them to make better decisions in responding to provocative situations, and provides them with alternatives to violent behavior. Through participation in SCARE, students first learn to recognize the problem of anger and violence in our society, and then learn the necessary skills to cope with their own feelings of anger and aggression, and finally learn strategies to prevent violence and aggression from escalating in others. Because the SCARE program is the prototype for other psychoeducation programs, we will return to it later for further discussion.

The other GOPEP programs include SOAR, or Students' Optimistic Attitudes and Resiliency Program (Gilboy, McWhirter, & Wallace, 2002); ART, or Anxiety Reduction Training (Boewe & McWhirter, 2002, November); and BLOCKS, or Building Lives on Companion Knowledge Skills (Fair & McWhirter, 2002, August). These are all based on supporting evidence that various social competencies can be directly and deliberately taught to reduce negative risk factors and to increase positive protective ones, and that educating young people in psychological foundations will help to prevent negative events. The group-oriented aspect of this program is based on psychoeducational group methodology. Psychoeducational group work is a common delivery method in comprehensive prevention programs where it is intended to maximize the potential for students' healthy development and success. Thus GOPEP uses a group format to deliver the skills, although sometimes the group is a classroom-sized group.

In these GOPEP prevention programs, we have targeted children and young adolescents mostly using a cognitive-behavioral approach. As discussed earlier, research indicates that at-risk children are overly sensitive to negative interpersonal interactions. They tend to have more negative beliefs about the intentions of others and to minimize their own responsibility for problems. They also frequently misunderstand and then mislabel their own affective arousal (emotions) so that feelings such as hurt, fear, frustration, and anger become confused. Higher-risk youth then subsequently respond to their own misperceived emotions, oftentimes in aggressive ways. Their solutions to perceived problems are often excessively action oriented and nonverbal, which typically worsens the problems they experience. The cognitive-behavioral training provided in GOPEP is designed to improve poor self-understanding, change frequent distortions of emotions and of perceptions around events, and enhance better problem solving.

The GOPEP programs are user-friendly prevention and intervention curriculums that provide leaders with easy-to-follow, step-by-step instructions. Currently, the four interventions focus on reducing anger, depression, and anxiety and on increasing hope and optimism, empathy, and positive relationships. Each curriculum consists of 15 group sessions with each session lasting approximately 1 hour. We designed the programs to be used by teachers, counselors, social workers, psychologists, law enforcement officers, detention center staff, scout leaders, senior citizen volunteers, and any other caring and dedicated adult who is committed to bringing about positive change in the lives of young people. The four packages deal with anger and empathy (SCARE); optimism, hope, and depression (SOAR); building and negotiating relationships (BLOCKS); and anxiety (ART) (see P. T. McWhirter & J. J. McWhirter [2011] for a more complete description of the GOPEP programs).

Anger Management

Learning to deal with anger and other emotions is an important component of an antibullying program and plays an important role in juvenile delinquency (Sigfusdottir, Gudjonsson, & Sigurdsson, 2010). Unfortunately, most anger reduction programs have not been empirically validated. Without validation, practitioners do not know whether their interventions are effective. More important is the possibility that the intervention is doing more harm than good. Most interventions are designed to put young people together in a group to help them reduce their anger and aggression, but this can be risky if youth are given unstructured time in which they may reinforce each other's aggression. Few anger programs have dealt with this issue, and few have been directed at the roots of aggressive and violent behavior in younger, middle-school-aged populations.

One exception is the SCARE program (Herrmann & J. J. McWhirter, 2001), which the Safe and Drug-Free Schools and Communities Agency in the U.S. Department of Education has identified as a "promising" program. The SCARE program was specifically developed to prevent violence and aggression through appropriate management of anger for early adolescents. A growing body of literature has consistently indicated that these years are critical to a young person's social development, and this time period is potentially one of the best times for prevention programs for at-risk youth. As there are a lack of aggression replacement and anger management packages available to teachers, counselors, and youth workers for this age group (J. J. McWhirter et al., 1995), the curriculum was designed for broad-scale implementation by such individuals.

One premise of the SCARE program is that negative actions perceived as intentional will elicit anger, and anger in turn motivates hostile behavior. Therefore, the SCARE program focuses on the reattribution of perceived offenses and the control and management of resulting anger. High levels of anger result in negative social consequences, including an increased propensity to cause physical damage to oneself and others and increased psychological and school-related problems. Anger can be effectively reduced through therapeutic intervention, which the SCARE program has demonstrated (Bundy et al., 2011; P. T. McWhirter & J. J. McWhirter, 2011). SCARE was constructed as a meta-theoretical treatment package focusing on anger management and coping skills for adolescents and young adults. Primary objectives embraced by the SCARE program include: (a) teaching young people about emotions, including aggression and anger; (b) helping young people to recognize alternatives to violent behavior and aggressive responses; and (c) encouraging young people to make good decisions in response to provocative situations. The 15 different sessions are clustered in three distinct yet related areas: (a) recognizing anger and violence in the community; (b) managing and reducing self-expressions of anger; and (c) defusing anger and violence in others.

In recognizing anger and violence in the community, primary objectives include: (a) providing a clear definition of anger and violence; and (b) introducing the topic of anger and violence in a way that promotes intrigue and interest for acquiring anger management and coping skills. We know that learning is facilitated among youth who have cultivated an interest for a particular subject and who feel that the material presented to them is relevant to their lives. By combining national statistics with descriptive images obtained from popular media resources, this section aims to stimulate motivation for learning anger reduction skills and cultivates awareness that such skills are vitally important to all adolescents.

The second section, managing and reducing anger in the self, was developed to inform youth about effective prosocial strategies for managing their own aggressive impulses and feelings of anger. This section is based on Novaco's (1975, 1979) adaptation of Michenbaum's (1972) stress inoculation model, and it consists of three separate phases: (a) education and cognitive preparation; (b) skill acquisition; and (c) application training. Education and cognitive preparation provides youth with information about the cognitive, physiological, and behavioral interactions of anger arousal. They learn about internal triggers that can provoke anger and about steps they can take to effectively manage their expression of anger. Skill acquisition consists of training adolescents in cognitive-behavioral coping skills to effectively manage situations involving anger and aggression. Application training consists of practicing newly acquired skills within the context of experiential group sessions or role plays until such skills are mastered. In studies assessing the efficacy of this model, Novaco (1975, 1979) reported evidence in support of stress inoculation training for reducing anger, whereas others have reported the effectiveness of this model with adolescent populations (Hains & Ellmann, 1994; Wilcox & Dowrick, 1992).

Finally, the third section, defusing anger and violence in others, draws on an eclectic model involving skills and techniques for (a) preventing situations involving anger and violence from developing and (b) promoting peaceful resolutions to hostile situations that have developed. To promote these objectives in as many different ways as possible, this section is not grounded in any one theoretical orientation but combines techniques from different schools of thought. In a review of the treatment literature, the multimodal approach combines several treatment modalities (e.g., cognitive skills, relaxation skills, and social skills training), which is usually more efficacious than unimodal approaches. In addition, multimodal approaches are of special value when treating behaviorally disordered and "acting-out" youth. Several sessions in the defusing anger and violence in others section draw upon diverse yet complementary theoretical tenants, including sessions on verbal and paraverbal techniques, body language training (proxemics and kinesics), identifying creative alternatives to aggression, diversity appreciation training, and no-violence contracting.

Hope, Optimism, Depression

SOAR (Student's Optimistic Attitudes and Resiliency Program; Gilboy et al., 2002) is a proactive program that is also multitheoretical in foundation and multimodal, utilizing humanistic, cognitive, and behavioral intervention techniques. The program also addresses the diversity of learning styles and works to engage the whole child in the process of learning. The humanistic approach creates the context for SOAR. The program builds largely on the positive foundations of students, emphasizing self-development, understanding, and positive regard for each student in a supportive community. The program uses stories, metaphors, and activities to increase hope and optimism and reduce depression. The purpose of the program is to build on the strengths of every child, increasing the child's sense of control over his or her thoughts, attitudes, and attributions. It builds resiliency and promotes well-being. The SOAR program seeks to explore healthy functioning not as the absence of something wrong but as a positive and definable entity in and of itself. The cognitive-behavioral approach also plays a prominent role in SOAR as many of the sessions engage students in learning new concepts, cognitive reframing, and activities that reinforce their learning.

The program was developed to highlight principles of positive psychology, and its theoretical foundations lie in learned optimism (Seligman, 1990) and hope theory (Snyder, 1994). In the simplest sense, optimism is a process by which one looks at a glass as half full (positive) as opposed to half empty (negative). It is the meanings that we give to the events in our lives that cause us to see them as positive or negative. The theory of learned optimism posits that our attributions are a function of the permanence, pervasiveness, and personalization of our thoughts. The optimist sees failure as a unique event that does not generalize and poison other areas of personal competence. This person will see the cause in the situation (external) as opposed to being a personal deficit (internal). The pessimist's failure is viewed as a permanent flaw that generalizes to all areas of life and is the result of some internal shortcoming. A wealth of research demonstrates a predictive relationship between optimism and psychological and physical well-being in children and adults (Buchanan & Seligman, 1995). The efficacy of the learned optimism intervention has been demonstrated in research with significantly fewer depressive symptoms in the intervention group than in a comparison group. An extremely important finding from this research was that the preventive effect, in terms of decreased depression, actually grew after the program had ended (Gillham, Reivich, Jaycox, & Seligman, 1995).

The second theoretical anchor is hope theory (Snyder, 1994). Hope is generically defined as having positive expectations or the lack of negative expectations about the future (Snyder et al., 1996). More specifically, hope is operationalized by three components: (1) the process of continual internal goal setting; (2) the ability to generate multiple paths to the goals; and (3) the perseverance to reach the goals (Snyder et al., 1996). The hopeful individual will see the path options and have the wherewithal to pursue the paths. The theory states that hope can be instilled through an improved view of one's future and skills acquisitions (i.e., techniques of optimistic thinking).

The sequence of the programming entails three broad areas. First, it is important to place the sessions in a meaningful context that will engage the students. Second, all students are taught how to think optimistically for themselves and how to modify other thoughts and behaviors to accommodate the new skills of hope and optimism. Third, students are made aware of the relevance of their newfound optimistic strategies. The students internalize the concepts and then apply them to their interactions with others, which ultimately positively affect their identity as members of the classroom and the larger community. These three areas are integrated into the sequence with key components practiced throughout. Implementation of this program predicts a decreased incidence of depressive symptoms and, concurrently, an increase in hope.

Relationships

BLOCKS (Building Lives on Cooperation Knowledge Skills; Fair & McWhirter, 2002) is designed to increase students' ability to negotiate successful interactions with others. Developing social skills to create successful relationships is one of the most important accomplishments of childhood (Durlak et al., 2015). This is especially important with students with differences in social skill functioning. BLOCKS focuses on increasing skills such as cooperation, assertion, responsibility, empathy, and self-control. The program is multitheoretical and utilizes multimodal interventions. BLOCKS promotes interpersonal and friendship skills, leading to better social adjustment.

The framework for this program is based on the theory of multiple intelligence (Gardner, 1983) and social learning theory (Bandura, 1993). Multiple intelligence theory, in essence, is a multiplied way of understanding intellect. According to Goleman (1995), IQ is not the only measure for success and counts for only 20% of the variance, with emotional and social "intelligence" accounting for the rest. Research demonstrates a positive relationship between social intelligences and academic performance (Elias, Gara, Schuyler, Branden-Muller, & Sayette, 1991). More important, research has shown that the acquisition of social skills can positively affect academic achievement during the time they are taught as well as in the long term.

Social learning theory (Bandura, 1973, 1993) is the second theoretical base for BLOCKS. Social learning theory explains that new skills are acquired through a complex interaction between the environment in relationship to individuals' behavioral and cognitive abilities.

Anxiety

ART (Anxiety Reduction Training; Boewe & J. J. McWhirter, 2002) is designed to reduce fear and anxiety in participants. Anxiety and fear can either be directed toward a specific object or can be a general negative feeling of worry. Anxiety inhibits cognitive abilities as well as emotional and social development. Anxiety may go undetected because it sometimes operates at a low level, yet it still influences many areas of daily functioning.

In the ART program young people reduce anxiety through a series of activities involving the creation of art. Using several different media, students create an art product and discuss their thoughts and feelings related to their productions. Each ART session activity has specific instructions that involve student reflection on specific components such as identity, feelings, environment, coping skills, and fears. The art skills involved are quite basic, and projects can be accomplished based on students' current levels of visual art skills: simple figures, simple abstract drawings, or collages of photos or magazine illustrations.

After each project, students discuss their respective pieces and what they represent. The exercises are nonthreatening while encouraging self-disclosure, connecting with group members, and cultivating feedback and support. Students recognize and confront certain fears while finding support and comfort from their peers.

CONCLUSION

The comprehensive prevention, early intervention, treatment framework presented in this chapter highlights how interventions are related to and modified by the developmental sequence as young people become increasingly troubling and troublesome. Prevention efforts include universal approaches for all children as well as selected programs that attend to issues of concern that are identified early on. As children come to be increasingly at risk, they may require indicated intervention or treatments focused on specific problem areas. For youth already engaged in an at-risk category activity, treatment that includes second-chance programs may be necessary. Each of these interventions, provided for children and teenagers at a specified level of risk, can be offered in social services settings in the community and in schools, serving families, groups, and individual youth. Antibullying programs and GOPEP represent two examples of effective prevention interventions.

Core Components of Programs for Prevention and Early Intervention

CHAPTER 12

It's three a.m. again and she wakens full of dread

Another day coming

another endurance test to mark

how many taunts, snubs, stares

a girl can bear in silence.

The clock ticks on relentlessly

then in its rhythm she begins to hear

"I think I can I think I can"

She smiles, remembering stories and laps, comfort

Smiles at herself for this lapse into silly optimism

Smiles at the thought of her teacher—

trying so hard to push this "positive thinking"

That no one will ever use ...

Sleep finds her

Still smiling.

CHAPTER OUTLINE

- **Coping Ability**
  - Relaxation
  - Progressive, Deep Muscle Relaxation
  - Benson's Relaxation Response
  - Guided Visual Imagery
  Procedures for Guided Imagery
  A Safe Place
  - Affirmations

- **Control: Strategies for Cognitive Change**

- Control of Decisions
- Self-Management and Self-Control
  Self-Assessment
  Self-Monitoring
  Self-Reinforcement
- Control for Learning

- **Conclusion**

Specific cognitive and behavioral skills and affective responses and awareness play a large part in a young person's personal and social success. Resilient youth develop social competencies that help them to negotiate life's vicissitudes and to emerge as healthy, strong, and contributing individuals. High-risk youth who do not develop such competencies may frequently find themselves on a downward spiral of lowered expectations, destructive behavior, rejection by society, and a dead-end future. These young people have not mastered the fundamental life skills that allow them to survive and thrive in the world.

In Chapter 5 we discussed resiliency and how some young people have the ability to thrive despite exposure to severe risk factors. To be considered "resilient," children must both experience significant negative life events that ensure their status as "high risk" and demonstrate successful and positive adaptations to that risk. We also highlighted five major areas—the Five Cs of Competency—that appear to be important in the lives of young people who are resilient. The Five Cs often separate youth who are at high risk and youth who are at low risk.

Indeed, increasing the Five Cs of competency provides a method to build at least some of the 40 Developmental Assets (see Search Institute, 2006). Developmental Assets are supports, strengths, and noncognitive skills young people experience in themselves, their families, their schools, and their communities. Young people need these positive opportunities, relationships, experiences, and personal qualities to be caring, healthy, and responsible. The 40 Assets are divided into 20 External and 20 Internal Assets: External Assets include such factors as family support, positive family communication, and positive peer influence; Internal Assets involve planning and decision making, interpersonal competence, self-esteem, sense of purpose, and similar qualities. Surveys of 89,000 middle and secondary school youth (Search Institute, 2006, 2013) suggest that assets have a powerful influence on youth behavior—promoting positive attitudes and behaviors and protecting them from problem behaviors. The more assets young people have, the more likely they are to do well—and the less likely they are to engage in risky behaviors. The converse is equally true. Evidence suggests that youth from all socioeconomic, multicultural, and racial backgrounds benefit or suffer similarly (Search Institute, 2006 2013).

In this chapter we lay out a series of prevention and early intervention strategies that are core components in improving resiliency and developing assets among young people. In presenting these various programs, we use the general framework of the Five Cs. This serves as a useful guide for our thinking, although an intervention to improve one specific competency is likely to improve others as well.

Most of these prevention and early intervention programs are designed to be implemented with young people early in their school careers, in some instances even in preschool. The reason for this, of course, is that most problem behavior develops according to an orderly progression from less serious to more serious. Nothing precludes implementing these programs later in a young person's life if the person has not developed the competency. Although some competency skills seem to tie in directly with specific problem behaviors presented in Chapters 6 through 10, specific problems usually do not exist in isolation from others. For example, youth engaged in delinquent behavior are likely to have reading problems, use drugs, engage in risky sex, and join gangs—behaviors reflecting so-called problem-behavior theory (Donovan, 2005; Jessor, 1993). In addition, a specific problem behavior tends to weaken protective factors such as commitment to school or attachment to significant adults, like parents. Improving the Five Cs by using some of the programs identified here will help to strengthen and increase protective factors. Of course, building the Five Cs does not focus on reducing risk alone but simultaneously fosters protective factors and enhancing skills (American Psychological Association, 2014; Hawkins, et al., 2014a).

CRITICAL SCHOOL COMPETENCIES

Critical school competencies consist of both basic academic skills and academic survival skills. Good academic skills are essential, including core reading, writing, mathematics skills, cognitive problem solving, and so forth. Exposing young people to high-quality education is critical for developing basic academic skills. Unless schools are funded to capably do this, we are fighting against ourselves. Academic survival skills include social competency, which is critical for school survival initially and later for survival in life.

Social competence can be described as the ability to make use of personal resources to influence the environment and to achieve a positive outcome. Social competence is made up of a variety of skills that provide effective ways of being with others. Such skills include behaving appropriately in the classroom, the formation of relationships and friendships, nonviolent resolution of conflicts, assertiveness and resistance to peer pressure, and negotiation of relationships with adults. Without these essential skills, children and adolescents are susceptible to high-risk problem behaviors. Deficits in personal, cognitive, and social skills are some of the underlying causes of social incompetence (Durlak, Domitrovich, Weissberg, & Gullotta, 2015; Monastra, 2015; Social and Character Development Research Consortium [SCDRC], 2010). So young people, especially those at risk, need specific help to acquire

---

Box 12.1 | **The Birthday Party**

As we walked up the sidewalk to the front porch, the front door opened and Mary exclaimed, "Grama, Papa ... Thank you for coming to my birthday party!" She said this in a clear, precise, and thoroughly rehearsed voice that only a 3-year-old can muster.

At 3 years old, Mary's social and interpersonal skills were in stark contrast to those of an older group of children I had worked with all that afternoon. Too bad all children don't have a parent who teaches them what to say and when to say it. But if parents don't, teachers must.

---

the social competence necessary to cope with academic work, to make good decisions about life's options, to adopt health-promoting behaviors, to form stable human relationships, and to maintain hope about their future (McKown, Gumbiner, Russo, & Lipton, 2010).

Training in Life Skills/Social Skills

Life-skills training—also known as social skills training—emphasizes the acquisition of generic social and cognitive skills. From the perspective of problem-behavior theory, deviant behaviors are seen as socially learned, functional behaviors that result from the interplay of personal and environmental factors (Jessor, 2014). The growing multidisciplinary field of social and emotional learning (SEL) has expanded greatly in the last 10 years and encompasses life/social skills and many of the Five Cs (Durlak et al., 2015). Skill-building training programs typically employ some combination of interpersonal communication and social skills, strategies for cognitive change, and coping mechanisms.

The Life/Social Skills Model

Life/social skills training is not a specific curriculum, but rather a collection of practices that use a behavioral approach for teaching young people age-appropriate social skills and competencies, including communication, problem solving, decision making, self-management, and peer relations (Monastra, 2015). With its emphasis on education and training rather than counseling and therapy, the life/social skills model is ideal for use in elementary, middle, and secondary schools. Programs that include a few core elements are useful, but comprehensive programs are more effective (SCDRC, 2010; Simon, 2016).

The SEL model can enlist the efforts of mental health counselors, psychologists, social workers, school nurses, nurse practitioners, and teachers in such varied fields as physical education, home economics, and health education. School counselors, psychologists, and special education teachers are key participants in this plan. Life/social skills modules can be incorporated into the curriculum at all developmental levels, from kindergarten through high school and in a variety of course content areas (Monastra, 2015). Life/social skills training can also be included in adult and continuing education programs and in parent education programs offered by the school system as well as by community colleges and community service agencies.

Training Model

Procedures for teaching life skills resemble those used in teaching any other skill. The overall task is broken down into small stages or component parts, which are taught systematically, step by step, from the simple to the more complex. Related to the SAFE model (sequenced, active, focused, and explicit) (Durlak, 2015), training in each session follows a five-step model: (1) instruction (teach), (2) model (show), (3) role-play (practice), (4) feedback (reinforce), and (5) homework (apply). Specific tasks are presented in sequence, and frequent rewards are given for desired behavior. In this model, directed practice and an emphasis on influential models play equal parts. Although the order may vary somewhat, all five training steps are important in teaching specific skills.

1. Teach. Explanations and instructions are provided. A rationale for the skill is provided, and students are given oral instructions on how to perform it.
2. Show. The specific skill is modeled for the student. The skill can be "shown" by videotape, or the trainer or another child can demonstrate it.
3. Practice. The child is encouraged to imitate and use the skill by role-playing in the training session. The performance is evaluated with emphasis on the correct aspects of the student's imitative behavior.
4. Reinforce. As the child role-plays additional problem situations, feedback and encouragement are given. Further coaching is provided as needed to shape and refine the performance.
5. Apply. Students are requested to perform the newly acquired skill in various real-life situations. They record their experiences and report back at the next session. The characteristics of successful and unsuccessful performances are reviewed, and refinements are introduced as needed.

Components of the life-skills program can be included in regular and special education classes and in a program designed for use throughout a school or a district. To be most effective, these skills programs should start early in a child's life, such as in preschool, and continue to be reinforced throughout the young person's school career. Many students learn this through family and school interactions; some do not. Ideally, such SEL programs would be universally applied so as not to stigmatize students with limited or deficient skills. Students who possess these skills from natural family and parent interaction will be reinforced and not hurt by such instruction. Of course, focused provision needs to be made to teach or reteach skills to children who miss or otherwise do not get them (Monastra, 2015; Simon, 2016). This is the reason that indicated programs are needed.

Prevention Strategy for Children: Interpersonal Cognitive Problem Solving

There are several useful models for academic survival, life, and social problem-solving skills that include "think aloud" (Camp & Bash, 1985a, 1985b, 1985c), the "skill streaming" programs (McGinnis, 2011, 2012a, 2012b), "activities for building character and social-emotional learning (Petersen, 2012a, 2012b, 2012c, 2012d), and "I can problem solve" (Shure, 1992a, 1992b, 1992c). This last program includes the interpersonal cognitive problem solving or "I can problem solve" (ICPS) manuals for preschool, kindergarten and primary grades, and intermediate elementary grades. This cognitive problem-solving program is the result of more than 30 years of research by Spivack and Shure and their colleagues at Hahnemann University (Shure, 2006). ICPS is designed to enhance interpersonal thinking skills that reduce or prevent high-risk behaviors. The underlying goal of the program is to help children learn how to think, not what to think. It continues to be supported by more recent research with some evidence of positive impact on neuropsychological functions (Pokhrel et al., 2013).

Rebelliousness, aggressive and antisocial behavior, poor peer relationships, and poor academic achievement are important early predictors of later delinquency, alcohol and substance abuse, psychopathology, and school dropout (Shure, 2006, 2007; Shure & Aberson, 2005). Often by the third grade, schoolchildren with poor academic survival and life skills exhibit behavior that indicates a high-risk pattern for subsequent behavioral maladjustment, special school placement, academic problems, and grade retention. Considerable evidence exists to suggest that some children do not have adequate problem-solving skills. Available evidence suggests that problem solvers draw on (or are limited by) their repertoire of social behavioral and social-cognitive competencies (e.g., role taking and assertiveness skills) as well as their store of social knowledge (e.g., familiarity with social roles and conventions) in generating, evaluating, and applying potential solutions to social and interpersonal dilemmas that confront them.

Shure (2006) investigated how these cognitive interpersonal skills might be taught and how early they could be successfully absorbed. They assumed that the earlier these skills could be learned, the greater the cumulative benefit and the broader their usefulness for confronting life challenges. Focusing on African American inner-city nursery school children, these researchers found that children as young as 4 years old benefit from the program. The interpersonal cognitive problem-solving program (ICPS), later nicknamed by the children "I can problem solve," was the result.

The researchers also investigated whether the level of effective problem solving was correlated with level of intelligence, asking, in essence: Do smarter people make better problem solvers? Results suggest that general verbal skills and IQ scores are not related to effective problem solving (Spivack, Platt, & Shure, 1976). Another investigation focused on how overly impulsive (i.e., impatient and quick to act) or overly inhibited (i.e., passive and very shy) children would respond to problem-solving training. Both of these extremes are examples of children's deficits in the ability to foresee the consequences of their actions and limits in recognizing potential solutions to interpersonal problems. Both impulsive and shy children responded well to training in interpersonal problem solving. The ICPS program has even been successfully implemented with parents being trained to work with their children on problem solving (Shure, 1996a, 1996b). The program is applicable to different age groups, social classes, and to children of diverse ethno-cultural (ethnic and racial) backgrounds. More recent work supports the ICPS model with a similar process. Mothers who learned the CIPP (Context, Input, Process, Product) Evaluation Model, a problem-solving approach, demonstrated improved maternal self-esteem and sustained improvement of their knowledge and function regarding children's growth and development (Shams, Golshiri, & Najimi, 2013).

Program Description

The format of the preschool program is a script which is upgraded in sophistication for use in kindergarten and early elementary school (Shure, 1992a, 1992b) and further upgraded for intermediate grades (Shure, 1992c). The program has a particularly strong advantage as an intervention strategy in that teachers in a typical classroom, mixing quiet and talkative children and youth in smaller groups, can easily implement it. Ideally, teachers work with small groups of 6 to 10 students for about 20 minutes per day.

As a school-based program, the ICPS intervention includes all the children in a class because even good problem solvers can get better. The classroom-based, universal approach has several advantages: No student is left out because children who are initially competent in problem solving help avoid group silences; the approach can help identify children who need support but who might otherwise be identified incorrectly as being at low risk; and more youth can be reached in a shorter period of time.

This formal classroom curriculum should be implemented on a daily basis for 4 months. However, informal use of the approach should continue throughout the time children are in school. The ICPS manuals (Shure, 1992a, 1992b, 1992c) include formal lessons as well as specific suggestions for incorporating problem-solving approaches into ongoing classroom curricula and interactions. Each lesson includes a stated purpose, suggested materials, and a teacher's script. The teacher's script is intended to be a flexible guideline for implementing the basic steps of the lesson. Lessons are grouped into two major categories: pre-problem-solving skills and problem-solving skills.

Pre-Problem-Solving Skills

Pre-problem-solving concepts set the stage for the acquisition of problem-solving skills by teaching the ICPS vocabulary; teaching cause-and-effect relationships, encouraging listening and paying-attention skills, and helping children identify feelings.

The first and second weeks of the program focus on basic word concepts that lay a foundation for problem solving. For example, the words "different" and "same" help children develop a habit of thinking about a variety of alternatives in forming solutions. "Kicking" and "hitting" are the same in that they both hurt; "asking" is different from "hurting." The words "all" and "some" help children learn to recognize that certain solutions may not be successful with all people but with some. The word "or" helps children think about more than one way to solve a problem: "I can do this" or "I can do that."

Cause-and-effect relationships are also taught. For example, "Lidia hit Rachel" because "Rachel hit Lidia first." Children learn to understand cause and effect but also to think in such a way that they will see the cause-and-effect connection between an act and its consequence. The words "because" and "why," "might" and "maybe," "now" and "later," and "before" and "after" are all included and set the stage for problem-solving consequences that come later in the program.

Approximately 20 lessons are included that teach children the concept of emotions and about how people feel. Empathy development is central to all subsequent social skills. Children are encouraged to identify another's feelings in a problem situation; they learn to be sensitive to feelings. Obviously, they must learn a language for emotions. They are encouraged to learn "if … then" logic. For example, a child learns to identify and label emotions: "If he is crying, then he is sad." Teaching feelings is important; if people's feelings are to be considered in decision making, it is necessary to identify, understand, and verbalize them.

Problem-Solving Skills

Problem-solving skills are taught through lessons on alternative solutions, consequences, and solution–consequence pairs. The intermediate grade school program also includes a section on means–ends thinking, which is believed to be too advanced for younger students.

Alternative solutions lessons are designed to help children recognize problems and generate possible solutions. The goal is to stimulate children to think of as many different solutions as possible to everyday interpersonal problem situations that are presented to them. All solutions are accepted equally. Solutions are never evaluated for being "good" but are praised for being "different." Later, the children evaluate for themselves whether an idea is good or not, and why.

The objective of the consequences sessions is to help children learn to think sequentially and to engage in consequential thinking. Children are guided to think about what might happen next if a particular solution is carried out. Children are encouraged to identify consequences for their own solutions and then to decide whether the idea is good or not.

The lessons for solution–consequence pairs are designed to give children practice in linking solutions with consequences. Children are encouraged to suggest a solution to a problem and then follow it up with a consequence.

They then return to the same problem for a second solution and look at the consequence of that solution, and so on. These exercises provide experience in linking a variety of pairs of solutions and consequences. For example, in trying to get a friend to leave the room, a child might say "Push him if he won't go" (solution), "but he might hit me back" (consequence), or "If I ask him" (solution), "he might go" (goal).

The curriculum for older children includes means–ends thinking. Means–ends thinking is a higher order skill that does not emerge until sometime in middle childhood. In these sessions, children are taught to elaborate or plan a series of specific actions to attain a given goal. They are encouraged to recognize and devise ways around potential obstacles. They are helped to develop a realistic time frame in constructing a means to the goal.

In addition to the formal curriculum, the teacher is encouraged to extend the approach from helping children think about hypothetical situations and their problems to helping them think about actual problems that arise during the day, including those that occur in the classroom. This informal problem-solving dialogue technique, which focuses on the real-life world of the child, contributes to another advantage of the program—generalization—that is built in as an integral part of ICPS.

In addition to the preschool and elementary school programs, ICPS curriculums have been developed for adolescents through high school and young adulthood. Taken as a whole, available findings suggest that ICPS training has beneficial effects going beyond improved cognitive test performance (Shure, 2006, 2007). Changes in social behavior have been noted, including decreases in aggressive and impulsive behavior and increases in cooperative and prosocial behavior. Behavioral gains have been achieved with numerous groups, ranging from preschoolers showing early signs of behavioral maladjustment to disturbed schoolchildren in residential treatment to juvenile delinquents. Long-term follow-up data are sparse, but initial findings suggest substantial holding power for behavioral treatment effects, at least in the early years. ICPS helps instill academic survival skills and has the potential to prevent serious behavioral problems later on (Pokhrel et al., 2013).

CONCEPT OF SELF

In Chapter 5 we identified self-concept, self-esteem, and self-efficacy as the second "C" of competency. We pointed out that generally high-risk young people tend to struggle with negative self-concepts and with low self-esteem and self-efficacy. We do know that high-risk young people have biased attributions and that these biased attributions influence their perceptions, including self-perceptions. Providing interventions to modify biased attributions is a reasonable prevention approach. This is especially important because less attention has been paid to prevention of mental health problems than to their treatment (Rishel, 2007). One of the best early primary prevention programs was developed by Seligman and colleagues (Peterson,

Maier, & Seligman, 1993; Seligman, 1990, 1993, 1994, 1995) at the University of Pennsylvania.

Training to Prevent Depression

For more than 30 years, Seligman has been a major researcher in the general area of depression, with his first contributions identifying, clarifying, and establishing the concept of learned helplessness. He also devoted major effort and energy to the opposite side of the coin, learned optimism, establishing a robust link between pessimism and eventual depression (Seligman, Schulman, DeRubeis, Hollon, 1999). The Penn Prevention Program (PPP) sought to inoculate children against the effects of pessimism—with spectacular results. The children in the PPP spent a total of 24 hours learning and practicing cognitive-behavioral skills. They were also asked to practice the skills in homework assignments. Because the PPP worked so well in preventing depression when it was taught to children in schools, Seligman (1995) developed an approach to teach it to parents. This program is primarily a depression prevention program, but it helps youth improve their concept of self more generally, which is strongly related to depression.

In this intervention, children who reported parental conflict, depressive symptoms, or both were targeted because these factors increase children's risk for future depression and is one of a number of prevention programs (Catalano, Berglund, Ryan, Lonczak, & Hawkins, 2004; Weissberg, Kumpfer, & Seligman, 2003). Children who participated in the prevention program reported fewer depressive symptoms than did children in the control group immediately after the program and at a 6-month follow-up. A later study explored the program's effects after a 2-year delay (Gillham, Reivich, Jaycox, & Seligman, 1995). The effects of the prevention program actually grew stronger after the program was over, suggesting that psychological immunization against depression can occur by teaching social and cognitive optimism skills to children. These findings have held up over time with a meta-analysis of 17 separate studies significantly reducing depressive symptoms through at least one-year post intervention (Brunwasser, Gillham, & Kim, 2009).

The PPP contains two major components: a social problem-solving component and a cognitive component. The social problem-solving component focuses on interpersonal and conduct problems that are often associated with depressed children. Children are taught to think about their goals before acting. They generate lists of possible solutions for various problems and are encouraged to make decisions by weighing the pros and cons of all the options. The cognitive component is based on the theories developed by Ellis (Ellis & Ellis, 2011), Beck (2014), and Seligman (1990). Briefly, children are taught to identify negative beliefs and to evaluate these beliefs by examining the evidence for and against them. Children are taught explanatory style and how to identify pessimistic explanations. They learn to generate alternative explanations that are more realistic and more optimistic. Finally, children are also taught behavioral techniques to enhance assertiveness, negotiation, and relaxation, as well as techniques for coping with parental conflict. The PPP also focuses on the concept of optimism, which we discussed in Chapter 11 as a component of the GOPEP program.

Optimism

Optimism is an ability to think positively about one's situation and future, even in the face of difficulty. People who are optimistic believe that they can achieve their desired goals and make the changes in their lives necessary to achieve their goals. Optimism includes positive self-talk skills, so that when one experiences a setback, he or she is able to reason through it and not catastrophize the outcome. When people do badly, they typically ask themselves, "Why?" There are three components to the answer to this question: Who is to blame? How much of life will be undermined? How long will it last? The first component attaches blame to the self or to the world. The second and third questions—how pervasive is the cause and how permanent is the cause—govern what people do to respond to failure. Feeling bad about oneself does not directly cause failure. However, the belief that problems undermine everything in life and problems will last forever cause people to stop trying. Giving up leads to more failure, and more failure leads to an even more pessimistic explanatory style. Thus, in the face of a bad event, someone who is pessimistic characteristically thinks that a problem is pervasive and permanent and that he or she is personally at fault for the problem. For example, a child may attribute a poor school performance to a personal failure or inability and begin to believe that all school efforts will result in failure. This explanatory style leads to destructive actions and becomes a kind of self-fulfilling negative prophecy. Positive events are believed by pessimists to be temporary, limited, and caused by something other than their own actions.

By contrast, optimists characteristically employ an explanatory style in which they think the bad event is temporary, limited to the specific event, and with many possible causes other than themselves. This cognitive mindset saves the person from stress and mobilizes energy toward constructive goals. When a positive event occurs, an optimist characteristically thinks that he or she had a personal hand in causing the outcome and that it is pervasive and permanent. Thus the three critical dimensions used to explain why any particular good or bad event happens are personal, permanent, and pervasive.

Internal versus External: Personal

When events happen, children either blame themselves (internal) or blame circumstances or other people (external). Pessimistic children have a habit of blaming themselves when bad things happen and frequently explain good events by attributing them to other people or to the situation. To change the explanatory style from pessimism to optimism, and thus inoculate against future depression, children need to learn both to take appropriate responsibility for events that occur in their lives and to refrain from blaming themselves when things go wrong—because most problems are caused by a complex set of contributing factors. Some children shoulder the entire blame and think of things in black-and-white terms. This leads to overwhelming feelings of worthlessness and guilt, causing them to withdraw and further increasing their risk for depression.

Sometimes versus Always: Permanent

Pessimistic and depressed children believe the cause of bad events and the reasons for their failure are permanent. Because the cause will persist forever, bad events are always going to occur. Optimistic children believe that the causes for bad events are temporary; this serves to inoculate them against depression. For the pessimistic child, mistakes, rejections, failures, and so forth are thought of in terms of forever and always. The optimistic child explains bad events with words such as sometimes or lately or another time-limiting term.

Pessimistic and optimistic children react differently to positive events in their lives as well. Children who believe that good events have temporary causes tend to be more pessimistic than children who believe that good events have permanent causes. This is just the opposite of the explanation for bad events.

Specific versus Global: Pervasive

If the cause of the event is pervasive, its effect is distributed across many different situations in life and becomes global. Children who focus on global explanations for bad events give up on everything when they fail in one area. Pessimistic and depressed children tend to let a bad situation expand into all parts of their lives. This limits the number of positive outlets available to them and catastrophizes everything.

Children who attribute global causes to bad events need to learn to be more specific in their explanations. Instead of a test failure meaning "I am stupid," children can learn to say, "I didn't prepare very well this time." Children who think about good events as having more global causes do better in more areas of their lives. When it comes to good events, the optimist believes that the causes enhance everything they do. Pessimists believe that good events are caused by specific factors: "That just happened because she felt sorry for me." Global negative causes are pervasive and lead to despair and passivity. Seligman (1995) argues that the dimension of pervasiveness is not easily taught to children, although it is routinely taught to adults and may be used for middle and secondary school students.

Basic Skills of Optimism

The PPP has incorporated the main techniques of cognitive therapy (CT) for depression into a prevention program for people who are not depressed. The

PPP helps individuals develop new skills of optimistic thinking. There are four basic skills of optimism:

Thought Catching

People must first learn to catch the negative things they say to themselves, about themselves, and about events that occur. These almost imperceptible thoughts affect behavior and mood. By learning to recognize thoughts, they can then be changed.

Evaluation

The second skill is to evaluate the automatic and habitual thoughts or beliefs that have been identified. These can be acknowledged as being hypotheses that need to be tested rather than "Truths," and evidence can be gathered and considered to determine the accuracy of the beliefs.

Accurate Explanations

When bad events happen, more accurate explanations can be developed to challenge the automatic thoughts. By interrupting the chain of negative explanations, attitudes and mood can improve.

Decatastrophizing

Catastrophizing, or thinking about the worst possible case, is counterproductive. Most often, the worst case is very unlikely. Ruminating on potential terrible implications and the worst possible consequences creates frustration, drains energy, and interferes with correcting problems.

Identifying automatic thoughts, searching for evidence, generating alternatives, and decatastrophizing are extremely important in developing optimism and lowering pessimism and depression in children.

Application for Problem Prevention

Early primary prevention programs can be very helpful to children. Skills for optimism can serve as a means of problem prevention. Children, who drop out, and even children who attend school but have given up on themselves academically and personally, lack hope that school will benefit their future or that they can succeed in school. They may internalize their lack of success as their own fault, due to pervasive personal characteristics ("I'll never be able to read. I'm stupid."), or blame it on pervasive global factors ("Teachers don't care." "School is useless."). Teachers or school counselors could initiate classroom discussions to identify thoughts students face in response to negative school experiences (thought catching). The class can assist in evaluating sample thoughts, helping to generate accurate explanations to substitute for sample negative thoughts. Decatastrophizing can be illustrated. When working individually with students, the same series of steps can be followed, reinforcing and further personalizing optimism skills. With practice, students will begin to utilize these skills to encourage each other.

Teaching these skills to children is important, but it is equally important for the helping adults to learn and practice these skills themselves. Using these skills may improve the mental health of the helper—not an unimportant consideration given the nature of the work, the consistent drain of personal resources and energy, and the constant stress of budget cuts and limited resources. Increased optimism gives the helper more energy and greater influence as well.

Optimism can also be taught to parents. Parental (and other adult) criticism often reflects the bad habits and biases of the adult and contributes to increased pessimism in children. If parents are aware of their children's attributions, parents can provide more helpful feedback and criticism to their children. Children view ability as permanent, so blaming failure on lack of ability fosters pessimism. In contrast, blaming lack of success on conduct, effort, or attention is less malignant because these are temporary and changeable. Children can be challenged and supported in their efforts to improve conduct, increase effort, or focus attention. If they believe they lack ability, they will be at greater risk of dropout and other problems. Please see the description of the SOAR program related to enhancing optimism (Gilboy, McWhirter, Wallace, 2002) described in Chapter 11.

Cognitive Restructuring

The term *cognitive restructuring*, as we use it here, simply means modifying, changing, or restructuring one's beliefs. A belief is a rule that a person applies to all situations regardless of his or her current experiences. When the belief is maladaptive, it can be unlearned to produce a new and better belief. As more adaptive beliefs replace incomplete or faulty ones, behavior changes too. For example, cognitive-behavioral skills training programs have been recommended to increase empathy and decrease impulsiveness in bullies (Farrington & Baldry, 2010).

The best-known approaches to changing maladaptive beliefs or cognitive patterns are rational-emotive behavioral therapy (REBT; David, 2013; DiGiuseppe, Doyle, Dryden, & Backx, 2013; Ellis & Ellis, 2011) and cognitive therapy (CT; Beck, 1976, 1991). Both approaches are based on the assumption that faulty cognitions cause detrimental self-evaluations and emotional distress and that these experiences lead to behavioral problems. The goal is to help people develop their cognitive ability to recognize faulty self-statements and to substitute more positive ones. Children and adolescents can understand the principles of REBT and CT.

Rational-Emotive Behavior Therapy (REBT)

Ellis's rational-emotive behavior therapy, the oldest and probably best known of the cognitive therapies, is based on the belief that people need to change their faulty thinking and correct irrational beliefs to lead healthier, happier lives. Emotional disturbances are the result of illogical and irrational thinking in the form of internalized beliefs and arise from cognitive or thinking processes around an activating event. However, emotion is complex and is tied to a variety of sensing and response processes and states (Ellis & Ellis, 2011).

The major assumption of REBT is that thoughts create feelings. In other words, it is not events or other people that make one feel upset or inadequate but one's belief about them. A young boy who does not succeed at football and feels depressed, for example, may assume that his poor performance has caused the depressed feeling. REBT postulates, however, that it is the assumptions about the event or the failure—the thoughts about it, not the event itself—that cause the depressed feeling.

Ellis (Ellis & Ellis, 2011) proposes an A-B-C-D-E model as a cognitive intervention strategy. The child or adolescent learns to recognize the activating event (A), the corresponding belief (B) about the event, and the emotional and behavioral consequences (C). The counselor then helps the young person to dispute (D) the old belief system and attend to the new emotional and behavioral effects (E) of more rational thinking.

At-risk children and adolescents develop many irrational ways of thinking. These irrational thoughts lead to maladaptive behavior. Cognitive restructuring efforts are designed to help young people recognize and change these irrational beliefs into more rational ones. Attainment of this goal requires a supportive counselor who is able to actively engage and confront the client (David, 2013).

Cognitive Therapy

Beck, for 40 years, has provided an evidence-based cognitive model with a set of common principles to treat psychological disorders (Beck, 2014; Clark & Beck, 2011). Like Ellis, he believes that an individual's cognition about an event determines the affective response to the event. If cognitions are distorted or inaccurate, the individual's emotional response will be inappropriate.

Three elements are central to Beck's CT model: the cognitive triad, cognitive schemas, and cognitive errors. The cognitive triad is composed of thoughts that focus on three major aspects of life: view of the world, the self, and the future. When the cognitive triad is negative, the individual views the world, self, and future as negative, and depression and despair result.

A schema is like a personality trait; it is a stable cognitive pattern that an individual creates from the cognitive triad. Schemas are underlying cognitive structures that help the individual organize and evaluate information, events, and experiences. At-risk children and adolescents develop schemas that distort environmental stimuli in a negative way. Often their schemas include a derogatory self-image. Because these schemas are a person's "core beliefs," they influence both behavioral and affective responses to an event.

Dysfunctional or negative schemas are often maintained and exacerbated by faulty information processing or consistent errors in logic. These are called cognitive errors. At-risk young people make these automatic cognitive errors when they evaluate events. These errors—negativistic, categorical, absolute, judgmental—cause the person to consistently misread or misinterpret even benign experiences.

Treatment and training strategies flow directly from Beck's cognitive model. His CT has both behavioral and cognitive components that are designed to reduce automatic negative cognitions. The client learns to challenge the assumptions that maintain the faulty cognitions. Behavioral strategies are used first in the therapeutic or training process. Positive activities are established and augmented through role-playing, graduated task assignments, activity schedules, assertiveness training, and behavioral rehearsal. After these strategies are successfully used, cognitive interventions are introduced to identify, test, and modify the cognitive distortion (Weersing & Brent, 2010). Clients are taught (a) to recognize the connections between cognitions, affect, and behavior; (b) to monitor negative automatic thoughts; (c) to examine evidence related to distorted automatic cognitions; (d) to substitute more realistic interpretations for distorted cognition; and (e) to learn to identify and modify dysfunctional beliefs.

CT is dedicated to the goal of helping clients discover maladaptive thoughts, recognize their negative impact, and replace them with more appropriate and positive thought patterns (Weersing & Brent, 2010). Cognitive restructuring techniques have been successfully applied in clinical settings and are used increasingly in training modules to help at-risk young people make cognitive changes so that they can lead more productive lives.

Tyrone Baker (of Chapter 2) could benefit from cognitive change strategies. Interpersonal problem solving could help him make better decisions. Self-assessment, self-monitoring, and self-reinforcement could provide him with tools to help him delay gratification. Through cognitive restructuring, he could modify his irrational thoughts, the nature of his cognitive triad, and his negative schemas. Cognitive errors could be corrected to modify and improve his negative behavior.

CONNECTEDNESS

Connectedness with others is critical in people's lives (Lieberman, 2013; Smith & Sandhu, 2004; Townsend & McWhirter, 2005) and is a major goal of more effective and comprehensive life-skills training programs. Researchers have demonstrated that environmental conditions can support the development of positive, prosocial behaviors or conversely reinforce the development of negative, antisocial behaviors (Catalano, Berglund, Ryan, Lonczak, & Hawkins, 2004; Hawkins et al., 2000; Lonczak, Abbott, Hawkins, Kosterman, & Catalano, 2002; Walton, & Cohen, 2011; Walton, Cohen, Cwir, & Spencer, 2012). Connectedness is dependent upon an individual having the skills, opportunities, and recognition for engaging in successful behaviors. Connectedness involves both intrapersonal awareness and interpersonal skills. Both have to do with understanding self and others. The interpersonal communication skills that are core to connectedness are sometimes termed social skills, social competence, or human relations skills. Such skills in interpersonal communication are necessary for people to have effective and healthy interpersonal relationships. As we mentioned in Chapter 5, interpersonal communication skills are necessary for responsive, confident, and mutually beneficial relationships. A lack of good communication skills often leads to social isolation and rejection, which in turn results in poor psychological adjustment and a lack of connectedness (Mikulincer & Shaver, 2014). Positive adult reactions and peer acceptance are related to friendly, positive interpersonal communication and this forms a sense of connectedness that is critical for sustained happiness in people's lives (Townsend & McWhirter, 2005).

Training in Interpersonal Communication

Acquisition of basic communication skills begins in early childhood; by adolescence, teens have acquired a complex repertoire of social skills. Most programs designed to promote communication skills offer training in verbal and nonverbal communication, creation of healthy friendships, avoidance of misunderstandings, and development of long-term love relationships.

Programs to promote interpersonal communication should be developmentally appropriate. The variables that seem to play a role in the development and maintenance of interactions from age 1 to 3 years are attention to the listener, to the speaker, or to the object of interest; proximity and turn-taking with others; relevance of content; and provision of feedback from the listener. From age 3 to 5 years, behaviors that may be incorporated in training programs include the use of attention-getting cues, listener responses, reinforcement of turn-taking and mutual attention, and the use of routines to maintain attention. Mutual attention and feedback are still important skills for 6- to 8-year-olds and appropriate role taking is developed during this age period. From ages 9 to 12, the use of positive, cooperative, and helpful communication, as opposed to negative, is important. Clearly, interpersonal communication is included in social/emotional programs that stress emotion identification, responsible decision-making, perspective taking, and other effective interpersonal skills (Brown, Corrigan, & Higgins-D'Alessandro, 2012; SCDRC, 2010). Interpersonal communication skills represent the major component of many prevention programs. A particularly useful package is an integrated program of training in communication skills for adolescents (McGinnis, 2011), elementary school students, McGinnis, 2012a), and younger children (McGinnis, 2012b). Other useful programs have been developed for elementary school and older students and a quick online review will reveal a number of effective programs. Stephens's (1992) social skills program, for instance, is appropriate for both children and adolescents. Communication skills training used in prevention include the work of Cummings and Haggerty (1997), Dupaul and Eckert (1994), and Jones, Sheridan, and Binns (1993).

Jason Carter (of Chapter 3) could profit from training in communication skills. As described, he is disconnected from most other children and from most adults. His difficulty in dealing with his dysfunctional family has extended to his classroom interactions. Although parent training and family counseling approaches are probably necessary to help modify the family dysfunction, Jason's ineffective interpersonal communication is contributing to the aversive nature of his school experience. Better interpersonal communication skills would allow him to interact more positively with classmates and adults at school. This improvement could bring greater acceptance by Jason's peers and increase his self-esteem.

Assertiveness Skills

Some at-risk young people get into trouble because they are timid and withdrawn and appear to be incapable of dealing with other students, teachers, and family members in effective ways. Others express themselves in hostile, angry, aggressive ways that cause problems for people around them and ultimately for themselves. Still others find themselves going along with the crowd because they are overly susceptible to influence by their peers. They do not recognize pressure or have the skills to resist it. Many at-risk children and youth need training in general assertiveness and in specific ways to resist peer pressure.

General Assertiveness Training

Assertiveness training is a psychoeducational procedure designed to reduce deficits in specific social skills and to help the individual interact more effectively with others. Assertiveness training also reduces the maladaptive anxiety that prevents young people from expressing themselves directly, honestly, and spontaneously.

Assertiveness training usually includes modules on the expression of positive feelings, the expression of negative feelings, and the ability to initiate, continue, and terminate conversations. Besides these basic interpersonal communication skills, assertiveness training focuses on limit setting and self-initiation. The person who knows how to set limits can say no to unreasonable requests. Self-initiators have the capacity to ask for what they want and to actively seek opportunities for enjoyment, advancement, and intimacy.

Nonverbal communication is also an important aspect of assertiveness training. The way a message is delivered is given as much attention as the message itself. Loudness of voice, fluency of spoken words, facial expression, body expression, interpersonal distance, and method and degree of eye contact all deliver their own messages. Students are taught to look others squarely in the eye during both positive and negative social confrontations. Looking people in the eye is a sign that one is sure of one's position, knowledge, or attractiveness in mainstream U.S. culture. Students are taught that passive behavior can be replaced by assertive techniques and that assertive responses are more adaptive than aggressive ones in handling conflict and anger. All assertiveness training programs should attend to students from cultural backgrounds in which direct eye contact is considered disrespectful or aggressive. Rather than exclude "eye contact," this component of the program as well as others should acknowledge cultural differences and provide guidance in exploring when using assertive behavior may be more or less effective.

One school-based assertiveness training program has been reported to yield extremely positive results (Smith, 1986). The children trained in assertiveness had better school attendance records than their untrained counterparts, were ill less often, scored higher in reading and math, had better self-images, and showed positive changes in those negative attitudes that predict future drug abuse. Three years after completing the program, the trained students were more resistant to peer pressure to use tobacco, alcohol, and illicit drugs. The assertiveness-trained youth also achieved higher grades than the students who were not trained in assertiveness. This social thinking and reasoning program, called STAR (Benn, 1981), provides techniques and methods to train children from grades 3 through 5 in how to respond more effectively in social conflict situations. Another program for promoting learning and understanding of self, called PLUS (Benn, 1982), is an adaptation of STAR for high school students and has demonstrated similar success.

Resistance and Refusal Training

Specific resistance and refusal skills help at-risk students resist negative social influences (Herrmann & McWhirter, 1997). Resistance training focuses on helping young people (a) identify and label social influences and pressure situations and (b) develop behavioral skills to resist such influences. Skills are needed to resist various types of pressures, from those exerted by the entertainment media and advertising to those of peers. Students are taught to identify and label various forms of pressure. Peer pressure, for instance, can take the form of teasing, friendly pressure, tricks, dares, lies, physical threats, social threats, or silence. Typical examples of each kind of pressure are demonstrated.

Students are then taught strategies for resisting pressure and for refusing to succumb to it. Particular techniques are described, demonstrated, and modeled. Students practice and observe others practicing each resistance or refusal strategy. They engage in role-playing to develop competence in each technique. All of them are given opportunities to rehearse and refine their performances so that in real-life situations they can respond with confidence. Students who are trained in assertiveness develop skills to avoid the use of tobacco, alcohol, and marijuana (Herrmann & McWhirter, 1997, 2000). They are less willing to use drugs after resistance training, which provides youth with the skills needed to recognize and resist the external pressures to use drugs. But developing refusal skills alone, such as the "just say 'No'" campaign, is not effective. Young people need to enhance interpersonal skills, develop better self-awareness, remain free of drug-using peers, and be assisted in developing social networks and friendships with low-risk peers for intervention to be successful in the long term.

Allie Andrews (of Chapter 1) might well profit from assertiveness and resistance training. Her interaction with her stepfather suggests that she has few ways to respond to stress, mostly acting-out and self-defeating responses. Her peer interaction hints that she may be turning to her friends for the acceptance she does not receive at home. Thus, her resistance to drug use is probably quite low. Assertiveness and resistance training might help her develop the skills she needs to change her self-defeating patterns and prevent substance use.

COPING ABILITY

The fourth "C" identified in Chapter 5 is coping ability. Many at-risk young people are affected by stress and anxiety (Durlak et al., 2015). Anxiety is associated with a number of undesirable intrapersonal and interpersonal characteristics: lack of responsiveness, inability to perform independently, overdependence on conformity, excessive concern about evaluations, and self-critical and self-defeating attitudes. Anxiety from such sources leads to chronic stress. Because many aspects of the educational process are greatly affected by anxiety and stress, providing coping methods to deal with them is particularly beneficial. Mounting evidence suggests that school-based prevention and early intervention programs have the potential of reducing future instances of serious anxiety disorders. Earlier, in Chapter 5 we presented the concept of "mindfulness" as a prevention and intervention program (Cook-Cottone, Tribole, Tylka, & Tracy, 2013; Goyal et al., 2015; Kuyken et al., 2013; Simkin & Black, 2014). Mindfulness does, indeed, provide a major coping approach. Here we focus specifically on underlying techniques that are contained in mindfulness but in western psychology developed from a different tradition and which can be implemented separately from a purely mindfulness approach.

Relaxation, imagery, and affirmations are helpful tools to offset some of the negative aspects of anxiety and stress. These techniques are combined in a training model of relaxation and imagery training (RIT), an approach that promises to help at-risk children realize more of their potential and improve students' test anxiety, study skills, and academic self-esteem. RIT also helps young people deal with psychological distress and improve emotional well-being.

Relaxation

Relaxation techniques alone can reduce stress and many of its negative psychological and physical effects. Relaxation has been reported to help clients overcome fatigue, avoid negative reactions to stress, reduce anxiety, improve social skills and interpersonal relationships, and improve self-assurance. Relaxation can also help to reduce depression and improve self-esteem (Tavousi, 2015). Relaxation is both effective and efficient in helping students to behave more appropriately in school, to think more positively about themselves, and to interact more positively with their peers. Relaxation also reduces anxiety—an especially important effect because anxiety is associated with dependence, hostility, low peer status, poor relationships with teachers, and aggression (McReynolds, Morris, & Kratochwill, 1989).

Relaxation techniques are useful in learning school material as well as in the social arena. Studies have demonstrated the positive effects of relaxation techniques on a variety of classroom subjects probably by counteracting stress that interferes with learning and performance. In addition to improving social and academic performance, relaxation has been used successfully as an intervention strategy for hyperactivity. Relaxation is a viable tool for increasing attention to task and decreasing impulsiveness. And relaxation training teaches young people to use the relaxation response when anxiety and fear arise.

Relaxation training promotes anxiety reduction by teaching the individual to reduce muscle tension. Essentially, relaxation training accomplishes two objectives. First, it is a means to counter the anxiety associated with a stressful environment. Second, it is a self-management tool. Through the self-regulation training of relaxation, children can increase their control over their lives, be responsible for their behavior, and improve their academic performance. This tool has a spin-off effect. As children gain confidence in the ability to become calm in learning and social situations, they gain approval from adults and peers, improve their attention span, are less distractible, and learn more. This procedure shows considerable promise for improving the self-regulations skills of children and adolescents, which contributes to their resilience (Dishion & Connell, 2006).

Progressive, Deep Muscle Relaxation

Several techniques are useful in relaxation training, including biofeedback, autogenic training, meditation, the quieting reflex, and progressive relaxation. Most training in relaxation uses a procedure originally outlined by Jacobson (1938), which he referred to as progressive (deep muscle) relaxation. Merely telling an individual to relax is not enough. After a tough day do you ever get a headache and then later realize your shoulder muscles are all tight and stiff? RIT helps you identify where and how and eventually, then, in what situations you physically carry your stress. Jacobson developed a more structured and concrete procedure by which the individual achieves a state of deep muscular relaxation. To achieve relaxation in a specific muscle or muscle group, the client lies down comfortably and alternately tenses and relaxes the major muscle groups noting the different level of tension in the muscles. This process continues over several sessions until the individual develops muscle awareness and can release muscle tension purposefully and consciously (Tavousi, 2015).

In the relaxation technique used in RIT, the student or client is taught to tense and then relax various muscle groups in order. This procedure continues until the person is clearly aware of the contrast between a tense and a relaxed state. Early in relaxation training it is necessary to repeat the tension and relaxation phases several times during several sessions. Eventually, the need for tensing is eliminated and the individual achieves relaxation quickly. Once students develop this technique, they can relax on their own without instructions from the adult, thereby exercising a greater degree of self-control. With practice, most individuals can learn to achieve a relaxed physical and mental state within a few minutes. This procedure helps the individual learn and be more aware of the tension throughout the muscles and in the body. Once one becomes more aware of the body's contribution to stress, other relaxation techniques can be more easily applied. One of these is Benson's Relaxation Response.

Benson's Relaxation Response

The term *relaxation response* was used by Dr. Herbert Benson, a Harvard cardiology professor, to describe the process that helps muscles and organs slow down and that increases blood flow to the brain. In his first book, he highlights the scientific benefits of relaxation as an effective treatment for a wide range of stress-related disorders (Benson, 2000). Originally modeled on the changes produced by the Transcendental Meditation, more recent research (Benson & Proctor, 2010) has expanded the applications of the technique to a very wide range of physical and psychological problems and provided an even greater scientific and research foundation. Like progressive deep muscle relaxation, this technique is closely related to mindfulness, as discussed in Chapter 6. There are a number of steps that lead to the relaxation response:

- Sit in a comfortable position, eyes closed, back straight, with your feet flat on the floor. Breathe comfortably for a few seconds to get into a comfortable rhythm.
- Relax your body starting at your feet and gradually working your way up to your head. Then (or alternatively), imagine a large warm cloud moving from the top of your head down your body causing an even deeper relaxed state.
- Become aware of your breathing. Then as you breathe out, say the word "one" silently to yourself. (Benson used the word "One" in his early studies at Harvard although any melodious, soothing sounding word is acceptable.) Some people use the word "Calm"; some clients prefer counting to four when they breathe in and counting to eight when they breathe out.
- Breathe in and then breathe out, and repeat the selected word as you do so. After saying it silently several times, stop saying it, and "enter the silence."
- Continue to breathe easily and naturally for 10 to 20 minutes: You may open your eyes to check the time, but a bell or an alarm works against relaxation.

- It is not unusual for your mind to wander off into an internal, chattering dialogue. This is a cue to repeat "one" or "calm," or count to 4/8 again several times and then return to the silence.
- Do not try to force or worry about achieving a deep level of relaxation. Maintain a passive attitude and permit relaxation to occur at its own pace.
- When you finish, sit quietly for several minutes, first with your eye closed and then with your eyes open.

As with any skill the technique needs to be practiced daily, but the response should come with little effort especially if one is aware of muscle tension. Some clients practice first thing in the morning of just before bed (avoid two hours after meals, since digestion interferes with the response).

At least some of the problems faced by Paul Andrews (of Chapter 1) can be attributed to his stressful environment. The tension in his dysfunctional family and his intense dislike of school have led to angry, hostile, aggressive acting out. Adults' reactions to his behavior increase his stress. His aggressiveness and anger appear to be methods for coping with underlying anxiety. Relaxation training would enable him to cope better with his own emotional reactions to his situation. Deep muscle relaxation and the relaxation response would provide Paul with the skill needed to redirect his aggression and attend to his underlying apprehension and anxiety.

Guided Visual Imagery

Guided visual imagery is a relaxation technique as well as an important adjunct to relaxation training. It is used to lessen tension and to enhance comfort, to engage various muscle groups, and to cue a relaxation response. Guided imagery uses the process of visualization to intentionally redirected thoughts in order to achieve a positive, desired outcome such as stress relief, sleep, performance enhancement, and so forth. Because guided imagery is an active form of daydreaming, children and teens usually respond to it easily.

Guided fantasies allow the young person to confront areas of difficulty, to learn tasks, and to develop self-control. Through imagery, the individual is guided through an event as if the activity were actually happening. The child enters a rich world of internal experiences in his or her "mind's eye" where imagination is recruited to promote specific psychological and physiological changes to aid performance or behavior. In addition, imagery should include positive suggestions, especially when the person is anticipating a negative outcome or condition. Positive imagery is obviously important for an at-risk child or adolescent such as Paul Andrews, who has come to expect failure and negative reactions from others.

Procedures for Guided Imagery

Several key elements go into guided imagery scripts for young people. The scripts should be as realistic and focused as possible and incorporate words, phrases, and situations that apply to the individual. Paul Andrews's counselor might enlist other adults as collaborators. Paul's mother could become a technical consultant and suggest words, language, and fantasies as well as key events and details that would make the fantasy a rich and realistic experience. If we were to construct a fantasy for Paul, we would follow these guidelines:

1. Help Paul use all his senses—touch, smell, taste, and sound as well as vision. Internal emotional and muscular cues that are experienced before and during a scene should not be neglected.
2. Set the scene as vividly as possible by describing it clearly. If specific details are available, provide them. If not, ask Paul to supply them.
3. Work from the outside environment (the classroom, the home) to the inside environment or the emotional state.
4. Guide the image from Paul's viewpoint, as if he were actually in the situation. Paul is not simply observing himself as a spectator but is actually participating in the event—feeling the emotion it arouses, thinking about it, observing others in the situation, and so forth.
5. Use positive statements and autosuggestions to help Paul develop self-reinforcing statements. Be sure to close the fantasy with a positive image.

Guided imagery can improve learning and retention of academic subjects. It seems to be useful in all areas of the curriculum as it can create an appropriate readiness and mental set for learning. In the sciences and mathematics, imagery aids creative problem solving and memory and in language arts by lending vitality to poetry and prose. In educational contexts, imagery: (a) creates a readiness to learn, (b) aids comprehension, (c) enhances memory and recall, and (d) facilitates problem solving and creative thinking by helping students prepare their minds, emotions, and bodies for learning the process may be as important as the instruction itself. Anticipation of a mental event and openness of mind create a state of readiness for whatever is to be learned.

Many excellent scripts and audiotapes are available to set imaginary scenes for students (Davis, Robbins-Eshelman, & McKay, 2008). Commercial tapes have music, narrative, and distinctive environmental sounds (bird songs, flowing water, rustling leaves). Of course, the subject matter of the tape or script must be appropriate to the age and environment of the targeted youth. For example, an ocean scene may be outside the experience of some students. Students must be given ample time and practice to develop skill in imagery.

A Safe Place

One very important application of visual imagery is a safe, special, happy place. The practitioner helps the child develop and imagine a scene where the child feels safe and peaceful. This can become a special place where the child is more calm, secure, and relaxed. The setting can be an imaginary place but most often it is an actual place where the child has experienced safety and peacefulness. Usually, it contains sights and sounds such as waves lapping on a shore at night, sitting in a park with a gentle wind, sitting in front of a warm fireplace, or listening to a soft breeze whisper through tree leaves. The major issue is that it creates a feeling of contentment in the child.

After providing a guided imagery of the special place, the counselor encourages the young person to use this place to regulate their emotions and focus on the positive.

Affirmations

In view of the generally negative cognitions that many young people experience, use of positive affirmation to acknowledge and increase personal strengths is critical. Affirmations impact academic performance and motivation in a positive way (Sherman et al., 2013). RIT provides an opportunity for the teacher or counselor to encourage the child by making positive affirmations. These affirmations should be used consistently and frequently throughout both the relaxation and imagery segments of the program. Most children know the story *The Little Engine that Could* with its refrain of "I think I can, I think I can, I think I can." This saying can be the basis of a class discussion of other positive sayings (see the reading at the opening of this chapter). Children repeat these sayings to themselves to reduce stress and to build confidence. Several phrases seem particularly useful: "I can do it"; "I've studied for this test, and I'll do my best"; "I am special because … "; "I can relax and remember the right answer"; "I have lots of strengths." Thoughts of being unworthy, not good enough, a step away from failure, the young person is sabotaging their physical health, mental stability, and their happiness. Specific phrases and sentences to offset these negative ruminations need to be developed by children and adolescents themselves. Affirmations represent one technique in a wide range of useful cognitive strategies. In the following section, we attend to a number of cognitive restructuring approaches known to be helpful to children and adolescents. With RIT and similar types of programs and interventions, children and youth will begin to understand that they have the power and self-control to overcome the effects of stress and anxiety and get on with living and learning. Counselors and other adults can facilitate the development of that power and that self-control.

CONTROL: STRATEGIES FOR COGNITIVE CHANGE

The final and fifth "C" denoted in Chapter 5 is control—control of decisions, control of self, and control of the future. A variety of cognitive-behavioral techniques have been devised to help children and young people develop control over their internal reactions and overt behavior (Weersing & Brent, 2010). Three points in cognitive-behavioral theory are particularly important in this respect: First, cognitive events mediate behavior; therefore, a focus on cognition can be an effective approach to changing behavior. Second, young people are active participants in their own learning and can exercise control over it. And third, cognition, behavior, and the environment are related: Each affects and is affected by the others. Among the cognitive-behavioral strategies with demonstrated utility in dealing with control are interventions to improve decision making.

Control of Decisions

At-risk young people are more likely to engage in rigid thinking and to perceive fewer alternatives to problems when they emerge. Thus their ability to generate and select from alternative choices of action needs to be improved. Good decision making requires that the benefits and consequences of, say, drug use or other risky behavior are clear and accurate. Unfortunately, neither all the benefits nor all the consequences of drug use (and drug abstinence) are known. Nevertheless, decision-making strategies help users to (a) define the nature of their choice, (b) enlarge the number of alternatives under consideration, (c) identify all benefits and consequences of each alternative, and (d) implement their desired alternative. Because these steps are effective with many of the root problems, they represent a valuable resource for at-risk youth as does the DECIDE model that we present next.

Early models of problem solving and decision making were based on the assumption that adequate and accurate information would lead to better choices. There was an implicit assumption that prudent choices would flow from a rational review of options. We now know that accurate information is necessary but not sufficient for effective decision making. Even for adults with substantial life experience and mature cognitive skills and abilities, the processes of problem solving and decision making are far less rational than they were once thought to be (Krieshok, Black, & McKay, 2009). Children and adolescents are at least as irrational as adults in their problem solving and decision making.

At the same time, young people have the potential to make competent decisions. Children who accurately perceive and effectively solve interpersonal problems use a five-stage sequential problem-solving, decision-making process. In stage one, they attend to relevant environmental cues. In stage two, they accurately encode and interpret these cues. In stage three, they generate many and varied solutions to the problems. In stage four, they accurately evaluate each of the solutions and determine the best possible solution. Finally, in stage five, they plan the steps necessary to carry out and actually perform the favored solution. For high-risk youth, several things stand in the way of effective problem solving and decision making. These include the emotional component of most problems, the tendency to appraise situations from an egocentric perspective, the perception of limited alternatives, and failure to use systematic decision-making procedures. For example, social-cognitive deficits in aggressive children interfere in the area of social attention and recall (stage 1), generating multiple solutions to interpersonal problems (stage 3), and performance of favored responses (stage 5). Social-cognitive distortions in antisocial children occur when errors are made in the interpretation of social stimuli (stage 2) and misjudgments are made concerning the consequences of hostile acts (stage 4).

Explicit instruction in problem-solving and decision-making processes helps to avert problems and overcome areas of limitation. The steps involved in problem solving require specific skills, which need to be learned and practiced. We have borrowed Krumboltz and Hamel's (1977) decision-making model called "DECIDES" and adapted it for general problem-solving training as "DECIDE."

The DECIDE model can be used for improving the skills in general problem solving for at-risk children and adolescents. DECIDE stands for the steps to be taken: (1) Define the problem, (2) Examine variables, (3) Consider alternatives, (4) Isolate a plan, (5) Do action steps, and (6) Evaluate effects. Teaching at-risk children and adolescents these six problem-solving steps will contribute to a more internal locus of control—that is, students will feel that their behavior is under their own control—and will help modify impulsive, self-defeating behavior. An internal locus of control, in turn, can improve self-esteem, increase a sense of self-efficacy, and strengthen resistance to problem behaviors. Let's look at each of these steps.

1. Define the problem. The problem is defined as clearly as possible and is stated as a goal to be achieved. This goal is assessed: Will it address the problem? If it is attained, does it help the individual achieve satisfaction?
2. Examine variables. The specifics of the total situation are examined. Background issues and environmental factors are considered, so it may be necessary to gather and appraise additional information. It is particularly important to identify the feelings and thoughts of the young person at this step. Both here and in step 1, questions and suggestions from other students in the classroom or the group are useful.
3. Consider alternatives. Various means of solving the problem are considered. The strengths and weaknesses of each possibility are evaluated. Again, the teacher or the counselor may call for brainstorming to generate ideas from other students about alternatives and strategies.
4. Isolate a plan. The alternatives are gradually narrowed down until what seems like the best response or solution remains. A plan for carrying out this alternative is prepared, and the potential consequences are considered in more detail.
5. Do action steps. After a plan is decided upon, action must be taken to implement it. Youngsters are systematically encouraged to follow through on the necessary steps to carry out their plan. They perform the behaviors that make up the solution plan.
6. Evaluate effects. Finally, children and adolescents need to evaluate the effectiveness of the solution. Teaching them to look for effects in their thoughts and feelings is important. They analyze and evaluate the outcome, review the decision, and if necessary develop another plan to achieve their goal.

Self-Management and Self-Control

Self-management and self-control are related. Self-management is the ability to maintain or alter goal-directed behavior without depending on discernable external forces. Young people with good self-management skills are able to respond to situations based on their internal standards. Self-control is an important component of self-management and refers to control over one's affective, cognitive, and behavioral reactions. It is particularly important for high-risk children and adolescents because it helps them prevent problem situations, limit negative emotional reactions, resist problematic behaviors, and delay gratification. Conversely, as we mentioned in Chapter 11, lack of self-control and self-discipline is a major contributor to youth delinquency (Buker, 2011; Hirschi, 2004; Hirschi & Gottfredson, 2004). Lack of self-control is closely related to the inability to delay gratification—a significant risk factor for many problems.

Over 40 years ago Walter Mischel, then a psychologist at Stanford now at Harvard, received a "Golden Fleece Award" from Senator Proxmire (R., Wisconsin) for a series of grant-funded studies that Proxmire considered a waste of federal research dollars. Termed the "Marshmallow Experiment," Mischel tested the concept of delayed gratification. His researchers offered children one marshmallow immediately, or if they were able to wait 15 to 20 minutes the child received two marshmallows. Some children immediately ate the offered marshmallow. Others delayed for a while but eventually gave into temptation. Some were able to wait the entire time and receive their two marshmallow reward.

Researchers followed the original participants periodically during the subsequent 40 years, including Mischel and his graduate students Peake and Shoda. What they found was that, in the long term, children who could not wait or stop themselves from gobbling up the first marshmallow in order to enjoy two marshmallows also had significantly higher difficulty delaying gratification later on as adults. They had a harder time finding and keeping a job and were more likely to abuse drugs. Those who showed greater self-control and delay gratification as children had better SAT scores and generally a lower Body Mass Index. Brain imaging demonstrated that the part of the brain that responds to rewards during adolescence were different between the adults who as children could not wait to get two marshmallows and those who could delay gratification for a greater reward (Casey, 2015; Casey et al., 2011). The ability to delay gratification has a significant impact in one's success in life. Based on this body of research, in 2015 Mischel was awarded the "Golden Goose Award" (Jaffe, 2015), an award based on unique research that provides substantial and surprising results (and that was named in part to mock the mocking "Golden Fleece Award" initiated by Senator Proxmire 50 years earlier).

Training in self-management and self-control includes the following skills which can be subsumed under the general heading of self-regulation (McKown et al., 2010; Simon, 2016): (a) self-assessment (being able to compare present functioning with internal standards and evaluate significant differences between the performance and the standard); (b) self-monitoring (being attuned to and aware of one's present functioning); and (c) self-reinforcement (providing positive consequences when performance meets standards and negative consequences for failure to perform adequately).

Self-Assessment

Self-assessment is the systematic evaluation of one's own behavior to determine whether it has been adequate. Young people need to be able to evaluate and assess their behavior to improve it. Most young people evaluate themselves on the basis of standards acquired from significant others in their environment. Both parents and teachers provide young people with standards against which to evaluate their behavior in various situations. For a variety of reasons, many at-risk young people fail to acquire clear standards for self-evaluation.

Self-ratings can be used to teach youth to assess their behavior. First, the student and adult decide together which specific behavior needs to be changed. After a target behavior is identified, the next step is to devise a rating system—a scale of 0 to 10, say, or 0 to 100—by which the specific behavior can be assessed and evaluated. Paul Andrews of Chapter 1, for example, might be asked to rate his classroom outbursts by rating his underlying mood and behavior: 0 (no desire to hit or to explode) to 10 (several outbursts). Number 5 on this rating scale might be "resisted desire to hit or explode." Such a rating scale would provide Paul with a subjective measure of mood and behavior, and the self-assessment would help him to develop self-control. Although Paul has several behaviors that need to change, he needs to deal with only one behavior at a time. An attempt to change too many behaviors simultaneously would lower the probability of success and serve to confuse him. If he started out by attempting to change a single behavior, Paul's chance for success would be increased.

Self-Monitoring

Self-monitoring is focusing attention and awareness on one's characteristics, emotions, thoughts, or behavior and is closely related to self-assessment. Self-monitoring requires students to observe their own behavior and to record it. Essentially students are taught to collect data on their own behavior. Self-monitoring helps students become more aware of their own negative and positive behaviors, putting their behavior more firmly under their own control. Self-monitoring has also been supported as an effective tool in counseling (Baker et al., 2015).

Self-Reinforcement

Self-reinforcement is the act of supplying one's own consequences for performance. Such consequences may be intangible and intrinsic (such as silent self-praise for meeting a personal goal) or tangible and external (such as buying oneself a present after meeting a personal goal). Consequences may also be negative. A negative consequence might be self-criticism or forgoing a particular pleasure.

Self-reinforcement energizes the self-management process. People anticipate and work for possible positive consequences. Self-reinforcement keeps the person on the track of establishing and pursuing goals. The effects of self-reinforcement on school performance are found to be as beneficial as those of external reinforcement (Sherman et al., 2013). The self-reinforcement of behaviors conducive to learning works powerfully to improve school achievement and personal performance.

In summary, when young people are taught to assess their own behavior, to monitor their academic and personal performance, and to reinforce their improved behavior with positive consequences, their school performance is likely to improve and their personal problems are minimized.

Control for Learning

Self-management and self-control help in the educational process, too. Self-management training produces both short- and long-term gains in achievement. Students who can self-manage have been found to raise their levels of academic aspirations, increase their efforts on future tasks, improve their non-academic skills, and decrease their disruptive behaviors (Cleary, 2015). Self-control skills help students make adaptive attributions (McKown et al., 2010): Students are encouraged to take responsibility for their successes and failures by learning when failure is attributable to their own lack of effort and when success results from their own ability, efforts, and skills. These modified attributions result in enhanced efforts in similar tasks in the future.

One consistent difference between academically successful and unsuccessful students is their awareness of their own learning strategies. Many at-risk students are unaware that their learning strategies are limited or ineffective. Another way for adults to intervene in the learning process is to teach successful learning strategies to at-risk students. A learning strategy is a plan for merging cognitive skills and metacognitive ability in the process of acquiring information (Cleary, 2015; Wery & Thomson, 2013). In this educational approach, students are taught to observe, monitor, and think about their learning strategy or plan.

Children's awareness of their cognitive strategies is correlated with enhanced performance on reading measures. That is, children who can describe the thinking processes they use as they read are able to comprehend more than students who cannot; teachers should model their own mental processes to stimulate metacognitive skill in their students. The purpose of instruction in metacognitive strategies is to increase students' awareness of themselves as learners, place students in control of their own learning activity, and provide them with a method to use to improve their own learning.

Reciprocal teaching is a similar learning strategy that is successful with poor learners. To implement this strategy, the teacher and a small group of students talk about the texts they read. The students take turns being "teacher" and practicing the four components of reciprocal teaching: They (a) generate questions about the content of the reading material, (b) summarize the content, (c) clarify points, and (d) predict future content on the basis of prior knowledge or clues within the text. Reciprocal teaching has provided success for a variety of students (Meyer, 2014; Reichenberg & Lofgren, 2014).

CONCLUSION

Communication and life skills, cognitive change strategies, and coping techniques are critical elements in programs for prevention and early intervention. Young people who have acquired these tools have the ability to avoid problem behavior. Comprehensive training programs to teach these skills need to be instituted early and universally for all youth to prevent problems. For at-risk youth, indicated programs to teach these skills are needed as early as possible—ideally before third grade. For long-term benefits, young people need the skills reinforced over time and from a variety of people. Finally, for older children and adolescents who are at higher risk, these skills need to be included in special education classes, school counseling programs, and in community treatment programs.

School-based psychoeducational groups, peer (and cross-age) tutoring, and school mediation programs are strong environments in which to teach and reinforce these skills. By learning these skills, young people will improve their interactions with others, perform better in school, and realize their potential for a more positive future.

Peer Interventions

Dear Jenny,

I am really, really sorry that I did something to make you mad at me. If you would tell me what it is, I would change it, but you won't talk to me. Please be my friend again, I will try to be the best friend that I can be.

Kayla

Dear Jenny,

It has been 2 weeks that you won't talk to me, and I still don't know what I did. Did you tell Angie and Kara something about me, because now they won't talk to me either? I can't eat or sleep; this is making me very upset. I am going to go talk to the peer helper even though we think she is weird, that's how upset I am about all of this, so you should think about what you are doing to me. Your friend (still, even though you won't talk to me).

Kayla

Dear Jenny,

Jackie is actually nice, and she isn't weird at all. She asked me what a friend is, and I said that you are a friend. Hah! I would tell you more but I am going to go study with a FRIEND.

Kayla

Dear Jenny,

Well, I guess this is my last note to you because after all this time of wanting to be your friend and wanting to know what I did wrong, now it doesn't matter to me anymore. I liked being your friend and you are pretty and fun, but there are girls who don't act like you and they are my friends now. If that means I'm not cool, that's OK with me. A friend is someone who talks to you and listens to you, so we aren't really friends anymore. Maybe you should talk to Jackie too and tell her how mean you are, she could probably help you be a better friend, and then you wouldn't have to hang around girls that say mean things.

Kayla

P.S. I know you are going to show this to Kara and Angie, so don't think it will shock me.

In the previous chapter, we provided a series of core interventions designed to build personal resiliency and to increase the individual competencies of young people at risk. We presented prevention strategies to be implemented in curriculum-based developmental programs in schools. In this chapter, we present major prevention strategies that utilize the power of the peer group in helping young people decrease negative and increase positive behaviors. These interventions help prevent and reduce the negative behaviors discussed earlier in this book.

IMPORTANCE OF PEERS

The history of prevention of problem behaviors included educational and "scare" approaches during the 1960s, self-esteem and ego-enhancing approaches during the 1970s, and social skills training approaches during the 1980s and 1990s. Each of these approaches is necessary but not sufficient in preventing or decreasing problem behaviors. The core competency approaches described in Chapter 12, which include components of education (cognitive), self-esteem and optimism building (affective), and social skills training (behavioral), show great promise and characterize preventive interventions prevalent through the 2000s until now (American Psychological Association, 2014; Hawkins et al., 2015). Many of these interventions have proven efficacious in modifying the abuse of substances, in reducing teen pregnancy, and in preventing other problems. Adolescents improve their resilience and competencies more when interventions are specific, focused, and personalized.

Unfortunately, for many high-risk young people, learning to be competent is not enough. For example, young people can learn resistance and refusal skills, or to "just say no." However, knowing how to say "No" is very different from actually doing so. Any discussion of prevention must include consideration of the influences of peer pressure in encouraging and maintaining problem behavior (Trucco, Colder, & Wieczorek, 2011). Peer cluster theory provides one way to explain peer influence on problem behavior and models how to use peer influence to help young people overcome problems. Later in the chapter we highlight several prevention and intervention strategies designed to modify negative peer clusters and to engage youth in identifying more closely with positive peer clusters. For example, we examine cooperative learning groups with a particular emphasis on peer support networks. We also describe strategies that utilize peers to enhance academic and social success in school settings. We provide models for peer and cross-age tutoring, peer mediation programs, and other peer-assisted or peer-mediated interventions.

Peer Influence—For Good or Bad

As children grow older, the importance of parents decreases as a reference group and as a model for conformity (McGoldrick, Garcia-Preto, & Carter, 2015). Nevertheless, emotional closeness and agreement on values between parents and their children has been directly related to reduced problem behavior. Although parental influence is more important for some young people than for others, peer influence becomes the dominant factor for many teenagers. Peer influence clearly can be part of the problem (Trucco et al., 2011), but it also can be part of the solution.

Positive peer comments provide self-worth and self-esteem to young people. The peer group represents the transfer vehicle for transition from childhood to adulthood. It is within the peer group that the young person learns to relate to different roles and to experiment with interpersonal interaction skills that will eventually transfer to the world of adults.

The peer group exemplifies the world outside the home. Compliance, aggression, leadership, and need satisfaction are developed within peer group interaction. A teenager who is attracted to a peer group that values antisocial activity inevitably finds it insurmountable to resist group members' pressure to engage in negative behaviors. In this situation the adolescent is faced with a decision—either abandon the relationships that provide social support or capitulate to the dictates of peer pressure. A consistent risk factor for middle school students, for instance, is having friends who engage in problem behaviors. Meanwhile, the most powerful protective factor for a young person is to have an attitude that is intolerant of any deviant behavior. At the same time, research demonstrates that peer-mediated interventions produce positive academic outcomes for a wide range of students, including students with emotional and behavior disorders (EBD). Cross-age, same-age, and class-wide peer tutoring and cooperative learning are successful peer-mediated interventions across academic subject areas and grade levels (Ryan, Reid, & Epstein, 2004). The key is to enhance and engage positive peer interactions and reduce negative ones. Understanding peer cluster theory helps begin the steps for doing this.

Peer Cluster Theory

Peer cluster theory (Beauvais, Chavez, Oetting, Deffenbacher, & Cornell, 1996) provides a way to operationalize peer pressure, especially as it relates to problem behaviors. This theory suggests that antisocial behavior and school problems are major factors in creating deviant peer clusters. Young people who engage in troublesome behavior have a tendency to find one another. These individuals form peer cluster groups. These deviant peer cluster groups normalize, support, and encourage a wide range of deviant behaviors.

Peer cluster theory suggests that the dominant influences on an adolescent's drug use and other problem behaviors are the attitudes, beliefs, and behaviors of the young person's immediate peers (Beauvais et al., 1996; Dishion & Veronneau, 2012; Gardner & Steinberg, 2005; Rice, Milburn, Rotheram-Borus, Mallett, & Rosenthal, 2005; Zhen-Duan & Taylor, 2014). According to this theory, social and environmental factors such as poverty, prejudice, family, community, and the presence of emotional stressors, as well as personality traits, values, and beliefs, provide a framework that can increase or decrease adolescents' susceptibility to problem behaviors. Against this background, the peer cluster is a dominant influence on young people's behavior. A peer group can be a large or small reference group; a peer cluster is a small subset of a peer group in which each member influences the values, attitudes, and beliefs of other members of the cluster. In the case of a substance-using adolescent, for instance, associating peers who are in the same peer cluster are likely to use the same drugs, use them for the same reasons, and use them together. These characteristics are much more specific than those implied by the term *drug lifestyle*, which can refer to heavy and occasional drug users alike. Similarly, peer clusters influence sexual behavior, delinquency, gang membership, and school dropout (Dishion & Veronneau, 2012). Adolescents at risk of dropping out appear to have more friends who are dropouts, more working friends, and fewer school friends than adolescents at low risk of dropping out (Rosen & Chen, 2015). Peer pressure implies the heavy influence of a group on an individual, who usually has limited ability to resist it. Peer clusters are much more dynamic; every member of the peer cluster is an active participant in developing the norms and behaviors of the cluster. The cluster is an interactive whole. Although some members will wield more influence than others (as in any group), the group as a whole determines the behavior, attitudes, and beliefs of the entire cluster.

The dynamics of peer clusters may explain why many prevention and intervention treatments fail. Most adolescents who are pulled away for an intervention typically return to their original environment and former peer cluster after treatment. The norming influence of the peer cluster often can diminish or eliminate the treatment effects. Treatment strategies must consider peer clusters and provide alternatives for adolescents who may be drawn back into a peer cluster that engages in unproductive, unhealthy, or antisocial behavior. Sometimes merely removing a person from the peer cluster ameliorates the problem. Another alternative is providing treatment for the whole cluster; for example, in-school approaches that make use of the peer cluster. First, counselors can organize professionally led, weekly group counseling sessions for young people and their peers who use substances or show other risky behavior. Also, schools can assign young people to a form of in-school suspension that requires them to spend one or more days each week together as a group, learning why they have been having problems, learning the short- and long-term consequences, and developing the motivation and skills necessary to change. Both strategies are designed to engage the peer cluster and modify norms and attitudes that support negative behavior. But be cautious. The peer group may reinforce norms that adults cannot modify, especially if groups are provided with unstructured time. Researchers discuss the iatrogenic effect, whereby group interventions intended to help actually cause harm because peers within groups negatively influence one another and encourage antisocial behavior (Cho, Hallfors, & Sanchez, 2005; Gardner & Steinberg, 2005). This is particularly problematic in informal and unstructured groups. To reduce the potential harmful effects of a group intervention, it is wise to keep the group structured and to include in the group some young people with prosocial attitudes or, as we discuss later, trained peer or cross-age facilitators.

Interventions that provide group treatments to high-risk, aggressive youth are particularly problematic and can inadvertently exacerbate violent tendencies. In addition, interventions that fail to incorporate caretakers and focus exclusively on children tend to be less successful. A young person who returns from treatment into the same family dynamics, as well as the same peer cluster, is unlikely to be consistently reinforced for treatment gains that were made. Adolescent violence prevention programs offering intensive counseling for high-risk children and their families are more successful in deterring juvenile crime than "scared straight" or military-like boot camps. As predicted by peer cluster theory, young people with delinquent tendencies who are put together in camps or centers provide justification for criminal attitudes and values and teach one another how to commit more crimes (National Institutes of Health Consensus Development Program, 2004).

COOPERATIVE LEARNING AND PEER SUPPORT NETWORKS

Cooperative learning groups are a basic way to influence peer clusters. Any teacher can develop this approach, from the primary grades through high school and beyond. Children learn the skills of collaboration, manage conflicts and disputes, and develop a cooperative spirit with their classmates. Peer clusters lose some of their negative influence when this strategy is adopted.

The practice of grouping students by their ability to learn, as determined by some objective measure, has a negative effect on children in low-ability groups, and it tends to reinforce initial inequalities (Gamoran, 2009; Rubin, 2006). Teachers treat high-ability groups differently from low-ability groups. Students with lower ability receive fewer opportunities to answer analytical questions, are given less time to respond, and receive less praise than the students in high-ability groups. These students begin to think little of their own ability. Overall, ability grouping as a practice has decidedly negative effects for children with lower ability.

Cooperative Learning

The wide range of skills and abilities that teachers find in heterogeneous classrooms often frustrates them. Grouping procedures such as cooperative learning are one solution to this problem (Gamoran, 2009). Cooperative learning is implemented in various ways. First, it can vary in task structure. In some programs, students work independently on a task that has been divided up. In others, students work on the task as a group. The latter format encourages peer helping and a truly cooperative learning environment. Second, cooperative learning can vary according to incentives. For example, the group's grade or reward may be the sum or average of the individual members' performances or it may be contingent on the product that the group as a whole has created. In most cooperative learning implementations, students work in small, heterogeneous groups (usually numbering between four and six) and are rewarded according to the group's performance.

Cooperative learning groups also have the potential to provide at-risk students with a positive peer support group. Cooperative learning groups are a major intervention approach, and we discuss the deliberate adaptation of such groups to augment a peer support network. These networks are a counterpoint to negative peer clusters.

Positive Effects of Cooperative Learning Groups

Cooperative learning has several aims. First, a cooperative model is a healthy alternative to an individual competitive model. Individual competition can have devastating effects on the motivation of at-risk students.

Membership in a successful group permits students to experience success with all its attendant advantages—perceptions of themselves as able to perform well, satisfaction with their performance, and the esteem of their peers—regardless of each student's personal individual performance. This experience is of particular benefit to at-risk students who have known few academic successes (see Box 13.1).

In cooperative learning groups, students are encouraged to help and support one another rather than to compete. As in most athletic activities, individual excellence is encouraged because it benefits the whole team. Both high- and low-ability children profit from the experience. The low-ability children benefit from the assistance of their peers, and high-ability children achieve a higher level of understanding after providing that assistance (Gillies, 2014). Incidentally, high-ability students in cooperative learning situations, compared to those in individualistic or competitive ones, demonstrated higher achievement and high-level reasoning and had higher academic self-esteem (Roseth, Johnson, & Johnson, 2008).

Cooperative learning increases academic performance (Roseth et al., 2008). Whether students are questioning factual information, discovering new concepts, or solving problems, a cooperative learning approach has been shown to develop academic skills. Students, especially those from diverse linguistic and cultural backgrounds, make significant academic gains compared to student gains in traditional settings. Classroom interaction with peers offers students many chances to use language and improve speaking skills, especially important for English as a Second Language (ESL) or English Language Learners (ELL) students.

Cooperative learning encourages active learning. Extensive research and practice have indicated that students learn more when they are actively engaged in discovery and in problem solving. As students talk and reason together to solve a problem or complete a task, they become more involved in communicating and in thinking. These activities automatically engage a child in an active way that is quite different from the passive listening and learning required by most approaches.

Box 13.1	Getting Smart

One teacher recently experimented with cooperative learning groups. She joined two children of middle ability with one child of high ability and one of low ability for a social studies project. They worked together cooperatively on the reading material. When they were finished with their project, she quizzed each child on the material.

The next day, when the low-ability child received his score on the test, he looked perplexed and said, "I'm not this smart." The teacher smiled and replied, "I guess you must be." She decided to continue to organize cooperative learning groups in her classroom.

Cooperative learning helps prepare students for work in today's world. Team approaches to problem solving and individual efforts to accomplish group goals and aid interpersonal harmony in the work setting are all valued skills in today's society of interdependent workplaces. Cooperative learning teaches students how to work together and builds students' social nature, social understanding, and personal efficacy.

Finally, cooperative learning groups provide an opportunity to improve race relations in the school as well as acceptance of special education and LGBT students. Students who work together in cooperative learning groups are more likely to value mixed racial and ethnic acquaintances and friendships and develop a respect for diversity, including greater acceptance of students with physical and learning disabilities. When students cooperate to reach a common goal, they learn to respect and appreciate each other. Ms. Bassett, Carlos Diaz's social studies teacher (see Chapter 4), is working toward this goal by placing her students in cooperative learning groups. As her students of different ethnic backgrounds work with each other, prejudice diminishes. Consequently, Carlos is now establishing friendships with other students. Dividing a class into interracial learning teams reduces prejudice by undercutting stereotypes and encouraging group members to pull together.

Cooperative learning takes numerous forms. Programs are known by names such as Learning Together, Group Investigation, Team Assisted Individualization, Student Teams-Achievement Divisions, Teams-Games-Tournaments, and Jigsaw. A review of cooperative learning methods and specific classroom applications is provided by Hertz-Lazarowitz, Kagan, Sharan, Slavin, Webb, and Schmuck 2013. These strategies are a group of instructional methods that utilize interdependence among students in the learning of content.

Cooperative learning programs have demonstrated positive outcomes that directly address the needs of at-risk youth: motivation, peer support, self-attributions, and self-esteem (Slavin, Lake, Chambers, Cheung, & Davis, 2009). After 35 years of research the evidence is impressive (Gillies, 2014), supporting the claim that cooperative learning groups enhance academic achievement; increase positive self-esteem, internal locus of control, altruism, and perspective taking; improve intergroup relationships between students without and with disabilities, as well as the relationship between students of different cultural backgrounds; and provide positive peer support. Because they entail positive peer support, cooperative learning groups seem to be a natural way to promote feelings of connectedness among students at risk of dropping out or those who have other social and emotional problems. The potential to increase social capital and prosocial peer influence is especially important in cooperative peer learning groups.

Peer Support Networks

Grouping students together because they share a problem may increase interaction, mutual support, and camaraderie, but it can also have other unwanted effects: positive peer models and influences on academic performance and behavior may be drastically reduced; negative peer modeling may escalate; the entire group may perform according to anti-adult and antisocial norms. Nevertheless, to be successful, classroom interactions must foster caring communities in which students feel they belong and where they believe teachers and peers support them. Support networks for psychological well-being are well documented in the literature (Ali, Farrer, Gulliver, & Griffiths, 2015; Carter et al., 2013).

To increase their positive impact and to minimize their potential negative influence, we propose that cooperative learning groups be formed deliberately to increase the socioemotional supports for students. By purposefully and deliberately designing peer support networks, high-risk students are provided with positive peer support, which promotes their feelings of connectedness with other students and with the school (Carter, Cushing, Clark, & Kennedy, 2005). High-risk students are not identified in any formal or obvious way, but they are put in situations where they can maintain relationships with peers who provide positive models of academic performance and behavior. In this way, peer support networks are accessible to students regarded as being at risk. They also form a natural structure for psychoeducational, support, and counseling groups.

In developing peer support networks, first identify students at risk. Then identify students who are more grounded, resilient, and prosocial. The five Cs of competency (see Chapter 5) can be used to help identify both groups of students.

After students have been identified, the teacher or counselor deliberately structures a cooperative learning group that also functions as a peer support network. Students with the greatest support needs are targeted, and their names are put in one of the five slots in each cluster. If at all possible, only one high-risk student is included in any single group. Attempts should be made to avoid putting together individuals who form friendship bonds that are a negative influence on academic motivation, school achievement, and behavior. The other four students in each peer support network cluster should be chosen with the intent of making the group as heterogeneous as possible with regard to gender, ethnocultural group, ability, and achievement (e.g., European American, Latino, and African American; female and male; one low, one high, and three average achievers).

For each cooperative learning peer support group, include at least one student who is generally on task in group activities and, if possible, one student who is a peacekeeper diplomat. Also, include at least one group member who might be a potential friend to the student at risk. Ideally, students in the peer support cooperative groups would be very much like the student at risk with an important exception—the potential friends are positive influences. Try to avoid individual personalities that may create negative group combinations. For example, two physically aggressive, volatile students may create a potentially explosive group; or timid or quiet students may be manipulated or intimidated by peers who act in a dominant way.

These peer support cooperative learning groups should stay together for their class cooperative learning activities for at least a 9- or 12-week grading period. Although modifications may need to be made when group combinations are not working, the intent is to put together high-risk students with less risky students to provide a peer support network. Although there has been limited research on using the Good Behavior Game (GBG)—discussed later—with students older than first and second grade, the principles of the game should be helpful in a peer support network.

Elements of Cooperative Learning

After formation of the groups, it is important that the students engage in cooperative learning activities to help the interaction and mutual interdependent collaboration. In one study (Bassett, J. J. McWhirter, & Kitzmiller, 1997), we found that teachers who reported a commitment to cooperative learning groups were not really using the method. Many teachers believed that they were implementing cooperative learning when, in fact, they were missing its essence. Structured cooperative learning among students is more than just putting students into groups to learn. Students sitting together at the same table and talking with one another is not cooperative learning. Having one student do all the work on a group report while others simply put their names on it is not cooperative learning. A student who finishes a task early and helps slower students complete it is not involved in cooperative learning.

The five basic elements (Johnson, Johnson, & Holubec, 1990) discussed below are essential to cooperative learning groups. They are positive interdependence, individual accountability, face-to-face interaction, social skills, and group process. Slavin (1991, 2013) identifies similar elements and adds a sixth: group rewards. He argues that awards accruing to the whole group are useful and powerful in building the prestige and power of the cooperative learning group.

Positive Interdependence

Students are linked with others in such a way that one cannot succeed unless the other members of the group succeed and vice versa. Goal interdependence, role interdependence, shared rewards, dependence on one another's resources, and a distributed division of labor help ensure positive interdependence.

Individual Accountability

The performance of each individual student in the group is assessed, and the results are reported back to the student and to the group. Randomly selecting one student's work to represent the entire group or randomly asking one group member to explain a problem, solution, or concept are ways to accomplish this element. Students need to know that they can't "ride" on the backs of others.

Face-to-Face Interaction

This element exists when students assist, help, support, and encourage one another's efforts to learn. Discussion of strategies and concepts, explanations of how to solve problems, teaching knowledge, and making connections between past and present information fulfill this requirement.

Social Skills

Working cooperatively requires specific social and interactional skills. Leadership, communication, trust-building, decision-making, and conflict management skills are necessary components of effective cooperative learning groups. As we have made clear elsewhere in this book, these skills have to be taught just as purposefully and precisely as academic skills. Many students have never had an opportunity to work cooperatively in a group before, and they need the social skills to do so.

Group Process

Monitoring and discussing the interactional process of the groups is necessary. Students need to become aware and be encouraged to maintain effective working relationships in their groups and to consider whether they are achieving their goals. Group maintenance, feedback about participation, and other process issues need to be developed.

To develop and increase group cohesion, productivity, and interaction, ask the cooperative learning group members to respond to these two questions after each session: What was something that each member did that helped the group today? What can each person do at the next meeting to make the group better? The 10 minutes that this processing takes provides feedback for members on their collaborative skills, allows the group to focus on group maintenance, and reminds students to use their collaborative skills consistently.

Cooperative learning groups that are deliberately structured to provide a social support network can change the way young people experience school. The social support network provides high-risk students with systematic opportunities to develop positive interaction patterns and to form friendships with peers who have been carefully selected as potential supports and friends based on personal, cultural, and social characteristics. Teaching social skills, critical thinking, and academic content is integrated in the context of group support.

GOOD BEHAVIOR GAME

Considerable evidence (Helker & Ray, 2009) supports the position that teachers who teach relationship-building skills in the classroom improve student relationships and decrease students' externalizing behaviors. By improving positive childhood peer relations, externalizing outcomes are reduced (Witvliet, van Lier, Cuijpers, & Koot, 2009). Even more important are the long-term effects. A special issue of the *Journal of Drug and Alcohol Dependence* (Kellam, Reid, & Balster, 2008) provides evidence that suggests that developing positive relationships early in school using the GBG impacts a wide variety of long-term behavioral and mental health outcomes.

The GBG is a universal classroom-based preventive intervention using behavior management which helps children work together, learn the role and appropriate skills of being students, and master the key demands of the classroom, including paying attention, taking turns, sitting still, and completing school work. The model is team-based and encourages students to self-monitor their behavior as well as that of their classmates (Kellam et al., 2011).

Because teachers use GBG during the regular school day parallel with ongoing school curriculum, they have more time to devote to teaching due to less off-task, aggressive, and disruptive behavior. By the end of first grade, the program reduces students' aggressive and disruptive behavior and increases their on-task behavior.

The four components critical to the model include team membership, classroom rules, monitoring behavior, and reinforcing appropriate behavior. The teacher reads and posts the classroom rules to students, who are then divided into three heterogeneous groups or teams. When team members exhibit inappropriate and disruptive behavior, such as fighting, being out of their seat, talking out of turn, and similar behavior, their team receives a check mark. At the end of a specified time, 10 minutes at the beginning of the year to a half or full day later in the year, teams with four or fewer check marks receive a reward. In the beginning, tangible rewards are used, but as the year progresses more intangible rewards are provided. Strategies are included to make positive behaviors intrinsic and to generalize them. In addition, the teacher leads a weekly class meeting, focusing on the children's skills in social problem solving.

In addition to the results mentioned above, the GBG has produced a host of long-term benefits, including educational gains and longer schooling; improvement with emotional and behavioral problems; reduced smoking, alcohol, and other drug use; lower incidence of psychiatric and antisocial personality disorders; lowered violent or criminal behaviors; and reduced suicidal ideation and attempts (see, e.g., Bradshaw, Zmuda, Kellam, & Ialongo, 2009; Flower et al., 2013; Kellam et al., 2008, 2011; National Institutes of Drug Abuse, 2011; Wang, Iannotti, & Nansel, 2009). For example, students who had participated in the process as first and second graders were more likely as 13-year-old middle school students to have reduced aggressive and disruptive behavior compared to control group students; they were 26% less likely to have started smoking and less than half as likely to have used cocaine, crack, or heroin. Interestingly, there were no effects on the percent using alcohol, marijuana, or inhalants. At high school and later the GBG was associated with higher achievement test scores involving gains equal to one additional year of academic progress and reduced odds of special education involvement (36%). They were more likely to have graduated from high school or have received a General Educational Development (GED) (21%) and to have attended college (62%) (Bradshaw et al., 2009). Even in emerging and early adulthood, these young people had reduced use of mental and behavioral health services from through young adulthood. Males who participated in GBG, compared with their peers who did not participate, especially benefited: They had a 59% lower rate in smoking 10 or more cigarettes per day, 35% lower rate of lifetime alcohol abuse/dependence, and 50% lower rate of lifetime illicit drug abuse/dependence (Flower et al., 2014). The GBG also seems to delay or prevent onset of suicide ideation and suicide attempts (Wilcox et al., 2008).

PEER AND CROSS-AGE TUTORING PROGRAMS

Peer and cross-age tutors are students who teach other students in formal and informal learning situations that are delegated, planned, and directed by an educator (Nelson-Royes, 2015). Peer tutoring is a one-to-one teaching process in which the tutor is of the same academic age as the partner. Cross-age tutoring involves matching an older student tutor with a younger student learner. Peer tutoring alters the environmental and social climate in a school and can enhance and increase learning. It provides a cost-effective way to meet the individual needs of students and to improve the performance of students who need help with their studies. Tutoring programs are designed to aid at-risk children by improving their academic performance and their emotional well-being (Gerena & Keiler, 2011; Robinson, Schofield, & Steers-Wentzell, 2005). Peer tutoring improves social interactions, self-concept, motivation, attitudes toward the school (Lazerson, 2005), peer status, and overall school experience (Outhred & Chester, 2010). The concept of peer tutoring has deep roots in our educational system.

Systematic planning is a critical component of successful peer or cross-age tutoring programs. It improves thinking skills (Topping, Miller, Thurston, McGavok, & Conlin, 2011), use of mathematic and scientific words and concepts (Gosser, Kampmeier, & Varma-Nelson, 2010), and increases information on specialized subjects such as music, horticulture, health, safety, and social interactions (Bowman-Perrott et al., 2013). Administrators, teachers, students, and families more readily accept programs that attend to readiness, preparation, selection, implementation, supervision, and evaluation components, especially when cost-effective. Elements essential to implementing a successful peer or cross-age tutoring program include considerations of school readiness and teacher, student, and parent preparation.

Peer and cross-age tutoring has been found to be very cost-effective while at the same time producing better gains in math and reading scores for students than from computer-aided instruction, from reducing class size, or from extending the school day by 1 hour (see, e.g., Levin, Glass, & Meister, 1984). Information regarding the relative utility of peer or cross-age tutoring interventions is vital to administrators in a time of reduced resources, increased demands, and increased accountability. Young people make gains even with the brevity of contact and low cost in time and resources involved in peer tutoring (Nelson-Royes, 2015).

Readiness

Much of the success of peer tutoring depends on the readiness of the school to accept the program. Readiness is a function of both attitudinal factors and availability of resources to support the program. As administrator of the school, the principal is instrumental in allowing for program adjustments such as release time, schedule modifications, allocation of space, and active encouragement of peer tutoring. Teachers support the peer tutoring program by participating in peer selection, curriculum development, ongoing evaluation, and program development activities. Teacher readiness requires thorough training in peer tutoring methods through in-service training and ongoing consultation and supervision. Specialized training and instruction in peer and cross-age tutoring methods for teachers are often available from school psychologists and counselors. Counselors may encourage teachers to acquaint themselves with tutoring methods and materials through published resources (see, e.g., Gordon, Morgan, O'Malley, & Ponticell, 2007; Nelson-Royes, 2015).

Preparation

Sufficient preparation of participating individuals increases the likelihood that the peer or cross-age tutoring program will be successfully established and accepted in both the school and the community. Students may be readied for peer tutoring through written and oral information about the program. Because peer or cross-age tutoring is a nontraditional means of instruction, presenting the program and its participants in a positive light is important.

Teachers play a central role in determining the content to be taught. They also explain to tutors how to approach learning, monitor student progress, and facilitate students' interactions. To increase teachers' acceptance of and commitment to the program, training and preparation of teachers should encompass several components, including (a) understanding the purpose, advantage, and features of the peer tutoring program; (b) planning lessons and material preparation for student use; and (c) developing competence in teaching interactional and problem-solving skills to students. This training is accomplished through consultation, exposure to written material on peer tutoring, and in-service training. Teacher training includes instruction of tutoring methods, simulation exercises to familiarize teachers with student and teacher roles, modeling strategies for social and conflict resolution skills, and discussion of anticipated problems that may interfere with implementation. Our experience suggests that training programs developed for this purpose can accomplish these objectives in a minimum of three to five 40-minute training sessions if ongoing in-services, consultation, and coordination for maintenance purposes are provided.

The degree to which students are prepared to tutor is another critical element of an effective tutoring program. Children who have a fuller understanding of a task and its rationale are better prepared to perform the task themselves and better equipped to teach it to others. Students planning to tutor are better prepared when trained in various aspects of tutoring, including (a) developing and presenting instructional material; (b) recognizing and reinforcing correct learner responses appropriately; (c) providing corrective feedback effectively; (d) redirecting off-task behavior; (e) communicating with learners; and (f) working closely with teachers. Tutor preparation includes a mix of didactic instruction, practice in specific skills, and group discussion of possible problems. Tutors also benefit from ongoing training to strengthen their skills and reinforce the purpose of the program. Ongoing training can be accomplished through brief refresher training sessions offered periodically during the peer or cross-age tutoring program. Of course, tutoring provides a useful learning-by-teaching model for the tutor. In fact, one study showed that using a computer with a Virtual Tutee System prompted student tutors to engage deeper reflection, elaboration, and analysis with less boredom and greater enjoyment (Park & Kim, 2015).

Advance preparation of parents is essential to the program's acceptance. If not properly informed, parents may perceive their child's participation in the peer or cross-age tutoring program negatively. Advance preparation of participating parents in the form of written information, group discussions, and personal contact may convert potentially doubting parents to agents of support. Because peer tutoring activities involve individual students selected from the entire class, parental consent is needed. Parents should be provided with a clear explanation of the program, reasons for their child's involvement, and safeguards against possible negative effects. Parent preparation may be accomplished through letters to parents, meetings between parents and school personnel, and presentations at meetings such as the PTA and the PTSO.

Sample Method: Pause, Prompt, and Praise

To illustrate the nature of peer tutoring, we selected one method for fuller description. The "pause, prompt, and praise" method is very helpful for tutoring oral reading. The first part of the tutoring procedure, "pause," requires the tutor to delay attention to the student's reading error for more than 5 seconds or until the end of the sentence. The second part of the procedure, "prompt," requires the tutor to supply a prompt if no self-correction occurs. The prompts are the self-correction strategies that the student learner has already learned as part of program preparation. They are often graphic or contextual clues that provide meaning. If no correct response is elicited following two prompts, the tutor supplies the correct word and moves on. The final part of the procedure, "praise," requires the tutor to verbally reinforce positive behaviors and to encourage development of independent self-correcting skills. Therefore, in addition to the general praise for behaviors such as finishing a whole page, the tutor praises self-corrections and prompts corrections made by the learner.

This method supplies the tutor with a procedure for dealing with both correct and erroneous behavior by the reader. It encourages him or her to reinforce the desired behaviors. Perhaps more important, it allows the reader to develop independence and independent self-correction strategies. It is also a simple method for peer tutors to learn.

Program Implementations

Educational interventions such as peer or cross-age tutoring often emerge from a need to remediate students who are failing or at risk of failure. The impetus to develop new programs often reflects a sense of urgency. Initially, however, a modest peer or cross-age tutoring program is most viable. Avoid overtaxing available resources during the initial implementation stage of a program and expand later when the program is well established.

In spite of how thoroughly a program has been planned, unforeseen problems will arise. After initial startup, slight adjustments will be necessary. Administrative support is essential to the program. As well, teachers will need some release time and other forms of support to develop materials, assess and supervise program participants, and provide ongoing training (in-service and discussion groups) related to the program. Now let's take a closer look at the elements of a successful peer tutoring program.

Tutor Selection

In cross-age tutoring programs, older tutors are matched with younger partners. In peer tutoring programs, tutors and student learners (or partners) are the same age, class, or grade. When selecting tutors, consideration may be given to students with a variety of characteristics, including those who are academically accomplished and able to instruct, those who are positive role models and influential with their peers, and others who are at greater risk of school failure and may benefit academically and emotionally from their role as tutors. Each type of tutor offers a degree of assurance that the program will be accepted. The academically accomplished tutor will bring mastery of the subject matter to the tutoring session, the influential peer will popularize the program within the peer culture, and the at-risk tutor will provide evidence that the program is of benefit to those who tutor (Menesses & Gresham, 2009).

When choosing whom to include as student learners, educators might consider the degree of learning difficulties, motivation, and behavioral adjustment the learner presents. Learners with severe problems may not be good candidates for initial implementation of the program. These students may be introduced to the peer tutoring program in subsequent years, once introductory concerns are resolved and the program is established.

Once matched, it is advisable that tutor–learner interactions be observed and pairs assessed for compatibility. Supervising teachers or coordinating counselors should intervene in difficult relationships and reassign unworkable matches. This kind of support will prevent tutors and learners from feeling frustrated or discouraged with the program and will increase their enjoyment of the process.

Tutoring Sessions

The program coordinator, scheduling several 20- to 30-minute sessions each week, should develop a tutoring schedule. Tutoring schedules must be followed consistently. Failure to hold tutoring sessions at their scheduled times conveys the message that the program is unimportant relative to other activities.

Tutoring sessions typically are held in a designated area within the classroom, isolated somewhat from other student activities. This seating arrangement allows for privacy and reduces distractions but enables the teacher to directly monitor the tutoring session.

Materials

Tutoring materials are generated by the teacher or adapted from published sources. With supervision, experienced tutors can learn to develop materials for the learner, resulting in increased understanding of the materials by the tutor and decreasing the teacher's required time commitment somewhat.

Student Incentives

Students' motivation to participate in a peer or cross-age tutoring program will not be sustained without some form of incentive. Incentives for participating in the program can be provided for both tutors and their partners on a regular basis. Although most students are motivated through immediate praise and verbal approval, school personnel can recognize student involvement by making school-wide announcements and providing activities such as social events and learning games. Time set aside for personal reflection and discussion of students' experiences in the program is especially useful. In some schools, tutors receive elective credit for their participation in the program. Some programs recognize tutors and their partners by awarding certificates of completion and recognition. School newsletters and plaques hung in the central hallways are other ways to recognize students for their involvement. Schools can be very creative in developing incentives to enhance student involvement.

Teacher Supervision

Teachers need to meet with tutors before each session to review instructional materials. Prior to the session, the teacher ascertains that the tutor has a clear grasp of the content of the instructional material and the objectives for the learner. These meetings become shorter as the tutor demonstrates competence in the tutorial role.

Initially, after each session, the tutor meets with the teacher to discuss how the session went, the partner's progress, and any difficulties encountered. The teacher reinforces and instructs the tutor at this time. Postsession supervision is reduced as the tutor establishes competence. The motivational aspects of these meetings, however, must be kept in mind; reinforcement of tutors is an ongoing activity and is extremely important. As part of their supervisory role, teachers should directly observe the tutoring session in about one of every three or four sessions to monitor the tutoring process.

Evaluation

Program evaluation is important to a tutor program for several reasons. Ongoing evaluation of student progress can be used to motivate both the student receiving tutoring and the tutor. Also, feedback from student performance can be used to determine aspects of the program that are effective and those that could benefit from modification. Evaluation results can be used to demonstrate the value of the program to interested parties, such as administrators faced with decisions about funding special programs or parents who express doubts about the quality of alternative educational approaches. Evaluation activities should be linked to the goals and objectives of the program. Tutoring programs are often designed to improve the academic achievement of both the tutor and the student learner in the specific area tutored (Bowman-Perrott et al., 2013). Another common goal of tutoring programs is enhancing both students' academic self-concept. The effectiveness of a tutoring program may be gauged by whether the tutor and the learner have achieved gains in academic performance in the subject being tutored and in academic self-concept.

The use of global measures of academic achievement or self-concept for evaluating the effectiveness of the program may result in ambiguous feedback on student progress. Overall academic achievement is a composite of several academic areas (mathematics, reading, spelling, and so forth). It is unrealistic to expect change in overall academic achievement or in global self-concept through tutoring in only one specific academic area. Efforts to evaluate program effectiveness using global indices will underestimate the actual benefits of the program. The best way to measure the effect of the tutoring program is to evaluate academic and self-concept change specifically related to the subject tutored.

Students participating in the tutoring program should be assessed before, during, and after participating in the program. Academic achievement can be determined through teacher-developed, curriculum-based measures that are inexpensive, directly related to the academic subject matter, and sensitive to improvement in academic performance.

Several tests designed to measure children's self-concepts have academic self-concept factors (see, e.g., Harter, 1985; Piers, 1984). Each of these tests mixes academic self-concept items among the other self-concept items, which does not readily allow measurement of academic self-concept alone. The Multidimensional Self-Concept Scale (MSCS) is well suited to isolating academic self-concept because its 25 academic self-concept items, about a 5-minute test, are not woven into the body of the instrument; rather, they are presented on a separate page and may be administered, scored, and compared to national norms without including the entire test (Bracken, 1992).

PEER MEDIATION PROGRAMS

Mediation is a problem-solving process that enables individuals to resolve disputes that are troublesome. In addition to being effective in some marital relationships, it is used in contract disputes (Mareschal, 2005), legal disputes (Shestowsky, 2004), and child custody disagreements (Sanchez & Kibler-Sanchez, 2004). It also has great application in school settings (Samuels, 2014).

School peer mediation (Lane & McWhirter, 1992, 1996) is a mode of conflict management employed by students for the purpose of resolving conflicts. Trained peer mediators work as a team of two to facilitate problem solving between disputants. Students' involvement in the mediation process ensures practice with critical thinking, problem solving, and self-discipline. Students' participation in efforts to change their own and their peers' behavior is directly related to the developmental construct of self-regulation. Awareness of socially approved behaviors is a critical feature.

The setting for this mediation process is often the playground. Used in conjunction with traditional means of discipline, such as suspension for serious violent acts, peer mediation provides a structured forum for the resolution of in-school disputes. Students practice critical thinking, problem solving, and self-discipline directly related to the construct of self-regulation. Awareness of socially approved behaviors is a critical feature of self-regulation, which involves the ability to postpone acting on a desired object or goal. Self-regulation requires being able to generate socially approved behavior in the absence of external monitors. The ability to self-regulate is a developmental skill that must be practiced regularly. School peer mediation programs provide daily opportunities for reinforcement.

Background

School peer mediation programs have sprung up across the nation in the last three decades. Initially developed to deal with disputes between neighbors and businesses, they quickly were introduced as school-based programs. In most programs, students receive up to 16 hours of training and role-play practice. They eventually become team mediators on the playground and in the lunchroom. Programs now exist in many schools in almost all major cities in the United States. Models for children in schools promote conflict mediation through the application of communication skills, listening to evoke varying perspectives, eliciting mutual contributions to the problem's eventual solution, and attending to feelings—all in an atmosphere of respect for the parties involved.

Theoretical Assumptions

Advocates of peer mediation in the schools assume that "children helping children" is a valid perspective from which to view program implementation and outcomes (Bozeman & Feeney, 2008). A wealth of research literature supports this perspective. Peer leaders have been found to have greater credibility regarding student social interactions. They serve as potent role models and can demonstrate prosocial behaviors. Peers can create and reinforce norms supporting the notion that certain behaviors are deviant rather than acceptable, and they can promote alternatives to deviant behaviors. The student mediators who are the direct recipients of program training receive the most impact; students without direct training also benefit. Both student behavior and school discipline problems improve as a result of peer mediation (Samuels, 2014).

Such programs emphasize student involvement and student management. Thus participants tend to feel more committed to program goals and more interested in producing change among their peers. A more specific description of benefits follows.

Training Staff Members

The training sequence begins with presentation of the mediation program to the entire school staff. The school counselor and principal often conduct this introductory session. Given the time and resources required to implement a peer mediation program, it is very important that the initial presentation include evidence of the benefits to students and to the school. After the presentation, each staff member completes a level-of-interest questionnaire to determine his or her degree of commitment to the process. If staff support for mediation is adequate (usually 80%), training for teachers and support personnel is initiated. Elementary and middle school staff training usually requires about 8 hours. The content of this training includes communication skills that encompass active listening, reflection of feeling, message clarification, body language, giving "I" messages, brainstorming, types of questioning, and effective problem solving. The mediation sequence is identified, and adult responsibilities are delineated. Role play is used extensively with the adult staff members, as it is later with the students.

Training Student Peer Mediators

Once the adults have been trained, they plan and implement an orientation assembly to motivate students and to alert them to the qualities of a good mediator. Role plays and skits are used to outline aspects of the program and the process.

As the time for implementation nears, students who wish to become peer mediators nominate themselves or are nominated by others. Nominations may also come from counselors, teachers, and administrators. Final selection of mediators is completed by student vote. Adult staff members then train selected students. Training for elementary and middle school students consists of five half days. The adult staff members teach the communication skills that they reviewed in their own training. They guide the students through role plays not unlike those they engaged in during the adult training.

The mediation sequence is introduced and practiced until it becomes a comfortable process for the children. The simplicity of the peer mediation process contributes to its success. The student mediators can easily implement the steps. They also provide support for one another.

The sequence involves four basic stages: introduction, listening, wants, and solutions. In the first stage of the peer mediation sequence, the student mediators introduce themselves, offer their services ("Do you need a mediator?"), and walk to a different area to cause physical and psychological separation from the initial point of conflict. When the disputants and mediators are ready, the rules are reviewed and commitment to them is elicited. An assurance of confidentiality is given to disputants by the mediators.

In stage 2 of the mediation sequence, the peer mediators listen to each disputant in turn. They reflect and restate content and feelings as they address each disputant. Because no interruptions are allowed, disputants have the opportunity to hear the others' perspectives of the conflict and their resultant feelings.

With guidance from the peer mediators, disputants express their wants in stage 3 of the sequence. As the requests are heard and restated by mediators, clarity reduces anxiety about possible hidden agendas.

In stage 4, disputants are asked what they can contribute to the resolution of the problem. The peer mediators restate and check solutions for balance. Then each disputant is asked if the proposed solution is acceptable. An important step in this phase is asking if the problem is solved. Disputants may wish to express a need to receive or to give an apology to smooth hurt feelings. The mediators then ask disputants how such a conflict could be handled differently in the future. To reduce the potential for rumors, mediators ask disputants to tell their friends that the conflict has been solved. After congratulating the students on solving their problem, the peer mediators complete a mediation report form. In this last step of the sequence, the peer mediators have an opportunity to review the quality of their guidance because they do their record keeping together.

When training is complete, student mediators receive recognition and uniform T-shirts, banners, or hats at an assembly. They are then assigned to recess duty in pairs. They meet twice a week with a staff program coordinator to discuss their successes and problems, to maintain and build new skills, and to handle scheduling problems. School counselors often introduce classroom guidance curriculum activities to promote general student awareness of the peer mediators and the services they offer.

The Ripple Effect

Program implementation results in fewer playground problems and fewer referrals to the nurse or the principal's office. Families may also experience the program's impact; parents and students in peer mediation schools report that conflicts in the home are modified (Daunic, Smith, Robinson, Miller, & Landry, 2000).

Another ripple effect of peer mediation programs is a perceived improvement in school climate. For example, peer mediation programs have a sustained and significant impact on school climate at all educational levels—elementary, middle, and secondary. The program also increases students' perceptions of school as a healthy and safe environment.

Counseling Ramifications

Peer mediation helps youth develop self-regulation and other skills. When students are given an opportunity to participate in decisions relating to their own lives, more self-regulation and positive self-esteem are likely to result. School counselors can promote peer mediation programs (and are in a strong position to open up mediation training to parents as part of a school–community outreach program). Conflict resolution through peer mediation is a preventive program as well—in the form of leadership training. It is also an integral component of a school's discipline plan. Finally, it is a way to meet the communication objectives of a guidance curriculum. Regardless of its placement in the overall picture of pupil development, its importance for children and its implications for society are clear.

The conflict resolution model of peer mediation addresses the skills of listening, problem solving, oral language expression, and critical thinking. These essential skills are directly taught in the process of mediation training. They are modeled and reinforced by the peer mediators.

Carlos Diaz (of Chapter 4) would benefit in several ways from being trained as a peer mediator. The experience of being nominated by a peer, teacher, or counselor would bolster his confidence. The skills he learns as a mediator would help him to reduce the number of fights he has with peers. Providing a valuable service to his school would help him view himself as more a part of the school community. This participation might influence teacher perceptions, increasing the amount of support and positive feedback he receives from teachers. The verbal skills learned and utilized by peer mediators might enhance Carlos's language acquisition efforts. Finally, Carlos could be an effective mediator for monolingual Spanish-speaking children at the school. Given Carlos's responsibilities at home, however, staff would have to ascertain whether the time demand of the program would hinder Carlos more than the benefits would be an enhancement. Nevertheless, a young man reinforced for his contributions to the school community who is being supported in the development of useful life skills is a young man with a lowered risk of dropout.

PEER FACILITATION

Peer facilitation (sometimes referred to as peer leadership, helping, or counseling) is very helpful in increasing the impact and efficiency of professional counseling. Peer facilitation is a process in which trained and supervised students perform interpersonal helping tasks—listening, offering support, suggesting alternatives, and engaging in other verbal and nonverbal interactions—that qualify as counseling functions with similar-aged clients who either have referred themselves or have been referred by others. Like peer tutoring and peer mediation, peer facilitation appears to be a useful way to counter negative peer cluster influence (Karcher, 2007; Sheppard, Golonka, & Costanzo, 2012). It also reinforces and supports the use of life skills.

Peer facilitation programs generally have two major components: training and service. In the training phase, adult leaders provide designated peer helpers with intensive training. In the service or implementation phase, peer leaders offer direct service to other youth.

Training Phase

The training phase usually has certain common content. Communication skills, in particular, are emphasized. Active listening, empathetic understanding, and paraphrasing are included. Equally important are the nonverbal cues that the peer helper is projecting through his or her behavior.

In addition to basic communication skills, peer leaders almost always acquire skills in problem solving and decision making. These are useful skills that they can transfer to those whom they help, although peer facilitators are almost always prohibited from giving advice. Their role is to listen, to question, to reflect, and to be a friend.

The young people in training usually spend a fair amount of time learning about important community resources. For example, information on alcohol and drug use, crisis intervention programs, and treatment facilities are emphasized. Peer leaders are an important source of referrals to community agencies.

Service Phase

Peer leaders can be helpful in many areas. In addition to tutoring and mediation, discussed earlier, peer facilitators can help introduce new students to school, befriend lonely and alone children who seem to have no friends, and work with special education students. They can also provide classroom information on tobacco, alcohol, and drug abuse problems; on healthy lifestyles; and on many other topics. With training they can facilitate small discussion and support groups. Most important, they can provide supportive and caring listening to troubled youth. Peers are often the first to know when someone is considering suicide. As we discussed in Chapter 9, in every incident of school shootings, the event "leakage" was usually to another peer. Peer facilitators can make school safer by providing a link between troubled young people and caring adults.

The role of the adult supervisors is just as important in the service phase as it is in the training phase. In addition to being models of empathy, understanding, and caring, adults are necessary to coordinate and organize the program. They must be available to help the young leaders with the particularly difficult problems. Of course, problems of an extremely urgent or serious nature must be referred to responsible adults.

Successful facilitator programs attempt to involve a representative and diverse group of students as peer helpers. Using the natural helper method described earlier, students and school personnel are asked to identify those students who are perceived to be individuals other students talk to if they need help with a problem. If students perceive the peer helper group as only an elite collection of class leaders or high achievers, many of the students who are in most need of support will stay away.

Facilitation assignments can vary from helping other students with specific problems to being available to provide encouragement and support in a common office area, to assisting on a survey of student needs. Whatever the assignment, peer facilitation programs create a pool of helpers who are trained to be sensitive to student needs and concerns.

Need to Be Needed

One of the greatest human needs is to be needed. Young people can affirm their worth to themselves and to others by assuming meaningful roles. By doing too much for children, we can destroy their self-confidence and foster low self-esteem. Not infrequently, adults provide children with an environment that demands nothing of them. Then we criticize our children for not appreciating the lifestyle or the parents who provided it. In many instances, young people have been progressively denied the opportunity to be engaged in work that is important to others and therefore denied the rewards that such work produces. Children and adolescents who tutor their peers or younger children; who assist people with disabilities; who help to care for young children; who visit with the elderly; who mediate disputes; who help others to learn; and who participate in other programs to help their families, schools, and communities are filling the void that our age of technology and specialization has created in their lives. They are responding to real social needs, and they are assuming meaningful roles at the microsystemic and mesosystemic levels (McLeod, Jones, & Cramer, 2015). In so doing, they are satisfying their own need to be needed and are more likely to see themselves as contributing members of their communities, schools, and families.

CONCLUSION

In this chapter we have described several school-based peer programs designed to directly or indirectly prevent student problems. Such programs are an effective means of reducing some of the correlates of at-risk categories: depression, interpersonal conflict, communication deficiencies, loneliness, and lack of purpose. They can be also implemented at all levels of education—elementary, middle, and secondary settings—and can be organized within a single classroom, a whole school, or an entire district. Schools can also help mobilize peer groups as a force for good. When children are encouraged to work cooperatively in small groups, they are provided with a classroom community that encourages them to discuss their work with others, accept one another's viewpoints, weigh their options, and make decisions on the basis of reasoning.

Peer tutoring, mediation, and facilitation programs provide the direct help to at-risk young people in improving academic abilities, mastering new skills, and connecting to the school environment. The peer leaders also benefit by gaining confidence and increased self-esteem. Although requiring the assistance of teachers, counselors, and administrators in a time of increasing demands and fewer resources, peer-based programs have positive effects—both current and future—that clearly outweigh their costs.

Family Interventions

In some families words are like barbed wire, they cut and puncture.

In some families messages are like exploding shrapnel, they rip and tear.

In some families secrets are like land mines, step on one and they erupt in explosion.

In some families even love and affection are tools in the battle.

All war, especially the war in families, is at once horrible and dehumanizing and obscenely senseless.

CHAPTER OUTLINE

As discussed in Chapter 3, the nature of the family structure in the United States and elsewhere is shifting in response to changes in social, political, and economic conditions. More and more families deal with the stresses of separation, divorce, and single parenting, re-partnering and the complexities of blended families, the loss of extended family networks, migration, immigration, and acculturation, and the enduring effects of poverty and the Great Recession. Any one of these stresses can severely disrupt family life. Even negotiating the inevitable developmental changes that are part of the family life cycle can be highly stressful and can generate family conflict. Sometimes the symptoms of family distress emerge when a reasonably healthy family goes through a difficult transition, even a potentially positive transition, such as the marriage of the first child. In other cases, families reflect ongoing dysfunction that might emerge in response to a new stress. For example, a parent might abuse alcohol for several weeks following a layoff, then engage in productive coping strategies, adjust to the new situation, and return to his or her pre-layoff, nonproblematic level of drinking. In another family, someone may consistently go on drug use binges, driven by simple events, such as whenever the extended family gathers, when confronted, or when there is a lot of family conflict, or simply when the traffic is heavy. What is often sometimes difficult about family life is that, whatever the pattern of problematic behavior, family members each engage in their own coping strategies, and these strategies themselves often serve to maintain the symptoms of family dysfunction. Family members often assume particular roles to deal with the stresses of the family, such as chronic unemployment, violence, or drug and alcohol abuse (Adkison

et al., 2013; Kearns-Bodkin & Leonard, 2008). For example, one of the children might play the scapegoat role and act out (fighting in school, failing a class), thus drawing attention away from a marital problem. Parents temporarily unite while they deal with the "problem child." Sometimes the child or teen whose behavior appears self-destructive and irrational is actually driven by a desire to help another family member. And this also inadvertently serves to perpetuate dysfunction (see Box 14.1).

When teachers and counselors become frustrated by the destructive and aggressive behaviors of their students, it is helpful to keep in mind that these behaviors are often goal directed and represent attempts to meet needs (see our discussion of goals of misbehavior in Chapter 8). Much behavior originates in response to family dynamics to which the young person returns every night.

It is a mistake, however, to attribute all children and youth problems to some growing malevolence in the American family. As we have indicated, the family is changing in response to societal trends over which the individual family has little control. Society too often appears eager to blame families for individual problems, as evidenced by attempts to solve those problems by "fixing" families. Blaming families diverts attention from the facts that our society lacks a coherent national family policy and that the structural supports required for family life are grossly inadequate, especially in marginalized and economically despairing communities (Lott, 2002). In this chapter we describe interventions for individual families as one point of entry for addressing the problems of youth at risk. These interventions are family counseling, parent support groups, parent education, and parent training.

Box 14.1	The School Slut

He was always angry with her. Every aggressive retort, every call from the school, every violation of curfew drew his rage like flies to butter. But the failing grades, her reputation as the "school slut," and the constant battles were all worth it. Because as long as his attention was focused on his anger with her, it would not be directed at her sister, the "good" daughter. And he wouldn't come into her sister's bedroom. Her sister wouldn't be forced to endure those long nights, the hideous emptiness, the vomiting afterward. At least, this much she could control.

And that's one reason the rage overwhelmed and consumed her 10 years later; that's one reason the tears in my office were so torrential that her whole body convulsed with agony. Because 10 years later, her sister said, "It was happening to me too."

FAMILY COUNSELING

Working with the entire family is often the optimal approach for dealing with young people at risk for dropout, substance use, pregnancy, delinquency, suicide, and other problems. When a child or adolescent is contemplating or engaged in life-threatening behavior, it is of utmost importance that the family be involved in efforts to avert the problem. In general, family counseling is appropriate (a) when the presenting problems are affected by and affect the family system, (b) when the child or adolescent is living in the family or is working through unfinished business with the family and is in contact with them even though not living at home, and (c) when both the counselor and the client agree that family counseling is an appropriate intervention.

Family counseling is not always a viable option. The following questions are often considered in exploring the option of family counseling: Does the family have resources such as transportation? What about child care for younger children? Are there any language or cultural factors that might prohibit or discourage the family members from availing themselves of counseling services? Is the family willing and able to commit to attending counseling sessions? Is there a family member who has access to counseling services through an employee assistance program or some other work benefit? Discussion of these questions and familiarity with community resources will set the stage for appropriate referrals.

Referring the Family for Counseling

For many family members, attending a counseling session is tantamount to acknowledging severe mental illness within the family. When a teacher or counselor believes that a particular family might benefit from family counseling, several steps can be taken to lay a foundation for success. First, the family needs to know why. On what basis has the referring professional made this decision? The identified problem—that is, the behavior of the child that attracted attention—should be explained in specific and concrete terms. For example, Lidia Diaz's teacher (see Chapter 4) might say: "For three weeks now, Lidia has been withdrawn and quiet. She seems to be avoiding her school friends, she's refusing to participate in class, and she has cried at school three or four times this week. When I asked her how things were going at home, she simply stared at the floor and said, 'It's probably my fault anyway.' This is so different from Lidia's usual behavior that I thought it was important to contact you to talk about some possible ways to help her." Notice that Lidia's teacher does not assign blame or sound judgmental, nor does she draw conclusions from her observations.

A second step in family referral is to help the family understand that family counseling may help in the achievement of mutual goals. Counseling provides an opportunity for the family to work as a cohesive unit; the needs of all family members are considered in developing solutions to problems. Potential benefits include more appropriate behavior by the "problem child," increased responsibility among family members for voicing their opinions and feelings, better grades for the children, and more support and less stress for all family members. The teacher or counselor who knows the general nature of the problem can identify the benefits appropriate to the specific situation.

Family members are often more accepting of recommendations for counseling if they have a sense of what to expect. Thus, psychoeducation about services, including information about session frequency and the role of various participants, is important (Becker et al., 2015). When Jason Carter (of Chapter 3) was first seen as a client, he asked the family counselor, "Where's your black couch? Aren't you going to write down everything I say?" Adults, too, may have misconceptions. The teacher or counselor can dispel some of the mystique surrounding counseling by discussing some of the common reasons families go to a counselor and what the process might be like. Common reasons include problems with discipline and communication; lack of trust among family members; school problems; tension related to divorce or separation, dating, or remarriage of a parent; and grief and loss related to death of a family member. There are many approaches to family counseling, and individual therapists vary in style even if they ascribe to the same approach.

Families should be encouraged to ask potential counselors, "What do you expect of your clients?" "How long have you been practicing, and what are your credentials?" "What can we expect of you?" "How do you structure your counseling sessions?" "How can we make best use of our time and money here?" "Do you have experience working with families like ours?" A family that has a sense of its own role in the therapeutic process may be more willing to consider the option of counseling.

Some families resist counseling because they are unsure how to begin the process. Let them know that once they call for an appointment, it may

---

Box 14.2   In the Waiting Room

A tragedy occurred a few years ago in one of Kansas City's local hospitals. A woman of Hmong descent was standing in the waiting room of the hospital with her seriously ill infant. As she stood reticent in a corner waiting to be helped, the baby died in her arms. When the staff behind the reception desk realized what had just happened, they were aghast. They wondered why she had not approached them to ask for assistance.

The simple truth was this: Hmong people do not approach a majority group without first being summoned (Maltbia, 1991).

---

be anywhere from a day to a month or more before they have their first session. This first session may be an intake session during which a counselor gathers information about the family's background and history. The family may work with the intake counselor and in later sessions may be assigned to a different counselor. If families are unprepared for this sometimes drawn-out process, they may become frustrated and discontinue prematurely. Client-sensitive practices such as collaborative information sharing, open conversation about roles and expectations, modeling treatment, change strategies, and facilitating positive expectations at the beginning and throughout treatment convey respect and may increase retention and commitment (Becker et al., 2015).

Some parents may want to meet with the counselor first without their children. Some counselors may request such an arrangement; others may refuse it. This decision depends on the theoretical orientation and judgment of the counselor. Encourage parents to let the counselor know their preference.

Teachers and counselors are more likely to be successful in referring families for counseling if they are knowledgeable about a variety of local counseling agencies and practitioners. It is especially important to make referrals that are consistent with the family's cultural and language needs. The importance of multicultural competence is central in nearly all professional ethics codes and accreditation standards, but all counselors do not have sufficient multicultural training. And certainly many agencies do not have counselors fluent in languages other than English. When a counselor or teacher approaches a family from a minority ethnocultural group, it is important to consider that counseling as we know it has historically been a Western, White, middle- and upper-class phenomenon. Recent immigrants, in particular, will need a thorough explanation of the nature of counseling and may need time to consider whether it is consistent with their cultural values and practices (see Box 14.2).

When referrals are made for family counseling, the family should be provided with accurate information about agencies and practitioners, including addresses, phone numbers, specializations, and whether the agency adjusts fees to the client's ability to pay. Follow up with the family and find out what might help them to take action if they haven't followed through with the referral. For those who follow through, ask for feedback regarding the counseling facility for the benefit of future families.

The Nature of Family Counseling

In family counseling, problems are examined within the context of the family interactions, or system. Problems are viewed not as the result of individual issues but as the consequence of the complex dynamics that characterize every family system. Often, the family comes to a counselor expecting that the "problem child" will be fixed. The family counselor's first task is to assist family members to recognize that a family system is composed of a number of both positive and negative interlocking relationships. Family members must be helped to understand their contribution to the maintenance of the identified client's symptoms. Finally, the family must agree to work together to change their situation.

Working with the entire family is advantageous in many ways. It enables the counselor to gain a more accurate perspective on the problem. The counselor may discover, for example, that what a 15-year-old son has described as cruel authoritarianism is a belated attempt by his parents to impose control over curfew limits and homework completion. A mother who describes herself as loving and affectionate, and who truly believes she is so, may not be aware that her family members see her as unavailable and hostile. Sharing together the perspectives of her family is a way to clarify the words *loving* and *affectionate* and the expectations that surround them. Watching arguments in progress in the counseling session also provides the counselor with an essential picture of the family's interaction. In addition to enhancing problem identification, working with the whole family makes problem solving more cohesive, efficient, and timely. The outcome of family counseling depends on many variables, including the therapist's skill, the willingness of family members to exert effort and take risks, their willingness and ability to take responsibility for their behavior, and the range of coping skills they possess.

Strategies in Family Counseling

In the 1950s, Gregory Bateson and others at the Mental Research Institute (MRI) developed a communication framework for working with families. Focusing on the family as a system (see Chapter 3), family counseling attends to the interactional styles of family members. Interestingly, this perspective and many of the following scholars and theorists were also behind the development of the brief solution-focused approach that we discussed in Chapter 6 (Murphy, 2015). Notable members of this group include Paul Watzlawick, John Weakland, and Don Jackson, as well as Virginia Satir and Jay Haley. Jackson, Satir, and Haley, and to some extent Murray Bowen, Salvador Minuchin, and most other system family theorists, share four core concepts: (1) Two major tasks are involved in the process of forming and maintaining a relationship, deciding what the rules of the relationship are and negotiating who actually makes the decisions regarding the rules; (2) the exchange of messages is accomplished through the task of setting rules and negotiating who has control over the rules; (3) the basic elements of the interactional process are the messages that form the substance of communications between people in the relationship; and finally (4) messages have two major aspects, the communication (the content of the message) and the metacommunication (the message about the message).

Thus family counselors attempt to understand the family by analyzing the communication and metacommunication of the interactions. They identify problems through observation of the family's interactions, including such behaviors as seating arrangement, control of the children, who speaks most and least frequently, and so forth. Family counselors also sometimes employ techniques that include "paradoxical messages" and "prescribing the symptom." Paradoxical messages direct the family to do something that seems opposite to the stated goal; they are particularly useful with resistant families. For example, a family might be directed to refuse to cooperate during a session. The family has the choice of either cooperating (to maintain control vis-à-vis the counselor) or continuing their lack of cooperation and thereby giving the counselor therapeutic leverage because they are following a directive.

The counselor who prescribes the symptom asks the family to continue their problem behavior, perhaps because "I don't yet understand it well enough." This technique is also beneficial with families who seem to resist change because it allows family members to see more clearly the behaviors and interactions that contribute to problems. Relabeling or reforming consists of describing the problem behavior in such a way that makes it sound positive. A therapist might relate an adolescent's use of foul language, for example, as a way of directing her parents' attention away from her school performance. After establishing that the teen is being purposeful, the therapist can draw upon her purposefulness to help her devise more effective means of getting what she wants.

Other family counselors focus on the structural context of family interactions. They examine the organizational dynamics and boundaries both within the family system and between the family and the environment. Boundaries can be seen as a manifestation of the rules and regulations governing the system and separating the system from its environment. How the family regulates and modifies these boundaries is of interest to the family counselor. Two fundamental concepts are "differentiation of self" and "triangulation." A chronic high level of anxiety within a family causes tension to escalate. If unchecked, this tension eventually exceeds the capacity of the family's normal coping mechanisms, and a variety of family symptoms result. Differentiation of self is the individual's ability to discriminate between emotional and cognitive processes and to achieve independence from the emotional climate of the family. Highly differentiated family members can respond to conflict on a cognitive level on the basis of conscious beliefs and values, whereas the undifferentiated individual responds in an emotional and unstable manner. The greater the differentiation of self, the more effectively the family member can cope with anxiety. The failure of family members to differentiate is termed "fusion." Fusion, that is, a low level of differentiation, is characterized by inability to separate emotional from intellectual interaction.

Poorly differentiated family members are more likely to be part of a family triangle. Triangulation occurs when the anxiety in a two-person system is more than the system can handle and a third person is engaged in the system to diffuse the tension. Triangulation is a specific type of enmeshment (see Chapter 3). For example, to diffuse marital tension, the mother establishes a close "friendship" with her daughter and together they exclude the father. Triangulation generally increases problematic communication within a family.

As a family moves through the stages of the family life cycle (see Chapter 3), it changes structurally to accommodate changing roles and tasks. Such adaptation occurs through the renegotiation and modification of boundaries. Clear boundaries fall between enmeshed and disengaged boundaries and allow for optimal functioning. Family subsystem boundaries that are pervasively enmeshed or consistently rigid, especially those between the parent and child subsystems, are the primary basis for family dysfunction.

By identifying the boundaries and transactional patterns within the family system and subsystems, the family counselor can meet the goal of therapy, which is to change the structure of the family so that it is more consistent with the developmental needs of its members. One technique to do this is to present the family with a scenario and assign roles to the individual members. The roles require them to act out new patterns of behavior. This changes the behavior patterns that support the symptom and alters the sequences between family members, thereby restructuring the family system.

There are several ways in which a family counselor might work with the Carter family of Chapter 3. For example, the counselor might help the Carter family identify the sequence of acts in which the family's problems are embedded. The counselor would note the relationships among Lois's constant negative emotions, lack of eye contact with her husband, fatigue, and refusal to ask for what she wants and needs; Doug's telling Jason, "If you ..., I'll...." without ever following through, his black-and-white views of Jason, the "bad one," and Christie, the "good one," and his sarcastic tone when he talks to his wife; Jason's feeble attempts to cheer up his mother, his belligerence toward his father, and his rapt attention whenever his parents interact; Christie's subtle teasing of Jason, her aloof primness when asked a question, and her fingernail biting. The counselor might attempt to understand how these behaviors maintain or threaten the power balance in the family and might view each symptom as a tactic employed by one person to deal with the others. He or she would see Jason's acting out as his way of defining his relationship with his parents: Jason sets the pace and they respond. The counselor might direct Jason to continue to misbehave at school and at home (assuming his misbehaviors are not dangerous or harmful) and ask him to keep a log of all misbehaviors, noting why he chose each behavior when he did. This use of symptom prescription gives

Jason the choice of cooperating with the others, setting the stage for change, or resisting the therapist by reducing his symptoms.

In another approach the counselor would focus on helping each of the Carters to separate emotionality from objective thinking. He or she would begin by looking for clear and well-defined boundaries between family members. The counselor might view Doug's anger at his wife and his feelings of inadequacy as overriding his cognitive knowledge of the importance of consistency and consequences in discipline. He or she might view Lois's guilty feelings as an indication of her inability to separate her own feelings and behavior from those of her son. The unexpressed anger between Lois and Doug is diffused and focused on Jason, with the result that Doug feels excluded by both his wife and his son. The counselor might help the couple to express and explain their feelings to each other objectively. As the process of triangulation diminished, the members of the family would achieve a greater degree of differentiation.

Another approach would acknowledge the sociocultural context in which the Carter family operates. The counselor might conceptualize the problem in terms of two stressors: a developmental transition (Jason is entering adolescence) and an idiosyncratic problem (Lois is chronically depressed). The family's dysfunction is a result of their failure to renegotiate boundaries in response to these stressors. In light of the enmeshed boundaries between Jason and his mother and the lack of a defined parental subset, the counselor might work to increase the strength of the parental subset by engaging Doug and Lois in tasks together. He or she might ask Jason and Christie to reverse roles as a means of unbalancing the homeostasis and creating an opportunity for change.

Each of these strategies or techniques shares an emphasis on the family as a system. A systems framework is often a major foundation for family counseling. Although often helpful for a number of reasons, family counseling is not always the best way to pursue change. Families can gain the support, knowledge, and skills they need to address their problems through a number of other channels. But in what other ways might we be helpful to families with youth at risk? We now consider alternatives to family counseling.

ALTERNATIVES TO FAMILY COUNSELING

As we note in Chapter 11 and throughout this book, all interventions used should be based on evidence of success and/or have empirical support, especially with the specific population with whom they are being applied (e.g., Van Ryzin, Kumpfer, Fosco, & Greenberg, 2016). Kumpfer and Alder (2003; see Box 14.3), in an extensive review of reviews, identified a number of principles of effective family-focused programs to help practitioners judge whether a program is worth selecting. In this section we describe a number of empirically supported alternatives to family counseling that follow most of the principles highlighted in Box 14.3. Later, we discuss several alternatives to family counseling that may be more helpful to families than more traditional family counseling.

Box 14.3	Principles of Effective Family-Focused Interventions

1. *Recruitment and Retention.* Family recruitment and retention (in the range of 80% to 85%) is possible with the use of incentives—food, child care, transportation—plus rewards for homework completion, attendance, and graduation.

2. *Scope and Content.* Comprehensive, multicomponent interventions that address family relations, communication, and parental monitoring are more effective in modifying risk or protective factors than are single-component programs.

3. *Target.* Family-focused programs that emphasize family strengths, resilience, and protective factors are more effective for improving family relationships than child-focused or parent-focused programs.

4. *Focus.* Family programs tailored to the cultural traditions of the family are most effective when they produce cognitive, affective, and behavioral changes in family dynamics or the environment.

5. *Training Methods.* Skills training methods that use interactive techniques—role play, active modeling, family and skill practice sessions—along with homework activities and videos or CDs of effective and ineffective parenting skills increase client satisfaction and program effectiveness compared to didactic lecturing and simple discussion.

6. *Trainer or Leader.* The effectiveness of the program is highly tied to the trainer's personal efficacy and confidence, affective characteristics of genuineness, warmth, humor, and empathy, and ability to structure sessions and be directive.

7. *Parent/Family Dysfunction.* When parents are very dysfunctional, interventions beginning early in the life cycle are more effective. In addition, increased dosage or intensity (25 to 50 hours of intervention) is necessary with higher-risk families than with low-risk families (5 to 24 hours).

8. *Timing and Development.* Family programs should be age and developmentally appropriate with new versions available as children mature; they need to address appropriate risk and protective factors when the family is receptive to change.

9. *Empowerment.* Developing a collaborative process where family members are encouraged to find their own solutions is effective and also builds a supportive relationship and reduces parent resistance and dropout.

Source: Adapted from Kumpfer and Alder, 2003.

The EcoFIT Model and the Family Check-Up

EcoFIT, an ecological approach to family treatment, highlights the environment of young people and is designed for families experiencing mild to severe problems (Dishion & Stormshak, 2007). In the EcoFIT model, the child or adolescent, parents, siblings, neighborhood, teachers, and peers are considered. A major component is the Family Check-up (FCU), a brief family intervention (Dishion & Maurico, 2016; Stormshak et al., 2011) based on principles of motivational interviewing (Arkowitz, Miller, & Rollnick, 2015; see also Chapter 7).

The FCU consists of three sessions conducted by the counselor or parent consultant with the parents and the children. These sessions allow the counselor/parent consultant to tailor interventions to the specific needs of the family, especially the children and adolescents.

The first session is an interview that takes place in the home when possible so that the family is observed in its usual and familiar setting. This hour-long intake session provides an opportunity for the family and the counselor to get to know each other and is helpful to the counselor to better understand the family's concerns, mental health, and educational and social needs. The family also completes a brief questionnaire.

The second session consists of an ecological assessment of multiple dimensions of the family, including communication, discipline and monitoring, other aspects of parenting, characteristics of each family member, functioning in home and in school, and peer relationships. Usually, the family members' interactions at home are videotaped to help understand relationship and communication patterns. Family strengths are also assessed because a strengths-based focus provides examples of positive adjustment that might aid in helping families change. A careful assessment of the family members' experiences is important before recommending intervention options.

In the third session, which is designed to provide feedback and make recommendations, the family is presented with feedback designed to facilitate several goals. These include supporting and enhancing positive parenting by identifying strengths and weaknesses in parenting; reducing harm by identifying impending, serious events, such as a suicide attempt or school expulsion, and preventing such problems through provision of concrete recommendations; tailoring feedback to maximize motivation for change; and supporting motivation for change through identification of family strengths and resources. During the feedback session, parents provide a self-assessment of their family, and the clinician clarifies and contributes to this assessment using the information gained through the prior assessment stage. This session culminates in the collaborative development of a menu of options that emerge logically from the assessment and feedback. The menu of options targets changes that the family perceives as important and includes specific behaviors that the parents want to engage in on their own (e.g., meeting the parents of the children's friends and initiating Family Game Night once a week). The "service menu" may also include parent education, parent training, support groups; individual child, parent or couples counseling; brief family-centered interventions or family therapy; and school-based interventions.

Because this three-step model places a strong emphasis on forming a trusting relationship with the family and collaborative identification of concerns, families who may have initially resisted a recommendation for family therapy are often willing to pursue family therapy after an FCU; the families themselves have helped to identify targets for change in the family and are more motivated to create that change. There are multiple positive outcomes associated with the FCU, including reductions in family conflict, increased parental monitoring, and reduced substance use and problem behavior over time (Dishion & Maurico, 2016; Stormshak et al., 2011; Van Ryzin, Stormshak, & Dishion, 2012). Two other interventions are associated with the EcoFIT model: the Teen Check-Up (TCU) and the Adolescent Transitions Program (ATP).

Teen Check-Up

The TCU is for adolescents between 13 and 18 and includes four components: assessment, engagement, feedback, and a follow-up menu. First, the young person responds to a series of questions focusing on family, school, and peers. Ecological variables, self-strengths, and healthy choices that contribute to positive and risky behaviors are also assessed. Students are invited to receive feedback, including an appraisal summary, along with a motivation to change estimation. Teens are also engaged through a discussion of their strengths regarding handling problems. In the feedback section, self-strengths and strengths in the areas of academics, support systems (family and peers), and healthy choices are provided. Goals and ways of achieving them are identified. The follow-up menu includes options for skill building, including proven curricula and brief family-centered intervention—two or three sessions dealing with family skills and processes.

Adolescent Transitions Program

The Adolescent Transitions Program (ATP) was the predecessor to EcoFIT and FCU and is a multilevel family-centered intervention that has demonstrated long-term reductions in truancy, school failure, substance use, and arrest rate. This program has been shown to improve family relationships and parental monitoring (e.g., Dishion & Kavanagh, 2003).

Multisystemic Therapy

Multisystemic therapy (MST) has emerged as a leading intervention for responding to adolescent problematic and delinquent behavior (Henggeler & Schoenwald, 2011) as well as a helpful intervention for ethnic minority youth with asthma (Naar-King et al., 2014). Working from an ecological model of human development, MST counselors focus on providing parents with skills to effectively monitor and discipline their children and on increasing family cohesion. MST discourages continued contact with peers who provide reinforcement for delinquent behavior; it promotes contact with prosocial peers (Gatti, Tremblay, & Vitaro, 2009; Henggeler & Schoenwald, 2011). When treating conduct problems in young people, helpers must involve multiple systems in treatment and should attend to negative or positive roles that peers play in undermining or facilitating intervention.

Functional Family Therapy

Functional Family Therapy (FFT) is a family-based intervention that addresses supervision and monitoring and effective discipline for children and adolescents from 10 to 18 (Sexton & Turner, 2010). The program focuses on aggressive and defensive communication patterns and seeks to encourage supportive interaction in the family.

The effectiveness of FFT is well established, especially when the therapists delivering the intervention adhere to the treatment model. Particularly noteworthy is that the intervention improves positive emotions as key elements of the short- and long-term outcomes of systematic change (Sexton & Schuster, 2008).

Multidimensional Treatment Foster Care

Research supports that interventions targeted first toward the family but that also engage other parts of the family environment are highly effective. Behavior modification procedures used in halfway houses, for instance, have had immediate results but produce few long-lasting changes after teenagers return to their natural environments. Having youth associate with prosocial peers and be included in a functional, well-adjusted family are both key factors in socializing youth well. On the other hand, youth who have close interactions with deviant peers, even while in a treatment program, often increase their problematic behavior (Gatti et al., 2009). Youth outside of a functional family system are also less likely to thrive. The Multidimensional Treatment Foster Care (MTFC) program combats these two risk factors by recruiting community foster families to be members of a treatment team that monitors daily family and child activities, monitors peer associations, and tracks school behavior of high-risk delinquent youth in the program (Henggeler & Schoenwald, 2011; Smith, Chamberlain, & Eddy, 2010). These high-risk young people might otherwise be placed in institutional settings with little intervention or monitoring. The program illustrates how multidimensional and ecologically oriented interventions can be very effective for some of our most at-risk adolescents. The program responds to the whole ecology of children's lives and in so doing appears to help ameliorate nonclinical conduct problems (Kerr, DeGarmo, Leve, & Chamberlain, 2014).

In MTFC, foster parents receive increased financial compensation for participation in comparison to general foster parents and are considered to be primary members of the treatment team. They receive more than 20 hours of preservice training, attend weekly trainings and technical assistance meetings, and have 24-hour, 7-days-a-week on-call access to psychological support staff. The children and adolescents in the program, who would otherwise be placed in an institutional setting, receive services within a structured, supportive, teaching-oriented family environment; are closely supervised with regard to their whereabouts, activities, and peer associations; receive daily monitoring of their participation and progress in school; receive social skills building from a skills trainer; and receive individual therapy. The young person's family of origin receives intensive training and support; has 24-hour, 7-days-a-week access to program staff; receives family therapy; and is provided with aftercare services as well (e.g., ongoing support and consultation).

The young person's school is involved in a collaborative support meeting to set up a system before the youth is enrolled. Identified school personnel, such as the homeroom teacher, receive support in monitoring the child or young adolescent's behavior at school through use of a school "card" on which attitude, homework completion, and attendance are all evaluated. The performance ratings on the school card are checked nightly by MTFC foster parents and are linked with a three-level point system to reinforce positive behavior and decrease problematic behavior. In follow-up studies MTFC youth spent 60% fewer days incarcerated than control participants, had 50% fewer subsequent arrests, ran away from the program three times less often, returned to live with parents or relatives more often, and had significantly less hard drug use than same-age foster youth peers outside of the program (Smith et al., 2010). The program cost (nearly $130 per day) is substantially less than standard youth detention.

Family Effectiveness Training

José Szapocznik and his associates (2000; Bamatter et al., 2010; Robbins et al., 2011) present a prevention model for Hispanic families of preadolescents who are at risk for drug misuse and abuse. This program is based on the premise that intergenerational family conflict related to the acculturation process may exacerbate existing maladaptive patterns of interaction in families and contribute to drug use. The three components of family effectiveness training (FET) are designed to change maladaptive interactional patterns and to enhance the family's ability to resolve intergenerational and intercultural conflict.

The first component, family development, helps the family to negotiate their children's transition to adolescence. Family members learn constructive communication skills and take increased responsibility for their own behaviors. Parents develop the skills to direct their children in a democratic rather than an authoritarian style. This component also includes drug education for the parents so that they can effectively teach their children about drugs.

The second component, bicultural effectiveness training (BET), is designed to bring about family change by temporarily placing the explanation for the family's problems on the cultural conflict within the family. Alliances are established between family members through the development of bicultural skills and mutual appreciation of the values of the two cultures present among two different generations. BET helps the family handle cultural conflicts more effectively and reduces the likelihood that conflicts will occur. As a component of the larger FET, BET is itself an excellent program of value to families of diverse ethnocultural backgrounds.

The third component of FET is brief strategic family counseling (Robbins et al., 2011), the most experiential aspect of this model. The FET counselor meets with the family for thirteen 2-hour sessions and assists the family in addressing conflicts and improving relationships. The FET model may be modified to deal with issues other than drug use.

The final parent education and training program described is based on European American norms, but has potential benefits for other cultural groups as well.

Parent Effectiveness Training

Parent effectiveness training (PET; Gordon, 2006) is a method of parent training based on two principles stressed by the psychologist Carl Rogers: unconditional positive regard and empathy. A fundamental premise of the method is that everyone in the family can "win," with power negotiated and shared by parents and children. Although the program was originally designed for parents of problem children, its contents are also valuable for parents of well-functioning children. The PET program teaches parents skills in confrontation, conflict resolution, active listening, and giving "I-messages." Training provides parents with an opportunity to practice and refine those skills throughout the sessions. These skills enable parents to communicate more effectively with their children and to resolve problems constructively.

Gordon taught the first PET class in 1962 and in the 50-plus years of its use, it has had an enormous impact on many parents, children, and families. Because the concepts behind good parenting are so helpful in most interpersonal relationships, Gordon and his students and colleagues extended PET with books and training programs in Leader Effectiveness Training, Sales Effectiveness Training, Teacher Effectiveness Training, Effectiveness Training for Women, Youth Effectiveness Training, and others. PET also generated a large number of parent training programs, some with similar philosophy and approaches. Adams (2009; retrieved October 4, 2015, at http://www.gordontraining.com/thomas-gordon/) has compared PET with a number of other well-known, current parenting programs, including Nonviolent Communication (NVC); How to Talk so Kids Will Listen and Listen so Kids Will Talk; Systematic Training for Effective Parenting (STEP); Active Parenting; Positive Discipline; Love and Logic; Triple P (Positive Parenting Program); and Dare to Discipline. Although essentially supporting PET, Adams (2009) provides useful information on the other programs as well. A PET course is typically 24 hours in duration, ordinarily presented in eight weekly 3-hour sessions. Brief presentations, group discussions, audiotapes, dyads for skill practice, role playing, workbook assignments, and textbook reading are among the training methods used. Later, Gordon published a home study version of his program (Gordon, 2000). Core components of the program, described next, include problem ownership, active listening, using "I-messages," and mutual problem solving.

Problem Ownership

In accord with the PET model, parents are trained to identify whether the parent, the child, or the relationship (both parent and child) has ownership of the problem. Determining who owns the problem sets the stage for problem resolution. The child owns the problem when he or she is blocked in satisfying a need, but his or her behavior does not interfere with the satisfaction of the parent's needs. A parent owns the problem when the child's attempts to satisfy a need interfere with the parent's needs. The relationship owns the problem when neither the child nor the parent is able to satisfy his or her needs. Problem solving is achieved via three different pathways; the choice of pathway depends on problem ownership. Active listening is used when the child owns the problem, "I-messages" are used when the parent owns the problem, and mutual problem solving is used when both own the problem.

Active Listening

The purpose of active listening is to communicate a deep sense of acceptance and understanding to the child. The parent tries to understand what the child is feeling and to communicate empathy to the child. The affective and emotional dimensions of the communication process are reflected in eye contact, tone of voice, and body movement. If parents reflect their children's feelings accurately, the children will feel understood, freed from the emotion of the problem, and better able to deal with the problem. When children amplify and fully express their thoughts and feelings at the heart of the problem, they are moving toward the desired goal and often are able to suggest their own solutions. Sometimes active listening helps children accept an unchangeable situation (e.g., the family must move to a new apartment) and gives them a chance to get their feelings out and experience genuine acceptance.

Active listening requires getting inside the child, viewing the world through his or her eyes, and communicating that understanding. Essentially, then, the parent must respond to both the words that the child uses and the feelings that lie behind the words. The following examples demonstrate the skill:

Child 1 (crying): Daniel took my truck away from me.

Parent 1: You sure feel bad about that. You don't like it when he does that.

Child 1: Yeah, it makes me mad.

Child 2: I have a dumb teacher this year. I don't like her. She's mean.

Parent 2: Sounds like you are really disappointed with your teacher.

Child 2: I am; I miss being in Mrs. Chang's class. She liked me.

In each illustration, the parent has accurately understood the child, and the child has responded by verifying the parent's accuracy and elaborating on the feeling. Each interchange sets the stage for a continued and meaningful conversation.

Parents should never use active listening to draw out and then put down the child ("Oh, so you want to flunk and go back with Mrs. Chang, do you?"). Parents sometimes begin active listening but subsequently slam the door shut because their own attitudes get in the way or because of lack of time. At other times, parents simply echo a message to the child without empathy. Over time, this will result in demoralization and mistrust.

Using I-Messages

When the parent determines that he or she owns the problem—that is, his or her needs are directly and tangibly affected—there are several possible responses. For example, the parent can modify the environment, himself or herself, or the child directly. With younger children, changing the environment often promotes a change in the child's behavior and solves the parent's problem. Such changes may include enriching the environment (bringing out crayons and paper or scheduling times for friends to come over and play), simplifying the environment (turning down or turning off the television or requiring that one activity be cleaned up before another is initiated), or substituting one activity for another (tag on the front lawn instead of wrestling in the living room).

Parents who own the problem may also decide to change themselves. For example, a father might decide that he will work on becoming more tolerant of noise in the house and will follow through and supervise his children more after asking them to do a task; a mother might reduce the amount of pressure she puts on her children to behave in a particular manner.

Finally, the parent can seek to modify the child directly. Sometimes parents use spanking or some other form of punishment, which may produce short-term compliance but is detrimental in the long term. For example, corporal punishment is related to and actually predicts dating violence (Foshee & Reyes, 2009). Verbal punishment is also ineffective; it typically consists of derogatory labeling or put-down statements: "You are so lazy." "You are a real pest." "You are no good; you just want to be mean!" This kind of communication is called "you-messages" and communicates blame and shame.

Rather than using punishment or ineffective "you-messages," a simple "I-message" is a powerful tool in modifying a child's behavior. In an "I-message" the adult clearly expresses to the child the problem and the feelings about the problem while letting the child know that the adult owns the problem. Often the child is willing to modify behavior based on the adult's feelings. An "I-message" is less apt to provoke rebellion and resistance, and it places the responsibility on the child for changing behavior. The following examples demonstrate the contrast between "you-messages" and "I-messages."

> *You-message*: You didn't do your chores this morning. You are being lazy and irresponsible!
>
> *I-message*: I'm angry because you didn't do your chores.

The focus of the "I-message" is on the problem of the chores and the feeling it creates in the adult and not on the character or personality of the child. The parent's feelings of annoyance and anger are not directly expressed in the "you-message"; the anger is clear and direct in the "I-message."

You-message: Stop being such a problem. You're always interrupting your mother and me when we are talking.

I-message: I am frustrated with you because I want to finish my conversation with your mother and you keep interrupting us; this has been happening a lot lately.

The "I-message" communicates the parent's feelings, puts responsibility on the child for the behavior, but does not shame the child or attack the child's self-esteem.

By sending an "I-message," the adult anticipates that the child will understand the adult's problem, respect the adult's needs, and therefore discontinue acting in a negative way. Frequently an "I-message" is adequate for modifying the child's behavior. Occasionally it is necessary to follow it with a change in the environment. For example, after communicating frustration at being interrupted, the father could require the child to go play in another room until he has finished the conversation with the child's mother.

Mutual Problem Solving

Mutual problem solving is the PET strategy used when the problem is owned by both child and parent; that is, when the needs of both the child and the adult are being blocked by a problem. Too often solutions to problems and conflicts result in a win–lose situation. The loser (adult or child) feels defeated, and regardless of who loses, the child is denied opportunities to develop behavior that is self-disciplined, sensitive to others, and inner directed.

Gordon (2006) recommends following a six-step, no-lose method whenever an adult and a child encounter a conflict-of-needs situation. In this way the parent and the child can construct a solution that is acceptable to both of them. These steps are common to many problem-solving models.

1. *Identify and define the conflict.* It is important to determine whether the disagreement is actually over the issue at hand. Sometimes the conflict is really over a different matter and the current problem reflects another concern. Both parent and child need to be clear on the nature of the conflict.

2. *Generate possible solutions.* Both parent and child need to indicate as many alternative solutions as possible. The child should be encouraged and praised for identifying solutions even when they don't seem feasible.

3. *Evaluate the alternative solutions.* The feasibility and potential effectiveness of each solution is critically evaluated. Both the adult and the child should consider the consequences of the various solutions and decide which solutions they can live with. The parent does not stop being the parent at this step. For example, the parent should not enter into false "equal" arrangements in which the child also picks out the mother's clothes or the child gets to use profanity every time the parent does.

4. *Decide on and get commitments for the most acceptable solution.* Both must agree to commit themselves to the solution, including modifying their own behavior as needed.
5. *Work out ways of implementing the solution.* The adult and the child must agree upon who is going to do what and when it is to be done.
6. *Follow up and evaluate how the solution worked.* After an agreed-upon time limit, parent and child review the solution to determine satisfaction with it. If the parent is consistent about following up when the problem and the solution are "easy," the child will be more trusting and willing to try out solutions that demand more risk or effort on the child's part.

By engaging the child in the process of mutually solving the problem, over time, both parent and child will be more satisfied, and the child will learn to anticipate problems and generate solutions independently. Thus conflicts can be resolved in a healthy manner that builds a relationship that is mutually satisfying, constructive, and loving.

Effective parenting derives from a philosophy in which respect for the child is uppermost. This means respecting individuality, uniqueness, complexity, idiosyncratic potential, and capacity for making choices. This philosophy is expressed in effective communication. Of course, these skills are just as important to the effective teacher or counselor as they are to parents. The PET program, like all parent training programs, reflects a particular set of values and assumptions. Exploration of parent values is an important prerequisite to carrying out any parent training program.

In addition to the multiple parent education and training programs just reviewed, it is important to consider programs specifically for other caretakers—such as guardians and foster parents—who are often underrepresented in the family intervention treatment literature. Foster parents and foster families play key roles in many young people's lives and can play a critical role in the lives of high-risk youth.

ADJUNCTS TO FAMILY COUNSELING AND PARENT TRAINING: PARENT PSYCHOEDUCATION

All of the programs presented above have evidence of success and most have been empirically supported. They are also relatively expensive, although not as expensive as letting problems linger and get worse. For many practitioners, they are hard to implement without special training and other resources. So what is the alternative? Well-implemented parent education (psychoeducation), including coaching in child management, is a promising family intervention strategy (Scott & Dadds, 2009). It is most effective, however, if parents learn to recognize and deal with the signs of risk before their child reaches adolescence. Training in behavior modification, in management of rewards and consequences, and in communication skills is most effective with younger children whose behavioral problems have not yet developed into serious misbehavior. If children are already engaged in negative, destructive, and self-destructive behavior, parent training is relatively less effective. In this case, problem behavior may have already become part of the young persons' repertoire. Also, youth may have already identified with a negative peer group or may have achieved a high level of autonomy. Parent education refers to programs, support services, and resources offered to parents and caregivers that are designed to provide support and increase skills and efficacy for raising a family in a healthy and constructive manner. Teachers, counselors, and other human service professionals can often provide effective prevention and intervention in the form of parent education. The parents of a student who is acting out sexually may shy away from discussing sex, birth control, and sexually transmitted infection. The parents of a student who doesn't turn in homework may lack a consistent system for monitoring school progress. The parents of a student who is belligerent and aggressive may have lost control of their child at home. These issues and others may be effectively addressed by educating parents on dealing with specific aspects of their children's behavior. Family-oriented programs designed to prevent drug use and dependence and to strengthen families by teaching parents behavioral management, effective discipline, sex education, nutrition, and family budgeting can be very effective (Webster-Stratton & Reid, 2010).

Culture and Coaching

Cultural appropriateness is critical to the success of parent psychoeducation programs (Schwartz, Unger, Zamboanga, & Szapocznik, 2011). An important focus for the parent-trainer in getting acquainted with the family is to understand the family culture, values, identity, and practices. Expectations regarding child behavior and accepted modes of child discipline are culturally embedded (Chao & Kanatsu, 2008). Consequently, cultural appropriateness is important to the success of parent programs (Schwartz et al., 2011) and cultural adaptations need to be made to parent training programs that have been validated for use with the dominant culture so that these same programs appropriately address the needs of families from diverse ethnocultural groups (Ortiz & Del Vecchio, 2013).

Parent programs that include coaching in specific strategies have greater effects on child behavior than programs without coaching (Barnett, Niec, & Acevedo-Polakovich, 2014). Immediate and specific feedback to parents by the interventionist, while the parent practices new skills with the child, most effectively changes parents' behaviors and improves children's behavior. Supportive coaching feedback seems to be the best way to assure the use of effective behavior management skills (Barnett et al., 2014). There are a few basic principles of parenting that can go a long way to help parents be more effective. Three very useful strategies are: the Premack principle, logical and natural consequences, and use of time-out.

The Premack Principle

The Premack principle, or Grandma's Rule, is a relatively simple and highly effective guide that parents can quickly put to good use. The Premack principle indicates, "for any pair of responses, the more probable one will reinforce the less probable one" (Premack, 1965, p. 132). In other words, behaviors that kiddos are quite likely to perform (playing video games, riding a bike, watching television, talking on the telephone) can serve as reinforcements for those behaviors that they are less likely to perform (completing homework, washing the dishes, caring for younger siblings, cleaning their rooms). As Grandma's might put it: "First you work; then you play." The parents' task is to identify what their child wants to do and then require that a less-favored activity occur first: "Clean your desk and then we can play a game." "Pick up the room before you go out to play." Or "Do the dishes before you play your video game." A recent web posting labeled "21st century parenting" demonstrated the modern application of Grandma's Rule. The image showed a post-it note on a bulletin board with the message: Reward—For today's Wifi password. Listed below were: (1) Empty dishwasher; (2) Fold laundry; (3) Vacuum downstairs; (4) Take out trash. Old ideas, newly applied—Grandma would approve!

Application of the Premack principle is most effective when parents break down tasks into subtasks (e.g., clean desk; put away all loose books and papers; put away all pens and pencils; dust desktop), and sometimes it is also helpful to reward the performance of each subtask. Frequent small rewards provide more effective reinforcement than infrequent, large rewards. Parents should provide rewards immediately after the behavior is accomplished, reward the behavior only after it occurs, and the reward should always be accompanied with verbal praise. Parents will hear arguments and rationalizations ("But my friends will be playing online before I can finish the dishes!"), but they are guaranteed to hear even more if they give in to them.

Logical and Natural Consequences

Carrying out a system of logical and natural consequences (see Chapter 8) not only encourages children to take responsibility for their behavior but can also greatly reduce the amount of arguing (see Box 14.4). Consider the Carter family of Chapter 3. Doug Carter is unhappy with the fact that Jason stays up very late on weekends watching television. Because he stays up so late, Jason sleeps late the following morning, leaving his chores undone until the afternoon. Sometimes he forgets them altogether. Jason's behavior is only one of the problems here; the other problem is that his behavior has no logical consequences. A logical consequence of staying up very late is to be tired when one is roused from sleep to do one's chores. By allowing Jason to sleep late, his parents condone his late-night TV habits. By requiring Jason to get up and do his chores no matter what time he goes to bed, his parents would give Jason responsibility for deciding how late to stay up (reducing the likelihood of a "But I'm 13 years old!" argument) and still have the satisfaction of knowing his work is done (reducing the likelihood of a "You live in this house too" argument).

If logical consequences are to work, parents must be prepared to apply them without fail. Some sample behaviors and their logical/natural consequences are in the Instructor/Student e-manual of this book. Each

> ## Box 14.4   Eat Your Dinner!
>
> Parents once brought a 4-year-old to us who stubbornly clenched her teeth and refused to eat when she didn't like the dinner she was served. She often threw her food on the floor. Her parents responded in a number of ways—arguing with the little girl, arguing with each other, threatening the girl, or rewarding each bite—and typically concluded by cleaning up the mess and providing an alternative meal. Mealtime had become "a living hell."
>
> At first the parents were horrified when we informed them that the logical consequence of such behavior was to let her go without eating until the next meal was served. But finally they conceded that she really would not be harmed by her hunger pains and agreed to try this approach. Upon their daughter's next refusal to eat, they explained to her that if she threw her dinner on the floor, she would get nothing to eat until breakfast. When she promptly and predictably flipped her dinner to the floor, her parents were prepared. They didn't yell or argue or rush to clean it up. Instead, they calmly reminded her that it would be a long time until breakfast and finished their own dinner before attending to the mess she had made. She kept them awake most of the night with her tearful cries, but they didn't back down.
>
> The next day she ate breakfast and lunch without incident (lunch, eaten at day care, had never been a problem), and dinner the next evening was relatively peaceful. She complained about the food, but she ate most of it. The next evening she once again overturned her plate and endured the same logical consequence. She cried for only 2 hours that night. Two months later her parents reported that she had never again overturned her plate and was eating at least a small portion of everything they served her.

consequence is modified according to the severity of the misbehavior and the number of times the behavior recurs after consequences have been applied. If a child continues to leave toys around the house, for example, the parents may remove the toys for 2 or more days at a time. Children should always know the logical consequences of their misbehaviors and be informed when the consequences are changing. With older children, parents may draw up a contract that specifies, for example, rules for using the family car and consequences of failure to follow those rules. By signing the contract, families formalize the agreement and establish a clear standard of conduct.

Time-Out

The behavioral intervention "time-out," if applied accurately, is a very useful and effective child management technique for modifying child behavior. The problem is that it is frequently not used correctly. At its heart, time-out is a removal from reinforcement that gives the child an opportunity to calm him- or herself. Technically, it is not a punishment. Some parents remove the child from interaction; put him or her in the bedroom full of toys, TV, and electronic gadgets; and call it time-out. It is not.

For correct use of time-out, there are important evidence-based parameters to follow (Drayton et al., 2014). Among them are (1) The regular environment or caregiver and child interaction (i.e., the "time-in") must be reinforcing; (2) time-out is implemented immediately after misbehavior or after only one command or one verbal warning; (3) consistency, especially between parents, is critical; (4) almost no reinforcement, stimuli, or activities are available in the location of time-out or during time-out; (5) time-out is enforced and the child is returned to time-out if he/she leaves or receives a consequence for escaping from time-out; (6) time-out ends when the child is calm and the adult determines release from time-out; (7) follow-through requires the child to comply with the original command after time-out has ended. To be clear, with younger children time-outs should be relatively brief, typically one minute per year of age.

Time-out works when the above procedures are followed. Unfortunately, the interventionist has to teach and perhaps model these parameters because parents often need specific reinforcement and support to learn how to apply them. Referring parents to review websites will likely provide poor information about the procedure. In one study, none of the websites on use of time-out provided accurate information about the above parameters. In fact, inaccurate and inconsistent information was provided on 59% of the reviewed websites on the strategy of time-out (Drayton et al., 2014).

This last finding raises serious concerns about information available on the Internet. Another study also raised concerns. Websites providing specific information on anxiety disorders in children, for example, were found to be variably accurate, and the majority of websites that provide information on anxiety medications for children do not address dosages, duration, and side effects of the medications discussed (Reynolds, Walker, Walsh, & The Mobilizing Minds Research Group, 2014). As professionals, these problems support our need to provide direct parent education, psychoeducation, and coaching to families, and to assure that information and resources we recommend are accurate and up to date.

Parent Support Groups

Parent support groups are very useful to support parents and others serving in primary caretaking roles. Many parents would benefit from experiencing a sense of accompaniment with other parents who have "been there." Each new generation of parents deals with issues that their own parents never imagined. Your grandparents, for example, are unlikely to have had a son (i.e., your father) who came home with a pierced nipple. Many of the underlying issues are the same, however, and are related to the movement through the family life cycle: dealing with stress, change, loss, and anger; problems of communication, discipline, and authority; and passing down values and traditions. Especially in light of the decline of the extended family network, a parent support group is an ideal way for parents to express their concerns and learn what other parents have experienced and attempted. It also allows parents to share the pain and frustration as well as the joys and successes of raising children. Parent support groups are available through local churches, YMCAs, schools, counseling agencies, day-care centers, and workplaces. Many areas of the country also have local parent crisis lines or Parents Anonymous groups, which can provide information about parent support groups.

One parent support group that is active throughout the United States is ToughLove. ToughLove is a self-help group for parents and guardians of teenagers who are experienced by parents as uncontrollable, addicted, abusive, or otherwise in trouble with the school or the law. With more than 1,500 groups, this organization provides ongoing support, assistance in crises, and referrals to professionals, as well as many practical ideas for helping teenagers stop their self-destructive behavior. Parents are encouraged to make their own plans for addressing their teenager's behavior. The group functions as a sounding board, a source of suggestions, and a backup support team. One ToughLove mother we know enlisted the help of other ToughLove parents in planning a constructive confrontation with her drug-abusing daughter. One of the other couples provided an alternate place for the daughter to stay for a week in case she decided she could not stay with her mother after the confrontation. The same mother had just posted fliers for a ToughLove parent in another part of the country whose runaway son had been seen locally. Social media, like Facebook, has expanded the reach of support groups like ToughLove.

Alateen and Al-Anon family groups are broad-based teen and family support groups that operate throughout the country. Teens or families of alcoholics meet together much like the members of Alcoholics Anonymous. Participating teens and families learn about alcoholism and are helped to achieve a loving detachment from the alcoholic, to increase their self-esteem and independence, and to rely on the group for encouragement and support. Through sharing their common problems, members of alcoholics' families discover that they are not alone and that they have the ability to cope with their situation.

Parent support groups can provide invaluable information and support for parents and guardians who feel hopeless, angry, and alone in dealing with the problems of their troubled children and youth. ToughLove, Alateen, and Al-Anon provide support for family members who may feel trapped in an impossible situation. These are only three such groups; there are literally thousands of others. There are support groups for parents of children with problems ranging from spina bifida and cerebral palsy to bipolar disorder and schizophrenia. Teachers and counselors can assist families by keeping informed about these resources and by encouraging families to contact local chapters of these support groups. Refer to our website for more information, e-mail, and web addresses for many of the organizations mentioned.

CONCLUSION

A family systems framework is a realistic and viable way to view the problems of troubled children and adolescents. Too often work with an individual provides only partial solutions. All young people live in a montage of overlapping systems: families, schools, neighborhoods, larger communities, and the nation. Family counselors address the family as a system in order to change dysfunctional patterns of behavior and communication. Parent training and parent support groups provide alternatives and adjuncts to family counseling. Counselors, teachers, and other helping professionals can be of invaluable assistance by providing these services or by helping families gain access to such programs.

Abeysekera, L., & Dawson, P. (2015). Motivation and cognitive load in the flipped classroom: Definition, rationale, and a call for research. *Higher Education Research & Development*, 34(1). Retrieved from http://www.tandfonline.com/doi/abs/10.1080/07294360.2014.934336#.VduhupdrO8B

Abrego, L. J., & Gonzales, R. G. (2010). Blocked paths, uncertain futures: The postsecondary education and labor market prospects of undocumented Latino youths. *Journal of Education for Students Placed at Risk*, 15, 144–157.

Adachi, P. J. C., & Willoughby, T. (2011). The effect of violent video games on aggression: Is it more than just the violence? *Aggression and Violent Behavior*, 16(1), 55–62.

Adams, H. E. (2013). *Comprehensive handbook of psychopathology*. New York: Springer Science & Business Media.

Adams, L. (2009). How P.E.T. compares to other parent training programs. In *How to choose the right parenting program for you*. Retrieved from http://www.gordontraining.com/thomas-gordon/

Adkison, S. E., Grohman, K., Colder, C. R., Leonard, K. E., Orrange-Torchia, T., Peterson, E., & Eiden, R. D. (2013). Impact of fathers' alcohol use on the development of effortful control in early adolescence. *Journal Studies on Alcohol and Drugs*, 74(5), 674–683.

Adler, A. (1930). *The education of children*. South Bend, IN: Gateway.

Adler, A. (1964). *Social interest: A challenge to mankind*. New York: Capricorn.

Advocates for Youth. (2015). Retrieved from http://www.advocatesfor-youth.org/index.php

Afterschool Alliance. (2014). *America after 3PM: Afterschool Programs in Demand*. Washington, DC. Retrieved from http://www.after-schoolalliance.org/documents/AA3PM-2014/AA3PM_National_Report.pdf

Alan Guttmacher Institute. (2011). *Facts on American teens' sexual and reproductive health*. In Brief: Fact Sheet. Retrieved from http://www.guttmacher.org/pubs/FB-ATSRH.html

Albee, G. W. (1995, February). The answer is prevention. *Psychology Today*, 19, 60–64.

Albert, B. (2010). *With one voice 2010: America's adults and teens sound off about teen pregnancy*. Washington, DC: The National Campaign to Prevent Teen and Unplanned Pregnancy. Retrieved from http://www.thenationalcampaign.org/resources/pdf/pubs/wov_2010.pdf

Albright, K., & LaFromboise, T. D. (2010). Hopelessness among White- and Indian-identified American Indian adolescents. *Cultural Diversity and Ethnic Minority Psychology*, 16(3), 437–442. doi:10.1037/a0019887

Alexander, M. (2010). *The new Jim Crow: Mass incarceration in the age of color-blindness*. New York: The New Press.

Algozzine, B., Daunic, A. P., & Smith, S. W. (Eds.). (2010). *Preventing problem behaviors: Schoolwide programs and classroom practices* (2nd ed.). Thousand Oaks, CA: Corwin Press.

Ali, K., Farrer, L., Gulliver, A., & Griffiths, K. M. (2015). Online peer-to-peer support for young people with mental health problems: A systematic review. *Journal of Medical Internet Research Mental Health*, 2(2). Retrieved from http://mental.jmir.org/2015/2/e19/. doi: 10.2196/mental.4418

Allen, M., & Ashbaker, B. Y. (2004). Strengthening schools: Involving paraprofessionals in crisis prevention and intervention. *Intervention in School and Clinic*, 39(3), 139–146.

Alliance for Excellent Education. (2015). High school teaching for the twenty-first century: Preparing students for college. Alliance for Excellent Education. Retrieved from http://all4ed.org/reports-factsheets/high-school-teaching-for-the-twenty-first-century-preparing-students-for-college/

Alvord, M. K., Zucker, B., & Grados, J. J. (2011). *Resilience builder program for children and adolescents: Enhancing socialcompetence and self-regulation*. Champaign, IL: Research Press.

Allwood, M. A., & Widom, C. S. (2013). Child abuse and neglect, developmental role attainment, and adult arrests. *Journal of Research in Crime and Delinquency*, 50(4), 551–578. doi:10.1177/0022427812471177

Ambrosio, T., & Schiraldi, V. (1997). *From classrooms to cellblocks: A national perspective*. Washington, DC: The Justice Policy Institute.

American Academy of Child and Pediatric Psychiatry. (2012). When children have children #31. Retrieved from http://www.aacap.org/App_Themes/AACAP/docs/facts_for_families/31_when_children_have_children.pdf

American Academy of Pediatrics. (2015). Media and children. Retrieved from https://www.aap.org/en-us/advocacy-and-policy/aap-health-initiatives/pages/media-and-children.aspx

American Psychiatric Association. (2013). *Diagnostic and statistical manual of mental disorders-5* (5th ed.). Washington, DC: Author.

American Psychological Association. (2012). *Facing the school dropout dilemma*. Washington, DC: Author. Retrieved from http://www.apa.org/pi/families/resources/school-dropout-prevention.aspx

American Psychological Association Presidential Task Force on Violence and the Family. (1996). *Violence and the family*. Washington, DC: Author.

American Psychological Association Task Force on Psychological Intervention Guidelines. (1995). *Template for developing guidelines: Interventions for mental disorders and psychological aspects of physical disorders*. Washington, DC: Author.

American Psychological Association. (2014). Guidelines for prevention in psychology. *American Psychologist*, 69(3), 285–296. doi:10.1037/a0034569

American Psychological Association. (2015). Intimate partner violence facts and resources. Retrieved from http://www.apa.org/topics/violence/intimate-partner-violence.pdf

Amrein, A. L., & Berliner, D. C. (2002, March 28). High-stakes testing, uncertainty, and student learning. *Education Policy Analysis Archives*, 10(18). Retrieved from http://epaa.asu.edu/epaa/v10n18/

Anderson, S., Cavanagh, J., Hartman, C., & Leonard-Wright, B. (2001). *Executive excess 2001: Layoffs, tax rebates, the gender gap*. Boston, MA: Institute for Policy Studies and United for a Fair Economy.

Anderson, C. A., & Dill, K. E. (2000). Violent video games can increase aggression. *Journal of Personality and Social Psychology*, 78(4), 772–790.

Anderson, C. A., Shibuya, A., Ihori, N., Swing, E. L., Bushman, B. J., Sakamoto, A., …, Saleem, M. (2010). Violent video game effects on aggression, empathy, and pro-social behavior in eastern and western countries: A meta-analytic review. *Psychological Bulletin*, 136(2), 151–173.

Andrews, J. A., Hampson, S., & Peterson, M. (2011). Early adolescent cognitions as predictors of heavy alcohol use in high school. *Addictive Behaviors*, 36(5), 448–455.

Annetta, L. (2010). The "I's" have it: A framework for serious educational game design. *Review of General Psychology*, 14, 105–112.

Annie E. Casey Foundation. (2012). Kids Count: Data Snapshot on High-poverty communities. Retrieved from http://www.aecf.org/m/resourcedoc/AECF-ChildrenLivingInHighPovertyCommunities-2012-Full.pdf

Annie E. Casey Foundation. (2014). KIDS COUNT Data book: State trends in Child Well-being. Retrieved from http://www.aecf.org/m/databook/aecf-2014kidscountdatabook-embargoed-2014.pdf

Annie E. Casey Foundation. (2015). KIDS COUNT datacenter. Retrieved from http://datacenter.kidscount.org/data/

Anooshian, L. J. (2005). Violence and aggression in the lives of homeless children: A review. *Aggression and Violent Behavior*, 10, 129–152.

Arbona, C. (2000). The development of academic achievement in school aged children: Precursors to career development. In R. Lent & S. Brown (Eds.), *Handbook of counseling psychology* (3rd ed., pp. 270–309). New York: Wiley.

Arciaga, M., Sakamoto, W., & Fearbry Jones, E. (2010). *Responding to gangs in the school setting*. No. 5, Gang Center Bulletin, 2, 1–15. November 2010. Institute for Intergovernmental Research® (IIR) Washington, DC: Office of Juvenile Justice and Delinquency Prevention.

Arkowitz, H., Miller, W. R., & Rollnick, S. (2015). *Motivational interviewing in the treatment of psychological problems* (2nd ed.). New York: Guilford Press.

Assessment Capacities Project [ACAPS]. (2014). Other situations of violence in the Northern Triangle of Central America: Invisible borders, vicious spirals, and the normalisation of terror. Retrieved from http://acaps.org/resourcescats/downloader/other_situations_of_violence_in_the_northern_triangle_of_central_america_executive_summary_may_2014/230

Au, W. (2013). Hiding behind high-stakes testing: Meritocracy, objectivity and inequality in U.S. education. *The International Education Journal: Comparative Perspectives*, 12(2), 7–19.

Aud, S., & Hannes, G. (Eds.). (2010). *The condition of education 2010 in brief* (NCES 2010-029). Washington, DC: National Center for Education Statistics, Institute of Education Sciences, U.S. Department of Education. Retrieved from http://nces.ed.gov/

Baams, L., Grossman, H., & Russell, S. T. (2015). Minority stress and mechanisms of risk for depression and suicidal ideation among lesbian, gay, and bisexual youth. *Developmental Psychology*, 51(5), 688–696. doi: 10.1037/a0038994

Baer, J.S., Beadnell, B., Garrett, S.B., Hartzler, B., Wells, E.A., Peterson, P.L. (2008). Adolescent change language within a brief motivational intervention and substance use outcomes. Psychology of Addictive Behaviors, 22, 570–575.

Baker, S. B., Tyler, R. E., Lupton-Smith, H. S., Wang, A. B., Allen, A. H., Wapner, K. H., …, Isaac, S. T. (2015). Self-monitoring as a counseling technique and an accountability strategy. *VISTAS Online 2015*. Retrieved from http://www.counseling.org/knowledge-center/vistas

Balfanz, R. (2007). *What your community can do to end its dropout crisis: Learning from research and practice*. Center for Social Organization of Schools and Johns Hopkins University. Retrieved from http://civilrightsproject.ucla.edu/research/k-12-education/school-dropouts/the-dropout-crisis-in-the-northwest-confronting-the-graduation-rate-crisis-in-all-communities-with-special-focus-on-american-indian-and-alaska-native-students/legters-what-your-community-can-do.pdf

Bamatter, W., Carroll, K. M., Añez, L. M., Paris, M., Ball, S. A., Nich, C., ..., Martino, S. (2010). Informal discussions in substance abuse treatment sessions with Spanish-speaking clients. *Journal of Substance Abuse Treatment*, 39(4), 353–363.

Band, S. R., & Harpold, J. A. (1999, September). School violence: Lessons learned. *FBI: Law Enforcement Bulletin*, 68, 9–16.

Bandura, A. (1973). *Aggression: A social learning analysis*. Englewood Cliffs, NJ: Prentice-Hall.

Bandura, A. (1993). Perceived self-efficacy in cognitive development and functioning. *Educational Psychologist*, 28(2), 117–148.

Bandura, A., Pastorelli, C., Barbaranelli, C., & Caprara, G. V. (1999). Self efficacy pathways to childhood depression. *Journal of Personality and Social Psychology*, 76, 258–269.

Bardack, S. (2010). *Common ELL terms and definitions*. Washington, DC: American Institutes for Research. Retrieved from http://www.air.org/files/NEW_Common_ELL_TERMS_AND_DEFINITIONS_6_22_10.pdf

Bargiel-Matusiewicz, K., Grzelak, S., & Weglinska, M. (2010). Factors protecting against risk behavior concerning the psychoactive substances used by adolescents. *International Journal of Adolescent Medicine and Health*, 22(4), 503–510.

Barnett, M. L., Liec, L. N., & Acevedo-Polakovich, I. D. (2014). Assessing the key to effective coaching in parent-child interaction therapy: The therapist-parent interaction coding system. *Journal of Psychopathology and Behavioral Assessment*, 36(2), 211–223.

Bassett, C., McWhirter, J. J., & Kitzmiller, K. (1997). Teacher implementation of cooperative learning groups. *Contemporary Education*, 71(1), 46–50.

Bassuk, E. L., Richard, M. K., & Tsertsvadze, A. (2015). The prevalence of mental illness in homeless children: A systematic review and meta-analysis. *Child & Adolescent Psychiatry*, 54(2), 86–96.e2.

Battin-Pearson, S., Newcomb, M. D., Abbott, R. D., Hill, K. G., Catalano, R. F., & Hawkins, J. D. (2000). Predictors of early high school dropout: A test of five theories. *Journal of Educational Psychology*, 92(3), 568–582.

Bauman, L. J., Silver, E. J., & Stein, R. E. K. (2006). Cumulative social disadvantage and child health. *Pediatrics*, 117(4), 1321–1328.

Baumeister, R. F., Bushman, B. J., & Campbell, W. K. (2000). Self-esteem, narcissism, and aggression: Does violence result from low self-esteem or from threatened egotism? *Current Directions in Psychological Science*, 9(1), 26–29.

Bearman, P., & Moody, J. (2004). Suicide and friendships among American adolescents. *American Journal of Public Health*, 94, 89–95.

Beauvais, F., Chavez, E. L., Oetting, E. R., Deffenbacher, J. L., & Cornell, G. R. (1996). Drug use, violence, and victimization among White American, Mexican American, and American Indian dropouts, students with academic problems, and students in good academic standing. *Journal of Counseling Psychology*, 43(3) 292–299.

Beck, A. T. (1976). *Cognitive therapy and emotional disorders*. New York: International Universities Press.

Beck, A. T. (1991). Cognitive therapy: A 30 year retrospective. *American Psychologist*, 46(4), 368–375.

Beck, A. T. (2014). Advances in cognitive theory and therapy. *Annual Review of Clinical Psychology*, 10, 1–24.

Beck, A. T., Kovacs, M., & Weissman, A. (1979). Assessment of suicidal intention: The scale for suicidal ideation. *Journal of Clinical and Consulting Psychology*, 47, 343–352.

Beck, A. T., Weissman, A., Lester, D., & Trexler, L. (1974). The measurement of pessimism: The hopelessness scale. *Journal of Consulting and Clinical Psychology*, 42, 861–865.

Becker, E. (1981). *The denial of death*. New York: Free Press.

Becker, K. D., Lee, B. R., Daleiden, E. L., Lindsey, M., Brandt, N. E., & Chorpita, B. F. (2015). The common elements of engagement in children's mental health services: Which elements for which outcomes? *Journal of Clinical Child & Adolescent Psychology*, 44, 30–43. doi:10.1080/15374416.2013.814543

Beets, M. W., Flay, B. R., Vuchinich, S., Snyder, F. J., Acock, A., Li, K., ..., Durlack, J. (2009). Use of a social and character development program to prevent substance use, violent behaviors and sexual activity among elementary-school students in Hawaii. *American Journal of Public Health*, 99(8), 1438–1445.

Bellanti, C. J., & Bierman, K. L. (2000). Disentangling the impact of low cognitive ability and inattention on social behavior and peer relationships. *Journal of Clinical Child Psychology*, 29(1), 66–75.

Bender, W. N., Shubert, T. H., & McLaughlin, P. J. (2001). Invisible kids: Preventing school violence by identifying kids in trouble. *Intervention in School and Clinic*, 37(2), 105–111.

Benn, W. (Ed.). (1981). *STAR: Social thinking and reasoning*. Irvine, CA: Irvine Unified School District.

Benn, W. (Ed.). (1982). *PLUS: Promoting learning and understanding of self*. Irvine, CA: Irvine Unified School District.

Bennouna-Greene, M., Bennouna-Greene, V., Berna, F., & Defranoux, L. (2011). History of abuse and neglect in patients with schizophrenia who have a history of violence. *Child Abuse & Neglect*, 35(5), 329–332.

Benson, H. (2000). *The relaxation response*. New York: HarperCollins Publisher.

Benson, H., & Proctor, W. (2010). *Relaxation revolution: The science and genetics of mind body healing*. New York: Scribner.

Bergmann, J., & Sams, A. (2012). *Flip your classroom: Reach every student in every class every day*. Washington, DC: International Society for Technology in Education.

Berkovich, I. (2014). A socio-ecological framework of social justice leadership in education. *Journal of Educational Administration*, 52(3), 282–309.

Berliner, D. (2001, January 28). Our schools vs. theirs: Averages that hide the true extremes. Education Policy Project CERAI-01-02, Center for Education Research, Analysis, and Innovation. Milwaukee: University of Wisconsin–Milwaukee.

Berliner, D. C., & Biddle, B. J. (1995). *The manufactured crisis: Myths, fraud, and the attack on America's public schools.* Reading, MA: Addison-Wesley.

Bernstein, M. (2013, September 12). Kip Kinkel loses bid for new sentencing hearing in Thurston High shooting. *The Oregonian.*

Berry, E. H., Shillington, A. M., Peak, T., & Hohman, M. M. (2000). Multi-ethnic comparison of risk and protective factors for adolescent pregnancy. *Child and Adolescent Social Work, 17,* 79–96.

Bertram, C. C., Crowley, M. S., & Massey, S. (Eds.). (2010). *Beyond progress, beyond marginalization: LGBTQ youth in and out of schools.* New York: Peter Lang Publishing.

Bess, R., Leos-Urbel, J., & Green, R. (2001). *The cost of protecting vulnerable children II: What has changed since 1996?* The Urban Institute. Retrieved from http://newfederalism.urban.org/html/op46/coca46.html

Bethell, C. D., Newacheck, P., Hawes, E., & Halfon, N. (2014). Adverse childhood experiences: Assessing the impact on health and school engagement and the mitigating role of resilience. *Health Affairs, 33,* 2106–2115. doi:10.1377/hlthaff.2014.0914

Bickel, R., Howley, C., Williams, T., & Glascock, C. (2001). High school size, achievement equity, and cost: Robust interaction effects and tentative results. *Education Policy Analysis Archives, 9*(40). Retrieved from http://epaa.asu.edu/epaa/v9n40.html

Bierman, K. L., Nix, R. L., Heinrichs, B. S., Domitrovich, C. E., Gest, S. D., Welsh, J. A., & Gill, S. (2014). Effects of Head Start REDI on children's outcomes 1 year later in different kindergarten contexts. *Child Development, 85*(1), 140–159.

Bizot, E. (1999, May). *K–8 Educational system as a context for career decision-making.* Paper presented at conference of the Society for Vocational Psychology, Division 17, American Psychological Association, Milwaukee, WI.

Blake, J. J., Lund, E. M., Zhou, Q., Kwok, O., Benz, M. R. (2012). National prevalence rates of bully victimization among students with disabilities in the United States. *School Psychology Quarterly, 27*(4), 210–222. doi:10.1037/spq0000008

Blake, C., Wang, W., Cartledge, G., & Gardner, R. (2000). Middle school students with serious emotional disturbances serve as social skills trainers and reinforcers for peers with SED. *Behavioral Disorders, 25,* 280–298.

Boewe, M. I., & McWhirter, J. J. (2002, November). *ART: Anxiety reduction training. Trainer's manual and student workbook.* (Treatment Manual) Tempe, AZ: Arizona State University.

Boonstra, H. D. (2014). What is behind the declines in teen pregnancy rates? *Guttmacher Policy Review, 17*(3), 15–21.

Bor, W., & Sanders, M. R. (2004). Correlates of self-reported coercive parenting of preschool-aged children at high risk for the development of conduct problems. *Australian and New Zealand Journal of Psychiatry, 38,* 738–745.

Bowman-Perrott, L., Davis, H., Vannest, K., Williams, L., Greenwood, C., & Parker, R. (2013). Academic benefits of peer tutoring: A meta-analytic review of single-case research. *School Psychology Review, 42*(1), 39–55.

Bozeman, B., & Feeney, M. K. (2008). Mentor matching: A "Goodness of Fit Model." *Administration & Society, 40*(5), 465–482.

Bracken, B. A. (1992). *Multidimensional self-concept scale.* Austin, TX: Pro-Ed.

Bradshaw, C. P. (2014). The role of families in preventing and buffering the effects of bullying. *Journal of the American Medical Association Pediatrics, 168,* 991–993. doi:10.1001/jamapediatrics.2014.1627

Bradshaw, C. P. (2015). Translating research to practice in bullying prevention. *American Psychologist, 70,* 322–332.

Bradshaw, C. P., Pas, E. T., Bloom, J., Barrett, S., Hershfeldt, P., Alexander, A., …, Leaf, P. J. (2012). A state-wide partnership to promote safe and supportive schools: The PBIS Maryland Initiative. *Administration and Policy in Mental Health and Mental Health Services Research, 39,* 225–237. doi:10.1007/s10488-011-038 4-6

Bradshaw, C. P., Zmuda, J. H., Kellam, S. G., & Ialongo, N. S. (2009). Longitudinal impact of two universal preventive interventions in first grade on educational outcomes in high school. *Journal of Educational Psychology, 101*(4), 926–937. doi:10.1037/a0016586

Brady Center to Prevent Gun Violence. (2015). *The truth about kids & guns: 2015.* Retrieved from www.brady-campaign.org

Bridge, J. A., Goldstein, T. R., & Bren, D. A. (2006). Adolescent suicide and suicidal behavior. *Journal of Child Psychology and Psychiatry, 47,* 372–394.

Brock, S. E., Sandoval, J., & Lewis, S. (2001). *Preparing for crises in the schools: A manual for building school crisis response teams* (2nd ed.). New York: Wiley.

Bronfenbrenner, U. (1979). *The ecology of human development: Experiments by nature and design.* Cambridge, MA: Harvard University Press.

Bronfenbrenner, U. (1989). Ecological systems theory. *Annals of Child Development, 6,* 187–249.

Bronfenbrenner, U. (1994). *The ecology of human development.* Cambridge, MA: Harvard University Press.

Brook, T. V. (2014). Army commanders: White men lead a diverse force. *USA Today.* Retrieved from http://www.usatoday.com/story/news/nation/2014/09/11/army-officer-corps-dominated-by-white-men/14987977/

Brown, A. (2015). *US immigrant population projected to rise, even as share falls among Hispanics, Asians.* Washington, DC: Pew Research Center. Retrieved from http://www.pewresearch.org/fact-tank/pages/4/

Brown, P., Corrigan, M. W., & Higgins-D'Alessandro, A. (Eds.). (2012). *Handbook of prosocial education.* Lanham, MD: Rowman & Littlefield.

Brown, J. D., Halpern, C. T., & L'Engle, K. L. (2005). Mass media as a sexual super peer for early maturing girls. *Journal of Adolescent Health, 36,* 420–427.

Brown, S. D., & Krane, N. R. (2000). Four (or five) sessions and a cloud of dust: Old assumptions and new observations about career counseling. In S. D. Brown & R. W. Lent (Eds.), *Handbook of Counseling*

Psychology (3rd ed., pp. 740–766). New York: Wiley.

Brown, S. D., Lamp, K., Telander, K. J., & Hacker, J. (2011). Career development as prevention: Toward a social cognitive model of vocational hope. In E. M. Vera (Ed.), *The Oxford handbook of prevention in counseling psychology* (pp. 374–392). NewYork: Oxford University Press.

Brown, B., & Marin, P. (2009). Adolescents and electronic media: Growing up plugged in. In J. Brooks-Gunn & E. H. Donahue (Eds.), *The future of children: Children and The electronic media*, 18(#2009-29). Retrieved from http://www.futureofchildren.org

Brown, A. P., Marquis, A., & Guiffrida, D. A. (2013). Mindfulness-based interventions in counseling. *Journal of Counseling & Development*, 91, 96–104. doi:10.1002/j.1556-6676. 2013.00077.x

Brown, T., & Swenson, S. (2005). Identifying basic needs: The contexual needs assessment. *International Journal of Reality Therapy*, 24, 7–10.

Brown-Iannuzzi, J. L., Adair, K. C., Payne, B. K., Richman, L. S., & Fredrickson, B. L. (2014). Discrimination hurts, but mindfulness may help: Trait mindfulness moderates the relationship between perceived discrimination and depressive symptoms. *Personality and Individual Differences*, 56, 201–205.

Brunnwasser, S. M., Gillham, J. E., & Kim, E. S. (2009). A meta-analytic review of the Penn Resiliency Program's effect on depressive symptoms. *Journal of Consulting and Clinical Psychology*, 77(6), 1042–1054. doi:10.1037/a0017671

Brutsch, E. (2015). Protective environmental influences against suicidal ideation in youth. *Injury Prevention*, 21, 31. doi:10.1136/injuryprev-2015-041602.77

Bryan, J. (2009). Engaging clients, families, and communities as partners and mental health. *Journal of Counseling & Development*, 87(4), 507–511.

Bryan, C. J., Corso, K. A., Neal-Walden, T. A., & Rudd, M. D. (2009). Managing suicide risk in primary care: Practice recommendations for behavioral health consultants.

Professional Psychology: Research and Practice, 40, 148–155.

Buchanan, G. M., & Seligman, M. E. P. (Eds.). (1995). *Explanatory style*. Hillsdale, NJ: Erlbaum.

Buchman, D. D., & Funk, J. B. (1996). Video and computer games in the '90s: Children's time commitment and game preference. *Children Today*, 24, 12–16.

Buckholtz, J. W., Treadway, M. T., Cowan, R. L., Woodward, N. D., Li, R., Ansari, M. S., ..., Zald, D. H. (2010). Dopaminergic network differences in human impulsivity. *Science*, 329(5991), 532–532. doi: 10.1126/science.1185778

Buehler, C., & Gerard, J. M. (2013). Cumulative family risk predicts increases in adjustment difficulties across early adolescence. *Journal of Youth and Adolescence*, 42(6), 905–920.

Buhi, E. R. (2010). Quality and accuracy of sexual health information web sites visited by young people. *Journal of Adolescent Health*, 47(2), 206–208.

Buker, H. (2011). Formation of self-control: Gottfredson and Hirschi's general theory of crime and beyond. *Aggression and Violent Behavior*, 16(3), 265–276.

Bundy, A. (2004). *Efficacy of booster session maintenance in an anger prevention program and an optimistic resiliency program* (Doctoral dissertation). Arizona State University.

Bundy, A., McWhirter, P. T., & McWhirter, J. J. (2011). Anger and violence prevention: Enhancing treatment effects through booster sessions. *Education and Treatment of Children*, 34(1), 1–14.

Bureau of Labor Statistics. (2014). Labor force characteristics by race and ethnicity 2013. Retrieved from http://www.bls.gov/opub/reports/ cps/race_ethnicity_2013.pdf

Burrow-Sanchez, J. J., Call, M. E., Zheng, R., & Drew, C. J. (2011). How school counselors can help prevent online victimization. *Journal of Counseling and Development*, 89(1), 3–10.

Burrow-Sanchez, J., & Hawken, L. (2013). *Helping students overcome substance abuse: Effective practices for prevention and intervention*. New York: Guilford Press.

Bushman, B. J., & Anderson, C. A. (2001). Media violence and the American public: Scientific facts versus media misinformation. *American Psychologist*, 56(6/7), 477–489.

Bushman, B. J., Rothstein, H. R., & Anderson, C. A. (2010). Much ado about something: Violent video game effects and a school of red herring: Reply to Ferguson and Kilburn (2010). *Psychological Bulletin*, 136(2), 182–187.

Byers, E. S. (2011). Beyond the birds and the bees and was it good for you? Thirty years of research on sexual communication. *Canadian Psychology*, 52(1), 20–28.

Cabrera, N. L., Meza, E. L., Romero, A. J., & Rodriguez, R. C. (2013). "If there is no struggle, there is no progress": Transformative youth activism and the school of ethnic studies. *The Urban Review*, 45(1), 7–22.

Cammarota, J., & Romero, A. (2014). *Raza studies: The public option for educational revolution*. Tucson: University of Arizona Press.

Camp, B. W., & Bash, M. S. (1985a). *Think aloud: Increasing social and cognitive skills—A problem-solving program for children, classroom program grades 1–2*. Champaign, IL: Research Press.

Camp, B. W., & Bash, M. S. (1985b). *Think aloud: Increasing social and cognitive skills—A problem-solving program for children, classroom program grades 3–4*. Champaign, IL: Research Press.

Camp, B. W., & Bash, M. S. (1985c). *Think aloud: Increasing social and cognitive skills—A problem-solving program for children, classroom program grades 5–6*. Champaign, IL: Research Press.

Campaign High School Equity/CHSE. (2015). Plan for success: Communities of color define policy priorities for high school reform. Campaign for CHSE High School Equity. Retrieved from http:// inpathways.net/PlanforSuccess.pdf

Campfield, K. M., & Hills, A. M. (2001). Effects of timing of critical incident stress debriefing (CISD) on posttraumatic symptoms. *Journal of Traumatic Stress*, 14, 327–340.

Capaldi, D. M., Kim, H. K., & Pears, K. C. (2009). The association between partner violence and child maltreatment: A common conceptual framework. In D. Whitaker & J. Lutzker (Eds.), *Preventing partner violence: Research and evidence-based intervention strategies* (pp. 93–111). Washington, DC: American Psychological Association.

Caplan, G. (1964). *Principles of preventive psychiatry.* New York: Basic Books.

Carey, J. C., Dimmitt, C., Hatch, T., Lapan, R., & Whiston, S. (2008). Report of the National Panel on Evidence-Based School Counseling: Outcome research coding protocol and evaluation: Student Success Skills and Second Step. *Professional School Counseling, 11,* 197–206.

Carhill, A., Suárez-Orozco, C., & Páez, M. (2008). Explaining English language proficiency among adolescent immigrant students. *American Educational Research Journal, 45,* 1155–1179.

Carlock, A. L., & Lizotte, A. J. (2015). Gangs, guns, and violence: Synergistic effects. In S. H. Decker & D. C. Pyrooz (Eds.), *The handbook of gangs* (pp. 178–192). Malden, MA: Wiley & Sons.

Carson, E. A. (2014). Prisoners in 2013. U.S. Department of Justice Office of Justice Programs Bureau of Justice Statistics. September 2014, NCJ 247282. Retrieved from http:// www.bjs.gov/content/pub/pdf/p13. pdf

Carter, E. W., Asmus, J., Moss, C. K., Cooney, M., Weir, K., Vincent, L., ..., Fesperman, E. (2013). Peer network strategies to foster social connections among adolescents with and without severe disabilities. *Teaching Exceptional Children, 46*(2), 51–59.

Carter, E. W., Cushing, L. S., Clark, N. M., & Kennedy, C. H. (2005). Effects of peer support interventions on students' access to the general curriculum and social interactions. *Research and Practice for Persons with Severe Disabilities, 30,* 15–25.

Carville, J. (1996). *We're right, they're wrong: A handbook for spirited progressives.* New York: Random House.

Casey, B. J. (2015). Beyond simple models of self-control to circuit-based accounts of adolescent behavior. *Annual Review of Psychology, 66,* 295–319. doi: 10.1146/annurev-psych-010814-015156

Casey, B. J., Somerville, L. H., Gotlib, I. H., Ayduk, O., Franklin, N. T., Askren, M. K., ..., Shoda, Y. (2011). Behavioral and neural correlates of delay of gratification 40 years later. *Proceedings of the National Academy of Sciences, 108,* 14998–15003.

Castellanos-Ryan, N., & Conrod, P. J. (2011). Personality correlates of the common and unique variance across conduct disorder and substance misuse symptoms in adolescence. *Journal of Abnormal Child Psychology, 39*(4), 563–576.

Castle, S. (2009). Cyberbullying on trial: The computer fraud and abuse act and United States v. Drew. *Journal of Law and Policy Review, 17,* 579–607.

Catalano, R. F., Berglund, M. L., Ryan, J. A. M., Lonczak, H. S., & Hawkins, J. D. (2004). Positive youth development in the United States: Research findings on evaluations of positive youth development programs. *The ANNALS of the American Academy of Political and Social Science, 591*(1), 98–124.

Cattaneo, L. B., & Chapman, A. R. (2010). The process of empowerment: A model for use in research and practice. *American Psychologist, 65*(7), 646–659. doi:10.1037/ a0018854

Center for Innovative Public Health Research. (2015). Retrieved from https://innovativepublichealth.org/ category/press-releases/

Center on the Developing Child at Harvard University. (2009). *Maternal depression can undermine the development of young children* (Working Paper No. 8). Retrieved from http://www.developingchild. harvard.edu

Centers for Disease Control. (2015). Unmarried childbearing. Retrieved from http://www.cdc.gov/nchs/fastats/unmarried-childbearing.htm

Centers for Disease Control and Prevention. (2005). Associations of body mass index and perceived weight with suicide ideation and suicide attempts among U.S. high school students. Retrieved from http://archpedi.amaassn.org/cgi/ content/short/159/6/513

Centers for Disease Control and Prevention. (2010). *Web-based Injury Statistics Query and Reporting System (WISQARS)* [Online]. National Center for Injury Prevention and Control, Centers for Disease Control and Prevention (producer). [cited 2010 June 23]. Retrieved from www.cdc.gov/ injury/wisqars/index.html

Centers for Disease Control and Prevention (2014a). Understanding intimate partner violence fact sheet 2014. Retrieved from: http://www. cdc.gov/ViolencePrevention/pdf/ IPV-FactSheet.pdf

Centers for Disease Control and Prevention (2014b). Understanding teen dating violence fact sheet 2014. Retrieved from: http://www. cdc.gov/violenceprevention/pdf/ teen-dating-violence-factsheet-a.pdf

Centers for Disease Control and Prevention. (2011a). School health programs and academic achievement. National Center for Chronic Disease Prevention and Health Promotion, Division of Adolescent and School Health.

Centers for Disease Control and Prevention/CDC. (2013). The National intimate partner and sexual violence survey. Retrieved from http://www.cdc.gov/mmwr/preview/ mmwrhtml/ss6308a1.htm? s_cid=ss6308a1_e

Centers for Disease Control and Prevention. (2015a). Division of violence prevention. Suicide prevention. Retrieved from http:// www.cdc.gov/

Centers for Disease Control and Prevention. (2015b). Unmarried childbearing. Retrieved from http:// www.cdc.gov/nchs/fastats/unmarried-childbearing.htm

Cepukiene, V., & Pakrosnis, R. (2011). The outcome of solution-focused brief therapy among foster care adolescents: The changes of behavior and perceived somatic and cognitive difficulties. *Children and Youth Services Review, 33*(6), 791–797.

Cerel, J., Roberts, T. A., & Nilsen, W. J. (2005). Peer suicidal behavior and adolescent risk behavior. *Journal of Nervous and Mental Disease, 193*(4), 237–243.

Ceranoglu, T. A. (2010). Video games in psychotherapy. *Review of General Psychology, 14,* 141–146.

Chaffin, S. M. (2008). The new playground bullies of cyberspace: Online peer sexual harassment. *Howard Law Journal, 51*, 773–818.

Chambless, D. L., & Hollon, S. D. (1998). Defining empirically supported therapies. *Journal of Consulting and Clinical Psychology, 66*(1), 7–18.

Chandra, A. (2008). Does watching sex on television predict teen pregnancy? Findings from a national longitudinal survey of youth. *Pediatrics, 122*(5), 1047–1054.

Chao, R., & Kanatsu, A. (2008). Beyond socioeconomics: Explaining ethnic group differences in parenting through cultural and immigration processes. *Applied Developmental Science, 12*(4), 181–187.

Chapman, C., Laird, J., & KewalRamani, A. (2010). *Trends in high school dropout and completion rates in the United States: 1972–2008* (NCES 2011-012). Washington, DC: National Center for Education Statistics, Institute of Education Sciences, U.S. Department of Education. Retrieved from http://nces.ed.gov/pubsearch

Child Care Aware. (2014). Parents and the high cost of child care: 2014 Report. Child Care Aware of America. Retrieved from www.usa.childcareaware.org

Child Trends. (2013). Home computer access and Internet use. Retrieved from http://www.childtrends.org/wp-content/uploads/2012/07/69_Computer_Use.pdf

Chin, H. B., Sipe, T. A., Elder, R., Mercer, S. L., Chattopadhyay, S. K., Jacob, V., ..., Santelli, J. (2012). The effectiveness of group-based comprehensive risk-reduction and abstinence education interventions to prevent or reduce the risk of adolescent pregnancy, human immunodeficiency virus, and sexually transmitted infections: Two systematic reviews for the guide to community preventive services. *American Journal of Preventive Medicine, 42*(3), 272–294.

Chisler, A., Smischney, T. M., & Villarruel, F. A. (2014). Research brief: Positive development of LGBT youth. Military Research and Outreach (REACH) Laboratory, The University of Minnesota. Retrieved from https://reachmilitaryfamilies.umn.edu/sites/default/files/rdoc/Promoting%20Positive%20Development%20of%20LGBT%20Youth.pdf

Cho, H., Hallfors, D. D., & Sanchez, V. (2005). Evaluation of a high school peer group intervention for at-risk youth. *Journal of Abnormal Child Psychology, 33*, 363–374.

Christenson, S. L., & Thurlow, M. L. (2004). School dropouts: Prevention considerations, interventions, and challenges. *Current Directions in Psychological Science, 13*(1), 36–39.

Chronister, K. M. (2006). The intersection of social class and race in community intervention research with women domestic violence survivors. *American Journal of Community Psychology, 37*, 75–182. doi:10.1007=s10464-006-9017-8

Chronister, K. M., & Davidson, M. M. (2010). Promoting distributive justice for intimate partner violence survivors with group intervention. *The Journal for Specialists in Group Work, 35*(2), 115–123. doi: 10.1080/01933921003705958

Chronister, K. M., Linville, D., & Palmer, K. (2008). Domestic violence survivors' access of career counseling services: A qualitative investigation. *Journal of Career Development, 34*, 339–361.

Chronister, K. M., Marsiglio, M. C., Linville, D., & Lantrip, K. R. (2014). The influence of dating violence on adolescent girls' educational experiences. *The Counseling Psychologist, 42*(3), 374–405. doi: 10.1177/0011000012470569

Chronister, K. M., & McWhirter, E. H. (2006). An experimental examination of two career counseling programs for battered women. *Journal of Counseling Psychology, 53*, 151–164. doi:10.1177=0894845308316291

Claes, L., Luyckx, K., Baetens, I., Van de Ven, M., & Witteman, C. (2015). Bullying and victimization, depressive mood, and non-suicidal self-injury in adolescents: The moderating role of parental support. *Journal of Child and Family Studies, 3*, 1–9.

Clark, D. A., & Beck, A. T. (2011). *Cognitive therapy of anxiety disorders: Science and practice.* New York: Guilford Press.

Cleary, T. J. (2015). *Self-regulated learning interventions with at-risk youth: Enhancing adaptability, performance, and well-being.* Washington, DC: American Psychological Association.

Clough, B. A., & Casey, L. M. (2011). Technological adjuncts to enhance current psychotherapy practices: A review. *Clinical Psychology Review, 31*(3), 279–292.

CNN Money. (2015). Education vs. Prison costs. Retrieved from http://money.cnn.com/infographic/economy/education-vs-prison-costs/

Coleman, J. S., & Hoffer, T. (1987). *Public and private high schools: The impact of communities.* New York: Basic Books.

Collier, L. (2015, March). Helping immigrant children heal. *Monitor on Psychology, 46*(4), 50–54.

Commission on Adolescent Suicide Prevention/CASP. (2005). Youth suicide. In D. L. Evans, E. B. Foa, R. E. Gur, H. Hendin, C. P. O'Brien, M. E. P. Seligman, & B. T. Walsh (Eds.), *Treating and preventing adolescent mental disorders* (pp. 433–496). New York: Oxford University Press.

Conchas, G. Q. (2001). Structuring failure and success: Understanding the variability in Latino school engagement. *Harvard Educational Review, 71*(3), 579–589.

Contreras, J., & Kerns, K. A. (2000). Emotion regulation processes: Explaining links between parent–child attachment and peer relationships. In K. A. Kerns, J. M. Contreras, & A. M. Neal-Barnett (Eds.), *Family and peers: Linking two social worlds* (pp. 1–25). Westport, CT: Praeger.

Conyne, R. K. (2004). Prevention groups. In J. L. DeLucia-Waack, D. A. Gerrity, C. R. Kalodner, & M. T. Riva (Eds.), *Handbook of group counseling and psychotherapy* (pp. 621–629). Thousand Oaks, CA: Sage.

Conyne, R. K. (2015). *Counseling for Wellness and Prevention: Helping People Become Empowered in Systems and Settings* (revised). New York: Routledge.

Conyne, R., & Horne, A. (Eds.). (2012). *Prevention practice kit: Action guidelines for mental health professionals.* Thousand Oaks, CA: Sage.

Cook, C. R., Williams, K. R., Guerra, N. G., Kim, T. E., & Sadek, S.

(2010). Predictors of bullying and victimization in childhood and adolescence: A meta-analytic investigation. *School Psychology Quarterly, 25*(2), 65–83.

Cook-Cottone, C. P., Tribole, E., Tylka, T. L. (2013). *Healthy eating in schools: Evidence-based interventions to help kids thrive.* School psychology series (pp. 123–141). Washington, DC: American Psychological Association.

Cornelius, J. R., Douaihy, A., Bukstein, O. G., Daley, D. C., Wood, S. D., Kelly, T. M., & Salloum, I. M. (2011). Evaluation of cognitive behavioral therapy/motivational enhancement therapy (CBT/MET) in a treatment trial of comorbid MDD/AUD adolescents. *Addictive Behaviors, 36*(8), 843–848.

Cornell, D. G. (2004). Student threat assessment. In E. R. Gerler (Ed.), *Handbook of school violence* (pp. 115–135). Binghamton, NY: Haworth Press.

Cornell, D. G., & Williams, F. (2006). Student threat assessment as a strategy to reduce school violence. In S. R. Jimerson & M. J. Furlong (Eds.), *Handbook of school violence and school safety: From research to practice* (pp. 587–601). Mahwah, NJ: Lawrence Erlbaum.

Cowley, C., & Tillman, F. (2001). Adolescent girls' attitudes toward pregnancy: The importance of asking what the boyfriend wants. *Journal of Family Practice, 50*(7), 603–607.

Crone, D. A., Hawken, L. S., & Horner, R. H. (2015). *Building positive behavior support systems in schools* (2nd ed.). New York: Guilford Publications.

Crowe, L. M., Beauchamp, M. H., Catroppa, C., & Anderson, V. (2011). Social function assessment tools for children and adolescents: A systematic review from 1988 to 2010. *Clinical Psychology Review, 31*(5), 767–785.

Cummings, C., & Haggerty, K. P. (1997). Raising healthy children. *Educational Leadership, 54*(8), 28–30.

Cushing, C. C., Jensen, C. D., Miller, M. B., & Leffingwell, T. R. (2014). Meta-analysis of motivational interviewing for adolescent health behavior: Efficacy beyond substance use. *Journal of Consulting and Clinical Psychology, 82*, 1212–1218. doi:10.1037/a0036912

Dancy II, E. (2014). (Un)Doing hegemony in education: Disrupting school-to-prison pipelines for black males. *Equity & Excellence in Education, 47*(4), 476–493.

Daniel, S. S., & Goldston, D. B. (2009). Interventions for suicidal youth: A review of the literature and developmental considerations. *Suicide and Life-Threatening Behavior, 39*(3), 252–268.

Daniels, J. A., & Bradley, M. C. (2011). *Preventing lethal school violence.* New York: Springer.

Daniels, J. A., Bradley, M. C., Cramer, D. P., Winkler, A., Kinebrew, K., & Crockett, D. (2007a). In the aftermath of a school hostage event: A case study of one school counselor's response. *Professional School Counseling, 10*, 482–489.

Daniels, J. A., Bradley, M. C., Cramer, D. P., Winkler, A., Kinebrew, K., & Crockett, D. (2007b). The successful resolution of armed hostage/barricade events in schools: A qualitative analysis. *Psychology in the Schools, 44*, 601–613.

Daniels, J. A., Bradley, M. C., & Hays, M. (2007a). The impact of school violence on school personnel: Implications for psychologists. *Professional Psychology: Research & Practice, 38*, 652–659.

Daniels, J. A., Buck, I., Croxall, S., Gruber, J., Kime, P., & Govert, H. (2007b). A content analysis of news reports of averted school rampages. *Journal of School Violence, 6*, 83–99.

Daniels, J. A., & Page, J. W. (2013). Averted school shootings. In N. Böckler, T. Seeger, P. Sitzer, & W. Heitmeyer (Eds.), *School shootings: International research, case studies, and concepts for prevention* (pp. 421–439). New York: Springer.

Daniels, J. A., Volungis, A., Pshenishny, E., Gandhi, P., Winkler, A., Cramer, D. P., & Bradley, M. C. (2010). A qualitative investigation of averted school shooting rampages. *The Counseling Psychologist, 38*(1), 69–95. doi:10.1177/0011000009344774

Dank, M., Lachman, P., Zweig, J., & Yahner, J. (2014). Dating violence experiences of lesbian, gay, bisexual, and transgender youth. *Journal of Youth and Adolescence, 43*(5), 846–857.

Darlington, E., McWhirter, B. T., & McWhirter, E. H. (2012, March). *Risky behaviors in Chilean female adolescents: The role of mother-daughter connectedness.* Paper presented at the 14th Biannual Conference of the Society for Research on Adolescence, Vancouver, BC, Canada.

Daunic, A. P., Smith, S. W., Robinson, T. R., Miller, M. D., & Landry, K. L. (2000). School-wide conflict resolution and peer mediation programs: Experiences in three middle schools. *Intervention in School and Clinic, 36*(2), 94–100.

David, D. (2013). *Rational emotive behavior therapy in the context of modern psychological research.* New York: Albert Ellis Institute.

David-Ferdon, C., & Simon, T. R. (2014). *Preventing youth violence: Opportunities for action.* Atlanta, GA: National Center for Injury Prevention and Control, Centers for Disease Control and Prevention.

Davis, L., Johnson, S., Miller-Cribbs, J., & Saunders, J. (2002). A brief report: Factors influencing African-American youth decisions to stay in school. *Journal of Adolescent Research, 17*, 3.

Davis, M., Robbins-Eshelman, E., & McKay, M. (2008). *The relaxation and stress reduction workbook* (6th ed.). Oakland, CA: New Harbinger.

Dearing, E., McCartney, K., & Taylor, B. (2009). Does higher quality early child care promote low-income children's math and reading achievement in middle childhood? *Child Development, 80*(5), 1329–1349.

Deci, E. L., & Ryan, R. M. (2000). The "what" and "why" of goal pursuits: Needs and the self-determination of behavior. *Psychological Inquiry, 11*(4), 227–268.

Deci, E. L., Vallerand, R. J., Pelletier, L. G., & Ryan, R. M. (1991). Motivation and education: The self-determination perspective. *Educational Psychologist, 26*(3 & 4), 325–346.

Decker, M. D. (2009). Unexcused absence: A review of the need, costs, and (lack of) state support for peer mediation programs in U.S. schools. *Journal of Dispute Resolution, 2*(9),

1–19. Retrieved from http://scholarship.law.missouri.edu/jdr/vo12009/iss2/9

Decker, S. H., & Pyrooz, D. C. (2015). *The handbook of gangs*. Malden, MA: Wiley & Sons.

Delligatti, N., Akin-Little, A., & Little, S. G. (2003). Conduct disorder in girls: Diagnostic and intervention issues. *Psychology in the Schools, 40*, 183–192.

De Shazer, S., Nolan, Y., & Korman, H. (2007). *More than miracles*. Haworth: London.

De Witte, K., Cabus, S., Thyssen, G., Groot, W., & van den Brink, H. M. (2013). A critical review of the literature on school dropout. *Educational Research and Reviews, 10*, 13–28.

DiCola, L. A., Gaydos, L. M., Druss, B. G., & Cummings, J. R. (2013). Health insurance and treatment of adolescents with co-occurring major depression and substance use disorders. *Journal of the American Academy of Child and Adolescent Psychiatry, 52*, 953–960. doi: 10.1016/j.jaac.2013.06.012

Diemer, M. A. (2009). Pathways to occupational attainment among poor youth of color. *The Counseling Psychologist, 37*(1), 6–35.

Diemer, M., McWhirter, E. H., Ozer, E. J., & Rapa, L. (in press). Advances in the conceptualization and measurement of critical consciousness. *The Urban Review*. doi:10.1177/10690727 15599535

Diemer, M. A., Wang, Q., Moore, T., Gregory, S. R., Hatcher, K. M., & Voight, A. M. (2010). Sociopolitical development, work salience, and vocational expectations among low socioeconomic status African American, Latin American, and Asian youth. *Developmental Psychology, 46*(3), 619–635.

DiGiuseppe, R., Doyle, K. A., Dryden, W., & Backx, W. (2013). *A practitioner's guide to rational-emotive therapy* (3rd ed.). New York: Oxford University Press.

Dinkes, R., Kemp, J., & Baum, K. (2009). *Indicators of school crime and safety: 2009* (NCES 2010–012/NCJ 228478). Washington, DC: National Center for Education Statistics, Institute of Education Sciences, U.S. Department of Education, and Bureau of Justice Statistics, Office of Justice Programs, U.S. Department of Justice.

Dino, G., Kamal, K., Horn, K., Kalsekar, I., & Fernandes, A. (2004). Stage of change and smoking cessation outcomes among adolescents. *Addictive Behaviors, 29*(5), 935–940.

Dishion, T. J., & Bullock, B. M. (2001). Parenting and adolescent problem behavior: An ecological analysis of the nurturance hypothesis. In J. G. Borkowski, S. L. Ramey, & M. Bristol-Power (Eds.), *Parenting and the child's world: Influences on academic, intellectual, and social-emotional development* (pp. 231–249). Hillsdale, NJ: Erlbaum.

Dishion, T. J., & Connell, A. (2006). Adolescents' resilience as a self-regulatory process: Promising themes for linking intervention with developmental science. *Annals of the New York Academy of Sciences, 1094*, 125–138.

Dishion, T. J., & Kavanagh, K. (2003). *Intervening in adolescent problem behavior: A family-centered approach*. New York: Guilford Press.

Dishion, T. J., & Maurico, A. M. (2016). The Family Check-Up model as prevention and treatment of adolescent drug (ab)use: The intervention strategy, outcomes, and implementation model. In M. J. Van Ryzin, K. L. Kumpfer, G. M. Fosco, & M. T. Greenberg (Eds.), *Family-based prevention programs for children and adolescents: Theory, research, and large-scale dissemination* (pp. 86–106) New York: Psychology Press.

Dishion, T. J., & Veronneau, H. (2012). An ecological analysis of the effects of deviant peer clustering on sexual promiscuity, problem behavior, and childbearing from early adolescence to adulthood: An enhancement of the life history framework. *Developmental Psychology, 48*, 703–717. doi:10.1037/a0027304

Dishion, T. J., & Stormshak, E. (2007). *Intervening in children's lives: An ecological, family-centered approach to mental health care*. Washington, DC: American Psychological Association.

Dittus, P. J., & Jaccard, J. (2000). Adolescents' perceptions of maternal disapproval of sex: Relationship to sexual outcomes. *Journal of Adolescent Health, 26*(4), 268–278.

Dixon, A. L., Scheidegger, C., & McWhirter, J. J. (2009). The adolescent mattering experience: Gender variations in perceived mattering, anxiety, and depression. *Journal of Counseling & Development, 87*(3), 302–310.

Domenech Rodriguez, M. M., Donovick, M. R., & Crowley, S. L. (2009). Parenting styles in a cultural context: Observations of "protective parenting" in first-generation Latinos. *Family Process, 48*(2), 195–210.

Domitrovich, C. E., Gest, S. D., Jones, D., Gill, S., & DeRousie, R. M. S. (2010). Implementation quality: Lessons learned in the context of the Head Start REDI trial. *Early Childhood Research Quarterly, 25*, 284–298.

Donovan, J. E. (2005). Problem behavior theory. In C. B. Fisher & R. M. Lerner (Eds.), *Encyclopedia of applied developmental science* (Vol. 2, pp. 872–877). Thousand Oaks, CA: Sage.

Doren, B., Murray, C., & Gau, J. M. (2014). Salient predictors of school dropout among secondary students with learning disabilities. *Learning Disabilities Research & Practice, 29*(4), 150–159.

Dorgan, B. L. (2010). The tragedy of Native American youth suicide. *Psychological Services, 7*(3), 213–218.

Dotterer, A. M., Katie Lowe, K., & McHale, S. M. (2014). Academic growth trajectories and family relationships among African American youth. *Journal of Research on Adolescence, 24*(4), 734–747.

Drayton, A. K., Andersen, M. N., Knight, R. M., Felt, B. T., Fredericks, E. M., & Dore-Stites, D. J. (2014). Internet guidance on time out: Inaccuracies, omissions, and what to tell parents instead. *Journal of Developmental and Behavioral Pediatrics, 35*, 239–246.

Dreikurs, R. (1964). *Children: The challenge*. New York: Hawthorne.

Dreikurs, R. (1967). *Psychology in the classroom*. New York: Harper & Row.

Duncan, G. J., Kalil, A., & Ziol-Guest, K. M. (2015). Early childhood poverty and adult productivity and health. In A. J. Reynolds, A. J. Rolnick, & J. A. Temple (Eds.), *Health and education in early childhood: Predictors, interventions, and policies* (pp. 52–65). Cambridge: Cambridge University Press.

DuPaul, G. J., & Eckert, T. L. (1994). The effects of social skills curricula: Now you see them, now you don't. *School Psychology Quarterly, 9*(2), 113–132.

Duran, E., & Duran, B. (1995). *Native American post-colonial psychology.* Albany: State University of New York Press.

Durlak, J. A. (2015). What everyone should know about implementation. In J. A. Durlak, C. E. Domitrovich, R. P. Weissberg, & T. P. Gullotta (Eds.), *Handbook of social and emotional learning: Research and practice* (pp. 395–405). New York: Guilford.

Durlak, J. A., Domitrovich, C. E., Weissberg, R. P., & Gullotta, T. P. (2015). *Handbook of social and emotional learning: Research and practice.* New York: Guilford Press.

Durlak, J. A, Mahoney, J. L., Bohnert, A. M., & Parente, M. E. (2010). Developing and improving afterschool programs to enhance youth's personal growth and adjustment: A special issue of AJCP. *American Journal of Community Psychology, 45*(3–4), 285–293.

Durlak, J. A., Weissberg, R. P., & Pachan, M. (2010). A meta-analysis of after-school programs that seek to promote personal and social skills in children and adolescents. *American Journal of Community Psychology, 45*(3–4), 294–309.

Duvall, E. M., & Miller, B. C. (1985). *Marriage and family development* (6th ed.). New York: Harper & Row.

Dynarski, M., Clarke, L., Cobb, B., Finn, J., Rumberger, R., & Smink, J. (2008). *Dropout prevention: A practice guide* (NCEE 2008–4025). Washington, DC: National Center for Education Evaluation and Regional Assistance, Institute of Education Sciences, U.S. Department of Education. Retrieved from http://ies.ed.gov/ncee/wwc

Economic Policy Institute. (2015a). Poverty rates of various types of families, 1959–2013. Retrieved from http://www.stateofworkingamerica.org/chart/swa-poverty-figure-7e-poverty-rates-types/

Economic Policy Institute. (2015b). Average family income growth, by income group, 1947–2013. Retrieved from http://www.stateofworkingamerica.org/charts/realannual-family-income-growth-byquintile-1947-79-and-1979-2010/

Education World. (2015, March 28). Common elements of effective schools. Retrieved from http://www.educationworld.com/a_issues/schools/schools005.shtml#sthash.YwaOSOzJ.dpuf

Educause. (2012). 7 things you should know about flipped classrooms. Retrieved from http://www.educause.edu/library/resources/7-things-youshould-know-about-flippedclassrooms

Egley, A., Jr., Howell, J. C., & Moore, J. P. (2010). *Highlights of the 2008 National Youth Gang Survey.* Washington, DC: U.S. Department of Justice, Office of Justice Programs, Office of Juvenile Justice and Delinquency Prevention.

Ekstrom, R. B., Goertz, M. E., Pollack, J. M., & Rock, D. A. (1986). Who drops out of high school and why? Findings from a national study. *Teacher's College Record, 87,* 356–373.

Elias, M. J., Gara, M. A., Schuyler, T. F., Branden-Muller, L. R., & Sayette, M. A. (1991). The promotion of social competence: Longitudinal study of a preventative school-based program. *American Journal of Orthopsychiatry, 61,* 409–417.

Ellis, A., & Ellis, J. D. (2011). *Rational emotive behavior therapy.* Washington, DC: American Psychological Association.

Epstein, J. A. (2011). Adolescent computer use and alcohol use: What are the roles of quantity and content of computer use? *Addictive Behaviors, 36*(5), 520–522.

Erickson, S. J., Gerstle, M., & Feldstein, S. W. (2005). Brief interventions and motivational interviewing with children, adolescents, and their parents in pediatric health settings: A review. *Archives of Pediatrics and Adolescent Medicine, 159,* 1173–1180.

Ersche, K. D., Turton, A. J., Pradhan, S., Bullmore, E. T., & Robbins, T. W. (2010). Drug addiction endophenotypes: Impulsive versus sensationseeking personality traits. *Biological Psychiatry, 68*(8), 770–773. doi: 10.1016/j.biopsych.2010.06.015

Evans, G. W., & Cassels, R. C. (2014). Childhood poverty, cumulative risk exposure, and mental health in merging adults. *Clinical Psychological Science, 2*(3), 287–296.

Evans, S. D., Kivell, N., Haarlammert, M., Malhotra, K., & Rosen, A. (2014). Critical community practice: An introduction to the special section. *Journal for Social Action in Counseling and Psychology, 6*(1). Retrieved from http://www.psysr.org/jsacp/Evans-v6n1-14_1-15.pdf

Evans, W. P., Marte, R., Betts, S., & Silliman, B. (2001). Adolescent suicide risk and peer related violent behaviors and victimization. *Journal of Interpersonal Violence, 16*(12), 1330–1348.

Eysenck, S. B. G., & Eysenck, H. J. (1980). Impulsiveness and venturesomeness in children. *Personality and Individual Differences, 1*(1), 73–78. doi:10.1016/0191-8869(80)90006-9

Fad, K. S. (1990). The fast track to success: Social-behavioral skills. *Intervention in School and Clinic, 26*(1), 39–43.

Fair, C. A., & McWhirter, J. J. (2002, August). *BLOCKS: Building lives on cooperative knowledge skills. Trainer's manual and student workbook.* (Treatment Manual) Tempe, AZ: Arizona State University.

Farkas, M. S., Simonsen, B., Migdole, S., Donovan, M. E., Clemens, K., & Cicchese, V. (2011). Schoolwide positive behavior support in an alternative school setting: An evaluation of fidelity, outcomes, and social validity of tier 1 implementation. *Journal of Emotional and Behavioral Disorders.* doi: 10.1177/1063426610389615

Farrington, D. P., & Baldry, A. C. (2010). Individual risk factors for school bullying. *Journal of Aggression, Conflict and Peace Research, 2*(1), 4–16.

Farrington, D. P., Loeber, R., Ttofi, M. M. (2012). Risk and protective factors for offending. In B. C. Welsh & D. P. Farrington (Eds.), *The Oxford handbook of crime prevention* (pp. 46–69). New York: Oxford University Press.

Farrington, D. P., & Ttofi, M. M. (2010). Effective methods to reduce school bullying. Campbell Collaboration. Retrieved from http://www.campbellcollaboration.org/selected_presentations/index.php

Fassinger, R. E. (2000). Gender and sexuality in human development: Implications for prevention and advocacy in counseling psychology. In S. D. Brown & R. W. Lent (Eds.), *Handbook of counseling psychology* (3rd ed., pp. 346–378). New York: Wiley.

Federal Interagency Forum on Child and Family Statistics. (2010). *America's children in brief: Key national indicators of well-being*. U.S. Department of Education. Washington, DC: U.S. Government Printing Office. Retrieved from http://childstats.gov

Federal Interagency Forum on Child and Family Statistics. (2015). *America's children: Key national indicators of well-being, 2015*. America's Children at a Glance. Washington, DC: U.S. Government Printing Office. Retrieved from http://www.childstats.gov/americaschildren/glance.asp

Feder, J., Levant, R. F., & Dean, J. (2010). Boys and violence: A gender-informed analysis. *Psychology of Violence, 1*(S), 3–12.

Feinberg, M. E., Jones, D., Greenberg, M. T., Osgood, D. W., & Bontempo, D. (2010). Effects of the communities that care model in Pennsylvania on change in adolescent risk and problem behaviors. *Prevention Science, 11*, 163–171.

Feingold, A., Kerr, D., & Capaldi, D. (2008). Associations of substance use problems with intimate partner violence for at-risk men in long-term relationships. *Journal of Family Psychology, 22*, 429–438.

Feliz, J. (2011). Support and resources for parents dealing with teen drug and alcohol abuse. The partnership at drugfree.org. Retrieved from http://www.drugfree.org/

Ferguson, C. J. (2010). Blazing angels or resident evil? Can violent video games be a force for good? *Review of General Psychology, 14*, 68–81.

Ferguson, E. D. (2001). Adler and Dreikurs: Cognitive-social dynamic innovators. *Journal of Individual Psychology, 57*(4), 324–341.

Fergusson, D. M., Boden, J. M., & Horwood, L. J. (2009). Situational and generalized conduct problems and later life outcomes: Evidence from a New Zealand birth cohort. *Child Psychology & Psychiatry, 50*(9), 1084–1092.

Fergusson, D. M., & Woodward, L. J. (2002). Mental health, educational, and social role outcomes of adolescents with depression. *Archives of General Psychiatry, 59*(3), 225–231.

File, T., & Ryan, C. (2014). *Computer and Internet use in the United States: 2013*. American Community Survey Reports, ACS-28, U.S. Census Bureau, Washington, DC, 2014.

Finkel, E. (2012, November). Flipping the script in K12. District Administration. Retrieved from www.districtadministration.com/article/flipping-script-k12

Finn, J. D., Gerber, S. B., & Boyd-Zaharias, J. (2005). Small classes in the early grades, academic achievement, and graduating from high school. *Journal of Educational Psychology, 97*(2), 214–223.

Fiske, S. T. (2010). Envy up, scorn down: How comparisons divide us. *American Psychologist, 65*(8), 698–706.

Flipped Learning Network. (2012). Improve student learning and teacher satisfaction with one flip of the classroom. Retrieved from http://flippedlearning1.files.wordpress.com/2012/07/classroomwindowinfographic7-12.pdf

Flores, E., Cicchetti, D., & Rogosch, F. A. (2005). Predictors of resilience in maltreated and nonmaltreated Latino children. *Developmental Psychology, 41*, 338–351.

Flower, A., McKenna, J. W., Bunuan, R. L., Colin, S., Muething, C. S., & Vega, R. Jr. (2013). Effects of the Good Behavior Game on challenging behaviors in school settings. *Review of Educational Research, 84*(4), 546–571.

Foley-Nicpon, M., & Assouline, S. G. (2015), Counseling considerations for the twice-exceptional client. *Journal of Counseling & Development, 93*, 202–211. doi: 10.1002/j.1556-6676.2015.00196.x

Fong, R., Dettlaff, A., James, J., & Rodriquez, C. (2015). *Addressing racial disproportionality and disparities in Human Services*. New York: Columbia University Press.

Forgatch, M., Patterson, G. R., Degarmo, D. S., & Beldavs, Z. G. (2009). Testing the Oregon delinquency model with 9-year follow-up of the Oregon Divorce Study. *Development and Psychopathology, 21*(2), 637–660.

Foshee, V. A., Bauman, K. E., Ennett, S. T., Suchindran, C., Benefield, T., & Linder, G. F. (2005). Assessing the effects of dating violence prevention program "Safe Dates" using random coefficient regression modeling. *Prevention Science, 6*(3), 245–257.

Foshee, V. A., Mcnaughton Reyes, H. L., Ennett, S. T., Cance, J. D., Bauman, K. E., & Bowling, J. M. (2012). Assessing the effects of families for safe dates, a family-based teen dating abuse prevention program. *Journal of Adolescent Health, 51*(4), 349–356.

Foshee, V. A., & Reyes, H. L. (2009). Primary prevention of dating abuse perpetration: When to begin, whom to target, and how to do it. In D. J. Whitaker & J. R. Lutzker (Eds.), *Preventing partner violence: Research and evidence-based intervention strategies* (pp. 141–168). Washington, DC: American Psychological Association.

Foshee, V. A., Reyes, L. M., Agnew-Brune, C., Simon, T. R., Vagi, K. J., Lee, R. D., & Suchindran, C. (2014). The effects of the evidence-based safe dates dating abuse prevention program on other youth violence outcomes. *Prevention Science, 15*(6), 907–916.

Fry, R., & Taylor, P. (2013). Young Hispanics dropping out of high school. Retrieved from http://www.pewhispanic.org/2013/05/09/iii-young-hispanics-dropping-out-of-high-school/

Gallagher, M., Prinstein, M. J., Simon, V., & Spirito, A. (2014). Social anxiety symptoms and suicidal ideation in a clinical sample of early adolescents: Examining loneliness and social support as longitudinal mediators. *Journal of Abnormal Child Psychology, 42*, 871–883.

Gamoran, A. (2009). *Tracking and inequality: New directions for research and practice* (WCER

Working Paper No. 2009-6). Madison: University of Wisconsin–Madison, Wisconsin Center for Education Research. Retrieved from http://www.wcer.wisc.edu/publications/workingPapers/papers.php

Garbarino, J. (1998). The stress of being a poor child in America. *Child and Adolescent Psychiatric Clinics of North America*, 7(1), 105–119.

Garcia, M., & McDowell, T. (2010). Mapping social capital: A critical contextual approach for working with low-status families. *Journal of Marital Family Therapy*, 36(1), 96–107.

Gardner, H. (1983). *Frames of mind: The theory of multiple intelligences*. New York: Basic Books.

Gardner, M., & Steinberg, L. (2005). Peer influence on risk taking, risk preference, and risky decision making in adolescence and adulthood: An experimental study. *Developmental Psychology*, 41, 625–635.

Garland, E., Pettus-Davis, C., & Howard, M. O. (2013). Self-medication among traumatized youth: Structural equation modeling of pathways between trauma history, substance misuse, and psychological distress. *Journal of Behavioral Medicine*, 36, 175–185. doi:10.1007/s10865-012-9413-5

Gatti, U., Tremblay, R. E., & Vitaro, F. (2009). Iatrogenic effect of juvenile justice. *Journal of Child Psychology and Psychiatry*, 50(8), 991–998.

Gayes, L. A., & Steele, R. G. (2014). A meta-analysis of motivational interviewing interventions for pediatric health behavior change. *Journal of Consulting and Clinical Psychology*, 82, 521–535. doi:10.1037/a0035917

Gendron, B. P., Williams, K. R., & Guerra, N. G. (2011). An analysis of bullying among students within schools: Estimating the effects of individual normative beliefs, self-esteem, and school climate. *Journal of School Violence*, 10(2), 150–164.

Gerena, L., & Keiler, L. (2011). *Supporting English language learners in urban at risk secondary schools: Using literacy strategies to support ELL learning of science in a peer enhanced restructured classroom*. Honolulu, HI: Proceedings of the Hawaii International Conference on Education.

Gil, L., & Bardack, S. (2011). *Common assumptions vs. the evidence: English language learners in the United States*. Washington, DC: American Institutes for Research.

Gilboy, S. F., McWhirter, J. J., & Wallace, R. (2002). *SOAR: Students' optimistic attribution and resiliency program: A depression prevention and amelioration program*. Unpublished manuscript, Arizona State University.

Gillham, J. E., Reivich, K. J., Jaycox, L. H., & Seligman, M. E. P. (1995). Prevention of depressive symptoms in schoolchildren: Two-year follow-up. *Psychological Science*, 6, 343–351.

Gillies, R. M. (2014). Cooperative learning: Developments in research. International *Journal of Educational Psychology*, 3(2), 125–140. doi: 10.4471/ijep.2014.08

Girls Study Group. (2010). *Causes and correlates of girl's delinquency*. U.S. Department of Justice, Office of Juvenile Justice and Delinquency Prevention. Retrieved from http://permanent.access.gpo.gov/gpo11499/226358.pdf

Glasser, W. (1965). *Reality therapy: A new approach to psychiatry*. New York: Harper & Row.

Glasser, W. (1972). *The identity society*. New York: Harper & Row.

Glasser, W. (1990). The quality school. *Phi Delta Kappan*, 72, 425–435.

Glasser, W. (1998). *Choice theory: A new psychology of personal freedom*. New York: HarperCollins.

Glasser, W. (2001). *Counseling with choice theory: The new reality therapy*. New York: HarperCollins.

Glasser, W. (2002). *Unhappy teenagers: A way for parents and teachers to reach them*. New York: HarperCollins.

Gleason, P., Clark, M., Tuttle, C. C., & Dwoyer, E. (2010). *The evaluation of charter school impacts: Final report* (NCEE 2010-4029). Washington, DC: National Center for Educational Evaluation and Regional Assistance, Institute of Education Sciences, U.S. Department of Education. Retrieved from http://ies.ed.gov/ncee/pubs/20104029/pdf/20104029.pdf

Glenn, C. R., Franklin, J. C., & Nock, M. K. (2015). Evidence-based psychosocial treatments for self-injurious thoughts and behaviors in youth. *Journal of Clinical Child & Adolescent Psychology*, 44, 1–29. doi:10.1080/15374416.2014.945211

Goleman, D. P. (1995). *Emotional intelligence: Why it can matter more than IQ for character, health and lifelong achievement*. New York: Bantam Books.

Gonzales, R. G., Suárez-Orozco, C., & Dedios-Sanguineti, M. C. (2013). No place to belong: Contextualizing concepts of mental health among undocumented immigrant youth in the United States. *American Behavioral Scientist*, 57(8), 1174–1199.

Goodnight, J. A., Lahey, B. B., Van Hulle, C. A., Rodgers, J. L., Rathouz, P. J., Waldman, I. D., & D'Onofrio, B. M. (2012). A quasi-experimental analysis of the influence of neighborhood disadvantage on child and adolescent conduct problems. *Journal of Abnormal Psychology*, 121, 95–108. doi:10.1037/a002507

Goodwin, B., & Miller, K. (2013, March). Research says: Evidence on flipped classrooms is still coming in. *Educational Leadership*, 70, 78–80.

Gordon, E. E., Morgan, R. R., O'Malley, C. J., & Ponticell, J. (2007). *The tutoring revolution*. Lanham, MD: Rowman & Littlefield.

Gordon, R. (1987). An operational classification of disease prevention. In J. A. Steinberg & M. M. Silverman (Eds.), *Preventing mental disorders*. Rockville, MD: U.S. Department of Health and Human Services.

Gordon, T. (2000). *Parent effectiveness training: The proven program for raising responsible children*. New York: Three Rivers Press.

Gordon, T. (2006). *Parent effectiveness training: The tested new way to raise responsible children*. New York: Wyden.

Gosser, D., Kampmeier, J. A., & Varma-Nelson, P. (2010). Peer-led team learning: 2008 James Flack Norris award address. *Journal of Chemical Education*, 87(4), 374–380.

Gould, M. S., Greenberg, T., Velting, D. M., & Shaffer, D. (2003). Youth suicide risk and preventive interventions: A review of the past

10 years. *Journal of American Academy of Child and Adolescent Psychiatry, 42*(4), 386–405.

Gould, M. S., & Kramer, R. A. (2001). Youth suicide prevention. *Suicide and Life Threatening Behavior, 31*(Suppl.), 6–31.

Goyal, M., Singh, S., Sibinga, E. S., Gould, N. F., Rowland-Seymour, A., Sharma, R., …, Haythornthwaite, J. A. (2014). Meditation programs for psychological stress and well-being: A systematic review and meta-analysis. *JAMA Internal Medicine, 174*(3), 357–368. doi:10.1001/jamainternmed.2013.13018

Gragg, K. M., & McWhirter, E. H. (2003). Women, domestic violence, and career counseling: An application of social cognitive career theory. *Journal of Counseling & Development, 81*(4), 418–424.

Granata, K. (2015, March 28). Reports find 'small gains' after common core implementation. Education World. Retrieved from http://www.educationworld.com/a_news/repots-find-small-gains-after- common-core-implementation-2145468248#sthash.BbU95W4e.dpuf

Granello, D. H. (2010). The process of suicide risk assessment: Twelve core principles. *Journal of Counseling and Development, 88*(3), 363–372.

Gray, L., & Taie, S. (2015). *Public school teacher attrition and mobility in the first five years: Results from the first through fifth waves of the 2007–08 beginning teacher longitudinal study.* NCES 2015337. Retrieved from https://nces.ed.gov/pubsearch/pubsinfo.asp?pubid=2015337

Green, R., Waters Boots, K., & Tumlin, C. (1999). The cost of protecting vulnerable children. The Urban Institute. Retrieved from http://www.urban.org

Greene, D. C., Britton, P. J., & Fitts, B. (2014). Long-term outcomes of lesbian, gay, bisexual, and transgender recalled school victimization. *Journal of Counseling & Development, 92,* 406–417. doi:10.1002/j.1556-6676.2014.00167.x

Greenberg, M. T., & Harris, A. R. (2012). Nurturing mindfulness in children and youth: Current state of research. *Child Development Perspectives, 6,* 161–166.

doi:10.1111/j.1750-8606.2011.00215.x

Greenberg, B., Medlock, L., & Stephens, D. (2011). *Blend my learning: Lessons from a blended learning pilot.* Oakland, CA: Envison Schools, Google, & Stanford University D.School. Retrieved from http://blendmylearning.files.wordpress.com/2011/12/lessons-learned-from-a-blended-learning-pilot4.pdf

Grossman, A. H., & D'Augelli, A. R. (2007). Transgender youth and life-threatening behaviors. *Suicide and Life-Threatening Behaviors, 37*(5), 527–537.

Grossman, D. C., Mueller, B. A., Riedy, C., Dowd, M. D., Villaj-Prodzinski, J., Nakagawara, J., …, Harruff, R. (2005). Gun storage practices and risk of youth suicide and unintentional firearm injury. *JAMA: Journal of the American Medical Association, 293*(6), 707–714.

Gunasekera, H., Chapman, S., & Campbell, S. (2005, October 10). Sex and drugs in popular movies: An analysis of the top 200 films. *Journal of the Royal Society of Medicine, 10,* 464–470.

Gutierrez, P. M., Osman, A., Kopper, B. A., Barrios, F. X., & Bagge, C. L. (2000). Suicide risk assessment in a college student population. *Journal of Counseling Psychology, 47*(4), 403–413.

Guttmacher Institute. (2012). *Facts on American teens' sources of information about sex* (In Brief: Fact Sheet). Retrieved from https://www.guttmacher.org/pubs/FB-Teen-Sex-Ed.html

Gysbers, N. C., & Henderson, P. (2012). *Developing and managing your school guidance and counseling program* (5th ed.). Alexandria, VA: American Counseling Association.

Hacker, J. S., & Pierson, P. (2010). *Winner-take-all politics: How Washington made the rich richer—and turned its back on the middle class.* New York: Simon & Schuster.

Hains, A. A., & Ellmann, S. W. (1994). Stress inoculation training as a preventative intervention for high school youths. *Journal of Cognitive Psychotherapy, 8*(3), 219–232.

Hale, D. R., Fitzgerald-Yau, N., & Viner, R. M. (2014). A systematic review of effective interventions for reducing multiple health risk

behaviors in adolescence. *American Journal of Public Health, 104*(5), e19–e41.

Hall, B. C., Stewart, D. G., Arger, C., Athenour, D. R., & Effinger, J. (2014, January 27). Modeling motivation three ways: Effects of MI metrics on treatment outcomes among adolescents. *Psychology of Addictive Behaviors.* Advance online publication. doi:10.1037/a0033845

Halpern, D. F. (2005, July–August). Psychology at the intersection of work and family: Recommendations for employers, working families, and policymakers. *American Psychologist, 60*(5), 397–409.

Hamdan, N., McKnight, P., McKnight, K., & Arfstrom, K. M. (2013). A review of flipped learning. Retrieved from http://flippedlearning.org/cms/lib07/VA01923112/Centricity/Domain/41/LitReview_Flipped Learning.pdf

Hamilton, E., & Klimes-Dougan, B. (2015). Gender differences in suicide prevention responses: Implications for adolescents based on an illustrative review of the literature. *International Journal of Environmental Research and Public Health, 12,* 2359–2372. doi:10.3390/ijerph120302359

Harper, A., & Singh, A. (2014). Supporting ally development with families of trans and gender nonconforming (TGNC) youth. *Journal of LGBT Issues in Counseling, 8*(4), 376–388.

Harter, S. (1985). *Manual for the self-perception profile for children* (revision of the Perceived Competence Scale for Children). Denver, CO: University of Denver.

Hartman, L. B., Shafer, M., Pollack, L., Wibbelsman, C., Changa, F., & Tebb, K. (2013). Parental acceptability of contraceptive methods offered to their teen during a confidential health care visit. *Journal of Adolescent Health, 52,* 251–254.

Hatzenbuehler, M. L. (2011). The social environment and suicide attempts in lesbian, gay, and bisexual youth. *Pediatrics, 127*(5), 896–903.

Hawkins, J. D., Brown, E. C., Oesterle, S., Arthur, M. W., Abbott, R. D., & Catalano, R. F. (2007). Early effects of communities that care on targeted risks and initiation of delinquent behavior and substance use. *Journal of Adolescent Health, 43,* 15–22.

Hawkins, J. D., Herrenkohl, T. I., Farrington, D. P., Brewer, D., Catalano, R. F., Harachi, T. W., & Cothern, L. (2000). *Predicators of youth violence.* Washington, DC: U.S. Department of Justice, Office of Juvenile Justice and Delinquency, Juvenile Justice Bulletin.

Hawkins, J. D., Jenson, J. M., Catalano, R., Fraser, M. W., Botvin, G. J., Shapiro, V., ..., Stone, S. (2015). *Unleashing the power of prevention.* Discussion Paper, Institute of Medicine and National Research Council, Washington, DC.

Hawkins, J. D., Oesterle, S., Brown, E. C., Abbott, R. D., & Catalano, R. F. (2014). Youth problem behaviors 8 years after implementing the communities that care prevention system: A community-randomized trial. *JAMA Pediatrics, 168*(2), 122–129.

Hawkins, J. D., Oesterle, S., Brown, E. C., Arthur, M. W., Abbott, R. D., Fagan, A. A., & Catalano, R. F. (2009). Results of a type 2 translational research trial to prevent adolescent drug use and delinquency. *Archives of Pediatrics and Adolescent Medicine, 163*(9), 790–798.

Healy, K. L., & Sanders, M. R. (2014). Randomized controlled trial of a family intervention for children bullied by peers. *Behavior Therapy, 45,* 760–777. doi:10.1016/j.beth.2014.06.001

Heilbron, N., Goldston, D., Walrath, C., Rodi, M., & McKeon, R. (2013). Suicide risk protocols: Addressing the needs of high risk youths identified through suicide prevention efforts and in clinical settings. *Suicide and Life-Threatening Behavior, 43,* 150–160. doi: 10.1111/sltb.12004

Helker, W. P., & Ray, D. C. (2009). Impact of child teacher relationship training on teachers' and aides' use of relationship-building skills and the effects on student classroom behavior. *International Journal of Play Therapy, 18*(2), 70–83. doi: 10.1037/a0014456.

Henggeler, S. W., & Schoenwald, S. K. (2011). Evidence-based interventions for juvenile offenders and juvenile justice policies that support

them. *Society for Research on Child Development Social Policy Report, 25*(1), 3–28. Retrieved from http://mstservices.com/files/SPR.pdf

Henrichson, C., & Delaney, R. (2012). *The price of prison: What incarceration costs taxpayers.* Center on Sentencing and Corrections. The Vera Institute. Retrieved from http://www.vera.org/sites/default/files/resources/downloads/price-of-prisons-updated-version-021914.pdf

Henry, K. L., Stanley, L. R., Edwards, R. W., Harkabus, L. C., & Chapin, L. A. (2009). Individual and contextual effects of school adjustment on adolescent alcohol use. *Prevention Science, 10*(3), 236–247.

Herreid, C. F., & Schiller, N. A. (2013). Case studies and the flipped classroom. *Journal of College Science Teaching, 42,* 62–66.

Herrmann, D. S., & McWhirter, J. J. (1997). Refusal and resistance skills for children and adolescents: A selected review. *Journal of Counseling and Development, 75,* 177–187.

Herrmann, D. S., & McWhirter, J. J. (2000). *SCARE: Student created aggression replacement education* (2nd ed.). Trainer's manual and student workbook. Dubuque, IA: Kendall/Hunt.

Herrmann, D. S., & McWhirter, J. J. (2001). *The SCARE Program: Student created aggression replacement education.* Dubuque, IA: Kendall Hunt Publishing Company.

Herrmann, D. S., McWhirter, J. J., & Sipsas-Herrmann, A. (1997). The relationship between dimensional self-concept and juvenile gang involvement: Implications for prevention, intervention, and court referred diversion programs. *Behavioral Sciences and the Law, 15,* 181–194.

Hilton, J., Desrochers, S., & Devall, E. L. (2001). Comparison of role demands, relationships, and child functioning in single-mother, single father, and intact families. *Journal of Divorce & Remarriage, 35*(1/2), 29–56.

Himmelstein, K. E., & Brückner, H. (2011). Criminal-justice and school sanctions against nonheterosexual youth: A national longitudinal study. *Pediatrics, 127*(1), 49–57.

Hinduja, S., & Patchin, J. W. (2015a). *Bullying beyond the schoolyard: Preventing and responding to cyberbullying* (2nd ed.). Thousand Oaks, CA: Sage Publications (978-1483349930).

Hinduja, S., & Patchin, J. W. (2015b). What to do when your child cyberbullies others: Top tips for parents. Cyberbullying Research Center. Retrieved from http://cyberbullying.us/tips-for-parents-when-your-child-cyberbullies-others.pdf

Hinduja, S., & Patchin, J. W. (2015c). What to do when your child is cyberbullied: Top ten tips for parents. Cyberbullying Research Center. Retrieved from http://cyberbullying.us/tips-for-parents-when-your-child-is-cyberbullied/

Hirschi, T. (2004). Control theory of delinquency. In J. Jacoby (Ed.), *Classics of criminology* (pp. 294–301). Long Grove, IL: Waveland Press Inc.

Hirschi, T., & Gottfredson, M. (2004). A general theory of crime. In J. Jacoby (Ed.), *Classics of criminology* (pp. 1–567). Long Grove, IL: Waveland Press Inc.

Hockaday, C., Crase, S. J., Shelley, M. C., & Stockdale, D. F. (2000). A prospective study of adolescent pregnancy. *Journal of Adolescence, 23,* 423–438.

Holden, K., McGregor, B., Thandi, P., Fresh, E., Sheats, K., Belton, A., ..., Satcher, D. (2014). Toward culturally centered integrative care for addressing mental health disparities among ethnic minorities. *Psychological Services, 11*(4), 357–368.

Holleran, L. K., & Jung, S. (2005). Acculturative stress, violence, and resilience in the lives of Mexican-American youth. *Stress, Trauma, and Crisis: An International Journal, 8*(23), 107–130.

Hölzel, B. K., Lazar, S. W., Gard, T., Schuman-Olivier, Z., Vago, D. R., & Ott, U. (2011). How does mindfulness meditation work? Proposing mechanisms of action from a conceptual and neural perspective. *Perspectives on Psychological Science, 6,* 537–559.

Hong, J. S., Cho, H., Allen-Meares, P., & Espelage, D. L. (2011). The social ecology of the Columbine High School shootings. *Children and*

Youth Services Review, 33(6), 861–868.

Howell, J. C., & Griffiths, E. (2015). *Gangs in America's communities* (2nd ed.). Los Angeles: Sage.

Huesmann, L. R. (2010). Nailing the coffin shut on doubts that violent video games stimulate aggression: Comment on Anderson et al. *Psychological Bulletin, 136*(2), 179–181.

Hull-Blanks, E. E., Kerr, B. A., & Kurpius, S. E. (2004). Risk factors of suicide ideation attempts in talented, at-risk girls. *Suicide & Life Threatening Behavior, 34*(3), 267–276.

Human Rights Campaign Foundation. (2004). Gay teens and school. Retrieved from http://www.hrc.org

Hunt, J., & Moodie-Mills, A. (2012). The unfair criminalization of gay and transgender youth: An overview of the experiences of LGBT youth in the Juvenile Justice System. Retrieved from https://www.americanprogress.org/wp-content/uploads/issues/2012/06/pdf/juvenile_justice.pdf\

Hunt-Morse, M. C. (2002). *Adolescent mothers' psychosocial development: Implications for parenting* (Unpublished doctoral dissertation), University of Oregon.

Hyldahl, R. S., & Richardson, B. (2011). Key considerations for using no-harm contracts with clients who self-injure. *Journal of Counseling & Development, 89*(1), 121–127.

Jacob, S., Ouvrard, L., & Bélanger, J. (2011). Participatory evaluation and process use within a social aid organization for at-risk families and youth. *Evaluation and Program Planning, 34*(2), 113–123.

Jacobson, E. (1938). *Progressive relaxation* (2nd ed.). Chicago: University of Chicago Press.

Jaffe, E. (2015, July/August). The Golden Goose Award. *Observer, 28*(6).

Jaffee, S. R. (2002). Pathways to adversity in young adulthood among early childbearers. *Journal of Family Psychology, 16*, 38–49.

James-Burdumy, S., Dynarski, M., Moore, M., Deke, J., Mansfield, W., & Pistorino, C. (2005). *When schools stay open late: The national evaluation of the 21st Century Community Learning Centers Program*. Final Report. Document No. PR05-12. Princeton, NJ: Mathematica Policy Research, Inc.

Janosz, M., LeBlanc, M., Boulerice, B., & Tremblay, R. E. (2000). Predicting different types of school dropouts: A typological approach with two longitudinal samples. *Journal of Educational Psychology, 92*(1), 171–190.

Jennings, P. A., Frank, J. L., Snowberg, K. E., Coccia, M. A., & Greenberg, M. T. (2013). Improving Classroom Learning Environments by Cultivating Awareness and Resilience in Education (CARE): Results of a Randomized Controlled Trial. *School Psychology Quarterly, 28*(4), 374–390. doi: 10.1037/spq0000035

Jessor, R. (1991). Risk behavior in adolescence: A psychosocial framework for understanding and action. *Journal of Adolescent Health, 12*, 597–605.

Jessor, R. (1993). Successful adolescent development among youth in high-risk settings. *American Psychologist, 48*, 117–126.

Jessor, R. (2014). Problem behavior theory: A half century of research on adolescent behavior and development. In R. M. Lerner, A. C. Petersen, R. K. Silbereisen, & J. Brooks-Gunn (Eds.),*The developmental science of adolescence: History through autobiography* (pp. 239–256). New York: Psychology Press.

Jeynes, W. (2002). The relationship between the consumption of various drugs by adolescents and their academic achievement. *American Journal of Drug Alcohol Abuse, 28*, 15–35.

Jiang, Y., Ekono, M., & Skinner, C. (2015). Basic facts about low-income children: Children under 18 years, 2013. National Center for Children in Poverty. Retrieved from http://www.nccp.org/publications/pub_1100.html

Jimerson, S., Egeland, B., Sroufe, L. A., & Carlson, B. (2000). A prospective longitudinal study of high school dropouts: Examining multiple predictors across development. *Journal of School Psychology, 38*(6), 525–549.

Jimerson, S. R., Swearer, S. M., & Espelage, D. L. (Eds.). (2009). *Handbook of bullying in schools: An international perspective*. London: Routledge.

Jitendra, A. K., Dupaul, G. J., Someki, F., & Tresco, K. E. (2008). Enhancing academic achievement for children with Attention-Deficit Hyperactivity Disorder: Evidence from school-based intervention research. *Mental Retardation and Developmental Disabilities Research Reviews, 14*(4), 325–330.

Joe, S., Baser, R. S., Neighbors, H. W., Caldwell, C. H., & Jackson, S. J. (2009). 12-Month and lifetime prevalence of suicide attempts among black adolescents in the National Survey of American Life. *Journal of American Academy Child and Adolescent Psychiatry, 48*(3), 271–282.

Johnson, D. W., Johnson, R., & Holubec, E. (1990). *Circles of learning: Cooperation in the classroom*. Edina, MN: Interaction.

Johnson, A. D., Martin, A., & Brooks-Gunn, J. (2011). Who uses child care subsidies? Comparing recipients to eligible non-recipients on family background characteristics and child care preferences. *Children and Youth Services Review, 33*(7), 1072–1083.

Johnston, L. D., O'Malley, P. M., Bachman, J. G., & Schulenberg, J. E. (2011). *Monitoring the future national results on adolescent drug use: Overview of key findings, 2010*. Ann Arbor, MI: Institute for Social Research, University of Michigan. Retrieved from http://www.monitoringthefuture.org/pubs.html

Johnston, L. D., O'Malley, P. M., Miech, R. A., Bachman, J. G., & Schulenberg, J. E. (2014). *Monitoring the future: National survey results on drug use 1975–2013: 2013 Overview: Key findings on adolescent drug use*. Ann Arbor, MI: Institute for Social Research, University of Michigan.

Johnson, R. W., & Butrica, B. A. (2012). *Age disparities in unemployment and reemployment during the Great Recession and recovery*. Brief #3. Urban Institute. Retrieved from http://www.urban.org/sites/default/files/alfresco/publication-pdfs/412574-Age-Disparities-in-Unemployment-and-Reemployment-During-the-Great-Recession-and-Recovery.PDF

Joiner, T. E., Jr., Van Orden, K. A., Witte, T. K., Selby, E. A., Ribeiro, J. D., Lewis, R., & Rudd, M. D. (2009). Main predictions of the Interpersonal-psychological theory of suicidal behavior: Empirical tests in two samples of young adults. *Journal of Abnormal Psychology, 118*, 634–646.

Jones, D. E., Greenberg, M., & Crowley, M., (2015). Early social-emotional functioning and public health: The relationship between kindergarten social competence and future wellness. *American Journal of Public Health, 105*(11), 2283–2290. doi:10.2105/AJPH.2015.302630

Jones, R. N., Sheridan, S. M., & Binns, N. R. (1993). Schoolwide social skills training: Providing preventive services to students at-risk. *School Psychology Quarterly, 8*(1), 57–80.

Jones, T. S. (1998). Research supports effectiveness of peer mediation. *The Fourth R, 82*, 1–25.

Juhnke, G. (1997). After school violence: An adapted critical incident stress debriefing model for student survivors and their parents. *Elementary School Guidance & Counseling, 31*(3), 163–170.

Justice Policy Institute. (2015). *Sticker shock: Calculating the full price tag for youth incarceration.* Washington, DC: Author.

Juvonen, J., Graham, S., & Shuster, M. A. (2003). Bullying among young adolescents: The strong, the weak, and the troubled. *Pediatrics, 112*(6), 1231–1237.

Kabat-Zinn, J. (1994). *Wherever you go there you are: Mindfulness meditation in everyday life.* New York: Hyperion.

Kabat-Zinn, J. (2013). *Full catastrophe living (Revised Edition): Using the wisdom of your body and mind to face stress, pain, and illness.* New York: Bantam Books.

Kahn, D. J., Kazimi, M. M., & Mulvihill, M. N. (2001). Attitudes of New York City high school students regarding firearm violence. *Pediatrics, 107*(5), 1125–1132.

Kaiser Family Foundation. (2005). Sex on T.V. 4. Retrieved from http://www.Kaisernetwork.org/

Kaiser Family Foundation. (2006). *Generation M: Media in the Lives of 8–18 year olds.* Menlo Park, CA: Henry J. Kaiser Family Foundation.

Kaminer, Y. (2005). Cognitive group therapy for aggressive boys. *Journal of the American Academy of Child & Adolescent Psychiatry, 44*, 843.

Kamps, D., & Kay, P. (2001). Preventing problems through social skills instruction. In R. Algozzine & P. Kay (Eds.), *What works: How schools can prevent behavior problems* (pp. 57–84). Thousand Oaks, CA: Corwin Press.

Kann, L., Kinchen, S. A., Shanklin, S. L., Flint, K. H., Hawkins, J., William A., ..., Zaza, S. (2014, June). *Youth risk behavior surveillance—United States, 2013.* Surveillance Summaries. (Report number 63 (SS04); 1-168). Washington, DC: U.S. Government Printing Office. Retrieved from http://www.cdc.gov/mmwr/pdf/ss/ss6304.pdf

Kann, L., O'Malley, O. E., McManus, T., Kinchen, S., Chyen, D., Harris, W. A., Wechsler, H., & Centers for Disease Control and Prevention (CDC). (2011). Sexual identity, sex of sexual contacts, and health risk behaviors among students in grades 9–12—youth risk behavior surveillance, selected sites, United States, 2001–2009. *Morbidity and Mortality Weekly Report, 60*(7), 1–133.

Karcher, M. J. (2004). Connectedness and school violence: A framework for developmental interventions. In E. Gerler (Ed.), *Handbook of school violence* (pp. 7–42). Binghamton, NY: Haworth Press.

Karcher, M. (2007). Cross-age peer mentoring. Research in Action, 7, 8. Alexandria, VA: MENTOR/National Mentoring Partnership.

Karoly, L. A., Kilburn, M. R., & Cannon, J. S. (2005). *Early childhood interventions: Proven results, future promise.* RAND Labor and Population Research Brief (MG-341-PNC, 2005). Retrieved from http://www.rand.org/pubs/research_briefs/2005/RAND_RB9145.pdf

Kato, P. M. (2010). Video games in health care: Closing the gap. *Review of General Psychology, 14*, 113–121.

Kayama, M., Haight, W, Gibson, P. A., & Wilson, R. (2015). Use of criminal justice language in personal narratives of out-of-school suspensions: Black students caregivers, and educators. *Children and Youth Services Review, 51*, 26–35.

Kearns-Bodkin, J. N., & Leonard, K. E. (2008). Relationship functioning among adult children of alcoholics. *Journal of Studies on Alcohol and Drugs, 69*(6), 941–950.

Kellam, S. G., Ling, X., Merisca, R., Brown, C. H., & Ialongo, J. (1998). The effect of the level of aggression in the first grade classroom on the course and malleability of aggressive behavior into middle school. *Development and Psychopathology, 10*, 165–185.

Kellam, S. G., Mackenzie, A. C. L., Brown, C. H., Poduska, J. M., Wang, W., Petras, H., & Wilcox, H. C. (2011). The good behavior game and the future of prevention and treatment. *Addiction Science & Clinical Practice, 6*(1), 73–84.

Kellam, S. G., Reid, J., & Balster, R. L. (2008). Effects of a universal classroom behavior program in first and second grades on young adult outcomes. *Drug and Alcohol Dependence, 95*, 1–104.

Kelley, M. L., Lawrence, H. R., Milletich, R. J., Hollis, B. F., & Henson, J. M. (2015). Modeling risk for child abuse and harsh parenting in families with depressed and substance-abusing parents. *Child Abuse & Neglect, 43*, 42–52.

Kemple, J. J. (2004). *Career Academies: Impacts on labor market outcomes and educational attainment.* New York: Manpower Demonstration Research Corporation.

Kena, G., Musu-Gillette, L., Robinson, J., Wang, X., Rathbun, A., Zhang, J., ..., Dunlop Velez, E. (2015). *The condition of education 2015* (NCES 2015-144). U.S. Department of Education, National Center for Education Statistics. Washington, DC. Retrieved from http://nces.ed.gov/pubs2015/2015144.pdf

Kerr, D. C., DeGarmo, D. S., Leve, L. D., & Chamberlain, P. (2014). Juvenile justice girls' depressive symptoms and suicidal ideation 9 years after multidimensional treatment foster care. *Journal of Consulting and Clinical Psychology, 82*(4), 684–693. doi:10.1037/a0036521

Kessler, R. C., Wang, P., & Zaslavsky, A. M. (2005). Prevalence and treatment of mental disorders: Reply. *New England Journal of Medicine, 353*(11), 1184.

Key, J. D., Barbosa, G. A., & Owens, V. J. (2001). The second chance club: Repeat adolescent pregnancy prevention with a school-based intervention. *Journal of Adolescent Health, 28,* 167–169.

Khoury-Kassabri, M. (2011). Student victimization by peers in elementary schools: Individual, teacher-class, and school-level predictors. *Child Abuse & Neglect, 35*(4), 273–282.

Khurana, A., Romer, D., Betancourt, L. M., Brodsky, N. L., Giannetta, J. M., & Hurt, H. (2012). Early adolescent sexual debut: The mediating role of working memory ability, sensation seeking and impulsivity. *Developmental Psychology, 48*(5), 1416–1428.

Khurana, A., Romer, D., Betancourt, L. M., Brodsky, N. L., Giannetta, J. M., & Hurt, H. (2013). Working memory ability predicts trajectories of early alcohol use in adolescents: The mediational role of impulsivity. *Addiction, 108*(3), 506–515.

Khurana, A., Romer, D., Betancourt, L. M., Brodsky, N. L., Giannetta, J. M., & Hurt, H. (2014). Early experimentation vs. Progression in drug use: A test of an emerging neurobehavioral imbalance model. *Development and Psychopathology,* 1–13.

Khurana, A., Romer, D., Betancourt, L. M., Brodsky, N. L., Giannetta, J. M., & Hurt, H. (2015). Stronger working memory reduces sexual risk Taking in adolescents, even after controlling for parental influences. *Child Development, 86,* 1125–1141. doi:10.1111/cdev.12383

Kiernan, K. E., & Mensah, F. K. (2009). Poverty, maternal depression, family status and children's cognitive and behavioral development in early childhood: A longitudinal study. *Journal of Social Policy, 38*(4), 569–588.

Kirisci, L., Vanyukov, M., & Tarter, R. (2005). Detection of youth at high risk for substance use disorders: A longitudinal study. *Psychology of Addictive Behaviors, 19,* 243–252.

Kirby, D. (2001). *Emerging answers: Research findings on programs to reduce teen pregnancy.* Washington, DC: National Campaign to Prevent Teen Pregnancy.

Kirby, D. B. (2007). *Emerging answers 2007. Research findings on programs to reduce teen pregnancy and sexually transmitted diseases.* Washington, DC: National Campaign to Prevent Teen and Unwanted Pregnancy. Retrieved from http://www.thenationalcampaign.org/EA2007/

Kitts, R. L. (2010). Barriers to optimal care between physicians and lesbian, gay, bisexual, transgender, and questioning adolescent patients. *Journal of Homosexuality, 57*(6), 730–747.

Klein, J. (2012). *The bully society: School shootings and the crisis of bullying in America's schools.* New York: NYU Press.

Klein, K., Forehand, R., & the Family Health Project Research Group. (2000). Family processes as resources for African American children exposed to a constellation of sociodemographic risk factors. *Journal of Clinical Child Psychology, 29*(1), 53–65.

Knoester, C., & Haynie, D. L. (2005). Community context, social integration into family, and youth violence. *Journal of Marriage and Family, 67,* 767–780.

Knudson, J, Shambaugh, L., & O'Day, J. (2011). *Beyond the school: Exploring a systemic approach to school turnaround.* Washington, DC: Policy and Practice Brief, California Collaborative on District Reform, American Institutes for Research. Retrieved from http://www.cacollaborative.org/Portals/0/CA_Collaborative_School_Turnaround.pdf

Kochhar, R., & Morin, R. (2014). Despite recovery, fewer Americans identify as middle class. Pew Research Center. Retrieved from http://www.pewresearch.org/fact-tank/2014/01/27/despite-recovery-fewer-americans-identify-as-middle-class/

Kohl, P. L., Jonson-Reid, M., & Drake, B. (2011). Maternal mental illness and the safety and stability of maltreated children. *Child Abuse & Neglect, 35*(5), 309–318.

Kosciw, J. G., Greytak, E. A., Bartkiewicz, M. J., Boesen, M. J., & Palmer, N. A. (2012). *The 2011 National School Climate Survey: The experiences of lesbian, gay, bisexual and transgender youth in our nation's schools.* Gay, Lesbian & Straight Education Network. Retrieved from http://files.eric.ed.gov/fulltext/ED535177.pdf

Kosciw, J. G., Greytak, E. A., Palmer, N. A., & Boesen, M. J. (2014). *The 2013 National School Climate Survey: The experiences of lesbian, gay, bisexual and transgender youth in our nation's schools.* New York: GLSEN. Retrieved from https://www.glsen.org/

Kozol, J. (2005). *The shame of the nation.* New York: Crown.

Kumpfer, K. L., & Alder, S. (2003). Dissemination of research-based family interventions for the prevention of substance abuse. In Z. Sloboda & W. J. Bukoski (Eds.), *Handbook of drug abuse prevention* (pp. 75–119). New York: Kluwer Academic/Plenum.

Krahn, G. L., Walker, D. K., & Correa-De-Araujo, R. (2015). Persons with disabilities as anunrecognized health disparity population. *American Journal of Public Health, 105*(S2), 198–206.

Kraus, M. W., Côté, S., & Keltner, D. (2010). Social class, contextualism, and empathic accuracy. *Psychological Science, 21*(11), 1716–1723.

Kremer, K. P., Maynard, B. R., Polanin, J. R., Vaughn, M. G., & Sarteschi, C. M. (2015). Effects of after-school programs with at-risk youth on attendance and externalizing behaviors: A systematic review and meta-analysis. *Journal of Youth and Adolescence, 44*(3), 616–636.

Krieshok, T. S., Black, M. D., & McKay, R. A. (2009). Career decision making: The limits of rationality and the abundance of nonconscious processes. *Journal of Vocational Behavior, 75*(3), 275–290.

Krinsky, M. A. (2010). Disrupting the pathway from foster care to the justice system—A former prosecutor's perspectives on reform. *Family Court Review, 48*(2), 322–337. doi: 10.1111/j.1744-1617.2010.01313.x

Krugman, P. (2008, February 18). Poverty is poison. *New York Times.* Retrieved from http://www.nytimes.com/2008/02/18/opinion/18krugman.html

Krumboltz, J. D., & Hamel, D. A. (1977). *Guide to career decision making skills.* New York: College Entrance Examination Board.

Kumpfer, K. L., & Summerhays, J. F. (2006). Prevention approaches to enhance resilience among high-risk youth: Comments on the papers of Dishion & Connell and Greenberg. *Annals of the New York Academy of Science, 1094*, 151–163.

Kumpfer, K. L., & Tait, C. M. (2000). *Family skills training for parents and children*. Bulletin of the Office of Justice Programs, pp. 1–11. Washington, DC: U.S. Department of Justice, Office of Juvenile Justice and Delinquency Prevention.

Kuyken, W., Weare, K., Ukoumunne, O. C., Vicary, R., Motton, N., Burnett, R., …, Huppert, F. (2013). Effectiveness of the Mindfulness in Schools Program: Nonrandomized controlled feasibility study. *The British Journal of Psychiatry, 203*, 126–131. doi:10.1192/bjp.bp.113.126649

Labouliere, C., Kleinman, M., & Gould, M. (2015). When self-reliance is not safe: Associations between reduced help-seeking and subsequent mental health symptoms in suicidal adolescents. *International Journal of Environmental Research and Public Health, 12*(4), 3741–3755. MDPI AG. doi:10.3390/ijerph120403741

Lanctot, N., & Smith, C. A. (2001). Sexual activity, pregnancy, and deviance in a representative urban sample of African-American girls. *Journal of Youth and Adolescence, 30*, 349–372.

Landale, N. S., Hardie, J. H., Oropesa, R. S., & Hillemeier, M. M. (2015). Behavioral functioning among Mexican-origin children: Does parentallegal status matter? *Journal of Health and Social Behavior, 56*(1), 2–18. doi:10.1177/0022146514567896

Lane, P. S., & McWhirter, J. J. (1992). A peer mediation model: Conflict resolution for elementary and middle school children. *Elementary School Guidance and Counseling, 27*(1), 15–24.

Lane, P. S., & McWhirter, J. J. (1996). Creating a peaceful school community: Reconciliation operationalized. *Catholic School Studies, 69*(2), 31–34.

Langman, P. (2015). *School shooters: Understanding high school, college, and adult perpetrators*. Lanham, MD: Rowman & Littlefield.

Lannie, A. L., & McCurdy, B. L. (2007). Preventing disruptive behavior in the urban classroom: Effects of the good behavior game on student and teacher behavior. *Education and Treatment of Children, 30*(1), 85–98.

Larzelere, R. E., Morris, A. S., & Harrist, A. W. (2013). *Authoritative parenting: Synthesizing nurturance and discipline for optimal child development*. Washington, DC: American Psychological Association.

Laursen, E. K., & Birmingham, S. M. (2003). Caring relationships as a protective factor for at-risk youth: An ethnographic study. *Families in Society, 84*(2), 240–246.

Layton, L. (2014, April 28). National high school graduation rates at historic high, but disparities still exist. *The Washington Post*. Retrieved from https://www.washingtonpost.com/local/education/high-school-graduation-rates-at-historic-high/2014/04/28/84eb0122-cee0-11e3-937f-d3026234b51c_story.html

Lazerson, D. B. (2005). Detention home teens as tutors: A cooperative cross-age tutoring pilot project. *Emotional & Behavioural Difficulties, 10*, 7–15.

Lee, R. M., & Robbins, S. B. (2000). Understanding social connectedness in college women and men. *Journal of Counseling and Development, 78*, 484–491.

Lemberger, M. E., & Clemens, E. V. (2012). Connectedness and self-regulation as constructs of the Student Success Skills program in inner-city African American elementary students. *Journal of Counseling & Development, 90*, 450–458. doi:10.1002/j.1556-6676.2012.00056.x

Lemberger, M. E., Selig, J. P., Bowers, H., & Rogers, J. E. (2015). Effects of the Student Success Skills Program on executive functioning skills, feelings of connectedness, and academic achievement in a predominantly Hispanic, low-income middle school district. *Journal of Counseling & Development, 93*, 25–37. doi:10.1002/j.1556-6676.2015.00178.x

Lemstra, M., Bennett, N., Nannapaneni, U., Neudorf, C., Warren, L., Kershaw, T., & Scott, C. (2010). A systematic review of school-based marijuana and alcohol prevention programs targeting adolescents aged 10–15. *Addiction Research & Theory, 18*(1), 84–96. doi:10.3109/16066350802673224

Lenhart, A. (2015). *Teen, social media and technology overview 2015*. Washington, DC: Pew Research Center. Retrieved from http://www.pewinternet.org/2015/04/09/teens-social-media-technology-2015

Lenhart, A., Madden, M., MacGill, A., & Smith, A. (2007). *Teens and social media*. Washington, DC: Pew Internet and American Life Project.

Levin, H., Glass, G., & Meister, G. (1984). *Cost effectiveness of four educational interventions*, Project Report No. 84-A11. Stanford, CA: Institute for Research on Educational Finance and Governance.

Lewis, M. A., Neighbors, C., Lindgren, K. P., Buckingham, K. G., & Hoang, M. (2010). *Social influences on adolescent and young adult alcohol use*. Hauppauge, NY: Nova Science Publishers.

Lieberman, M. (2013). *Social: Why our brains are wired to connect*. New York: Crown.

Lindstrom, L., Harwick, R., Poppen, M., & Doren, B. (2012). Gender gaps: Career development for young women with disabilities. *Career Development and Transition for Exceptional Individuals, 35*(2), 108–117

Liu, R. T., & Mustanski, B. (2012). Suicidal ideation and self-harm in lesbian, gay, bisexual, and transgender youth. *American Journal of Preventive Medicine, 42*(3), 221–228.

Livingston, G. (2014). Four in ten couples saying "I Do" again. Pew Research Center. Retrieved from http://www.pewsocialtrends.org/2014/11/14/four-in-ten-couples-are-saying-i-do-again/

Livingston, G., & Parker, K. (2010). *Since the start of the great recession, more children raised by grandparents*. Washington, DC: Pew Research Center. Retrieved from http://pewsocialtrends.org/assets/pdf/764-children-raised-by-grandparents.pdf

Lloyd-Richardson, E. E. (2010). Non-suicidal self-injury in adolescence. *The Prevention Researcher, 17*(1), 3–7.

Lonczak, H. S., Abbott, R. D., Hawkins, J. D., Kosterman, R., & Catalano, R. F.

(2002). Effects of the Seattle social development project on sexual behavior, pregnancy, birth, and sexually transmitted disease outcomes. *Archives of Pediatrics and Adolescent Medicine, 156*(5), 438–447.

Longoria, V., Adams, E., & Hitter, T. (2014, October). *Contemplating culture: Exploring the use of mindfulness therapies with diverse groups.* Presented at biennial conference of the National Latino Psychological Association, Albuquerque, NM.

Lott, B. (2002). Cognitive and behavioral distancing from the poor. *American Psychologist, 57,* 100–110.

Low, S., Frey, K. S., & Brockman, C. J. (2010). Gossip on the playground: Changes associated with universal intervention, retaliation beliefs, and supportive friends. *School Psychology Review, 39*(4), 536–551.

Luginbuhl, P. J., McWhirter, E. H., & McWhirter, B. T. (2016). Sociopolitical development, autonomous motivation, and education outcomes: Implications for low-income Latina/o adolescents. *Journal of Latina/o Psychology, 4*(1), 43–59. http://dx.doi.org/10.1037/lat0000041

Luthar, S. S., & Barkin, S. H. (2012). Are affluent youth truly "at risk"? Vulnerability and risk across three diverse samples. *Developmental Psychopathology, 24*(2), 429–449.

Lynch, M. (2015). Cause and effect: The high cost of high school dropout. Huff Post Education. Retrieved from huffingtonpost.com

Macdonald, A. (2011). *Solution-focused therapy: Theory, research and practice* (2nd ed.). Sage: London.

MacSwan, J., & Pray, L. (2005). Learning English bilingually: Age of onset of exposure and rate of acquisition of English among children in a bilingual education program [Online]. *Bilingual Research Journal, 29*(3). Retrieved from http://brj.asu.edu/

Madden, G. J., & Bickel, W. K. (Eds.). (2010). *Impulsivity: The behavioral and neurological science of discounting.* Washington, DC: American Psychological Association.

Madill, R. A., Gest, S. D., & Rodkin, P. C. (2014). Students' perceptions of relatedness in the classroom: The roles of emotionally supportive teacher-child interactions, children's aggressive-disruptive behaviors, and peer social preference. *School Psychology Review, 43*(1), 86–105.

Mahatmya, D., & Lohman, B. (2011). Predictors of late adolescent delinquency: The protective role of after-school activities in low-income families. *Children and Youth Services Review, 33*(7), 1309–1317.

Maine, S., Shute, R., & Martin, G. (2001). Educating parents about youth suicide: Responses to suicidal statements, attitudes, and intention to help. *Journal of Suicide and Life Threatening Behavior, 31,* 320–332.

Mainhard, M. T., Brekelmans, M., den Brok, P., & Wubbels, T. (2011). The development of the classroom social climate during the first months of the school year. *Contemporary Educational Psychology, 36*(3), 190–200.

Mallet, C. A. (2014). The "learning disabilities to juvenile detention" pipeline: A case study. *Children & Schools, 36*(3), 147–154.

Maltbia, G. (1991). Cultural diversity as a labor management issue. *Employee Assistance Program Exchange, 21*(5), 26.

Maples, M. F., Packman, J., Abney, P., Daugherty, R. F., Casey, J. A., & Pirtle, L. (2005, Fall). Suicide by teenagers in middle school: A post-vention team approach. *Journal of Counseling & Development, 83*(4), 397–405.

Mares, S. H. W., van der Vorst, H., Engels, R. C. M. E., & Lichtwarck-Aschoff, A. (2011). Parental alcohol use, alcohol-related problems, and alcohol-specific attitudes, alcohol-specific communication, and adolescent excessive alcohol use and alcohol-related problems: An indirect path model. *Addictive Behaviors, 36*(3), 209–216.

Mareschal, P. M. (2005). What makes mediation work: Mediators' perspectives on resolving disputes. *Industrial Relations: A Journal of Economy & Society, 44,* 509–517.

Markey, P. M., & Markey, C. N. (2010). Vulnerability to violent video games: A review and integration of personality research. *Review of General Psychology, 14*(2), 82–91. doi:10.1037/a0019000

Mars, B., Collishaw, S., Hammerton, G., Rice, F., Harold, G. T., Smith, D., ..., Thapar, A. (2015). Longitudinal symptom course in adults with recurrent depression: Impact on impairment and risk of psychopathology in offspring. *Journal of Affective Disorders, 182,* 32–38.

Martin, J. A., Hamilton, B. E., Osterman, M. J. K., Curtin, S. C., & Mathews, T. J. (2015). National Vital Statistics Report. Division of Vital Statistics Center for Disease Control and Prevention Vol. 62 No. 1. Retrieved from http://www.cdc.gov/nchs/data/nvsr/nvsr64/nvsr64_01.pdf

Martin, J. A., Hamilton, B. E., & Ventura, S. J. (2015). *Births: Final Data for 2013.* Hyattsville, MD: National Center for Health Statistics. Retrieved from http://www.hhs.gov/ash/oah/adolescent-health-topics/reproductive-health/teen-pregnancy/trends.html

Martin-Storey, A., & Crosnoe, R. (2012). Sexual minority status, peer harassment, and adolescent depression. *Journal of Adolescence, 35,* 1001–1011.

Martinez, G., Abma, J., & Casey, C. (2010). Educating teenagers about sex in the United States, National Center for Health Statistics Data Brief, No. 44. Retrieved from http://www.cdc.gov/nchs/

Mason, M. J., & Mennis, J. (2010). An exploratory study of the effects of neighborhood characteristics on adolescent substance use. *Addiction Research & Theory, 18*(1), 33–50. doi:10.3109/16066350903019897

Massey, O. T., Armstrong, K., Boroughs, M., Henson, K., & McCash, L. (2005). Mental health services in schools: A qualitative analysis of challenges to implementation, operation, and sustainability. *Psychology in the Schools, 42,* 361–372.

Mather, M. (2010). U.S. children in single-mother families. Population Reference Bureau. Retrieved from http://www.prb.org/pdf10/single-motherfamilies.pdf

Mayer, K. H., Garofalo, R., & Makadon H. J. (2014). Promoting the successful development of sexual and gender minority youths. *American Journal of Public Health, 104*(6), 976–981. doi:10.2105/AJPH.2014.301876

Mayou, R. A., Ehlers, A., & Hobbs, M. (2000). Psychological debriefing for road traffic accident victims: Three year follow-up of a randomized controlled trial. *British Journal of Psychiatry, 176,* 589–593.

Mazza, J. J., & Eggert, L. L. (2001). Activity involvement among suicidal and non-suicidal high-risk and typical adolescents. *Suicide and Life-Threatening Behavior, 31*(3), 265–281.

McCambridge, J., Day, M., Thomas, B. A., & Strang, J. (2011). Fidelity to Motivational Interviewing and subsequent cannabis cessation among adolescents. *Addictive Behaviors, 36*(7), 749–754.

McCreanor, T., & Watson, P. (2004). Resiliency, connectivity and environments: Their roles in theorizing approaches to promoting the well-being of young people. *International Journal of Mental Health Promotion, 6*(1), 39–42.

McGinnis, E. (2011). *Skillstreaming the adolescent. A guide for teaching prosocial skills.* Champaign, IL: Research Press.

McGinnis, E. (2012a). *Skillstreaming the elementary school child. A guide for teaching prosocial skills.* Champaign, IL: Research Press.

McGinnis, E. (2012b). *Skillstreaming in early childhood: A guide for teaching prosocial skills.* Champaign, IL: Research Press.

McGloin, J. M., & Widom, C. S. (2001). Resilience among abused and neglected children grown up. *Development and Psychopathology, 13,* 1021–1038.

McGoldrick, M., Garcia-Preto, N., & Carter, B. (2015). *The expanded family life cycle: Individual, family, and social perspectives* (5th ed.). Old Tappan, NJ: Pearson.

McKown, C., Gumbiner, L. M., Russo, N. M., & Lipton, M. (2010). Social-emotional learning skill, self-regulation, and social competence in typically-developing and clinic-referred children. *Journal of Clinical Child and Adolescent Psychology, 38*(6), 858–871.

McLaughlin, M., & Overturf, B. J. (2012). The common core: Insights into the K–5 standards. *The Reading Teacher, 66*(2), 153–164. doi: 10.1002/TRTR.01115

McLeod, D. A., Jones, R., & Cramer, E. P. (2015). An evaluation of a school-based, peer-facilitated, healthy relationship program for at-risk adolescents. *Children & Schools,* doi:10.1093/cs/cdv006

McMahon, H. G., Mason, E. C. M., Daluga-Guenther, N., & Ruiz, A. (2014). An ecological model of professional school counseling. *Journal of Counseling & Development, 92,* 459–471. doi:10.1002/j.1556-6676.2014.00172.x

McReynolds, R. A., Morris, R. J., & Kratochwill, T. R. (1989). Cognitive-behavioral treatment of school-related fears and anxieties. In J. N. Hughes & R. J. Hall (Eds.), *Cognitive-behavioral psychology in the schools* (pp. 434–465). New York: Guilford Press.

McWhirter, B. T., & Burrow-Sanchez, J. J. (2004). Preventing and treating affective disorders in children and adolescents. In D. Capuzzi & D. Gross (Eds.), *Youth at risk: A prevention resource for counselors, teachers, & parents* (4th ed., pp. 147–179). Alexandria, VA: American Counseling Association.

McWhirter, B. T., & McWhirter, E. H. (2007). Toward an emancipatory communitarian approach to counseling psychology training: The University of Oregon program. In E. Aldarondo (Ed.), *Promoting social justice through mental health practice* (pp. 391–416). New York: Lawrence Erlbaum and Associates.

McWhirter, E. H. (1994). *Counseling for empowerment.* Alexandria, VA: American Counseling Association.

McWhirter, E. H. (1997, April). Empowerment, social activism, and counseling. *Counseling & Human Development, 29*(8), 1–11.

McWhirter, E. H., & McWhirter, B. T. (in press). Critical consciousness and vocational development among Latina/o high school youth: Initial development and testing of a measure. *Journal of Career Assessment, 26*(3). doi:10.1177/10690727 15599535

McWhirter, E. H., & McWhirter, B. T. (2007). Grounding clinical training and supervision in an empowerment model. In E. Aldarondo (Ed.), *Promoting social justice through mental health practice* (pp. 417–442). New York: Lawrence Erlbaum and Associates.

McWhirter, E. H., Ramos, K., & Medina, C. (2013). ¿Y ahora qué? Immigration status barriers and Latina/o high school students' future expectations. *Cultural Diversity and Ethnic Minority Psychology, 19,* 288–297.

McWhirter, E. H., Valdez, M., & Caban, A. R. (2013). Latina adolescents' plans, barriers, and supports: A focus group study. *Journal of Latina/o Psychology, 1*(1), 35–52.

McWhirter, J. J. (2002). Will he choose life? In L. B. Golden (Ed.), *Case studies in child and adolescent counseling* (3rd ed., pp. 81–89). New York: Merrill/Prentice-Hall.

McWhirter, J. J., Herrmann, D. S., Jefferys, K., & Quinn, M. M. (1995). *Violence prevention programs.* Phoenix: Prudential Securities/City of Phoenix.

McWhirter, J. J., McWhirter, B. T., McWhirter, A. M., & McWhirter, E. H. (1995). Youth at-risk: Another point of view. *Journal of Counseling and Development, 73*(5), 567–569.

McWhirter, P. T. (2006). Community therapeutic intervention for women healing from trauma. *Journal for Specialists in Group Work, 31*(4), 1–14.

McWhirter, P. T. (2007). Domestic violence and chemical dependency co-morbidity: Promoting eclectic responses to concomitant mental health concerns. *International Journal of Mental Health Promotion, 9*(1), 34–42.

McWhirter, P. T. (2008a). An empirical evaluation of a collaborative child and family violence prevention and intervention program. In G. R. Walz, J. C. Bleuer, & R. K. Yep (Eds.), *Compelling counseling interventions* (pp. 221–228). Alexandria, VA: Counseling Outfitters, American Counseling Association.

McWhirter, P. T. (2008b). Therapeutic interventions for children who have witnessed domestic violence. In G. R. Walz, J. C. Bleuer, & R. I. Yep (Eds.), *Compelling counseling interventions* (pp. 31–38). Alexandria, VA: Counseling Outfitters, American Counseling Association.

McWhirter, P. T. (1998). Risk factors associated with adolescent alcohol, tobacco, marijuana, solvent inhalant, and cocaine use. *National Institute on Drug Abuse Research Monograph, 179,* 202.

McWhirter, P. T., & McWhirter, J. J. (2010). Community and school violence and risk reduction: Empirically supported prevention. Special Issue on Prevention Groups: Evidence-Based Approaches to Advance the Field. *Group Dynamics: Theory, Research & Practice, 14*(3), 242–256.

McWhirter, P. T., & McWhirter, J. J. (2011). Community and school violence and risk reduction: Empirically supported prevention. Special Issue on Prevention Groups: Evidence-Based Approaches to Advance the Field. *Journal of Group Dynamics: Theory, Research & Practice, 14*(3), 242–256. doi: 10.1037/a0020056

McWhirter, R. J. (2007). *The citizenship flowchart.* Chicago: American Bar Association.

The Media Project. (2015). Teen Health and the Media. Retrieved from http://depts.washington.edu/thmedia/view.cgi?section=medialiteracy&page=fastfacts

Medline Plus. (2011). Adolescent pregnancy. Retrieved from https://www.nlm.nih.gov/medlineplus/ency/article/001516.htm

Mehta. M. (2015). Escaping the shadow: A Nation at Risk and its far-reaching influence. *American Educator, 39*(2), 20–26.

Meier, D., Kohn, A., Darling-Hammond, L., Sizer, T. R., & Wood, G. (2004). *Many children left behind: How the No Child Left Behind Act is damaging our children and our schools.* New York: Beacon Press.

Menesses, K. F., & Gresham, F. M. (2009). Relative efficacy of reciprocal and nonreciprocal peer tutoring for students at-risk for academic failure. *School Psychology Quarterly, 24*(4), 266–275. doi:10.1037/a0018174

Mermelstein, L. C., & Garske, J. P. (2014). A brief mindfulness intervention for college student binge drinkers: A pilot study. *Psychology of Addictive Behaviors.* doi:10.1037/adb0000040

Meyer, K. (2014). Making meaning in mathematics problem-solving using the reciprocal teaching approach. *Australian Journal of Language & Literacy, 37*(2), 7–14.

Michenbaum, D. (1972). *Clinical implications of modifying what clients say to themselves.* Research Reports in Psychology, 42. Waterloo, ON: University of Waterloo.

Mikulincer, M., & Shaver, P. R. (2014). *Mechanisms of social connection: From brain to group.* Washington, DC: American Psychological Association.

Miller, M., Azrael, D., & Hemenway, D. (2002). Firearm availability and unintentional firearm deaths, suicide, and homicide among 5–14 year olds. *Journal of Trauma, 52*(2), 267–275.

Miller, M., Borges, G., Orozco, R., Mukamal, K., Rimm, E. B., Benjet, C., & Medina-Mora, M. E. (2011). Exposure to alcohol, drugs and tobacco and the risk of subsequent suicidality: Findings from the Mexican Adolescent Mental Health Survey. *Drug and Alcohol Dependence, 113*(2–3), 110–117.

Miller, W. R., & Rollnick, S. (2012). *Motivational interviewing: Helping people change* (Applications of Motivational Interviewing). (3rd ed.). New York: Guilford Press.

Miranda, R., DeJaegere, E., Restifo, K., & Shaffer, D. (2014). Longitudinal follow-up study of adolescents who report a suicide attempt: Aspects of suicidal behavior that increase risk of a future attempt. *Depression and Anxiety, 31*, 19–26. doi:10.1002/da.22194

Mitsopoulou, E., & Giovazolias, T. (2015). Personality traits, empathy and bullying behavior: A meta-analytic approach. *Aggression and Violent Behavior, 21*, 61–72.

Mojtabai, R., Stuart, E. A., Hwang, I., Eaton, W. W., Sampson, N., & Kessler, R. C. (2015). Long-term effects of mental disorders on educational attainment in the National Comorbidity Survey ten-year follow-up. *Social Psychiatry and Epidemiology, 50*(10), 1577–1591. doi:10.1007/s00127-015-1083-5

Monastra, V. J. (2015). *Teaching life skills to children and teens with ADHD: A guide for parents and counselors.* Washington, DC: American Psychological Association.

Montgomery, K. L., Thompson, S. J., & Barczyk, A. N. (2011). Individual and relationship factors associated with delinquency among throwaway adolescents. *Children and Youth Services Review, 33*(7), 1127–1133.

Moon, M., McFarland, M. W., Kellogg, T., Baxter, M., Katz, M., MacKellar, D., & Valleroy, L. (2000). HIV risk behavior of runaway youth in San Francisco: Age of onset and relation to sexual orientation. *Youth and Society, 32*(2), 184–201.

Moore, J. (2005, July). Quality in after-school programs: After-school project of the Robert Wood Johnson Foundation. *Youth Today.* (For a free 79-page copy contact JoAnne Vellardita at vellardita@theafterschoolproject.org.)

Moran, K., & Milsom, A. (2015). The flipped classroom in counselor education. *Counselor Education & Supervision, 54*, 32–43. doi:10.1002/j.15566978.2015.00068.x

Morgan, R. E., Kemp, J., Rathbun, A., Robers, S., & Synder, T. D. (2014). *Indicators of school crime and safety, 2013.* National Criminal Justice Reference Service (NCJRS) NCJ 243209. Retrieved from http://www.bjs.gov/content/pub/pdf/iscs13.pdfhttps://www.ncjrs.gov/yviolence/statistics.html

Morin, R. (2011). The public renders a split verdict on changes in family structure. Pew Research Center's Social & Demographic Trends. Retrieved from http://www.pewsocialtrends.org

Morin, R., & Kochhar, R. (2010). Lost income, lost friends—and loss of self-respect. The impact of long-term unemployment. Pew Research Center's Social & Demographic Trends Project. Retrieved from http://pewsocialtrends.org

Morris, D. S., Fiala, S. C., & Pawlak, R. (2012). Opportunities for policy interventions to reduce youth hookah smoking in the United States. *Preventing Chronic Disease, 9*, 120082. doi:10.5888/pcd9.120082

Moskos, M. A., Achilles, J., & Gray, D. (2004). Adolescent suicide myths in the United States. *Crisis: The Journal of Crisis Intervention and Suicide Prevention, 25*(4), 176–182.

Moule, R. K., Pyrooz, D. C., & Decker, S. H. (2014). Internet adoption and online behaviour among American street gangs: Integrating gangs and organizational theory. *British*

Journal of Criminology, 54(6), 1186–1206. doi:10.1093/bjc/azu050

Mrazek, P. J., & Hagerty, R. J. (Eds.). (1994). *Reducing risks for mental disorders: Frontiers for preventive intervention research*. Washington, DC: National Academy Press.

Mulvey, E. P., Schubert, C. A., & Chassin, L. (2010). *Substance use and delinquent behavior among serious adolescent offenders*. Washington, DC: Office of Justice Programs Office of Juvenile Justice and Delinquency Prevention U.S. Department of Justice.

Murphy, J. J. (2015). *Solution-focused counseling in schools* (3rd ed.). Alexandria, VA: American Counseling Association.

Murphy, J., & Tobin, K. (2011). *Homelessness comes to school*. Thousand Oaks, CA: Corwin Press.

Murry, V. M., Simons, R. L., Simons, L. G., & Gibbons, F. X. (2013). Contributions of family environment and parenting processes to sexual risk and substance use of rural African American males: A 4-year longitudinal analysis. *American Journal of Orthopsychiatry, 83*(2–3), 299–309. doi:10.1111/ajop.12035

Naar-King, S., Ellis, D., King, P. S., Lam, P., Cunningham, P., Secord, E., ..., Templin, T. (2014). Multisystemic therapy for high-risk African American adolescents with asthma: A randomized clinical trial. *Journal of Consulting and Clinical Psychology, 82*, 536–545. doi: 10.1037/a0036092

Naar-King, S., & Suarez, M. (2011). *Motivational interviewing with adolescents and young adults*. New York: Guilford Press.

Nakkula, M. J., Foster, K. C., Mannes, M., & Bolstrom, S. (2010). *Building healthy communities for positive youth development*. New York: Springer Science Business Media. doi:10.1007/978-1-4419-5744-3

National Alliance for Public Charter Schools. (2014). A growing movement: America's largest charter school communities. Retrieved from http://publiccharters.org/publication/?id=902

National Alliance for Public Charter Schools. (2015). *Estimated number of public charter schools & students, 2014–2015*. Washington, DC:

Author. Retrieved from http://publiccharters.org/publication/?id=902

National Alliance to End Homelessness. (2014). The state of homelessness in America 2014. Retrieved from http://www.endhomelessness.org/library/entry/the-state-ofhomelessness-2014

National Campaign to Prevent Teen Pregnancy. (2001, May). *Emerging answers: Research findings on programs to reduce teen pregnancy*. Washington, DC: Author.

National Campaign to Prevent Teen Pregnancy. (2005). The What if? project: What if teen birth rates in each state had not declined between 1991 and 2002? Retrieved from www.teenpregnancy.org/whycare/whatif.asp

National Campaign to Prevent Teen Pregnancy/Child Trends. (2005). *Not yet: Programs to delay first sex among teens*. Retrieved from www.teenpregnancy.org/works/pdf/NotYet.pdf

National Campaign to Prevent Teen Pregnancy. (2001). *Halfway there: A prescription for continued progress in preventing teen pregnancy*. Washington, DC: Author

National Campaign to Prevent Teen Pregnancy. (2002). *Not just another single issue: Teen pregnancy prevention's link to other critical social issues*. Washington, DC.

National Center for Education Statistics. (2006). *Internet access in U.S. public schools and classrooms: 1994–2005* (NCES 2007-020). Washington, DC: U.S. Department of Education. Retrieved from http://nces.ed.gov/

National Center for Education Statistics. (2010). *America's children in brief: Key national indicators of well-being, 2010*. National Assessment of Educational Progress. Washington, DC: U.S. Department of Education. Retrieved from http://nces.ed.gov/

National Center for Education Statistics. (2014). Charter school enrollment. Condition of Education 2014. Retrieved from http://nces.ed.gov/programs/coe/

National Center for Family Homelessness. (2015). Retrieved from http://new.homelesschildrenamerica.org/mediadocs/275.pdf2015

National Center on Addiction and Substance Abuse. (2005). *Criminal neglect: Substance abuse, juvenile*

justice and the children left behind. Retrieved from www.casacolumbia.org/pdshopprov/files/JJreport.pdf

National Commission on Excellence in Education. (1983). *A nation at risk: The imperative for educational reform*. Washington, DC: U.S. Government Printing Office.

National Council of Teachers of English. (NCTE /2014). Why class size matters. Position statement, National Council of Teachers of English. Retrieved from http://www.ncte.org/positions/statements/why-class-size-matters

National Gang Center. (2013). National Youth Gang Survey Analysis. Retrieved from http://www.nationalgangcenter.gov/Survey-Analysis

National Institutes of Drug Abuse. (2011). Behavior game played in primary grades reduces later drug-related problems. *NIDA Notes, 23*(1), 6–9. Retrieved from http://www.drugabuse.gov

National Institute of Drug Abuse. (2015). DrugFacts: Marijuana. Retrieved from http://www.drugabuse.gov/publications/drugfacts/marijuana

National Institute on Drug Abuse. (2015). High school and youth trends. Retrieved from http://www.drugabuse.gov/publications/drugfacts/high-school-youth-trends

National Institutes of Health Consensus Development Program. (2004). *Preventing violence and related health-risking social behaviors in adolescents* (Draft Statement). Retrieved from http://consenses.nih.gov/ta/023/youthviolence DRAFTstatement101504.pdf

National Low Income Housing Coalition. (2013). *Out of reach 2013*. Washington, DC: Author. Retrieved from http://nlihc.org/oor/2013

National Organization for Human Services. (2015). *Social justice standards*. Washington, DC: Author. Retrieved from http://www.nationalhumanservices.org/about-us-page

Neihart, M., Reis, S. M., Robinson, N. M., & Moon, S. M. (2002). *The social and emotional development of gifted children: What do we know?* Washington, DC: National Association for Gifted Children.

Neimeic, C. P., & Ryan, R. M. (2009). Autonomy, competence, and relatedness in the classroom: Applying self-determination theory to educational practice. *Theory and Research in Educational Practice*, 7(2), 133–144.

Nelson, T. S., & Thomas, F. N. (2012). *Handbook of solution-focused brief therapy: Clinical applications* (2nd ed.). New York: Routledge.

Nelson-Royes, A. M. (2015). *Why tutoring?: A way to achieve success in school*. Lanham, MD: Rowman & Littlefield.

Newman-Carlson, D., & Horne, A. M. (2004). Bully-busters: A psychoeducational intervention for reducing bullying behavior in middle school students. *Journal of Counseling & Development*, 82(3), 259–267.

Noell, J. W., & Ochs, L. M. (2001). Relationship of sexual orientation to substance use, suicidal ideation, suicide attempts, and other factors in a population of homeless adolescents. *Journal of Adolescent Health*, 29(1), 31–36.

Noer, M. (2012). One man, one computer, 10 million students: How Khan Academy is reinventing education. *Forbes*. Archived from the original on June 29, 2015–.

Novaco, R. W. (1975). *Anger control: The development and evaluation of an experimental treatment*. Lexington, MA: Heath.

Novaco, R. W. (1979). Anger and coping with stress. In J. Foreyt & D. Rathjen (Eds.), *Cognitive behavior therapy: Therapy, research and practice* (pp. 135–161). New York: Plenum Press.

Nowotny, K. M., & Graves, J. L. (2013). Substance use and intimate partner violence victimization among White, African American, and Latina women. *Journal of Interpersonal Violence*, 28(17), 3301–3318. doi:10.1177/0886 260513496903

O'Connell, M. E., Boat, T., & Warner, K. E. (2009). *Preventing mental, emotional, and behavioral disorders among young people: Progress and possibilities*. Washington, DC: National Academies Press.

Organization for Economic Co-operation and Development [OECD]. (2014). Country notes: United States. Programme for international student assessment (PISA) results from PISA 2012. Retrieved from http://www.oecd.org/unitedstates/PISA-2012-results-US.pdf

Organization for Economic Co-operation and Development [OECD]. (2015). *In it together: Why less inequality benefits all*. Paris: OECD Publishing. Retrieved from http://www.oecd-ilibrary.org/employment/in-it-together-why-less-inequality-benefits-all_978926 4235120-en

Oesterle, S. J., Hawkins, J. D., Fagan, A. A., Abbott, R. D., & Catalano, R. F. (2013). Variation in the sustained effects of the communities that care prevention system on adolescent smoking, delinquency, and violence. *Prevention Science*, 15 (2), 138–145.

Office of Juvenile Justice and Delinquency Prevention. (2005). *Juvenile arrests 2002*. Retrieved from http://www.ncjrs.org/pdffiles1/ojjdp/204608.pdf

Office of Juvenile Justice and Delinquency Prevention. (2010). *America's children in brief: Key national indicators of well-being, 2010*. Retrieved from http://www.child-stats.gov/pdf/ac2010/ac_10.pdf

Office of Juvenile Justice and Delinquency Prevention. (2014). School crime victimization. Retrieved from http://www.ojjdp.gov/ojstatbb/victims/qa02203.asp?qaDate=2010

Office of Management and Budget. (2015). Fiscal Year 2015 Budget of the U.S. Government. Retrieved from http://www.gpo.gov/fdsys/pkg/BUDGET-2015-BUD/pdf/BUDGET-2015-BUD.pdf

Office of Program Policy Analysis & Government Accountability. (2010). *Juvenile justice students face barriers to high school graduation and job training*. Report No. 10-55. Retrieved from http://www.oppaga.state.fl.us/MonitorDocs/Reports/pdf/1055rpt.pdf

Oh, S. S., & Cooc, N. (2011). Immigration youth and education. *Harvard Education Review*, 81(3), 397–406.

O'Keeffe, G. S., & Clarke-Pearson, K. (2011). Clinical Report: The impact of social media on children, adolescents, and families. American Academy of Pediatrics. Retrieved from http://pediatrics.aappublications.org/content/127/4/800.full.pdf+html

Olfson, M., Shaffer, D., Marcus, S. C., & Greenberg, T. (2003). Relationship between antidepressant medication treatment and suicide in adolescents. *Archives of General Psychiatry*, 60, 978–982.

Opperman, K., Czyz, E. K., Gipson, P. Y., & King, C. A. (2015). Connectedness and perceived burdensomeness among adolescents at elevated suicide risk: An examination of the Interpersonal Theory of Suicidal Behavior. *Archives of Suicide Research*, 19(3), 385–400. doi:10.1080/13811118.2014. 957451 Online publication date: 4-mar-2015

Organization for Economic Co-operation and Development. (2010). *Growing unequal? Income distribution and poverty in OECD countries*. Retrieved from http://www.oecd.org/els/s

Organization for Economic Co-operation and Development. (2014). Program for International Student Assessment (PISA), Institute of Educational Science, National Center for Education Statistics. Washington, DC.

Organization for Economic Co-operation and Development. (2015). *In it together: Why less inequality benefits all*. OECD Publishing: Paris. Retrieved from http://www.oecd-ilibrary.org/employment/in-it-together-why-less-inequality-benefits-all_978926 4235120-en

Ortega, R., & Sánchez V. (2011). Juvenile dating and violence. In C. P. Monks & I. Coyne (Eds.), *Bullying in different contexts* (pp. 113–136). New York: Cambridge University Press.

Ortiz, C., & Del Vecchio, T. (2013). Cultural diversity: Do we need a new wake-up call for parent training? *Behavior Therapy*, 44, 443–458. doi:0005-7894/44/443-458

Outhred, T., & Chester, A. (2010). The experience of class tutors in a peer tutoring programme: A novel theoretical framework. *Australasian Journal of Peer Learning*, 3(1), 12–23.

Page, J. W., Daniels, J. A., & Craig, S. J. (2015). School violence: Correlates, interventions, and prevention. Monograph for the Springer Behavioral Criminology Series, V. Van Hasselt, Editor. New York: Springer.

Pajares, F., & Urdan, T. (Eds.). (2006). *Self-efficacy beliefs of adolescents.* Greenwich, CT: Information Age.

Paquette, K., & Bassuk, E. (2009). Parenting and homelessness: Overview and introduction to the special section. *American Journal of Orthopsychiatry, 79,* 292–298.

Park, S. W., & Kim, C. M. (2015). *Boosting learning-by-teaching in virtual tutoring. Computers & Education, 82,* 129–140. doi:10.1016/j.compedu.2014.11.006

Patterson, G. R., Crosby, L., & Vuchinich, S. (1992). Predicting risk for early police arrest. *Journal of Quantitative Criminology, 8*(4), 335–355.

Patterson, G. R., De Baryshe, B. D., & Ramsey, E. (1989). A developmental perspective on antisocial behavior. *American Psychologist, 44*(2), 329–335.

Pattij, T., & Vanderschuren, L. J. M. J. (2008). The neuropharmacology of impulsive behaviour. *Trends in Pharmacological Sciences, 29*(4), 192–199. doi:10.1016/j.tips.2008.01.002

Paul, K. I., & Moser, K. (2009). Unemployment impairs mental health: Meta-analyses. *Journal of Vocational Behavior, 74,* 264–282.

Pedlow, C. T., & Carey, M. P. (2004). Developmentally appropriate sexual risk reduction interventions for adolescents: Rationale, review of interventions, and recommendations for research and practice. *Annals of Behavioral Medicine, 27,* 172–184.

Pelligrini, A. D. (2002). Bullying, victimization, and sexual harassment during the transition to middle school. *Educational Psychologist, 37*(3), 151–163.

Peters, E. N., Khondkaryan, E., & Sullivan, T. P. (2012). Associations between expectancies of alcohol and drug use, severity of partner violence, and posttraumatic stress among women. *Journal of Interpersonal Violence, 27*(11), 2108–2127. doi:10.1177/0886260511432151

Petersen, K. (2012a). *Activities for building character and social-emotional learning: Grades 1–2.* Minneapolis, MN: Free Spirit.

Petersen, K. (2012b). *Activities for building character and social-emotional learning: Grades 3–5.* Minneapolis, MN: Free Spirit.

Petersen, K. (2012c). *Activities for building character and social-emotional learning: Grades 6–8.* Minneapolis, MN: Free Spirit.

Petersen, K. (2012d). *Activities for building character and social-emotional learning: Grades Pre K–K.* Minneapolis, MN: Free Spirit.

Peterson, C., Maier, S., & Seligman, M. (1993). *Learned helplessness.* New York: Oxford.

Pew Research Center. (2011). *Twenty to one: Wealth gaps rise to record highs between whites, blacks and Hispanics.* Retrieved from http://www.pewsocialtrends.org/files/2011/07/SDT-Wealth-Report_7-26-11_FINAL.pdf

Piers, E. V. (1984). *Piers-Harris children's self-concept scale* (Rev. ed.). Nashville, TN: Counselor Recordings and Tests.

Planned Parenthood. (2014). Last updated January 2014 © 2013 Planned Parenthood Federation of America, Inc. Retrieved from https://www.plannedparenthood.org/files/9313/9611/7194/Planned_Parenthood_By_The_Numbers.pdf

Plunk, A. D., Tate, W. F., Bierut, L. J., & Grucza, R. A. (2014). Intended and unintended effects of state-mandated high school science and mathematics course graduation requirements on educational attainment. *Educational Research, 43*(5), 230–241.

Plunkett, M., & Mitchell, C. M. (2000). Substance use rates among American Indian adolescents: Regional comparisons with monitoring the future high school seniors. *Journal of Drug Issues, 30,* 575–592.

Pokhrel, P., Herzog, T. A., Black, D. S., Zaman, A., Riggs, N. R., & Sussman, S. (2013). Adolescent neurocognitive development, self-regulation, and school-based drug use prevention. *Prevention Science, 14*(3), 218–228. doi: 10.1007/s11121-012-0345-7

Pong, S., & Ju, D. (2000). The effects of change in family structure and income on dropping out of middle and high school. *Journal of Family Issues, 21*(2), 147–169.

Ponnet, K. (2014). Financial stress, parent functioning and adolescent problem behavior: An actor-partner interdependence approach to family stress processes in low-, middle-, and high-income families. *Journal of Youth & Adolescence, 43*(10), 1752–1769. doi:10.1007/s10964-014-0159-y.

Ponterotto, J. G. (2010). Multicultural personality: An evolving theory of optimal functioning in culturally heterogeneous societies. *The Counseling Psychologist, 38*(5), 714–758.

Povich, D., Roberts, B., & Mather, M. (Winter, 2014–15). Low-income working families: The racial/ethnic divide. The Working Poor Families Project. Retrieved from http://www.workingpoorfamilies.org/wp-content/uploads/2015/03/WPFP-2015-Report_Racial-Ethnic-Divide.pdf

Powell, S. R., Fuchs, L. S., & Fuchs, D. (2013). Reaching the mountaintop: Addressing the Common Core Standards in mathematics for students with mathematics difficulties. *Learning Disabilities Research & Practice, 28,* 38–48. doi:10.1111/ldrp.12001

Powers, C. J., Bierman, K. L., & the Conduct Problems Prevention Research Group. (2013). The multifaceted impact of peer relations on aggressive-disruptive behavior in early elementary school. *Developmental Psychology, 49*(6), 1174–1186. doi:10.1037/a0028400

Premack, D. (1965). Reinforcement theory. In D. Levin (Ed.), *Nebraska symposium on motivation: 1965.* Lincoln: University of Nebraska Press.

Preston, A. S., Heaton, S. C., McCann, S. J., Watson, W. D., & Selke G. (2009). The role of multidimensional attentional abilities in academic skills of children with ADHD. *Journal of Learning Disabilities, 42*(3), 240–249.

Prilleltensky, I. (1997). Values, assumptions and practices: Assessing the moral implications of psychological discourse and action. *American Psychologist, 52*(5), 517–535.

Prochaska, J. O. (2013). *Transtheoretical model of behavior change.* Encyclopedia of Behavioral Medicine. New York: Springer

Prochaska, J. O., & DiClemente, C. C. (1992). Stages of change in the modification of problem behaviors. In J. O. Prochaska (Ed.), *Progress in behavior modification* (pp. 184–218). New York: Academic Press.

Prothrow-Stith, D. (2001). Youth, risk, and resilience: Community approaches to violence prevention. In J. M. Richmond & M. W. Fraser (Eds.), *The context of youth violence: Resilience, risk, and protection* (pp. 97–114). Westport, CT: Praeger.

Public Agenda. (2005). *All work and no play? Listening to what kids and parents really want from out-of-school time.* Retrieved from http://www.publicagenda.org/research/pdfs/all_work_no_play.pdf

Pugh, K. L., & Farrell, A. D. (2012). The impact of maternal depressive symptoms on adolescents' aggression: Role of parenting and family mediators. *Journal of Child and Family Studies, 21,* 589–602. doi: 10.1007/s10826-011-9511-y

Pyrooz, D. C., Decker, S. H., & Webb, V. J. (2014). The ties that bind: Desistance from gangs. *Crime & Delinquency, 60,* 491–516. doi: 10.1177/0011128710372191

Ragatz, L. L., Anderson, R. J., Fremouw, W., & Schwartz, R. (2011). Criminal thinking patterns, aggression styles, and the psychopathic traits of late high school bullies and bully-victims. *Aggressive Behavior, 37*(2), 145–160.

Ramey, H. L., Busseri, M. A., Khanna, N., & Rose-Krasnor, L. (2010). Youth engagement and suicide risk: Testing a mediated model in a Canadian community sample. *Journal of Youth and Adolescence, 39,* 243–258.

Ramírez García, R., Jorge, I., Manongdo, J. A., & Cruz-Santiago, M. (2010). The family as mediator of the impact of parent–youth acculturation/enculturation and inner-city stressors on Mexican American youth substance use. *Cultural Diversity and Ethnic Minority Psychology, 16*(3), 404–412.

Randell, B., Eggert, L. L., & Pike, K. (2001). Immediate post intervention effects of two brief youth suicide prevention interventions. *Suicide and Life-Threatening Behavior, 31*(1), 41–61.

Rapee, R. M. (2009). Early adolescents' perceptions of their mother's anxious parenting as a predictor of anxiety symptoms 12 months later. *Journal of Abnormal Child Psychology, 37,* 1103–1112.

Ratcliffe, C., & McKernan, S-M. (2010). *Childhood poverty persistence: Facts and consequences Brief 14.* Washington, DC: The Urban Institute. Retrieved from http://www.urban.org

Reddy, M., Borum, R., Berglund, J., Vossekuil, B., Fein, R., & Modzeleski, W. (2001). Evaluating risk for targeted violence in schools: Comparing risk assessment, threat assessment, and other approaches. *Psychology in the Schools, 38*(2), 157–172.

Reichenberg, M., & Lofgren, K. (2014). An intervention study in Grade 3 based upon reciprocal teaching. *Journal of Education and Learning, 8*(2), 122–131.

Reupert, A., Maybery, D., Nicholson, J., Gopfert, M., & Seeman, M. V. (Eds.). (2015). *Parental psychiatric disorder: Distressed parents and their families* (3rd ed.). Cambridge: Cambridge University Press.

Reyes, M. R., Brackett, M. A., Rivers, S. E., White, M., & Salovey, P. (2012). Classroom emotional climate, student engagement, and academic achievement. *Journal of Educational Psychology, 104*(3), 700–712. doi: 10.1037/a00272668

Reynolds, A. J., Rolnick, A. J., & Temple, J. A. (2015). *Health and education in early childhood: Predictors, interventions, and policies.* Cambridge, England: Cambridge University Press.

Reynolds, K. A., Walker, J. R., Walsh, K., & The Mobilizing Minds Research Group. (2014). How well do websites concerning children's anxiety answer parents' questions about treatment choices? *Clinical Child Psychology and Psychiatry.* Advanced online publication. doi: 10.1177/ 1359104514534948

Rice, E., Milburn, N. G., Rotheram-Borus, M. J., Mallett, S., & Rosenthal, D. (2005). The effects of peer group network properties on drug use among homeless youth. *American Behavioral Scientist, 48,* 1102–1123.

Rigby, K. (2011). *The method of shared concerned.* Melbourne: Australian Council for Educational Research (ACER Press).

Rishel, C. W. (2007). Evidence-based prevention practice in mental health: What is it and how do we get there? *American Journal of Orthopsychiatry, 77*(1), 153–164.

Rivers, I., & Noret, N. (2010). Participant roles in bullying behavior and their association with thoughts of ending one's life. *Crisis: The Journal of Crisis Intervention and Suicide Prevention, 31*(3), 143–148.

Robbins, M. S., Feaster, D. J., Horigian, V. E., Puccinelli, M. J., Henderson, C., & Szapocznik, J. (2011). Therapist adherence in brief strategic family therapy for adolescent drug abusers. *Journal of Consulting and Clinical Psychology, 79*(1), 43–53.

Robinson, D., Schofield, J. W., & Steers-Wentzell, K. L. (2005). Peer and cross-age tutoring in math: Outcomes and their design implications. *Educational Psychology Review, 17*(4), 327–362.

Robinson Kurpius, S. E., Kerr, B., & Harkins, A. (Eds.). (2005). *Handbook for counseling girls and women: Ten years of gender equity research at Arizona State University. Vol. 1:* Talent, risk and resiliency. Vol. 2: Talent development. Mesa, AZ: MTR Nueva Science.

Rodkin, P. C., & Hodges, E. V. E. (2003). Bullies and victims in the peer ecology: Four questions for psychologists and school professionals. *School Psychology Review, 32,* 384–400.

Rohde, P., Lewinsohn, P. M., Klein, D. N., & Seeley, J. R. (2005). Association of parental depression with psychiatric course from adolescence to young adulthood among formerly depressed individuals. *Journal of Abnormal Psychology, 114,* 409–420.

Romano, J. L. (2014). *Prevention psychology: Enhancing personal and social well-being.* Washington, DC: APA Books.

Romano, J. L., & Hage, S. M. (2000). Prevention and counseling psychology: Revitalizing commitments for the 21st century. *The Counseling Psychologist, 28,* 733–763.

Romer, D., Duckworth, A. L., Sznitman, S., & Park, S. (2010). Can adolescents learn self-control? Delay of gratification in the development of control over risk taking. *Prevention Science, 11*(3), 319–330. doi: 10.1007/s11121-010-0171-8

Rose, S., Bisson, J., & Wessely, S. (2001). Psychological debriefing for preventing post traumatic stress disorder (PTSD) (Cochrane Review) [Abstract]. Cochrane Library, 4.

Rosen, J. A., & Chen, X. (2015). High school dropouts and stopouts: Demographic backgrounds, academic experiences, engagement, and school characteristics. Institute of Education Sciences. U.S. Department of Education. Retrieved from nces.ed.gov/pubs2015/2015066.pdf

Roseth, C. J., Johnson, D. W., & Johnson, R. T. (2008). Promoting early adolescents' achievement and peer relationships: The effects of cooperative, competitive, and individualistic goal structures. *Psychological Bulletin, 134*(2), 223–246.

Rosser, R., Stevens, S., & Ruiz, B. (2005). Cognitive markers of adolescent risk taking: A correlate of drug abuse in at-risk individuals. *Prison Journal, 85,* 83–86.

Rotheram-Borus, M. J., & Langabeer, K. A. (2001). Developmental trajectories of gay, lesbian, and bisexual youths. In A. R. D'Augelli & C. J. Patterson (Eds.), *Lesbian, gay, and bisexual identities and youth* (pp. 97–128). New York: Oxford University Press.

Rothstein, R. (2004). *Class and schools: Using social, economic and educational reform to close the Black-White achievement gap.* Washington, DC: Economic Policy Institute.

Rubin, B. C. (2006). Tracking and detracking: Debates, evidence, and best practices for a heterogeneous world. *Theory into Practice, 45*(1), 4–14. ERIC Document # EJ733833.

Rudolph, K. D., Lambert, S. F., Clark, A. G., & Kurlakowsky, K. D. (2001). Negotiating the transition to middle school: The role of self-regulatory processes. *Child Development, 72*(3), 929–946.

Ruedy, M. C. (2008). Repercussions of a MySpace teen suicide: Should anti-cyberbullying laws be created? *North Carolina Journal of Law and Technology, 9,* 323.

Rumberger, R., & Ah Lim, S. (2008). Why students drop out of school: A review of 25 years of research. California Dropout Research Project Policy. Brief 15. Retrieved from www.lmri.ucsb.edu/dropouts

Russell, S. T., & McGuire, J. (2008). The school climate for lesbian, gay, bisexual, and transgendered (LGBT) students. In M. Shinn & I. Yoshikawa (Eds.), *Towards positive youth development: Transforming schools and community programs* (pp. 133–149). New York: Oxford University Press.

Russell, S. T., Toomey, R. B., Ryan, C., & Diaz, R. M. (2014). Being out at school: The implications for school victimization and young adult adjustment. *American Journal of Orthopsychiatry, 84*(6), 635–643.

Rüütel, E., Sisask, M., Värnik, A., Värnik, P., Carli, V., Wasserman, C., …, Wasserman, D. (2014). Alcohol consumption patterns among adolescents are related to family structure and exposure to drunkenness within the family: Results from the SEYLE project. *International Journal of Environmental Research and Public Health, 11,* 12700–12715. doi: 10.3390/ijerph111212700

Ryan, R. M., & Deci, E. L. (2000). Self-determination theory and the facilitation of intrinsic motivation, social development, and well-being. *American Psychologist, 55*(1), 68–78.

Ryan, R. M., Lynch, M. F., Vansteenkiste, M., & Deci, E. L. (2011). Motivation and autonomy in counseling, psychotherapy, and behavior change: A look at theory and practice. *The Counseling Psychologist, 39*(2), 193–260. doi: 10.1177/0011000009359313

Ryan, J. B., Reid, R., & Epstein, M. H. (2004). Peer-mediated intervention studies on academic achievement for students with EBD: A review. *Remedial & Special Education, 25*(6), 330–341.

Sadker, D. M., Zittleman, K., & Sadker, M. P. (2010). *Teachers, schools, and society* (9th ed.). New York: McGraw-Hill.

Santiago, C. D., Wadsworth, M. E., & Stump, J. (2011). Socioeconomic status, neighborhood disadvantage, and poverty-related stress: Prospective effects on psychological syndromes among diverse low-income families. *Journal of Economic Psychology, 32,* 218–230.

Salami, T. K., Brooks, B. A., & Lamis, D. A. (2015). Impulsivity and reasons for living among African American youth: A risk-protection framework of suicidal ideation. *International Journal of Environmental Research and Public Health, 12*(5), 5196–5214.

Sanchez, E. A., & Kibler-Sanchez, S. (2004). Empowering children in mediation: An intervention model. *Family Court Review, 42,* 554–575.

Sander, J. B., & McCarty, C. A. (2005). Youth depression in the family context: Familial risk factors and models of treatment. *Clinical Child and Family Psychology Review, 8*(3), 203–219.

Sargalska, J., Miranda, R., & Marroquin, B. (2011). Being certain about an absence of the positive: Specificity in relation to hopelessness and suicidal ideation. *International Journal of Cognitive Therapy, 4,* Special Section: Cognitive-Behavioral and Neuroscientific Approaches to Obsessive-Compulsive and Related Phenomena, 104–116. doi: 10.1521/ijct.2011.4.1.104

Schlam, T. R., Wilson, N. L., Shoda, Y., Mischel, W., & Ayduk, O. (2013). Preschoolers' delay of gratification predicts their body mass 30 years later. *The Journal of Pediatrics, 162,* 90–93.

Schliebner, C. T., & Peregoy, J. J. (1994). Unemployment effects on the family and the child: Interventions for counselors. *Journal of Counseling & Development, 72*(4), 368–372.

Schott Foundation for Public Education. (2012). *The urgency of now: The Schott 50 state report on public education and black males.* Retrieved from http://www.blackboysreport.org

Schultz, D., Izard, C. E., Ackerman, B. P., & Youngstrom, E. A. (2001). Emotion knowledge in economically disadvantaged children: Self-regulatory antecedents and relations to social difficulties and withdrawal. *Development and Psychopathology, 13*, 53–67.

Schuyler Center for Analysis and Advocacy. (2008). Teenage births: Outcomes for young parents and their children. Retrieved from http://www.scaany.org/documents/teen_pregnancy_dec08.pdf

Schwartz, S. J., Unger, J. B., Zamboanga, B. L., & Szapocznik, J. (2011). How selective is acculturation? Broadening our perspective. *The American Psychologist, 66*(2), 155–157.

Schwinn, T. M., & Schinke, S. P. (2014). Alcohol use and related behaviors among late-adolescent urban youths: Peer and parent influences. *Journal of Child and Adolescent Substance Abuse, 23*, 58–64. doi: 10.1080/1067828X.2012.735561

Scott, S., & Dadds, M. (2009). Practitioner review: When parent training doesn't work: Theory-driven clinical strategies. *The Journal of Child Psychology and Psychiatry, 50*(12), 1441–1450.

Scruggs, T. E., Brigham, F. J., & Mastropieri, M. A. (2013). Common Core Science Standards: Implications for students with learning disabilities. *Learning Disabilities Research & Practice, 28*, 49–57. doi:10.1111/ldrp.12002

Search Institute. (2006). *The Asset Approach: 40 elements of healthy development*. Minneapolis, MN: Search Institute. Retrieved from http://www.search-institute.org

Search Institute. (2013). A fragile foundation: The state of Developmental Assets among American youth SURVEY: Profiles of student life: Attitudes and behaviors, search institute. Minneapolis, MN; Retrieved from www.search-institute.org

Seligman, M. (1990). *Learned optimism*. New York: Knopf.

Seligman, M. (1993). *Helplessness: On depression, development, and death*. San Francisco: Freeman.

Seligman, M. (1994). *What you can change and what you can't*. New York: Knopf.

Seligman, M. E. P. (1995). *The optimistic child: A revolutionary program that safeguards children against depression and builds lifelong resilience*. New York: Houghton Mifflin.

Seligman, M. E. P., Schulman, B. S., DeRubeis, R. J., & Hollon, S. D. (1999). The prevention of depression and anxiety. *Prevention & Treatment, 2*, article 8. Retrieved from http://journals.apa.org/prevention/volume2/pre0020008a.html

Senn, T. E., Carey, M. P., & Coury-Doniger, P. (2011). Self-defining as sexually abused and adult sexual risk behavior: Results from a cross-sectional survey of women attending an STD clinic. *Child Abuse & Neglect, 35*(5), 353–362.

Sewell, K. W., & Mendelsohn, M. (2000). Profiling potentially violent youth: Statistical and conceptual problems. *Children's Services: Social Policy, Research, and Practice, 3*, 147–169.

Sexton, T. L., & Schuster, R. A. (2008). The role of positive emotion in the therapeutic process of family therapy. *Journal of Psychotherapy Integration, 18*(2), 233–247.

Sexton, T., & Turner, C. W. (2010). The effectiveness of functional family therapy for youth with behavioral problems in a community practice setting. *Journal of Family Psychology, 24*(3), 339–348.

Shams, B., Golshiri, P., & Najimi, A. (2013). The evaluation of Mothers' participation project in children's growth and development process: Using the CIPP evaluation model. *Journal of Educational Health Promotion, 2*, 21.

Sharkey, J. D., Shekhtmeyster, Z., Chavez-Lopez, L., Norris, E., & Sass, L. (2011). The protective influence of gangs: Can schools compensate? *Aggression and Violent Behavior, 16*(1), 45–54.

Shedler, J., & Block, J. (1990). Adolescent drug use and psychological health: A longitudinal inquiry. *American Psychologist, 45*, 612–630.

Sherman, D. K., Hartson, K. A., Binning, K. R., Purdie-Vaughns, V., Garcia, J., Taborsky-Barba, S., ..., Cohen, G. L. (2013). Deflecting the trajectory and changing the narrative: How self-affirmation affects academic performance and motivation under identity threat. *Journal of Personality and Social Psychology, 104*, 591–618.

Sheppard, C., Golonka, M., & Costanzo, P. (2012). Evaluating the impact of a substance use intervention program on the peer status and influence of adolescent peer leaders. *Prevention Science, 13*, 75–85. doi: 10.1007/s11121-011-0248-z

Shestowsky, D. (2004). Procedural preferences in alternative dispute resolution: A closer, modern look at an old idea. *Psychology, Public Policy, and Law, 10*, 211–249.

Shubert, T. H., Bressette, S., Deeken, J., & Bender, W. N. (1999). Analysis of random school shootings. In W. N. Bender, G. Clinton, & R. L. Bender (Eds.), *Violence prevention and reduction in schools* (pp. 97–101). Austin, TX: Pro-Ed.

Shure, M. B. (1992a). *I Can Problem Solve (ICPS): An interpersonal cognitive problem solving program (preschool)*. Champaign, IL: Research Press.

Shure, M. B. (1992b). *I Can Problem Solve (ICPS): An interpersonal cognitive problem solving program (kindergarten/primary grades)*. Champaign, IL: Research Press.

Shure, M. B. (1992c). *I Can Problem Solve (ICPS): An interpersonal cognitive problem solving program (intermediate elementary grades)*. Champaign, IL: Research Press.

Shure, M. B. (1996a). *Raising a thinking child: Help your young child to resolve everyday conflicts and get along with others*. New York: Pocket Books.

Shure, M. B. (1996b). *Raising a thinking child workbook*. New York: Pocket Books.

Shure, M. B. (2006). I Can Problem Solve (ICPS): An interpersonal cognitive problem solving approach for children. In M. J. Elias & H. Arnold (Eds.), *The educators guide to emotional intelligence and academic achievement: Social-emotional learning in the classroom* (pp. 92–101). Thousand Oaks, CA: Corwin Press.

Shure, M. B. (2007). Bullies and their victims: A problem-solving approach to treatment and prevention. In S. Goldstein & R. B. Brooks (Eds.), *Understanding and managing children's classroom behavior* (2nd ed., pp. 408–431). Hoboken, NJ: Wiley.

Shure, M. B., & Aberson, B. (2005). Enhancing the process of resilience through effective thinking. In S.

Goldstein & R. Brooks (Eds.), *Handbook of resilience in children* (pp. 373–394). New York: Kluwer Academic/Plenum.

Sieh, D. S., Visser-Meily, J. A., & Meijer, A. M. (2013). The relationship between parental depressive symptoms, family type, and adolescent functioning. *PLoS ONE, 8*(11), 1–9.doi:10.1371journal.pone0080 699.

Sigfusdottir, I. D., Gudjonsson, G. H., & Sigurdsson, J. F. (2010). Bullying and delinquency. The mediating role of anger. *Personality and Individual Differences, 48*(4), 391–396.

Simkin, D. R., & Black, N. B. (2014). Meditation and mindfulness in clinical practice. *Child and Adolescent Psychiatric Clinics of North America, 23*(3), 487–534.

Simon, D. J. (2016). *School-centered interventions: Evidence-based strategies for social, emotional, and academic success.* Washington, DC: American Psychological Association.

Slavin, R. E. (1991). Cooperative learning and group contingencies. *Journal of Behavioral Education, 1*(1), 105–115.

Slavin, R. E. (2013). An introduction to cooperative learning research. In R. Hertz-Lazarowitz, S. Kagan, S. Sharan, R. Slavin, C. Webb, & F. Schmuck (Eds.), *Learning to cooperate, cooperating to learn* (pp. 5–15). New York: Springer.

Slavin, R. E., Lake, C., Chambers, B., Cheung, A., & Davis, S. (2009). *Effective beginning reading programs: A best-evidence synthesis.* Baltimore, MD: The Johns Hopkins University School of Education's Center for Data-Driven Reform in Education.

Smith, D. K., Chamberlain, P., & Eddy, J. M. (2010). Preliminary support for multidimensional treatment foster care in reducing substance use in delinquent boys. *Journal of Child and Adolescent Substance Abuse, 19,* 343–358.

Smith, D. C., & Sandhu, D. S. (2004). Toward a positive perspective on violence prevention in schools: Building connections. *Journal of Counseling & Development, 82*(3), 287–293.

Smith, D. L., & Smith, B. J. (2006). Perceptions of violence: The views of teachers who left urban schools. *The High School Journal, 89*(3), 34–42.

Smith, K. (2002). *Who's minding the kids? Child care arrangements: Spring 1997.* Current Population Reports. Washington, DC: U.S. Census Bureau.

Smith, M. J. (1986). *Yes, I can say no.* New York: Arbor House.

Smith, S. W., & Daunic, A. P. (2002). Using conflict resolution and peer mediation to support positive behavior. In B. Algozzine & P. Kay (Eds.), *Preventing problem behaviors: A handbook of successful prevention strategies* (pp. 162–182). Thousand Oaks, CA: Sage.

Snyder, C. R. (1994). *The psychology of hope: You can get there from here.* New York: Free Press.

Snyder, C. R., Sympson, S. C., Ybasco, F. C., Borders, T. F., Babyak, M. A., & Higgins, R. L. (1996). Development and validation of the State Hope Scale. *Journal of Personality and Social Psychology, 2,* 321–335.

Social and Character Development Research Consortium. (2010). *Efficacy of schoolwide programs to promote social and character development and reduce problem behavior in elementary school children* (NCER 2011–2001). Washington, DC: National Center for Education Research, Institute of Education Sciences, U.S. Department of Education.

Social Security Administration/SSA. (2014). Fast facts & figures about Social Security, 2014. Retrieved from http://www.ssa.gov/policy/docs/chartbooks/fast_facts/2014/fast_facts14.html#pagei

Society for Public Health Education. (2012). Lesbian, gay, bisexual, and transgender youth: Embracing diversity and promoting inclusion. Adolescent Health: Planting Seeds for a Healthier Generation. Society for Public Health Education. Retrieved from http://www.sophe.org/Sophe/PDF/LGBT_Youth.pdf

Solantaus, T., Leinonen, J., & Punamaki, R. L. (2004). Children's mental health in times of economic recession: Replication and extension of the family economic stress model in Finland. *Developmental Psychology, 40*(3), 412–427.

Sparks, S. D. (2011, April). Study: Third grade reading predicts later high school graduation. *Education Week.* Retrieved from http://blogs.edweek.org/edweek/inside-school-research/2011/04/the_disquieting_side_effect_of.html

Spence, I., & Feng, J. (2010). Video games and spatial cognition. *Review of General Psychology, 14,* 92–104.

Spinazzola, J., Hodgdon, H., Liang, L. J., Ford, J. D., Layne, C. M., Pynoos, R., …, Kisiel, C. (2015, July/August). Unseen Wounds. *Monitor on Psychology, 46*(7), 68–73.

Spivack, G., Platt, J. J., & Shure, M. B. (1976). *The problem solving approach to adjustment.* San Francisco: Jossey-Bass.

Stanger-Hall, K. F., & Hall, D. W. (2011). Abstinence-only education and teen pregnancy rates: Why we need comprehensive sex education in the U.S. *PLoS ONE, 6*(10), e24658–. doi:10.1371/journal.pone.0024658

Starbuck, D., Howell, J. C., & Lindquist, D. (2001, December). *Hybrid and other modern gangs.* Bulletin of the Office of Juvenile Justice and Delinquency Prevention. Washington, DC: U.S. Department of Justice, Office of Justice Programs.

Stephens, T. M. (1992). *Social skills in the classroom* (2nd ed.). Odessa, FL: Psychological Assessment Resources.

Stephens, J., Heffner, J., Adler, C., Blom, T., Anthenelli, R., Fleck, D., …, Del Bello, M. (2014). Risk and protective factors associated with substance use disorders in adolescents with first-episode mania. *Journal of the American Academy of Child & Adolescent Psychiatry, 53,* 771–779. doi:10.1016/j.jaac.2014.04.018

Sterling, S., Weisner, C., Hinman, A., & Parthasarathy, S. (2010). Access to treatment for adolescents with substance use and co-occurring disorders: Challenges and opportunities. *Journal of the American Academy of Child & Adolescent Psychiatry, 49*(7), 637–646.

Stiglitz, J. (2011). Inequality: Of the 1%, by the 1%, for the 1%. Retrieved from http://www.vanityfair.com/news/2011/05/top-one-percent-201105

Stormshak, E. A., Connell, A. M., Véronneau, M. H., Myers, M. W., Dishion, T. J., Kavanagh, K., & Caruthers, A. S. (2011), An ecological approach to promoting early adolescent mental health and social adaptation: Family-centered intervention in public middle schools. *Child Development, 82*, 209–225. doi: 10.1111/j.1467-8624.2010.01551.x

Straussner, S. L. A., & Fewell, C. H. (2015). Children of parents who abuse alcohol and other drugs. In A. Reupert, D. Maybery, J. Nicholson, M. Gopfert, & M. V. Seeman (Eds.), *Parental psychiatric disorder: Distressed parents and their families* (3rd ed.). (pp. 138–153). Cambridge: Cambridge University Press.

Suárez-Orozco, C., Gaytán, F. X., Bang, H. J., Pakes, J., O'Connor, E., & Rhodes, J. (2010). Academic trajectories of newcomer immigrant youth. *Developmental Psychology, 46*(3), 602–618.

Substance Abuse and Mental Health Services Administration. (2012). Preventing suicide: A toolkit for high schools. HHS Publication No. SMA-12-4669. Rockville, MD: Center for Mental Health Services, Substance Abuse and Mental Health Services Administration.

Sue, D. W., & Sue, D. (2013). *Counseling the culturally diverse: Theory and practice* (6th ed.). Hoboken, NJ: John Wiley & Sons.

Suh, S., Suh, J., & Houston, I. (2007). Predictors of categorical at-risk high school dropouts. *Journal of Counseling and Development, 85*(2), 196–203.

Sullivan, M., & Wodarski, J. S. (2002). Social alienation in gay youth. *Journal of Human Behavior in the Social Environment, 5*(1), 1–17.

Sussman, S., Sun, P., Rohrbach, L. A., & Spruijt-Metz, D. (2012). One-year outcomes of a drug abuse prevention program for older teens and emerging adults: Evaluating a motivational interviewing booster component. *Health Psychology, 31*(4), 476–485.

Sutton, M. J., Brown, J. D., Wilson, K. M., & Klein, J. D. (2002). Shaking the tree of knowledge for forbidden fruit: Where adolescents learn about sexuality and contraception. In J. D. Brown, J. R. Steele, & K. Walsh-Childers (Eds.), *Sexual teens, sexual media* (pp. 25–55). Hillsdale: NJ: Erlbaum.

Tang, M., & Cook, E. P. (2001). Understanding relationship and career concerns of middle school girls. In P. O'Reilly, E. M. Penn, & K. deMarrais (Eds.), *Educating young adolescent girls* (pp. 213–229). Mahwah, NJ: Erlbaum.

Taqi-Eddin, K., Macallair, D., & Schiraldi, V. (1998). *Class dismissed: Higher education vs. corrections during the Wilson years.* San Francisco, CA: Justice Policy Institute.

Tavousi, M. N. (2015). The effectiveness of progressive relaxation training on daily hassles: Moderating role of hardiness and self-esteem. *Procedia-Social and Behavioral Sciences, 190*(21), 54–60.

Taylor, R. D. (2010). Risk and resilience in low-income African American families: Moderating effects of kinship social support. *Cultural Diversity and Ethnic Minority Psychology, 16*(3), 344–351.

Taylor, P. (2011). The decline of marriage and rise of new families. Pew Research Center's Social & Demographic Trends project. Retrieved from http://www.pewsocialtrends.org

Terrion, J. L. (2006). Building social capital in vulnerable families: Success markers of a school-based intervention program. *Youth & Society, 38*(2), 155–176.

Thomas, S. P., & Smith, H. (2004). School connectedness, anger behaviors, and relationships of violent and nonviolent American youth. *Perspectives in Psychiatric Care, 40*(4), 135–148.

Thompson, W. E., & Bynum, J. E. (2016). *Juvenile delinquency: A sociological approach* (10th ed.). Lanham, MD: Rowman & Littlefield.

Thompson, E. A., & Eggert, L. L. (1999). Using the suicide risk screen to identify suicidal adolescents among potential high school dropouts. *Journal of the American Academy of Child and Adolescent Psychiatry, 38*(12), 1506–1514.

Tolan, P. H., Gorman-Smith, D., & Henry, D. B. (2006). Family violence. *Annual Review of Psychology, 57*, 557–583.

Tolan, P., Gorman-Smith, D., Henry, D., & Schoeny, M. (2010). The benefits of booster interventions: Evidence from a family-focused prevention program. *Prevention Science, 10*(4), 287–297.

Topitzes, J., Mersky, J. P., & Reynolds, A. J. (2012). From child maltreatment to violent offending: An examination of mixed gender and gender specific models. *Journal of Interpersonal Violence, 27*(12), 2322–2347. doi:10.1177/08862 60511433510

Toporek, R. L., Lewis, J., & Crethar, H. C. (2009). Promoting systemic change through Advocacy Competencies. Special Section on ACA Advocacy Competencies. *Journal of Counseling and Development, 87*, 260–268.

Topping, K., Miller, D., Thurston, A., McGavok, K., & Conlin, N. (2011). Peer tutoring in reading in Scotland: Thinking big. *Literacy, 45*, 3–9. doi: 10.1111/j .1740-4369.2011.005 77.x

Townsend, K. C., & McWhirter, B. T. (2005). Connectedness: A review of current literature, with implications for counseling, assessment, and research. *Journal of Counseling & Development, 83*(2), 191–201.

Trepal, H. C. (2010). Exploring self-injury through a relational cultural lens. *Journal of Counseling & Development, 88*(4), 492–499.

Trevor Project. (2015). Facts about suicide. Retrieved From thetrevorproject.org

Trucco, E. M., Colder, C. R., & Wieczorek, W. F. (2011). Vulnerability to peer influence: A moderated mediation study of early adolescent alcohol use initiation. *Addictive Behaviors, 36*(7), 729–736.

Tuttle, C., Teh, B., Nichols-Barrer, I., Gill, B., & Gleason, P. (2010, June). *Student characteristics and achievement in 22 KIPP middle schools.* Washington, DC: Mathematica Policy Research. Retrieved from http://www.mathematica-mpr.com/publications/pdfs/education/kipp_fnlrpt.pdf

U.S. Census Bureau. (2001). Census 2000 Supplementary Survey. Washington, DC: Demographic Surveys Division.

U.S. Conference of Mayors. (2014). *Hunger and homelessness survey of 25* cities: A status report on Hunger and Homelessness, A 25 city survey. Retrieved from http://www. usmayors.org/pressreleases/uploads/ 2014/1211-report-hh.pdf

U.S. Department of Agriculture. (2015). Rural poverty & well-being. Economic Research Service. Retrieved from http://www.ers. usda.gov/topics/rural-economy-population/rural-poverty-well-being/poverty-overview.aspx

U.S. Department of Education. (2000). *Safeguarding our children: An action guide.* Washington, DC: U.S. Government Printing Office.

U.S. Department of Education. (2009). Race to the top program: Executive summary. Retrieved from https:// www2.ed.gov/programs/racetothe-top/executive-summary.pdf

U.S. Department of Education. (2010). *Evaluation of evidence-based practices in online learning: A meta-analysis and review of online learning studies.* Retrieved from http://www2.ed. gov/rschstat/eval/tech/evidence-based-practices/finalreport.pdf

U. S. Department of Health and Human Services. (2008). *Child maltreatment 2006.* Washington, DC: Author.

U.S. Department of Health and Human Services. (2015). Tobacco facts and figures. Retrieved from http://beta-baccofree.hhs.gov/about-tobacco/ facts-figures/

U.S. Department of Health and Human Services; Office of Adolescent Health. (2015). Retrieved from http://www.hhs.gov/ash/oah/adoles-cent-health-topics/reproductive-health/stds.html

U. S. Office of Juvenile Justice and Delinquency Prevention. (2005). Overcoming barriers to school re-entry. Retrieved from www.ncjrs. org/pdffiles1/ojjdp/fs200403.pdf

U.S. Surgeon General Report. (2014). Smoking-attributable morbidity, mortality, and economic costs. Retrieved from http://www.surgeon-general.gov/library/reports/50-years-of-progress/sgr50-chap-12.pdf

Vago, D. R., & Silbersweig, D. A. (2012). Self- awareness, self-regulation, and self-transcendence (S-ART): A framework for under-standing the neurobiological mechanisms of mindfulness. *Frontiers in Human Neuroscience, 6,* 1–30.

Vandell, D. L., Belsky, J., Burchinal, M., Steinberg, L., Vandergrift, N., & NICHD Early Child Care Research Network. (2010). Do effects of early child care extend to age 15 years? Results from the NICHD study of early child care and youth develop-ment. *Child Development, 81*(3), 737–756. doi:10.1111/j.1467-8624. 2010.01431.x

Van Orden, K. A., Witte, T. K., Cukrowicz, K. C., Braithwaite, S. R., Selby, E. A., & Joiner, T. E. (2010). The interpersonal theory of suicide. *Psychological Review, 117*(2), 575–600. doi:10.1037/ a0018697

Van Ryzin, M. J., Kumpfer, K. L., Fosco, G. M., & Greenberg M. T. (2016). *Family-based prevention programs for children and adolescents: Theory, research, and large-scale dissemination.* New York: Psychology Press.

Van Ryzin, M. J., Stormshak, E. A., & Dishion, T. J. (2012). Engaging parents in the family check-up in middle school: Longitudinal effects on family conflict and problem behavior through the high school transition. *Journal of Adolescent Health, 50*(6), 627–633.

Ventura, S. J., Matthews T. J., & Hamilton, B. E. (2002). *Teenage births in the United States: State trends, 1991–2000, an update.* National Vital Statistics Reports, 50. Atlanta: Centers for Disease Control.

Villanueva, M., Tonigan, J. S., & Miller, W. R. (2007). Response of Native American clients to three treatment methods for alcohol dependence. *Journal of Ethnicity in Substance Abuse, 6*(2), 41–48.

Vitiello, B., Brent, D., Greenhill, L., Emslie, G., Wells, K., & Walkup, J., ..., Zelazny, J. (2009). Depressive symp-toms and clinical status during the treatment of adolescent suicide attempters. *Journal of the American Academy of Child and Adolescent Psychiatry, 48*(10), 997–1004.

Vitiello, B., Silva, S., Rohde, P., Kratochvil, C., Kennard, B., Reinecke, M., ..., March, J. (2009). Suicidal events in the treatment for adolescents with depression study (TADS). *Journal of Clinical Psychiatry, 70*(5), 741–747.

Voight, A., Austin, G., & Hanson, T. (2013). *A climate for academic success: How school climate distin-guishes schools that are beating the achievement odds (Full Report).* San Francisco: WestEd. Retrieved from https://www.wested.org/online_ pubs/hd-13-10.pdf

Wade, L. A. (2015). Illegal immigra-tion and education. The National Law Review. Retrieved from http://www.natlawreview.com/ article/illegal-immigration-and-education

Walmsley, R. (2011). *World's prison population list* (8th ed.). King's College London: International Centre for Prison Studies. Retrieved from http://www. prisonstudies.org/

Walton, G. M., & Cohen, G. L. (2011). A brief social-belonging interven-tion improves academic and health outcomes of minority students. *Science, 331,* 1447–1451.

Walton, G. M., Cohen, G. L., Cwir, D., & Spencer, S. J. (2012). Mere belonging: The power of social connections. *Journal of Personality and Social Psychology, 102,* 513–532.

Wanberg, C. R. (2012). The individual experience of unemployment. *Annual Review of Psychology, 63,* 369–396.

Wang, J., Iannotti, R. J., Nansel, T. R. (2009). School bullying among adolescents in the United States: Physical, verbal, relational, and cyber. *Journal of Adolescent Health, 45*(4), 368–375.

Wang, M. T., & Fredricks, J. (2014). The reciprocal links between school engagement, youth problem beha-viors, and school dropout during adolescence. *Child Development, 85*(2), 722–737.

Washington State Institute for Public Policy. (2014). *Early childhood education for low-income students: A review of the evidence and benefit-cost analysis.* Olympia WA: Author. Retrieved from http:// www.wsipp.wa.gov/ReportFile/ 1547/Wsipp_Early-Childhood-Education-for-Low-Income-Students-A-Review-of-the-Evidence-and-Benefit-Cost-Analysis_Full-Report.pdf

Watts, R. J., Diemer, M. A., & Voight, A. M. (2011). Critical conscious-ness: Current status and future directions. In C. A. Flanagan &

B. D. Christens (Eds.), *Youth civic development: Work at the cutting edge*. New Directions for Child and Adolescent Development, *134*, 43–57.

Wayne, A. (2002, June 13). Teacher inequality: New evidence on disparities in teachers' academic skills. *Education Policy Analysis Archives*, *10*(30). Retrieved from http://epaa.asu.edu/epaa/v10n30/

Webb, L., & Brigman, G. A. (2007). Student success skills: A structured group intervention for school counselors. *The Journal for Specialists in Group Work*, *32*(2), 190–201. doi:10.1080/019339207012277257

Webster-Stratton, C., & Reid, M. J. (2010). Adapting the incredible years, an evidence-based parenting programm, for families involved in the child welfare system. *Journal of Children's Services*, *5*(1), 25–42.

Webster-Stratton, C., Reid, M. J., & Hammond, M. (2001). Preventing conduct problems, promoting social competence: A parent and teacher training partnership in Head Start. *Journal of Clinical Child Psychology*, *30*(3), 283–302.

Weersing, V. R., & Brent, D. A. (2010). Treating depression in adolescents using individual cognitive-behavioral therapy. In J. R. Weisz & A. E. Kazdin (Eds.), *Evidence-based psychotherapies for children and adolescents* (2nd ed., pp. 126–139). New York: Guilford Press.

Weissberg, R. P., Kumpfer, K. L., & Seligman, M. E. P. (2003). Special issue: Prevention that works for children and youth: An introduction. *American Psychologist*, *58*, 425–432.

Weist, M. D., Lever, N. A., Bradshaw, C. P., & Owens, J. (2014). Further developing school mental health: Reflecting on the past to inform the future. In M. D. Weist, N. A. Lever, C. P. Bradshaw, & J. Owens (Eds.), *Handbook of school mental health: Advancing practice and research* (2nd ed., pp. 1–14). New York: Springer. doi:10.1007/978-1-4614-7624-5_1

Welner, K. G., & Mathis, W. J. (2015, February). National Education Policy Center Policy Memo:

Reauthorization of the Elementary and Secondary Education Act: Time to Move beyond Test-Focused Policies. Retrieved from http://nepc.colorado.edu/files/nepc-policy-memo-esea.pdf

Werch, C. E., & DiClemente, C. C. (1994). A multi-component stage model for matching drug prevention strategies and messages to youth stage of use. *Health Education Research: Theory & Practice*, *9*, 37–46.

Werner, E. E. (1995). Resilience in development. *Current Directions in Psychological Science*, *4*(3), 81–82.

Wery, J., & Thomson, M. M. (2013). Motivational strategies to enhance effective learning in teaching struggling students. *Support for Learning*, *28*, 103–108. doi:10.1111/1467-9604.12027

Whisenhunt, J. L., Chang, C. Y., Flowers, L. R., Brack, G. L., O'Hara, C., & Raines, T. C. (2014). Working with clients who self-injure: A grounded theory approach. *Journal of Counseling & Development*, *92*, 387–397. doi:10.1002/j.1556-6676.2014.00165.x

Whitebook, M., Phillips, D., & Howes, C. (2014). *Worthy work, STILL unlivable wages: The early childhood workforce 25 years after the National Child Care Staffing Study*. Berkeley, CA: Center for the Study of Child Care Employment, University of California, Berkeley.

Whitaker, D., & Lutzker, J. (2009). *Preventing partner violence: Research and evidence-based intervention strategies*. Washington, DC: American Psychological Association.

Whiteman, T. L., Borkowski, J., Keogh, D., & Weed, K. (2001). *Interwoven lives: Adolescent mothers and their children*. Mahwah, NJ: Erlbaum.

Whitlock, J., Muehlenkamp, J., Eckenrode, J., Purington, A., Baral Abrams, G., Barreira, P., & Kress, V. (2013). Nonsuicidal self-injury as a gateway to suicide in young adults. *Journal of Adolescent Health*, *52*(4), 486–492. doi:10.1016/j.jadohealth.2012.09.010

Whitlock, J, Purington, A., & Gershkovich, M. (2009). Influence of the media on self injurious behavior. In M. K. Nock (Ed.), *Understanding non-suicidal self-injury: Origins, assessment, and*

treatment (pp. 139–156). Washington, DC: American Psychological Association.

Whitney, S. D., Renner, L. M., Pate. C. M., & Jacobs, K. A. (2011). Principals' perceptions of benefits and barriers to school-based suicide prevention programs. *Children and Youth Services Review*, *33*(6), 869–877.

Widom, C. S., Czaja, S., & Dutton, M. A. (2014). Child abuse and neglect and intimate partner violence victimization and perpetration: A prospective investigation. *Child Abuse & Neglect*, *38*(4), 650–663.

Wiehe, S. E., Garrison, M. M., Christakis, D. A., Ebel, B. E., & Rivara, F. P. (2005). A systematic review of school-based smoking prevention trials with long-term follow up. *Journal of Adolescent Health*, *36*(3), 162–169.

Wilcox, D., & Dowrick, P. W. (1992). Anger management with adolescents. *Residential Treatment for Children and Youth*, *9*(3), 29–39.

Wilcox, H. C., Kellam, S. G., Brown, C. H., Poduska, J. M., Ialongo, N. S., Wang, W., & Anthony, J. C. (2008). The impact of two universal randomized first- and second-grade classroom interventions on young adult suicide ideation and attempts. *Drug and Alcohol Dependence*, *95*(1), 60–73.

Wilens, T. E., Biederman, J., Bredin, E., Hahesy, A. L., Abrantes, A., Neft, D., …, Spencer, T. J. (2002). A family study of high-risk children of opiod- and alcohol-dependent parents. *American Journal on Addictions*, *11*(1), 41–51.

Witte, J. F., Cowen, J. M., Fleming, D. J., Wolf, P. J., Condon, M. R., & Lucas-McLean, J. (2010). *The MPCP Longitudinal Educational Growth Study third year report* (SCDP Milwaukee Evaluation Report #15). Fayetteville, AK: University of Arkansas, School Choice Demonstration Project.

Witvliet, M., van Lier, P. A. C., Cuijpers, P., & Koot, H. M. (2009). Testing links between childhood positive peer relations and externalizing outcomes through a randomized controlled intervention study. *Journal of Consulting and Clinical Psychology*, *77*(5), 905–915.

Wolak, J., Finkelhor, D.,. Mitchell, K., & Ybarra, M. (2011). Online 'predators' and their victims: Myths, realities, and implications for prevention and treatment. *American Psychologist, 63,* 111–128.

Wolak, J., Mitchell, D., & Finkelhor, D. (2011). Online victimization of youth: Five years later. National Center for Missing & Exploited Children. Retrieved from http://www.missingkids.com/en_US/publications/NC167.pdf

Wolchik, S. A., Schenck, C. E., & Sandler, I. N. (2009). Promoting resilience in youth from divorced families: Lessons learned from experimental trials of the New Beginnings Program. *Journal of Personality, 77*(6), 1833–1868.

Wolfe, D. A., Wekerle, C., Scott, K., Straatman, A. L., & Grasley, C. (2004). Predicting abuse in adolescent dating relationships over 1 year: The role of child maltreatment and trauma. *Journal of Abnormal Psychology, 113*(3), 406–415.

Wu, C., & Eamon, M. K. (2011). Patterns and correlates of involuntary unemployment and underemployment in single-mother families. *Children and Youth Services Review, 33*(6), 820–828.

Wubbolding, R. E. (2000). *Reality therapy for the 21st century.* Philadelphia: Brunner-Routledge.

Wubbolding, R. (2006). *Reality therapy training manual.* Cincinnati, OH: Center for Reality Therapy.

Wubbolding, R. E. (2007). Glasser quality school. *Group Dynamics: Theory, Research, and Practice, 11*(4), 253–261. doi:10.1037/1089-2699.11.4.253

Youngstrom, E., Wolpaw, J. M., Kogos, J. L., Schoff, K., Ackerman, B., & Izard, C. (2000). Interpersonal problem solving in preschool and first grade: Developmental change and ecological validity. *Journal of Clinical Child Psychology, 29*(4), 589–602.

Yoshikawa, H., Aber, J. L., & Beardslee, W. R. (2012). The effects of poverty on the mental, emotional, and behavioral health of children and youth: Implications for prevention. *American Psychologist, 67,* 272–284. doi:10.1037/a0028015

Yoshikawa, H., Weiland, C., Brooks-Gunn, J., Burchinal, M. R., Espinosa, L. M., Gormley, W. T., …, Zaslow, M. J. (2013). *Investing in our future: The evidence base on preschool education.* Washington, DC: Society for Research in Child Development and the Foundation for Child Development. Retrieved from http://fcd-us.org/sites/default/files/Evidence%20Base%20on%20Preschool%20Education%20FINAL.pdf

Zajacova, A., Montez, J. K., & Herd, P. (2014). Socioeconomic disparities in health among older adults and the implications for the retirement age debate: A brief report. *Journals of Gerontology, Series B: Psychological Sciences and Social Sciences,* 1–6. Retrieved from http://psychsocgerontology.oxfordjournals.org/content/early/2014/05/07/geronb.gbu041.full.pdf+html

Zald, D. H., Cowan, R. L., Riccardi, P., Baldwin, R. M., Ansari, M. S., Li, R., …, Kessler, R. M. (2008). Midbrain dopamine receptor availability is inversely associated with novelty-seeking traits in humans. *The Journal of Neuroscience, 28*(53), 14372–14378. doi:10.1523/JNEUROSCI.2423-08.2008

Zenner, C., Herrnleben-Kurz, S., & Walach, H. (2014). Mindfulness-based interventions in schools—A systematic review and meta-analysis. *Frontiers in Psychology, 5,* 603. Retrieved from http://journal.frontiersin.org/article/10.3389/fpsyg.2014.00603/abstract

Zhen-Duan, J., & Taylor, M. J. (2014). The use of an ecodevelopmental approach to examining substance use among rural and urban Latino/a youth: Peer, parental, and school influences. *Journal of Ethnicity in Substance Abuse, 13*(2), 104–125. doi:10.1080/15332640.2013.873

NAME INDEX

SUBJECT INDEX